1994

POLITICS IN DEVELOPING COUNTRIES

POLITICS IN DEVELOPING COUNTRIES

Comparing Experiences with Democracy

edited by
Larry Diamond
Juan J. Linz
Seymour Martin Lipset

Lynne Rienner Publishers   Boulder & London

Published in the United States of America in 1990 by
Lynne Rienner Publishers, Inc.
1800 30th Street, Boulder, Colorado 80301

and in the United Kingdom by
Lynne Rienner Publishers, Inc.
3 Henrietta Street, Covent Garden, London WC2E 8LU

Library of Congress CIP number: 90-31540

ISBN: 1-55587-212-3

A Cataloguing in Publication record for this book is also
available from the British Library.

Printed and bound in the United States of America

5 4

• Contents •

· Illustrations ·

· MAPS ·

· TABLES AND FIGURES ·

• CHAPTER ONE •

Introduction:
Comparing Experiences with Democracy

LARRY DIAMOND
JUAN J. LINZ
SEYMOUR MARTIN LIPSET

The ten case studies in this book analyze the political development of a selection of countries from Africa, Asia, Latin America, and the Middle East—or what we term, for lack of a better label, "developing countries." While analyzing the full sweep of regime evolution and change, we focus on a particular issue in political development that can justifiably be called the preeminent political issue of our times: the struggle for democracy. Beginning from a common theoretical agenda, we seek to explain whether, why, and to what extent democracy has evolved and taken root in the vastly different cultural and historical soils of these countries.

The larger (twenty-six–nation) comparative study from which these cases derive was undertaken at a time of tremendous democratic ferment in the developing world.[1] The movement toward democracy that witnessed, in the mid-1970s, the toppling of Western Europe's last three dictatorships—Greece, Portugal, and Spain—moved on through Latin America. In the ensuing decade, most Latin American military dictatorships collapsed or withdrew, defying predictions of a longer reign for these "bureaucratic-authoritarian" regimes. By the end of the 1980s, the transition to democracy was nearing completion in Chile, and the world was transfixed by the campaign for democratization in China, the growing demands for national autonomy and further political liberalization in the Soviet Union, and the stunning collapse of Communist rule throughout Eastern Europe. The latter developments showed the diversity of paths to democracy—even within the seemingly homogeneous Communist world—ranging from reform from above to negotiation to the violent overthrow of a regime that combined Communist with personalistic (sultanistic) rule in Romania.[2]

In East Asia, democratic progress was apparent in the dramatic transitions in the Philippines and South Korea, and in the incremental but considerable movement in Taiwan and Thailand. In the old British South Asian raj, Pakistan completed a transition to democracy, but India experienced serious and persistent challenges to its democratic institutions and Sri Lanka descended into an ethnic civil war.

1

Among the states of Africa, which found it difficult to establish new nationhoods and democratic regimes, there were also some signs of democratic emergence or renewal. Uganda, for example, struggled to put an end to decades of anarchy, tyranny, and civil strife in order to fulfil its hopes for democracy and human rights. Despite intense repression (somewhat diminished by 1990), the black and colored peoples of South Africa continue their struggle for a nonracial democracy through multiple forms of nonviolent action, including an increasingly powerful trade union movement. Nigeria instituted an elaborate timetable for democratic transition from military rule, beginning with local government elections and the formation of two political parties, to be followed in stages by partisan elections at the local and state and then federal levels. In North Africa, processes of political liberalization were launched in the late 1980s in Tunisia and Algeria, and a partially competitive, partially liberal, multiparty system persists in Egypt.

The 1980s witnessed an unprecedented growth of international concern for human rights—including, prominently, the rights to choose democratically the government under which one lives and to express and organize around one's political principles and views. As torture, disappearances, and other grave human rights violations became more widespread but also more systematically exposed and denounced around the world, there developed a renewed and deeper appreciation for democratic institutions which, with all their procedural messiness and sluggishness, nevertheless protect the integrity of the person and the freedoms of conscience and expression. The growth of democratic norms throughout the world is strikingly evidenced in the degree to which authoritarian regimes find it necessary to wrap themselves in the rhetoric and constitutional trappings of democracy, or at least to state as their goal the eventual establishment of democracy.

The global advance of democracy in the 1980s was assisted by the demise of its historic ideological rivals. Fascism was destroyed as a vital force in World War II. The appeals of Marxism-Leninism have declined with the harsh repressiveness, glaring economic failures, and loss of revolutionary idealism of the existing Communist regimes. More-limited, quasi-socialist or mass mobilizational models—the Mexican, Yugoslav, and Nasserite—have also lost their aura. Military regimes almost universally lack ideological justification and legitimacy beyond a temporary intrusion to correct political and social problems. With the important but still-indeterminate exception of the Islamic fundamentalist state—for that large portion of the world from Indonesia to West Africa wherein Islam is a major or dominant religion—democracy is the only model of government with any broad ideological legitimacy and appeal today.

It is a sign of the changes in our world, politically and intellectually, that the normative question—Why study democracy?—now seems, at the start of the 1990s, much less contentious and problematic than it did in the 1960s. Nevertheless, previous historical cycles warn that the 1990s may bring setbacks and even a renewed crisis of confidence in democracy. Some critics suggest that political democracy is the wrong problem and ask: Are there not more pressing issues of survival and justice facing developing societies? Others contend our choice of topic betrays a misplaced value bias for democracy. They ask (or assert): If in some societies democracy in our (liberal) sense has to work against so many odds, as our research unveils, is it worth striving for, or are there alternatives to democracy that should be considered?

We wish to state quite clearly here our bias for democracy as a system of government. For any democrat, these questions carry serious implications: The former suggest that economic and social rights should be considered more important than civil and political liberties; the latter implies granting to some forms or cases of authoritarian rule the right to use coercive measures, in the name of some higher good, to suppress democratic opposition. For ourselves, neither of these normative suppositions is tenable.

If there were many undemocratic governments (now and in the past) committed to serving collective goals, rather than the interests of the rulers, and ready to respect human rights (to refrain from torture and indiscriminate violence, to offer due process and fair trial in applying laws that, even if antiliberal, are known in advance, to maintain humane conditions of imprisonment), we might find these questions more difficult to answer. However, no undemocratic regime meets these two requirements, and even those that begin with a strong ideological commitment to the collectivity and a professed sensitivity to human rights often become increasingly narrow, autocratic, and repressive, although these trends, too, are subject to reversal.

Even where authoritarian rulers (whether civilian or military, bureaucratic or charismatic) strive to serve collective goals, why should we assume that their conception of the collective good is better than that of any other group in society? Only if we were totally certain that one ideological conception is the expression of historical reason—true and necessary—would we be forced to accept such an authoritarian alternative as better than democracy. To do so, as we know, justifies any sacrifices and ultimately terrible costs in freedom and human lives. Democracy—with its relativism and tolerance (so disturbing to those certain of the truth), and its "faith" in the reasonableness and intelligence of the common people, deciding freely (and with a chance to change their minds every four or five years) and without the use of force—seems still a better option.

• THE ORGANIZATION OF THE STUDY •

Despite the growth of political and intellectual interest in democracy in developing countries, there remain huge gaps in our understanding of the factors that foster or obstruct the emergence, instauration (establishment), and consolidation of democratic government around the world. The contributions to this book are distinctive in that they deal with the entire history of a country's experience with democracy: establishment, breakdown, reequilibration and consolidation of democratic government; periods of democratic persistence, crisis, authoritarianism, and renewal; and all of the ambivalences and oscillations in between. We consider each country's early cultural traditions, analyze (where relevant) the colonial experience, and consider all of its postindependence history, giving special emphasis to post–World War II developments. Whereas most other works cut horizontally through the history of countries to focus on limited time spans and particular processes (usually ignoring the phenomena of democratic consolidation and stability),[3] we cut vertically through historical phases in order to explain the overall path of a country's political development.

While it can be enormously fertile, this historical approach is not without methodological problems. In particular, it runs the risk of attributing contemporary political patterns to antecedents far removed in time, without clearly demonstrating that those factors (or characteristics resulting from them) are operating at a later time and account for the failure or success of democracy. To overcome this risk, each case study author reviews the country's political history, describing its major experiences with democratic and undemocratic governments, including the structure, nature, and characteristic conflicts and tensions of each regime; and explains the fate of each regime (especially each democratic one)—why it persisted, failed, or evolved as it did, and why successive regimes emerged as and when they did. Finally, each author offers a summary theoretical judgment of the factors that have been most important in determining the country's overall degree of success or failure with democratic government, and considers its prospects for democracy, along with any policy implications he or she might wish to derive. Each country's overall experience is assessed along a six-point scale of ideal types, ranging from stable and consolidated democratic rule to the failure or absence of democracy.[4] Our readers are cautioned, however, that the case studies provide no more than capsulized surveys of a country's experience, which will hopefully inspire wider study.

Culturally, the cases in this book encompass much of the enormous variation in the developing world: Brazil, Chile, and Mexico—Christian (largely Catholic) societies of Latin America; India with its mosaic of traditions, including the distinctive Hindu culture; two largely Islamic societies—Senegal and Turkey (whose secularization is linked historically with its democratization); largely Buddhist Thailand; South Korea with its mixture of Buddhism, Confucianism, and Christianity; multiethnic Zimbabwe; and a major example—Nigeria—of what Ali Mazrui calls the "triple heritage" of Christianity, Islam, and traditional African religion and culture.

One of the most complex and intractable problems in our world is the tension between the model of ethnically, linguistically, and culturally homogeneous societies that satisfy the ideal of the nation-state and the multiethnic, multilingual societies that face the difficult task of nation- or state-building in the absence of the integration and identification we normally associate with the idea of the nation-state. Even in Europe, before the massive and forced transfers (if not destruction) of populations, most states did not satisfy that ideal, but outside of Europe, even fewer do. Virtually no African or Asian countries and only a few Latin American countries (in this book, only Chile) seem to satisfy that model. Others, such as Brazil and Mexico, include not only descendants of the *conquistadores* and European immigrants but also substantial populations (intermixed to varying degrees with the above) of Indians and descendants of black slaves. To the list of the relatively homogeneous countries could be added South Korea and Turkey (with some significant minorities, such as the long-suffering Kurds). Our remaining cases confront us with the problem of democracy in ethnically and culturally divided societies. In some of our cases, most prominently India and Nigeria, these cultural divisions have generated conflicts that have cost dearly in terms of political trauma and human bloodshed, and that continue to endanger the prospects for democracy and political stability.

One experience that almost all of these countries share is a previous history of domination by an outside imperial power. Only Turkey and Thailand have been continuously independent and only in the latter do we find a continuity with a premodern traditional monarchy. Our study therefore does not cover a sufficient number of countries to deal with the question: Does continuous legitimacy of rule by an indigenous state facilitate both modernization and, ultimately, democratization, by contrast with the historical trauma of conquest and colonial domination?

For those who have raised the question of the relation between size and democracy,[5] our larger, twenty-six–country study includes the largest (most populous) democracy—India—and some of the smallest. Because the larger countries are generally of wider interest for classroom consideration of cross-regional comparisons, we have tended to favor them in the selection of cases for this book. Unfortunately, this required us to exclude the fascinating and theoretically informative cases of several small countries that have experienced unusual democratic success (Costa Rica, Uruguay, Botswana) or crisis (Sri Lanka). Since the major countries—with their political influence and their capacity to serve as models—occupy a special position in their respective areas, leading some to speak of subimperialisms, we feel our selection on this account is justified.

Save for the deliberate exclusion of countries with no prior democratic or semidemocratic experience, or no prospect of an opening to freedom, our study encompasses virtually every type of democratic experience in the developing world. As the decade turns, several of the cases in this book can be classified as democratic, albeit with some important qualifications (India, Turkey, Brazil, and South Korea); some are semidemocratic but moving in different directions (Thailand toward greater democracy, Zimbabwe toward less); and two are authoritarian military regimes embarked on transitions to democracy, with Chile transferring power to an elected civilian president (but not yet fully repealing military prerogatives), while Nigeria is not scheduled to reach the same point until October 1992. Although its democratic institutions and cultural commitments have been wearing thin over the past twenty years, India's democracy has persisted for four decades (interrupted only by Indira Gandhi's emergency rule from 1975 to 1977). The democracies in Turkey, Brazil, South Korea, and now Chile, are only recently renewed after long, traumatic periods of authoritarian rule or, in Turkey's case, unstable alternation between civilian-democratic and military regimes. From these cycles of regime change, Turkey has managed to emerge with a generally longer and more-successful democratic experience than has Thailand or Nigeria, although the increasing historical and political distance from its last successful coup in 1977 suggests that Thailand may be well on the road to the institutionalization of a stable (if not yet fully democratic) parliamentary regime.

• CONCEPTS, DEFINITIONS, AND CLASSIFICATIONS •

Depending on the individual, ideology, paradigm, culture, or context, democracy may mean many different things. It is reflective of the political climate of our time that the word is used to signify the desirable end-state of many social, economic, and political pursuits, or else to self-designate and thus presumably legitimate many existing structures. Hence, it is imperative to be as precise as possible about exactly what is being studied.

The term *democracy* is used in this book to signify a political system, separate and apart from the economic and social system to which it is joined. Indeed, a distinctive aspect of our approach is to insist that issues of so-called "economic and social democracy" be separated from the question of governmental structure. Otherwise, the definitional criteria of democracy will be so broadened and the empirical reality narrowed to a degree that makes study of the phenomenon very difficult. In addition, unless the economic and social dimensions are kept conceptually distinct from the political, there is no way to analyze how variation on the political dimension is related to variation on the others. Most of all, we distinguish the concept of political democracy out of a clear and frankly expressed conviction that it is worth valuing—and hence worth studying—as an end in itself.

In this book, then, democracy—or what Robert Dahl terms *polyarchy*—denotes a system of government that meets three essential conditions: meaningful and extensive *competition* among individuals and organized groups (especially political parties) for all effective positions of government power, at regular intervals and excluding the use of force; a "highly inclusive" level of *political participation* in the selection of leaders and policies, at least through regular and fair elections, such that no major (adult) social group is excluded; and a level of *civil and political liberties*—freedom of expression, freedom of the press, freedom to form and join organizations—sufficient to ensure the integrity of political competition and participation.[6]

While this definition is, in itself, relatively straightforward, it presents a number of problems in application. For one, countries that broadly satisfy these criteria nevertheless do so to different degrees (and none do so perfectly, which is why Dahl prefers to call them polyarchies). The factors that explain this variation at the democratic end of the spectrum in degrees of popular control and freedom is an important intellectual problem, but it is different from the one that concerns us in this book, and so it is one we have had largely to bypass. We seek to determine why countries do or do not evolve, consolidate, maintain, lose, and reestablish more or less democratic systems of government, and even this limited focus leaves us with conceptual problems.

The boundary between democratic and undemocratic is sometimes blurred and imperfect, and beyond it lies a much broader range of variation in political systems. We readily concede the difficulties of classification this variation has repeatedly caused us. Even if we look only at the political, legal, and constitutional structures, several of our cases appear to lie somewhere on the boundary between democratic and something less than democratic. The ambiguity is further complicated by the constraints on free political activity, organization, and expression, and the substantial remaining political prerogatives of military authorities, that may in practice make the system much less democratic than it might appear. In all cases, we have tried to pay serious attention to actual practice in assessing and classifying regimes. But still, this leaves us to make difficult and in some ways arbitrary judgments. The decision as to whether Thailand and Zimbabwe, for example, may today be considered full democracies is replete with nuance and ambiguity. Even in the case of Brazil, which was generally presumed democratic after the election of a civilian president in 1985, Alfred Stepan cautions that the extent of military prerogatives to participate in government and wield autonomous power put the country "on the margin of not being a democracy."[7] With the direct presidential election of December 1989, the transition may now be considered closed, but serious problems of democratic consolidation remain.

We have alleviated the problem somewhat by recognizing various grades of distinction among less than democratic systems. While isolated violations of civil liberties or modest and occasional vote-rigging should not disqualify a country from broad classification as a democracy, there is a need to categorize separately those countries that allow greater political competition and freedom than would be found in a truly authoritarian regime but less than could justifiably be termed "democratic." Hence, we classify as *semidemocratic* those countries in which the effective power of elected officials is so limited, or political party competition so restricted, or the freedom and fairness of elections so compromised, that electoral outcomes, while competitive, still deviate significantly from popular preferences; or where civil and political liberties are so limited that some political orientations and interests are unable to organize and express themselves. In different ways and to different degrees, Senegal, Zimbabwe, and Thailand fit this category (so would the electoral but still heavily military-dominated regimes in Guatemala and Honduras, for example).

Still more restrictive is a *hegemonic party system,* in which opposition parties are legal but denied, through pervasive electoral malpractices and frequent state coercion, any real chance to compete for power. Such a system has long prevailed under the domination of the Partido Revolucionario Institucional (PRI) in Mexico, but the political reforms of the 1980s and especially the unprecedented gains of both right and left opposition parties in the 1988 elections, discussed by Daniel Levy in his chapter, justify a reclassification of the Mexican system as a "semidemocracy."

Descending further on our scale of classification, *authoritarian* regimes permit even less pluralism, typically banning political parties (or all but the ruling one) and most forms of political organization and competition, while being more repressive than liberal in their level of civil and political freedom. Paying close attention to actual behavior, one may distinguish a subset of authoritarian regimes that we call *pseudodemocracies* because the existence of formally democratic political institutions, such as multiparty electoral competition, masks (often in part to legitimate) the reality of authoritarian domination. Central America has long lived under such regimes. While this regime type overlaps in some ways with the hegemonic regime, it is less institutionalized and typically more personalized, coercive, and unstable.

Democratic trappings aside, authoritarian regimes vary widely in the degree to which they permit independent and critical political expression and organization. Judging by the level of what the regime allows, one can distinguish between what Guillermo O'Donnell and Philippe Schmitter call "dictablandas," or liberalized autocracies, and "dictaduras," harsher dictatorships that allow much less space for individual and group action.[8] Classifying by the level of what groups in the society recurrently demand (which may or may not overlap with what the regime allows), one can distinguish between authoritarian situations with strong democratic pressures and those with weak democratic pressures. In selecting cases for this book, our bias was toward the former.

Finally, of course, are the *totalitarian* regimes, which not only repress all forms of autonomous social and political organization, denying completely even the most elementary political and civil liberties, but also demand the active commitment of citizens to the regime.[9] With the decay, collapse, or at least partial liberalization of most of the world's Communist regimes in the late 1980s, it is debatable whether the totalitarian distinction is any longer salient. Nevertheless, the totalitarian legacy shapes in distinctive ways the possibilities and conditions for democratization even in a post-totalitarian age, and what seemed in 1984 the dim possibilities for imminent transitions from communism led us to exclude all of these systems from our larger comparative study.[10]

The "dependent variable" of our study was concerned not only with democracy but also stability—the persistence and durability of democratic and other regimes over time, particularly through periods of unusually intense conflict, crisis and strain. A *stable* regime is one that is deeply institutionalized and consolidated, making it likely to enjoy a high level of popular legitimacy. *Partially stable* regimes are neither fully secure nor in imminent danger of collapse. Their institutions have perhaps acquired some measure of depth, flexibility, and value, but not enough to ensure them safe passage through severe challenges. *Unstable* regimes are, by definition, highly vulnerable to breakdown or overthrow in periods of acute uncertainty and stress. New regimes, including those that have recently restored democratic government, tend to fall in this category.

• FACILITATING AND OBSTRUCTING FACTORS FOR DEMOCRATIC DEVELOPMENT •

Legitimacy and Performance

All governments rest on some mixture of coercion and consent, but democracies are unique in the degree to which their stability depends on the consent of a majority of those governed. So intimately is legitimacy tied to democratic stability that it is difficult to know where definition ends and theorizing begins. Almost as a given, theories of democracy stress that democratic stability requires a widespread belief among elites and masses in the legitimacy of the democratic system: that it is the best form of government (or the "least evil"), "that in spite of shortcomings and failures, the existing political institutions are better than any others that might be established," and hence that the democratic regime is morally entitled to demand obedience—to tax and draft, to make laws and enforce them, even "if necessary, by the use of force."[11]

Democratic legitimacy derives, when it is most stable and secure, from an instrinsic value commitment rooted in the political culture at all levels of society, but it is also shaped (particularly in the early years of a democracy) by the performance of the democratic regime, both economically and politically (through the "maintenance of civil order, personal security, adjudication and arbitration of conflicts, and a minimum of predictability in the making and implementation of decisions").[12] Historically, the more successful a regime has been in providing what people want, the greater and more deeply rooted tends to be its legitimacy: A long record of successful performance tends to build a large reservoir of legitimacy, enabling the system better to endure crises and challenges.[13] As Arturo Valenzuela shows here in the case of Chile, however, such a long accumulation of democratic legitimacy does not confer immunity from breakdown and can be squandered with great speed by a combination of poor leadership, wrong choices, and outmoded political institutions.

Regimes that lack deep legitimacy depend more precariously on current performance and are vulnerable to collapse in periods of economic and social distress.[14] This has been a particular problem for democratic (as well as undemocratic) regimes in the developing world, given especially their tendency to experience an interaction of low legitimacy and low effectiveness. Because of the combination of widespread poverty and the strains imposed by modernization, regimes that begin with low legitimacy also find it difficult to perform effectively, and regimes that lack effectiveness, especially in economic growth, find it difficult to build legitimacy. Our own studies and many others caution against drawing too deterministic a linkage between the economic performance of democratic regimes and the probability of their survival. Nevertheless, the correlation remains both obvious and understandable.

While they have not been immune to problems of recession, inflation, and corruption, the more successful democracies in our study have generally experienced relatively steady economic growth, which in turn has benefited their legitimacy. Often this is traceable not (just) to sound policies but to the bounty of highly marketable natural resources, but the dangers of such dependence (and the free-wheeling, populist neglect of savings and investment to raise productive capacities that often accompanies it) are substantial. These were revealed in Venezuela, for example, in early 1989 when the public erupted into violent rioting over the imposition by President Carlos Andres Pérez of harsh austerity measures, necessitated by the decline in oil revenues and by decades of overspending and overborrowing.[15]

An important determinant of steadily successful economic performance, however, is policy. Botswana has benefited from great natural resources and high levels of foreign aid, but underlying its development performance have been sound policies and effective management (which have helped attract foreign aid). State policies have not strangled producers of agricultural exports (in this case, cattle) as they did in much of the rest of tropical Africa. The state has prudently invested in basic infrastructure, and the elite has kept an effective lid on political and administrative corruption. Parastatals have been managed efficiently, and efforts have been made to distribute growth through state investment in education, housing, health, and other social services; unusually effective food distribution programs to relieve the effects of drought; and improvement of wages in the formal sector.[16] This record of performance contrasts markedly with the bloated, predatory state structures, widespread corruption, and ill-designed, poorly implemented development policies that sucked the economic breath from putative democratic republics in Nigeria and elsewhere in Africa.

Although it is often presumed to have done poorly in delivering material progress, India has actually achieved significant, if incremental, socioeconomic development, and would have done much better had its population not doubled in the past three decades to 800 million people. As Jyotirindra Das Gupta observes, since independence India has "experienced a partial renovation of agricultural production leading to self-sufficiency in food, developed a structure of industrialization that produces most products that the country needs, expanded the supply of educated and technical personnel . . . , consistently held down the level of inflation to one of the lowest in the world, and in the process ensured a level of self-reliance and payment ability that kept it away from debt crisis." Ample evidence for these claims may be found in Table 1.1, which demonstrates the steady economic and social gains India has continued to make since the mid-1960s, significantly improving such crucial social indicators as education and life expectancy (to among the highest levels for low-income countries) while restraining inflation and foreign borrowing (as a percentage of gross national product (GNP), India's foreign debt burden is the lowest of any of the ten cases in this book). High levels of poverty and inequality remain, along with a need to rationalize the highly inefficient public sector, but such economic prudence and steady development progress, which has dramatically expanded the size of the middle class in a generation, may be one of the least appreciated foundations of India's democratic persistence.

It appears that consistency, prudence, and moderation in economic policy, as in politics, are conducive to democratic stability. In Colombia, eclectic, pragmatic, undoctrinaire economic policies produced steady economic growth with low inflation, following the transition to democracy in 1957. Colombia's flexibility and pragmatism, which motivated a relatively early partial reorientation of the economy from import substitution to export promotion, enabled it to avoid some of the disastrous experiences in import substitution and sharp pendular swings in policy (between populism and radical neoliberalism) that so devastated the economies of Chile, Argentina, Peru, and Uruguay.[17]

As Table 1.1 suggests, a similar emphasis on prudent and consistent economic policies, and on controlling inflation, fiscal deficits, and foreign borrowing (with a particular emphasis on export promotion) has produced an impressive record of economic growth in Thailand, which at the beginning of the 1990s ranks as one of the most dynamic economies in the world, growing at an annual rate of 9–10 percent. While it is accentuating problems of corruption and inequality, rapid economic growth in Thailand is producing many of the same social forces for democratization that arose in South Korea and Taiwan during the 1960s, 1970s, and 1980s: the expansion of autonomous (and increasingly politically conscious) entrepreneurial and professional middle classes (including social scientists and intellectuals); the movement of labor into manufacturing, furthering the differentiation and organization of the urban sector; and improvements in literacy, education, and communication, which bring much wider circulation of people,

Table 1.1. Selected Development Indicators, 1965–1987[a]

	Chile 1965	Chile 1987	Brazil 1965	Brazil 1987	Mexico 1965	Mexico 1987	Turkey 1965	Turkey 1987
Civil and Political Liberties, 1975 & 1989[b]	12	7	8	4	7	7	5	6
Population in Millions, 1966 & 1987	8.7	12.5	86.5	141.4	44.9	81.9	31.9	52.60
Population Growth Rate, 1965–1980 & 1980–1987	1.7	1.7	2.4	2.2	3.1	2.2	2.5	2.3
Projected Rate of Population Growth, 1987–2000		1.4		1.8		1.9		1.9
Projected Population in Millions, 2000 & 2025	15	19	178	234	105	141	67	90
Current GNP per Capita in US Dollars,[c] 1966 & 1987	740	1310	280	2020	490	1830	310	1210
Average Annual Growth Rate, GNP per Capita, in Percentages, 1965–1987		0.2		4.1		2.5		2.6
Average Annual Growth Rate of GDP, 1965–1980 & 1980–1987	**1.9**	**1.0**	**9.0**	**3.3**	**6.5**	**0.5**	**6.3**	**5.2**
Average Annual Rate of Inflation, 1965–1980 & 1980–1987	129.9	20.6	31.3	166.3	13.0	68.9	20.7	37.4
Urban Population as Percentage of Total[d]	**72**	**85**	**50**	**75**	**55**	**71**	**34**	**47**
Percentage of Labor Force in Agriculture, 1965 & 1980	27	17	49	31	50	37	75	58
Life Expectancy at Birth								
Male	**56**	**68**	**55**	**62**	**58**	**65**	**52**	**63**
Female	**62**	**75**	**59**	**68**	**61**	**72**	**55**	**66**
Infant Mortality Rate per 1,000 Births	103	20	105	63	82	47	165	76
Percentage Enrolled in Primary School, 1965 & 1986[e]	**124**	**110**	**108**	**105**	**92**	**114**	**101**	**117**
Percentage Enrolled in Secondary School, 1965 & 1986	34	70	16	36	17	55	16	44
Total External Public Debt as Percentage of GNP, 1970 & 1987	**25.8**	**89.4**	**8.2**	**29.1**	**8.7**	**59.5**	**14.7**	**46.6**

Sources: World Bank, *World Development Report 1983, 1987, 1989* (New York, Oxford University Press, 1983, 1987, 1989); World Bank, *World Tables 1987*, 4th ed. (Washington, DC: World Bank, 1987); and (for the ratings of political and civil liberties) Raymond D. Gastil, *Freedom in the World: Political Rights and Civil Liberties 1987–88* (Lanham, MD: University Press of America, 1988), and *Freedom at Issue* 112 (January–February 1990), with permission of Freedom House.

a The figures are for the years 1965 and 1987, unless otherwise indicated in the labels for each row.

b Combined score of civil and political liberties, each rated on a 1 to 7 scale with 1 being freest and 7 least free. A score of 5 or less (with a 2 on political rights) is regarded as "free," 6 to 11 as partly free, and 12 to 14 as "not free."

India 1965	India 1987	Thailand 1965	Thailand 1987	South Korea 1965	South Korea 1987	Nigeria 1965	Nigeria 1987	Senegal 1965	Senegal 1987	Zimbabwe 1965	Zimbabwe 1987
5	5	8	5	11	5	10	11	11	7	11	10
498.8	797.5	32.0	53.6	29.5	42.1	60.0	106.6	4.0	7.0	4.5	9.0
2.3	2.1	2.9	2.0	2.0	1.4	2.5	3.4	2.5	2.9	3.1	3.7
	1.8		1.5		1.0		3.0		3.1		3.0
1010	1365	65	82	48	56	157	286	10	20	13	22
90	300	150	850	130	2690	70	370	210	520	220	580
	1.8		3.9		6.4		1.1		-0.6		0.9
3.7	**4.6**	**7.2**	**5.6**	**9.5**	**8.6**	**6.9**	**-1.7**	**2.1**	**3.3**	**4.4**	**2.4**
7.6	7.7	6.3	2.8	18.8	5.0	13.7	10.1	6.5	9.1	6.4	12.4
19	**27**	**13**	**21**	**32**	**69**	**17**	**33**	**33**	**37**	**14**	**26**
73	70	82	71	55	36	72	68	83	81	79	73
46	**58**	**53**	**63**	**55**	**66**	**40**	**49**	**40**	**46**	**46**	**56**
44	**58**	**58**	**66**	**58**	**73**	**43**	**53**	**42**	**49**	**49**	**60**
151	99	90	39	64	25	179	105	172	128	104	72
74	**92**	**78**	**99**	**101**	**94**	**32**	**92^f**	**40**	**55**	**110**	**129**
27	35	14	29	35	95	5	29^f	7	13	6	46
14.7	**15.1**	**4.6**	**29.6**	**20.3**	**20.7**	**3.4**	**109.8**	**11.9**	**68.3**	**15.5**	**36.2**

[c] GNP per capita is expressed in current U.S. dollars for each year. Comparison between 1966 and 1987 figures therefore is not controlled for (U.S.) inflation.

[d] Because these estimates (taken from UN data) are based on different national definitions of what is urban, cross-country comparisons should be interpreted with caution.

[e] In some countries with universal primary education, the gross enrollment ratios may exceed 100 percent because some pupils are younger or older than the country's standard primary school age.

[f] Figure is for 1983.

information, and ideas. Together, these changes increase the proportion of the population desiring political liberalization, draw the country increasingly into contact and exchange with the advanced, industrialized democracies, and enhance the resources and skills necessary for people to organize autonomously to pursue their interests, as Sung-joo Han explains for the case of South Korea.[18]

Such changes help us to understand why authoritarian (especially military) regimes do not derive from successful economic performance the same enduring benefits for their legitimacy that democratic regimes do. Unlike democratic regimes, most authoritarian regimes are not intrinsically applauded and admired for their organization of power. Rather, their monopoly of power, and their limitation and repression of political and civil liberties, is accepted by the people only to achieve some higher good (economic growth, socialism, the Islamic society, utopia). Such regimes, therefore,

> face a legitimacy contradiction, a kind of catch-22. If they do not perform, they lose legitimacy because performance is their only justification for holding power. However, like South Korea or Peru (under Valasco's reformist military rule), if they do perform in delivering socioeconomic progress, they tend to refocus popular aspirations around political goals for voice and participation that they cannot satisfy without terminating their existence. Similarly, if they succeed in meeting the critical threat or challenge (e.g., subversion, terrorism, political violence) that justified their seizure of power, they become dispensable, just as the generation of new challenges and interests with the passing of time makes them, with their inability to adapt, irrelevant.[19]

At the same time, democracies also have their peculiar vulnerabilities. One of these is the particularly corrosive effect of corruption on the legitimacy of democratic regimes, even more than of authoritarian ones. This is so in part because under conditions of freedom, with competitive elections, an independent judiciary, an opposition in parliament, and a free press, corruption is likely to be more visible than under authoritarianism. Its scale and its extension to the whole democratic political class—as has repeatedly occurred in Ghana and Nigeria, for example—delegitimize the whole political system rather than disqualifying a particular politician or party. Further, the prevalence of political corruption as the primary motive for the pursuit of power (because of the dominance of the state over economic life) reduces the political process to a struggle for power rather than a debate about policies, and taints the electoral process while generating cynical and apathetic responses in the electorate (or at least the bulk of it outside patronage networks). Such widespread corruption also undermines economic development and is one of the major arguments used by the military to justify its overthrow of elected governments, even though its own corruption will likely be as great or greater in time.[20]

Political Leadership

While our theoretical orientation gives substantial emphasis to the importance of various structural factors in shaping the prospects for democracy, these are never wholly determinative. As we have just seen, regime performance and viability, not only economically but politically, are the outcome in part of the policies and choices that political leaders make—acting, to be sure, within the constraints of the structural circumstances they inherit. Even structures and institutions, especially political ones, are shaped by the actions and options of political leaders. The more constraining and unfavorable are the structural circumstances, the more skillful, innovative, courageous, and democratically committed must political leadership be for democracy to survive. Even where the obstacles are formidable, democratic breakdowns are not inevitable but are accelerated by poor leadership and bad choices.[21]

In this book, we see the way in which inefficacious, weak, and often militant and uncompromising political leadership has contributed to democratic breakdown in Chile, Brazil, Turkey, South Korea, Thailand, and Nigeria. In some of these cases, it could be argued that structural circumstances were highly unfavorable, but often this was due in part to the failure of politicians to produce needed economic reforms and institutional innovations. Certainly, Valenzuela and Ergun Ozbudun show, for the breakdowns in Chile (1973) and Turkey (1980), how much the miscalculations and intransigence of political leaders contributed.

We see also the importance of strong democratic commitments on the part of political leaders—what Juan Linz calls "loyalty" to the democratic system. Democratically loyal leaders reject the use and rhetoric of violence and illegal or unconstitutional means for the pursuit of power, and they refuse to condone or tolerate antidemocratic actions by other participants.[22] The Nigerian case portrays graphically how electoral violence and fraud, thuggery, demagoguery, and widespread political corruption delegitimated and destroyed the Second Republic—even in the absence of the polarized ethnic conflict that further contributed to the failure of the First Republic. In the case of India, we see the central role of Indira Gandhi's equivocal commitment to democratic values in motivating not only her declaration of emergency rule in 1975 but her centralization and personalization of political power in the preceding years and after her return to power in 1980. Throughout Africa and Asia, the erosion or destruction of democratic institutions has come through the actions of self-aggrandizing, authoritarian elected leaders such as Marcos in the Philippines, Syngman Rhee in South Korea, Nkrumah in Ghana, and Obote in Uganda. This confirms G. Bingham Powell's generalization that democratic breakdown (by executive or military coup) is commonly preceded by "renunciation of the democratic faith by its elected leaders."[23]

The story, of course, is not all negative. Throughout the developing world, flexible, accommodative, consensual leadership styles have contributed notably to democratic development, as in the early years of institution-building under Gandhi and Nehru and a gifted crop of Congress party leaders in India. Accommodating and shrewd political leadership, showing keen timing and some political courage, by Roh Tae Woo in South Korea and Chiang Ching-kuo in Taiwan must be partially credited for the democratic transformations of those two countries in recent years. Similarly, the personal leadership decisions and skills of Leopold Senghor and Abdou Diouf were important, as Christian Coulon shows, in opening up Senegal's politics to more democratic pluralism and competition. Democracy in Colombia and Venezuela came into being as the result of creative negotiation among contending party elites who, learning from past political mistakes, agreed to transcend their rivalries and arrange a sharing of power.[24] Valenzuela shows how important able, democratically committed, and even visionary political leadership was in the founding of democracy in Chile in the early nineteenth century, its adaptation and expansion during periods of turbulent change and growth, and its maintenance during the Great Depression of the 1930s. Demonstrating a different, corollary rule, Levy shows in his case study of Mexico how consistently skilled and effective leadership, with many undemocratic values, contributed to the stability of an undemocratic regime for several decades.

Political Culture

One important dimension of regime performance is the management of conflict. As Seymour Martin Lipset has argued, in a long theoretical tradition dating back to Aristotle, "a stable democracy requires relatively moderate tension among its contending political forces."[25] Here again, democratic regimes require an unusually high degree of effectiveness. As institutionalized systems of competition and conflict, they are especially liable to witness the disintegration of competition into enmity, of conflict into chaos. If political freedom and competition are not to descend into extremism, polarization, and violence, there must be mechanisms to contain conflict within certain behavioral boundaries. One of the most important factors in this regard is a country's political culture; that is, the beliefs and values concerning politics that prevail within both the elite and the mass.

Theorists in the pluralist or liberal tradition identify several values and beliefs as crucial for stable democracy: belief in the legitimacy of democracy; tolerance for opposing parties, beliefs, and preferences; a willingness to compromise with political opponents, and, underlying this, pragmatism and flexibility; some minimum of trust in the political environment, and cooperation, particularly among political competitors; moderation in political positions and partisan identifications; civility of political discourse; and political efficacy and participation—tempered by the addition of two other roles—the subject (which gives allegiance to political authority) and the primordial (which involves the individual in traditional, nonpolitical pursuits).[26] Dahl in particular emphasizes the importance of such a democratic culture among the political elite, especially early on.

Our larger study provides considerable evidence that such presumed features of democratic culture are closely correlated with democratic stability. Those countries that have been the most strongly and stably democratic also appear to have the most democratic political values and beliefs. In Venezuela, survey data on mass beliefs "show consistently strong support for democracy as a political system" and for such basic democratic principles as the legitimacy of elections, open opposition, and open criticism. Moreover, peasants and political leaders alike commonly stress the need for caution, compromise, and conciliation in politics.[27] Similarly, survey data in Costa Rica show broad support for democratic institutions within both elites and masses, and a striving toward compromise and consensus. In particular, the political elite disavows violence and responds to protest and confrontation with moderation and conciliation. Costa Rica also manifests unusually high levels of mass political participation, interest, and awareness, comparable in many respects to the world's most-developed democracies.[28]

Democratic success in developing countries may be traced not only to the growth of democratic values but also to their roots in a country's historical and cultural traditions. Das Gupta points out that from the time of the founding of the Indian National Congress a century ago, "democratic rules of procedure, tolerance of adversaries and reconciliation of conflicting claims became part of the political education of the participants." This liberal tradition was further deepened by Gandhi's emphasis on accommodation, compromise, and nonviolence. In Botswana, the political culture of public discussion, community consensus, and nonviolence is a major foundation of democratic stability. John Holm traces this to the cultural tradition of popular consultation and pursuit of consensus known as the *kgotla*, which the ruling party has amplified through the practice of discussing "all new policies with the local community in *kgotla* before any local implementation."[29]

Ambivalence in a country's political culture is also associated with ambivalence in its experience with democracy. Turkey, Ozbudun tells us, has been torn between a strong consensus on the legitimacy of popular, elective government and the continuing predilection (dating back to Ottoman rule) for organic theories of state, which spawn excessive fear of division, intolerance of political opposition and individual deviation, and a tendency to see politics in absolutist terms. The behavioral manifestations of these values have figured prominently in Turkey's democratic breakdowns. Similarly, as Larry Diamond shows, Nigeria has been torn between a deep and broadly based commitment to political freedom with popular, accountable government, and a weak inclination toward tolerance and accommodation. Twice this contradiction has made for political chaos, violence, and democratic breakdown. In both countries, these cultural tendencies have been shaped in part by the overbearing state.

Coulon shows the correspondence between the "mixed" political culture of Senegal and the semidemocratic character of the regime. Traditional political cultures in Senegal balanced authoritarian values with "a propensity for debate, political game-playing," and constitutional limits on monarchical authority. Liberal, Western cultural influences further press in a democratic direction, but this is undermined by the lack of support for democracy among the neglected and alienated lower classes and the growing interest in authoritarian Islamic doctrines felt by a segment of the elite. Chai-Anan Samudavanija suggests that repeated military intervention in the politics of Thailand derives in part from a military conception of democracy that values "national security, stability, and order" over freedom and participation, and dislikes pressure groups and conflict. And, as Masipula Sithole demonstrates, the violence and instability of democratic politics in postindependence Zimbabwe owes much to a political culture that, despite its appreciation in principle for democratic institutions, bears the scars of the "intolerant, violent, and commandist" culture of the liberation struggle.

Strong democratic currents in a country's political culture may make it very difficult for an authoritarian regime to institutionalize its rule. The instability of dictatorial rule in Nigeria can be traced in part to the popular devotion to political freedom, which has made it impossible for any military regime to survive long in power without committing itself to a firm date for transition to civilian, elected government. Authoritarian rule was never really accepted in the Philippines as a long-term proposition because of that country's commitment to democratic values and traditions—in contrast to Indonesia and Thailand, for example.[30] In Uruguay, the military's failure to perpetuate authoritarian rule was due in part to "the resilience of the democratic political culture permeating even the armed forces, and the inhospitable climate for authoritarian discourse."[31] A similar observation could be made of Chile.

Social Structure and Socioeconomic Development

The favorable effects of a democratic political culture are reinforced by social structures that minimize the possibility of social and political polarization. In particular, many theorists have argued that socioeconomic development changes fundamentally the way in which individuals and groups relate to the political process. An advanced level of economic development, producing greater economic security and more-widespread education, is assumed to reduce socioeconomic inequality and mitigate feelings of relative deprivation and injustice in the lower class, thus reducing the likelihood of extremist politics.[32] Increased national wealth also tends to enlarge the middle class, which has long been associated in political theory with moderation, tolerance, and democracy.[33]

Over the past three decades, a large number of quantitative analyses have supported the thesis of a positive relationship between socioeconomic development and democracy. Theoretically, the more interesting question now is not whether the relationship exists but how it is manifested over time. As Samuel Huntington has argued, while modernity tends eventually to bring democratic stability, the process of modernization may be destabilizing: "Social and economic change—urbanization, increases in literacy and education, industrialization, mass media expansion—extend political consciousness, multiply political demands, broaden political participation."[34] Political institutions must expand and adapt to incorporate this increasing (and increasingly autonomous) participation or risk breaking down. Thus, the relationship is best framed in probabilistic terms: "As countries develop economically, they can be conceived of moving into a zone of transition or choice, in which traditional forms of rule become increasingly difficult to maintain and new types of political institutions are required to aggregate the demands of an increasingly complex society."[35] Whether the new institutions chosen are democratic—and whether, if chosen, democratic institutions can be maintained—depends on a host of other factors.

The evidence indicates that the most common and in the long run probably the most important effect of rapid socioeconomic development under authoritarian rule has been to generate pressures and create social structural conditions more conducive to democracy. At different historical periods and to different degrees, this has been true of Brazil, Costa Rica, the Dominican Republic, Peru, Thailand, Taiwan, and South Korea. In addition, an important foundation for democracy in Peru and especially (much earlier) in Taiwan was generated by land reforms and other steps that reduced socioeconomic inequality, eliminated semifeudal relations, and created a significant middle peasantry. (Because Peru's reforms were insufficiently extensive and sustained, however, poverty and regional and class inequalities continue to threaten its democratic future). Similarly, in South Korea the social reform and substantial improvement in the welfare of lower-income groups that accompanied rapid growth stimulated political consciousness and democratic opposition. Of course, slow or negative growth has also helped to destabilize and bring down authoritarian regimes, as in the Philippines and Haiti, but changes made under such conditions do not bode so well for the future of democracy.

Socioeconomic inequality. Comparative evidence supports the proposition that democracy and socioeconomic equality are related. In particular, deep, cumulative social inequalities represent a poor foundation for democracy. Historically, this has been a contributing factor to the instability of democracy in much of Latin America, including the Dominican Republic and Peru, and most of Central America. By contrast, the historic absence of *hacienda* agriculture and large landholdings in Costa Rica, and the shortage of agricultural labor that kept rural wages high, bred an egalitarian social culture and what John Booth terms an "interdependence among classes" that helped significantly to foster the development of democracy.[36]

Perhaps nowhere in the coming years will inequality pose a more acute and urgent problem for democracy than in Brazil, where the wealthiest tenth of the population controls a higher percentage of income (about half) than in any other country for which the World Bank reports data.[37] Bolívar Lamounier shows that the marked failure to reduce inequality was an important structural factor weakening the democratic system and contributing to its breakdown in 1964. As Brazil has become even more urbanized and socially mobilized in the past quarter-century—while income inequality and, by some accounts, even absolute poverty worsened, despite the stunning overall rates of economic growth under military rule—"deconcentration" of wealth has become imperative, Lamounier maintains, for democratic consolidation. And yet, policies to reduce inequality, such as land reform, carry serious short-term political risks, while reducing absolute poverty requires long-term policy commitments that may be politically difficult to sustain. The potential polarizing effects of inequality in Brazil have recently been evidenced in the growth of urban labor militancy and strife, violent rural land conflicts, and electoral support for populist and radical candidates, including labor leader Luis Inácio (Lula) da Silva, who finished second to free-market advocate Fernando Collor de Mello in the December 1989 run-off presidential election.

Population growth.   A socioeconomic problem that is often overlooked in evaluating democratic performance and prospects is that of rapid population growth. Although birthrates do tend to decline with higher standards of living and improved socioeconomic opportunities for women (as suggested by the data in Table 1.1), population growth rates nevertheless remain high in most of Asia, Latin America, and, especially, Africa. Even if countries reduce these annual growth rates down toward 2 percent, as Brazil, Mexico, Turkey, Thailand, and India (nearly) managed to do in the 1980s, populations will *double* in thirty-five years or less. With populations growing annually at rates closer to 3.5 percent, as in Nigeria, Zimbabwe, and some other African countries, the doubling time is reduced to about twenty years. In countries with such rapid growth rates, the age structure is heavily tilted toward children and adolescents, with 40 to 50 percent of the population typically under fifteen years of age.[38] Thus, not only is there a much larger dependent population to be cared for, schooled, and ultimately somehow gainfully employed, but there is a hidden momentum to population growth that will only be fully felt when these children in turn bear children of their own—even if social, economic, and cultural conditions are by then transformed so that they do so only at the rate of replacement fertility (i.e., two children per couple).

The political consequences of such rapid population growth follow closely, but not entirely, from the economic ones. To the extent that its population is growing rapidly, a country's economic growth each year is absorbed in providing for its additional people at existing levels of nutrition, schooling, health care, and so on, rather than improving per capita standards. Thus, improvement in per capita income and services—in *real* standard of living—lags well behind the gross gains in national income. The annual increments of population are often quite large in absolute terms: at current growth rates, more than 3 million additional people each year in Nigeria and Brazil; more than a million a year in Turkey and Thailand; more than 16 million annually in India. And increasingly, as these countries also become more urbanized, these burgeoning numbers are concentrated in the cities. To the extent that economic growth is rapid enough to provide adequate schooling, training, jobs, and opportunities for these young populations, political stability may not be affected, and population growth rates will decline to the more manageable levels (1 percent or less) found in the advanced industrial countries. But only in South Korea, among our cases, is this projected to occur in the next decade, although birthrates are forecast to approach this reduced level in Chile and Thailand as well (see Table 1.1). In the seven other cases in this book, population growth in the next decade is expected to remain near 2 percent or higher, generating exploding economic and political demands and expectations that these systems will be hard pressed to meet. The problem is exacerbated by substantial economic inequality, since the poor typically have higher birthrates while being less able to provide for their children's future.

If current assumptions are not altered, the resulting stagnation, frustration, and political turmoil may be blamed on economic mismanagement, but rapid population growth should not be overlooked as a contributing factor. National programs to foster family planning and population consciousness must be accelerated—along with efforts to improve health care and education for women and the poor—if population growth rates are to be slowed sufficiently to allow these developing countries a reasonable chance to consolidate and maintain stable democratic government.

Associational Life

Both theoretical work, going back to Alexis de Tocqueville, and empirical evidence argue strongly for the importance to stable democracy of a pluralistic, autonomous, vigorously organized civil society that can balance and limit state power while providing additional channels for the articulation and practice of democratic interests. A rich associational life can supplement the role of political parties in stimulating political participation, increasing citizens' efficacy, recruiting and training political leaders, and enhancing commitment to the democratic system.[39] In each of the three countries in our twenty-six–nation study that have enjoyed the most successful experience with democracy in the past few decades—India, Costa Rica, and Venezuela—a vigorous network of autonomous and increasingly sophisticated voluntary associations has been an important foundation of democratic stability and robustness.

From its earliest beginnings in the nationalist mobilization against colonial rule a century ago, democracy in India has been invigorated by the presence of a rich array of voluntary associations directed to language reform, legal reform, educational modernization, defense of press freedom, civil liberties, and women's rights. While strong trade unions and peasant, student, and business associations today often align with political parties, they also act autonomously to pursue their own interests, and this political autonomy has increased as new leadership groups within them give greater emphasis to economic issues. In addition, notes Das Gupta, the Indian scene is today replete with a vast network of issue-oriented movements, "bringing together various parties, groups, and concerned publics" in aggressive campaigns for social and political reform. Indeed, as formal political institutions have deteriorated in the past two decades, India's associational life has become an increasingly crucial resource for democratic articulation and accountability.

Where associational life is dense, institutionalized, and autonomous, it may also undermine authoritarian rule and generate effective pressure for democratization, as was dramatically evidenced during 1985–1986 in the Philippines. There (where 95 percent of the population is Catholic) the Catholic church was the one institution that Marcos was not able to co-opt in his two decades in power, and it proved to be a vital source of protest against government repression and abuse of power. Associations of lawyers, intellectuals, and students also helped to keep democratic aspirations alive and, with key segments of the modern business community, joined the church in the broad popular mobilization that ultimately brought down the Marcos dictatorship. Throughout Latin America in the 1970s and 1980s, the Catholic church has played a similar role in opposition to political tyranny and in defense of social and political pluralism. And in South Korea, the Protestant denominations, along with the much smaller but still-influential Catholic church, endorsed and gave encouragement to the campaign for an end to authoritarian rule. One asset of religious institutions in the struggle for political freedom and pluralism is the special moral legitimacy they have almost by definition, but religious institutions may also be advantaged by the fact that they are less explicitly politically self-interested in character than are other types of interest groups that seek rewards and resources from the state.

In Nigeria, efforts to sustain authoritarian rule in the 1970s, and to deepen its repressive character under the military regime of General Buhari (1984–1985), were frustrated by the vigilance and organizational strength of the press, the bar association, student groups, trade unions, business associations, and intellectuals and opinion leaders. These groups were responsible for the popular resistance to authoritarian decrees that helped precipitate Buhari's downfall in a coup, and they have exerted similar pressure on his military successor, Ibrahim Babangida, for liberal and accountable government. The assertive and extensively organized civil society is probably the single most-important force holding the military regime to its stated commitment to withdraw from power in 1992. More generally, sub-Saharan Africa has been experiencing a promising, and in some countries prodigious, efflorescence of informal participation as a result of the growth of independent associational life. Although this development has come in response to the pervasive abuse of state power and what Naomi Chazan calls the disengagement of the state from society, it has important democratic implications. Many of the emerging popular organizations provide "small-scale settings for meaningful political participation," constitutional means for the transfer and rotation of power, consultative processes of decisionmaking, and "innovative means of information collection and communication."[40] Collectively, they constitute a major means for the creation of an informed, efficacious, and vigilant citizenry, and for the reconstruction—from the ground up—of democratic political processes.

As a strong and autonomous associational life may buttress or foster democracy, so the absence of a vigorous sector of voluntary associations and interest groups, or the control of such organizations by a corporatist state, may reinforce authoritarian rule and obstruct the development of democracy. Perhaps the classic demonstration of this in our study is Mexico, where, as Levy points out, the early encapsulation of mass organizations (especially of peasants and workers) by a hegemonic ruling party has been an important foundation of the stability of the authoritarian regime, and where the struggle of labor and other popular movements to break free of corporatist controls is now critical to the struggle for democracy. In Thailand, and many other Asian countries as well, state corporatist controls have stunted the development of autonomous associational life, and thus of democracy.

State and Society

One of the crucial problems for democratic theory is how to restrain the power of the state so that its incumbents remain responsive and accountable to the people. This is why so much emphasis is appropriately given to the need for a pluralistic, independent associational life. But, as with other factors, the relationship between state and society must manifest a certain balance if democracy is to be viable. The state must not become too powerful and autonomous, but if it is too weak and easily penetrated it may be unable to deliver the social and economic goods that groups expect or to maintain order in the face of conflicting group demands. The state bureaucracy must be subjected to democratic control by elected politicians, but at the same time the relative autonomy and continuity of the bureaucracy constitute an important check on the potential for patronage and corruption, and for absolute and arbitrary power, by party politicians.

A problem for democracy in some Asian countries, such as Thailand and

South Korea, has been the excessive power of the state, and its bureaucratic and coercive institutions, in relation to civil society. In Thailand, the dominance for the past half-century of central and highly centralized bureaucratic institutions—with the military in an increasingly ascendant position—discouraged the development of strong and autonomous interest groups, village associations, and political parties. When these did begin to emerge, they were co-opted or overrun by the bureaucracy and by the military, which extended its control into vast sectors of society, including the mass media, rural development, and civic education. A similar historical process was at work in South Korea, with a similar effect: The weakness of independent civic institutions created both the opportunity and the justification for continued military-bureaucratic intervention and control. Although the trend abated in both countries during the late 1980s, as the process of socioeconomic development gives new organizational resources and momentum to independent interests, repealing state corporatist controls over the flow of information and the expression and organization of diverse interests remains an important priority for the thorough and lasting democratization of these societies.

Among the most important dimensions of the state-society relationship is the strong tendency we find for state dominance over the economy and society to undermine democratic politics in developing countries. In the least developed region, sub-Saharan Africa, this tendency has been most powerful because there the state's extensive ownership and mediation of socioeconomic resources and rewards is not counterbalanced by private means of economic accumulation and opportunity. Hence, upward social mobility and the accumulation of personal wealth depend on getting and maintaining control of, or at least access to, the state.[41] This raises the premium on political power to the point where no competing party or candidate is willing to entertain the prospect of defeat. The result is a zero-sum game—the politics of intolerance, desperation, violence, and fraud.[42]

This zero-sum character of politics in the swollen African state has heavily motivated the postindependence drive by ruling parties and elites to monopolize power in such countries as Senegal and helps to explain the current unwillingness of the political bosses of Senegal's ruling Socialist Party to allow the opposition parties a fully free and fair chance to compete for power. In Nigeria, where most of the country's wealth is mediated through government contracts, jobs, licenses, development projects, and other state largesse, it has been a primary factor underlying the failure of both the First and Second republics. Ozbudun notes a similar effect in Turkey, where public enterprises proliferated to the point where they produced about half of Turkey's industrial output. The ruling party's access to such immense resources in relation to the resource base of society, and the clientelistic traditions that give the political class wide scope in distributing state resources, made being out of power in Turkey very costly. This in turn helped to generate the political polarization and unwillingness to compromise that have repeatedly destabilized democratic regimes. Statism also intensifies ethnic political conflict in Africa and Asia. The fact that the state is the biggest employer in Sri Lanka, for example, has heightened the stakes in the ethnic struggle and made accommodation (and so the reequilibration of democracy) more difficult.[43]

Excessive state control over the economy and society may also reduce democratic regime performance in two important respects. As we have already implied, it feeds corruption. And, throughout the world, the evidence is accumulating that huge public sectors and pervasive state subsidies and controls have hampered economic efficiency and come to represent a major obstacle to vigorous economic growth. This has become increasingly apparent in India, where state ownership has led to higher waste of capital and labor, to corruption, and to a heavy drag of unprofitable, inefficient state enterprises, depressing growth potential. Similar problems exist in many other countries, including such prominent examples as Turkey, Mexico, Nigeria, Senegal, the Philippines, and Argentina. It is probably no coincidence that the country in Latin America that has done the most to prune back state control of its economy and open it to national and international market forces—Chile—also showed the most robust economic performance in the final years of the 1980s; a fact not lost on its neighbors or even on the bulk of the democratic opposition to the dictatorship.

One must be cautious, however, about drawing blanket conclusions. There are cases, such as Costa Rica, Botswana, and Uruguay, where extensive state economic ownership and control has not had such destructive consequences for democracy. But each of these countries has had institutional mechanisms or sociocultural traditions (like those in the European social democracies) that have tended to insulate the state from brazen partisan abuse and widespread corruption.

Political Institutions

Constitutional and party structures play an important role in shaping the conflict-regulating capacity of democratic systems. While these conditions of political structure are not intrinsically necessary for stable democracy, they become particularly significant as social, cultural, and economic conditions become less favorable.

Parties and party systems.   Political scientists have long debated the ideal number of parties for stable democracy. Lipset considers the two-party system most likely to produce moderation, accommodation, and aggregation of diverse interests because it compels each party to fashion broad political appeals, in contrast to the strident and ideological appeals small parties tend to make in a multiparty system in order to consolidate and mobilize their limited bases.[44] However, the two-party system requires crosscutting cleavages; if the two-party cleavage coincides with other accumulated cleavages (such as ethnicity and religion), it might so further polarize conflict as to produce democratic breakdown and civil strife.[45] Linz and Giovanni Sartori draw the distinction instead between moderate (with fewer than five relevant parties) and extreme, polarized multiparty systems, the latter increasing significantly the probability of democratic breakdown.[46] Yet Powell argues, from empirical examination of twenty-nine democracies over time, that a "representational" party system, in which numerous parties exhibit strong linkages to distinct social groups, may contribute to democratic stability by facilitating the involvement of potentially disaffected groups in legitimate politics—provided that extremist parties are unable to gain significant support.[47]

It is difficult and probably inadvisable to derive a single, general rule about the ideal number of parties, since this depends in important ways on the social structure and related institutional arrangements. Because the party system is a crucial institutional device not only for representation but for conflict management, what appears most important is that the party system suit the social and cultural conditions, and that it articulate in a coherent way with other political institutions. Thus, if the constitutional system is designed to induce a two-party system—as tends strongly to result from a presidential system with election of legislators from single-member districts, by simple plurality and single ballot[48]—it makes sense to have in place other institutional inducements to crosscutting cleavage, such as federalism or even, as in the Nigerian case, specific laws requiring parties to establish transethnic organizations, bases, and symbols. If the "representational" system is sought, proportional representation (in a parliamentary system) is its electoral means, and the encouragement of crosscutting cleavages becomes a less pressing concern.[49]

Our twenty-six–nation study does offer some support for the proposition that a system of two or a few parties, with broad social and ideological bases, may be conducive to stable democracy. Of the five most-stable democratic systems in our study, two (Venezuela and Costa Rica) have two-party systems composed of broad, multiclass parties, in societies that lack deep social cleavages; two (India and Botswana) have had one-party dominant systems in which the ruling parties incorporate and aggregate a wide range of ethnic and social interests (although with the displacement of the Congress party from power in December 1989, India's system appears to have broken down); and one (Papua New Guinea) has a moderate multiparty system in which two parties are dominant. Certainly, fragmentation into a large number of parties—as has occurred historically in Thailand, as well as Pakistan and Indonesia—is associated with democratic instability and breakdown. This is not only because such party systems tend toward the conditions of polarized pluralism outlined by Linz and Sartori but also because parties in such systems are poorly institutionalized.

A critical consideration for democracy is not just the number of political parties but their overall institutional strength, as indicated by Huntington's criteria of coherence, complexity, autonomy, and adaptability.[50] Among the twenty-six cases of our larger study, we find that where at least one and eventually two or more parties were able to develop some substantive coherence about policy and program preferences, some organizational coherence and discipline, some complexity and depth of internal structure, some autonomy from dominance by individual leaders or state or societal interests, and some capacity to adapt to changing conditions—incorporating new generations and newly emergent groups—democracy has usually developed considerable durability and vitality. The early and deep institutionalization of the Congress party became an important foundation for democratic consolidation in India, just as the personalization of party power and decay of party organization under Indira Gandhi reflected and heightened the overall deterioration of democratic institutions since the mid-1960s. The strength of Chilean parties likewise contributed for many decades to stable democracy, with breakdown resulting not from their institutional deterioration but from the polarization of relations among them. In Brazil, the "deinstitutionalization" of the party system that began in the mid-1950s, fragmenting or dividing each of the major parties and so undercutting their capacity to respond to and harness changing economic and social forces, heavily contributed, as Lamounier shows, to the democratic breakdown in 1964.

Thailand shows vividly the linkage between extreme party fractionalization and the institutional weakness of parties and the party system. With 143 parties crossing the Thai political stage between 1946 and 1981, political elites have been unable to build strong bases of popular support, to articulate, aggregate, and mobilize political interests, to incorporate emerging interests into the political process, and to cooperate with one another in achieving policy innovations. As a result, the military and bureaucracy have been able to claim many of these functions, making it more difficult for independent democratic forces to establish themselves. The weakness and fragmentation of Thailand's party system was a leading factor in the failure of past democratic attempts (notably the 1974–1976 regime), and, with fifteen parties having won legislative seats in the 1988 elections, remains an obstacle to the evolution and consolidation of a fully democratic system today.

Democratic consolidation requires in part the consolidation of a reasonably stable and workable party system. In two important efforts at engineering the reconstruction of democracy, the Turkish military—seeking to prevent the classic conditions of polarized pluralism that brought down democracy in 1980—adopted measures (a 10 percent electoral threshold for representation in parliament; banning of extremist, religious, and separatist parties) to encourage a two- or three-party system that would yield stable parliamentary majorities and preclude centrifugal pulls. The Nigerian military mandated that the new Third Republic would have two and only two parties. When none of the parties that vied for recognition in 1989 proved to the liking of Nigeria's Armed Forces Ruling Council, it took the further, and unprecedented, step of establishing two new parties by fiat.[51]

Constitutional structure. Although presidential government is associated with the world's longest and most successful democratic experience, in the United States, its record in the developing world exhibits several characteristic problems. For one, a presidential system tends to concentrate power and legitimacy in the executive branch, which may be unhealthy for nascent democracies where the separation of powers and checks and balances are not well established. Second, presidentialism, with its "winner-take-all" distribution of power, "tends to make democratic politics a zero-sum game, with all the potential for conflict such games portend."[52] Third, presidentialism, with its fixed terms, rigidifies outcomes, possibly sticking a nation, even for several years, with a government that has utterly lost public confidence and support.

The advantages of a parliamentary system lie in its greater flexibility. An executive who has lost popular support can be turned out of office before his term is up. Coalitions can be formed to reach across significant political divisions, and these can be reformed in light of shifting political issues and fortunes, making for a more than zero-sum game. Because they are associated with a greater number of parties, parliamentary systems are somewhat less conducive to the polarization of politics between two or three major political parties, each identified with major class or ethnic cleavage groups. Moreover, presidential coalitions typically have little incentive to cohere (and often real incentives to fragment) after the election, while in a parliamentary multiparty system the parties have to assume responsibility in supporting a government that would otherwise fall.[53]

The theoretical case for these advantages lies largely with the experience of parliamentary democracy in Western Europe and the disastrous experience with presidentialism of some Latin American countries, especially Chile. Valenzuela demonstrates the lack of fit between a highly polarized and competitive multiparty system—which, because it could not generate electoral majorities, necessitated bargaining and coalition-making—and a presidential system of centralized authority, zero-sum outcomes, and fixed terms. The contradictions "came to a tragic head in the Allende years," culminating in 1973 in a breakdown of democracy that could have been avoided. In the late 1980s, the debilitating rigidities of presidentialism became manifest in Brazil and Peru, where presidents whose programs had failed catastrophically and whose political support had evaporated were forced to limp through their remaining terms with virtually no capacity to respond effectively to the deepening economic and political crises.

We also stress the importance to democracy of a strong and independent judiciary. A powerful judiciary can be the bulwark of a democratic constitution, defending both its integrity (and hence political freedom and due process) and also its preeminence as the source of democratic legitimacy.

More generally, the judiciary is the ultimate guarantor of the rule of law, and thus of the accountability of rulers to the ruled, which is a basic premise of democracy. During the authoritarian emergency in India, "a beleaguered and partially 'captured' Supreme Court still struck down a constitutional amendment, enacted by parliament, that would have destroyed an 'essential feature' of the constitution."[54] Similarly, in Zimbabwe an independent and sophisticated judiciary has at times played an important role in the defense of human rights and democracy as they have come under increasing pressure.[55]

Ethnic and Regional Conflict

One of the stronger generalizations emerging from our larger study is the danger for democracy of excessive centralization of state power. Where there are major ethnic or regional cleavages that are territorially based, the relationship is by now self-evident and axiomatic: The absence of provisions for devolution and decentralization of power, especially in the context of ethnoregional disparities, feeds ethnic insecurity, violent conflict, and even secessionist pressures. These, in turn, are poisonous to democracy.

Secessionist pressures carry a dual threat. Unless resolved by political means, through institutions such as autonomy, federalism, or—in the extreme—separate statehood, they can lead to the imposition of authority by force and the deterioration or breakdown of democratic rule. Alternatively, a democratic center may be questioned for its inefficiency in creating or its weakness in handling the secessionist crisis, opening the way for military intervention. In differing ways and to differing degrees, these dangers have threatened or damaged democratic regimes in recent years not only in Peru and Sri Lanka but in India, the Philippines, and Sudan (contributing in no small way to the failure of that democratic experiment in 1989). Historically, they figured prominently in the failure of Nigeria's first democratic attempt in the 1960s. And though India benefits in some ways from the multiple, complex character of religious, linguistic, and regional identities—fragmented and crosscut by caste and class formations—its more recent failure to integrate diverse ethnic communities (especially Sikhs and Muslims) into the national polity, or at least to find some stable formula for accommodating and managing diversity, has been a major source of instability. Das Gupta's conclusion from the Indian experience is confirmed by our wider evidence: "When ethnic leaders are allowed to share power, they generally act according to the rules of the regime," but when the state responds to ethnic mobilization with exclusion and repression, violence festers.

Democracy in plural societies requires not just a federal structure but a properly balanced one. An important reason for the failure of the First Nigerian Republic, and for the subsequent descent into civil war, was the gross inadequacy of the three-region federal system, which reified the major tripartite ethnic cleavage while assuring one group political hegemony. By contrast, the nineteen-state federal structure in the Second Republic went a long way toward giving Nigeria's many ethnic groups a much greater sense of political security and also crosscut ethnicity to some extent. Moreover, as in India—where federalism has functioned, even in a context of virtually continuous one-party dominance, to give opposition parties a stake in the system and to expand access to new groups—federalism in Nigeria disperses the stakes in electoral competition and so reduces the fixation on the center.

It is not only to manage ethnic and regional cleavage that decentralization is important to democracy. Centralization of power, by its very nature, tends to undermine democracy and thus constitutes an important obstacle to democratization in several of our cases. In Mexico, centralization and strong presidentialism have been important pillars of one-party hegemony and have become major targets of groups seeking democratic reform. In Turkey, state centralization—as reflected in the absence of any tradition of autonomous municipalities and the dependence of municipal and provincial administrations on the central government—has increased the stakes riding on control of the central government, and so the tendency toward violence and intolerance in the electoral struggle. In Thailand, a highly centralized state bureaucracy manifests cynicism and suspicion of democratic politics. In Senegal, the unresponsiveness to popular concerns and distance from popular reach of a highly centralized state have not only fueled a sometimes violent resistance movement in the geographically isolated and culturally distant Casamance region, but have also undermined the legitimacy of the semidemocratic regime throughout the country. By contrast, the substantial power of local elected councils over community development and services can be a source of democratic vitality, as it has been in Botswana, where opposition party control of some local councils has mitigated somewhat the effect of continuing one-party dominance at the center and so enhanced commitment to the system.

The Military

In most of the countries in our larger study, democracy is threatened and in the past has been overturned by military establishments that regard themselves "as the privileged definers and guardians of the national interest."[56] However, the military variable is not independent of political ones. Typically, military role expansion is induced by the corruption, stagnation, and malfunctioning of democratic institutions, to the point where the military is increasingly called upon to maintain order and comes to see itself as the only salvation of the country. In virtually every country considered here that has experienced democratic breakdown by military coup, these interventions have come in the wake of manifest political and, often, economic crises: This is true for the military coups in Brazil in 1964, in Chile in 1973, in Turkey in 1960 and 1980 (and the "half-coup" in 1971), in South Korea in 1961, in Thailand in 1976, and in Nigeria in 1966 and

1983. The military's size, autonomy, professional doctrine, and role conception may determine its threshold for intervention but do not constitute an independent cause of democratic breakdown.

This is not to say that factors external to the political process do not shape the military disposition to intervene. External Communist threats, or perceptions of Communist support for indigenous insurgencies, have heightened the military's readiness to intervene and rule on behalf of "national security" not only in much of Latin America, but in Thailand and, especially, in South Korea. In fact, the "militarized" nature of South Korean society was, as Han explains, a major factor creating a political setting conducive to authoritarian rule. The contemporary problem, however, is that repeated interventions in politics over decades have shaped the mentality of many officers, and the formal role conception and organization of the armed forces, in ways that generate a higher probability of future intervention at a lower threshold of civilian malfunctioning (witness the four serious coup attempts in Argentina during 1987–1988).

As Stepan has shown, once military role expansion occurs, it tends to endure and advance, diminishing not only the stability but also the authenticity of democracy, as numerous areas of public policy pass from elected civilian to unaccountable military control. It is thus imperative that newly restored democracies reorient the military role around external defense; reduce military prerogatives to control or influence vast reaches (military and nonmilitary) of the state, the political system, and even civil society; and assert civilian control and oversight even over strictly military functions. These steps require, Stepan forcefully argues, "democratic empowerment." By this process, civilian scholars and policy specialists acquire credible expertise in military and intelligence affairs, legislatures develop the institutional capacity to monitor military and intelligence systems effectively and routinely, and democratic state leaders implement "a well conceived, *politically* led strategy" to narrow military involvement in conflict regulation, enhance military professional capacities, and build effective procedures for civilian control.[57]

International Factors

In an influential theoretical movement that dominated academic thinking in the 1970s, various dependency theorists maintained that political exclusion and repression of popular mobilization were inevitable concomitants of peripheral status in the global division of labor and the dependent character of economic development.[58] The authors of the case studies in this book reject that assumption and attribute the course of political development and regime change primarily to internal structures and action. Nevertheless, they do recognize how structures have been been shaped historically by a variety of international factors, including colonial rule, cultural diffusion, and demonstration effects from abroad.[59]

Any accounting of the colonial legacy has to include not only the authoritarian and statist character of the colonial state, which heavily influenced indigenous norms and models (especially in Africa), but also the liberal and democratic values communicated by the French and, especially, British colonizers that provided India and, to a lesser extent, countries such as Nigeria and Senegal some preindependence experience in self-governance and scope for democratic, pluralist expression and organization.[60] In the postcolonial period, and for Turkey and Thailand, which were never colonized, cultural diffusion of democratic norms and models has remained an important stimulant of democratic progress. Regional demonstration effects have also helped to induce waves of change, such as the military coups in South America of the late 1960s and early 1970s, inspired by doctrines of national security; the Latin American redemocratizations of the 1980s; and the sudden collapse of Communist regimes throughout Eastern Europe in 1989. In East Asia, the transition to democracy in South Korea was spurred on by the demonstration of "people power" toppling Marcos in the Philippines, but the more potent international pressure may have come from the sense that full acceptance into the club of advanced, capitalist nations required a democratic political system (this has helped to motivate the democratic opening in Taiwan as well).

Under certain circumstances (including questionable or eroding internal legitimacy), democratic and authoritarian regimes in developing countries can be vulnerable to direct international political and military pressures. International pressure alone cannot effect democratic change, but the potential for democratic influence from the United States or other external actors should not be underestimated. Of course, neither should one overlook past Western and U.S. support for authoritarian regimes, and willingness to conspire against, sabotage, or even overthrow popularly elected regimes that seemed threatening.[61] One supporting factor in the consolidation of democracy in Venezuela was the fact that the Kennedy administration "bet heavily on democracy in Venezuela, the kind of bet later administrations have made all too rarely."[62] In Argentina, U.S. human rights pressure under the Carter administration did not force the withdrawal of the military, but it "saved many victims of indiscriminate repression in the late 1970s and was a factor in the international isolation of the military regime."[63] By the same token, the absence of pressure can be taken as a sign of tacit support from which an authoritarian regime may draw strength. During the later 1960s and 1970s, the lack of U.S. pressure for democratization was an important "permissive" factor in the construction and consolidation of authoritarian rule in South Korea, yet U.S. diplomatic pressure may have played a critical role in dissuading President Chun Doo Hwan from unleashing massive repression against the popular mobilization for democracy during the tense days of mid-1987 when democratic transition was almost aborted. U.S. support for multilateral loans to Chile—$2.2 billion between 1980 and 1986—helped perpetuate the Pinochet regime, "yet on the one occasion when substantive pressure was threatened—the 1985 multilateral loan abstentions—the dictator quickly lifted the state of siege."[64]

Of course, there are still more direct forms of foreign influence. As Dahl observes, many of the world's now-established democracies were imposed by foreign powers through armed conquest or colonization.[65] Needless to say, external military intervention can help rescue a democratic government threatened by coup—such as Aquino's in the Philippines—or topple a dictatorship such as Noriega's, but such actions often have deleterious consequences for the legitimacy of the democratic government so saved or installed—especially when, as in the Philippines and Panama, the external intervention is unilateral and by a nation whose previous interventions have historically been viewed with resentment and suspicion by indigenous actors. It remains to be seen whether these dramatic U.S. actions at the close of 1989 will contribute to real and lasting democracy in these two countries.

External military pressure or insecurity can affect the democratic prospect by strengthening the military establishment and its claim to power, as we have already noted in the case of South Korea. In Thailand, the Communist insurgency heightened the military's fear of competitive politics, so that, as Chai-Anan tells us, "any democratic movement that aimed at mobilizing and gaining support from the masses was usually suspected of being communist-inspired."

At the current time, however, and no doubt in many previous decades, the most important international influences on the prospects for democracy in developing countries appear to be economic ones. While we reject the argument that international economic dependence or capitalist industrialization is incompatible with democracy, we cannot ignore the degree to which international economic constraints—severe indebtedness, weak or obstructed export markets, sluggish growth and demand in the industrialized countries, and steep balance of payments crises—may severely limit the maneuverability and damage the legitimacy of democratic regimes, especially relatively new ones, in developing countries.

To be sure, democratic legitimacy rests on other foundations than short-term economic performance, and the task of democratic consolidation is, to a substantial degree, a matter of what Linz and Stepan term "political crafting."[66] Thus, even in a recently established democracy such as Spain, the consolidation of democracy may proceed for a time in the face of relatively weak economic performance and sharply declining belief in the socioeconomic efficacy of democracy.[67] However, there is always some danger in extrapolating from one historical case to another. The recently reestablished democracies of Latin America, the Philippines, and Pakistan, and the liberalizing regimes of Africa face even deeper economic crises and social tensions, with less working capital of system legitimacy and without the benefits of being part of the democratic community of Europe (something from which the Eastern European countries, even with all their unique problems of transition from bankrupt socialist economies, are nevertheless uniquely poised to benefit). The new democracies of the developing world are deeply threatened by grave and urgent economic crises, the relief (not to mention resolution) of which depends in part on a host of factors in the world economy over which they can have only very limited if any influence—interest rates, growth rates, trade barriers, levels of economic assistance, and so on.

Consolidating these new democracies requires skilful political crafting and courageous and wise policy choices by their leaders. Economies must be reoriented to compete in international markets, state economic ownership and control must be reduced, and the enormous inequalities between rich and poor must be considerably narrowed. Foreign capital must find it attractive to invest, at a time when there are still many investment opportunities in the advanced industrial countries as well as new ones emerging in Eastern Europe. At the same time, democratic consolidation will demand considerable patience and forbearance from their publics and interest groups. But, it is also likely to depend on the flexibility and vision of powerful international economic actors, and especially the major industrialized democracies, in dealing with the critical issues of developing countries' debt and trade. The more hostile and inflexible is this international environment, the more heroic must be the performances and compromises of leaders and the sacrifices and forbearance of publics. History suggests that heroism and sacrifice are not promising conditions on which to depend for the survival, much less consolidation, of new democratic regimes.

• NOTES •

1. For all twenty-six case studies, see Larry Diamond, Juan J. Linz, and Seymour Martin Lipset, eds., *Democracy in Developing Countries,* vols. 2, *Africa*; 3, *Asia*; and 4, *Latin America.* (Boulder, CO: Lynne Rienner Publishers, 1988 and 1989). Vol. 1, containing the theory and conclusions of the project and subtitled *Persistence, Failure, and Renewal* is forthcoming from the same publisher

2. Although the larger comparative project does not incorporate cases from the Communist world, these recent regime changes in Eastern Europe indicate the salience of the kind of variables we consider—including historical traditions, political culture, state-society relations, and regime type—for explaining the types of processes of democratization that occur, and their likelihood of success.

3. This neglect is to some extent overcome in Arend Lijphart's creative and enterprising study, *Democracies: Patterns of Majoritarian and Consensus Government in Twenty-One Countries* (New Haven, CT: Yale University Press, 1984). However, Lijphart's focus is mainly on political structure, and the comparison is limited to the continuous and stable democracies of the advanced, industrial countries.

4. Specifically, the points on this scale are: (1) *high success*—stable and uninterrupted democratic rule, with democracy now deeply institutionalized and stable; (2) *progressive success*—the consolidation of relatively stable democracy after one or more breakdowns or serious interruptions; (3) *mixed success*—democratic and unstable (e.g., democracy has returned following a period of breakdown and authoritarian rule but has not yet been consolidated); (4) *mixed success—partial or semidemocracy;* (5) *failure but promise*—democratic rule has broken down, but there are considerable pressures and prospects for its return; (6) *failure or absence*—democracy has never functioned for any significant period of time, and there is little prospect that it will in the coming years.

5. See Robert A. Dahl and Edward Tufte, *Size and Democracy* (Stanford, CA:Stanford University Press, 1973).

6. Robert A. Dahl, *Polyarchy: Participation and Opposition* (New Haven, CT: Yale University Press, 1971), pp. 3–20; Joseph Schumpeter, *Capitalism, Socialism and Democracy* (New York: Harper and Row, 1942); Seymour Martin Lipset, *Political Man,* expanded and updated ed. (Baltimore, MD: Johns Hopkins University Press, 1981), p. 27; Juan Linz, *The Breakdown of Democratic Regimes: Crisis, Breakdown and Reequilibration* (Baltimore, MD: Johns Hopkins University Press, 1978), p. 5.

7. Alfred Stepan, *Rethinking Military Politics: Brazil and the Southern Cone* (Princeton, NJ: Princeton University Press, 1988), p. 123.

8. Guillermo O'Donnell and Philippe C. Schmitter, *Transitions from Authoritarian Rule: Tentative Conclusions about Uncertain Democracies* (Baltimore, MD: Johns Hopkins University Press, 1986).

9. The distinction between authoritarian and totalitarian regimes has a long intellectual history. See Juan J. Linz, "Totalitarian and Authoritarian Regimes," in *Handbook of Political Science,* ed. Fred I. Greenstein and Nelson W. Polsby (Reading, MA: Addison-Wesley, 1975), vol. 3, pp. 175–411.

10. The possibilities and conditions for transition from communism to democracy are quite different in Eastern Europe—particularly in Hungary, Czechoslovakia, Poland, and East Germany, with their previous, pluralist party traditions and the heavy dependence of their Communist regimes on the prop of Soviet troops. The time is clearly now ripe for a comparative study of transitions from communism.

11. Linz, *Breakdown of Democratic Regimes,* pp. 16–17. See also Lipset, *Political Man,* p. 64; and Dahl, *Polyarchy,* pp. 129–131.

12. Linz, *Breakdown of Democratic Regimes,* p. 20.

13. Lipset, *Political Man,* pp. 67–71.

14. Ibid., pp. 64–70; Dahl, *Polyarchy,* pp. 129–150; and Linz, *Breakdown of Democratic Regimes,* pp. 16–23

15. For insights into the problems such populist political strategies have generated for Venezuela's democratic institutions, see Anibal Romero, "The Political Culture of Democratic Populism: The Case of Venezuela," in *Political Culture and Democracy in Developing Countries,* ed. Larry Diamond (forthcoming).

16. John D. Holm, "Botswana: A Paternalistic Democracy," in Diamond, Linz, and Lipset, *Democracy in Developing Countries: Africa,* pp. 196–199.

17. Jonathan Hartlyn, "Colombia: The Politics of Violence and Accommodation," in Diamond, Linz, and Lipset, *Democracy in Developing Countries: Latin America,* pp. 310–311.

18. For evidence and analysis of how rapid social and economic change has ultimately contributed to democratization in Taiwan, see Tun-jen Cheng,"Democratizing the Quasi-Leninist Regime in Taiwan," *World Politics* 41, no. 4 (July 1989): esp. 480–483; Tun-jen Cheng and Stephan Haggard," Regime Transformation in Taiwan: Theoretical and Comparative Perspectives," in *Political Change in the Republic of China on Taiwan,* ed. Cheng and Haggard (forthcoming); and (with particular reference to the democratizing effects on political culture) Ambrose Y. C. King, "A Non-Paradigmatic Search for Democracy in a Post-Confucian Culture: The Case of Taiwan, R.O.C.," in Diamond, *Political Culture and Democracy in Developing Countries.*

19. Larry Diamond, "Beyond Authoritarianism and Totalitarianism: Strategies for Democratization," *The Washington Quarterly* 12, no. 1 (Winter 1989): 150.

20. New or newly restored democracies are particularly vulnerable in this regard. Her inability to control the widespead venality around her—despite her own integrity and honorable intentions—was, for example, a key factor not only in the erosion of Corazón Aquino's base of political support during 1989, but in the coup that almost toppled the Philippines' democratic system near the end of the year.

21. Juan J. Linz and Alfred Stepan, eds., *The Breakdown of Democratic Regimes,* 4 vols. (Baltimore, MD: Johns Hopkins University Press, 1978).

22. Linz, *Breakdown of Democratic Regimes,* pp. 27–38. For extensive evidence of the role of violence and terror, and party reactions to them, in the breakdown or persistence of democracies, see G. Bingham Powell, Jr., *Contemporary Democracies: Participation, Stability, and Violence* (Cambridge, MA: Harvard University Press, 1982), pp. 155–170.

23. Ibid, p. 174.

24. Daniel H. Levine, "Venezuela: The Nature, Source, and Future Prospects of Democracy,"

and Hartlyn, "Colombia," in Diamond, Linz, and Lipset, *Democracy in Developing Countries: Latin America*, pp. 247–290, 291–334, respectively.

25. Lipset, *Political Man*, pp. 78–79.

26. Gabriel A. Almond and Sidney Verba, *The Civic Culture* (Princeton, NJ: Princeton University Press, 1963); Sidney Verba, "Conclusion: Comparative Political Culture," in *Political Culture and Political Development*, ed. Lucian W. Pye and Sidney Verba (Princeton, NJ: Princeton University Press, 1965), pp. 512–560; Dahl, *Polyarchy*, pp. 129–162; Lipset, *Political Man*; and Seymour Martin Lipset, *The First New Nation* (New York: W. W. Norton, 1979), part 3.

27. Levine, "Venezuela," pp. 278–279.

28. John A. Booth, "Costa Rica: The Roots of Democratic Stability," in Diamond, Linz, and Lipset, *Democracy in Developing Countries: Latin America*, pp. 402–404.

29. Holm, "Botswana," p. 195.

30. Karl Jackson, "The Philippines: The Search for a Suitable Democratic Solution, 1946–1986," in Diamond, Linz, and Lipset, *Democracy in Developing Countries: Asia*.

31. Charles Gillespie and Luis Eduardo Gonzales, "Uruguay: The Survival of Old and Autonomous Institutions," in Diamond, Linz, and Lipset, *Democracy in Developing Countries: Latin America*, p. 223.

32. Lipset, *Political Man*, p. 45.

33. Ibid., p. 51; Dahl, *Polyarchy*, p. 81.

34. Samuel P. Huntington, *Political Order in Changing Societies* (New Haven, CT: Yale University Press, 1968), p. 5.

35. Samuel P. Huntington, "Will More Countries Become Democratic?" *Political Science Quarterly* 99, no. 2 (Summer 1984): 201.

36. Booth, "Costa Rica," pp. 389–391.

37. World Bank, *World Development Report 1989* (New York: Oxford University Press, 1989), table 30, pp. 222–223. For more-extensive discussion of the comparative data, see Larry Diamond and Juan J. Linz,"Introduction: Politics, Society, and Democracy in Latin America," in Diamond, Linz, and Lipset, *Democracy in Developing Countries: Latin America*, pp. 40–41.

38. Michael P. Todaro, *Economic Development in the Third World*, 2d ed. (New York: Longman, 1981), p. 165.

39. Levine, "Venezuela," pp. 279–280.

40. Naomi Chazan, "The New Politics of Participation in Tropical Africa," *Comparative Politics* 14, no. 2 (January 1982): 174–176. For her analysis of the state's disengagement from society, and society's subsequent disengagement from the state, see Chazan, "Ghana: Problems of Governance and the Emergence of Civil Society," in Diamond, Linz, and Lipset, *Democracy in Developing Countries: Africa*, pp. 93–140. An important theoretical and comparative treatment of the problem is found in Victor Azarya and Naomi Chazan, "Disengagement from the State in Africa: Reflections on the Experience of Ghana and Guinea," *Comparative Studies in Society and History* 29, no. 1 (1987): 106–131.

41. Richard L. Sklar, "The Nature of Class Domination in Africa," *Journal of Modern African Studies* 17, no. 4 (December 1979): 531–552.

42. Larry Diamond, "Class Formation in the Swollen African State," *Journal of Modern African Studies* 25, no. 4 (December 1987): 567–596.

43. Urmila Phadnis, "Sri Lanka: Crises of Legitimacy and Integration," in Diamond, Linz, and Lipset, *Democracy in Developing Countries: Asia*, pp. 143–186.

44. Lipset, *First New Nation*, pp. 307–308.

45. Ibid., pp. 308–310; Linz, *Breakdown of Democratic Regimes*, p. 24.

46. Linz, *Breakdown of Democratic Regimes*, pp. 25–27; Giovanni Sartori, *Parties and Party Systems: A Framework for Analysis* (Cambridge: Cambridge University Press,1976), pp. 131–140. From this perspective, to be relevant a party must be potentially useful in the formation of a coalition government or have "power of intimidation" politically. Polarized pluralism encompasses not just extreme multipartyism but such other factors as antisystem parties, irresponsible oppositions, outbidding between parties, and ideological polarization.

47. Powell, *Contemporary Democracies*, pp. 154–157, 206, 222–223.

48. Maurice Duverger, *Political Parties: Their Organization and Activity in the Modern State* (New York: John Wiley and Sons, 1954), pp. 217–228; Lipset, *First New Nation*, pp. 307–308; and Powell, *Contemporary Democracies*, pp. 82–83.

49. Electoral systems, of course, have other consequences as well, sometimes unintended. The single-member district, plurality method of election enables a dominant party, such as the

Congress in India for so long, to muster a disproportionate share of seats, greatly exaggerating its political power beyond its real level of support. By allocating seats with minimal or lesser distortion, and making it easier for smaller parties to win representation, systems of proportional representation are viewed by many as inherently more democratic. However, when the small parties who win entry into the parliament have extremist agendas and the capacity to blackmail large but not dominant competitors, the consequences may be undemocratic.

50. Huntington, *Political Order in Changing Societies,* pp. 12–24.

51. Despite President Babangida's vow not to copy foreign models, the two new parties were dubbed the Social Democratic Party and the National Republican Convention. The National Electoral Commission was charged by the military with the task of synthesizing, from the submissions of the various aspiring parties, constitutions and manifestos for the Democrats and Republicans. Nigerians were then invited to join the party of their choice, with party leaderships to emerge by successive elections beginning at the local level.

52. Juan J. Linz, "The Perils of Presidentialism," *Journal of Democracy* 1, no. 1 (January 1990): 56.

53. For a full analysis of these issues, see ibid., pp. 51–69, and a forthcoming enlarged version of that article to appear in a volume edited by Arturo Valenzuela and Juan Linz on parliamentary versus presidential government.

54. Richard L. Sklar, "Developmental Democracy," *Comparative Studies in Society and History* 29, no. 4 (October 1987): 694.

55. Ibid., p. 695.

56. Carlos H. Waisman, "Argentina: Autarkic Industrialization and Illegitimacy," in Diamond, Linz, and Lipset, *Democracy in Developing Countries: Latin America,* pp. 59–110.

57. Stepan, *Rethinking Military Politics,* especially ch. 8. Quoted passage is from p. 137 (emphasis in the original).

58. See the review in Peter Evans, *Dependent Development: The Alliance of Multinational, State, and Local Capital in Brazil* (Princeton, NJ: Princeton University Press, 1979), pp. 25–54.

59. For theoretical consideration of these factors, see Dahl, *Polyarchy,* pp. 171–175, and Huntington, "Will More Countries Become Democratic?" p. 207.

60. For an analysis of the impact of colonial rule on subsequent political development in Africa, see L. H. Gann and Peter Duignan, *Burden of Empire: An Appraisal of Western Colonialism in Africa South of the Sahara* (Stanford, CA: Hoover Institution Press, 1967), pp. 253–272; Robert Jackson and Carl Rosberg, "Popular Legitimacy in African Multi-Ethnic States," *Journal of Modern African Studies* 22, no. 2 (June 1984): 177–198; Michael Crowder,"Whose Dream Was it Anyway? Twenty-five Years of African Independence," *African Affairs* 86, no. 342 (January 1987): 11–18; and Larry Diamond, "Introduction: Roots of Failure, Seeds of Hope," in Diamond, Linz, and Lipset, *Democracy in Developing Countries: Africa,* pp. 6–10.

61. For an analysis of "political development doctrines" in U.S. foreign policy between 1947 and 1968, and the frequent conflict between the goals of fighting the expansion of communism and promoting democracy abroad, see Robert Packenham, *Liberal America and the Third World: Political Development Ideas in Foreign Aid and Social Science* (Princeton, NJ: Princeton University Press, 1973).

62. Levine, "Venezuela," p. 281.

63. Waisman, "Argentina," pp. 98–99.

64. Pamela Constable and Arturo Valenzuela, "Is Chile Next?" *Foreign Policy* 63 (1986): 74–75.

65. Dahl, *Polyarchy,* p. 197.

66. Juan Linz and Alfred Stepan, "Political Crafting of Democratic Consolidation or Destruction: European and South American Comparisons," in *Democracy in the Americas: Stopping the Pendulum,* ed. Robert A. Pastor (New York: Holmes and Meier, 1989), pp. 41–61.

67. Ibid., pp. 43–46.

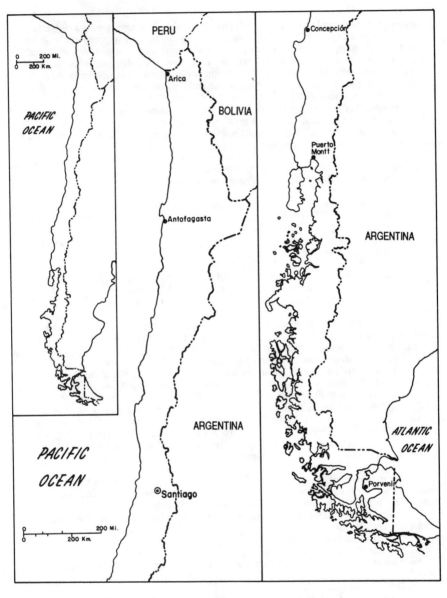

CHILE

CHAPTER TWO

Chile: Origins, Consolidation, and Breakdown of a Democratic Regime

ARTURO VALENZUELA

Chile, under the rule of General Augusto Pinochet Ugarte, experienced the longest single government in the nation's history and one of the harshest dictatorships of the contemporary world. For years after the military coup of September 11, 1973, elections for public office, and even elections within private organizations and associations were circumscribed or monitored by the authorities. The doors of Congress were closed, and all major public decisions were made by the general, officials appointed by him, or a junta consisting of the commanders of the four military services.

Elected local governments, which had dated back to colonial times, were replaced by mayors who served at the pleasure of the commander-in-chief of the army and president of the republic. Even the nation's universities were not spared. Soon after the coup, high-ranking army officers were appointed to head both private and public institutions of higher education, with a mandate to purge government opponents and administer with an iron hand. Political parties were banned or dismantled, and their leaders persecuted. Rights of assembly and free speech were restricted. The press was severely censored, while the authorities made ample use of television to project their own vision of the world. An elaborate security apparatus operating with broad formal and informal powers sent regime opponents into internal and external exile without trial. Thousands were arrested, "disappeared," or killed.[1]

Despite serious economic difficulties and international isolation, Chile's authoritarian regime resisted the trend in Latin America back to democratic forms of government. A new constitution, written by a handful of government advisers and ratified in a highly suspect plebiscite in 1980, extended Pinochet's term until 1989 and made it legally possible for him to continue in office until 1997 or beyond. Although the constitutional framework specified the return to elective politics in 1989, the document contained many features that sharply restricted democratic practices and the accountability of government authorities to popular will. It created a powerful executive and a weak Congress and gave the commanders-in-chief of the armed forces veto power over public-policy issues. The Constitution also declared illegal all political parties that advocate philosophical doctrines based on class struggle.[2]

This state of affairs, though not uncommon in the Third World, was a sharp and historic departure for Chile. Before the 1973 breakdown, the country would have been classified, following the criteria used in this book, as a high success, a stable and uninterrupted case of democratic rule. For most of the preceding one hundred years, Chilean politics had been characterized by a high level of party competition and popular participation, open and fair elections, and strong respect for democratic freedoms. Indeed, Bollen, in one of the most comprehensive cross-national efforts to rank countries on a scale of political democracy, placed Chile in the top 15 percent in 1965, a score higher than that of the United States, France, Italy, or West Germany. For 1960, Chile's score was higher than that of Britain.[3]

However, synchronic studies such as Bollen's fail to account for the fact that Chile's democratic tradition was not a recent phenomenon but goes back several generations. In the nineteenth century, Chile developed democratic institutions and procedures, setting the country apart from many of its European counterparts, as well as its Latin American neighbors. As Epstein has noted, in Europe "political power was not often effectively transferred from hereditary rulers to representative assemblies no matter how narrow their electorates until late in the nineteenth century."[4] By contrast, Chile had, by the turn of the century, experienced several decades in which political authority was vested in elected presidents, and Congress wielded substantial influence over the formulation of public policy.[5] Indeed, from 1830 until 1973, all Chilean presidents were followed in office by their duly elected successors. Deviations to this pattern occurred only in 1891, in the aftermath of a brief civil war, and in the turbulent period between 1924 and 1932, when four chief executives felt pressured to resign in an atmosphere of political and social unrest and military involvement in politics. In 143 years, Chile experienced only thirteen months of unconstitutional rule under some form of junta, and only four months under a junta dominated exclusively by the military. And, though the executive was preeminent in the decades after independence, Congress gradually increased its prerogatives, becoming an important arena for national debate and one of the most powerful legislatures in the world.

Dahl has noted that the development of democracy entails not only establishing institutions for public contestation and leadership renewal, but also popular sovereignty.[6] In nineteenth-century Chile, citizenship was sharply restricted, first to men who owned property and later to those who were literate. Thus, Chile was only a partial democracy, according to the definition used here, until well into the twentieth century, when women's suffrage was established, the literacy requirement abolished, and 18-year-olds given the right to vote.[7] It must be stressed, however, that Chile did not deviate substantially from other nascent democracies in extending citizenship. In 1846, only 2 percent of the Chilean population voted, but this figure was comparable to that in Britain in

1830, Luxembourg in 1848, the Netherlands in 1851, and Italy in 1871. In 1876, two years after it had abolished the property requirement, Chile had 106,000 registered voters, compared to 84,000 in Norway for a comparable adult male population. Secret voting was established in Chile shortly after its adoption in Britain, Sweden, and Germany, and before its adoption in Belgium, Denmark, France, Prussia, and Norway.[8]

Reflecting the profound social changes brought about by urbanization, incipient industrialization, and a booming export economy, Chile's middle- and then working-class groups were incorporated into the democratic political game by the second decade of the twentieth century. With the rise of an organized Left, Chilean politics became sharply polarized between vastly different conceptions of what the country's future should be. This division, articulated by powerful and institutionalized parties functioning within the framework of Chile's presidential system, placed increasing strains on democracy. In the 1970s, these strains contributed to the the breakdown of democracy soon after the first leftist candidate in Chilean history had been elected to the nation's highest office.

In the aftermath of the defeat of President Pinochet in a plebiscite prescribed by his own constitution, Chile can be characterized as a democratic failure with promise according to the terminology employed by the editors of this volume. Ironically, though authoritarian rule and the sharp divisions that persist in Chilean politics, and the complexities of partisan relationships, have made the transition to democracy unusually difficult, there is reason to believe that because of Chile's long history of democratic practices, once a transition is instituted it may be more durable than in many other countries of the Third World.

The historical overview provides a sketch of the major trends in Chilean politics. It is not intended to cover all periods in equal depth; rather, it gives disproportionate attention to those historical developments that are especially important to making analytical arguments about the development and breakdown of Chilean democracy. Following this is a theoretical assessment of the applicability to the Chilean case of several leading hypotheses generated by social scientists to account for the emergence of democratic politics. The third part analyzes the breakdown of democracy, highlighting those variables that best explain the complex process resulting in the 1973 military coup. The fourth gives an overview of military rule in Chile, explaining how authoritarian politics was first institutionalized and why the transition back to democracy was so slow and painful. It ends by speculating about the future course of Chilean democracy.

· HISTORICAL OVERVIEW ·

Origins and Consolidation of
Chilean Democracy, 1830s-1960s

As in the rest of Latin America, attempts in Chile to inaugurate republican institutions, based on democratic principles inspired by the framers of the U.S.
Constitution, met with resounding failure.[9] For a quarter-century after Chile's
declaration of independence from Spain in 1810, the new nation alternated between dictatorship and anarchy. The war of independence was a prolonged and
bloody civil "war to the death," as much as a war to end colonial rule, as many
Chileans supported the royalist cause. The final defeat of Spanish forces left the
territory's administrative and governing institutions in shambles, and local
elites bitterly divided by regional, family, ideological, and personal disputes.
Gone were the complex, far-flung patrimonial bureaucracy and the mediating
power of the crown, which for centuries had imposed a traditional style of political authority over a distant colony. In 1830, the clear military victory of one
coalition of forces permitted the inauguration of a concerted effort to institute
political order and encourage economic progress. However, despite the able
leadership of Cabinet Minister Diego Portales and military President Joaquín
Prieto, and the establishment of a new constitution in 1833, coup attempts and
conspiracies continued to plague Chile; Portales himself was assassinated in
1837 by troops he had thought loyal.

Portales' death was widely, though probably erroneously, blamed on interference in Chilean affairs by General Andrés Santa Cruz, the ruler of the Peru-
Bolivia Confederation and a powerful rival for hegemony in Pacific commerce.
The Bolivian dictator, after gaining control over Peru, had made no secret of his
ambition to extend his empire southward. In response, Portales engineered, in
1836, a declaration of war, an unpopular move widely condemned in political
circles. Ironically, Portales' death helped galvanize support for the war among
disparate Chilean political factions; incensed at foreign intervention, several
groups agreed to back an expeditionary force to Peru.

The war effort and the resounding victory achieved by the Chilean military
had a profound impact. Individuals of all stations enthusiastically welcomed
home the returning expeditionary force. The victory ball at the presidential
palace was attended by rival families who had not spoken to each other in years,
helping to heal long-standing wounds and forge a sense of common purpose. In
the wake of triumph, authorities decreed a broad amnesty and the restitution of
military ranks and pensions for those defeated in the civil war of 1830. As historian Encina notes, defeat of the Chilean forces would have magnified political
divisions and seriously imperiled the already tenuous governmental stability.
Military success gave the Prieto government and Chile's fledgling institutions a
new lease on life.[10]

The 1837-1838 war had another, equally important consequence for Chile's political development. It created a national hero, the first Chilean leader to rise unambiguously above factional disputes. General Manuel Bulnes, the embodiment of national unity, was easily able to succeed Prieto in the presidential elections of 1840, a transition facilitated by Prieto's willingness to leave office in favor of his nephew. In his two terms, Bulnes took two important steps to implement the principles set forth in the nation's republican Constitution, principles that were nothing less than revolutionary at the time.[11]

In the first place, Bulnes refused to rule autocratically, giving substantial authority to a designated cabinet carefully balanced to represent some of the most important factions of the loose governing coalition. And though executive power was paramount, Bulnes permitted growing autonomy of the courts and the legislature. In time, Congress became increasingly more assertive, delaying approval of budget laws in exchange for modifications in cabinet policy. The cabinet's response to growing congressional activism was not to silence the institution but to capture it by manipulating the electoral process. Ironically, while this practice was condemned by opponents as a perversion of suffrage, it contributed to reinforcing the legitimacy of the legislature as a full-fledged branch of government. Eventually, as presidents changed ministers or as political coalitions shifted, even legislatures originally elected through fraud became centers for the expression of opposition sentiments, reinforcing presidential accountability to legislative majorities.

In the second place, Bulnes firmly exchanged his role as commander-in-chief of the armed forces for that of civilian president. Under his guidance, the professional military was sharply cut back, its personnel thinned out, and many of its assets sold. Instead, and to the dismay of his former military colleagues, Bulnes poured resources into the National Guard, a force of citizen soldiers closely tied to the government patronage network, who served as a ready pool of voters for government-sponsored candidates. In his last presidential address to the nation, Bulnes proudly described the reduction of the regular army and the expansion of the militia as the most convincing evidence of his administration's fidelity to republican institutions.[12]

The transition to a new president, however, was not easy. Many of the country's elites rejected the candidacy of Manuel Montt, a civil servant and cabinet minister of middle-class extraction, to succeed Bulnes. His candidacy was also rejected by elements in the professional army, who believed Bulnes would support a revolt to prevent Montt's accession to power and thus ensure the continuity of leadership from his native area of Concepción. When a revolt was attempted, however, Bulnes personally led the National Guard to defeat the rebel forces.

With the mid-nineteenth–century development of a new class of government functionaries and political leaders who espoused the liberal creed, the state gained substantial autonomy from the traditional landed elite, the pillar of social and economic power. State autonomy was reinforced by the government's success in promoting economic progress, particularly the booming export trade in wheat and minerals, which encouraged economic elites to give the authorities substantial leeway in policy formulation and implementation. Just as important, however, the export-import trade gave the authorities a ready and expanding source of income from customs duties, without their having to make the politically risky decision to tax property or income. Ironically, had the Chilean economy been more balanced and less dependent on foreign trade, the state would have been much more vulnerable to the immediate and direct pressures of economic elites. In Chile, economic dependency contributed to strengthening, not weakening, the state.[13] From 1830 to 1860, customs revenues, which represented 60 percent of all revenues, increased sevenfold, enabling the Chilean state to undertake extensive public-works projects, including constructing Latin America's second railroad, and to invest large sums of money in education, which officials believed to be the key to prosperity and national greatness.

In time, however, the state, rapidly extending its administrative jurisdiction and public-works projects throughout the national territory and actively promoting domestic programs in education and civil registries, clashed sharply with landowners, the church, and regional interests. Discontent in the ranks of the conservative landed elite was such that it led to the formation of the country's first real party, the Conservative Party, in direct opposition to Montt's administration. The Conservatives were committed to preserving the traditional order, and defending the values and interests of the church. At the same time, and also in opposition to the state, a group of ideological liberals, influenced by the Revolution of 1848 in France, pressed to accelerate secularization and decentralization and to expand suffrage and democratization. The secular-religious issue, with state elites taking a middle ground, would become the most salient political cleavage in nineteenth-century Chile, and the basis for crystalizing partisan alignments.

By 1859, discontent with the government from various quarters was such that a disparate coalition, composed of aristocratic Conservatives, regional groups, and the newly formed Radical Party representing the anticlerical and mining interests, challenged the government by force. In particular, the dissidents objected to the widespread state intervention in the 1858 congressional election, in which the government obtained a large majority in the Chamber of Deputies. Once again, however, state officials, with strong support from provincial interests and urban groups, were able to make use of the National Guard to put down the revolt. In the process, they put to rest the lingering center-periphery cleavages that had challenged central authority from the days of independence. The new president, following earlier precedents, granted a national amnesty and incorporated many dissidents into policymaking positions. Even the Radical Party obtained congressional representation in the next election.

The monopoly that the government had obtained over the country's most effective fighting forces made it difficult for Conservatives and other opposition elements to contemplate victory through armed challenge. Because of official intervention in the electoral process, moreover, opponents were unable to wrest control of the state from incumbents. Ironically, Conservatives soon realized that they had no choice but to push for expanded suffrage if they were to succeed in capturing the state. Even more oddly, in opposing the government they structured alliances of convenience in Congress with their nemeses, the staunchly ideological liberals, who were worried about electoral intervention and the authorities' refusal to press for increased democratization. This strategic adoption of a "liberal" creed by Conservative forces in a traditional society explains one of the most extraordinary paradoxes of Chilean history: the legislative alliance of ultramontane Catholics and radical liberals, both seeking for different reasons the fulfilment of democratic ideals.

Clearly, the Conservatives did not become democrats because of an ideological conversion, though many with close ties to England had come to believe that parliamentary government was a requirement for any civilized nation-state. But they correctly perceived that representative institutions were in their best interest, and the only real alternative once military solutions to domestic conflicts no longer seemed viable. Conservatives were forced to make the liberal creed their own precisely because they had lost ground to a new political class, which had gained strength by dominating the state. In turn, the pragmatic "liberals" (known as the Montt-Varistas) were not acting irrationally when they resisted attempts to expand suffrage and bar official manipulation of the electoral process. They fully realized that in an overwhelmingly rural society, with traditional landlord-peasant relationships, the Conservatives would beat them at the polls and challenge their monopoly of power.[14]

Under the leadership of Conservative José Manuel Irarrazaval, who became a champion of electoral reform, the Right sought to advance its interests through the democratic electoral process, rather than through military conspiracies or direct ties with elements of the central bureaucracy, as was the case in many other countries at the time. As a result, the church, hostile to electoral democracy in much of Latin Europe, also came to accept the legitimacy of suffrage in generating public officials. From a position of strength in Congress, the Conservatives, together with Radicals and ideological liberals and over the objections of the executive, successfully pressed for a series of reforms that restricted presidential power. The president was limited to a single 5-year term, and his veto power was restricted. The adoption of the Electoral Reform Act in 1874 tripled the electorate from 50,000 to 150,000 voters over the 1872 total.[15]

Nevertheless, official intervention in the electoral process did not end with electoral reform, and the stakes in controlling the state continued to increase. With its victory in the War of the Pacific (1879–1883), Chile gained vast new territory and rich nitrate deposits. Customs duties climbed to over 70 percent of government income, eliminating the need for property taxes and swelling state coffers. President José Manuel Balmaceda (1886–1891) refused to give in to congressional demands that ministers serve with congressional approval. He also balked at proposals that local governments be given substantial autonomy from the central administration, and that local notables be given control of the electoral process. When his cabinet was censured, Balmaceda sought to govern without congressional approval, adopting the national budget by decree. Finally, a civil war broke out between Congress, backed by the navy, and the president, backed by the army; Balmaceda was defeated in August 1891 and committed suicide.

With the country in disarray and the president dead, a junta headed by a navy captain, the vice-president of the Senate, and the president of the Chamber of Deputies assumed control of the government for three months. This marked the first time since 1830 that political power had been exercised in a manner not prescribed by the Constitution. But the brief period of unconstitutional rule did not involve imposing an authoritarian regime, nor did the military as an institution involve itself in politics except to take orders from civilian leaders. The cabinet continued to be a civilian cabinet, and Congress remained in session with virtually no interruption.

The victory of the congressional forces ushered in almost four decades of parliamentary government (1891–1927), in which the center of gravity of the political system shifted from the executive to the legislature, from the capital to local areas, and from state officials and their agents to local party leaders and political brokers. Politics became an elaborate log-rolling game centered in Congress, in which national resources were divided for the benefit of local constituents. Democratization, implied by these changes, had important effects on the political system. With the expansion of suffrage and local control of elections, parliamentary parties expanded beyond the confines of congressional corridors and became national networks with grassroots organizations.

Just as significant, however, was the emergence of parties outside the congressional arena (in Duverger's terms) in response to increased democratization and to other dramatic changes taking place in Chilean society.[16] While the Conservatives initially gained from electoral reform and were able to dominate the politics of the Parliamentary Republic, they did not foresee that the country's social structure would change so quickly in a quarter-century, and that electoral reform would soon benefit a new group of parties with far different agendas. The urban population, which accounted for 26 percent of the total in 1875, had soared to 45 percent by 1900. Nitrate production, employing between 10 and 15 percent of the population, spawned a host of ancillary industries and created a new working class, which soon found expression in new political parties when the traditional parties, particularly the modern Radicals, failed to provide the leadership required to address its grievances.

Both the state and private employers were slow to recognize the legitimacy of working-class demands and often brutally repressed the infant labor movement. But the openness of the political system, and the sharp competition among traditional parties searching for alliances to maximize electoral gain, permitted the development of electorally oriented class-based parties. By 1921, the year the Chilean Communist Party was officially founded, it had elected two members to Congress; four years later, it achieved representation in the Senate. Thus, to the secular-religious cleavage of the nineteenth century was added the worker-employer cleavage of the early twentieth century—generative cleavages that would shape the basic physiognomy of Chile's contemporary party system.

The 1920s were years of considerable political upheaval. The invention of synthetic nitrates during World War I led to the collapse of the Chilean nitrate industry, with far-reaching ramifications for the whole economy. The cumbersome and venal Parliamentary Republic fell increasingly into disrepute, criticized by the Right for allowing politics to become corrupt and overly democratic; denounced by the Center and Left for its inability to address national problems. President Arturo Alessandri (1920–1924) violated political norms by becoming an activist president and pressing for change in the face of congressional inaction and opposition. In September 1924, a group of young military officers unsheathed their swords in the congressional galleries, demanding reforms and the defeat of a congressional pay increase. Bowing to the unprecedented pressure, Alessandri resigned his post and left the country in the hands of a military junta—the first time in over 100 years that military men had played a direct role in governing the nation.

Senior officers, however, objected to the reform agenda of their younger colleagues; uncomfortable with the responsibility of governing, they soon began to defer to civilian leaders of the Right. This prompted a national movement to have Alessandri return, backed by younger officers who identified with the September *pronunciamiento*. In January 1925, the president resumed his position, marking the end of the first extraconstitutional government since 1891. During Alessandri's term, the 1925 Constitution was adopted with the expectation that it would increase the power of the president. It was the first full reform of the basic document since the Constitution of 1833, but it also embodied many elements of continuity.

Alessandri's elected successor, Emiliano Figueroa, proved unable to stand up to political pressures and the growing influence of Minister of War Colonel Carlos Ibañez, a military officer who had participated in the 1924 movement. In 1927 Figueroa resigned, and Ibañez was elected with broad support from all major parties, who sensed the country's and the military's demand for a "nonpolitical" and forceful chief executive. During his administration, Ibañez sought to alter fundamentally Chilean politics by introducing "efficient and modern" administrative practices, disdaining the role of Congress in cabinet appointments and resorting to emergency and executive measures, such as forced exile, in attempting to crush labor and opposition political parties. It is important to stress, however, that Ibañez's government was not a military dictatorship. While his authority derived in large measure from support in the barracks, army officers did not govern. The vast majority of cabinet officials were civilians, though most were newcomers to politics who criticized the intrigues of the traditional political class.

Ibañez soon discovered that he, too, could run out of political capital. His inability to curb the influence of parties, and his growing isolation, combined with the catastrophic effects of the Great Depression (in which Chilean exports dropped to a fifth of their former value) and mounting street unrest, finally led the demoralized president to submit his resignation in July 1931. After a period of political instability, which included the resignation of yet another president and the 90-day "Socialist Republic" proclaimed by a civil/military junta that attempted to press for social change, elections were scheduled in 1932. Once again, Arturo Alessandri was elected to a full constitutional term, thereby restoring the continuity of Chile's institutional system. During his second administration, Alessandri was far more cautious than during his first, successfully bringing the country out of the depression with firm austerity measures and reaffirming the value of institutions based on democratic values and procedures at a time when they were under profound attack in Europe.

The 1938 presidential election represented another major turning point in Chilean politics and a vivid confirmation of the extent to which ordinary citizens had become the fundamental source of political authority. In an extremely close election, the Center, in an alliance with the Marxist Left called the Popular Front, captured the presidency, and Radical Pedro Aguirre Cerda was elected. Despite the often-bitter opposition of the Right, the government for a decade expanded social-welfare policies, encouraged the rise of legal unionism, and actively pursued import-substituting industrialization through a new Corporación de Fomento de la Producción (Corporation for the Development of Production). The trend toward urbanization continued: in 1940, 53 percent of the population lived in cities; by 1970, that figure had increased to 76 percent.

By 1948, the new Cold War climate abroad and the increased local electoral successes of the Communist Party were making both Socialists and Radicals increasingly uneasy. Encouraged by Radical leaders, President Gabriel González Videla dissolved the Popular Front, outlawed the Communist Party, and sent many of its members to detention camps. These actions, combined with the wear of incumbency and general dissatisfaction with the opportunistic Radicals, contributed to the election of Carlos Ibañez as president in 1952 on an anti-party platform. But Ibañez, unable to govern without party support, was forced to shift his initial populist programs to a severe austerity plan that contributed to wage and salary declines. He was succeeded in 1958 by Conservative businessman Jorge Alessandri, the former president's son, who edged out Socialist Salvador Allende by only 2.7 percent of the vote. Alessandri applied more austerity measures, provoking cries for profound reform from a populace tired of spiraling inflation and economic stagnation. In the 1964 presidential elections, fear of the growing strength of the Left led Chile's traditional rightist parties to reluctantly support Eduardo Frei, the candidate of the new Christian Democratic Party, which had replaced the Radicals as the largest party in Chile and the most powerful party of the Center. With massive financial assistance from the United States, the Frei government attempted to implement far-reaching reforms, but after dissolving their tacit alliance with the Right, the Christian Democrats were unable to increase their share of the vote. In 1970, claiming to have been betrayed by Frei's reformist policies, the Right refused to support Christian Democratic candidate Radomiro Tomic, making possible the election of leftist candidate Salvador Allende and his Popular Unity coalition, with only 36.2 percent of the vote. The Christian Democratic and Popular Unity governments are treated in more detail in the discussion of the breakdown of Chilean democracy, below.

Characteristics of Chilean Politics at Mid-Century[17]

By the 1930s, with the rise of Marxist parties at a time of electoral expansion, the Chilean party system, in Lipset and Rokkan's terms, had become complete.[18] In addition to the traditional Conservative and Liberal parties that had emerged from church-state cleavages in the early nineteenth century, and the Radical Party that had developed later in that century out of similar divisions, Communist and Socialist parties had now developed in response to a growing class cleavage. The only new party to emerge after the 1930s, the Christian Democratic Party, was an offshoot of the Conservatives, which sought to address social and economic issues from the vantage point of reform Catholicism.

Yet this "complete" system was characterized by sharp social polarizations in which the organized electorate was divided almost equally among the three political tendencies. Although numerous small parties appeared after 1932, the six major parties continued to dominate politics, commanding over 80 percent of the vote by the 1960s. Elections and politics became a national "sport," as parties became so deeply ingrained in the nation's social fabric that Chileans would refer to a Radical or a Communist or a Christian Democratic "subculture." Parties helped to structure people's friendships and social life. Partisan affiliation continued to be reinforced by both class and religion, so that Christian Democratic elites were more likely to go to Catholic schools and universities and come from upper-middle-class backgrounds, while Socialist elites went to public schools and state universities and came from lower-middle-class backgrounds. Communist strength was heavily concentrated in mining communities and industrial areas, Christian Democrats appealed to middle-class and women voters, while the Right retained substantial support in rural Chile.

The major parties framed political options not only in municipal and congressional elections but also in private and secondary associations. The penetration of parties into Chilean society was such that even high school student associations, community groups, universities, and professional societies selected leaders on party slates. Political democracy helped democratize social groups and erode historic patterns of authoritarian social relations.

It is crucial to stress that there were no giants in the Chilean political system. No single party or tendency could win a majority and impose its will. This pattern had clear implications for the functioning of Chile's presidential system.

Since majorities were impossible to achieve, Chilean presidents were invariably elected by coalitions or were forced to build governing coalitions with opposing parties in Congress after the election. However, because preelection coalitions were constituted primarily for electoral reasons, in an atmosphere of considerable political uncertainty, they tended to disintegrate after a few months of the new administration.

Ideological disputes were often at the root of coalition changes, as partisans of one formula would resist the proposals of opponents. But narrow political considerations were also important. Since a president could not succeed himself, leaders of other parties in his coalition often realized they could best improve their fortunes in succeeding municipal and congressional elections by disassociating themselves from the difficulties of incumbency in a society fraught with economic problems. In the final analysis, only by proving their independent electoral strength in nonpresidential elections could parties demonstrate their value to future presidential coalitions.

Since Chilean presidents could not dissolve Congress in case of an impasse or loss of congressional support, they needed to build alternative alliances in order to govern. Parties assured their influence by requiring that candidates nominated for cabinet posts seek their party's permission (*pase*) to serve in office. Presidents, required continually to forge working coalitions, were repeatedly frustrated by the sense of instability and permanent crisis that this bargaining process gave Chilean politics.

An image of Chile's party system as excessively competitive and polarized, however, is incomplete and inaccurate. The collapse of party agreements, the censure of ministers, and the sharp disagreement over major policy issues captured the headlines and inflamed people's passions. But the vast majority of political transactions were characterized by compromise, flexibility, and respect for the institutions and procedures of constitutional democracy. Over the years, working agreements among political rivals led to implementing far-reaching policies, including state-sponsored industrialization; comprehensive national health, welfare, and educational systems; agrarian reform; and copper nationalization. Agreements were also structured around the more mundane aspects of politics. Congressmen and party leaders of different stripes would join in efforts to promote a particular region or to provide special benefits to constituency groups and individuals.[19]

This pattern of give-and-take can be attributed to three mutually reinforcing factors: a pragmatic center; the viability of representative arenas of decision-making and neutrality of public institutions; and the imperatives of electoral politics. Compromise would have been difficult without the flexibility provided by Center parties, notably the Radical Party, which inherited the role of the nineteenth-century Liberals as the fulcrum of coalition politics. The Radicals supported, at one time or another, the rightist presidencies of the two Alessandris in the 1930s and 1960s and governed with support of the Right in the late 1940s. In the late 1930s and through most of the 1940s, however, they allied with the Left to form Popular Front governments under a Radical president, and in the 1970s, a substantial portion of the party supported Salvador Allende, though by then the party's strength had been severely eroded.

Accommodation and compromise were also the hallmarks of democratic institutions such as the Chilean Congress, whose law-making, budgetary, and investigatory powers provided incentives for party leaders to set aside disagreements in matters of mutual benefit. Indeed, the folkways of the legislative institution, stemming from years of close working relationships in committees and on the floor, contributed to the development of legendary private friendships among leaders who were strong public antagonists. Just as significant, however, were such prestigious institutions as the armed forces, the judiciary, and the comptroller general, respected for their "neutrality" and remoteness from the clamor of everyday politics. These institutions provided an important safety valve from the hyperpoliticization of most of public life. The legitimacy of public institutions was further reinforced by a strong commitment to public service, which extended from the presidential palace to the rural police station. Although electoral fraud and vote-buying by political party machines were common, financial corruption remained very rare in Chilean public life, and the vigilance of the Congress and the courts helped prevent wrongdoing for personal gain by public office–holders.

Finally, the press of continuous elections forced political leaders to turn away from ideological pursuits and attend to the more mundane side of politics, such as personal favors and other particularistic tasks inherent in a representative system. Congressmen and senators had to look after their party brokers in municipalities and neighborhoods, making sure to provide public funds for a local bridge or jobs for constituents. Often political leaders from different parties joined in advancing the common interests of their constituencies, setting aside acrimonious, abstract debates over the role of the state in the economy or Soviet policy in Asia. In Chile, the politics of ideology, rooted in strong social inequalities, was counterbalanced by the clientelistic politics of electoral accountability reinforced by that same inequality. As will be noted below, many of these elements disappeared during the later 1960s and early 1970s, putting the democratic system under great strain and ultimately contributing to its total collapse.

• ORIGINS OF CHILEAN DEMOCRACY:
A THEORETICAL ASSESSMENT •

Because it is one of the few cases in which a democratic government was successfully established in the mid-nineteenth century, and an especially dramatic example of democratic failure, Chile constitutes a valuable paradigmatic case in the effort to construct theoretical propositions explaining the origins, consolidation, and breakdown of democratic regimes. Its theoretical utility is enhanced by the fact that there are no comparable cases of democratic development outside the Western European–North American context, or among primarily Catholic or export-oriented countries. As a deviant case, which has been largely neglected in scholarly literature, Chile can serve as a useful test for the validity of theoretical propositions generated by observing the experience of other countries, primarily European.[20]

The most prominent theses aimed at explaining the development of democracy assume that political practices and institutions can be understood by reference to a series of historical, cultural, or economic determinants. It is the central argument of this chapter that such approaches fall short in accounting for Chilean exceptionality, and that the Chilean case can be best explained by considering political factors as independent variables in their own right. This section will review the "determinants" of democracy embodied in what can be called the colonial-continuity thesis, the political-culture thesis, and the economic–class-structure thesis.[21] It will then turn to an analysis of those political variables that are most helpful in understanding Chile's political evolution, variables that can add to the development of theoretical propositions to be tested in other contexts.

Naturally, any hypotheses derived from the Chilean case or any single case will remain tentative until subjected to systematic comparative analysis drawing on a broader sample of carefully chosen observations. Without comparative evidence it would be difficult to identify those factors that are generalizable and constitute necessary conditions for the development of democratic practices and institutions, and those that are unique to and ultimately incorrect for explaining the single case.

The Colonial-Continuity Thesis

According to the colonial-continuity thesis, democratic practices will flourish in postcolonial regimes if institutions for self-rule, even if limited, were in place for several generations during colonial times, and if the transition from colony to independent state was accomplished without too much violence and destruction of those institutions. Both these conditions figure prominently in accounts of the outcome of the British decolonization experiences of the eighteenth and twentieth centuries.[22] It is clear that this thesis cannot account for the Chilean case. Although Chile was a more isolated colony than the major centers of Spanish rule in the new world, there is no evidence that the colony was able to gain the necessary autonomy to develop institutions of self-rule that would carry it into the postindependence period. Chile was subject to the same patrimonial administration and mercantilistic policies that discouraged expressions of political or economic independence and frowned on participatory institutions as contrary to the fundamental conception of monarchical rule. The colonies were the personal property of the king, subject to his direct control. Moreover, the Chilean wars of independence were profoundly disruptive of the previous political order, plunging the nation into a fratricidal conflict that tore asunder institutions and political practices that had been in place for generations. Although Chileans later established democratic rule, this accomplishment had little to do with the political experiences gained in colonial times.[23]

There is, however, a variant of the continuity thesis that must be addressed because it constitutes the principal explanation found in the historiographical literature dealing with Chilean exceptionality. According to this thesis, Chile deviated from the pattern that held sway in nineteenth-century Latin America not because its colonial institutions were more liberal, but because its post-independence institutions were more conservative. This argument holds that Diego Portales, the cabinet minister who dominated the government of President Prieto during the 1830s, helped to establish firm and authoritarian rule equivalent to that of the Spanish crown during the colonial era, thus rescuing Chile from misguided liberals enamored with unrealistic federal formulae and excessive freedoms.[24] Chile succeeded not because it broke from the colonial past, this argument holds, but because it reimposed that past. Morse articulates the point:

> Chile was an example perhaps unparalleled of a Spanish American country which managed, after a twelve-year transitional period, to avoid the extremes of tyranny and anarchy with a political system unencumbered by the mechanisms and party rhetoric of exotic liberalism. . . . [T]he structure of the Spanish patrimonial state was recreated with only those minimum concessions to Anglo-French constitutionalism that were necessary for a nineteenth century republic which had just rejected monarchical rule.[25]

It is disingenuous to argue, as most Chileans do, that Portales forged Chile's institutions singlehandedly. The minister was in office for only a total of three years, had little to do with drafting the 1833 Constitution, and died in office at a time when his government was under serious challenge.[26] Regardless of Portales' role, it is also profoundly mistaken to argue that Chile's concessions to Anglo-French constitutionalism were minimal. The political system established by the Constitution of 1833 was qualitatively different from the colonial system of the past, bearing far greater resemblance to the institutions and practices followed in the North American colonies, and the compromises struck at the constitutional convention in Philadelphia, than to the institutions set up by the Castilian rulers.

In Weberian terms, Chile's new constitutional formula substituted rational-legal authority for traditional authority; that is, it replaced the authority of an hereditary monarch, whose power was inherent in his person by virtue of divinely ordained practices going back generations, with the authority of an elected president whose power derived from the office as defined by law. Moreover, rather than recreating colonial patterns of political domination, nineteenth-century Chilean politics from the outset expanded the concept of citizenship (a radical notion at the time) and affirmed the legitimacy of elected assemblies to claim political sovereignty equally with the chief executive.

When viewed in this light, the achievements of the forgers of Chilean institutionality are very significant in contrast to those of their North American counterparts, who fashioned their institutions and practices by drawing on generations of experience with self-rule within the political framework of Tudor England.[27]

The Political-Culture Thesis

Perhaps the most influential set of propositions associated with the development of democratic institutions are those that hold that democracy requires a country's citizens, or at the very least its politically active elites, to share the liberal beliefs and values that are the hallmark of the Enlightenment. These include values conducive to accepting the equality of all people and their fundamental worth, values tolerating opposition and the free expression of ideas, and values celebrating the legitimacy of moderation and compromise. In short, they are the values associated with participatory politics as opposed to authoritarian patterns of governance. These political-culture variables have figured prominently in efforts to explain the general failure of democracy in Latin America and in Latin Europe, and the success of democracy in Protestant Europe and the United States. Democracy succeeded in the United States, this argument holds, because the British colonies were populated by settlers already imbued with more egalitarian values stemming from the Enlightenment and the Protestant Reformation. By contrast, the colonizers of Latin America brought aristocratic and feudal values reinforced by a Catholic faith stressing the importance of hierarchy, authority, corporativism, and the immutability of the traditional social order.[28]

But if the absence of democracy in Latin America is explained by the lack of appropriate beliefs, how can we account for the Chilean case? Were Chileans, located in one of the most remote colonies of the empire and dominated by an aristocracy of Basque descent, less tied to royal institutions? Or was the Chilean church more liberal or less influential in the social and political life of the colony? None of the historical evidence supports these contentions. To the contrary, Chile's isolation had made the colony one of the most traditional on the continent. Royalist sentiment was as strong in Chile as anywhere else, and troops who fought with the Spaniards to suppress the insurrection were recruited locally. Similarly, the church was as conservative as in other countries and retained the strong backing of the local aristocracy despite its close ties with the colonial power. Chilean elites were no less Catholic than the political elites of other former colonies.[29]

A variant of the political-culture thesis holds that it is not so much the religious traditions or political practices of the past that condition political beliefs and attitudes, but the authority relations found in secondary spheres of society: the workplace, the family, or the educational system.[30] Of particular importance in a predominantly agricultural society are the social relations of production resulting from the country's land-tenure system. Where land is concentrated in a small number of estates with traditional patron-client authority relations, this thesis argues, political values will be hierarchical and authoritarian. Where land is divided more equally and exploited by family farmers and contract labor, political values will be more egalitarian and democratic, facilitating the development of democratic politics. This is the argument that Booth makes in attempting to account for democratic development in Costa Rica.[31] Dahl echoes this approach when he suggests that the Chilean case can be explained by "considerable equality in distribution of land and instruments of coercion, reinforced by norms favoring social and political equality."[32]

However, Dahl's argument also fails to stand up to historical scrutiny. Chile's system of social relations and stratification was one of the most rigid and traditional on the continent, based on large landed estates and semifeudal relationships of authority between landlord and peasant. Authority relations in the family and in the educational system, still under church tutelage, were also authoritarian and hierarchical.[33] The wars of independence disrupted the country's social structure less than they did elsewhere. As Dominguez notes, "Chile lagged behind the other colonies, although it had experienced economic growth and mobilization. Its society had been transformed the least. The social bonds within it remained strong. Centralization had not been advanced nor had society been pluralized. Traditional elites remained strong, and traditional orientations prevailed."[34] Throughout the nineteenth and well into the twentieth century, the traditional nature of social relations in the countryside remained one of the most striking features of the Chilean social structure. Despite the rise of an urban working class and the democratization of other spheres of social life, rural social relations were not significantly altered until the 1960s, when agrarian reform was finally undertaken as national policy.[35]

There is no reason to assume that the evolution of democratic politics in Chile in the nineteenth century was due to more "favorable" political-culture variables. The failure of cultural explanations to account for the Chilean case raises serious questions about the underlying assumption that there is a direct fit between societal values and political institutions. It is very unlikely that Chile had societal values comparable to those of Norway, Australia, or the United States (though they may not have been too dissimilar to those found in class-concious Britain), yet the political outcomes were not dissimilar. Several students of democracy have argued that "stable" democracy is the product not only of liberal and participatory values, but of a mixture of participatory and deferential ones. However, in the absence of a clearly defined set of values that relate to democracy, it is difficult to ascertain which mix is appropriate. As a result, there is a real temptation to engage in circular reasoning: If a particular regime was stable or had the requisite democratic characteristics, it was assumed it had *ipso facto* the appropriate value structure.

Although egalitarian and democratic values were not necessary to structure democratic institutions and procedures, the Chilean case suggests that the exercise of democratic practices over a period of time encourages the development of certain norms of political conduct and reinforces belief in the legitimacy of the rules of the game. As early as the 1850s, Chilean political elites of different ideological persuasions worked together in Congress to advance common objectives, thus developing habits of flexibility and compromise. The Radicals, who were excluded from decisionmaking roles in Argentina until after the 1912 Saenz Peña law, were invited to serve in cabinets fifty years earlier in Chile.

As an industrial working class developed, moreover, Chilean elites, despite serious objections to accepting the principle of collective bargaining at the workplace and brutal repression of the incipient labor movement, accepted the legitimate role of working-class parties in the arena of electoral competition and eventually in the corridors of power. Democratic institutions came to be accepted by most Chileans as the best way to resolve disagreements and set national policy. By mid-twentieth century, ordinary Chileans took great pride in their civic duties, participating enthusiastically in an electoral process that made Chile distinctive among Third World nations. In sum, Chilean democracy emerged without strongly held democratic values. But the practice of democracy itself instilled norms of give-and-take, tolerance, and respect for fundamental liberties that were widely shared by the population as a whole.[36]

This does not mean that democratic politics in Chile were centrist-oriented and devoid of sharp conflict. In 1891, after thirty years of domestic tranquility, the strongly felt political anatagonisms generated by the executive-congressional impasse spilled onto the battlefield, a conflict that nonetheless pales by comparison with the U.S. Civil War, which also took place eighty years after the Declaration of Independence. The deep ideological disagreements of twentieth-century Chile continuously challenged the country's institutions and practices. The Chilean case and those of other highly polarized political systems like Italy, France, and Finland show that consensus on the fundamentals of public policy can be relatively low, while consensus on the rules and procedures for arriving at policy decisions can be high.

It was not moderation that made Chilean democracy function; It was Chilean democracy that helped moderate political passions and manage deep-seated divisions. A democratic political culture is not an abstract set of beliefs or psychological predispositions governing interpersonal relations in the body politic, but practical and ingrained traditions and working relations based on regularized patterns of political interaction in the context of representative institutions. As will be noted below, with the breakdown of democracy, Chile lost not only representative rule, but the institutional fabric that helped define many of the values of democratic human conduct.

The Economic–Class-Structure Thesis

While there is broad variation in studies emphasizing the economic determinants of democracy, they can be divided into two categories: those relating democracy to overall levels of economic development; and those focusing on the contribution to the creation of democratic institutions of particular groups or classes that emerge as a result of economic transformations in society.

The first group draws on the insights of "modernization" theory, arguing that economic development leads to more complex, differentiated, secularized, and educated societies, opening the way for the rise of new groups and institutions that find expression in democratic practices.[37] In addition, economic growth is said to provide channels for upward mobility and for ameliorating the sharp social disparities found in poor societies, disparities that undermine democratic performance. Empirical evidence for these propositions was advanced in a host of cross-national studies conducted in the late 1960s, inspired by Lipset's classic article on the "economic correlates of democracy."[38] The main difficulty with these studies in explaining the Chilean case is that they are ahistorical. Chile in the nineteenth century, like most incipient democracies of the time, was a rural, pre-industrial society with very low levels of personal wealth and literacy, yet it met many of the criteria for democratic performance. In the twentieth century, as several authors have noted, Chile was clearly an outlier, exhibiting many of the characteristics of economic underdevelopment while boasting high scores on democratic performance.[39] As Linz has argued, explanations that draw on levels of economic development do not contribute much to our understanding of the origins and development of democratic politics.[40]

Scholars writing in a Marxist tradition have argued that the most important variable is not overall economic development, but the rise of rural and urban middle classes capable of challenging the monopoly of landed elites and breaking their political power. Based on his reflections on the European case, Therborn attributes the rise of democracy to the emergence of agrarian bourgeois groups, giving particular emphasis to "the strength of these agrarian classes and the degree of their independence from the landowning aristocracy and urban big capital."[41] Moore goes further, presenting a more complex argument. For Moore, as for Therborn, the development of a bourgeoisie was central to the development of democracy. However, whether a country actually followed a democratic path depended on how agriculture was commercialized, whether or not it became "labor repressive" or "market commercial."[42]

As with the political-culture thesis, it is difficult to accept the applicability of the economic–class-structure thesis to the Chilean case. As noted earlier, Chilean agriculture remained "labor repressive" well into the twentieth century, retaining a high concentration of land ownership. And though, as Dominguez notes, Chilean agriculture was geared by the eighteenth century to the export of wheat, wheat production was never commercialized as in North America. As in czarist Russia, it was expanded with only minimal modifications to the traditional manorial system.[43] By the same token, and despite some interpretations of Chilean history that stress the rise of an urban bourgeoisie as the key liberalizing force, Chile did not develop a strong and independent urban-based bourgeoisie before the development of democratic rules and procedures. Although mining interests became powerful and some of the most prominent mine owners were identified with the Radical Party, it is mistaken to identify Chilean mining interests as representatives of a new and differentiated bourgeois class. Other, equally prominent mine owners had close ties to the Conservative Party, and many members of the Chilean elite had both mining and agricultural interests.[44]

However, the most telling argument against the economic–class-structure thesis has already been anticipated in the historical discussion at the beginning of this chapter. The rise of democracy in Chile—including the limitations on presidential authority, the expansion of legislative prerogatives, and the extension of suffrage—took place not over the objections of the conservative landed elites but, as in Britain, at their instigation. If the traditional landowning class, which championed the Roman Catholic church, decided to support suffrage expansion and the development of democratic institutions, then theoretical explanations that hold that democracy emerges only with the destruction of that class are less than adequate. This is a central point, to which we will return.

The Political-Determinants Thesis

An examination of various theses dealing with the historical, cultural, and economic "determinants" of democracy suggests that they are not particularly useful in explaining the Chilean case. What is more, the Chilean case, as one of successful democratic development that does not conform to the principal arguments of those theses, raises serious questions about their overall validity. However, from this evidence alone it would be clearly mistaken to argue that these factors play no substantial role in democratic development. A "liberal" colonial tradition, egalitarian values, economic development, and a variegated social structure are undoubtedly conducive to the implementation and acceptance of institutions of self-governance. Indeed, a perspective such as the one advocated here, the political-determinants thesis, which stresses the importance of discrete political variables and even historical accidents as independent variables, need not eschew the economic and cultural constants nor shy away from developing generalizations that relate socioeconomic to political variables. The point is that these cultural and economic variables are hardly determinants of democratic practices. They may very well be important contributory or even sufficient conditions; but they are not necessary ones.

A historical review of the development of Chilean political institutions immediately suggests the utility of the "political-crisis" literature developed by political scientists. According to this literature, all countries face severe challenges in developing democratic institutions and, depending on the timing and sequence of those challenges, have greater or lesser success in achieving democratic stability.[45] Although the challenges vary in kind and number, most authors view the crises of national identity (creating a sense of national community over parochial loyalties), authority (establishing viable state structures), and participation (incorporating the citizenry into the political system) as crucial.

In addition, the sequence and timing of the appearance of these problems on the historical scene can seriously affect the political outcome. As Nordlinger puts it, "the probabilities of a political system developing in a nonviolent, non-authoritarian, and eventually democratically viable manner are maximized when a national identity emerges first, followed by the institutionalization of the central government, and then the emergence of mass parties and mass electorate."[46] It can be argued that Chile followed this "optimal" sequence and that the timing was also favorable, particularly with respect to the emergence of the participation crisis, which did not become a critical issue until after central authority structures had been consolidated.[47]

National identity.   It is doubtful that Chileans considered themselves a nation before independence, because there were far fewer mechanisms of social communication and exchange than in North America and a far more ubiquitous set of colonial authority structures.[48] However, the clear-cut military victory in the war against the Peru-Bolivia Confederation, a victory without parallel in Latin America, gave the small, divided nation a powerful new sense of confidence and purpose, creating tangible symbols of patriotism and nationality. These feelings were reinforced with the victory of Chilean forces in the War of the Pacific, which led to the incorporation of large portions of Peruvian and Bolivian territory into national boundaries.

Political authority.   Rustow has noted the importance of distinguishing between establishing and consolidating institutions of democracy. Consolidation involves a lengthy process of "habituation," which is not necessarily unilinear; there can be reversals and even breakdown.[49] In consolidating political authority in Chile, five factors were critically important: leadership; state autonomy; government efficacy; civilian control of the armed forces; and conservative support for democratic rules.

The first important element was leadership. General Bulnes, drawing on his command of the most powerful armed forces in the country and his widespread popularity, could have easily used his position to establish personal rule, following the pattern of notable Latin American *caudillos* such as Paez in Venezuela, Rosas in Argentina, or Santa Ana in Mexico. Instead, like Washington in the United States, he insisted on working within the framework of established political institutions and chose to leave office at the end of his term, making way for his successor. His willingness while in office to underscore the autonomy of the courts, accept the role of Congress in policy, and allow ministerial cabinets to formulate the government's program set a precedent for his successor and future administrations, and helped to establish the legitimacy of democratic institutions.[50]

The second important factor was state autonomy. A crucial legacy of Bulnes' and, later, Montt's respect for constitutionally mandated institutions was the development of politics and government service as a vocation. An impressive group of functionaries and legislators emerged who were committed to strengthening and expanding the secular state. By 1860, more than 2,500 people worked for the state, not including local officials, construction workers, and members of the armed forces. All of Chile's nineteenth-century presidents save one had extensive congressional experience before being elected to office, and five who took office before 1886 began their careers in the Bulnes administration. Between Bulnes and Pinochet, only two of Chile's twenty-two presidents were career military officers, and both of those were freely elected with political-party support in moments of political crisis.[51]

The third element was governmental efficacy. Under the leadership of the first three presidents to serve after 1830, the Chilean economy performed relatively well. This not only brought credit to the new institutions and leaders of the independent nation, but more importantly, it gave the government elites time and autonomy to begin state consolidation. By the time important interests sought to stop the expansion of the secular state, it had garnered significant political, financial, and military strength.[52]

The fourth factor was control of the armed forces by civilian governmental leaders. By deliberately refusing until after the War of the Pacific to create a professional military establishment, while retaining close political control over an effective national militia, Chilean officials were able to establish a monopoly over the control of force and a tradition of civilian supremacy over the military. The military challenges of 1851 and 1859 were defeated, discouraging dissident elites from gathering their own military force to challenge national authority structures.

The fifth factor was conservative support for democratic rules. This factor is directly related to the development of state autonomy and control of the military. Control of the military prevented aggrieved sectors of the elites from resorting to insurrectionary movements in order to prevent state action or to capture the state by force. Thus such elites, including conservative landholders, were forced to turn to democratic procedures already in place, and indeed to seek their expansion, in order to preserve and advance their interests. Far from being a minor footnote in history, this support of the Chilean conservatives for liberal rules was of central importance. It led to the creation of a Conservative Party, committed to representative institutions, which had no exact parallel in Latin America or Latin Europe.

This leads to a basic proposition: that the origins and evolution of democratic institutions and procedures are determined more by the choices made by key elites seeking to maximize their interests within the framework of specific structural and political parameters, than they are by abstract cultural or economic factors. Chilean elites, initially hostile to democracy, came to embrace democratic rules as a conscious choice for political survival, in the process contributing to the strengthening of those institutions over the years.[53] Where political elites have fewer incentives to support democratic institutions, and, in particular, where resorting to force to prevent the distribution of power through the expansion of citizenship is a viable option for those elites, the consolidation of democratic authority structures is seriously jeopardized.

Participation. Perhaps the greatest challenge to the consolidation of stable democracy is the expansion of citizenship rights to nonelite elements, and the incorporation into the political process of new groups and classes. Like Britain and Norway, but unlike Latin Europe, the consolidation of democratic institutions in Chile benefited from a gradual extension of suffrage, less in response to pressures from below than as a consequence of interelite rivalries and strategies to maximize electoral gain. Like Britain, but unlike Latin Europe, Chile found in the elites of the Conservative Party the driving force in the first pivotal extension of suffrage in 1874. This took place a dozen years before the French Third Republic teetered on the brink of collapse with Boulangisme, and twenty-five years before the French Right, still resisting republicanism and democracy, became embroiled in the Dreyfus Affair. It also took place forty years before the pope lifted the *non-expedit* that barred Catholics from participating in Italian elections.

The extension of suffrage in Chile clearly benefited the Conservatives who controlled the countryside, but it also benefited middle-class sectors who identified with the growing urban-based Radical Party. Forty-two years before the adoption of the Saenz Peña Law in Argentina, which forced reluctant Conservatives to suddenly expand the electoral system to permit the Radical Party's eruption on the political stage, Chile had initiated the gradual expansion of suffrage, permitting middle-class sectors to become full participants in ministerial and congressional politics.

In a classic case of what Merton calls the unanticipated consequences of purposive social action, the expansion of suffrage in Chile also soon benefited the growing working class.[54] But the entry of the working class into politics in Chile was also gradual, coming both after the consolidation of parliamentary institutions and after middle-class parties had become full actors in the political process. Indeed, in the 1910s, suffrage expansion was actually limited by complex electoral rules and byzantine electoral pacts in which the working-class parties became full participants.

The gradual expansion of suffrage and incorporation of new groups in Chile had some clear implications for the country's democratic development. Had the pressure for full participation coincided with attempts to set up democratic institutions, it is difficult to see how these could have survived. At the same time, however, it is important to stress that in Chile, suffrage expansion and party development occurred prior to the growth of a powerful and centralized state bureaucracy. The growth of the public sector was consequently shaped by organizations whose primary goals were electoral success and accountability. This reinforced the viability of representative institutions. Where strong bureaucracies emerged before strong parties or legislatures, as in Brazil or Argentina, informal or officially sponsored linkage networks without popular representation were much more likely to develop, encouraging corporatist and authoritarian patterns of interest representation.[55]

In sum, the political-determinants thesis suggests that the development of democracy must be understood as a complex process that owes much to fortuitous events and variables, such as leadership, that defy quantification and precise definition. It is a long and difficult course, subject to challenges and reversals as societal conditions and the correlations of political forces change. Its chances of success are better in some contexts than others and may depend on the timing and sequence of fundamental societal challenges.

In the final analysis, however, democracy involves human choice by competing groups and leaders who must determine whether peaceful mechanisms for the resolution of conflict, based on the concept of popular sovereignty, provide them with the best possible guarantees under the circumstances. More often than not, this choice may stem from an inconclusive struggle for power; a situation of stalemate where there are no clear winners. That being so, democracy can be understood as resulting from a set of compromises—second-preference choices—in which the concurrence of nondemocrats may be as important as the support of democrats. Once democracy is structured, it provides the key rules of the game, defining the parameters for action and the strategies to be pursued by relevant actors. In time, democratic rules may be accepted as the only proper norms for political conduct, but only if democracy continues to provide guarantees to all players, even if it is not the preferred system of all.

• THE BREAKDOWN OF CHILEAN DEMOCRACY •

Chilean Politics and the Dialectic of Regime Breakdown

The breakdown of Chilean democracy did not occur overnight. Several developments contributed to the erosion of the country's system of political compromise and accommodation, even before the 1970 election of President Salvador Allende. These included the adoption of a series of reforms aimed at making Chilean politics more "efficient," and the rise of a new and more ideological Center, less willing to play the game of political give-and-take.[56]

In 1958, a coalition of the Center and Left joined in enacting a series of electoral reforms aimed at abolishing what were considered corrupt electoral practices. Among the measures was the abolition of joint lists, a long-established tradition of political pacts that permitted parties of opposing ideological persuasions to structure agreements for mutual electoral benefit. While this reform succeeded in making preelection arrangements less "political," it also eliminated an important tool for cross-party bargaining. More important were reforms aimed at curbing congressional authority, promulgated in the guise of strengthening the executive's ability to deal with Chile's chronic economic troubles. Congressional politics were viewed by chief executives and party elites of various political persuasions as excessively incremental and old-fashioned; the antithesis of modern administrative practices. In the name of modernity, the executive was given control of the budgetary process in 1959, and Congress was restricted in its ability to allocate fiscal resources. Indeed, under the Christian Democratic administration (1964–1970), government technocrats pushed strongly to restrict entirely congressional allocations of funds for small patronage projects, even though these represented an infinitesimal portion of the total budget.

The most serious blow to congressional authority came with the constitutional reforms enacted in 1970, this time through a coalition of the Right and Center. Among other provisions, the reforms prohibited amendments not germane to a given piece of legislation and sanctioned the use of executive decrees to implement programs approved by the legislature in very broad terms. More significantly, it barred Congress from matters dealing with social security, salary adjustments, and pensions in the private and public sectors—the heart of legislative bargaining in an inflation-ridden society.[57]

These reforms went a long way toward cutting back on many of the traditional sources of patronage and log-rolling, reducing the most important political arena for compromise in Chilean politics. Again, the principal motivation was to strengthen executive efficiency. It is clear, however, that the 1960 reformers were also convinced they would be able to win the 1970 presidential election and did not want to have to deal with a difficult Congress in which the Left had a strong presence. Ironically, it was the Left that won the presidency, leaving a legislature with reduced powers in the hands of the Right and Center.

Although these changes were significant, they were symptomatic of other far-reaching changes in Chilean politics, the most notable of which was the rise in the 1960s of a new Center party with a markedly different political style. Unlike their predecessor, the pragmatic Radicals, the Chilean Christian Democrats conceived of themselves as a new and vital ideological force in Chilean politics, a middle road between Marxist transformation and preservation of the status quo. The Christian Democrats believed they would be capable of capturing the allegiance of large portions of the electorate from both sides of the political divide, and become a new majority force. In the early 1960s, they began an unprecedented effort at popular mobilization, appealing to women and middle-class voters, as well as factory workers and especially shanty-town dwellers. Their determination to transform the physiognomy of Chilean politics was strengthened by their success in capturing the presidency under the leadership of Eduardo Frei in 1964, in an electoral coalition with the Right, and by their impressive victory in the 1965 congressional race, the best showing by a single party in Chile's modern history. Their success presented a serious challenge to the parties of both the Right and Left. The Right was practically obliterated in the 1965 election, while the Left redoubled its efforts to maintain its constituents and to appeal with a more militant cry to Chile's most destitute citizens.

Once in office and heartened by their electoral success, the Christian Democrats sought to implement their "revolution in liberty" by disdaining the traditional coalition politics of the past. They were particularly hard on the now-diminished Radicals, refusing any overtures for collaboration. Unlike the Radicals, they were unwilling to tolerate clientelistic and log-rolling politics or to serve as an effective bridge across parties and groups. Although they enacted critical copper "Chileanization" legislation in concert with the Right, and agrarian reform in coalition with the Left, the Christian Democrats went out of their way to govern as a single party and refused to deal with opponents unless they had to. At the same time, they expended large amounts of state resources and vast amounts of U.S. foreign-aid funds on programs that were clearly designed to enhance their electoral superiority at the expense of both Right and Left.[58]

The Christian Democrats' rigid posture added to the growing radicalization of elites on the Left (particularly the Socialist Party), who feared the electoral challenge of the Center party, and to profound resentment among elites on the Right, who felt betrayed by the reforms, especially in land redistribution, enacted by their erstwhile coalition partners. Radicalization of the Left was also profoundly affected by international events, notably the Cuban Revolution, which set a new standard for the Latin American Left to emulate.

Had the Christian Democrats succeeded in becoming a genuine Center majority, the increased ideological tension would not have had such serious institutional repercussions. But despite vast organizational efforts and extraordinary levels of foreign aid from the Johnson administration in Washington, which was anxious to promote Chile as a showcase of democracy on a continent fascinated by Cuba, they did not succeed in breaking the tripartite deadlock of Chilean politics.

As a result, even when it became apparent that the Christian Democrats would not be able to win the 1970 presidential election in their own right, they were unable to structure preelection coalitions with either the Right or the Left. The bulk of the Radical Party joined in supporting Salvador Allende, who stunned most observers by edging out rightist Jorge Alessandri by a plurality of 36.2 percent to 34.9 percent of the vote. Christian Democratic candidate Radomiro Tomic received only 27.8 percent of the vote.

The election of Allende was not the result of growing radicalization or political mobilization. Nor was it due, in Huntington's terms, to the inability of Chile's political institutions to channel societal demands. Allende won even though he received a smaller percentage of the vote than he had received in his loss to Frei in the two-way race of 1964. Electoral analysis suggests that a greater percentage of newly mobilized voters voted for the Right than for the Left. The election results simply underscored the repercussions of the failure of the Right and Center to structure a preelection coalition.[59]

Because no candidate received an absolute majority, the election had to be decided in Congress, forcing the creation of a postelection coalition. Christian Democrats joined legislators of the Left in confirming Allende's accession to the highest office in the nation. But the president's minority status, and his lack of majority support in Congress, meant that like other presidents before him, he would have to tailor his program to the realities of coalition politics in order to succeed, even though the very reforms that the Right and the Christian Democrats had enacted made such compromises more difficult. But compromise was easier said than done. Important elements in the Unidad Popular (Popular Unity, UP) coalition, including Allende's own Socialist Party, were openly committed to a revolutionary transformation in the socioeconomic order and the institutional framework of Chilean politics. Furthermore, the coalition was unwieldy and fractious, with parties and groups competing as much with one another for spoils and popular support as with the opposition.

At the same time, Allende's election touched off an extraordinary reaction from other sectors of Chilean society, who feared a pro-Moscow, Marxist-Leninist system might be established in Chile, to their detriment. They encouraged sabotage, subversion, and foreign intrigue. On both sides of Chile's divided party system, the commitment to change or preservation of the status quo now exceeded the commitment to the principles and practices of Chile's historic democracy.

Under these circumstances, structuring a Center coalition committed to social change within the framework of traditional liberties and democratic guarantees was crucial to the system's survival. However, like the Christian Democrats before them, many leaders of the UP coalition became convinced that bold use of state power could break the political deadlock and swing the balance to the Left. This misconception led them to enact a host of ill-conceived redistributive and stimulative economic measures, which aggravated inflation and generated serious economic difficulties. When combined with measures of questionable legality to bring private business under state control, these policies alienated not only Chile's corporate elite, but also small businessmen and much of Chile's middle class.

In an atmosphere of growing suspicion and violence, the lines of communication between leaders and followers of opposing parties eroded, accentuating the polarization of Chilean politics. At several key junctures, and despite pressures from both sides, attempts were made to forge a Center consensus and structure the necessary compromises that would have saved the regime. But Center groups and moderate politicians on both sides of the political divide abdicated their responsibility in favor of narrower group stakes and short-term interests. The involvement of "neutral" powers, such as the courts and the military, only served to politicize those institutions and pave the way for the military coup—a coup that undermined the very institutions of compromise and accommodation moderate leaders had professed to defend. With the failure of Congress, parties, the courts, and other state institutions to serve as viable arenas to resolve conflict, politics became more and more confrontational; contending groups resorted to mobilizing ever greater numbers of their followers to "prove" their power capabilities. Politics spilled out of the chambers of government onto the streets, exacerbating an atmosphere of fear and confrontation.[60]

The Chilean breakdown was a complex and dialectical process, in which time-tested patterns of accommodation were eroded by the rise of a Center unwilling to bridge the gap between extremes, by the decline of institutional arenas of accommodation in the name of technical efficiency, and by the hardening of ideological distance between leaders with radically different conceptions of a good society. It was also the product of gross miscalculations, extremism, narrow group stakes, and the lack of courage in key circumstances. Breakdown was not inevitable. While human action was severely circumscribed by the structural characteristics of Chilean politics and by the course of events, there was still room for choice for a leadership willing to prevent the final denouement. Nor did most Chileans want a military solution to the country's problems. Surveys taken in the weeks before the coup indicated an overwhelming support for democracy and a peaceful outcome of the political crisis.[61]

Political Structures and Regime Breakdown:
A Critique of Presidentialism

Although it was not inevitable, the breakdown of Chilean democracy raises serious questions about the viability of particular institutional forms of governance in democratic regimes. It is a premise of this chapter that in Chile there was an inadequate fit between the country's highly polarized and competitive party system, which was incapable of generating majorities, and a presidential system of centralized authority.[62]

The starting point for this argument must be a recognition that through much of the twentieth century, presidentialism in Chile was in crisis. By definition, a presidential election is a zero-sum game that freezes the outcome for a fixed period of time. In Chile, the winner invariably represented only a third of the electorate, and yet, as the head of government and head of state, he felt responsible for the national destiny as the embodiment of popular sovereignty. As minority presidents, however, Chilean chief executives received weak legislative support or outright congressional opposition. And since they could not seek reelection, there was little incentive for parties, including the president's, to support him beyond mid-term. The fixed terms for both president and Congress contributed to an atmosphere of ungovernability and a feeling of permanent crisis, alleviated only by the willingness of centrist parties or politicians to provide last minute reprieves to beleaguered presidents in exchange for ambassadorial appointments or concessions on policy.

Paradoxically, the response to this problem of governance was to seek an increase in presidential power. The resolution of the country's pressing social and economic problems required strong leadership, it was argued, and such leadership should not be thwarted by ideological wrangling and the narrow partisan interest of the parties and the legislature. However, increased presidential power only aggravated the problem by further reducing arenas for accommodation and by making executive-legislative relations more bitter. Indeed, the stronger the power of the presidency as a separate constitutional actor, the greater were the disincentives for structuring presidential support among parties and groups jealous of their autonomy and future electoral prospects.

In Chile, there was an inverse correlation between the power of the presidency and the success of presidential government. The stronger the president, the weaker the presidential system—a perverse logic that came to a tragic head in the Allende years. A parliamentary system of government would have defused the enormous pressures for structuring high-stakes coalitions around a winner-take-all presidential option, which only reinforced political polarization. At the same time, it would have eliminated the stalemate and confrontation in executive-legislative relations. Had Chile had a parliamentary regime in the early 1970s, Allende's government might have fallen, but democracy would have survived. The working majority in Congress that elected Allende to the presidential post would have had to continue for him to have retained his position. This was not out of the question. The Christian Democrats were close to the UP government on many key points of substance, as attested by the near-agreements at several key junctures of the unfolding drama of the UP years. And, had the coalition collapsed, it is quite likely that a Christian Democrat, or perhaps a member of the small Leftist Radical Party, would have formed a new government with support from elements on the Right.

It is important to stress that parliamentary politics would have had the opposite effect of presidential politics on party distance. It would have contributed to moderating Chilean politics by reinforcing the time-honored traditions of give-and-take honed by generations of politicians. Moderate leaders on both sides of the congressional aisle would have gained strength, encouraging centripetal drives toward coalition and compromise, rather than being outclassed by maximalist leaders who thrived in the public arenas of high-stakes electoral battles. Moreover, legislators of all parties would have thought twice about abandoning hard-fought coalition arrangements if they had faced the prospect of immediate reelection, and the greater accountability of having been part of an agreement to structure executive authority.

The considerations should be borne in mind by political leaders of both Right and Left in discussing the transition back to democracy after military rule. Ironically, as will be noted in the next section, the very prospect of a presidential election is one of the principal obstacles in structuring a return to democracy in Chile.

• MILITARY RULE IN CHILE
AND THE PROSPECTS FOR REDEMOCRATIZATION •

With the collapse of democracy, Chile was abruptly tranformed from an open and participatory political system into a repressive and authoritarian one. Few

Chileans could have imagined in September 1973 that military intervention would lead to a government so alien to institutions and traditions dating from the nation's founding. Fewer still would have believed that Chile would produce an authoritarian regime capable of outlasting other contemporary military governments on the continent, or that General Pinochet, the obedient commander who assured President Allende of his undivided loyalty, would achieve a degree of personal power rare in the annals of modern dictatorship. How could this transformation have taken place? What has happened to Chilean institutions under military rule? What are the prospects for transition back to stable democracy?

Soon after the coup, it became clear that Chile's military commanders, with no personal experience of direct involvement in politics, were not about to turn power back to civilian leaders after a brief interregnum. From the outset, they articulated two basic aims.[63] The first was to destroy the parties of the Left and their collaborators. The Chilean military did not interpret its intervention as a simple military coup aimed at replacing a government, but as an all-out war to crush an enemy that it believed had infiltrated close to half the population. However, military leaders were convinced that it was not only foreign Marxists who were to blame for Chile's predicament. They thought the Left had been able to make inroads because of the inherent weaknesses of liberal democracy, which they saw as encouraging corruption and demagoguery. Thus, their second objective was to engineer a fundamental restructuring of Chilean political institutions and political life, aimed at "cleaning" impurities from the body politic while creating a new political order of committed and patriotic citizens, dedicated to modernizing the country and projecting its grandeur to a hostile world.

The junta had a clear idea of how to pursue its first objective; it simply took the years of training, awesome firepower, and many contingency plans that had been developed to protect the constitutional government, and applied them to the new task of finding and neutralizing the enemy. Military units moved in to "clean up" neighborhoods that were strongholds of the Left, as if they were securing enemy territory during wartime.[64] Thousands of party leaders, trade-union officials, and community activists associated with the parties of the Left were "neutralized" through arrests, exile, and, in some cases, death. Labor unions were sharply circumscribed, parties were banned or declared in "recess," and internal elections were prohibited or closely monitored in all private organizations including professional associations and nonprofit agencies. Citizens, who during the Allende years and before had been repeatedly enlisted for one cause or another, now turned inward and avoided public affairs entirely, either out of fear of reprisals or outright support for military rule. Politics, which for generations had revolved around parties and interest groups that penetrated all levels of society, was now confined to small groups of individuals and cabals in the inner corridors of power. One of the most highly mobilized societies in the world became one of the most demobilized.

The junta, however, had a much hazier conception of how political power should be structured, no experience in governing, and no precise blueprint for its foundational program. In the first months and years, the military governed in an *ad hoc* and arbitrary fashion, at times racked by internal tension. Gradually, however, the commanders succeeded in establishing a degree of national political authority rare among Latin American military regimes. Ironically, a major reason for this achievement was that, in contrast to other bureaucratic authoritarian regimes in the Southern Cone, the Chilean military successfully invoked Chile's tradition of political stability and concern for legality to reinforce its own political control. By drawing on the ubiquitous power of the Chilean state and utilizing constitutional principles from Chile's presidentialist tradition, while, at the same time, restoring the principle of military obedience to constituted authority, Chile's commanders were able to structure efficient, if not fully legitimate, governing institutions. An important ingredient of this process was elevating General Pinochet to the role of president of the republic, while he retained his posts as commander-in-chief of the army and a voting member of the four-man junta. Further aiding the consolidation of political rule by Pinochet and his colleagues was the successful effort to implement far-reaching socioeconomic transformations of a more revolutionary nature than those attempted by their elected predecessors.[65]

It should be stressed that Pinochet did not resort to populist or charismatic rule, as did Juan Perón in Argentina and Getúlio Vargas of Brazil, nor was power based on developing a corrupt political machine like those of Paraguay's Alfredo Stroessner or the Somoza clan of Nicaragua. In Chile, the consolidation of political power and one-man rule was due to four fundamental factors. First, Pinochet and his advisers were able to draw on the framework of traditional constitutional legality to justify one-man rule. Second, they could rely on the disciplined and hierarchical nature of the armed forces and the growing power of the secret police. Third, they enjoyed the strong and uncritical support of much of the business community and sectors of the middle class. And fourth, they were able to take advantage of continued sharp divisions in the opposition, which continued to fuel widespread fear among influential Chileans that an end to military rule would permit the Left to resurge and once again challenge the socioeconomic status quo.

Constitutional Tradition and the Rise of Pinochet

In the immediate aftermath of the coup, the commanders of the army, navy, and air force, and the director general of the Carabineros (Chile's paramilitary police) constituted themselves as a governmental junta, which would exercise executive, legislative, and constitutional authority through unanimous agreement of its members. General Pinochet was selected to be junta president by virtue of his position as leader of the oldest military branch. He argued initially, however, that the junta presidency would rotate on a periodic basis among the commanders. Junta members also agreed to divide up policy areas so that each of the services would handle the affairs of different ministries. Even the appointment of university presidents was parceled out among the services, so that Pinochet named the army general who became president of the University of Chile, while Admiral Merino appointed one of his own colleagues to the top post at the Catholic University.

Pinochet, however, moved swiftly to assert his position as more than *primus inter pares*. Although Air Force General Gustavo Leigh was, in the early days, the most articulate, visible, and hardline member of the junta, Pinochet proved to be more politically skillful and ambitious.[66] But, Pinochet owed his ascendancy to more than his personal qualities. Ministers and other governmental officials automatically turned to the junta leader for direction, as they had always done to Chile's constitutional presidents. Soon, Pinochet was far better informed than the other junta members about government issues and began to make day-to-day decisions, including top government appointments, without consulting his colleagues. The growing junta staff, which he "generously" provided the junta from the ranks of the army, and the increasingly assertive secret police, both reported directly to Pinochet.

At the same time, key Conservative civilian and military legal advisers, even some of those who worked for other junta members, became increasingly uncomfortable with the concept of collegial rule, fearing that divided authority would lead to incoherent policies and regime instability. Ironically, they were profoundly influenced by Chilean constitutional law and the traditional practices of a strong presidential system. They could not conceive of a system of authority that did not reproduce the structure of Chile's presidential constitution, with its clear separation of powers between executive, legislative, and judicial branches. Working directly with Pinochet, they gradually proposed to the junta, which was overwhelmed by legislative detail and legal and policy complexities, the adoption of several measures aimed at "rationalizing" military rule in conformity with constitutional doctrine.

The most important of these was Decree Law 527 of June 26, 1974, which directly took the constitutional framework of the 1925 Constitution and applied it to the military government. It specified that the junta would exercise legislative and constitutional powers, while the junta president would have executive power as "Supreme Chief of the Nation."[67] The judiciary, which had shown a strong willingness to support the coup and defer to the armed forces on issues of personal liberties, would remain independent though subject to funding authorizations provided by the junta. Although the other commanders objected to Pinochet's new title, they went along with the measure, persuaded that it was necessary for the efficient administration of a country whose legal corpus was designed for a presidential regime. They were startled and displeased when Pinochet unexpectedly called a ceremony in which he donned the presidential sash.

Although the new statute was designed to institutionalize military authority by providing it with the legitimacy of Chile's presidentialist constitution, it failed to institute a genuine separation of powers. While Pinochet became the nation's chief executive, he continued to serve as one of the four junta members. Since all junta measures required a unanimous vote for adoption, any junta member could block legislation he did not approve of. Because Pinochet could resort to widespread executive authority to implement policy initiatives, the unanimity rule clearly worked in his favor. He could either work with the junta or ignore it; but the junta could not function without his consent. As the chief executive to whom ministers, government officials, and an expanding presidential staff reported, Pinochet had incomparably better information than did his colleagues. The junta soon became a weak legislature overwhelmed by initiatives from a large and complex state, ably administered by political and economic advisers and a growing secret police—all of whom owed exclusive loyalty to the president.

As Pinochet's powers grew, his relationship with the junta became more and more conflictive. General Leigh in particular bitterly opposed Pinochet's ambitions and growing prerogatives, as well as the growing influence over public and economic policy of a group of free-market economists protected by Pinochet. Leigh blocked, in mid-1977, Pinochet's proposal to have junta laws approved by a majority rather than by unanimity. At the end of that year, he also blocked Pinochet's request for junta approval of a referendum endorsing "President Pinochet in his defense of the dignity of Chile" in the face of widespread international criticisms of Chilean human-rights policy. Leigh perceived this as a move on the president's part to gain popular legitimacy for his mandate and to increase further his supremacy over the junta. Pinochet, in the face of junta objections, called the referendum anyway, invoking executive authority.

The tension between Pinochet and Leigh worsened as the two men continued to clash. But the president, making use of his now-considerable powers of persuasion, was able to get the other junta members to side with him against General Leigh. On July 28, 1978, with the support of the other two junta members, he forcibly and illegally removed General Leigh from office, risking an open and armed confrontation with the air force in order to accomplish his ends.[68] With this coup within the coup, Pinochet resolved his principal obstacle to unipersonal control of the Chilean state, control that was formally embodied in a legal foundation that reflected the constitutional practices of the past and gave the general the authority of Chile's traditional presidents without the constraints of a democratic political order.

With the defeat of opposition within the government, Pinochet moved with more confidence to design a new constitutional framework for the country's and his own future. In early 1980, a group of conservative legal advisers sent a constitutional draft to the Council of State for approval and revision. The draft, though based on the 1925 Constitution, called for a further increase in presidential authority, including a provision that reduced the autonomy of legislative bodies, and another that enabled the president to appoint several members of the Senate. The Constitution also created a National Security Council, composed primarily of the armed forces commanders, with the authority to rebuke any governmental institution, elected or nonelected, if its actions were deemed to be a threat to the national security. Finally, it outlawed parties and politically banned individuals for supporting doctrines that are based on the notion of "class struggle" or that "violate the integrity of the family."[69]

The Council of State also proposed a number of transitional provisions, calling for a return to democracy and open presidential elections by 1985. Although a Congress would be named before then, Pinochet would be allowed to continue as president until that date. However, Pinochet rejected these proposals. He made it clear to his advisers that he wanted a document that would enable him to stay in office at least until 1997, or through two more 8-year "constitutional" terms. When his advisers hesitated on the grounds that such a formula would be widely rejected even by the political Right, Pinochet agreed to a compromise whereby the four armed forces commanders (including himself) would select his successor in late 1988 or early 1989, subject to ratification in a popular plebiscite. But he managed to alter the Constitution in one way that made it easier for him to remain in office: The document specifically exempts him, by name, from the provision barring Chilean presidents from succeeding themselves in office.[70] In a 1980 plebiscite, held without electoral registration and in a climate that gave opponents few opportunities to challenge the government publicly, the new Constitution was approved by the voters, establishing Pinochet *de jure* as the most powerful leader in Chilean history.

Military Obedience to Authority

Ironically, military obedience to governmental authority, a second important factor in Chile's long democratic tradition, also abetted Pinochet's efforts at consolidating dictatorial supremacy. During the UP years, Chile's armed forces had become increasingly politicized, as officers openly called for the resignation of commanders unwilling to move to overthrow the constitutional government. Pinochet himself was forced to shift at the last minute from a position of loyalty to the elected government to support for a coup when he realized that "his" generals were in open revolt. In the immediate aftermath of the coup, military leaders moved quickly to reestablish the lines of authority within the institution and to stress the professional and "nondeliberative" character of the armed forces.

Pinochet proved his shrewdness by retiring those members of his cohort who had led in planning the coup, while at the same time promoting officers who had remained loyal to the institutional chain of command. He thus eliminated potential rivals among officers who had, ironically, forced the military to intervene, while seeking to mold the officer corps into a loyal group of followers completely beholden to Pinochet for their careers. All colonels promoted to the rank of generals were required to provide the army commander with a signed letter of resignation, which Pinochet could use at any moment to end a general's career.

But, loyalty was assured with more than the threat of sanctions. Under military rule, officers enjoyed privileges that they had never dreamed of. In addition to increases in pay and fringe benefits, officers could look forward to attractive rewards such as ambassadorships or membership on boards of public and semipublic corporations. Government service provided military men with responsibility and status they had never before enjoyed in the nation's history.[71]

More important for regime stability than the privileges accorded officers was the reestablishment of traditional norms of obedience to authority and hierarchy of rank, practices that had eroded in the turbulent final months of the Allende government. This meant that to a degree unheard of in other military regimes the Chilean authorities were able to establish a sharp separation between the military as institution and the military as government.[72] High-ranking officers were often brought into governmental positions that ranged from cabinet posts, heads of state agencies, and ambassadorships, to university presidencies and local governorships.[73]

However, once in government service, officers no longer took orders from their immediate military superiors but reported instead to their superiors in government, either military or civilian. As government officials, they could discuss policy with their military and civilian counterparts but were barred from discussing these matters with military colleagues serving a strictly military command. Indeed, officers in the military line of duty could be dismissed from the services for discussing politics or policy with fellow officers or with civilians. And for the duration of the Pinochet years, military men were not allowed to remain for long periods of time in governmental duties, continuously being rotated back to military command. Officers who were not deemed to be completely reliable found that their careers were terminated, cutting short a chance for a lucrative and prestigious post and retirement with high pensions. By serving both as president and commander-in-chief of the army with direct responsibility over the institution, and by strictly observing the separation of the military as government from the military as institution, Pinochet avoided the inherent tensions that develop in military regimes between officers occupying government positions and those serving in the institution itself.[74]

Aiding the general's ascendancy and ability to control the armed forces in the early years was the growing power of the secret police. The DINA (Dirección de Inteligencia Nacional or National Bureau of Intelligence), under the direction of Colonel Manuel Contreras, a close friend of the Pinochet family, soon became a law unto itself. It eliminated with efficient brutality the clandestine leadership of leftist parties in Chile and carried out with impunity a series of high-risk political assassinations abroad, aimed at silencing prominent critics of the regime. But DINA's power extended beyond its role in fighting the resistance movement. The secret organization came to be feared in military and governmental circles as DINA agents reported on the personal lives and political proclivities of prominent officers and advisers. It soon developed its own cadres of experts in fields including economic policy, as DINA officers sought to take control of sectors of the Chilean state, particularly the nationalized industries. Pinochet made use of Contreras' services to counter other advisory groups and to strengthen his hand vis-à-vis the junta and the military.[75]

Regime Support in the Business Community

The durability of Chile's military regime cannot be understood without underscoring the strong support for the military in key sectors of Chilean society. Business groups have been profoundly affected by economic policies that have transformed the Chilean economy from a state-supported, import-substituting industrialization model to an export-oriented economy with low tariff barriers and few government subsidies. Although many Chilean businessmen went bankrupt because of these policies and became bitter opponents of the regime, the bulk of the business community remained a strong pillar of the military government. In particular, the government gained powerful new supporters in a new breed of dynamic business leaders who flourished with the opening of Chile's economy to the world market. For Chile's business leaders, democracy had meant the electoral triumph of political forces bent on destroying them. No matter how objectionable the Pinochet government was, it remained a far preferable alternative to the uncertainties of democratic politics. Many people in Chile's middle classes, despite serious reverses, shared these views.

It should be stressed that the business community, while supporting the government, had little direct influence in the formulation of public policy. Policies were made by an economic team that had the complete confidence of the president, and substantial latitude to implement policies without consulting affected groups. The use of a group of neutral technocrats with no strong constituency support, but with a clear and sophisticated understanding of economic policy, helped insulate the president from societal pressures and demands, contributing further to state autonomy and to his increasing powers.

Political Polarization and a Fragmented Opposition

The coup that ended Chile's long trajectory of democratic politics was applauded by many sectors of society, while condemned by others. Chile's rightist parties welcomed the new authorities and soon agreed to disband, confident that the military would represent their interests. The Christian Democrats, Chile's largest party, reluctantly accepted the coup as the inevitable result of the Popular Unity government's policies. However, Christian Democrats were not prepared to accept the diagnosis of the country's new rulers that democracy was also at fault and that military rule should be maintained for an indefinite period of time. Soon, the Christian Democrats began to join the parties of the Left in strong criticisms of the regime's human-rights abuses and its redrafting of the nation's institutional structures. By the late 1970s, Christian Democrats were able to begin a dialogue with elements on the Left, as both groups attempted to come to terms with their collective responsibility in the failure of Chile's political order.

It was not until 1983, however, that Chile's political parties reasserted themselves, signaling that the regime's efforts to obliterate them from national life had failed.[76] The spontaneous protest movement, begun at the urging of a group of labor leaders, surprised the party leadership as much as it surprised the regime. The government's swift repressive measures against labor, rendered vulnerable by high levels of unemployment, opened the door for the party leadership to gain control over the burgeoning opposition movement. In the moderate opposition, the Christian Democrats sought to create a broad alliance with small groups on the Right and Left in order to structure a proposal for an alternative government that would press the armed forces to negotiate. On the Left, the Communist Party, which had countenanced an armed strategy against the regime, sought to mobilize popular discontent through increasingly militant protests in the expectation that the regime would capitulate.

This division, between those that sought peaceful mobilization in order to engage in negotiations with the authorities and those that sought sharp and even violent confrontations in order to render the country ungovernable, is the key to understanding the paralysis of Chile's opposition after 1983.[77] When the regime's intransigence led important sectors on the Right to join with the center and moderate Left and sign a National Accord for Transition to Democracy in 1985, calling for free elections and significant modifications in the 1980 Constitution, the fragile alliance failed. Some groups accused the Right of trying to halt political mobilization in Pinochet's favor; others accused the Left of trying to undermine possible negotiations with the armed forces while alienating middle-class support for the opposition.

At the root of this division is the continued polarization of Chilean politics between a strong Marxist Left, which advocates far-reaching socioeconomic reforms, and a rejuvenated Right, which refuses to have any of the economic gains of authoritarianism threatened. While significant political learning took place in broad quarters of Chilean party life, with Socialists embracing democratic practices as important ends in their own right, and Christian Democrats vowing not to pursue single-party strategies for their own gain, mistrust remains high as elements on both extremes press for radically divergent solutions.

Antidemocrats on both sides made it difficult for centrist forces to pursue concerted policies. Moderate Socialists feared that too many concessions to the regime would lead to a loss of support among the faithful, who might be attracted by the more militant line of the Communist Party or socialist groups affiliated with them. Democratic rightists have feared that they would be isolated and outflanked by Pinochet supporters who argued that any compromise with the opposition is nothing but an opening to the Communist Party. The Christian Democrats, in turn, were immobilized by sharp internal divisions over fears that the party might move too close to either the Left or the Right. The same logic of polarization that made it difficult to maintain a Center consensus and finally helped bring Chilean democracy crashing down in 1973 conspired against structuring a broad and coherent opposition movement to force the military from power. Widespread rejection of the Pinochet regime as illegitimate could not translate into an early return to democracy for lack of a clear alternative.[78]

• PROSPECTS FOR REDEMOCRATIZATION •

Paradoxically, it was the regime that provided the opposition with a rationale for unity and a means to define the transition process in its favor. Although no opposition leader accepted the legitimacy of the plebiscite formula spelled out in the 1980 Constitution, calling instead for open and fair presidential elections as soon as possible, by 1987 most seemed resigned to accepting the plebiscite as a fact of political life. At first, opposition leaders called on Chileans to register in the electoral roles, while still pressing for open presidential elections. Gradually and reluctantly, they began to call on their followers to register to vote NO in the plebiscite that would ratify the individual chosen by the armed forces chiefs to serve the next 8-year presidential term beginning on March 11, 1989.[79]

The Communist Party and sectors of the socialist Left strongly objected to this "participation in the legality of the regime." They were convinced that registering and voting would simply serve further to legitimize the regime, since they felt that the authorities would not permit a negative result and would resort to fraud if necessary to impose their candidate.

Moderate opposition leaders, on the other hand, argued that the plebiscite represented a valuable tool for popular mobilization and an important opportunity to try to defeat the regime at its own game—the only viable alternative for an opposition that had not succeeded in overthrowing the dictatorship through other means. Reluctantly they agreed to go further than asking citizens to vote: They also proceeded to register their political parties according to government regulations, which limited in several ways the autonomy of party organizations and forced them to engage in a national campaign to collect signatures from potential members, many of whom feared committing themselves publicly to a particular party or movement. Party registration was necessary to entitle opposition groups to name poll watchers to monitor the fairness of the election. The principal groups to register were the Christian Democrats and a loose coalition of Left-of-Center groups that called itself the Party for Democracy.

By December 1987 it became clear Chileans were prepared to register and vote in large numbers, forcing party leaders to structure a united effort in an attempt to win the NO vote in the plebiscite. A massive television campaign on the part of the authorities and growing evidence of the use of public resources to bolster the official candidate helped further to galvanize opposition groups into action. The Communist Party soon became isolated as its allies on the Left decided to join the NO command.

In governmental circles there was considerable speculation that Pinochet might not be the candidate selected by the four commanders-in-chief (including Pinochet as commander of the army). Many leaders on the Right felt that the government needed to project its institutions into the future without being tied to the figure of one man. They also feared that Pinochet was too controversial a leader, one around whom the opposition could unite in a simple zero-sum decision. An alternative candidate, preferably a civilian, would contribute to dividing the opposition and depersonalizing the regime. Two of the four commanders shared this view.

In late August 1988, however, Pinochet was named the candidate. He was determined to be selected and used the force of his personality and the weight of his office to obtain the designation. Leaders on the Right had not been willing to go too far in proposing an alternative for fear of antagonizing the chief executive. Businessmen who were still heavily indebted to the state were not about to jeopardize key loans by coming out publicly for an alternative. Without strong vocal support from the Right for another candidate, the dissenting commanders were not able to press for an alternative, particularly since Pinochet's supporters argued effectively that he was the country's most prominent figure and could win popular support.

Government and military leaders were confident that an improved economy, a massive housing and public-works program, and a saturation television campaign would tip the balance in favor of the regime. In particular, they felt that most Chileans did not want uncertainty and the fear of a return to a Marxist government; that television and other media could effectively remind them of the dangers of not supporting the regime. Furthermore, key government officials and advisers in both the military and civilian sectors repeatedly stressed that their evidence pointed to a strong victory for Pinochet as the only candidate to appear on the ballot. They noted that the disarray and divisions in the opposition would only strengthen the government's position.

The Chilean authorities came under considerable pressure internally and internationally to stage a fair contest, even though the plebiscite formula was widely criticized as undemocratic. Chile's tradition of fair and free elections, combined with the military regime's own desire to assert its legitimacy, contributed to the structuring of virtually fraud-proof voting procedures. The contest was unequal, however, because the government used substantial resources for media efforts on behalf of its "record" and made ample use of the authority of provincial leaders and mayors to give an advantage to the YES campaign. The opposition was able to turn to television only in the last month, after Pinochet had been officially nominated, and then was restricted to fifteen minutes of free air time a day, to be shared in equal amounts with the YES campaign.

To the surprise of most people, particularly in the government, the opposition groups mounted an extraordinarily successful media and door-to-door campaign in the last few weeks before the elections. With limited resources and relying on volunteer workers, they successfully countered the "fear" campaign of the government by stressing a positive and upbeat message. NO came to denote happiness and the future, while the YES campaign remained mired in the past. The drive to produce advertisements, recruit poll watchers, to set up an effective parallel vote count, and to conduct door-to-door campaigns cemented further the unity of the sixteen parties that formed the NO command. International support, particularly through the U.S. National Endowment for Democracy, channeled through the National Democratic Institute for International Affairs, contributed important resources for the media campaign and for the computer system designed to monitor the electoral count.

The victory of opposition forces by a 12-percent margin was a stunning achievement. Ninety-seven percent of the registered voters (representing 92 percent of the eligible population) went to the polls, and the opposition won in all but two of the country's twelve regions. Pinochet lost among most categories of voters, including women and provincial dwellers.

Two elements were critical in making it possible for the NO vote to win and to derail plans by some elements close to Pinochet to create a climate of violence that they hoped would lead to canceling the plebiscite. First, elements in the military and in the civilian political Right expected a fair contest and would not have tolerated any disruption of the process. Pinochet was the most powerful person in the country, but Chile's institutions were not "personalized." Even in the army, institutional loyalties and respect for "legality" were more important factors than allegiance to the ambitions of the commander-in-chief. Second, opposition leaders were successful in persuading voters to stay home, waiting calmly for results on election night, and to celebrate peacefully the next day. The violence that some elements in the regime had expected simply did not materialize. The Communist Party played an important role by insisting that its own militants refrain from organizing street demonstrations.

The election showed clearly how easy it is for an authoritarian regime to engage in collective self-delusion. Countless polls and newspaper accounts suggested that once the voters got over their skepticism about the election's fairness, the NO vote stood a good chance of winning. And yet, Pinochet, his advisers, and his supporters in the military and the business community were absolutely convinced that the government could not lose. All the information transmitted up the chain of command was designed to reinforce the president's wishes, to the point that negative information was filtered out. Often, however, it was difficult for the authorities to perceive such information; citizens were for the most part not forthcoming when asked their views by individuals with official credentials. A generalized contempt for politics and politicians, even those supporting the regime, made it difficult for officials to sense the mood of the country.

The victory of the NO vote in the plebiscite augurs well for Chile's democratic future. Had Pinochet been ratified for another 8-year term the country might have become ungovernable. A large percentage of the population would not have accepted the plebiscite as legitimate, and some sectors, in the aftermath of the opposition failure, would have renewed their calls for violence. At the same time, Pinochet would have had to govern with an elected Congress, one in which the opposition would have played a substantial role. The evolution of Pinochet from military commander and authoritarian leader to civilian president, albeit with strong executive powers, would not have been easy.

With the opposition victory, the country will hold open presidential elections at the end of 1989. What is unclear at this writing is whether, before the election, opposition leaders and government officials will be able to agree on some fundamental changes in a Constitution that is not accepted as democratic by opposition leaders. Although opposition leaders hope to obtain those changes, arguing that the victory represents not only a defeat for Pinochet but also for his "constitutional itinerary," fundamental changes are unlikely precisely because the military sees the Constitution as one of its principal legacies to the country. Changes will come only with the election of a democratic president and a Congress with constituent powers, and provided that the opposition is able to gain majorities in those elections. An opposition majority is more likely if the parties that structured the NO campaign can agree on a presidential candidate and a transition formula. Such an opposition, which would represent the reconstruction of a Center consensus in Chilean politics, would permit a return to democratic practices with broad majority support.

Should the coalition of the Center-Left, which supported the NO vote in the plebiscite, fail to present a common program and candidate, Chileans will face a presidential contest with candidates representing each of the traditional "thirds" of Chilean politics: a Marxist Left, a social democratic Center, and a pro-business Right. The country would thus run the risk of being governed once again by a president without majority support, facing hostile majorities in the Congress—a formula that might lead to decisional paralysis and political confrontation and place significant pressures on the armed forces to resolve the conflict through extraconstitutional measures. Given the strength of the three political tendencies of the Chilean electorate, constitutional experts should seriously entertain the option of creating a parliamentary form of government, where Center coalitions can more easily be formed and where the country's future is not at the mercy of a president who was either elected for a fixed term without a majority mandate or who has lost a majority mandate.

Despite the continued polarization of Chilean politics, the transition may be easier than that of other countries for several reasons. In the first place, the strong tradition of democratic rule that existed before the regime breakdown and was so eloquently manifested in the plebiscite will help Chileans return to democratic practices. Institutions of democratic governance in Chile do not have be new-forged as they do in many other Latin American countries; they need to be restored. Second, Chile's armed forces, even after a decade and a half of military rule, have not become politicized. The sharp separation of the political from the institutional roles of the military under Pinochet makes it possible for the institution to return to its professional pursuits without becoming involved in the daily political tug of war of a democratic regime. This does not mean that the Chilean armed forces would be reluctant to intervene in politics again should they feel that "national security" is threatened. There is strong evidence that the Chilean officer corps is less committed than in the past to respecting democratic rules and procedures. However, the institution itself is not fragmented and politicized and is likely to intervene only in a serious crisis. Third, the Chilean armed forces retain substantial prestige despite deep resentment against the authorities in some sectors. Of particular importance is the fact that the institution was not directly compromised by the "dirty war" of the security police that led to the most flagrant human-rights abuses. Demands for an accounting for human-rights abuses and justice for the guilty will not create a serious rift between civilian authorities and military leaders. Finally, Chile begins its transition with a relatively good economic picture compared to that of its neighbors. Chilean economic planners succeeded in reordering the Chilean state so that it operates more efficiently. They have also encouraged an impressive new class of entrepreneurs able to compete in world markets. Although these economic successes were made possible by strong authoritarian practices, including curbing labor rights and imposing policies with strong regressive tendencies, planners under a democratic regime will not face the same intractable economic problems that their Argentine neighbors faced when coming to power. The challenge to maintain growth and efficiency, while at the same time tending to the real demands for greater social justice, will tax the abilities of the most skilled leaders. But, Chileans in the aftermath of the 1988 plebiscite seem determined to return to their historic democratic practices with a renewed realism and hope for the future.

• NOTES •

1. There are few general treatments of the military regime in Chile. The best single study is Manuel Antonio Garretón, *El proceso político chileno* (Santiago: Facultad Latinoamericana de Ciencias Sociales, 1983). Useful edited volumes are those by Manuel A. Garretón et al., *Chile: 1973–198?* (Santiago: Facultad Latinoamericana de Ciencias Sociales, 1980); and J. Samuel Valenzuela and Arturo Valenzuela, eds., *Military Rule in Chile: Dictatorship and Oppositions* (Baltimore, MD: Johns Hopkins University Press, 1986). The literature on the human-rights situation under the Chilean military government is voluminous. The most complete record is that provided by the publications of the Vicaría de la Solidaridad, dependent on the Archbishopric of Santiago (see the annual reports). The most comprehensive and authoritative overview of the human-rights record of the Chilean government is provided by the Commission on Human Rights, Organization of American States, in its *Informe sobre la situación de los derechos humanos en Chile* (Washington, DC: Organization of American States, 1985). The commission estimates that approximately 1,500 people were killed after the coup (see *Informe*, p. 54). The Vicaría has documented 668 cases of individuals who disappeared after being arrested in the period 1973–1985. The number killed in Chile may be closer to 3,500, as many deaths and disappearances may not have been reported, particularly in rural areas. Most rural towns visited by the author appear to have lost a few people after the coup, in some cases because of private feuds or reprisals on the part of landowners.
2. A valuable sourcebook on the 1980 Constitution is Luz Bulnes Aldunate, *Constitución política de la República de Chile: Concordancias, anotaciones y fuentes* (Santiago: Editorial Jurídica de Chile, 1981). For a "legislative history" of the Constitution see Sergio Carrasco Delgado, *Génesis y vigencia de los textos constitucionales chilenos* (Santiago: Editorial Jurídica de Chile, 1980).

3. Kenneth A. Bollen, "Comparative Measurement of Political Democracy," *American Sociological Review* 45, no. 3 (June 1980): pp. 370–390. See also Robert W. Jackman, "On the Relations of Economic Development to Democratic Performance," *American Journal of Political Science* 17, no. 3 (August 1973): pp. 611–621; and his "Political Democracy and Social Equality: A Comparative Analysis," *American Sociological Review* 39, no. 1 (February 1974): pp. 29–44.

4. Leon Epstein, *Political Parties in Western Democracies* (New York: Praeger, 1967), p. 192. For a discussion of the rise of parliamentary opposition in Western Europe, see the excellent collection in Robert Dahl, ed., *Political Oppositions in Western Democracies* (New Haven, CT: Yale University Press, 1966). See also Dahl's *Polyarchy: Participation and Opposition* (New Haven, CT: Yale University Press, 1971).

5. Some countries, including Britain and Norway, developed political contestation with parliamentary responsibility before Chile did. Others, such as Belgium and the Netherlands, began to develop parliamentary influence at around the same time. The Swedish king was able to choose ministers without regard to parliamentary majorities until 1917, though the parliament's views were taken into consideration earlier. Italy was not unified until the 1860s and did not establish a system of parliamentary rule until the 1880s. Republican France dates from 1871, and many observers, noting the importance of the Napoleonic bureaucracy, question the degree of authority wielded by the French parliament. Because of the importance of the monarchies in Europe, Chile comes closer to the United States in the origins and evolution of its political institutions. For historical discussions of these issues, see Dahl, *Political Oppositions;* and Stein Rokkan, *Citizens, Elections, Parties* (Oslo: Universitetsforlaget, 1970).

6. See Dahl, *Polyarchy,* ch. 1. Dahl's definition informs the discussion of democracy in Chapter 1 of this volume.

7. Women were able to vote in national elections for the first time in 1952. The voting age was reduced from 21 to 18 and illiterates were given the right to vote with the constitutional reforms of 1970. The best discussion of Chilean electoral practices can be found in Federico Gil, *The Political System of Chile* (Boston: Houghton Mifflin, 1966). The 1970 reforms are discussed in Guillermo Piedrabuena Richards, *La reforma constitucional* (Santiago: Ediciones Encina, 1970). The intricacies of the electoral system are described in Mario Bernaschina G., *Cartilla electoral* (Santiago: Editorial Jurídica de Chile, 1958). For an overview of electoral participation, see Atilio Borón, "La evolución del régimen electoral y sus efectos en la representación de los intereses populares: El caso de Chile." Estudio no. 24 (Santiago: Escuela Latinoamericana de Ciencia Política y Administración Pública, FLACSO, April 1971).

8. Voting data for Europe can be found in Stein Rokkan, *Citizens.* Voting data on Chile is found in J. Samuel Valenzuela, *Democratización vía reforma: La expansión del sufragio en Chile* (Buenos Aires: Ediciones del IDES, 1985). This is the best study of the critical decisions that led to suffrage expansion in Chile in the nineteenth century, underscoring the important role of the Conservatives in that process. As such, it is an important revisionary study in Chilean historiography.

9. This section draws extensively from J. Samuel Valenzuela and Arturo Valenzuela, "Chile and the Breakdown of Democracy." In *Latin American Politics and Development,* ed. Howard J. Wiarda and Harvey F. Kline (Boston: Houghton Mifflin, 1979), pp. 234–249. The author is grateful to J. Samuel Valenzuela for his contribution to this work and to much of the thinking that is reflected in this chapter. See also Arturo Valenzuela, *Political Brokers in Chile: Local Government in a Centralized Polity* (Durham, NC: Duke University Press, 1977), ch. 8.

10. Francisco Antonio Encina, *Historia de Chile,* vol. 9 (Santiago: Editorial Nacimiento, 1941–1942), p. 493; cited in Arturo Valenzuela, *Political Brokers,* p. 175.

11. This thesis is at variance with standard interpretations that attribute to Diego Portales a pivotal role in forming the Chilean institutional system. See Arturo Valenzuela, *Political Brokers,* ch. 8; and his "El mito de Portales: La institucionalización del régimen político chileno en el siglo XIX." In *La transición a la democracia en América Latina,* ed. Fernando Molina (Santiago: Universidad Católica de Chile, forthcoming).

12. Chile, *Documentos parlamentarios correspondientes al segundo quinquenio de la administración Bulnes, 1846–1850,* vol. 3 (Santiago: Imprenta del Ferrocarril, 1858), p. 795.

13. Some of the generalizations from the "world-system" and "dependency" literature to the effect that dependent capitalist development leads to weak states does not fully apply to the Chilean case.

14. This section draws heavily on Arturo Valenzuela and J. Samuel Valenzuela "Los orígenes de la democracia: Reflexiones teóricas sobre el caso de Chile," *Estudios públicos* 12 (Spring 1983): pp. 3–39; and J. S. Valenzuela, *Democratización.*

15. In 1863, the total electorate was about 22,000. By 1878, the electorate had expanded sevenfold. See J. S. Valenzuela, *Democratización*, pp. 118–119.

16. Maurice Duverger, *Political Parties* (New York: John Wiley, 1965), pp. xxiii–xxxvii.

17. This section draws heavily on Arturo Valenzuela, *The Breakdown of Democratic Regimes: Chile* (Baltimore, MD: Johns Hopkins University Press, 1978), ch. 1.

18. Seymour Martin Lipset and Stein Rokkan, *Party Systems and Voter Alignments* (New York: Free Press, 1967), pp. 50–56.

19. For a discussion of this, see Valenzuela, *Political Brokers*.

20. An exception to this generalization is Dahl's *Polyarchy*. Not only has Chile been neglected in the broader literature, Latin America in general has been left out. The volumes of the Committee on Comparative Politics of the Social Science Research Council had only a few studies dealing with Latin America, and Latin America did not figure prominently in the theoretical efforts of the 1960s. In his excellent study of parties in Western democracies, Epstein acknowledges that a few Latin American countries meet his criteria for inclusion but leaves them out "mainly because the whole of Latin America is *customarily* treated along with developing nations" (emphasis added). See Epstein, *Political Parties*, p. 4. For a discussion of the place of Latin America in the literature on comparative politics, see Arturo Valenzuela, "Political Science and the Study of Latin America." In *Windows on Latin America: Perspectives from Six Disciplines*, ed. Christopher Mitchell (Stanford, CA: Stanford University Press, forthcoming).

21. These terms are designed to group in analytically similar categories propositions that are sometimes advanced in more discrete fashion. They are drawn from previous work of the author on the subject, some of which has been done in collaboration with J. Samuel Valenzuela. I have attempted to address within each category the relevant variables advanced in this book. I do not treat what can be called the national-cohesiveness thesis because it is not as relevant to the Chilean case. Ethnic, regional, and center-periphery cleavages were defused in the early half of the nineteenth century.

22. The importance of gradual evolution without significant upheaval is stressed by Dahl in *Polyarchy*, pp. 40–47. The continuity of institutions from the colonial period is one of the points advanced by Seymour Martin Lipset in his provocative study of the United States, *The First New Nation* (New York: Doubleday, 1967), pp. 106–107. For a discussion of differences in the colonial experience, see Rupert Emerson's classic *From Empire to Nation* (Boston: Beacon Press, 1960).

23. Chile inaugurated a polyarchy through a struggle for independence that led to the collapse of the remnants of the old colonial regime, and not, as Dahl holds, through an evolutionary process comparable to that of England or Sweden. In this sense, the Chilean case is closer to that of France than England. See Dahl, *Polyarchy*, p. 42.

24. See Frederick Pike, *Chile and the United States, 1880–1962* (Notre Dame, IN: University of Notre Dame Press, 1963), p. 11. The literature on Portales is voluminous. An influential work that argues this thesis is Alberto Edwards Vives, *La Fronda aristocrática* (Santiago: Ediciones Ercilla, 1936), pp. 50–51. For a sampling of views, see B. Vicuña Mackenna, J. Victorino Lastarria, and R. Sotomayor Valdés, *Portales: Juicio histórico* (Santiago: Editorial del Pacífico, 1973).

25. Richard Morse, "The Heritage of Latin America." In *The Founding of New Societies*, ed. Louis Hartz (New York: Harcourt, Brace and World, 1964), pp. 163–164. See also Hartz's comments on the Chilean case on p. 88 of that work.

26. For an elaboration of this argument see Valenzuela, *Political Brokers*, ch. 8.

27. See Samuel P. Huntington, *Political Order in Changing Societies* (New Haven, CT: Yale University Press, 1968), ch. 2.

28. David Martin argues that "the incidence of pluralism and democracy is related to the incidence of those religious bodies which are themselves inherently pluralistic and democratic. . . . Such bodies . . . are much more prevalent in the Anglo-American situation than elsewhere. . . . In Russia and Latin America democratic and individualistic Protestantism arrived late in the process and could not have an important effect." See his *A General Theory of Secularization* (New York: Harper and Row, 1978), p. 25. For an influential essay dealing with Latin America along these same lines, see Seymour Martin Lipset, "Values, Education and Entrepreneurship." In *Elites in Latin America*, ed. Seymour Martin Lipset and Aldo Solari (New York: Oxford University Press, 1963). See also Howard Wiarda, "Toward a Framework for the Study of Political Change in the Iberic-Latin Tradition: The Corporative Model," *World Politics*, 25, no. 2 (January 1973): pp. 206–235. For a classic work that links liberal values stemming from the Protestant tradition with the growth of democracy in the United States, see Louis Hartz, *The Liberal Tradition in America* (New York: Harcourt, Brace and World, 1955).

29. See Jorge I. Dominguez, *Insurrection or Loyalty* (Cambridge, MA: Harvard University Press, 1979) for a discussion of some of these points.

30. Harry Eckstein, *Division and Cohesion in a Democracy: A Study of Norway* (Princeton, NJ: Princeton University Press, 1966).

31. See Booth's chapter on Costa Rica in this volume.

32. Dahl, *Polyarchy*, p. 140.

33. For a description of Chile's *hacienda* system, see George M. McBride, *Chile: Land and Society* (New York: American Geographical Society, 1936). For the origins, the classic study is Mario Góngora, *Origen de los inquilinos del Valle Central* (Santiago: Editorial Universitaria, 1960). See also Arnold J. Bauer, *Chilean Rural Society from the Spanish Conquest to 1930* (New York: Cambridge University Press, 1975).

34. Dominguez, *Insurrection*, p. 141.

35. See Robert Kaufman, *The Politics of Land Reform in Chile, 1950–1970* (Cambridge, MA: Harvard University Press, 1972); and Brian Loveman, *Struggle in the Countryside: Politics and Rural Labor in Chile, 1919–1973)* (Bloomington: Indiana University Press, 1976).

36. Chile is a good illustration of Dankwart Rustow's argument that democracies must go through a "habituation" phase before they are consolidated. See his "Transitions to Democracy: Toward a Dynamic Model," *Comparative Politics* 2, no. 3 (April 1970): pp. 337–363.

37. See Daniel Lerner, *The Passing of Traditional Society* (New York: Free Press, 1958). See also S. N. Eisenstadt, "Social Change, Differentiation and Evolution," *American Sociological Review* 29 (June 1964): pp. 375–387.

38. Seymour Martin Lipset, "Some Social Requisites of Democracy: Economic Development and Political Legitimacy," *American Political Science Review* 53, no. 1 (March 1959): pp. 69–105. For collections of articles on "empirical democratic theory," see J. V. Gillespie and B. A. Nesvold, eds., *Macroquantitative Analysis: Conflict, Development and Democratization* (Beverly Hills, CA: Sage Publications, 1971); and Charles Cnudde and Deane Neubauer, eds., *Empirical Democratic Theory* (Chicago: Markham, 1969). For an excellent review of this literature, see Leonardo Morlino, "Misure di Democrazia e di Libertá: Discusione di Alcune Analisi Empiriche," *Rivista Italiana di Scienza Política* 5, no. 1 (April 1975): pp. 131–166.

39. See, for example, Phillips Cutright, "National Political Development: Measurement and Analysis," *American Sociological Review* 28, no. 2 (April 1963): pp. 253–264; and Bollen, "Comparative Measurement of Political Democracy."

40. Juan Linz, "Totalitarian and Authoritarian Regimes." In *Handbook of Political Science*, vol. 3, ed. Fred I. Greenstein and Nelson W. Polsby (Reading, MA: Addison Wesley, 1975), p. 182. As Dahl notes, the United States in the nineteenth century did not meet the development criteria but met the political criteria. See Dahl, *Polyarchy*, p. 72.

41. Goran Therborn, "The Rule of Capital and the Rise of Democracy," *New Left Review* 103 (May-June 1977): p. 3–41. Therborn adds that the rarity of bourgeois democracy in capitalist Third World countries is due to the vulnerability of commodity-oriented economies, which give the "indigenous bourgeoisie little room for manoeuvre vis-à-vis the exploited classes." In such contexts there is an "intertwining of capitalist with feudal, slave or other pre-capitalist modes of exploitations . . . impeding the development of impersonal rule of capital and free labormarket, thereby seriously limiting the growth of both the labor movement and an agrarian petty bourgeoisie." Ibid., pp. 1, 32. Although he is not dealing with the development of democracy *per se*, Immanuel Wallerstein argues that peripheral states in the world system were much weaker in part because the social structure of export economies did not permit the development of bourgeois sectors. See his *The Modern World System*, 2 vols. (New York: Academic Press, 1974, 1980.)

42. Barrington Moore, *Social Origins of Dictatorship and Democracy: Lord and Peasant in the Making of the Modern World* (Boston: Beacon Press, 1966). As he notes, for democracy to emerge, "the political hegemony of the landed upper class had to be broken or transformed. The peasant had to be turned into a farmer producing for the market instead of for his own consumption and that of the overlord. In this process the landed upper class either became an important part of the capitalist and democratic tide, as in England, or, if they came to oppose it, they were swept aside in the convulsions of revolutions (France) or civil war (U.S.). In a word the landed upper classes either helped to make the bourgeois revolution or were destroyed by it." Ibid., p. 429–430. Moore's analysis, though brilliant in scope, leaves much to be desired in terms of clarity. For a valuable critique, see Theda Skocpol, "A Critical Review of Barrington Moore's Social Origins of Dictatorship and Democracy," *Politics and Society* 4 (Fall 1973): pp. 1–34. See also Joseph V. Femia, "Barrington Moore and the Preconditions for Democracy," *British Journal of Political Science* 2 (Janu-

ary 1972): pp. 21–46; and Ronald Dore, "Making Sense of History," *Archive Européenes de Sociology* 10 (1969): pp. 295–305.

43. See Dominguez, *Insurrection*, p. 131.

44. Influential works of Chilean historians in this vein include Julio César Jobet, *Ensayo crítico del desarrollo económico-social de Chile* (Santiago: Editorial Latinoamericana, 1965); and Hernán Ramirez Necochea, *Historia del movimiento obrero en Chile, antecedentes siglo XIX* (Santiago: Editorial Austral, 1956). The most fully developed version of this thesis is in Luis Vitale, *Interpretación marxista de la historia de Chile* (Frankfurt: Verlag Jugend und Politik, 1975). Maurice Zeitlin's *The Civil Wars in Chile: 1851 and 1859* (Princeton, NJ: Princeton University Press, 1984) draws uncritically from the work of Vitale and others.

45. See Leonard Binder et al., *Crises and Sequences in Political Development* (Princeton, NJ: Princeton University Press, 1971). For a volume of essays applying the framework to particular cases, see Raymond Grew, ed., *Crises of Political Development in Europe and the United States* (Princeton, NJ: Princeton University Press, 1978). Influential earlier studies that anticipate the arguments in these books include Dankwart Rustow, *A World of Nations* (Washington, DC: Brookings Institution, 1967); Lipset and Rokkan, eds., *Party Systems and Voter Alignments;* and Gabriel Almond, Scott Flanigan, and Roger Mundt, eds., *Crisis, Choice and Change: Historical Studies of Political Development* (Boston: Little, Brown, 1973). Although some of these works focus on political development more generally, and not on the development of democracy as such, their framework is oriented toward democratic regimes rather than other regime types.

46. Eric Nordlinger, "Political Development, Time Sequences and Rates of Change. In *Political Development and Social Change*, 2d ed., ed. Jason L. Finkle and Robert W. Gable (New York: John Wiley, 1971), p. 458. This argument is made in Rustow, *World of Nations*, pp. 120–123.

47. Of the three crises, the most difficult to deal with is that of national identity. Its definition is imprecise and in the absence of survey-research data it is virtually impossible to find empirical evidence to document its relative strength. Much of this analysis has to be speculative and informed by general historical accounts. Particularly useful in capturing the mood of Chile in the early period is the work of Diego Barros Arana, which is also an eyewitness account. In particular, see his *Un decenio de la historia de Chile*, 2 vols. (Santiago: Imprenta Universitaria, 1906.)

48. See Richard Merritt, "Nation-Building in America: the Colonial Years." In *Nation-Building*, ed. Karl W. Deutsch and William J. Foltz (New York: Atherton Press, 1966; and Karl Deutch, *Nationalism and Social Communication: An Inquiry into the Foundations of Nationality*, 2d ed. (Cambridge, MA: MIT Press, 1966). Lipset discusses the question of national identity in the United States in his *First New Nation*, ch. 2.

49. See Rustow, "Transitions to Democracy."

50. For a discussion of Washington's impact, see Lipset, *First New Nation*, pp. 18–23.

51. For lists of all Chilean presidents, cabinet officials, and members of Congress from independence until the 1940s, see Luis Valencia Avaria, *Anales de la república*, 2 vols. (Santiago: Imprenta Universitaria, 1951). Most presidents had extensive parliamentary experience.

52. On the question of efficacy, see the arguments of Juan J. Linz in *The Breakdown of Democratic Regimes: Crisis, Breakdown and Reequilibration* (Baltimore, MD: Johns Hopkins University Press, 1978), pp. 20–21.

53. For an elaboration of this argument, see Valenzuela and Valenzuela, "Orígenes de la democracia."

54. R. K. Merton, "The Unanticipated Consequences of Purposive Social Action," *American Sociological Review* 1936, 1: pp. 894–904.

55. This point is made in Arturo Valenzuela and Alexander Wilde, "Presidentialist Politics and the Decline of the Chilean Congress." In *Legislatures in Development: Dynamics of Change in New and Old States*, ed. Joel Smith and Lloyd Musolf (Durham, NC: Duke University Press, 1979), p. 194.

56. The material in this section is taken from the author's *Breakdown*. For other books on the Chilean breakdown, see Paul Sigmund, *The Overthrow of Allende and the Politics of Chile* (Pittsburgh, PA: Pittsburgh University Press, 1977); Ian Roxborough, Phil O'Brien, and Jackie Roddick, *Chile: The State and Revolution* (New York: Holmes and Meier, 1977); and Manuel A. Garretón and Tomás Moulian, *Análisis coyuntural y proceso político: Las fases del conflicto en Chile (1970–73)* (San José, Costa Rica: Editorial Universitaria Centro-Americana, 1978). The last-named is drawn from the comprehensive and detailed daily account of the most important events of the Allende administration, published in Manuel Antonio Garretón et al., *Cronología del período*

1970–73, 9 vols. (Santiago: Facultad Latinoamericana de Ciencias Sociales, 1978); an invaluable publication including extensive indices to parties, individuals, and events. In the immediate aftermath of the coup, a host of primarily more polemical works were published. For a review essay of thirty-one books, see Arturo Valenzuela and J. Samuel Valenzuela, "Visions of Chile," *Latin American Research Review* 10 (Fall 1975): pp. 155–176.

57. See Valenzuela and Wilde, "Presidentialism and Decline of Congress," pp. 204–210.

58. The most comprehensive study of U.S. involvement was conducted by the U.S. Select Committee to Study Govermental Operations with respect to Intelligence Activities (Church Committee) of the 94th Congress, 1st Session. See its *Covert Action in Chile 1963–1973* (Washington, DC: Government Printing, 1975).

59. The fact that Allende received fewer votes in 1970 than in 1964 suggests that his victory was not due to an increase in popular discontent and mobilization fueled by a worsening socioeconomic crisis. An examination of socioeconomic indicators in the late 1960s does not support the argument that the lot of the average Chilean was becoming worse or that political mobilization was exceeding historic levels. Survey data also supports the view that a majority of voters would have preferred a Center-Right to a Center-Left coalition. Huntington's thesis, in *Political Order*, that political order collapses when political institutions are too weak, is not supported by the Chilean case. Chile's parties prior to the election of Allende were very strong (perhaps too dominant), and political mobilization was the product of deliberate strategies on the part of the parties and the government to bring people into the political process, rather than the product of widespread discontent or anomic behavior. In Chile, the election of Allende and the economic and social crisis of the Allende years was more the product of the sharp political crisis rather than vice-versa. For a full elaboration of this argument, see my *Breakdown*, ch. 3. An article that argues that mobilization in Chile became excessive is Henry Landberger and Tim McDaniel, "Hypermobilization in Chile, 1970–73," *World Politics* 28, no. 4 (July 1976): pp. 502–543.

60. For the concept of neutral powers, see Linz, *Breakdown*, pp. 76–80. For a discussion of the growing confrontation, suggesting that mobilization was more the result of political crisis rather than its cause, see Valenzuela, *Breakdown*, p. 34.

61. Seventy-two percent of those polled thought Chile was living through extraordinary times, but only 27 percent of the respondents felt the military should be involved in the political process. See Valenzuela, *Breakdown*, p. 65. The Chilean case suggests that even where democratic norms are widespread and deeply rooted in a society, political crisis resulting from institutional struggles and competing claims can seriously erode democratic practices. A democratic political culture is no guarantee for the maintenance of democratic institutions.

62. This argument is elaborated in Arturo Valenzuela, "Orígenes y características del sistema de partidos políticos en Chile: Una proposición para un gobierno parlamentario," *Estudios Públicos* 18 (Fall 1985): pp. 87–154; and my "Hacia una democracia estable: la opción parlamentaria para Chile," *Revista de Ciencia Política* 7, no. 2 (1985): pp. 129–140. The author is grateful to Juan Linz for his reflections on this subject. See the suggestive discussion in Linz, *Breakdown*, pp. 71–74; and his "Democracy, Presidential or Parliamentary: Does It Make a Difference?" Paper presented at the 83rd Annual Meeting of the American Political Science Association, Chicago, IL, September 3–6, 1987.

63. This section draws on the author's forthcoming book with Pamela Constable, *By Reason or By Force: Pinochet's Chile*.

64. This section is based on interviews, conducted in August 1987, with high-ranking military officers who commanded troops during the coup and were responsible for "cleaning up" or "neutralizing" Santiago neighborhoods.

65. A valuable discussion of the neoconservative economic policies applied by the Chilean military regime is Pilar Vergara, *Auge y caída del neoliberalismo en Chile* (Santiago: FLACSO, 1985).

66. This section is based on extensive interviews with advisers close to the junta and General Pinochet in 1973–1978.

67. For the text of Decree Law 527, see Eduardo Soto Kloss, *Ordenamiento constitucional* (Santiago: Editorial Jurídica de Chile, 1980), pp. 145–153.

68. These observations are based on interviews conducted with General Leigh in Santiago, Chile, during November 1985. An excellent published interview is in Florencia Varas, *Gustavo Leigh: El general disidente* (Santiago: Editorial Aconcagua, 1979). Pinochet retired eighteen air force generals before finding one who would accept his action and replace Leigh on the junta. Had

Leigh had better intelligence, the conflict might have been much more dramatic.

69. See Chile, *Constitución de la República de Chile 1980* (Santiago: Editorial Jurídica, 1981). See Article 8, p. 13, for that language.

70. See transitional articles 16 and 27 in *Constitución*.

71. For an excellent study that gives a picture of rising military expenditures for personnel, see Jorge Marshall, "Gasto público en Chile 1969–1979," *Colección estudios cieplan* 5 (July 1981): pp. 53–84.

72. As such, the Chilean military regime was of the military, but not by the military. I am indebted to the excellent work of Genaro Arriagada for this insight. See his *La política militar de Pinochet* (Santiago: Salesianos, 1985).

73. For an article detailing the service of military men in government positions, see Carlos Huneeus and Jorge Olave, "Autoritarismo, militares y transición a la democracia: Chile en una perspectiva comparada" (Santiago: CERC, mimeo, 1986).

74. See Alfred Stepan's now classic elaboration of this problem in his *The Military in Politics: Changing Patterns in Brazil* (Princeton, NJ: Princeton University Press, 1971).

75. Senior officers such as General Oscar Bonilla, perhaps the most powerful general at the time of the coup, were not successful in their attempts to control Contreras. Bonilla died in an accident of suspicious nature. Many civilian advisers came to fear that Contreras could come to threaten Pinochet, though the general succeeded in playing various groups off against each other. Contreras was finally fired and the DINA restructured as relations between the United States and Chile deteriorated following U.S. demands for extradition of Contreras to the United States for his alleged involvement in the assassination of Orlando Letelier, Allende's foreign minister, in the streets of Washington. For studies that deal with the Letelier case and provide insights into the DINA, see John Dinges and Saul Landau, *Assassination on Embassy Row* (New York: Pantheon, 1980); and Taylor Branch and Eugene M. Propper, *Labyrinth* (New York: Viking, 1982).

76. For a discussion of political parties under authoritarianism, see Arturo Valenzuela and J. Samuel Valenzuela, "Political Oppositions under the Chilean Authoritarian Regime." In *Military Rule in Chile: Dictatorship and Oppositions,* J. Samuel Valenzuela and Arturo Valenzuela (Baltimore, MD: Johns Hopkins University Press, 1986).

77. See Pamela Constable and Arturo Valenzuela, "Is Chile Next?" *Foreign Policy* 63 (Summer 1986): pp. 58–75.

78. See Adam Przeworski's persuasive critique of the notion that the lack of legitimacy is a sufficient condition for the breakdown of a regime in his "Some Problems in the Study of the Transition to Democracy." In *Transitions from Authoritarian Rule,* ed. Guillermo O'Donnell, Philippe C. Schmitter, and Laurence Whitehead (Baltimore, MD: Johns Hopkins University Press, 1986).

79. This section is based on field research conducted by the author in Chile in 1987 and 1988. For a more detailed description of the events leading up to the plebiscite, see Pamela Constable and Arturo Valenzuela, "Plebiscite in Chile: End of the Pinochet Era?" *Current History* 87 (January 1988): pp. 29–33, 41; and Pamela Constable and Arturo Valenzuela, "The Victory of the No Vote in Chile: Implications for Democratic Transitions" *Current History* (forthcoming, 1989).

• CHAPTER THREE •

Brazil: Inequality Against Democracy

BOLÍVAR LAMOUNIER

Political scientists have repeatedly emphasized the advantages of viewing democracy as a political subsystem rather than as a total pattern of society. The study of democratic breakdowns has given them every reason to insist on that view, since it has showed that in many cases dictatorship could have been avoided through institutional change and conscious political effort. Observing processes of "opening" (*abertura*) or "decompression" in authoritarian regimes has certainly reinforced that preference, not least because the importance of prior institution-building came clearly to light during some of these processes. Democracy, then, is a political subsystem, not a total pattern of social organization. But how sharply can we draw the line between the development of political institutions and the substantive democratization of society? How should we approach the fact that enormous tensions develop between these concepts— especially when we move from the dilemmas of democratic opening to those of democratic consolidation?

The Brazilian case is certainly worth examining in this connection. Recall that on March 31, 1964, a military coup overthrew President Goulart and inaugurated the longest period of ostensible authoritarian rule in Brazil's history. More than two decades later, on January 15, 1985, the Electoral College instituted by the military to ratify their presidential nominations elected Tancredo Neves—a civilian and a moderate oppositionist since 1964—to the presidency of the republic. The Brazilian authoritarian regime was ending by peaceful means. Quite obviously, this is not the kind of change that takes place in countries without a fair degree of institutional development. Protest and popular resistance played an important role, of course, but there was also an element of flexibility among power holders and a weight of their own among traditional representative institutions.

Can we then say that the Brazilian Nova República is fully democratic or fully consolidated? The answer to this question transcends the Brazilian case. It depends on our evaluation of the historical record, but also on our conceptualization of democracy and on our models of consolidation. Our first step here should be an attempt to determine Brazil's position on the scale of democracy

BRAZIL

employed in this book. Few would have major doubts about Brazil's position; it is clearly not a case of high success or of extreme failure. The optimist would think of Brazil as a "mixed success," noting that we have some democratic tradition, despite many interruptions, and that civilian rule is again in place after twenty years of ostensible military domination. The pessimist will prefer to speak of "partial development," rejecting the view that democracy has been the dominant pattern. Mixed or partial, both will agree that we are a case of unstable democracy, since the democratic system cannot be said to be fully institutionalized in Brazil.

Facing sharp inequality and major social strains, a political system—democratic or authoritarian—can hardly be said to be institutionalized completely. In some cases, democracy succeeds in becoming accepted as a framework for an endless series of substantive changes. Not every contender accepts it as an end in itself, but all or at least the key ones trust that its continuing practice will make substantive outcomes more compatible at some future date. The distinction between state and democratic institutions properly so called is not as simple as it seems when one is still close to the historical process of state-building. Brazilian history can be told as a series of steps toward state formation or toward democracy, depending on one's viewpoint. This has an important bearing on the evaluation of democratic development and seems to demand some conceptual refinement.

• FROM GEISEL TO TANCREDO: OPENING THROUGH ELECTIONS •

Gradual and peaceful, the Brazilian *abertura* seems unique by virtue of a third characteristic: It was essentially an opening through elections. It was not a result of sharp mass mobilization and was not precipitated by dramatic or external events, as in Portugal, Greece, and Argentina. In this sense, Brazil must be distinguished even from Spain, if we consider that the death of Franco brought the Spanish political system to an inevitable moment of restructuring. The Brazilian process had no such moment. Here, a gradual accumulation of pressures was channeled through the electoral process. Election results functioned as indicators of the degree to which the authoritarian regime was losing legitimacy and, in turn, helped to aggregate further pressures against it.[1]

Taking the period 1964–1984 as a whole and ignoring for a while certain moments of authoritarian exacerbation, three important democratic formalisms seem to have been at work, channeling the opening process in the direction just described: (1) an element of self-restraint on the part of military institutions; (2) electoral rules and practices kept at an acceptable level of credibility, despite some manipulations; and (3) a clear (and after 1974 virtually unanimous) preference on the part of the opposition to play the electoral game and to avoid violent confrontation.

The Brazilian opening has a strong element of deliberate decompression, starting with the Geisel administration (1974–1978). It amounted, from this point of view, to recognition among the regime's power holders that an indefinite monopoly of power, or even "Mexicanization" by means of a hegemonic party, would not be viable. The opposition seems on the whole to have evaluated the situation correctly and to have sought to explore the political spaces that appeared at each moment. The formidable impact of the 1974 elections helped it to organize under the label of the Partido do Movimento Democrático Brasileiro (PMDB) for electoral purposes, while at the same time establishing bridges among a variety of social movements and associations then increasingly (re)politicizing.

It would be naive to gloss over the tensions inherent in these changes, as if the actors were simply following a previously conceived blueprint. The point is rather that both sides, government and opposition, found enough space to redefine their respective roles through several stages, since each perceived what it stood to gain from the continuity of the process. The opposition was capable of extracting important concessions while at the same time organizing itself as a powerful electoral force. The government also benefited in many ways. Most importantly, it saw a gradual reduction in the costs of coercion. Decompression helped it to contain the growing autonomy of the repressive apparatus, which had seriously compromised, as is well known, the country's image abroad. In short, the government could capitalize on the political benefits of an atmosphere of progressive "normalcy," as if exchanging losses of legitimacy arising from discontent with its past for gains based on the increasing credibility of its intentions as to the future. Paradoxically, the erosion of authoritarian legitimacy since 1974 amounted to a revitalization of governmental authority—since such authority was thus invested in the role of conductor of the decompression (later rebaptized normalization and eventually redemocratization).

We have said that the electoral game was the institutional expression of an implicit negotiation between the parliamentary opposition and the liberal sectors of the military—or of the regime as a whole. Three examples will make these arguments more concrete. All three refer to the legitimation, in practice, of a congressional majority that the government would hardly be capable of putting together if it did not have semidictatorial powers. The first is the so-called Pacote de Abril (April Package) of 1977. Using the "revolutionary" powers of the Institutional Act 5, President Geisel decreed several measures designed to preserve a majority for the Aliança Renovadora Nacional (ARENA, the government party) in the Senate, to make an oppositionist victory for the lower chamber unlikely, and to postpone the return to direct state gubernatorial elections from 1978 to 1982.[2] Despite the incredibly massive and arbitrary nature of this intervention, the opposition chose not to reject the electoral process and went confidently to the polls. In so doing it legitimized the new authoritarian parameters; the actual election results confirmed ARENA's majority, though by a small margin. This meant that the government, with an absolute majority in both houses and controlling all but one of the twenty-three states, kept a complete monopoly of the presidential succession and of the political initiative. On the other hand, because it had such a monopoly, the government agreed to relinquish the supraconstitutional powers of Act 5 in December 1978, and negotiated a fairly comprehensive amnesty law, finally approved the following August.

The second example is the party reform of 1979, which ended the compulsory two-party structure established by the first "revolutionary" government in 1965. Knowing that the continuity of the electoral disputes within the two-party framework would inevitably lead to a major defeat, perhaps forcing the regime to violate its own rules, the Figueiredo government (1979–1984) resorted to its majority in both houses and changed the party legislation, precipitating the return to a multiparty system. The ambiguity of the opening process was again brought to the surface. On one hand, the procedure was formally impeccable, since the government did have the majority, and the reform was demanded even by some sectors of the opposition; on the other, the evident intention was to break up the opposition party, the PMDB, in order to keep the agenda under control for a more extended period of time and to set the conditions under which the new party structure would be formed.

The third example is the imposition, in November 1981, of a new set of electoral rules, requiring a straight party vote at all levels (councilman, mayor, state and federal deputy, governor, and senator). This effectively prohibited any kind of alliance among the opposition parties in the 1982 elections. Care was thus taken to avoid a serious defeat for the government, since that election would affect the composition of the Electoral College that would choose the next president, in January 1985. Again, though the straight ticket helped the government's party in the overall count, many thought that it would (and certainly did) help the opposition in some key states. Also, despite its manipulative intent, this new set of rules was approved by a congressional majority that had, just a month before, broken up over two bills deemed essential to the government's interests.[3]

Although our focus in this chapter is mainly political and institutional, we must note as well the economic legitimation of the authoritarian governments up to 1984. With the exception of the first three years (1964–1966), the post-1964 governments gave an enormous impetus to modernization and economic growth. The rapid internationalization of the economy and the heavily regressive effect of government policies on income distribution eventually alienated many sectors initially favorable to the authoritarian experiment. However, during most of the post-1964 period, growth rates were high enough to grant the regime an important claim to legitimacy. Under the Médici administration, which was the most repressive and culturally stagnant, such rates were extremely high (the Brazilian "economic miracle").

Geisel, chosen for the presidency in 1973, started the decompression project exactly when the international environment began to become severely adverse. However, his economic policies were designed not only to sustain high rates of growth but, through an ambitious strategy of import substitution in basic sectors, to reduce Brazil's external dependency significantly. With the help of hindsight, it is not difficult to question some of these measures, which aggravated our external debt intolerably. However, this was not an authoritarian government lost in its internal contradictions and without any semblance of a project. On the contrary: in addition to engaging the opposition in gradual political decompression, Geisel's administration was sometimes praised by representatives of the opposition, who perceived his economic policies as nationalistic and antirecessionist.[4]

The first two years of Figueiredo's administration (1979–1980) can be regarded as a continuation of Geisel's strategy, but 1981 was a clear dividing line. On the economic side, sustaining high rates of growth became clearly impossible, after the second oil and the interest-rate shocks of 1979. Politically, Figueiredo's unwillingness to support a thorough investigation of a terrorist attempt against a May 1 artistic show in Rio de Janeiro struck a heavy blow to the credibility of the *abertura*. The attempt was seemingly planned by the information and security agencies. The lack of a thorough investigation thus brought to the surface with stunning clarity the suspicion that the whole process was subject to a military veto, regardless of electoral results or of public-opinion trends.

The election of 1982 inaugurated a fundamentally different situation. Together, the opposition parties made a majority (albeit small) in the lower chamber. Even more important, gaining a large number of local and ten of the twenty-three state governments, including São Paulo and Rio de Janeiro, the opposition now had significant bases of power. The only secure institutional instruments of containment at the disposal of the regime were now the Senate and the Electoral College, both severely questioned in their legitimacy.[5] This strange "diarchy," pitting the military-bureaucratic system against state governments and a lower chamber enjoying stronger popular legitimacy, was bound to affect the presidential succession, and thereby the fate of the regime. A proposed amendment to the Constitution, determining that Figueiredo's successor would be chosen by direct election, set the stage for a major popular campaign, led by the opposition parties and supported by the oppositionist state governments. This was the *diretas já* (direct elections now), marked by a series of impressive popular rallies, which not only revealed the further loss of regime legitimacy but also paved the way for a formal dissidence (the Frente Liberal) within the government party, the Partido Democrático Social (PDS). The proposed amendment failed to get the two-thirds majority in the Chamber, but after the vote the situation was close to irreversible. Combined, the Frente Liberal and the largest of the opposition parties, the PMDB, established the Democratic Alliance and led Tancredo Neves to victory in the Electoral College in January 1985. Tancredo died without taking office and was succeeded in the presidency by José Sarney, a PDS dissident who had been nominated for vice-president.

It can thus be said that the outcome of the opening process became clear only when the moving horizon that guided it during ten years became completely exhausted. Deep recession and the succession crisis combined to make the implicit negotiation virtually impossible after 1982; or rather, to make it possible only insofar as it was embodied in the already existing institutional rules, without further manipulation. The presidency, as an expression of military tutelage over the political system, was forced to stay neutral in the succession struggle.

This rather peculiar process of decompression was made possible because, in the initial stages, the opposition party was fighting for institutional positions almost totally emptied of real power. Up to 1982, the state governments were chosen indirectly, in effect appointed by the federal government. Congress had completely lost its main functions and prerogatives. The docility of the government party (ARENA) and of the (indirectly elected) "bionic" senators, one-third of the upper house, made it hopelessly weak. Hence, the return to civilian rule did not amount to a clear-cut return to a preexisting order. Congress, political parties, the federation: all of these regained some prestige and strength but did not automatically invest themselves in their traditional roles, first because the traditions themselves were modest, and second because the country had changed immensely under authoritarian rule. To understand the prospects for democracy in Brazil, one must appreciate these historical traditions and legacies.

• INSTITUTIONAL HISTORY: AN OVERVIEW •

Our interpretation of the Brazilian *abertura* stressed that the electoral process and conventional representative institutions had preserved their potential as vehicles for an orderly and peaceful transition. This element seems to have been missed by some academic theories and pieces of journalistic analysis that depicted a far more petrified authoritarian regime. Linz, one of the few scholars who did pay attention to this problem, correctly observed that the Brazilian authoritarian rulers would have a hard time if they had seriously decided to search for an alternative and durable legitimacy formula.

Our reconstruction of Brazilian institutional history starts with a view of the nineteenth-century empire as an extremely difficult and slow process of state-building. In fact, we look at that process as a Hobbesian construction, not in the vulgar sense of violent or tyrannical domination, but just the opposite way, meaning that certain legal fictions had to be established lest naked force become imperative—and even then, it might not be available in the requisite amount. Stretching it a little further, the empire will be regarded as a political system that developed in order to build a state, not the other way around.[6]

The concept of representation will help us bring the process of state-building into the analysis. In fact, the original or Hobbesian meaning of representation is simply formal authorization: It is the fiction that creates the state as an institution. It is prior to Dahl's legitimate contestation, since it corresponds to establishing the state framework within which contestation may later take place.[7] The democratic components of the concept appear at a more advanced stage. Social conflict and participation demands give rise to the descriptive image of representation; i.e., the notion that representative bodies should be like a sample or miniature, reflecting society's diversity. Increasing conflict and cultural strains may at the same time give rise to a demand for symbolic representation; i.e., institutions or charismatic leaders embodying a collective self-image of the nation. A fourth concept eventually emerges, focusing on the behavior of representatives. It expresses itself in the demand for faithfulness and relevance, for greater coherence in the party system, greater independence for unions and other associations, and the like. It corresponds, in short, to a more watchful state of public opinion. Let us now see what these ideas look like in historical perspective.[8]

The Empire: Hobbesian State Building

The only Portuguese colony in the New World, Brazil's political path after independence was completely different from that followed by her Spanish-speaking neighbors. Independence, obtained in 1822, was already marked by a unique feature: It came without a war against the Portuguese metropolis. A proclamation by the regent prince effected the separation and turned Brazil into an independent monarchy. After some years of instability, the monarchical form of government succeeded in establishing a stable political order and in keeping the integrity of the national territory.

The key factor accounting for stability during most of the nineteenth century was the existence of a cohesive political elite entrusted with the legal control of the country. The political system, considered more broadly, was a coalition of the rural aristocracy with the bureaucratic elite, but at the top these two sectors became strongly integrated. Recruited among landowners, urban merchants, and miners, this political elite was trained in the spirit of Roman law, Portuguese absolutism, and mercantilism.[9] The ideological unity of the elite helped it cope with threats to territorial integrity, despite the centrifugal tendencies inherent in our continental size, inadequate means of communication and transportation, the thinness of the economic linkages among provinces and regions, and the absence of a strong sense of national identity. Another important factor, in contrast with the old Spanish colonies, lies in the field of civil-military relations. During the empire, there was no threat to civil hegemony in Brazil. A parliamentary monarchy thus developed. The whole arrangement was elitist, no doubt, but the fact is that cabinets were elected and governed, liberals and conservatives rotated in office, and representative practices thus developed to some extent.

The "artificial" character of this political system has been frequently pointed out. Constitutional arrangements gave the emperor the so-called moderating power, which placed him above parties and factions, in fact allowing him to make and unmake majorities when he decided to dissolve parliament and call new elections. The two parties hardly differed, it is said, and had no significant roots in society. Elections not only tended to return the same people but were frequently fraudulent. This account is as correct as it is anachronic; it completely misses the fact that here we are not talking about descriptive representation in a highly differentiated society, but rather about Hobbesian authorization in the course of state-building. In order to understand this, we must take a broader look at the function of elections and at the way in which they were regulated up to 1930.[10]

The endless series of electoral reforms and the constant accusations of fraud were due primarily to the fact that there was no independent judicial organization to manage elections. The whole process, from voter registration (or rather, recognition) to counting ballots and proclaiming results was, in one way or another, subject to the interference of those involved and especially of police authorities subject to the provincial governors. To this extent, the importance of elections was indeed reduced. But local councils did affect the choice of state and national deputies. The government was thus constantly concerned with elections at all levels; in fact, it is said that the main function of the provincial governor, under the empire, was to win elections. From our Hobbesian standpoint, it may be deduced that losing them too frequently would force the central government to resort to its *ultima ratio*; i.e., open intervention.

Not a few observers have gone as far as to say that in Brazil, elections were totally farcical, and that more "authentic" results would have been achieved through a plain recognition of whomever held power in a given region or locality; or, on the other extreme, through complete centralization. The argument seems persuasive simply because it skips the difficult step. If recognition in this sense means granting a legal title to rule (as elections do), at that time it would have been tantamount to unleashing an endless series of small civil wars, since in each case public authority would be bestowed on a specifically named individual or faction, to the exclusion of others. The central government would thus be multiplying the conflicts it was seeking to avoid.

It is equally evident that the imperial government did not possess material capabilities to intervene everywhere and "centralize" power, as the recipe goes. Centralization did occur, but in a different sense. The representative mechanism of the empire operated by means of a highly aristocratic two-party system. Rotation between the two was partly a matter of elections, but it also had a lot to do with imperial inducement. The whole point of this courtly and apparently alien system was actually to control the processes of party formation. Monarchical government meant that, contrary to the United States, we did not have the formative impact of presidential elections. Formation through class conflict was out of the question, given the rudimentary state of the productive structure and the low level of social mobilization. But two other alternatives can still be imagined, and the empire carefully controlled both. One was parties of principle, in Burkean language; i.e., parties based on religious or otherwise doctrinal views. Some initiatives of this kind appeared toward the end of the century and were adequately controlled or repressed. The other, certainly more significant, was a gradual evolution from kinship groups (with their private armies) toward nationally organized parties. Something of this sort happened in Uruguay, for example. Brazil's territorial extension made it far less likely, but, in any case, it was prevented exactly by the flexible rotation allowed at the top of the pyramid and managed by the emperor.

The nineteenth-century constitutional monarchy was clearly not a democratic system. Its equilibrium rested largely on the bureaucracy, but this arrangement worked well only as long as it was attractive to a few key actors. When it ceased to be attractive to landowners and slave owners, and when new interests, most notably the military, became more differentiated, it fell without anyone to defend it and without violence.

The First Republic: Hobbes II

When Marshall Deodoro da Fonseca marched before the troops in Rio de Janeiro, on November 15, 1889, signaling the change of the regime, military discontent with the monarchy had already gone a long way. During most of the nineteenth century, the military had played virtually no role in Brazilian politics. The Paraguayan war (1865–1870), however, led to the development of a strong professional army. Victorious, the military decided to claim a share in power and greater respect from society. This was also the time when Comtean positivism and republican ideas began to penetrate military circles, starting a military circles, starting a long tradition of military politicization.[11]

Another major source of opposition to the political system of the empire were the São Paulo coffee growers. One of the links between the bureaucratic elite and the landowners under the empire was the underlying agreement to preserve slavery. But the coffee plantations of São Paulo, which developed rapidly during the last decades of the century, depended on wage labor, and indeed on the free labor of European migrants. Republican ideas thus became clearly linked to economic modernization. But the republic was, at the beginning, just as bad for the coffee growers; first because an inexperienced military exerted decisive influence and made the system potentially very unstable, and second because the unitary monarchy gave way to extreme federative decentralization. The republican Constitution of 1891, closely inspired by the U.S. model, gave a great deal of autonomy to the states, including extensive fiscal rights. The country thus faced a precocious "ungovernability" syndrome. The weakness of the central government affected, very adversely, the interests of the more dynamic sectors of the economy, which were exactly those located in São Paulo. For the *paulista* coffee growers, the fiscal and exchange policies were vital.

These elements do not exhaust the picture but go a long way to explain the changes that took place in the political system of the First Republic, producing a generalized feeling that the "real" Brazil had little to do with its liberal Constitution. First, the political leaders of the two major states, São Paulo and Minas Gerais, decided to establish between themselves the backbone of a functioning polity. A key aspect of the pact was that they would alternate controlling the federal executive. From this vantage point, they went on to develop a new "doctrine", called politics of the governors: They would support whichever oligarchy was dominant in each of the other states, in exchange for support for their arrangement at the federal level. The central government thus refrained from passing judgment on the quality of the political practices of each state.[12] This was the new guise of the Hobbesian construction. Needless to say, it went rather far to making liberal "formalities" indeed a farce. The legislative and judicial branches were decisively reduced to a secondary role; Congress became increasingly docile and lost its potential as a locus of party formation; and opposition was curbed in most of the states, so much so that statewide single parties became the rule.

The end of slavery and the extension of voting rights to large numbers of town dwellers and rural workers made it imperative for the federal government to be sure it would gain these votes. The governor's role thus became one of disciplining an extended electoral base, which he did by granting extensive extralegal authority to local bosses, in exchange for electoral support. This is the root of the phenomenon of *coronelismo,* which did so much to demoralize the electoral process in the eyes of the urban middle class up to 1930 and to generalize the notion that electoral institutions were somehow "alien" to Brazilian soil. Another result of this process of state-building was to make the relationship between political and private power—the latter based on land ownership—extremely transparent and resilient to change.

In exchange for the votes they garnered, the *coronéis* (backland bosses) received support from the oligarchy in control of the state machinery, thus reproducing further down the scale the arrangement between the states and the federal government. Control of the state machinery thus became rather literally a matter of life and death, since in addition to hiring and firing it could easily arrest or release.

Hobbes III: Getúlio Vargas

It is in many ways astounding that the political system of the First Republic did, after all, last forty-one years. In addition to the modest development of the urban middle strata and to the very incipient advances toward forming an industrial working class, that longevity was facilitated by the hierarchical character of nonurban politics, which was the real center of gravity of the whole construction. The votes of the peasants and other lower strata were controlled by rival factions of *coronéis,* who tended to be unified in a single pyramid because of the fied in a single pyramid because of the single-party structures in the states.

In October 1930, the First Republic was terminated by a revolutionary movement led by Getúlio Vargas, who until then was a rather conventional politician from the southernmost state, Rio Grande do Sul. The Revolution of 1930 cannot be described by a single set of causes. It was a reflection of regional cleavages as well as of urban middle-class and military discontent. It was made possible by the obsolescence of the political pact between the two major states, Minas Gerais and São Paulo. The rapid development of the latter toward modern capitalist agriculture and even toward industrialization gradually unbalanced the initial arrangements. However, São Paulo was hit hardest by the international crisis of 1929; other important states, Minas Gerais included, thus made a bid for greater power and influence.[13]

The main institutional result of the movement headed by Getúlio Vargas was an irreversible increase in central authority: The federative excesses of the First Republic were curtailed; government intervention in the economy was legitimized to a far greater degree; and, last but not least, important changes in representation concepts and practices were quickly introduced. Descriptive and symbolic meanings of representation finally made headway into the legal and political culture.

Descriptive representation is based on the notion that representative bodies ought somehow to look like a sample of society. It is therefore a demand that the Hobbesian process of formal authorization be enriched, in order to bring the diversity of social cleavages into those bodies. Perhaps we should stress the word *enriched*, since, for the 1930s, it is not always possible to speak of an articulate demand on the part of autonomous and identifiable social groups. A great deal of the legislation adopted must be understood as having a preemptive character (as was clearly the case of corporatism in the field of labor organization). In the electoral field, the introduction of a comprehensive scheme of proportional representation (through the Electoral Code of 1932), the design of which remains basically the same today, was intimately linked to other changes, in an overall design intended to enhance governmental authority. Indeed, the revolution rapidly moved to lower the voting age to eighteen, to extend the right to vote to women, to introduce the secret ballot, and to create an Electoral Court in charge of the whole process, from voter registration to certifying the victor.

These advances beg the question of how efficacious voting rights could be at that moment. But the point is that the First Republic had seriously degraded parliamentary and electoral institutions. To recover them would, of course, have a democratizing impact in the long run; but there was a pressing problem of reorganizing and reasserting authority in the short run. The revolution, after all, had decisively strengthened the federal executive vis-à-vis states and regions; signs of Left/Right polarization and especially resistance to a quick return to institutional normalcy were quite visible.

The provisional government was thus obliged to meet, and drew a great deal of legitimacy from meeting, the prior demand for "moralization of electoral practices." What most attracted Assis Brasil (the main author of the Electoral Code of 1932) to proportional representation (PR) was the enhancement he thought it would give to government legitimacy and stability, rather than the faithful representation of social diversity. Because it represented the (electoral) minority, PR strengthened its involvement with the state system and its acceptance of the majority. Also, PR was based on larger geographical divisions (actually, the states), thus making the mandate truly independent, in the Burkean sense, instead of the almost imperative mandate that resulted from small districts under the direct influence of landowners and local potentates. It should also be noted that Assis Brasil's model prevails even today insofar as the representation of the different states in the federal Chamber is concerned. The latter is based on the overrepresentation of the smaller and on the underrepresentation of the very large states (especially São Paulo), thus introducing considerations of federative equilibrium, and not simply of electoral justice, in the composition of the lower chamber. In recent years this has been much criticized, but at that time the logic was clearly the same that underlies Assis Brasil's reference to minority support.

It was also thought that PR on a broad geographical basis would practically force the consolidation of the other elements of the electoral reform, such as the secret ballot and administration of the electoral process by an independent Electoral Court. It is noteworthy that one of the most capable analysts of Brazilian institutional history, Nunes Leal, hardly emphasizes the element of proportionality when he discusses the reform of the early 1930s. The important aspect for him is the advance toward "moralization"; i.e., the Electoral Court. This is also remarkable in that Nunes Leal was deeply skeptical about the development of representative democracy in Brazil without a major change in the agrarian structure. Even so, he wrote, in 1948,

> despite the excesses and frauds that may have occurred here and there, most testimonies have been favorable to the electoral laws of the early thirties. The gravest accusations against our system of political representation ended simply as a consequence of the fact that those laws withdrew the prerogative of certifying who was elected from the chambers themselves. The *ins* ended up defeated in some states and a numerous opposition, later reinforced by contestation in the presidential election, found its way even to the Federal Chamber.[14]

One irony of modern Brazil is that these initial and decisive advances toward Dahlsian democratization were in part instrumental to the new Hobbesian/ Getúlian thrust. Moreover, they were in part effected under the auspices of protofascist thinking.[15] The forty-one years of the first republican Constitution had given rise to a deep strain in political culture: Liberal forms had come to be regarded as an alien factor, distorting or corrupting the "true" nature of Brazilian society. There arose a demand for "authentic" representation, for an institutional structure truly adapted to Brazilian reality. For some, this meant an improvement, but for others it meant the suppression of electoral, party, and parliamentary institutions. The Constitutional Congress of 1934 included a section of "corporatist" deputies, an experiment that did not take root and would never be repeated. But corporatist views of representation were widely propagated and became in fact the framework within which so-called social rights were extended to the urban working class.[16] Such views were part and parcel of the Getúlian thrust toward an authoritarian (as distinguished from totalitarian) integration of the political order. Under Getúlio Vargas' guidance, protofascist thinking quickly became *anti*fascist; i.e., an edge against the further development of mobilizational fascism. More than that, it became an ideological framework helping him effectively to repress the two extremes, *integralistas* and Communists, starting in 1935 and leading to the formal announcement of the dictatorial Estado Novo (1937–1945).

The two pillars of this move toward a far more centralized state structure must be considered, since they embody the presence, apparently for the first time in Brazilian history, of a comprehensive experiment in symbolic representation. One was the increasingly charismatic nature of the presidential office, with Getúlio Vargas in the role of founding father. At the time, however, this was a limited and cautious change, if we compare it with the more portentous events that would soon take place in Argentina with Perón. In Brazil, the charismatic presidency developed without a confrontation with the system's element of limited pluralism (in Linz's sense): A *de facto* federation continued to exist, with strongly oligarchical features within each state; the church's traditional legitimacy went on receiving a great deal of deference; and the elite (strange as this may sound) did not give up its reverence for legal culture and for the Brazilian legal tradition.

Another pillar in the emergence of Getúlian representation was the reinforcement, if not, indeed, a considered invention of certain symbols of national identity. It is surely possible to assert that at this time we witness the emergence of culture policy; that such policy was closely associated with a process of nation- (as opposed to state-) building; and finally that both would have long-range effects in crystallizing a whole new notion of representation in Brazilian political culture. This cultural construction vigorously asserted that zero-sum conflict cannot reasonably emerge in Brazilian society. This view became truly encompassing and persuasive in part because it was espoused by leading intellectuals and artists, but also because it reflected important historical and social traits. It was, first, a celebration of past success in keeping together such a vast territory; this in turn always associated with the notion of unlimited opportunity. Second, it suggested that Brazilian social structure had indeed evolved in the direction of increased equality and mobility, not least in the field of race relations.[17] Third, it was a view of Brazilian politics; it effectively retrieved the experience of the early empire, especially Conciliation, when elite restraint and skill put an end to regional and factional struggles. But in the 1930s, a subtle turn seems to have occurred: Instead of reinforcing its nascent negative image as oligarchical, intra-elite behavior, this cultural construction came to regard political flexibility and realism as an emanation of similar traits in the social system, implying that Brazilian politics at its best would always be flexible. Finally, it was a reassertion, on a grand scale, of the conservative (patriarchal) view of conflict as childish behavior: an image that could only be persuasive in a country that had virtually no experience with principled politics and that felt threatened by its emergence in the guise of communism and mobilizational fascism.

The Failure to Consolidate: 1945–1964

Getúlio Vargas was forced to resign on October 29, 1945. His fall and the subsequent developments had a lot to do with the changed international environment. The defeat of the Axis had discredited the Estado Novo internally and externally, despite the fact that it did not belong to the family of mobilizational fascism. At least at first sight, the democratic "experiment" that followed the fall of the Estado Novo had very favorable conditions to prosper and succeed. The international environment was certainly favorable; the domestic economy was not under unusual strain; the armed forces had developed a high decree of organization and an antipersonalistic outlook as a result of their close attention to the weakness of Italian fascism; and the Getúlian dictatorship had led to the emergence of a vigorous liberal opposition, with outstanding parliamentary leadership: the União Democrática Nacional (UDN). The deepest of all Brazilian evils, in the eyes of Nunes Leal, the sin of *governismo,* seemed to have ended.[18] The transition had once again been peaceful: If the lack of a clear break with the Estado Novo made further democratization more difficult later on, it is also true that the absence of bloody cleavages could have made it easier.

Why did the democratic system then fail to consolidate itself in the next twenty years? The first difficulty that comes to mind is the important institutional contradiction that had developed after 1930 and as a consequence of the Estado Novo. Authority now seemed to bifurcate in a truly charismatic image of the presidency on one side, and an enormous assertion of the parliamentary institution—not least because of the formation of the UDN in the struggle against Vargas—on the other. This was not an immediate threat, since Vargas withdrew to a silent role after his downfall, but became extremely serious when he came back, riding the tide of a direct presidential election in 1950. The political system was now torn between an executive with strong Caesarist overtones, and a parliamentary center of gravity that pulled toward some sort of congressional or party government. Needless to say, Vargas' second presidency was extremely tense, and the contradiction was aggravated instead of diluted by his suicide in August 1954.[19]

Second, this newly assertive and formally powerful Congress was essentially made up of notables. It understandably had not developed a technical substructure to speak of and was not supported by a modern party system. In order to appreciate this difficulty, it is necessary to recall that the scope of government intervention had been enormously enlarged since 1930. The bureaucracy, traditionally large by virtue of the patrimonial origins of the Brazilian state, had again been expanded and modernized after the revolution. The legislature had constitutional powers but lacked everything else it needed to supervise and check this massive amount of policymaking.[20]

Interpretations of the 1964 breakdown have diverged a great deal. Stating his preference for those that stress the "internal sociopolitical situation" rather than "causes exogenous to the polity," Merquior aptly summarizes this literature:

> government instability, the disintegration of the party system, virtual paralysis of legislative decision-making, equivocal attitudes on the part of President Goulart, not least with regard to his own succession; the threat of an ill-defined agrarian reform; military concern with government-blessed sergeants' mutinies; and mounting radicalism on both the right and the left . . . all of this compounded by soaring inflation and, of course, by the haunting ghost of the Cuban revolution.[21]

The fate of the party system should be specifically noted. We have suggested that from 1945 onward we had for the first time some basic conditions to develop a competitive party structure. Most observers seem to agree that the start was promising, but that the new party system underwent a sharp deinstitutionalization from the second half of the 1950s up to 1964. Some impute this to sheer erosion; i.e., rapid social mobilization in the wake of industrialization and urbanization, decreasing efficacy of traditional control mechanisms of the patron-client type, and so forth. Others place greater emphasis on institutional regulations, especially the electoral system based on PR and on the preferential vote (open party lists). The fact, however, is that from Jânio Quadros' presidential resignation (August 1961) to the military takeover (March 1964), the party system was overpowered by the worst of all worlds. It became highly factionalized and subject to increasing radicalization at the same time that each of the major parties was internally divided; the tide of antiparty populism became truly exponential (the election of Jânio Quadros to the presidency in 1960 being an example); and the party traditionally identified with moderation and equilibrium, the Partido Social Democrático (PDS) became fragmented.[22]

However, we must guard against an overly "politicistic" interpretation. On a broader canvas, the fragmentation of the party system was itself associated with the overall process of economic and social change. This relationship operated in two ways. On one hand, urbanization and social mobilization eroded traditional attachments and social-control mechanisms. On the other, the lack of substantial advance toward deconcentration (reduction of social inequality) left the parties, individually and as a system, without strong bases of popular support. This was the structural framework within which older ideological and institutional conflicts were acted out, setting the stage for the military takeover. On March 31, 1964, the incumbent president, João Goulart, Getúlio Vargas' political heir, was ousted from office and sent to exile.

It would thus seem that Brazil moved rapidly toward instituting the form of democracy—political contestation and participation—but failed to consolidate democracy by reducing socioeconomic inequality. Unable to channel social conflict toward concrete policies, the party system entered a cycle of deinstitutionalization, rather than of consolidation in the new democratic mold. Had there been substantial advances toward reducing inequality, we might have had major conflict among the parties and along class lines, but not the combination of radicalism and populism that took place in big cities, plus survival or even reassertion of basically clientelistic structures in the less developed areas of the country. The crisis of the party system was thus rather telling and cannot be understood simply in terms of the traditional view of those parties as being premodern, preideological, or otherwise not ripe for serious representative democracy. It was more in the nature of an induced suicide, by means of which the society seems to have expelled an extraneous body: a trend toward stronger political representation in the absence of any substantial deconcentration.

An Overview of the Overview

Brazilian institutional development was, so to speak, preeminently state-centered. It must be understood in terms of the prolonged process of state-building and the cautious strategies on which it was based, since a small central elite and state structure were confronted with the challenge of preserving territorial unity in a country of continental dimensions. Today's heavy bureaucratic machinery; the ponderous legalistic ethos, despite the fact that legal norms are frequently bypassed; the continuing weight of clientelism and of conservative interests based on land ownership, not to speak of the increasingly tutelary role of the military since the Estado Novo—all these can be traced to or partly explained by that fundamental thrust of our state formation. These aspects of state-building have also been held responsible for what is felt to be an absence of public authority, or a lack of differentiation of the political system vis-à-vis societal structures. This is often phrased as an absence of political institutions properly so-called. This chapter has argued, to the contrary, that there has been significant institution-building, though not necessarily of a formally democratic character. Certain aspects of the post-1964 regime, which are surely relevant for understanding the *abertura* process of the last decade, are clearly related to that prior institutional development.

The literature on the recent authoritarian experiment rightly stresses that its economic project was one of capitalist modernization and greater integration in the world capitalist system; and further, that this led, from 1967 on, to a strategy of accelerated industrial growth rather than of income redistribution or of reduction of absolute poverty. It is also correctly said that the initial perceptions led policymakers to curb labor unions and "progressive" organizations; and finally, that this overall thrust, combined with the need to repress guerilla activities, ended up engaging the regime, from 1968 to 1974, in a highly repressive phase, with very high costs in terms of human rights. Yet, two features of the post-1964 regime helped preserve institutional continuity, which in this context meant a chance for a peaceful resumption of democracy. The first is the impersonal concept of government, which materialized in: (a) tighter rules to contain politicization among the military; (b) conservation of the presidency as an elective office, at least through an Electoral College; and (c) keeping the traditional limits pertaining to the duration of the presidential mandate and the norm against reelection.[23]

The second feature was the preservation of the representative system. Needless to say, representation here meant formal authorization, in the Hobbesian sense; but it now took place within institutional parameters that not even the military could afford to ignore or distort completely. It is interesting to note, in this context, that the pre-1964 party structure was not immediately suppressed. The decision to terminate the old parties was made only in October 1965, one and one-half years after the coup, and was immediately followed by the creation of at least a "provisional" party structure; i.e., the two-party system that was to remain until 1979. The military governments obviously manipulated the conditions under which elections were held in the ensuing twenty years but did not try to do away with the electoral mechanism as such or replace it by a totally different doctrine of representation.

• THEORETICAL REVIEW •

State-building in Brazil left a highly contradictory legacy for contemporary democratic development. As a skillful extension of central regulatory capabilities, it was constantly oriented toward keeping intra-elite conflict at a low level and preventing the eruption of large-scale political violence. But this preemptive pattern of growth undoubtedly made Brazilian society too "backward" from the standpoint of autonomous associational participation. This, in turn, gave the elites and the bureaucracy an excessive latitude to define policy priorities, crystalized unjustifiable income differentials, and left the political system constantly exposed to a dangerous legitimacy gap.

Overall Historical Pattern

Brazil was a part of the Portuguese Empire from 1500 to 1822. During those three centuries, it was in essence a commercial (as opposed to a settlement) colony: mining and large-scale plantations based on slave labor. Even the colonizers were few, since the Portuguese population was pathetically small compared to the vast world empire it tried to build. These are some of the reasons why the colonial system left neither a powerful central authority nor an integrated national community in its wake.

The comparative question with respect to Brazil's colonial past, then, is not so much one of democratic tradition, imported or indigenous.[24] It is rather the relatively smooth transition to a process of political development that we see as consciously oriented toward long-range goals. Political competition and the appropriate institutions began to develop under the empire, at a time when mass political participation was totally absent. From then on, political changes became comparatively nonviolent, allowing enough room for the contending groups to accommodate their differences afterwards. Since the nineteenth century, large-scale violence has been increasingly controlled, and bitter memories have not accumulated, at least not among the political elite.

The theoretical judgment according to which democracy is better off when peaceful contestation among elites precedes mass participation may be accepted, but requires some qualifications in the Brazilian case. First, there is a matter of degree, since that process finally led to a state structure that seems excessively strong vis-à-vis civil society: too large and clientelistic to be effectively controlled by the citizenry and constantly reinforced by the constraints of so-called late industrialization. Second, the Dahlsian sequence seems to have left serious strains in terms of legitimacy and political culture, as indicated by the alleged excess of conciliation and elitist character of the political system.

State Structure and Strength

Historians who see a strong state in Brazil in the nineteenth century normally stress that the empire kept the country's territorial integrity, though compelled to use force against important separatist movements. Other analyses attempt to trace the bureaucratic organization of the Brazilian government directly back to the Portuguese absolutist state. But these arguments overstate the case, since they overlook the fact that state structures never became entirely distinguished *qua* public authority. Symbiotic arrangements with private power (e.g., landed wealth) were part and parcel of a gradual extension of regulatory capabilities. The effectiveness of the central authority in keeping public order and eventually in undertaking social changes is, then, recent in Brazilian history. It is difficult to see how it could exist at a time when the national army hardly existed, or even before it developed organizational responses to its own internal divisions.[25]

The organizational "maturity" of the army would appear only after the Revolution of 1930. From the 1930s onward, the armed forces developed an increasingly tutelary conception of their role vis-à-vis civilian institutions and society as a whole. Thus, in 1945 they pressured Getúlio Vargas out of office, on the understanding that the days of the Estado Novo were gone. Friction with elected presidents or with their ministers was evident throughout the 1950s and early 1960s. In 1961, following Jânio Quadros' resignation from the presidency, the military ministers actually vetoed the transfer of power to the elected vice-president, João Goulart. This move brought the country to the brink of civil war and was defeated only because the military ministers failed to achieve unitary backing for their position among the regional commanders. In 1964, with substantial popular support, the military overthrew Goulart and took power.

However, this tutelary role should not be taken to mean that the Brazilian military is quintessentially opposed to democratic principles and institutions. The tutelary self-conception clearly belongs to the broader authoritarian ideology that presided over the last phase of state-building; i.e., the Getúlian thrust of the 1930s. That ideology includes elements that, paradoxically, help sustain some of the institutional mechanisms of representative democracy. Being, at root, antipopulist and nonmobilizational, it stresses the distinction between private and public roles—hence the limits on the duration of mandates, the electoral calendar, and, more generally, the importance of keeping the legislature, at least as an institution, capable of being reactivated—all of these clearly practiced by the post-1964 regime.

Brazil's political development has also benefited from the fact that instances of direct armed challenge to the state have been few in this century and have been effectively repressed since the 1930s. Ethnic separatism has been virtually nonexistent in modern Brazil. From this point of view, too, state-building was brought to a conclusion that certainly favors democracy.

On the other hand, the procedures and justifications used to repress armed challenges, in the 1930s and again after 1964, led to threatening precedents. In both cases, those challenges were treated in terms of "internal war," far more than as unlawful behavior that perhaps could be dealt with by judicial or political means. The legislature, political parties, the judiciary: all of these came out clearly weakened vis-à-vis the executive (which in fact meant the military). With the military directly in power after 1964, this trend became far more serious. First there came the arrests, proscriptions, and similar measures designed to curb opposition and promote societal demobilization. From 1968 to 1974, confronting armed underground movements, the regime adopted widespread censorship and all sorts of cover-up repressive practices. The cost of this phase in terms of human rights was not as high as that faced by Argentina shortly afterwards, but it cannot be underestimated as a negative effect for democratic prospects. As argued in our first section, some of the military seem to have recognized that they had gone too far, when they opted (circa 1973) for a gradual "opening from above."

The description of the Brazilian military as exerting a tutelary role and as having directly established an authoritarian regime that would last for twenty-one years obviously does not square well with the emerging image of a vigorous "civil society." In fact, we think that there have been exaggerations in applying the latter concept to the Brazilian case. It is true, of course, that Brazilian society has not become highly differentiated and complex. Combined with resistance to the military regime, this has led to a rapid increase in associational politicization. But a more appropriate reading of this trend would be that of updating a society marked by unusually low participation and predominantly organized along corporatist, rather than along consociational, lines. The latter term refers to autonomous subcultures or subsocieties, which hardly exist in Brazil. Corporatist political organization, in contrast, is organization stemming from occupational criteria, directly controlled by the state (as in the case of labor unions) or, more frequently, aiming to keep differential privileges among professions, the gradient of such differences being guaranteed by the state.

After twenty years of military-authoritarian rule (1964–1984), no one will doubt that the Brazilian state is highly centralized vis-à-vis the federation, or that it directly controls a large proportion of the economy. Since the nineteenth century, the predominant concern with state-building, and the high degree of cohesion of the political elite contrasting with the dispersion and abysmal poverty of the general populace, meant that the central authorities enjoyed a wide margin of discretion to make choices in economic policy.

Development Performance

Disregarding redistributive issues for a moment, there can be no question that Brazilian governments have been consistently seeking to promote economic growth for a long time, and that their record is fairly impressive. The Brazilian economy now belongs among the ten or twelve largest in the world, roughly on a level with Italy and Canada. This rank is the result of continuously high rates of growth since the early 1930s, and especially of steady advances toward industrialization. The average growth rate of GDP during this whole period has been of the order of 6 to 7 percent a year, with a peak of 10 percent a year from 1968 to 1974. Industrial growth rates have been twice or thrice that of agriculture; in 1968, ten times higher. This growth pattern accounts for the vast scale of the structural changes the country has undergone (see Table 3.1), which Santos finds at least as impressive as that promoted by Meiji restoration in Japan or by the Soviet government in its initial two decades.[26]

Some structural aspects of Brazil's "late-developer" pattern of growth must be underlined if we are to understand its political implications. Far from deconcentrating state power, the growth record mentioned above has greatly reinforced it. Reacting to the constraints brought by World War I and by the crisis of 1929, subsequent governments assumed an increasingly direct role in the economic sphere. Starting with the Volta Redonda steel complex, in 1942, state and mixed enterprises were created to foster industrial infrastructure. Foreign trade was regulated not only through fiscal and exchange policies, but also through government entities specifically designed to supervise the commercialization of coffee, sugar, and other commodities. Four decades later, Hewlett could aptly describe the Brazilian state as "a significant producer of basic industrial goods and infra-structural items, an important agent of protection and subsidy, a powerful regulator of economic activity, and the determiner of the direction of national economic development."[27]

Needless to say, this record of growth underlies the proven ability of the Brazilian political system to avoid the generalization of zero-sum perceptions and expectations. But these successes have not been sufficient to dilute the illegitimacy syndrome that permanently surrounds the political system, if not authorities in general. In fact, the Brazilian state, having relied heavily on economic growth for legitimacy, has been reasonably successful in promoting growth but seems rather far from overcoming its legitimacy deficit. In theory,

Table 3.1. Socioeconomic Change in Brazil, 1940–1980

	1940	1950	1960	1970	1980
Population (in millions)	41.2	51.9	70.1	93.1	119.1
Percent of population in urban areas	31.2	35.1	45.1	55.9	67.6
Percent of population in metropolitan areas (nine largest cities)	15.2	17.9	21.5	25.5	29.0
Percentage of the labor force in:					
Agriculture	67.4	60.2	54.5	44.6	30.5
Industry	12.6	13.3	12.4	18.1	24.9
Services	19.9	26.4	33.1	37.8	44.6
Per-capita gross national product (GNP) (in U.S. dollars)	391[a]	444	640	960	1,708

Sources: For population data: *Fundação IBGE* (Censos Demográficos e Tabulações Avançadas de 1980). For GNP: *Conjuntura Econômica* 26, no. 11 (1972), and *Gazeta Mercantil* (1970–1985).

[a]Data for 1947.

the state can manipulate the supply of key inputs and thus start altering the many perverse aspects of the growth pattern, but it cannot readily do that in practice, as Hewlett points out, since interfering with the market conditions toward which major enterprises are oriented would often mean reducing the rate of growth—hence, losing legitimacy. Moreover, insufficient domestic savings, technological dependence, and other imbalances have increasingly led the country, since the 1950s, to a strategy of growth-*cum*-debt and inflationary financing. In the 1970s and early 1980s, as is well known, foreign debt sky-rocketed to over $100 billion and inflation rapidly moved to the three-digit altitude.

In conclusion, Brazilian development can thus be said to have very positive and very negative aspects. High rates of growth (hence variable-sum percep-tions among different strata of society) co-exist with dramatic imbalances—regionally, against the northeast; sectorally, against small-scale agriculture and rural labor; by class, against the poor in general. But there is no persuasive evi-dence that those positive or negative aspects are predominantly associated by the mass public with either democratic or authoritarian governments. Memories of high growth flash back on democratic (e.g., Kubitschek, 1955–1960) as well as on extreme authoritarian (e.g., Médici, 1969–1973) administrations.

A significant distinction emerged in the 1970s and early 1980s among the educated, urban middle class. In this segment, there undoubtedly was an in-crease in the proportion of those thinking that the military-authoritarian regime achieved growth at an unacceptable social cost: income concentration; neglect of welfare investments; denationalization of economy and culture; damage to the environment; corruption. This change was crucially important for the Brazil-ian political *abertura*, expressing itself in electoral mobilization as well as in the political activation of professional and civic associations of numerous types. How lasting this realignment will be is a moot question. Disappointment with the "New Republic" may induce further changes in the political value sys-tem of this segment.

A final word on corruption: up to 1964, corruption was clearly perceived in a patrimonial rather than in a capitalistic framework. The widespread feeling that politicians are corrupt was then primarily focused on clientelistic (patron-age) practices. Undue use of public funds for private enrichment was not un-known, of course, but it was perceived as associated with only a few practices (e.g., dubious credits to landowners and co-optation of union leaders). Under the military governments, the context and, therefore, the whole perception of corruption underwent an enormous change—perhaps we should say that both moved to an exponential scale. Accelerated industrialization, increasing inter-nationalization of the economy, the whole strategy of growth-*cum*-debt—all of these took place, we must recall, without any effective parliamentary oversight and often under the protection of pervasive press censorship. No wonder, then, that the idea of corruption became associated with financial scandals, alleged "commissions" in foreign dealings and so on; the number of known cases being sufficient, needless to say, to lend credence to the most extravagant generalizations.

The gradual and negotiated nature of Brazilian redemocratization made the exemplary investigation and punishment of major instances of corruption politically very difficult. The "new republic" thus failed to capitalize on one of the most potent sources of popular discontent with the previous authoritarian regime. Worse, it was quickly affected by a resurrection of the older "patrimonial" perception, since critics of the huge public deficit readily seized on patronage (*empreguismo*) as a target. Against a background of poverty and inequality, insufficient governability, and a political culture strongly affected by pervasive images of corruption, it comes as no surprise that even as remarkable a record of growth as the Brazilian may fall short of full legitimation for a democratic regime.

Class Structure, Income Distribution, and Social Organization

No matter how one measures them, levels of income inequality and mass poverty in Brazil are among the worst in the world. The main determinants of present income differentials and class structure undoubtedly have their roots in the pattern of land appropriation inherited from the colonial past. Concentration of landed wealth and use of the best land to produce export commodities have always been the major "push" factors behind the enormous supply of cheap labor constantly flocking to the cities.[28] Rapid industrial growth oriented toward a predominantly middle-class market, high rates of population growth, and the insufficiency of investment in basic welfare services have combined to maintain extreme inequalities and indeed to make a mockery of the "trickle-down" theory of indirect redistribution.[29] Needless to say, the full implications of Brazilian-size poverty and inequality for democratic prospects must also take into account that the country has now become highly urbanized and "mobilized" (in Deutsch's sense).

Throughout the empire and the First Republic, both working class and urban middle strata were numerically unimportant. The vast majority of the population lived in rural areas or in very small villages and towns, where society was steeply stratified. Here, there was no middle class worth speaking of. At the bottom were the peasants, a sprinkling of very poor independent farmers, and similar strata in the towns. At that time, a crisis in the coffee business was tantamount to economic recession, but it did not necessarily mean that a large number of laborers lost their jobs. From World War II onward, the picture started changing dramatically. Total population grew from 41 million in 1940 to 119 million in 1980; urban population, from 13 to 70 million; and metropolitan population (i.e., residents of the nine largest urban centers) from 6.3 to 35 million. These changes were accompanied by major shifts in the labor force out of agriculture and into industry and services (see Table 3.1).

Despite the impressive overall rates of economic growth during the "economic miracle" period of the military regime (the late 1960s and early 1970s), there is ample evidence that income differentials and some telling indicators of basic welfare (such as infant mortality) went on worsening. By the early 1970s, several studies were showing that income inequality had increased relative to the early 1960s. Writing in 1976, Graham offered the following summary of the evidence:

> (a) income concentration (as measured by the standard Gini index) increased over-
> all, and in all regions, during the sixties; (b) the rates of concentration were more
> pronounced in the more developed (and most rapidly growing) areas like Sao Paulo
> and the south than in the lesser developed regions; (c) real income increased in all
> areas; (d) average monthly real income per urban worker increased much more
> rapidly (43 percent) than income per agricultural worker (14 percent), thereby in-
> creasing the intersectoral income differentials during the decade; (e) these inter-
> sectoral income differentials stood out much more dramatically in the northeast
> than in Sao Paulo and the center and south.[30]

World Bank data on forty-four countries, including twenty-six less developed countries, shows Brazil to have the worst income inequality, as evidenced in the share of national income received in 1972 by the highest 20 percent and 10 percent of the population.[31] Using data from 1960 to 1980, Serra reports that concentration was still going on in the 1970s. The lowest 20% of the economically active population had gone from 3.9% of total income in 1960 to 3.4% in 1970, to 2.8% in 1980; the top 10%, from 39.6% to 46.7%, to 50.9%.[32] This means that the governmental policies practiced throughout this period, at best, did not counteract structural forces making for greater inequality; at worst they aggravated their effect. Combined with the massive character of absolute poverty that prevails in the northeast and in the outskirts of all major cities, this degree of income concentration is undoubtedly one of the steepest challenges to democratic consolidation.

Let us now look at this picture in terms of class structure, rather than of income distribution. The starting point here must be the corporatist order imposed from above in the 1930s.[33] This system can be seen as a highly successful attempt to control, not to say petrify, the process of class formation, by which we mean development of differentiated collective identities and autonomous political organization. The lowest extremity of the class structure, made up of landless peasants and very poor small farmers, was not regulated in a strict sense, since they lacked the occupational differentiation that formed the basis of the whole system; rather, they were excluded from it. The upper extremity, made up of large landowners, provided another parameter—untouchable property rights. But this should not be confounded with total political autonomy, much less with monolithic control of the state: The political sphere (embodied in the military, the bureaucracy, and in the political "class") retained considerable decisional discretion.

Between these two extremes, a corporatist gradient was imposed on the rest of society; i.e., on urban wage labor and middle-class independent occupations in general. The privilege of "representing" a given sector was thoroughly subjected to state (legal) control, as well as to effective means to circumscribe each sector's agenda-building and other overt political moves. This pattern applied even to industrial and commercial entrepreneurs, through corporatist pyramids exactly paralleling those of urban labor. As Santos points out, this whole structure remained virtually unchanged through the "democratic experiment" based on the Constitution of 1946. Attempts at self-organization on the part of rural labor, in the early 1960s, were quickly repressed by the post-1964 regime, obviously with full applause and cooperation from the landowners, who saw such attempts as outright subversion.

Ironically enough, serious and lasting "subversion" of the regulated order would occur, first as the result of the scale of the economic changes induced by the military governments; second, as an unintended by-product of some of their "modernizing" reforms; and finally, in that context of large-scale structural change, from the reactivation of "civil society" during the political opening. Development of large-scale industry led entrepreneurs, especially in the heaviest and most dynamic sectors, to organize in new types of associations, pulling themselves out of the traditional corporatist framework. Ousted, as it were, from the administration of social-security funds, labor leaders found themselves with nothing to offer their constituencies; nothing but more authentic leadership. This was the origin of so-called new unionism, which thrived in the most dynamic sectors of the economy and struck a major blow against the old corporatist structure. Trying to sidestep political clientelism in their attempt to extend social security to the rural areas, the military governments stimulated the formation of rural labor unions. From 1976 to 1983, unionized rural labor increased from slightly over 3 to more than 8 million, accounting now for more than half of total union membership in the country, even though rural labor accounts for only 30 percent of the economically active population. Needless to say, rural unions did not conform to the passive blueprint that the government probably conceived for them. In less than two decades, they had a national leadership, undertook successful strikes, and indeed placed land reform firmly on their agenda. The politicization of the urban middle strata has not lagged behind. White-collar unions, neighborhood organizations, and associations of numerous types quickly emerged, undoubtedly reflecting the increasing complexity and, in many ways the increasing technical and professional sophistication of Brazilian urban life.

The conclusion, then, is that, in Brazil, medieval economic inequalities exist side-by-side with a dynamic and increasingly sophisticated society. Heavy external dependency does not mean that an indigenous bourgeoisie failed to develop. There is, in fact, a modern entrepreneurial class, in industry as well as agriculture. This class has become much more affirmative in the last decade, profiting from the process of political opening. Perceiving that it could not unconditionally count on the military or on elected politicians, it became highly and autonomously organized. This process in fact underwent a remarkable acceleration under the new republic, first in view of the Constitutional Congress (elected in November 1986); and second, and perhaps more important, because the economic reforms of the Sarney government (the Cruzado Plan) politicized the economy to a far greater extent; for example, introducing generalized price controls.

We have so far emphasized the economic bases and the organizational aspects of class formation. Needless to say, the picture becomes much less politicized when we look at the rank-and-file and especially at class consciousness. A very large proportion of the urban working class is young, politically inexperienced, indeed made up of recent migrants. Wage strikes can be mobilized without much difficulty, but both unions and political parties must reckon with a great deal of instability, indeed of volatility, when it comes to broader electoral or ideological disputes.

Brazilian development, as we have repeatedly stressed, has been able to create a basically non–zero-sum perception of social conflict. Spatial mobility has been extremely high and has, in fact, meant better life chances for poor migrants. The belief in upward social mobility is probably not as deep today as it was in the 1950s, but access to education and to consumption has increased considerably with increases in total income. Some fashionable descriptions of Brazilian society as being rigidly hierarchical must, then, be taken with a grain of salt. The concentration of property, twenty-one years of authoritarian rule, and huge income inequalities have not meant petrification of status inequality.

On the other hand, socioeconomic inequalities do tend to cumulate to some extent. Although extremely high correlation among education, occupation, income, and, say, "honor," certainly does not exist, the overall structure of inequalities has an evident regional component. The southeast (where São Paulo is located) and the extreme south are "rich" regions, whereas the northeast, with 35 million inhabitants, is one of the major examples of mass poverty in the world. This regional disparity has an important overlap with the country's ethnic differentiation. Blacks and *pardoes* account for well over two-thirds of the northern and northeastern states, while the reverse proportion obtains in the southeast and the south. These definitions are known to be very imprecise in Brazilian population statistics, but the difference is large enough to merit attention.

Nationality and Ethnic Cleavages

Political conflict among language or religious groups is virtually nonexistent in Brazil. On these two dimensions, let alone nationality, the country is comparatively very homogeneous. The picture is much more complex in the field of race relations. Interpretations range from the belief in a genuinely "peaceful" evolution to the notion that underprivileged minorities (especially blacks) lack collective identity and organization as a consequence of white economic and political domination. The extremes do seem to agree that overt ethnic strife is not prevalent. There can be no doubt, however, that poverty and color are significantly correlated.[34] Blacks, and especially black women, are disproportionately locked in low-status and low-income occupations. The proportion of white men earning less than three minimum wages per month was 66% in 1976, while the comparable proportion was 82% for white women, 87% for black men, and 95% for black women. Educational data also show important differences (though not significantly between men and women). The proportion of illiterates among white men declined from 44% in 1950 to 24% in 1980; among black men, from 74% to 47%.[35] These figures clearly indicate diffuse racial barriers to social mobility.

But the country does have an overarching national identity. Living generations have virtually no memory of separatist movements or politically relevant subcultures, whether based on language, race, or religion. It can, of course, be said that this high degree of cultural uniformity reflects a process of authoritarian state-building under colonial and then imperial government. The fact, however, is that Brazil is not presently confronted with serious ethnic or cultural strife. Given the immense burden that socioeconomic cleavages place on the political agenda, this relative homogeneity is clearly a positive factor for democratic development.

Political Structure

The formal structure of the Brazilian state has varied a great deal since independence (see Table 3.2), but the concentration of power in the national executive has been a constant. Accepted as a hallmark of state-building and, more recently, as necessary for the sake of economic development and national security, that concentration was often carried out at the expense of state and local governments, of legislative and judicial powers, and even more clearly of the party system.[36]

The First Republic (1889–1930) tried to adapt the U.S. model, providing for a popularly elected president and granting extensive autonomy to the provinces, now called states, of the old unitary empire. The result was full of perverse effects, as the "politics of the governors" decisively weakened the national legislature and judiciary and seriously compromised elections and party competition. In practice, the government became as oligarchical and probably far less legitimate than the empire, in the eyes of the relevant strata. This process of political decay eventually led to the Revolution of 1930 (and, in 1937, to Vargas' Estado Novo), which again concentrated federal power, but now within a framework of nonmobilizational, partyless authoritarian rule.

The Revolution of 1930 is undoubtedly the "founding" mark of the modern Brazilian political system, but again with contradictory effects in terms of democratic prospects. In the short run, advances in "state-ness" (bureaucratic reach, military complexity, greater regulation of economy) were certainly favorable, since they reduced the scope of private power and made purely praetorian involution thenceforth unlikely. In the long run, however, some of those advances seem to have outlived their function. The corporatist system of labor relations has certainly been detrimental to the political organization of the working class. The conventional PR electoral system then established has clearly not contributed to developing a stable party system. Worse still, the presidential office became overloaded with contradictory expectations. For professional politicians, it became the ultimate distributor of patronage, credits, and public investments, and the arbiter among regional interests. For the newly mobilized urban masses, after 1945, it was the focal point of demands for better wages and improvements in living conditions. From the viewpoint of the military establishment, it came to be the very embodiment of national security, implying containment of both "oligarchical" and "mob" rule.

These cross-pressures and institutional deficiencies were clearly operative in the 1964 breakdown. The democratic experiment initiated in 1945 was based, in comparison with the earlier periods, on a far stronger representative system. The national legislature and the main political parties started as fundamental political actors. However, growing social mobilization and persistent inflation made it impossible for the two major parties (UDN and PSD) to retain their initially safe electoral advantage. As a typical "institutional" party, the PSD became increasingly vulnerable to a bipolar (Left and Right) opposition, roughly as suggested by Sartori's "polarized pluralism" model.[37]

The erosion of party and congressional support meant that Goulart (1961–1964) had to carry the full burden of maintaining institutional equilibrium exactly when the Caesarist ghost that surrounds Latin American presidentialism came, full-bodied, to the fore. The Caesarist dilemma stems from the need to cope with stringent and clearly defined contradictory situational constraints. Frustrating mass demands in the name of austerity or economic rationality alienates diffuse support and thus deprives the president of the one resource that makes him strong vis-à-vis elected politicians. If, on the contrary, he chooses to court those demands too closely, the specter of a mob-based dictatorship is immediately raised by the propertied classes and, often, by the military organization. The middle course is often unavailable because of the very weakness and inconsistency of the party system. When the difficulties inherent in these situational constraints are compounded by ambiguous personal behavior, as was evidently the case in the Goulart presidency, the breaking point is near.

Leadership

From 1961 to 1964, President Goulart proved unable to escape the Caesarist trap. He in fact made it more inexorable by allowing too much room for doubt as to his intention to abide by the constitutional rules that would govern his succession. Few analysts would dispute that Goulart's equivocal behavior was a crucial precipitating factor in the democratic breakdown.[38] The important question, then, is how does it come about that a country with an important institutional history and a fairly impersonal conception of governing falls prey to that sort of populistic retrogression and thence to breakdown.

Table 3.2. Brazilian Political Structure Since Independence

Regimes	Form of Government	Party System	Civil/Military Relations	Social Mobilization	Demise
EMPIRE (1822–1889)	Unitary state; parliamentary monarchy *cum* "moderating power"	Two parties (Liberal and Conservative) since the 1830s; district voting (very unstable rules)	Civil hegemony through National Guard; weak army	Extremely low	Republican military coup; no resistance
FIRST REPUBLIC (1889–1930)	Directly elected president; highly decentralized federation	One-party systems at state level; multimember district voting; unstable rules	Increasing tension between military (especially young officers) and politicians	Very low	Revolutionary movement headed by Getúlio Vargas; three weeks fighting
REVOLUTION OF 1930 (1930–1937)	Provisional government headed by Vargas; in 1934, Weimar-inspired constitution with strong corporatist leanings	Numerous, unstable party groupings; growing Fascist/Communist polarization	Army becoming dominant national institution	Growing significantly in urban areas	Vargas' coup, with military backing, leads to Estado Novo
ESTADO NOVO (1937–1945)	Authoritarian, nonmobilizational regime; Getúlio Vargas dictator	None; all parties and elections suppressed	Army identified with regime through national security ideology	Growing rapidly; population 31% urban in 1940	Senior army officers force Vargas to resign; 1945: controlled redemocratization

Table 3.2. Brazilian Political Structure Since Independence, cont.

DEMOCRATIC REGIME (1946–1964)	Directly elected president; weak federation and powerful national legislature	Multiparty system with 13 parties; increasing polarization at end of period; PR electoral system	Frequent friction between military factions and civilian governments; threats of military intervention	Fairly high, increasing even in rural areas; population 45% urban in 1960	Military coup with substantial popular backing in middle strata ousts President Goulart
MILITARY REGIME (1964–1985)	Republican form; presidency *de facto* monopoly of the military; nominations ratified by Electoral College only up to 1985; federation severely weakened	Compulsory two-party system from 1965 on; partial return to pluralism in 1979, still barring Communist parties; PR electoral system	Unmistakable hegemony of military as institution, guaranteeing "technocratic" governments	Very high; population 67% urban in 1980	Very gradual, negotiated transition culminating in election of Tancredo Neves (civilian, oppositionist) through Electoral College
NEW REPUBLIC (1985–)	Direct election of president reestablished as constitutional principle; growing influence of states and legislature; Constitutional Congress, 1987	Multiparty system; no legal restrictions on Marxist parties; moderates (PMDB) control both chambers, early 1987; PR electoral system	Civilian control formally guaranteed; military influence remains strong	(Very high)	

Part of the answer may indeed be an oversupply of leaders willing to violate the rules of the game. The pattern was set by Getúlio Vargas, in 1930 and especially with the Estado Novo coup of 1937. Liberal opposition to the *varguista* tradition, after 1945, often displayed the same ambiguous behavior of which Goulart was later accused. Prominent UDN leaders, like Carlos Lacerda, were not only *golpistas* but, in fact, strongly inclined to (and skillful at) impassioned demagogic rhetoric.

Yet, personalistic leadership has not been as successful as implied in the common lore. Getúlio Vargas did not establish a personality cult comparable to that of Perón in Argentina. Former president Juscelino Kubitschek (1955–1960) is remembered as a modernizer and a "nice guy," not as a power-seeking *caudillo*. Jânio Quadros ascended to the presidency in 1960, riding a protest vote that he cleverly mobilized by means of a rancorous, theatrical style. In August 1961, he resigned, claiming that the country was ungovernable (in his terms, of course). His decision was fateful in the ensuing years, but is it not a blessing for our hypothesis that the Brazilian political system has developed antibodies against wild personalism? His successful comeback as the elected mayor of São Paulo in 1985 would seem to deny our view, but it is noteworthy that Quadros has carefully confined his Poujade-like, protofascist appeal to the electoral arena, never daring to establish some sort of paramilitary apparatus.

The leadership problem cannot therefore be considered simply as a lack of men with the appropriate skills and civic virtues, and not even as an absence of antibodies against irresponsible demagogs. It is rather the inherent instability of democracy amid rapid social mobilization and extreme inequality, trying to escape the Scylla of Caesarist *caudillismo* and the Charybdis of uninspiring, clientelistic politics. A proper understanding of the leadership problem must then consider, in addition to the already cited situational constraints, some underlying cultural elements that contribute to shaping them.

Political Culture

Brazilian political culture is sometimes said to embody an unchanging Iberian propensity toward monolithism, and thus to be irreducibly inimical to democratic development. We argue that, on balance, the effects of political culture may indeed be negative, but hardly for that reason. The views that do operate in the political system (i.e., those put forward by influential writers, journalists, and the like) show a pervasive and persistent concern, indeed an obsession, with the alleged incongruence between elite and mass culture. Since the early decades of this century, outstanding writers of different persuasions have insisted that powerful cultural strains tend to undermine the idea of a Western-style democracy in Brazil. Alberto Torres was only one among hundreds who emphasized the discrepancy between the "legal" Brazil, expressed in political institutions, and the "real" one, embodied in actual social behavior.

Somehow, popular culture came to be seen as the only real thing, while political institutions became irremediably artificial. What is certainly disturbing in this dichotomous approach is that through it, we may be unconsciously demanding a degree of congruence among different spheres of society and especially between "center" and "periphery," which does not in fact exist anywhere among advanced democracies. The starting point is the Aristotelian ideal that social institutions (familial, educational, religious) must buttress and reinforce the overarching principle of legitimacy. But that ideal, petrified in a simplistic dichotomy, gradually comes to imply that democratic political principles are irrelevant or illegitimate when they fail to mold each and every subsystem. Even in the advanced democracies, we find, as in Brazil, that knowledge of and support for democratic rules of the game are undoubtedly correlated with education and other indicators of social status. In Brazil, this is hardly surprising, if we consider that elite political socialization has been closely associated, since the nineteenth century, with the law schools (hence with a reverence for legal culture) as well as with a free press and more recently with a sizable and reasonably cosmopolitan academic community.[39]

The dichotomous view just described derives historically from the state-centered pattern of political development and from the fact that elite contestation preceded, by far, the expansion of participation. In fact, elite culture became political at a time when the bulk of the populace, poor and widely dispersed over a large territory, was totally excluded from the system. In 1900, the illiteracy rate among the population over fifteen was 75 percent. There thus arose an excessive predominance of state over societal development and hence a deep anxiety, among opinion makers, that liberal-democratic development would not be viable under such conditions.

However, this picture has changed in surprising ways during the decompression process of the 1970s and now under the new republic. The Aristotelian craving for congruence remains, but its contents and ideas to correct incongruence have become more complex. Under the impact of high social mobilization (see Table 3.1), of repoliticization and, of course, of protest against income inequality, there appeared an Augustinian strand, according to which the people are good and the state is evil. Stimulated by religious movements and by abundant leadership coming from the now much larger wage-earning middle sectors, the implied correction is no longer to replace liberal by authoritarian politics, as in the 1920s, but rather to substitute some sort of Rousseauan "participatory" for representative democracy.

The historical sequence of institutional development, combined with persistently wide income differentials and other factors, thus seemed to have produced very negative cultural conditions for representative democracy. These negative effects do not derive from a would-be unitary worldview, but rather from a pervasive utopian standard against which democratic development is constantly measured by the leadership of some popular movements and by influential opinion makers. The impact of these trends on parliamentary politics has been so far modest, but may increase through the Workers' Party or even through the left wing of the PMDB.

The usual pessimistic account of Brazilian political culture must be qualified in many ways. Consideration of some positive developments that took place despite distant Iberian origins and recent authoritarian experiences may be useful as an antidote. First, since the establishment of the Electoral Court, in 1932, there has been unmistakable progress toward orderliness and fairness in administering the electoral process. On the side of the voters, sheer size (now about 75 million registered voters) allied to social mobilization have made the assumption of individual autonomy increasingly realistic. Despite abysmal poverty and the prevalence of patron-client relationships in many regions, there can be no doubt that the electoral process now operates with the requisite quantum of aggregate uncertainty.

Second, there is no monolithic domination, not even at the local level. This is in part a consequence of the overall changes in the electoral process and in part of local rivalries even among landowners. The image of monolithism has been frequently maintained by students of Brazilian social structure, but they tend to underestimate the impact of political and electoral competition when it is not linked to ideological or class cleavages.

Third, as we noted earlier, even the authoritarian ideology of the 1920s and 1930s (and hence the idea of military tutelage) has been tempered by anti-populist elements that help sustain some democratic institutions and practices. Hence, the limits on the duration of mandates, the electoral calendar, and, more generally, the importance of keeping the legislature as an institution capable of being reactivated—all these are clearly practiced by the post-1964 regime.

Fourth, as noted above, a significant degree of social mobility exists, despite severe income inequality. Here, the cultural process of modernization does seem to have an impact of its own, judging from the increasingly informal character of social relationships. Urban living and mass communications work massively in the direction of an egalitarian culture.

Finally, the development of representative institutions, in a general way, clearly implies that primitive *caudillismo* and unitary blueprints are not deemed desirable or realistic by the political elite—not even by authoritarian (military) elites. Three features seem to characterize the Brazilian "doctrine" of representation. One is the recognition of diversity among the elite. This should not be understood primarily in ideological terms and even less in terms of cultural or ethnic segmentation. It is rather an acceptance of the fact that politics involves constant division and disagreement, making monolithic rule inconceivable. This recognition is deeply rooted in the country's cultural and legal system because, if for no other reason, it was historically a *sine qua non* for holding the provinces and local governments together.

The second feature is the electoral process. Countless writers have seen a puzzle, or worse, a mimetic disease, in the Brazilian tendency to import such profoundly "alien" liberal institutions. But the fact is that electoral mechanisms, with many of the classical provisions for fair competition, have strong roots in Brazil. Despite the equally countless instances of violence, fraud, and manipulation that can be cited, it is perfectly legitimate to speak of a

Brazilian electoral tradition, and even more to recognize that the recent struggle against authoritarian rule has reinforced it.

The third feature, which has the military institution as its main guardian, is the notion that the government must be an impersonal entity. Hence the military's fundamental dislike for any kind of plebiscitarian *caudillismo* and their (reluctant, no doubt) understanding that elections are the ultimate safeguard against some sort of personalistic appropriation of the state.

Do these three features amount to "democratic" representation? Not quite: one indication that they do not are the powerful cultural strains that constantly delegitimize the representative process. Public debate is full of references to the "elitist" character of such institutions. The image of politicians is incessantly associated with clientelism, co-optation, and conciliation—the last being a reference to the early nineteenth century, but also a way of saying that our pluralism is still oligarchical, without substantive meaning for the average citizen. Indeed, what we can assume, in the Brazilian case, is the existence of strong state institutions, which are not necessarily democratic and which in many ways belong in the category of structural resistances in need of "deconcentration."

International Factors

The international environment is a positive factor for representative democracy in political, military, and cultural terms, but it is also an overwhelmingly negative condition on the economic dimension. Brazil is a fully Western nation in cultural terms, and a dependent (if you will) part of the world capitalist system. One (oft-neglected) consequence of this is that Brazilian elites, including the military, do not ignore the risks involved in toying with fundamentally different principles of political organization. Brazil's territory acquired its present shape a long time ago. Nature provided most of the solution to Brazil's frontier problem. Diplomatic efforts polished it up early in this century. Participation in foreign wars and military readiness are unknown to the vast majority of Brazilians. Were it otherwise, the weight of the military vis-à-vis civilian institutions would undoubtedly be much greater than it has been. Proper understanding of the negative effects of the economic dimension requires a broad historical perspective. Dependency on export commodities, with its attendant instability, was extremely high until the 1950s at least. Import-substituting industrialization began during World War I, but was until recently insufficient to alter that basic link to the external world.

An important change took place in the 1950s. Under Juscelino Kubitschek, the Brazilian government gave up its formerly cautious strategy and started emphasizing durable consumer goods as a means to accelerate industrial growth. The automobile industry was the driving force of that new phase. The impact of industrialization on the overall social structure became thenceforth much greater. A rapidly expanding population, large cities, and the demonstration effect of foreign consumption patterns now made for permanent tension, leaving no option but constantly high rates of growth. Major inflationary pressures, the need to increase exports at any price, and, of course, to attract investments and credits now became permanent features of the economic system. Internationalization had come to stay.

This, in a rough sketch, is the background of Brazil's deep involvement in the international debt crisis. Having again accelerated growth in the late 1960s and early 1970s, the military governments, especially under President Geisel (1974–1978), undertook major new steps toward import substitution, this time in basic or "difficult" sectors.[40] The premise of that effort, needless to say, was the easy credit situation of that decade. The oil- and interest-rate shocks of the late 1970s and early 1980s thus caught Brazil in an extremely vulnerable position.

Our judgment that the present international environment is negative for the consolidation of democracy goes far beyond the "normal" pattern of external dependency. When the country depended on export crops, the urban population was so small that even a sharp decline in economic activity did not affect the majority immediately and dramatically. Now it does. Massive transfer of real resources abroad to meet disproportionate debt obligations strangles the country's efforts to promote growth and aggravates already intractable political problems at home.

• PROSPECTS FOR DEMOCRATIC CONSOLIDATION •

Reconceptualizing Democratic Consolidation

Liberalization and participation are described by Dahl as distinct theoretical dimensions of democratization. However, when we think about consolidating democracies recently reinstated as a consequence of authoritarian demise, socioeconomic conditions must be incorporated more effectively into our models. It is a trivial observation that a large amount of genuine political democracy tends to be incompatible with a rigid or unequal society, or even with a low rate of change toward greater mobility and equality. Thus, when we think about consolidation, social and economic conditions cannot remain in the category of purely external correlates or prerequisites. They must be "politicized"; i.e., brought into the model, and this for two important reasons. The first is that, like liberalization and participation, those conditions will necessarily appear to political actors as objects of decision, and therefore as so many choices they will be forced to make. Land reform is the obvious example in Third World countries. Whether and how such choices are faced may make the difference between keeping and losing support; the loss may transcend individual leaders and parties and extend to the newly constituted democratic system as a whole. The second reason has to do with the change from procedural to substantive demands in the course of redemocratization. Cast in a different theoretical language, this means that, once achieved, formal democracy becomes an Olsonian collective good. Since it already exists and benefits everyone, the incentive to defend and protect it decreases sharply.[41] In Third World countries, the implications of this fact are obviously more dramatic, since elites have not completely consolidated pluralism among themselves, frequently perceive conflicts as zero-sum, and are vastly more threatened by the substantive demands of the masses.

If the assumptions just stated are correct, it seems clear that we need, not two, but three dimensions. The graphic representation of democratic consolidation would thus be a cube made up of Dahl's liberalization and participation plus another dimension referring to policy advances toward structural deconcentration, which means greater equality, social mobility, and the like. Taking all three dimensions at once, the dilemmas of democratic consolidation will, we believe, appear in a more realistic light. If our questions about the democratic character of the Brazilian new republic were to deal only with Dahl's two-dimensional scheme, the answer should probably be positive. Looking at the "liberalization" axis, we would find that most legal restrictions on political competition have been removed. If difficulties remain, they are somehow produced by hidden vetoes (e.g., expectations concerning military behavior), by the sheer weight of certain resources (e.g., bureaucratic power), and by other, "nonpolitical" determinants (e.g., those determining the concentration of power in the societal environment of the political system).

Probing somewhat further, it seems possible to compact Dahl's liberalization and participation into a single dimension, which would be representation; i.e., strength of the representative system. Where contestation becomes the nor-

Figure 3.1 Representation, Deconcentration, and Democratization

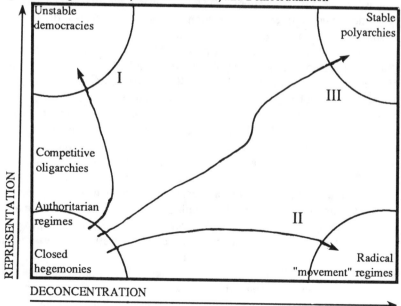

mal way of doing things among political elites and where such elites are regarded as adequate foci for support or as spokesmen for demands arising from participation, what we have is a strong representative system. We can thus come back to a two-dimensional space, with strength of the representative system on one axis and advances toward social change, or deconcentration, on the other (see Figure 3.1).

The first two years of the new republic have shown very clearly that the reinstatement of formal democracy is a far cry from real consolidation. On the horizontal axis of Figure 3.1, the new civilian government was faced with what might be called the vicious circle of transition. The prior authoritarian suppression of politics and the prolonged struggle for redemocratization dammed up enormous (substantive) expectations, which could not (in fact cannot) be met in the short run. Not meeting them at an adequate rate, the government quickly loses the support it needs in order to undertake more forceful policies, the lack of which reinforces the circle. The "moving horizon" that worked so well during the decompression process at the institutional level (i.e., on the vertical axis) thus seems far more difficult to sustain when it comes to our horizontal axis.

Toward Deconcentration?

The proposition that greater equality helps sustain democracy is certainly correct in the long run, but the concrete steps and policies that will reduce inequality may also undermine support for the democratic system in the short run. This is evident enough when we speak of deconcentrating income and wealth, and especially land ownership. Virtually any policy intended to achieve deconcentration produces visible and immediate losses and thus tends to change the basis of political support, often in the direction of undemocratic forces. But there is, in addition, the worst face of inequality, so-called absolute poverty. The problem here is that a truly substantial effort would have to be sustained over many years; this presupposes a degree of consistency in political support and implementation that seems unlikely in fragile, underdeveloped democracies. There is thus a tendency to avoid sweeping commitments of this kind, not least because they may raise expectations beyond a realistic level and eventually cause an antidemocratic backlash. And yet, the circle is truly demonic, because without a major effort, duly announced and symbolized, such basic welfare measures may not gain the allegiance of disadvantaged groups to the point of compensating losses of support among the well-to-do. Or they may compensate, but produce at the same time a threatening effect on the latter. In order to consolidate itself, a functioning democratic system should be capable not only of undertaking substantial measures to reduce inequality but, also, of conveying to the deprived majority that such measures are serious efforts undertaken on their behalf; and at the same time, that underdevelopment and the pattern of inequalities traditionally associated with it cannot be overcome on short notice.

The "new republic" clearly did not find a consistent answer to these problems in its first two years. The initial idea was to launch an "emergency program" of assistance (while at the same time designing alternative economic policies and starting a moderate, long-range land-reform project). There would be, for example, a milk program directed toward groups known to have a desperate nutritional deficit. The results of this phase could not have been more disastrous. Insufficient production, inadequate implementation networks, and political disputes all combined to paralyze such initiatives. Toward the end of 1985, these difficulties were compounded by the ghosts of hyperinflation and an unprecedented strike wave in the subsequent few months. The "illegitimate" origins of Sarney's presidency (i.e., the fact that he was the conservative side of the ticket, as Tancredo Neves' running mate, and that both had been elected indirectly) began to be recalled. Support for the government rapidly dwindled.

It is therefore probably correct to infer that the so-called Cruzado Plan had political as well as economic objectives. The stabilization plan and monetary reform introduced by President Sarney on February 28, 1986, were decisive in stopping a dangerous erosion of authority. Popular acquiescence to the plan immediately reinforced presidential leadership. But, clearly, such acquiescence was entirely due to the price freeze, the difficulties of which began to appear rather soon. In a country with tremendous income inequalities, the redistribution of money income implicit in the price freeze quickly led to an explosive demand for consumer goods of all kinds. Entrepreneurs responded to the price freeze by reducing supply and enhancing their political organization. To make things worse, a decisive election was scheduled to take place in November (state deputies and governors, and federal deputies and senators, the latter two making up the Constitutional Congress). Sarney's enormous popularity after the economic reforms of February was the one big asset of the governing Democratic Alliance, hence the enormous pressures to go on with the price freeze, despite the evident distortions to which it was giving rise. Confronted with an enlarged demand and a reduced internal supply, the government resorted to massive imports of food products. The result was that reserves fell sharply. By early 1987, readjustment measures had proved insufficient and the country had no alternative but to declare a partial default on foreign-interest payments.

The irony, or tragedy, is that the Cruzado Plan was the closest thing to actual income redistribution in several decades; it was also the one moment in which the government seemed capable of gaining widespread support. But short-run euphoria should not obscure the dark contours of the broader picture. To begin with, bold measures like the Cruzado Plan reflect the institutional weakness of the political system, not its sources of institutional strength. Presidential authority was reinforced by the populist, indeed Caesarist components of the situation, not by the denser substrata of the country's power structure. It is perhaps unnecessary to point out that not every government faces such an opportunity; that the gains were short-lived; and indeed that such a sweeping reform was introduced through a decree-law, and not by means of a prior amalgamation of party and congressional support.

On the economic side, a recovery of sorts, after three years of recession, had been taking place since 1984. The transition to civilian rule, in early 1985, thus began in a moment of relative relief. But, on a broader canvas, the country is clearly confronted with severe economic constraints. The balance sheet of twenty years of authoritarian rule includes, on the negative side, a staggering external debt that demands massive remittance of real resources abroad and internal debt that rivals in magnitude the external one. The Brazilian economy is thus besieged by multiple and contradictory requirements. It is imperative to grow, but growth constantly leads to perverse results in the balance of payments; it is necessary to promote exports, but that takes away some of the goods required for domestic consumption and refuels inflation; expanding imports to curb inflation quickly reduces reserves to a dangerous low point.

So far we have dealt with deconcentration of income and wealth, but the concept also involves the dimension of power, and particularly of bureaucratic power. In a country like Brazil, where the weight of the state is said to be a barrier to democratic development, welfare or antipoverty programs are often included among structures to be deconcentrated. However, the parts of the state that pose truly difficult problems of democratic control seem to be neither the traditional public service not the more modern welfare programs. It is, rather, the so-called entrepreneurial public sector, made up of state companies that directly control large economic assets and thus exert substantial influence in economic policymaking.[42] In order to understand the institutional problem involved here, it will be necessary to make a short theoretical detour.

Among the conceptual schemes presently available, one of the most appropriate to the problem at hand seems to be Lowi's distinction among three decisional arenas—the redistributive, regulatory, and distributive.[43] But it is not entirely clear how sensitive this scheme is to the political structure of societies like Brazil's, which have long had an inclusive and interventionist public sector—an "entrepreneurial state," as it is sometimes described. From this standpoint, Lowi's threefold classification seems incomplete, in fact truncated at the top, since it does not distinguish for separate treatment what might be called an accumulative arena; i.e., the locus par excellence of the main investment decisions, which ends up being responsible for the rate and for the overall direction of economic growth. This arena has not been and cannot easily be subject to "pluralistic" political competition—at least not as long as parliamentary and party structures remain fragmented and ineffectual as they have been in Brazil. Despite their broad disagreement on everything else, neoconservative entrepreneurs demanding "de-statization" and left-wing parties demanding "democratic control" over this arena seem to agree that a problem does in fact exist. Needless to say, this autonomous power, of vast proportions, was the technocratic spine of the post-1964 military regime. The idea of dismantling or deconcentrating it can be considered largely lyrical, since it embodies the model of economic growth that, for good or evil, changed the face of Brazil during the last thirty to forty years.

Dahl identifies the "centralized direction of the economy," regardless of the form of ownership, as a negative condition for democracy. He also says that "where the military is relatively large, centralized and hierarchical, polyarchy is of course impossible, unless the military is sufficiently depoliticized to permit civilian rule."[44] It is doubtful whether the Brazilian military is "sufficiently depoliticized"; and there is little doubt but that they keep a close watch on what we have called the accumulative arena. This leads to a particularly complex situation. Purely "praetorian" political decay seems unlikely, given the sheer weight of the military institution and its modern pattern of organization. But it is not certain how adaptable the institution is to open competitive politics, taking into account not only past ideological propensities but also the strategic links that bind it to these major economic concerns, deemed essential to economic growth and national security. This may be called a "Huntingtonian" weakness of the Brazilian political system, if we consider that political development has to do not only with the strength but also with the adaptability of organizations; and further, with the primacy of specialized political institutions, such as parliaments and political parties.

Institutional Options

The dualistic expression "state versus civil society" became quite common in Brazil, by virtue of the struggle against authoritarian rule during the 1970s. "State" became virtually synonymous with authoritarian mechanisms, in the mind of the intellectualized or militant opposition; "civil society" was sometimes understood as the opposition as a whole, but more often the ensemble of professional, university, religious, and other associations. The factual political importance of this distinction is undeniable, but if a dualistic characterization is necessary, it does not seem to run exactly along those lines. It is probably more appropriate to say that the completion of state-building and increasing social mobilization have made the Brazilian political system diarchical, the division running between state and democratic institutions properly so-called. The former has clearly identifiable clusters—the bureaucracy, public and semi-public economic concerns, and, of course, the military. These are not necessarily authoritarian in an absolute or doctrinaire sense, but they do certainly conceive of their role primarily in terms of ensuring stability, preventing an exaggerated escalation of social conflict, controlling the effort toward economic growth in its fundamental lines, promoting industrialization and technological development, and protecting national security.

The democratic half of the diarchy can be said to have comparable clusters in a purely formal sense—Congress, political parties, the press, universities, churches, and labor unions—but it is far from certain that all of these share a core conception of what democracy is about or what should be its long-range goals, mechanisms, and practices. For one thing, it is here above all that one feels the tensions between formal and substantive views of democracy. The latter often appear associated with more or less utopian conceptions of "participatory" democracy, aiming to replace or subordinate representation to a more "authentic" expression of the people's will. Part of the problem confronting the Constitutional Congress involves benefiting from this increased participation at the level of civil society as a means to enhance the democratic half. Can it realistically be done? An adequate answer must consider at least three levels: (*a*) the overall conception of democracy deemed viable for Brazil; (*b*) the form of government (i.e., presidential or parliamentary); and (*c*) the inability of the party structure to provide intermediation between the two halves of the diarchy.

A convenient starting point for the discussion of the overall conception is the contrast between consociational and majoritarian models of representative democracy. The majoritarian model can be described as a pattern of institutional organization that consistently leads to excluding minorities (sometimes large ones) from governing; the consociational model forces coparticipation in that process. In the Brazilian case, there can be little doubt that a pure majoritarian model would be disastrous. Brazil is not nearly as segmented culturally and religiously as the societies studied by Lijphart, but the depth of socioeconomic differences perhaps makes majoritarian organization even less advisable. If legitimizing the political system is difficult through more inclusive mechanisms, it can be easily surmised that the typical Westminster model, as Lijphart calls it, would simply not work in Brazil.

This is not to say, however, that the pure consociational model would work. The amount of decentralization and fragmentation of power that this idea implies can hardly be imagined in a country without consociational traditions, just recently emerged from a long-drawn process of state-building, and deeply confronted with the dilemmas of economic growth, income redistribution, and basic welfare.[45] Instead of collaboration among a myriad of autonomous subcommunities, the consociational model would more likely produce an exacerbation of corporatism, clientelism, regionalism, and the like—thus opening the breach for a major reassertion of authoritarian rule in the usual guise of the imperial presidency, bureaucratic power, and military tutelage.

Historically, the Brazilian political system can be described as standing somewhere half-way between Lijphart's two poles. If the preceding remarks make sense, the route to follow now is not a sharper inclination toward either of these broad models. It is rather a need for another major step toward institutionalization. In practice, this means reducing the distance and the potential for conflict between underlying and equally viable models of government. Since the 1930s, Brazil has been deeply torn between a hyperpresidential (virtually Caesarist) and a more typically parliamentary conception of what the political center of gravity should be. These two often conflict, and it is not inconceivable that they may develop into true *weltanschauungen*, since they are in many ways implicated with the substantive versus formal disagreement as to the nature of democracy. That is why further institutionalization will require reexamination of the form of government. Quite obviously, we cannot go from a hyperpresidential to a classical (i.e., British-type) parliamentary system. The latter would clash with the political culture and prevailing structures on many points. Assuming that the Constitutional Congress retains direct election of the president, we would have the additional difficulty of investing a head of state, elected by fifty or sixty million voters, in the role of the queen of England; not to speak of the proverbially weak party system that would be operating such a parliamentary system.

The search for a "mixed" formula is thus inevitable, and it must be conscious of the risks inherent, for example, in the French system, now facing the difficult issue of "cohabitation." The most promising lines would then seem to be either a slight attenuation of the separation of powers, as in the letter of the Finnish Constitution, where the prime minister is clearly submitted to the president; or a more clearly parliamentary system, where the cabinet is in fact responsible before the legislature, even though the president is elected directly and keeps substantial powers and prerogatives.[46]

Strengthening the party system is important in itself but becomes imperative in the parliamentary or semiparliamentary hypothesis. There can be little question that this will require a great deal of institutional "engineering," if we consider that Brazil has not known the historical processes that typically led to the crystalization of party systems. In Europe, such systems resulted either from class cleavages, which did not emerge as sharply in Brazil until recently, or from cultural, linguistic, or religious cleavages that simply do not have a Brazilian equivalent, and that were decidedly controlled by the central authority when they did come up in embryo. Anxiety over the need to assert central authority also explains why Brazil did not have strong nationwide parties based on an articulation among regional oligarchies—quite aside from the fact that federation and continental size made such parties unlikely. Brazil also lacked, except during the democratic experiment of 1945–1964, the formative impact of direct presidential elections.

This is to say that strong parties, in Brazil, will of necessity be a "work of art." The main instrument to bring them about will be the party and electoral legislation and other regulations pertaining to political representation. Given the inappropriateness for Brazil of the extreme Lijphartian models, such regulations should avoid the extreme majoritarian as well as the looser forms of proportional representation. The promising suggestion, here, would seem to be the electoral system practiced in West Germany, which attempts to combine the PR representative principle with the participatory principle of majoritarian elections.[47]

These hypotheses, as stated before, start from the notion that democratic consolidation in Brazil will depend on a major increase in institutionalization, which in turn will require deliberate efforts to enhance the party and parliamentary gravitation of the political system.[48] So-called participatory proposals, inspired by the new vigor brought to the political arena by labor, religious, and professional organizations, are here seen as a healthy updating of Brazilian politics, the overall trajectory of which was unusually oligarchical and/or concerned with the basic issue of state-building. It is, however, hardly realistic to conceive of a functioning democracy, on the Brazilian scale, in terms of a Rousseauan ideology. Carried to an extreme, such proposals will end up diluting rather than reinforcing political representation. Seeking Rousseau, we may again find Hobbes.

Conclusion

From 1986 to 1988, Brazil moved from an extreme of wild optimism to extreme pessimism. The dream of rapid growth without inflation gave way to virtual stagnation and severe inflation (20 percent a month during the first quarter of 1988); with these came a deep sensation that the country is rapidly losing its developmental edge and becoming ungovernable. If the final note we have struck was already a bit pessimistic, no improvement could be expected under such circumstances.

Yet, the real battle is the one the country is now fighting on the economic front, in the short run. The political and ideological "reading" of this crisis will probably be adapted *ex post factum* to success or failure in the attempt to curb inflation, and resume growth—and thus avoid another democratic breakdown. If we succeed, we will probably hear an ode to prudence. The gradual path to redemocratization will again be hailed as the best, or as the only one available; the politician's low prestige will be seen as inevitable or as a temporary phenomenon; even the signs of a "populistic revival" in the elections of 1985 and 1986 and wild clientelism in the federal government in 1987–1988 may be interpreted as the price to pay for mass democracy: our Jacksonian age?

If, on the contrary, hyperinflation leads the country into convulsion and thereby into another cycle of authoritarian rule, all "obvious" hypotheses will have been thoroughly confirmed. As in Jorge Luis Borge's story, Kafka's existence will lead to the discovery of an infinite chain of Kafka's "precursors." We will again discover that excessive gradualism does undermine legitimacy; that a large-scale democracy will not become stable in Brazil until we have strong political parties; that without organized and minimally ideological parties, we should not have embarked on a competitive process of constitution-making; that the Constitutional Congress showed the enormous strength of an obsolete set of institutions by keeping the presidential system, an overly permissive electoral system, nationalist rhetoric, paternalistic welfare provisions—and even confirmed, in the democratic way, with strong support from the labor unions, the corporatist system established by Vargas in the 1930s, which had been branded as "fascist" for over forty years!

The Constitutional Congress did confirm, as expected, a five-year term for President Sarney. Those who supported this decision believe it will give the country the stability it needs to face the economic crisis; those who didn't are convinced that we will face that crisis with a very weak president, recently confirmed in office, throughout 1989.

• NOTES •

Note: This chapter was largely written before the Constitutional Congress, which met during 1987 and 1988.

I am grateful to Luis Aureliano Gama Andrade for his collaboration in the initial version of this chapter. Wanderley G. Santas, Amavry de Sovzar, and my colleagues at IDESP also made very valuable suggestions.

1. The Movimento Democrático Brasileiro (opposition) elected sixteen of the twenty-two senators in 1974 (renovating one-third of the Senate), with a strong showing in the more urban and modernized states. An extended discussion of the structure of electoral competition as a factor capable of preventing authoritarian consolidation in Brazil can be found in Bolívar Lamounier, "*Authoritarian Brasil* Revisited." In *Democratizing Brazil*, ed. Alfred Stepan (Princeton, NJ: Princeton University Press, forthcoming).

2. One of these measures was the introduction of indirect elections for one-third of the senators. These senators were quickly nicknamed "bionic" and were never accepted as legitimate by public opinion. Another measure was the severe curtailing of electoral propaganda through radio and television, generalizing restrictions previously applied only in the municipal election of 1976.

3. One of these bills aimed at increasing contributions to finance the social-security system; the other attempted to extend the *sublegendas* (triple candidacies in each party) to the gubernatorial elections.

4. Cardoso was probably the first scholar to stress that the Brazilian authoritarian regime did not pursue stagnant economic policies; that it was, on the contrary, decidedly modernizing. See Fernando H. Cardoso, "Dependent-Associated Development: Theoretical and Practical Implications." In *Authoritarian Brazil: Origins, Outputs, Future*, ed. Alfred Stepan (New Haven, CT: Yale University Press, 1973). On economic policy in the 1970s, see Bolívar Lamounier and Alkimar R. Moura, "Economic Policy and Political Opening in Brazil." In *Latin American Political Economy: Financial Crisis and Political Change* ed. Jonathan Hartlyn and Samuel A. Morley (Boulder, CO: Westview Press, 1986); and Antônio Barros de Castro and Francisco E. Pires de Souza, *A Economia Brasileira em Marcha Forçada* (Rio de Janeiro: Editora Paz e Terra, 1985)

5. In addition to the "bionic" senators, created in 1977, the government majority increased the weight of the smaller states in the Electoral College through Constitutional Amendment 22 of 1982. The traditional but now controversial overrepresentation that those states enjoy in the federal chamber was thus unacceptably extended to the presidential succession. It is worth noting that the opposition assimilated even this change when it decided to present Tancredo Neves to the Electoral College as a presidential candidate.

6. Bureaucratic continuity has led many historians to accept the naive idea that Brazil inherited a ready-made state from the Portuguese at the time of independence in 1822. The more cautious view that Brazilian state-building was "completed" by 1860 or 1870 may be accepted, but even this with important qualifications. See J. G. Merquior, "Patterns of State-Building in Brazil and Argentina." In *States in History* ed. John A. Hall (London: Blackwell, 1986).

7. On the formation of a central power as a precondition for peaceful competition, see the excellent treatment of the English case in Harvey Mansfield, Jr., "Party Government and the Settlement of 1688," *American Political Science Review* 63, no. 4 (1964): pp. ; on the U.S. case, see Richard Hofstadter, *The Idea of a Party System* (Berkeley and Los Angeles: University of California Press, 1972).

8. Our treatment of these questions is evidently inspired by Hannah Pitkin's now-classic work. However, searching for different images of representation in the Brazilian case, we placed them in a historical sequence she may not have intended, at least not as a general rule. See Hannah Pitkin, *The Concept of Representation* (Berkeley and Los Angeles: University of California Press, 1972).

9. See José Murilo de Carvalho, *A Construção da Ordem* (Rio de Janeiro: Editora Campus, 1980).

10. The classic here is Victor Nunes Leal, *Coronelismo, Enxada e Voto: O Município e o Regime Representativo no Brasil* (Rio de Janeiro: Editora Forense, 1948). For a quick introduction to the history of electoral legislation in Brazil, see Toshio Mukai, *Sistemas Eleitorais no Brasil* (São Paulo: Instituto dos Advogados, 1985).

11. On the evolution of military institutions, see Edmundo Campos Coelho, *Em Busca da Identidade: O Exército e a Política na Sociedade Brasileira* (Rio de Janeiro: Editora Forense,

1976); José Murilo de Carvalho, "As Forças Armadas na Primeira República: O Poder Dese-stabilizador." Belo Horizonte, UFMG, *Cadernos do Departamento de Ciência Política* no. 1, March 1974. On the nineteenth-century National Guard, see Fernando Uricoechea, *O Minotauro Imperial* (São Paulo: Difel, 1978).

12. Control of the credentials commission (Comissão de Verificação de Poderes) of the federal chamber was the key to the system, since through it undesirable deputies eventually elected in the states would not be allowed to take up their position. This became popularly known as *degola* (beheading). Souza provides an excellent treatment of this question: "If the sedimentation of the [state] oligarchies was essential to consolidate the federation, it was also the reason for its future weakness. Contrary to the imperial framework, rotation in power among state oligarchies now became impossible." See Maria do Carmo Campello de Souza, "O Processo Político-Partidário na Velha República." In *Brasil em Perspectiva*, ed. Carlos Guilherme Mota (São Paulo: Difel, 1971), p. 203.

13. There is an extensive literature on the Revolution of 1930. Especially useful for our purposes is Campello de Souza, "Processo Político-Partidário". See also Boris Fausto, ed., *O Brasil Republicano*, 3 vols. (São Paulo: Difel, 1978, 1982, and 1983); Hélio Silva, *A Revolucão Traída* (Rio de Janeiro: Civilização Brasileira, 1966); and two volumes of conference proceedings: UFRGS, *Simpósio sobre a Revolução de 1930* (Porto Alegre: Universidade do Rio Grande do Sul, 1982); and UnB, *A Revolução de 1930: Seminário Internacional* (Brasília: Editora da Universidade, 1982).

14. Nunes Leal, *Coronelismo*, p. 170–171.

15. Protofascism is used here in the same sense given to it by James Gregor, *The Ideology of Fascism* (New York: Free Press, 1969), Ch. 2. He deals with important theoretical precursors, such as Gumplowicz, Pareto, and Mosca, stressing their antiparliamentarianism, their view on the relation between elite and mass, on the function of political myths, and the like.

16. On the corporatist "regulation" of citizenship, see Wanderley Guilherme dos Santos, *Cidadania e Justiça* (Rio de Janeiro: Editora Campus, 1979). Comprehensive accounts of the corporatist features of the labor relations system can be found in P. Schmitter, *Interest Conflict and Political Change in Brazil* (Stanford, CA: Stanford University Press, 1971); and Amaury de Souza, *The Nature of Corporatist Representation: Leaders and Members of Organized Labor in Brazil* (Ph.D. Diss., Massachusetts Institute of Technology, 1978).

17. The name of Gilberto Freyre comes readily to mind in connection with race relations and nationality in Brazil. On these themes, see T. Skidmore, *Black into White* (New York: Oxford University Press, 1974). The impact of these developments in Brazilian political culture was of course enormous in the 1930s and as a support to the Estado Novo. The factual importance of these core beliefs has been recognized quite broadly in the ideological spectrum since then. On intellectuals and culture policy in that period, see Simon Schwartzman et al., *Tempos de Capanema* (Rio de Janeiro: Paz e Terra, 1984): Sérgio Miceli, *Intelectuais e Classe Dirigente no Brasil (1920–1945)* (São Paulo: Difel, 1979); Lúcia Lippi de Oliveira, *Estado Novo—Ideologia e Poder* (Rio de Janeiro: Zahar Editores, 1982).

18. On the downfall of the *Estado Novo*, see Mario do Carmo Campello de Souza, *Estado e Partidos no Brasil* (São Paulo: Editora Alfa-Ômega, 1976): T. Skidmore, *Politics in Brazil: An Experiment in Democracy* (New York: Oxford University Press, 1968); Peter Flynn, *Brazil: A Political Analysis* (Boulder, CO: Westview Press, 1975). On the UDN, see Maria Vitória Benevides, *UDN e Udenismo* (Rio de Janeiro: Paz e Terra, 1981).

19. The literature on Vargas' second government is surprisingly small. In addition to the works of Flynn and Skidmore, already cited, see Maria Celina Soares D'Araujo, *O Segundo Governo Vargas, 1951–1954* (Rio de Janeiro: Zahar Editores, 1982); and Edgard Carone, *A República Liberal II* (São Paulo: Difel, 1985).

20. Useful data on bureaucratic growth under the Estado Novo can be found in Maria do Carmo Campello de Souza, *Estado e Partidos Políticos*. On economic policymaking from the 1930s to the mid-1950s, see John Wirth, *The Politics of Brazilian Development, 1930–1954* (Stanford, CA: Stanford University Press, 1970); and Luciano Martins, *Pouvoir et développement économique au Brésil* (Paris: Éditions Anthropos, 1976).

21. J. G. Merquior, "Patterns of State-Building," p. 284.

22. An overview of these hypotheses and of the relevant literature can be found in Bolívar Lamounier and Rachel Meneguello, *Partidos Políticos e Consolidação Democrática: O Caso Brasileiro* (São Paulo: Editora Brasiliense, 1986), sect. 4. Rigorous analysis of the crisis leading to 1964 was pioneered by Wanderley Guilherme dos Santos, *The Calculus of Conflict: Impasse in*

Brazilian Politics (Ph.D. Diss., Stanford University, 1974). Important works for the understanding of executive-legislative relations in the 1950s and early 1960s include: Celso Lafer, *The Planning Process and the Political System in Brazil* (Ph.D. Diss., Cornell University, 1970); Maria Vitória Benevides, *O Governo Kubitschek* (Rio de Janeiro: Paz e Terra, 1976): and Lúcia Hippolito, *PSD: De Raposas e Reformistas* (Rio de Janeiro: Paz e Terra, 1984).

23. On the ambiguities of military-directed institution-building after 1964, see Juan Linz, "The Future of an Authoritarian Situation or the Institutionalization of an Authoritarian Regime: The Case of Brazil." In Stepan, *Authoritarian Brazil;* Bolívar Lamounier, "*Authoritarian Brazil* revisited"; Wanderley Guilherme dos Santos, *Poder e Política: Crônica do Autoritarismo Brasileiro* (Rio de Janeiro: Forense, 1978). Roett synthesized those ambiguities as follows: "In Brazil, although the latitude given to the civilian political process is severely compromised, it does exist. The commitment to political participation—limited, elitist, and manipulable as it is—is strongly rooted in Brazilian constitutional history. Geisel's efforts at decompression were part of that historical belief that there should be a more open system". See Riordan Roett, "The Political Future of Brazil." In *The Future of Brazil,* ed. William Overholt (Boulder, CO: Westview Press, 1978).

24. Before independence and especially before the intensification of mining, in the early eighteenth century, the local chambers (*câmaras municipais*) were almost exclusively made up of landowners and had virtually unlimited authority, concentrating executive, legislative, and judiciary functions. Their members were chosen by means of a crude electoral system set forth in the *ordenações* of the Portuguese Crown. During the nineteenth century, detailed regulations were established to control local and statewide elections. Needless to say, the franchise was limited and voting was not secret. In addition, the empire kept the tradition of not allowing a clear distinction between legislative and executive functions at the local level; an elected local executive would appear only under the republic, and especially after 1930.

25. On bureaucratic continuity, see Raimundo Faoro, *Os donos do Poder* (Porto Alegre: Editora Globo, 1958); for a comparative analysis, see Merquior, "Patterns of State-Building"; on the military organization, see Coelho, *Em Busca da Identidade*

26. See Wanderley Guilherme dos Santos, "A Pós-'Revolução' Brasileira." In *Brasil: Sociedade Democrática,* ed. Hélio Jaguaribe (Rio de Janeiro: José Olympio Editora, 1985).

27. Sylvia A. Hewlett, "The State and Brazilian Economic Development." In Overholt, *Future of Brazil,* p. 150.

28. Russet calculated Gini coefficients for inequality in land tenure circa 1960 in forty-seven countries and found Brazil to be the thirty-sixth from low to high concentration. See Bruce M. Russet, "Inequality and Instability: The Relation of Land Tenure to Politics." In *Readings in Modern Political Analysis,* ed. Robert A. Dahl and Deanne E. Neubauer (Englewood Cliffs, NJ: Prentice-Hall, 1968), pp. 150–162. There is no reason to assume that landed property is less concentrated today than in the 1960s. What did happen was that agrarian social relations became thoroughly capitalist. Landed property in Brazil was never "feudal" in a technical sense. Land was essentially used for capitalist purposes; i.e., to produce for a market or to function as a reserve of value in a highly inflationary economy. True, social relations were often paternalistic and exploitative, but this, too, is now undergoing rapid change.

29. The literature on growth and income distribution in this period is, of course, voluminous. A convenient starting point is Ricardo Tolipan and Artur Carlos Tinelli, eds., *A Controvérsia sobre Distribuição de Renda e Desenvolvimento* (Rio de Janeiro: Zahar Editores, 1975); see also Edmar Bacha, *Os Mitos de uma Década* (Rio de Janeiro: Editora Paz e Terra, 1976); Clarence Zuvekas, Jr., "Income Distribution in Latin America: A Survey of Recent Research." Center Essay no. 6, Center for Latin America, University of Wisconsin, Milwaukee, July 1975; and World Bank, *World Development Report 1983* and *World Development Report 1986* (New York: Oxford University Press, 1986).

30. Douglas H. Graham, "The Brazilian Economy: Structural Legacies and Future Prospects." In Overholt, *Future of Brazil,* p. 122.

31. World Bank, *World Development Report 1986,* Table 24, pp. 226–227.

32. See José Serra, "Ciclo e Mudanças Estruturais na Economia Brasileira do Pós-Guerra." In *Desenvolvimento Capitalista no Brasil—Ensaios sobre a Crise,* no. 2, ed. L. G. Belluzzo and Renata Coutinho (São Paulo: Editora Brasiliense, 1983), p. 64.

33. The following account of class structure in relation to the corporatist system draws heavily on dos Santos' important essay, "Pós-'Revolução' Brasileira."

34. See dos Santos, "Pós-'Revolução' Brasileira," p. 258; see also Carlos A. Hasenbalg, *Discriminação e Desigualdades Raciais no Brasil* (Rio de Janeiro: Edições Graal, 1979).

35. Data from an unpublished paper by Carlos A. Hasenbalg and Nelson do Valle e Silva, as quoted in dos Santos, "Pós-'Revolução' Brasileira," pp. 258, 264.

36. On Brazilian party history, see Lamounier and Meneguello, *Partidos Políticos*.

37. See works cited in n. 22, above.

38. Alfred Stepan, "Political Leadership and Regime Breakdown: Brazil." In *The Breakdown of Democracies,* ed. Juan Linz and Alfred Stepan (Baltimore, MD: Johns Hopkins University Press, 1978).

39. The importance of law schools throughout the nineteenth century and up to 1945 is beyond dispute. Resistance to Vargas' Estado Novo and again to the post-1964 military governments gave them a new lease on life. The Brazilian Lawyers Association was a basic reference point for the opposition during the decompression period.

40. A detailed analysis of Geisel's economic and political strategies can be found in Lamounier and Moura, "Economic Policy and Political Opening".

41. Perhaps we can interpret in this light the familiar finding that support for the democratic "rules of the game" is often more a matter of elite ethos than of mass attitudes. On "collective goods" as a tool in political analysis, see Mancur Olson, Jr., *The Logic of Collective Action* (New York: Schocken Books, 1968).

42. Even more serious than the influence exerted by such companies is perhaps the lack of coordination that results from their autonomous power, which leads several authors to talk about Balcanization, or feudalization. See dos Santos, *Poder e Política*, p. 123; and Luciano Martins, *Estado Capitalista e Burocracia no Brasil Pós-64* (Rio de Janeiro: Paz e Terra, 1985), p. 81.

43. The redistributive arena affects income and wealth, consequently producing very visible and highly organized contenders; the regulatory deals with the conditions under which certain activities will be exercised; finally, the distributive is what, broadly, one would call clientelistic politics, based on highly divisible and thus rather invisible decisions. Theodore Lowi, "American Business, Public Policy, Case Studies and Political Theory," *World Politics* 16 (1964): pp.

44. Robert A. Dahl, *Polyarchy; Participation and Opposition* (New Haven, CT: Yale University Press, 1971); p. 50.

45. The important critique of Lijphart's consociational model by A. O. Cintra and Plínio Dentzien, In *A Ciência Política nos Anos 80,* ed. Bolívar Lamounier (Brasília: Editora da Universidade, 1982).

46. Article 2 of the Constitutional Act of Finland states that the legislative power shall be exercised by Parliament together with the president and that the supreme executive power is vested in the president of the republic.

47. The West German system is clearly proportional, but the principle has been operationalized so as to allow for a "personalized" (majoritarian) choice of half the seats allocated to each party. No less important from our point of view is the choice of the other half by means of closed lists, in order to enhance the authority of the party as such over individual candidates.

48. Of course, we are here discussing long-run prospects. The new Constitution (October 5, 1988) has lifted the restrictions that the military had imposed on congressional powers—including those pertaining to economic and budgetary matters. But a full appreciation of the new Constitutional structure and its possible impact on democratic development requires another essay.

CHAPTER FOUR

Mexico: Sustained Civilian Rule Without Democracy

DANIEL C. LEVY

Alone of the countries examined in this volume (and exceptional in the series, Democracy in Developing Countries) Mexico has had no significant twentieth-century experience (and precious little prior experience) with democratic rule. Instead, Mexican politics has displayed considerable disdain for the public competition and accountability integral to liberal democracy. Nevertheless, Mexico merits inclusion in our comparative study for three reasons: (1) the nation's overall importance; (2) theoretical insights distinguishing the bases of democratic and stable civilian rule; and (3) notable if uncertain democratizing developments in recent years. The first reason is obvious; this chapter will focus on the others, especially the second reason.[1]

The dominant theme here is that many factors commonly associated with good prospects for democracy have been present in Mexico without promoting that result. Moreover, the very achievement of Mexico's major political success—stability—has presented obstacles to democratization. Naturally, observers have long realized that democracy and stability are empirically and analytically separable. But a strong tendency lumps the two together as one desired outcome. Many of the hypotheses orienting this comparative project illustrate this tendency. Although distinct measures are developed for democracy and stability, democratic stability appears as the key dependent variable.

Among recent attempts to explore difficulties in achieving democracy and stability together, some have concentrated on why democracies fall. For other nations discussed in this volume, but not Mexico, we can analyze democratic periods, democratic breakdown (or consolidation), and "redemocratization." Another line of inquiry concerns the conditions under which authoritarian regimes become democratic.[2] But the literature on that process deals overwhelmingly with military regimes—typically very exclusionary and coercive—and to a limited extent with narrow personalistic regimes. Unlike either "bureaucratic-authoritarian" or personalistic rule, Mexico's authoritarianism has much of the institutionalization, breadth, forms, pacts, and legitimacy often associated with democratic government.

In fact, many factors associated with democratic stability have promoted,

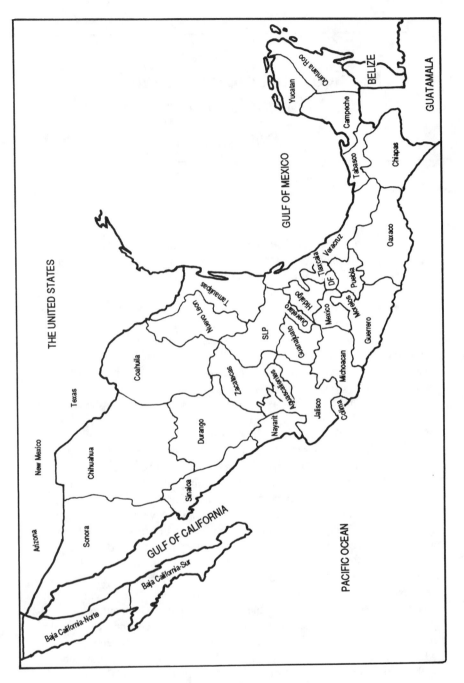

MEXICO

in Mexico, a civilian authoritarian rule that has managed the most impressive political stability in all Latin America regardless of regime type. No other major Latin American nation has sustained civilian rule throughout the postwar period; Mexico's predates that period. In terms of our measures of stability, no regime in the region matches Mexico's in durability and legitimacy built through periods of change, conflict, and challenge. Despite recent developments, including increased challenges and decreased support, efficacy, and effectiveness, Mexico has ranked in the category of stable polities, albeit bordering on partially stable. Unlike Latin American systems that are partially stable because they have not consolidated new regimes, Mexico's difficulty concerns erosion of previous consolidation.

Assessments of stability have been clearer than assessments of democracy in Mexico. The latter have been excessively influenced by dominant paradigms in comparative politics in general and Latin American studies in particular. An irony is that interpretations of Mexican politics have changed so much while the system itself has remained remarkably stable. In line with burgeoning literature on political development, Mexico was typically depicted in the 1950s and most of the 1960s as incompletely but increasingly democratic. Probably the most cited work emphasized an evolution toward Western democracy in rising interest-group activity, participation, inclusiveness, national identity, legitimacy, and functional specialization, alongside declining personalism. Mexico fell short on its citizenship base and leadership selection largely because the regime had pursued "suitable social and economic conditions" before democratic goals, but those conditions had made Mexico ready for democracy.[3] Subsequently, however, Mexico was almost consensually depicted as authoritarian, with democratic tendencies not ascendent. Linz's seminal work on authoritarianism was widely employed by Mexicanists, and Mexico was even overzealously tied to bureaucratic authoritarianism. Recently, interpretations of complex blends of authoritarianism and pluralist forces have been developed.[4]

From 1945 to 1985, Mexico ranked between third and seventh among twenty nations on the best-known (if controversial) ratings for Latin American democracy.[5] Mexico ranks much lower in this volume, however, as all the other cases except Chile currently fit our basic definition of democracy. Mexico falls far short on three elements of democracy, though some qualification is pertinent in each case: (1) Mexico has lacked meaningful and extensive competition among organized groups for major government office, though competition is increasing; (2) participation does not reliably extend to leadership selection through fair elections, though neither is that element entirely absent and elections are regular; and (3) civil and political liberties have been insufficient to guarantee the integrity of competition and participation, but they have been significant and variable rather than minimal. Similarly, Mexico falls into the lowest category (failure/absence) in this study's six-part "summary scale" of democratic experience because there has been no extended period of democracy, and little immediate prospect for it. However, democratic space has increased in recent years, and the future is far more uncertain than it has been for decades.

Regarding this study's classification of democratic stability, Mexico comes closest to the "hegemonic party" system. The dominant party does not tolerate genuine challenges (i.e., alternatives) to its rule, it claims almost all subfederal posts, and electoral fraud is common. Still, the party does not regularly take the high vote percentage cited for hegemonic systems. More broadly, our overall definition of democracy is heavily weighted toward electoral dimensions, long a weak area for Mexico. Thus, the Mexican case shows some significant features of "semidemocracies," including substantial room for expression, and suggests that hegemonies are not necessarily the least democratic of authoritarian nations.

This chapter identifies basic roots of Mexico's complex system of stable civilian rule without democracy, and more specifically considers the editors' hypotheses about stable democracy. Finally, it analyzes prospects for democratization and the role the United States might play.

First, however, a preliminary qualification must be inserted here. This chapter was written before the 1988 electoral campaign took shape and hurtled towards an exciting, unprecedented finish. In the election's immediate aftermath, no serious observer has more than questionable ideas about most of the implications for democracy. What is clear is that the elections were the most competitive in spirit and result of any in modern Mexican history and that they vastly increased uncertainty about the future of Mexican politics. Even if Mexican politics undergo transforming changes, however, it will be important to understand the long-standing reality that preceded (and undoubtedly would help shape) those changes.

• AN UNDEMOCRATIC PAST: REVIEW AND ANALYSIS •

Mexico's political heritage is authoritarian. There is less democratic precedent to analyze than in any other country considered in this volume; viable democratic rule has been virtually absent. A point highlighted by Wiarda in the Dominican case is particularly relevant in the Mexican case: Democratic experiments historically proved ineffective, in contrast to certain authoritarian periods.

Great precolonial civilizations, such as the Aztec, presaged a pattern of relatively strong authoritarian rule. Spain's centuries-long rule was similar in that respect. Some observers see not only precedent but causal roots in these experiences. According to Octavio Paz, the Aztec *tlatoani* introduced impersonal, priestly, institutional rule, and colonialism introduced Arabic-Hispanic reverence for the personal *caudillo:* "I repeat: there is a bridge that reaches from *tlatoani* to viceroy, viceroy to president."[6] And much has been made of the contrast between authoritarian and "liberal" colonizations by Spain and England, respectively.

Independence (1821) brought neither democracy nor stability. Federalist-centralist conflicts were among the most important. The lack of stability crippled hopes for economic growth, which in turn contributed to further instability. Despite examples of autonomous local rule, liberal projects were weak. Liberal rule was extremely short-lived, as was the presidency of Valentín Gómez Farías in the 1830s, until the Reform (1855–1876). The Reform is probably the closest Mexico has come to democracy. It featured a belief that democracy (however restricted) was compatible with stability and growth; a liberal constitution; substantial liberties; some significant elections; and some socioeconomic mobility and educational expansion alongside attacks on large landholders, including the church. On the other hand, the Reform was limited in mass inclusiveness and hostile to Indian communitarianism. Yet, democracy often begins with public contestation restricted to certain groups. Mexico's liberal experiment failed because it could not build sufficient strength. French imperial intervention, though eventually beaten back, was debilitating. Mostly, liberal democratic forms were used by antidemocratic forces. Regional *caciques* used decentralized authority to block reform. As it often has in Latin America, Congress represented *cacique* and other oligarchic interests in conflict with a liberal executive.[7] The weakness of liberal experiments with decentralized political authority would not go unnoticed by twentieth-century leaders.

Always fragile, the Reform faded after leader Benito Juárez's death (1872). A split over the 1876 presidential succession opened the way for a military coup. Porfirio Díaz became supreme dictator. For the first time, independent Mexico achieved political stability and economic growth. The regime was repressively authoritarian: Gone were free elections; diminished was freedom of the press. Commonly for Latin America, some democratic formalities were preserved, but Díaz's reference to Congress as his herd of tame horses was indicative of the basic realities. The *porfiriato*'s positivist notions of progress through permanent evolution, accompanied by economic growth without distribution and political stability without democracy, offer broad historical parallels to the contemporary regime.

Among factors ultimately bringing down the *porfiriato* (1910), contemporary optimists about democracy might speculate on both repressiveness and economic growth leading to calls for democracy; but the main reason for the regime's fall was its unwillingness to allow political mobility among the elite. In any case, Díaz's fall was precipitated by his quickly inoperative pledge not to seek reelection in 1910. Francisco Madero held Díaz to his rhetoric about free elections, and Díaz's attempts at electoral fraud were his end. Madero won Mexico's uniquely free (if still limited) election and became president (1911–1913). He led those whose agenda was "a return to '57," the Reform constitution, and "free suffrage, no reelection." Considerable democracy blossomed. For example, Congress was autonomous of the executive and the scene of powerful debates among very antagonistic forces. Division of power (federalism) and separation of power (including judicial review) were important for Madero.

But such democratization proved largely irrelevant for Mexico. Democratic, competitive structures did not lead to the destruction of Porfirian forces including *caciques,* governors, bureaucrats, the military, and a partially revitalized church. Madero even appointed former Díaz aides to government positions, while he tended to exclude revolutionary groups. In other words, this democratic leader, so popular in 1911, neither destroyed the old order nor constructed a viable new one. Although a good deal of the literature on transitions to democracy stresses the need for pacts among elites, probably the major weakness in Madero's approach, reflected in his inattention to socioeconomic problems, was failure to strengthen democratic forces by adding a mass base. Of course, whether Madero could have successfully done so is unknown. After his assassination (covertly aided by the United States), other leaders would incorporate the masses—undemocratically.

Years of revolutionary warfare among various armies brought mass mobilization and, especially, death and destruction. By 1916, a million Mexicans had died, and nearly as many had emigrated. Compared, for example, to Emiliano Zapata's peasant army and its demands for land reform, Venustiano Carranza's ultimately victorious constitutionalists were not committed to fundamental socioeconomic change. In subsequent years, some observers would even question whether a real revolution had occurred. In any case, the revolution would become a symbol of mass involvement, progressive change, and nationalism, skillfully manipulated by the regime to bolster its legitimacy. By 1940, the revolution would be "institutionalized," the fragile stability forged since 1916 safely deepened. Two crucial factors in building this postrevolutionary stability were pacts among those elites not destroyed by the revolution, and organized integration of mass groups.[8]

President Carranza only partly recognized these two necessities, but he accepted provisions that gave the 1917 Constitution strong mass appeal as a legacy of the revolution. These included a minimum wage, an 8-hour workday, workman's compensation, land reform, and notable nationalist measures. Equally significant, the Constitution ambiguously blended democratic aspirations with authoritarian realities: popular sovereignty; free elections; guarantees for individual rights; federalism; separation of powers; and a potent national government in general and presidency in particular.

Between them, Carranza's two powerful successors, Alvaro Obregón and Plutarco Elías Calles extended the state's ties to and control over mass agrarian and urban labor interests. Yet, when their terms ended (1928), the regime's stability was still much in doubt. All three presidents had plotted to rule beyond their constitutional terms; two had been assassinated. Major groups still competed violently; and none was powerful enough to end the nation's political stalemate.

At this point, Mexico experienced two moments of great political leadership, the kind in many ways associated with democratic consolidation. The leadership that stabilized Mexico's civilian rule would be undemocratic in means (not unusual in democratic consolidations) but also in ends. First, Calles engineered a grand pact among elite power-holders. Convincing them that without compromise they faced defeat or endless uncertainty, he brought them to support creation of a civilian institution (the party) that would centralize authority for the regime on the basis of bargains, including elite circulation through peaceful means. Second, ironically, Calles' successor had to block his personalistic attempt to regain and perpetuate his rule.[9] Although Calles had the edge among elites, Lázaro Cárdenas fortified the incorporation of the masses, as he won their allegiance not only to himself but to the regime. Critically, however, Cárdenas was not responding to autonomous demands from below. His modes were corporatist; he was in fact a proclaimed opponent of bourgeois democracy.

By the time the immensely popular Cárdenas peacefully relinquished power to a moderate successor (1940), the regime was sufficiently institutionalized to pave the way for more than a quarter-century of maximum strength and stability, followed finally by increasing weaknesses but not instability.

• CIVILIAN RULE WITHOUT DEMOCRACY •

This section analyzes four topics identified as crucial to democratic development. For each, I explore how basic features have evolved and operate, how they serve civilian stability but not democracy, and what challenges have recently emerged in Mexico.

State-Society Relations

State relations with mass groups approximate "state corporatism" much more than pluralism.[10] The regime has significant control over organizations that bring the masses into the system. Participation and interest-group demands are seriously limited. In fact, much of the Mexican population is unorganized and politically "marginal"; it does not express discontent, or it asks for help from a political mediator without demanding rights. Even formal, organized groups often react to more than participate meaningfully in policy formation.[11]

Encapsulating mass organizations obviously is antithetical to democracy. It also greatly limits the democratizing option available in Venezuela's *trienio* when the AD party could organize peasants and workers. Those groups have already been organized in Mexico, into an undemocratic party. On the other hand, the early incorporation of mass groups has promoted stability. It has given the regime a wide base, which has been used to boost the regime's autonomy from business. Mainly, however, incorporation has made organized dissent on the Left extremely difficult. Such dissent threatens other regimes, particularly when mass mobilization leads to elite fears and military coups. The Mexican regime has repeatedly been able to effect austere economic policies that would bring revolt in other nations.[12] Thus, the regime's mass base has sustained civilian rule even while it has been undemocratic. Additionally, because major threats have been forestalled in Mexico, the regime has been able to use less repressive force than have many other authoritarian regimes in Latin America.

As one of two major organized mass groups (the peasantry is the other), labor verifies the pattern of state corporatism. Labor power, including access to rewards, is concentrated in one dominating union, the Confederation of Mexican Workers (CTM), which Cárdenas carefully grafted onto the official party. Crucially, labor was incorporated and granted benefits from above, more than independently organized for the conquest of rights.[13] Labor leaders have helped make Mexican unions "moderate" but neither autonomous nor democratic. Occasionally, when independent labor movements have threatened to become powerful, the regime has resorted to severe repression (as in the late 1950s); but usually the regime has relied on the undemocratic internal structure of organized labor and its ties to the regime.[14] A big challenge has emerged, however, with the economic crisis of the 1980s. As Waisman points out in this volume, Argentine labor corporatism worked to give the government support only as long as the workers reaped the benefits of redistribution. In Mexico, the regime has long carefully funneled benefits to organized labor, but real wages have recently plummeted.

However formidable, corporatist controls are far from complete. Even official trade unions often bargain hard for benefits, and some leaders have increased their criticism of regime policies. Further, independent labor movements have precedent and recently became usually active, at least until economic setbacks in the 1980s. Attention has focused on the electrical workers' Tendencia Democrática and parallels for telephone workers, miners, and teachers. Third, the CTM's share of the organized work force is diminishing, and the regime's economic opening of the 1980s could further weaken it.

Whereas qualifications must be made to a corporatist view of state-labor relations, such a view is fundamentally inappropriate for state-business relations. Reasonable scholarly debate exists over past relations. Some "peak" business associations have been established by government, mandatory in inclusiveness, and dependent (on government) in matters ranging from subsidies to leadership selection. But a good case can be made that domestic business, even including older associations such as the Confederation of Industrial Chambers and the National Chamber of Manufacturing Industry, has long worked with government because of mutual self-interest and "inducements" more than coercion and "constraints"; has been economically strong and politically able to influence regulatory, trade, and other policies; and has expressed a "sectorial consciousness" involving some "adversary relationship with political elites."[15] In any case, this more pluralist view holds for newer associations, such as the Entrepreneurial Coordinating council and the Mexican Employers' Confederation, and increasingly for traditional ones. The economic populism of President

Luis Echeverría in the early 1970s weakened state-business ties by scaring and alienating business and by hurting the economy. Today, harsh and repeated business criticism of the regime simultaneously jeopardizes political stability and shows considerable freedom of expression.

Juxtaposition of business and labor relations with the state illustrates how the balance between freedom and corporatist controls usually depends on social class. Consider highly educated groups. Granted, dependency on the state goes far beyond what is found in the United States in terms of employment opportunities and professional associations. But intellectuals and other professionals have been much freer than workers to control their affairs and even to criticize the government. Despite the potential corporatist tie of depending almost fully on the state for income, Mexico's public universities have substantial though circumscribed autonomy from government. Furthermore, groups within the public universities have considerable freedom of expression and power to affect institutional policies, as the massive and successful student demonstrations against academic reforms proposed in 1986 illustrate.[16] Private universities, holding roughly 15 percent of the nation's more than 1 million enrolments, add significantly to state-society pluralism.[17]

What, then, of the infamous events of 1968, when the government killed hundreds of protesting university students? The slaughter was a watershed in views about Mexican democratization: It convinced many of the regime's unalterably repressive nature. But my view is that limits on protest are not so fixed. Behavior that lies within the "logic" of this authoritarian system is not inevitable behavior; at other times, other Mexican leaders have been more tolerant. To be sure, the student protests of 1968 were unprecedented for the widespread questions they so actively raised about the lack of democracy in Mexico. And 1968 serves as a chilling and restraining reminder of the state's possible violent response to protest, a response much more commonly visited on poorer groups.[18]

One rule demarking zones of permitted and unpermitted freedoms can be identified as central to Mexico's exclusion from the democratic category: Organized dissent that poses a realistic alternative to the regime is forbidden. Violations usually bring harsh repression along with co-optation. Even this formidable restriction leaves some room for pluralism and, especially, individual freedoms.[19] Religion provides an example of both the restrictions and the possibilities. After the revolution broke the church's tremendous political-economic power, a *modus vivendi* allowed it considerable autonomy in religious-cultural-educational affairs—beyond what the Constitution ostensibly permits. In turn, the church has not been allowed the opposition voice heard in Brazil, Chile, Nicaragua, and elsewhere in Latin America—though some Mexican church leaders have recently supported opposition party calls for democratization with free elections. Meanwhile, individuals are free to worship (or not) as they please, and several religious and ethnic minorities have significant group autonomy. Mexico has no official religion.

Of course, some such societal freedoms (e.g., private schooling and free-dom to travel) lack a direct political component or offer opportunity for the privileged only. Nonetheless, evidence of increased vibrancy and inclusiveness in political life abounds. As president, Echeverría criticized the nation's basic development model. Under José López Portillo (1976–1982), Mexico enjoyed an unusually open (though still partly managed) debate over whether to join the GATT. Under Miguel de la Madrid (1982–1988), the freedom to advocate alter-native policies reached new heights, though presidential claims that policy was often made through popular consultations were mere pretense. The 1988 elec-toral campaign then opened considerably more space for free expression.

While this tendency to use the increasing democratic space has been most evident among privileged groups (as in middle-class organizations on environ-mental issues), it also extends to popular sectors. A basic factor has been dis-enchantment with government, particularly given the consequences of continued economic crisis. (A catalyst was the earthquakes of 1985; the govern-ment appeared impotent in reacting.) Some see scars and challenges that go beyond 1968 and could promote "an initial democratization of Mexico's politi-cal institutions."[20] Individuals have formed associations to deal with urban problems such as homelessness, tenant conditions, schooling, and other public services. Although spontaneous association has considerable precedent in Mexico, one wonders whether a new era has begun. Recent behavior can be contrasted to Fagen and Tuohy's well-known depiction of "depoliticized" urban life, where management substitutes for politics and most people believe that government should or will handle their political affairs.[21] The new vibrancy in Mexican politics alters traditional state-society patterns associated with stabil-ity; indeed, it has resulted from both the state's success in modernizing and di-versifying society and from its declining legitimacy.

My points about societal freedom—its limits and growth—are illustrated by analysis of the media. First, outright repression and censorship exist. De-spite the pluralism apparently offered through the multiplicity of outlets, mostly private, dependence on government is insured through official control of news-print and the need for licenses. Mostly, however, smooth state-media relations reflect overlapping elite interests. Mutual interests on "macro" orientations such as growth and stability without major redistribution are supported by "micro" support through government advertising revenue, corrupt stipends for reporters, and the like. In return, government has counted on fairly favorable reporting and a lack of the information a citizenry needs for responsible democ-racy with accountability. Where the media come closest to escaping such restric-tions, we tend to see elite pluralism. Most independent publications, including newspapers (e.g., *Uno Más Uno* and *La Jornada*), magazines (e.g., *Proceso* and *Nexos*), and academic books are not only expensive but appeal to the edu-cated minority. Electronic media are much safer in content. Television's conser-vative banality is crucial. Thus, the most vigorous areas of contestation are the ones that reach the least inclusive audience. Additionally, considerable room exists for fundamental Marxist critiques of the immutable state but much less for practical critiques including policy alternatives.[22] Where coverage of such alternatives is found, it is often in the cautious form of citing what various officials and others have said, avoiding in-depth analysis.

Nevertheless, coverage of true dissent is increasing. Repression of the nation's leading independent newspaper in 1976 has been followed by the greatest media freedom contemporary Mexico has known. It has included investigative reporting and public opinion polls concerning increased cynicism about government, and prominent calls for widespread democratization. All this, however limited, contributes to a new era of democratic challenge.

Government Centralization

In turning now from state-society relations to the structure of the government, we turn from elements intrinsic to democracy to elements hypothetically associated with democracy. That is, a system with widespread freedoms and pluralism is more democratic than one in which state corporatism rules society, whereas decentralized governments can exist in undemocratic systems and centralized governments can exist in democratic systems.

The editors have hypothesized a strong association between decentralization and democracy. The Mexican case is perhaps supportive of the hypothesis, but only indirectly, as it combines centralization with the absence of democracy. Much clearer is that centralization—geographically and in the presidency—has been crucial to civilian stability. As González Casanova's classic analysis showed, Mexico's antiliberal government structure must be viewed in historical context. Mexico City–based presidentialism with a hegemonic party ended military and legislative conspiracies as well as divisively unstable rule by regional and other *caudillos*. "Respect for the balances of power would have been respect for the conspiracies of a semi-feudal society."[23]

Establishing central authority and national identity and security is a major problem for new nations. Mexico was unsuccessful in the nineteenth century. Into the 1920s and even 1930s, regional and village strongmen ruled outside the grasp of Mexico City. Such decentralized power had nothing to do with democracy; nor did the ensuing geographical centralization of power. Although aided by transportation and communication advances, a key was decisive political leadership by the likes of Obregón, Calles, and Cárdenas. Overcoming centrifugal antidemocratic forces is often a prerequisite to democratic consolidation. In Mexico, it proved crucial to stability but not democracy.

Mexico formally has a federalist structure with thirty-one states (plus the Federal District), which in turn are divided into over 2,000 supposedly free municipalities. State political structures parallel the national except that their legislatures are unicameral. In practice, a range of daily and other activities are handled by states, and the federal government usually intervenes only when conflicts are not locally contained. However. the very infrequency of explicit interventions reflects (as we saw in state-labor relations) ongoing national government control over basic policy. In essence, presidents appoint the official party's gubernatorial candidates and depose troublesome governors. National cabinet ministries have delegates in each state, and stationed military officers represent national authority. States have very limited funds and depend on the national government for most of them. Similarly, municipalities depend on states and the national government regarding leadership and funds, and funds are very unevenly disbursed; most municipalities lack income beyond very small appropriations and fees from licenses and fines. Political careers have been made in Mexico City, not at the grassroots.

Electoral patterns have illustrated the centralized hold.[24] First in 1958, then in 1967, and especially since the 1977 reform, several opposition victories have been allowed at the municipal level. But the opposition has not gained a single governorship. And the official party still holds roughly 95 percent of the municipalities. Sometimes, as after the leftist victory in Juchitán, Oaxaca, the regime uses violence to oust the municipal opposition. Usually, the centralized party-government structure itself limits the importance of municipal opposition victories.

Centralization has recently come under strong attack, however. Disaffection runs especially high in the industrial north, though Mexico does not face the separatist threats that undermine stability in some Third World nations. Many Mexicans consider decentralization necessary for increased participation and democratization (suggesting some parallel to what Hartlyn finds for Colombia). Decentralization in implementation and, more controversially, in decision-making is increasingly linked to regime effectiveness and stability as well. Latell even portrays a fundamental split between "federalists" and "centralists." The former include many business and conservative opposition party leaders joined by a minority of government officials. President de la Madrid, while duly citing the historical necessity of centralization, called it "a grave limitation": "Centralist mentalities have become obstacles that distort democracy."[25] His administration claimed to have expanded municipal autonomy and increased access to local resources. In its 1988 campaign, the official party made decentralization a major theme.

But obstacles to decentralization remain enormous. Centralization goes beyond political to economic and social realms; economic crisis makes it hard to invest in decentralization; party leaders, governors, and many other government official have vested interests in centralization; political traditions carry weight. Overall, decentralization involves risks. Even if overcentralization now threatens stability, sudden decentralization might threaten it more.

Centralization of power in Mexico City has meant centralization of power in the presidency. Constitutional provisions about the separation of powers within the federal government have had no more impact than provisions about the division of powers between federal and state governments. Mexico achieved stability not by defying authoritarian tendencies toward the enormous concentration of authority in one leader but by limiting the leader's term. Apt are references to Mexico's "king for six years." The president has been central to policymaking, agenda setting, conflict resolution, key appointments, control over the party, and so forth. He heads a vast network of federal agencies (employing 17 percent of the nation's workforce), including many "parastatals."[26]

Cardoso even called the Mexican president perhaps more powerful than any Southern Cone military president.[27] Such assessments probably underestimate three factors, however. One is the comparative limits of the Mexican state's control over society; the Mexican president can be no more powerful than his government. Second are the terrible disorders, rivalries, and duplications rampant in the Mexican federal bureaucracy. Third is the erosion of presidential strength in the last two decades, reflected in increasing attacks on presidents, once unthinkable, and widespread beliefs about the failures of at least the last three presidents. In fact, the last presidential "giant" was Miguel Alemán, who left office in 1952.

The presidency nonetheless has remained very powerful, largely because Congress and the judiciary have been so weak. Congressional debate and opposition continued into the 1920s but died with regime consolidation. Although token opposition reappeared in 1940, executive initiatives have been approved unanimously or overwhelmingly. A function of Congress has been to show the rule of law in legitimizing executive action. Since the 1970s, however, political reform has expanded opposition representation, and one sees some coalition building, revelations about unpopular government actions, and greatly expanded debate.[28] The opening has included the appearance of cabinet officers to answer questions posed by the legislative opposition. Still, the legislature has lacked the openness or, especially, the power found in democracies. I must add, however, that the opening may well have grown dramatically in 1988. Opposition parties gained nearly half the seats in the Chamber of Deputies (as Table 11.1 will show) plus its first Senate representation, and vigorous protests were seen. However cloudy the prospects for policymaking power remain, unprecedented openness seems certain.

The judiciary has played a more important role than has the legislature (until recently) but also a limited one. It has been a place for privileged actors to protect their interests even against executive initiatives, particularly in the case of landlords working against land reform. Although it has handled disputes among citizens, it has not limited executive authority by interpreting the Constitution or executive actions. Nor has it, for example, yet dealt seriously with electoral fraud. No parallel has emerged for the liberalization occurring in the legislature. "Judicial reform" refers basically to speeding up the decisionmaking process. It has not referred to increasing autonomy from the executive.[29]

Given common patterns of both Latin American politics and Mexican history from independence until roughly the 1930s, however, the main reason that government power is centralized in the presidency is that the military is subordinated. In the postwar era, only Costa Rica rivals Mexico in degree of subordination. Outside Mexico, subordination is generally associated with the establishment and defense of democracy, as in Costa Rica. But Mexico produced no Figueres, no democratic rule. Nonetheless, skilled political leadership was crucial in establishing civilian supremacy.

Presidents Obregón, Calles, and Cárdenas, themselves revolutionary generals (like all presidents until 1946, at least nominally) adeptly timed and executed measures to subordinate the military. These included: purges and other forced retirements and transfers (which minimized loyalty to given officers); welcome opportunities for corruption within the service and for business employment outside it; dependence on government salaries and social security; professionalization; cuts in military funding; creation of a viable political party; and incorporation of mass organizations into civilian structures. And since 1946, all presidents have been civilians.

Since the institutionalization of the regime, there have been no coups or serious threats of coups. The military has not been a powerful interest group blocking policies it does not like and forcing others. Its share of government expenditures has been famously low. The military has not been integrated with the civilian Right. All these factors distinguish Mexico from most of Latin America and help us understand the nation's stability.

Some signs of increasing military strength have recently appeared in role, stature, funding, modernization, and appointments of retired generals.[30] Still, a major change in the military's role remains very unlikely. The civilian regime would probably have to weaken so much as to need continual assistance to quell protests over austerity or electoral fraud. To this point, the Mexican military has loyally sustained rather than threatened civilian rule, but its loyalty is not to democracy.

The Party and Electoral Systems

Integral to both state corporatism and centralization is the dominance of the Institutional Revolutionary Party (PRI). The editors hypothesize that deeply institutionalized competitive parties are conducive to stable democracy. The PRI is deeply institutionalized. It has held power longer than any other party in Latin America and has reached widely into society. Yet this institutionalization has been conducive to a distinctly undemocratic stability. It has helped to encapsulate groups and to preclude alternative institutionalized parties.

From independence until the revolution, parties were mostly political clubs. The elections in which they participated "were not a mechanism of popular voting but a legitimization of military force."[31] Of seventy-one governments (1823–1911), only seventeen were elected by constitutional norms. Even these involved indirect elections, open balloting, and so forth. The elected president almost always came from the incumbent party or group. Nonetheless, all new governments felt obliged to seek popular-constitutional legitimization through elections. Again, democratic ideology is juxtaposed to undemocratic reality.

Even after the revolution, parties continued to be weak, transitory, dependent on a single leader, without mass bases, and multitudinous. Then, however, a new party, continually juggled and deepened from 1929 to 1946 (when it became the PRI), replaced anarchic conflict and made elites play by institutionalized and legal rules. From 1929 to 1933, the number of parties dropped from fifty-one to four.[32] Mass organizations were incorporated. Civilian rulers built a strong institution that could organize and distribute resources, thus helping to subordinate the military. Such developments are often associated with transitions to democracy, but in Mexico, competition among elites did not encompass open public contestation, and mass incorporation was corporatist.

Not surprisingly, then, the PRI has not concentrated on the functions expected of democratic parties. Its main mission has been neither to aggregate nor to articulate demands. It has not truly competed for power. Although it has always been—until now—"in power," the PRI has not had a major role in policymaking. Instead, it has concentrated on other party functions but has directed them to the service of the government of which it is really a part (even though party and government personnel are formally distinct). These functions include mobilizing support for the regime; suppressing dissent; gathering and manipulating information; distributing welfare and patronage; engaging in political socialization and recruitment; handling particularistic grievances; and providing an ideological rationale for government action. Unlike what one expects of democratic party systems, PRI's hegemonic rule has sustained socioeconomic inequalities, and the PRI wins its largest vote from the least privileged groups.

But the PRI has stumbled into critical difficulties. Once more, we see where new challenges to political stability suggest increased hopes for democratization. So integral is the PRI to the regime that all the regime difficulties already cited (e.g., the beleaguered presidency and the need for decentralization) are PRI difficulties as well. In fact, the PRI is crucial to the overall crisis of the "political class" that has so adeptly managed key aspects of Mexico's postrevolutionary affairs.[33] The party is not legitimizing the regime as it once did. Very high abstention rates (roughly 50 percent in 1979 and 1985) and the PRI's declining share of the votes cast illustrate the problem (see Table 11.1). In fact, PRI's decline suddenly accelerated in 1988 when even official tallies gave the party only a slim majority in the presidential vote and in congressional seats. One could imagine the PRI as the "party of pluralities," flanked by a powerful Right and Left. PRI's invincibility appears shattered.

PRI's crisis is a culmination of both relatively sudden problems, such as the imposition of austerity, and long-run problems. Perhaps a party built to handle a basically rural and uneducated society is ill-equipped for modern Mexico. Perhaps a party established without true democratic functions finds itself unprepared to compete openly for citizen support.[34] Efforts to reform the PRI naturally produce further tensions within the party.

In truth, most PRI reforms (at least until now) have been aimed less at democratizing *per se* than at reviving legitimacy and combating opposition parties.[35] Probably the most ambitious (pre-1980s) reform attempt, undertaken by PRI president Carlos Madrazo in the mid-1960s, envisioned primaries and some separation of party from government. It was beaten back by vested PRI interests. In 1986, a new "democratic tendency" was immediately denounced by party and labor leaders as disloyal, selfish, and misleading—since PRI is continually perfecting its democracy. Whatever its motives, the movement at first carefully stressed its party credentials and limited its call for reform. But from the outset it proposed increased dialog within the party and with groups outside it, and it challenged the key practice of presidential appointment of successors by suggesting that "precandidates" resign ministerial posts and campaign openly before the public. Even before it split from the PRI to run against it in 1988, the movement had received well over a year of extraordinarily extensive, daily media coverage, as it has energetically carried its message around the country. Nevertheless, during that time, de la Madrid followed traditional practice by handpicking the PRI's next candidate for president, and therefore the next president, Carlos Salinas de Gortari.

If democracy has been weak within the PRI, it has also been weak in the party system overall. Granted, opposition parties have existed and some have expressed considerable dissent. But until recently, they have served mostly to legitimize PRI–regime rule. In fact, opposition parties were largely government-created in the 1940s and 1950s. Co-optation was the norm at least until the 1970s.

On the Left, legal parties have usually been tied to the left wing of the PRI. The Popular Socialist Party, historically connected with mainstream labor, is the main example. Since the 1970s, however, independent leftist parties have arisen. The Communist Party, formed in 1919 but denied electoral registration from 1945 to 1979, has been the major party in recent socialist coalitions. But at least until 1988, the coalitions repeatedly split (as on whether to join rightist parties in pressing for free elections). Moreover, even when united, the electoral Left has had very little mass appeal.[36] This weakness reflects the lack of an organized independent Left in Mexican society, particularly given the state corporatism encapsulating labor and the peasantry. But in 1988 Cuauhtémoc Cárdenas (son of the revered ex-president) led dissident leftist PRI members into a powerful coalition with mostly leftist parties (although perhaps the campaign was as "populist" as "leftist"). The official count gave the coalition a startling second place with over three in ten votes. If (but it is not an easy if) the coalition could be solidified at local levels, and show itself not to be primarily a personalistic or protest phenomenon, Mexico could take a major step toward multiparty democracy.

As Table 4.1 shows, the Right has had a much stronger sustained electoral presence, concentrated almost fully in one party. The National Action Party (PAN), formed in 1939, has functioned mostly as an institutionalized opposition, not pressing seriously to defeat the PRI. Recently, though, a significant

Table 4.1 Electoral Support for the PRI and the PAN, 1946–1985

YEAR	% of Vote for Presidency		% of Vote for Chamber of Deputies		Seats in Chamber of Deputies		
	PRI	PAN	PRI	PAN	PRI	PAN	OTHER
1946[a]	78	—[b]	—	—	143	4	0
1952	74	8[b]	—	—	154	5	2
1958	90	9	—	—	152	6	3
1961	—	—	90	8	172	5	1
1964	89	11	86	12	175	20[c]	15
1967	—	—	83	12	176	20	16
1970	86	14	80	14	178	20	15
1973	—	—	70	15	189	25	20
1976	99	—[d]	80	9	196	20	22
1979	—	—	70[e]	11	296	43	61
1982	72	16	69	18	299	51	50
1985[f]	—	—	65	16	289	41	71

Sources: Pablo González Casanova, *Democracy in Mexico* tr. Danielle Salti (London: Oxford University Press, 1970), pp. 199–200; Secretaría de Gobernación, *Diario Oficial*, various; Comisión Federal Electoral; Dale Story, "The PAN, the Private Sector, and the Future of the Mexican Opposition." In *Mexican Politics in Transition*, ed. Judith Gentleman (Boulder, CO.: Westview Press, forthcoming), Table 11.3, drawing on various sources.

a. 1946 was the PRI's first year; PRI forerunners had claimed 98% and 94% of the vote in the 1934 and 1940 presidential elections, respectively.

b. The PAN was not the major opposition winner.

c. Since 1964, opposition seats have been based on outright district victories but overwhelmingly on PR; I show the total figures.

d. The PAN did not field a candidate.

e. Starting in 1979, the new PR procedure took effect; I report the simple plurality vote rather than the separate, but quite close, PR vote.

f. Preliminary results for 1988 show the PRI claiming just over half the presidential vote (51%) followed by the leftist Cárdenas coalition with nearly one-third of the votes (31%) and the PAN with just over one-sixth (17%), and claiming 260 of 500 Chamber seats (with 139 for the leftist coalition and 101 for the PAN).

portion of the party has favored all-out competition in a democratic setting. Joined by the independent Left, the PAN advocates honest elections. It takes the lead in championing federalism and the separation of powers. Unlike the PRI, it selects candidates rather openly. Like the PRI and the opposition in general, however, the PAN usually fails to offer specific alternatives to PRI–government policies. Indeed, its ideology (including links to Catholic thought) has usually been ambiguous, though a business orientation is increasingly marked. The PAN's appeal is limited to certain regions, particularly in the north and urban areas, and to privileged groups. It does not even run candidates in many districts around the nation. It does not attract a major portion of labor or the peasantry the way, for example, some Christian-democratic parties have done (e.g., in Chile and Venezuela). Much of its vote has been a protest vote.

Opposition parties have gained more freedom and importance with the reforms inaugurated in 1977 and modified in 1986. Previous electoral reform had been very limited. Universal suffrage was achieved in 1954 and 1973 reforms on a 1918 base. Since 1963, the regime has reversed a 1929–1954 trend that greatly inhibited opposition-party formation and representation. The 1977–1986 reforms went much further with democratization. They allowed parties to register more easily and granted public funds and free media time. Most dramatic, however, was the procedure for modified proportional representation in the Chamber of Deputies. While 300 seats were still determined by plurality vote by district, first 100 and then 200 seats were open to a PR system; whereas the 100 were reserved for minority parties, the 200 were not, but then the majority party was restricted to a 350-seat maximum.[37] Even critics on the Left and the Right have generally acknowledged that the electoral system now provides more freedom, information, exposure, and alternative positions. Indeed, the 1988 elections indicated how profound the changes facilitated by the reform might be.

Why the opening? Mostly, the regime tried to arrest its declining legitimacy and respond in a controlled way to cries for democratization. Moreover, the regime wanted to make sure that dissent is institutionalized, not spontaneous.[38] Possibly, the regime also hoped to strengthen the electoral Left a bit to offset the PAN's growth. Nonetheless, to understand the regime's purposes is to understand that it still contemplated no full-blown democratization. Thus, several "reform" provisions aimed at insuring the PRI a legislative majority even were it to gain fewer than half the votes; a major problem is continued PRI dominance on the electoral body that supervises elections. Additionally, certain PRI leaders have blocked measures such as imposing reform on states.[39]

The regime's disposition to increase freedom, choice, and competitiveness in the party system without democratically risking its rule has been verified in recent elections. Those of 1979, 1982, and 1983 were unusually clean. Opposition strength increased to where, in 1983, it captured mayoralties in five state capitals. Putting the best face on it, regime and PRI leaders claimed proof of competitiveness. Led on by presidential pledges to honor electoral results, and by foreign press and governmental attention stimulated by recent democratization in Latin America, many looked toward imminent elections for much further democratization (including opposition governorships). How unrealistic they appeared in the 1984–1987 period. Resorting to an unspecifiable but apparently ample degree of fraud, the PRI took all cities in question in 1984, and all governorships in the next two years. Regime officials denounced critics of the elections for promoting foreign models at the expense of national sovereignty.

The regime would strengthen oppositions but, unlike true democratizers of the Betancourt stripe, not to the point that those oppositions could win.[40] For the real function of Mexican elections is still not to select parties, leaders, and policies through open choice, but rather to offer the hope, mobility, and regularized renewal necessary to maintain support for the regime.

Increasingly, however, voices are being raised against ratifying rather than democratic elections. Protest intensified with the 1986 Chihuahua elections. Hunger strikes, roadblocks, demonstrations, boycotts, and repeated denunciations ensued. The bishop ordered church closed one Sunday (though the Vatican overruled him). Clearly, protest was not limited to the PAN. Nor was it transient. On the contrary, the imposed PRI rulers in Chihuahua have had a hard time. Nationally, civic groups, religious leaders, and independent leftist parties joined the PAN in an unprecedented national alliance. They focused their attention on one issue—free elections. They established a National Forum for Effective Suffrage. They made specific proposals, including ones dealing with electoral financing and supervision. The regime, they said, "has for many years paralyzed national democratic development."[41]

And all this preceded the 1988 elections. Pressures for free and honest elections have become (and will likely remain) stronger than ever before. In fact, debate over fraud brought Mexico near a constitutional brink in 1988 as repeated large demonstrations and severe confrontations emerged over ratifying the reported results, access to stored ballots (blocked by the military), and calls for immediate new elections. So hard did major oppositions press their claims that some believe the regime ultimately bought acquiescence largely by committing itself in negotiation to more democratic procedures in future elections. In sum, prospects for free, clean elections are stronger than ever, but they are still uncertain.

Performance and Support

Until the 1970s at least, Mexico's strong civilian rule brought widely envied economic success and societal support. Like many nations in Latin America, Mexico relied heavily on import substitution. Unlike others, Mexico achieved average annual economic growth of over 6 percent from 1940 to 1970, and held its inflation low (under 5 percent annually) in the latter half of the period.

Economic growth promoted enormous social change. Today, roughly two-thirds of the population live in urban communities of 2,500 or more. Only about one-third of the labor force remains in agriculture. A large middle class has developed, though it is still dwarfed by the lower class. Mexico has pulled itself to an average position among the larger, relatively developed Latin America nations with its 65-year life expectancy at birth, its infant mortality rate of fifty-six per 1,000 live births, its 83-percent adult literacy, and its dramatic improvements in caloric intake, access to primary schools, and energy consumption.[42] In turn, the regime has used economic growth in playing a prominent if selective role in social modernization. Even amid socioeconomic crisis in 1986, the president could point out that 86 million school textbooks were distributed free that year, while one in three Mexicans was in school, and that, from 1970 to 1986, the average number of years of schooling for the over-fifteen population had doubled (from three to six).[43]

Of course, even official national figures show not just progress but underdevelopment. Moreover, these figures obscure regional and class inequality, both tragically high in Mexico. Such outcomes have been consistent with Mexico's striking internal contrasts in the distribution of power and freedom. In fact, government policies have contributed to inequalities. Promotion of capital-intensive industrialization has brought severe problems for rural Mexico and for employment of the less privileged. Hyperurbanization often means urban dwellers also suffer from a lack of piped water and sewage systems, and from increasing water, soil, and air pollution. Government social expenditures and services have been very unequally directed, in ways that reward some potentially dangerous groups while repressing and marginalizing others. Health benefits for unionized workers are a good example. Consistent with Mexico's elite pluralism, a wide network of private organizations, including schools, universities, and hospitals are available for the privileged.[44] Consequently, economic successes under civilian rule have been compatible with what a World Bank study called one of the world's worst profiles of income distribution.[45] As Table 4.2 shows, the profile did not improve even during decades of growth and selective mobility.

Table 4.2   Income Distribution in Mexico, 1950–1977[a]

Income Group (deciles)	Percentage of Income Earned		
	1950	1963	1977[b]
1–2 (lowest 20 percent)	4.7	3.5	3.3
3–5	12.7	11.5	13.4
6–8	23.7	25.4	28.2
9–10 (highest 20 percent)	58.9	59.6	55.1

Source: Daniel C. Levy and Gabriel Székely, *Mexico: Paradoxes of Stability and Change*, 2nd ed. (Boulder, CO.: Westview Press, 1987): Table 5.6, based on data from ECLA for 1950 and 1963, and Mexico's Secretaría de Programación y Presupuesto for 1977.

a. Similar but even more extreme data are reported in Werner Baer, "Growth with Inequality: The Cases of Brazil and Mexico," *Latin American Research Review* 21, no. 2 (1986): p. 198.

b. 1977 is the last year for which data are available. Although debate exists over whether distribution improved in the immediately ensuing years, it has certainly worsened in the last few.

Thus, or at least thus far, hypotheses linking economic growth to the likelihood of democratic government are not supported in Mexico. Nor does Mexico fit the bureaucratic-authoritarian notion that dependent industrialized development leads at a certain point to instability followed by military rule. Instead, Mexican economic and social modernization has long reinforced stable, undemocratic civilian rule. Still, significantly, such modernization has also increased pressures for democratization.

However much long-term socioeconomic modernization brings pressures, it is probably the recent economic reversal that has most clearly brought pressures. Economic crisis dominated the 1980s. Many see its roots in policies designed for political, not economic, efficiency that built support from business, the middle class, organized labor, and even less privileged groups: protracted import substitution; a variety of credits and subsidies (e.g., for energy, universities, public transportation); low taxes; and bloated public employment. Unfortunately, the government's income increasingly failed to meet its expenditures and huge borrowing resulted. Added to all this, world oil prices fell sharply. And so, Mexico came to face a foreign debt of over $100 billion, blocked and even negative growth, inflation rates of roughly 100 percent, and socially devastating declines in employment and real wages.

No one knows how much economic disaster will undermine political strength. What we do know is that careful manipulation of the fruits of economic success has long been associated with political strength and high support levels. That manipulation long helped sustain a myth of continual progress, which provided legitimacy. In fact, Mexicans have taken pride in their political system and credited it for many of the social and personal material successes they have seen, despite cynicism about politicians and low evaluations of the daily performance of government. Even much of the Left has granted legitimacy for the regime's progressive record in some socioeconomic and particularly nationalist matters.[46]

A decline in long-standing legitimacy is illustrated by attitudes toward corruption; perhaps an increasingly modernized society has decreasing tolerance for it. In any case, corruption is a target of broadly rising popular discontent with a struggling system. And corruption is a target because it recently exceeded vaguely institutionalized limits, under President López Portillo. Thus, de la Madrid made what appeared to be the most serious in a line of presidential commitments to curb corruption. Some measures were taken, such as requiring financial statements from top government appointees and punishing a few ex-officials. By virtually all accounts, however, the clean-up campaign was disappointing. Explanations are varied but, historically, corruption has figured in the regime's performance and legitimacy. We have already seen that opportunities for corruption helped bring the military under civilian control. Additionally, corruption has provided some flexibility in an often unresponsive bureaucracy. It has provided an incentive for major and minor actors to seek rewards within the system and to rely on the peaceful turnover of personnel. It has provided glue for many implicit political pacts among elites and has been integral to patron-client and state-society relationships.

Whether corruption on the Mexican scale is compatible with significant democratization is uncertain. I think it is not. At the same time, corruption is illustrative of factors that may now increasingly undermine legitimacy even as the system has not yet found satisfactory alternatives, democratic or otherwise.

· THEORETICAL ANALYSIS ·

I have tried to show how several factors commonly associated with democratic stability have in Mexico long contributed to stable civilian rule that is not democratic. I have referred throughout to this study's hypotheses about democracy, but I now summarize the argument in the explicit context of those hypotheses. A major problem in so doing is that the hypotheses deal with factors that contribute to democracy, whereas Mexico is not a democracy. Repeatedly, we identify where Mexico has lacked a characteristic associated with democracy, but that offers only indirect evidence to sustain the hypothesis.

Political Culture and Legitimacy

We have seen that political legitimacy in Mexico has been high, though diminishing. Mexicans have been remarkably accepting of their political system. Whether because of a national trait of stoicism, or the fear of disorder, or belief in the regime's positive orientations, Mexicans have at a minimum not rebelled even when their aspirations have been long frustrated, and many have maintained pride in their system.[47]

With respect to democratic values, works on Mexico's "national character" have often depicted hierarchical, authoritarian, submissive, and other undemocratic inclinations. They suggest that such character traits help promote Mexico's authoritarian politics; political culture both explains and legitimizes the political system. On the other hand, most social scientists have been either skeptical or hostile to such interpretations. I am inclined to the Purcells' position: Political culture appears to reinforce the system but it is "striking how much of Mexican politics can be comprehended by a model of the rational political actor."[48] Others argue that the political culture is basically at odds with the political structure. They find that Mexicans support participation and dissent and oppose censorship.[49]

If evidence on deep values remains inconclusive, evidence on behavior is not. Mexico's regime has not been precariously superimposed on a society filled with democratic practices. The society never was so constituted, and the revolution brought new and strong but mostly undemocratic institutions. State corporatism goes hand-in-hand with hierarchical, authoritarian rule inside mass institutions such as unions. And it goes hand-in-hand with limited mass participation, encapsulated and restricted to official channels; patrimonial networks;

and petitions rather than aggregated demands. Allowing for recent signs of increased grassroots participation, the rule has been to hope that government acts. Efficacy increases with socioeconomic status, however.[50] Participation by elites is much freer and more influential, but elite institutions (media, intellectual publications, businesses, private schools, and universities) often operate undemocratically. Pluralism exceeds democracy.

Yet elites display a behavioral norm hypothesized (in this book and elsewhere) to be powerfully associated with democracy. This is the disposition to compromise. Ongoing politics confirm our historical (postrevolutionary) evidence of flexibility, bargaining, moderation, restraint, and pacts that avoid "fights to the finish."[51] In Mexico, acceptance of such norms has contributed to regime consolidation and stability without democracy. First, though elite pacts in democracies often limit mass participation, Mexico's corporatist mass inclusion is distinctly antidemocratic. Second, the restraint in the elite pacts has covered the exclusion of open, organized competition for rulership.

Overall, my view is that the Mexican case presents interesting information on the relationship between political culture and democracy, but not information that strongly confirms or disconfirms major project hypotheses.

Historical Sequences

Mexico scores low on the historical dimensions associated with democracy. Mexico lacks sustained, successful democratic precedents. In fact, it has had few experiments with democratic government. If the present regime has precedents, they are chiefly authoritarian. Where it democratizes, it innovates.

Moreover, Mexico has not followed Dahl's favored route of early liberal contestation followed by mass incorporation.[52] Rather, Calles, Cárdenas, and others adeptly incorporated mass organizations into a corporatist system. If elite pacts in nations like Venezuela have limited the masses' ability to obtain socioeconomic benefits, Mexico's pacts excluded democracy. Mexico's pacts were aimed at controlling masses mobilized by the revolution and established viable, perhaps ingenious, alternatives to open elite contestation for power. Such is the conventional scholarly wisdom on sequences, which I accept. However, if one were to highlight the persistent marginality of unorganized Mexico and perhaps the rise of new groups, or if one were to reserve "inclusiveness" for a more independent mass participation, then Mexico might rank low on that dimension. In that case, recent political reforms expanding contestation, coupled with longer-standing and expanding personal freedoms, might then give some sense of liberalization preceding inclusiveness.

Class, Ethnic, and Religious Cleavages

Key hypotheses on class structure and cumulative cleavages do not suggest favorable conditions for democracy in Mexico. The distribution of wealth is terribly unequal, as data on income show. Despite massive land reform, large agribusiness and an impoverished, massive peasantry divide the land very unequally in terms of both the size and desirability of plots. Mexican agriculture is not characterized by middle-class farming. Moreover, many cleavages are cumulative. A common disadvantaged profile would include low-income, Indian-Mestizo, peasant, and rural south.

Indians form the largest ethnic minority, perhaps 10 percent of the population (depending on definition), though ethnic diversity is largely determined by the "European-Indian" mixes among Mestizos. The revolution brought some respect for Indian identity, and pockets of self-governance exist (with some direct democratic selection of leaders and policies). Mostly, however, the Indian population continues to be either marginalized or integrated into a servile underclass, despite some mobility for individuals. In turn, the "rule of law" and the state are often seen as oppressive alien forces by Indian communities. Of interest are increasing signs of ethnically based political demands.[53] Overall, however, Indian distinctiveness hardly translates into pluralist politics.

The regime has been effective in defusing the destabilizing potential of great societal diversity and cumulative cleavages. One way has been to grant autonomy to groups and institutions (e.g., religious) that avoid mainstream politics. This, of course, fits Linz's now classic notion of authoritarian regimes.[54]

Second, the regime handles much of its politics in ways that cut across class cleavages—not on basic distributive policies but on symbolic and organizational ones. Symbolically, it has successfully used nationalism even if the concept means somewhat different things to different groups. Organizationally, it has structured itself on "vertical" patron-client relationships. This reinforces hierarchy and other undemocratic societal norms. The "formation of horizontal alliances based on common class interests is impeded" and the relationships serve "to maintain the separation between ideology and its social base."[55]

Third, as noted earlier, the regime has been sophisticated in managing privileged groups differently from other groups. Allowing for important flexibility, and other qualifications, state relationships with mass organizations are corporatist, whereas state relationships with elite groups are much more pluralist. But autonomous elite organizations have not usually been run democratically, nor, perhaps more to the point, have they pressured for democratization. Instead, they have normally accepted a stable nondemocracy that has granted them considerable material reward and a substantial if restricted degree of freedom.[56]

State Structure and Strength

Although state strength is a necessary condition for democratic stability, it is not sufficient. Lack of strength may doom a democratic experiment, but in Mexico state strength has meant the stability of an undemocratic system.

Building authority was a historic accomplishment of the postrevolutionary regime. The regime's stability is unique in both historical and comparative perspective. The regime has centralized power, maintained order, and preserved civilian rule. It has created an adept political class, while controlling mass groups and excluding organized challenges to its rule. Nonetheless, the state has not been the nearly omnipotent political force that much of the literature on Mexican authoritarianism has depicted. Its power has been limited by business and the middle class, and it has had to work out deals and make compromises with organized labor and even with less privileged groups. We have seen, for example, that the state lacked the capacity to tax sufficiently to pay for the political bargains it struck. A further qualification is that the regime's legitimacy and strength have substantially weakened in recent years.

One element in the regime's political strength was its early and sustained control over key parts of the economy. Unaccompanied by great bureaucratic professional autonomy from partisan politics, such statism is hypothesized to diminish prospects for democracy. However, it is simply impossible to know whether a causal relationship holds in Mexico, though the idea is in vogue in some business circles. What is clearer is that statism promoted civilian stability. It provided populist legitimacy; the nationalization of oil (1938) is a notable example. And it gave the regime tremendous political leverage.

Even though the Mexican economy has for the most part been privately owned, the state has owned such sectors as oil, mining, electricity, railroads, and, since 1982, banks. It has been heavily involved in regulation, subsidies, public investments, public credits, and so forth. It has established institutions such as the Central Bank (1925), the National Development Bank (1934), and a tremendous network of parastatal agencies. Measures such as the public expenditure's share of GDP show even a recently expanded state role (22 percent in 1970 to 44 percent in 1983).[57] But de la Madrid undertook a reversal. Citing counterproductive political effects of statism but concerned chiefly about economic crisis and inefficiencies, the president repeatedly cut state expenditures, employment, and subsidies. He sold off many state enterprises and brought Mexico into the GATT. His selection of Salinas de Gortari as his successor was apparently aimed at sustaining this historic change in economic policy. The consequences for democratization remain uncertain.

Political Structure and Leadership

The structural reality of Mexico's undemocratic civilian rule has been overwhelmingly centralized. Mexico's has been a presidential system with only limited roles for the judiciary, the legislature, and state and local government. More liberalism, though still restricted, has been evident regarding the rule of law, freedom of the media, and other liberties. But the party system was long characterized by PRI hegemony and integration with the regime. The PRI has generally been pragmatic. It has been at least somewhat inclusionary and has built a multiclass base. It has kept the vote for extremist parties very small. Yet, like other successes of the centralized party-regime, these have served civilian stability without democracy. Earlier interpretations of a political structure purposefully or ineluctably evolving into liberal forms have proved naive. On the other hand, the recent ineffectiveness of centralized forms has raised interesting speculations about future changes in Mexico's political structure.

Like the political structure, political leadership in postrevolutionary Mexico has proven unusually effective, and this effectiveness has been crucial to sustaining civilian rule without democracy. In fact, leadership and structure have been intertwined. Leaders have created and respected structures strong enough to condition behavior but flexible enough to allow for change and continual leadership.

Mexico takes second place to no nation in the skill and will of leadership to build a viable civilian system out of a past characterized mostly by weak political rule. I have highlighted the formative leadership acts of Carranza, Obregón, Calles, and Cárdenas in establishing legitimate, inclusive, centralized, civilian rule. Their acts provide powerful evidence for those political scientists who have championed the resurgence of "politics" and "choice" as major variables in studies of development. For example, Almond and Mundt write that a rational prediction from coalition theory would have pointed toward a military coup in the 1930s, but Cárdenas pulled off the "most striking" leadership success discussed in their volume featuring choice in a number of nations.[58] But unlike leaders in the Venezuelan case or in contemporary Argentina, Brazil, and other Latin American nations, Mexico's civilian leaders have not acted out of a commitment to democracy. On the contrary, some Mexican leaders have been hostile to democracy as a foreign, unworkable model, whereas others have been indifferent, and still others see democracy as an ideal too risky for Mexico today. Yet another view, however, is that realities have changed to where blocking democratization has become too risky.

Political learning has been crucial to Mexico's civilian success, but: (a) most of its leaders have not set democracy as their goal; and (b) the lessons have been undemocratic ones. Again, unlike Venezuela, with its *trienio,* not to mention Argentina, Brazil, and (at an extreme) Uruguay, Mexico has not had a modern liberal experiment that made headway before failing. Mexico would have to look back to the Reform for even a mixed record with liberal politics; the Madero interlude at the beginning of the revolution represents more recent failure. Most of the nineteenth century and the first two revolutionary decades suggested to elites the impracticality of decentralized systems and the dangers of excessive competition among elites. The revolution also impressed on them the need for elite pacts to forestall devastating actions by the masses.

By definition, an institutionalized system does not require continual acts of great formative leadership. Instead, Mexico managed to create a strong political class. This class has boasted many of the traits of successful professions: comparative autonomy, status, authority, and power; and control over training and rites of entry. Since the 1940s (with due qualifications for the deterioration elaborated above), Mexico's leaders have shaped politics in ways largely associated with establishing or even the smooth functioning of democracy. Yet for each aspect, the shaping has been distinctly undemocratic. The party has incorporated and legitimized but has also encapsulated. Sexennial rule has guaranteed mobility, turnover, renewal, and flexibility, but not public choice of leaders. Leaders have denounced disloyalty to the system and violence against the system, but have regarded some democratic dissent as disloyal and have used violence against peaceful dissenters. They have contained conflicts and managed crises enviably, but their tools have been predominantly undemocratic. Formative leaders shrewdly forged pacts among conflicting elites, and subsequent leaders have continually bargained, compromised, and disciplined themselves and their followers to accept less than optimal outcomes. Such procedures have excluded democratic opponents, limited mass participation, and often worked against mass material interests. Leaders have also subtly varied their approaches (depending on time, place, policy field, and constituency) in ways that show a greater sensitivity to and understanding of the public than most authoritarian regimes have, but such sophistication is not synonymous with democracy. Thus, we see corporatism mixed with pluralism, repression with cooptation and acquiescence, and continuity with flexibility.

Development Performance

Political leadership also played a major role in establishing Mexico's decades of high growth with low inflation. Legitimacy, stability, and incentives were crucial, though so were repression and sanctions. Why did sustained growth (inconsistency and reversal are recent phenomena) not produce democracy?

One explanation concerns Mexico's failure to attain the kind of sustained growth hypothesized to promote democracy, growth whose fruits are well distributed. Mexico's have been horribly maldistributed. A middle class has grown, but its commitment to democracy remains debatable (as it does in comparative politics generally), and much of Mexico's middle class has been dependent on the state. Moreover, the rise of the middle class has not been part of a generalized equalization of wealth or a broad movement involving coalitions with mass groups. In fact, a second possible explanation for the lack of democratization is that the growth argument is by itself irrelevant to democracy, or even that growth may serve the interests of reigning undemocratic regimes. In Mexico, growth has contributed to the legitimacy and power of such a regime. It has allowed it to manipulate, reward, and claim credit.

A third explanation, compatible with the first two, is that growth can help efforts at democratization (perhaps is even vital to them) but is just one factor and therefore insufficient.[59] I am inclined to believe that changes brought about by sustained growth in Mexico eventually promote pressures for broad democratization, that they in fact have contributed some to liberalization. In short, there is much to conventional development theses about an association between growth and social change, and between both and the chances for democracy.[60] Still, chances are far from certainties and it is difficult to gauge effects. The record shows that decades of growth produced comparatively limited pressures for democracy in Mexico, and more limited results. The strongest calls for democratization have come since growth was reversed.

To sum up, growth may well increase the chances for democracy eventually, but for a long time it may well shore up almost any regime. After all, the fall of Latin American authoritarian regimes, like Latin American democracies, has been tied to economic failure more than success. In Mexico, growth has been integral to the stability of civilian authoritarian rule.

International Factors

As with so many other variables in this comparative study, international factors hypothesized to be conducive to democratic stability have, in Mexico, long been conducive to stability without democracy. For one, Mexico has not been a significant target of external subversion since the regime consolidated power. But such fortune is much more likely to sustain than to create democracy. Second, the major source of diffusion—given realities of geography, continual back-and-forth migration, trade, investment, and cultural and media might— has long been the United States, a democracy. Third, Mexico has been a recipient of extraordinary foreign assistance from the United States and other democracies, though the emphasis is recent. Whereas the second and third realities are postulated to have democratizing influences even on undemocratic systems, Mexican leadership has limited the degree of political dependency and influence that accompany economic dependency on the United States.

Protecting itself from leftist subversion has been one reason for Mexico's progressive foreign policy. The only Latin American nation not to break diplomatic relations with Communist Cuba, Mexico was never targeted the way Bolivia, Venezuela, and others were. Comparatively sympathetic to the Sandinistas and to the guerrillas in El Salvador, Mexico again achieved an at least tacit agreement that leftists outside Mexico would not encourage independent leftists inside.

Into the bargain, such progressivism has enhanced legitimacy by demonstrating independence of the United States. Given a historical legacy of military conquest (costing Mexico much of her good land) and an ongoing contrast of wealth and culture, it is not surprising that Mexicans would feel alienation as well as respect for their neighbor. Something seen as a U.S. model—and liberal democracy as defined in this book fits here—is not simply seen positively. Moreover, to the degree that the United States has leverage stemming from its might, its priority for Mexico has been stability, not democratization. So, despite the fact that it has depended on the United States for almost two-thirds of its imports and exports, roughly 80 percent of its tourism, and roughly

70 percent of its foreign investment, Mexico has maintained a notable degree of independence from U.S. influence.[61]

• PROSPECTS AND POLICY IMPLICATIONS •

However much cited variables may have contributed to sustaining civilian stability without democracy, Mexican politics is changing. Of course, it has constantly changed, and one of the strengths of the system and its leadership has been the flexibility to modify a stable system. The question here is whether contemporary changes will add up to more than adaptation within a nondemocracy. In an important sense, factors that have reinforced stability have blocked democratization. That does not prove, however, that they will always do so. Nor does it suggest that instability is likely to produce democracy.[62] Major change is a necessary but insufficient condition for democratization.

Positive Prospects for Democratization

Numerous political uncertainties represent some hope for democratization. First, the erosion of undemocratic practices opens at least some possibility of democratic alternatives and strengthens opposition voices. Second, the regime's realization that traditional bases of stability are endangered can stimulate liberalizing moves aimed at protecting stability. Third, some of the uncertainties themselves involve a degree of opening. To be sure, the second and third points involve liberalization rather than transformation toward a democracy, as defined here. Nevertheless, just as Mexico has enjoyed several aspects of democracy, so it may increase the degree of democracy. Moreover, continued liberalization may, in turn, increase the pressures for such practices as free elections among truly competitive alternative parties. In fact, one can imagine the 1988 elections reinforcing many factors considered here as favorable to democratization.

The following recapitulates some of the major recent political changes that involve uncertainties. Regarding state-society relations, the degree of freedom (e.g., media freedom) has expanded. Middle-class, business, and even grassroots popular groups have organized more autonomously and become much more critical of the regime. Regarding centralized regime power, the presidency has been tarnished, the legislature is increasingly a forum of debate and dissent, and perceptions are widespread that geographical centralization is excessive, and that significant decentralization must somehow be achieved. Regarding the party system, the PRI (like the political class overall) has lost much of its strength, while an independent Left has appeared and the independent Right has grown substantially. For the middle class in particular, elections have become times of delegitimation more than popular affirmation. Pressures for honest elections are strong, perhaps undeniably so in the aftermath of the 1988 elections. The party and electoral reforms inaugurated in the 1970s have helped

open the system significantly but have not settled the issue of how far the opening will go. Regarding the regime's performance, legitimacy has eroded and the
economy—long central to the regime's strength—has fallen into crisis. Economic opening, even if ultimately successful in purely economic terms, might
well reduce the regime's tools of control.

Political reform, uncertainty, and (regime) weakness have contributed to
increased calls for democratization. Such calls are not new, of course. For
years, some observers argued that democratization was necessary for
socioeconomic development and, therefore, for political stability. These observations have not fared well, but perhaps they are valid in the long run. Or
perhaps circumstances have changed enough in Mexico that they are now becoming valid. At any rate, previous calls for democratization have not been
nearly as widespread and sustained as today's. Nor did they enjoy the degree of
free space for development that dissenters now have.

Naturally, proponents of democratization are not united. They do not hold
identical views of what democracy means, nor how to pursue it (though the
broad coalition formed, in 1986, reinforced in 1988, around the banner of truly
free elections is significant). Voices on the Right argue in terms partly consistent with major hypotheses of this project: a highly centralized state with massive power concentrated in an unchecked presidency, which exercises extensive
corporate controls over society and the economy, is incompatible with democracy. By contrast, most of the Left argues that democratization requires a large
and revitalized state assuming a central role in economic policy and social
change. But many on the Right want merely a return to a successful undemocratic state that grants concessions to business, suppresses labor, and so forth.
And many on the Left couple demands for a revitalized state with demands for
increased autonomy of societal organizations and for internal democratization
within labor unions, neighborhood organizations, and other institutions. Finally, one may question the sincerity of certain democratic banners on both the
Right and the Left. For some, such banners are but a tool in the play for power.
For others, democracy is a worthy pursuit, but principally a means toward
higher priorities. Thus, some business leaders see democracy largely as a way
to weaken government and achieve growth and profits, and some intellectuals
see democracy as a means of mass mobilization to achieve better socioeconomic distribution and, eventually, socialism.

Another way to see hopeful signs for democratization is to focus on the
many ways in which Mexico ranks high on variables associated with democracies. In terms of our variables, my thesis has been that Mexico shows that
many of the variables are compatible with a civilian rule that is effective, stable,
and undemocratic. That thesis has allowed, however, that Mexico's high standing on some of the variables may have built certain pressures for democratization. The notion of "zones" of lower and higher probabilities for democracy
may be useful in assessing Mexico's future. Economic growth, industrialization, urbanization, the growth of a middle class, increased education and other

indices of rising expectations among even the poorer classes, the persistence of at least formal structures of liberal government, growing if still inconclusive evidence of some political cultural affect for democracy—these and other factors put Mexico in a higher zone of probability for democracy than would have been the case even a couple of decades ago.[63]

Recent research on transitions to democracy also suggests some hopes for democratization in Mexico, though O'Donnell rightly labels Mexico "a type by itself" (largely because the regime is so institutionalized). First, authoritarian regimes constantly evolve. Second, transitions usually occur through evolution, not sudden overthrows. Third, democracy usually results from stalemate and dissensus, not from a clear plan based on consensus. Fourth, these transitions usually begin with elite calculations and initiatives, not independent mass mobilization. When the regime initiates liberalization, it runs risks of losing the initiative amid rising expectations and mobilizations, but it can sometimes control the pace of change, experiment, retreat, and so forth. Fifth, democratization often emerges from situations with seemingly low probabilities for it.[64] In sum, the lack of a clear or massive movement toward democracy in Mexico does not preclude democratization. And the experimental, evolutionary, regime-led notion of transition could allow further societal liberalizations involving press freedom, criticism (short of organized mass alternatives to the regime), and party and electoral reform. Reform within the PRI, expanded representation for oppositions, and opposition victories in localities and even states could occur without immediate threat to the regime's rule. Nor after the shock of 1988 does it seem naive to speculate on even the transfer of national government to the opposition, or at least on opposition appointments to cabinet positions.

The Brazilian case is particularly interesting for speculations on Mexico.[65] Brazilian authoritarian rule was comparatively long and economically successful on its own terms, with massive inequalities. Repression was comparatively limited in the years prior to transition. In fact, constitutional forms persisted almost throughout the dictatorial period, and the limited term of the presidency proved significant. Elections took on increasing importance even as the regime manipulated the rules. Transition was stimulated by long-term factors, but an economic downturn critically undermined support for the regime. Nonetheless, unlike some other cases, democratization was not precipitated by mass mobilizations but by elite accommodations. In short, the Brazilian case illustrates how democratization need not be an all-or-nothing proposition. This fact can make the prospect less threatening for the Mexican regime, which realizes that some political changes are necessary.

Negative Prospects for Democratization

But the factors that point away from full-blown democratization remain weighty. This is especially evident if we refer to democratization as a transition toward democratic government and not just further liberalization. Obviously, transformation is less common than continuity. Beyond that, Mexican authoritarianism has been uniquely long-lasting and institutionalized. Unlike other authoritarian regimes, Mexico's has always justified itself as permanent (albeit evolving) rather than transitory *en route* to democracy.

Whereas factors commonly associated with democracy are found in Mexico, others are not. Mexico lacks significant experience with democratic government (though I would emphasize the potential importance of increasing experience with liberalizing politics). Despite its declining legitimacy, the regime has not been discredited in the dramatic way that sometimes leads to democratic transitions (e.g., in Argentina) or that leads major actors to value democracy as an alternative system of rule. Not all the rising criticism of the Mexican regime concerns its lack of democracy. The political-cultural attachment of the masses to democracy is questionable, and elites have given uncertain evidence of such attachment. Opposition parties, indeed organized oppositions in general, have usually been limited. Corporatist controls have precluded both independent mass-based institutions (unions or parties) and sudden mobilization of the unorganized. The state retains a large role in politics and the economy. And poverty remains widespread, wealth painfully concentrated.

Prospects for any liberalization are also limited because of the risks of transition.[66] Fear is a central notion in the relevant literature; in Mexico, the fear of transition has dominated the perceived need for or benefits of transition. To be sure, even before the 1988 elections some in the regime, as well as critics, believed that the system required major changes. President de la Madrid spoke repeatedly of how changes in demographics, urbanization, education, communications, and class structure have created "a new vigor in society," a greatly expanded "civil society" that requires political changes. As in Colombia, a widespread perception is that conditions that called for structures of restricted, stable civilian rule have been superseded. But, also as in Colombia, powerful political incentives are built into the status quo. Even the "soft-liners" within the Mexican regime have focused on modernizing measures (including liberalizing ones) that would not produce a liberal democracy. Cornelius writes that the regime, and indeed the elites in general, regard two-party or multiparty competition for and alternation in power as an alien concept.[67] "Democracy" has meant the PRI as the "party of majorities," with opposition voice allowed. Some argue that a return to economic normalcy is all that is required for politics to return to normal. And many, whatever their ultimate hopes, believe that times of great economic change, and of some inevitable political change, require steadying reliance on established political structures and practices.

Crucially, fear of transition is not limited to the regime or even the elites overall. As Monsiváis has emphasized, the regime has succeeded in portraying alternatives to it as disasters, as fascism, communism, or anarchy.[68] Anarchy is perhaps particularly frightening to many Mexicans, perhaps because of the nation's history. Consequently, another point about democratization in nations like

Venezuela is relevant in Mexico, again with a twist. As Levine writes in this volume, a major reason for Venezuela's democratic stability is that citizens realize they "can afford little else," given authoritarian alternatives. In Mexico, many citizens have found that they could well afford something other than democracy: Their system has provided them with relative social peace and political tranquility, economic growth, mobility, selective rather than pervasive repression, a degree of political liberty, and substantial national pride.

In sum, the prospects for democracy are brighter than they have been since the revolution. And yet, they are very uncertain. The prospects for stability are perhaps dimmer than they have been for several decades. And yet, they are bright, remaining brighter than the prospects for democracy. Such contrasts reflect the way Mexico's strong, undemocratic political system has long functioned.

U.S. Policy

If democratization merits increasing serious attention, but democracy still appears only a possibility in Mexico, what should the United States do? The conventional scholarly wisdom has been: not much. I concur.

I do not believe that all attempts by one nation to encourage democracy in another are wrong, but I do believe that several demanding criteria ought to be present. They usually are not. First, a viable alternative to the present regime must exist. Second, that alternative should be more democratic than the present regime. Third, a rather limited role by the foreign nation should have a high probability of making a substantial positive impact.

None of these conditions has characterized the case of Mexico and the United States, although the first two points could be debated in light of the 1988 elections. Much of this chapter has concerned why no viable alternative to the regime has been organized. Leading opposition parties and groups have not proved their democratic credentials. And even if U.S. policymakers believed a viable and democratic alternative existed, their efforts would likely have either an insignificant or negative impact. For one thing, the Mexico–U.S. relationship is particularly sensitive, given historical, geographical, economic, and cultural realities. For example, President Wilson's military interventions and threats in the early revolutionary years contributed to turmoil, not democracy, and left a legacy of mistrust about the democratic giant to the north. In the early 1980s, perceptions that Ambassador John Gavin and U.S. Republican Party leaders supported the PAN probably hurt that opposition party, as the PRI identified it with a still-arrogant, interfering neighbor.

Beyond the particular sensitivities of Mexico–U.S. relations lie broader obstacles to government efforts to encourage democracy. Whitehead concludes that in peacetime, the overall international role in democratization is subordinate; U.S. efforts in Latin America have with reason been viewed as "showcase" and short-term.[69] Whether or not the United States deserves any credit for the wave of Latin American democratization in the 1980s, its clearest successes have come in protesting grievous human-rights abuses; such abuses have been less characteristic of Mexico than of the bureaucratic-authoritarian regimes. Moreover, this comparative study of Third World democracies reminds us of the variability, complexity, and uncertainty of the conditions that promote democracy. In any event, particular cases present their own dynamics, as we have repeatedly seen for Mexico. Even if we could identify clearly the factors associated with democracy, we would be left with a standard research-policy question: How do we move from the present to the desired future? Rallying cries of the U.S. Right and simplifications by both Democratic and Republican administrations to the contrary, we know little about this.

In reality, U.S. pressures have not concerned democratization, or most other aspects of Mexican domestic politics, as much as Mexican economic and foreign policy. Again, we really do not know what economic and foreign policies, against which the United States has brought pressure, have been identifiably associated with the stability of Mexico's civilian rule. Regarding foreign policy, for example, the United States should therefore recognize that Mexico has based its foreign policy not on naive leftist notions or anti-Americanism but on sober judgments about its own security from external threats and from domestic delegitimation. If U.S. pressure can "work"—in the sense of influencing Mexican foreign policy, and if times of Mexican economic weakness make some such influence possible—impacts on Mexico's political stability may be negative.

A more reasonable course for the United States is to support Mexico's political stability. This can be done in the hope that stability will allow for democratization, but mostly in the realization that instability is even less likely to produce democratization, and that stability is important on other grounds. If these admittedly debatable assumptions are accepted, several oft-cited measures to support stability make sense. Some, such as easing terms on debt payment, reducing protectionism, and providing economic aid, are not particular to Mexico but have special relevance there. Others are more particular to Mexico, such as guaranteeing the safety valve of migration and not discouraging tourism and investment by portraying Mexico as too lenient with drug dealers and Communists. Moreover, the United States should temper the arrogance that views Mexico's troubles as the simple result of poor policy, not to mention political-cultural backwardness. Instead, the United States should respect the successes of the Mexican political system and the enormous difficulties and dilemmas of meeting present challenges. And the United States should realize that many of these challenges result from factors for which Mexico is not solely responsible, such as excessive U.S. bank loans, high U.S. interest rates, and fallen oil prices.

None of this is to deny the U.S. government a right to express critical opinions about Mexican politics, including its markedly undemocratic aspects, but advocacy and heavy pressure are different matters. Nor is it to ignore the possible positive impact on democratization of some private actors. For example, recently increased foundation aid to academic institutions and scholarship recipients seems legitimate and hopeful, though effects would typically be indirect, long-term, and difficult to gauge.

To conclude, the possibilities of external influence on democratization are limited—and largely negative. And there is much to lose. Things can get worse. Regarding U.S. self-interest, this should be clear from the stability, markets, labor, resources, and so forth, that Mexico has provided. For Mexicans, there is also much to lose. On the political side, even restricted degrees of freedom and liberalization count. Unparalleled stability stands out more in Mexico. There is also much to criticize and work for politically. Democratization is a prime example, but perhaps major improvements remain less likely than major losses.

Should Mexico continue to liberalize and even democratize without shattering its stability, it will have achieved a truly historic and magnificent political feat. Our understanding of the conditions for Third World democracy would be profoundly affected. For most of the century, however, Mexican reality has shown how many conditions conducive to sustained civilian rule can have neutral or even negative implications for democracy.

• NOTES •

I thank John Bailey and Gabriel Székely, as well as their series editors, for the comments on drafts of this chapter.

1. Mexico's population, over 80 million, ranks second in Latin America and eleventh in the world; its economic size ranks roughly fifteenth among market economies; and its geography makes its fate vital for the United States. I use democracy in the sense of a desired result, democratization as movement in that direction, and liberalization as movement in terms of at least increased freedoms.

2. On breakdown, see Juan Linz and Alfred Stepan, eds., *The Breakdown of Democratic Regimes* (Baltimore, MD: Johns Hopkins University Press, 1978). On democratization, see Guillermo O'Donnell, Philippe C. Schmitter, and Laurence Whitehead, eds., *Transitions from Authoritarian Rule: Prospects for Democracy* (Baltimore, MD: Johns Hopkins University Press, 1986).

3. Robert Scott, *Mexican Government in Transition* (Urbana: University of Illinois Press, 1964), pp. 16, 300–301.

4. See, for example, the citations and analysis in Daniel C. Levy and Gabriel Székely, *Mexico: Paradoxes of Stability and Change*, 2nd ed. (Boulder, CO: Westview Press, 1987), ch. 4.

5. Kenneth F. Johnson and Philip L. Kelly, "Political Democracy in Latin America," *LASA Forum* 16, no. 4 (1986): pp. 19–22, has the most recent data and points the reader to earlier sources.

6. Octavio Paz, *The Other Mexico: Critique of the Pyramid*, tr. Lysander Kemp (New York: Grave Press, 1972), pp. 102, 111. Some Indian villages enjoyed self-government in the precolonial and colonial eras.

7. See, for example, Juan Felipe Leal, "El estado y el bloque en el poder en México: 1867–1914," *Latin American Perspectives* 11, no. 2 (1975): p. 38.

8. A standard work on the integration is Arnaldo Córdova, *La formación del poder en México*, 8th ed. (Mexico City: Serie Popular Era, 1980).

9. Two major accounts are Tzvi Medín, *Ideología y praxis político de Lázaro Cárdenas* (Mexico City: Siglo XXI, 1976); and Wayne A. Cornelius, "Nation Building, Participation, Distribution: Reform Under Cárdenas." In *Crisis, Choice, and Change: Historical Studies of Political Development*, ed. Gabriel A. Almond, Scott C. Flanigan, and Robert J. Mundt (Boston: Little, Brown, 1973), p. 394, 429–462.

10. I use the terms as elaborated in Philippe C. Schmitter's widely cited "Still the Century of

Corporatism?" In *The New Corporatism,* ed. Frederick Pike and Thomas Stritch (Notre Dame, IN: University of Notre Dame Press, 1974), pp. 93–105.

11. On political marginality, see Pablo González Casanova, *Democracy in Mexico,* tr. Danielle Salti (London: Oxford University Press, 1970), pp. 126–134; on reacting, see Susan Kaufman Purcell, *The Mexican Profit-Making Decision: Politics in an Authoritarian Regime* (Berkeley: University of California Press, 1975).

12. See Evelyn Stevens, *Protest and Response in Mexico* (Cambridge, MA: MIT Press, 1974), pp. 276–277, on how activists have been unable to attract mass followings. On the consequences of early incorporation, see Robert R. Kaufman, "Mexico and Latin American Authoritarianism." In José Luis Reyna and Richard S. Wienert, *Authoritarianism in Mexico* (Philadelphia: ISHI, 1977), pp. 220–221.

13. See, for example, Jesús Silva Herzog, *La revolución mexicana en crisis* (Mexico City: Ediciones Cuadernos Americanos, 1944), pp. 22–34; and for a similar point on peasants, see Gerrit Huizer, "Peasant Organization in Agrarian Reform in Mexico." In *Masses in Latin America,* ed. Irving Louis Horowitz (New York: Oxford University Press, 1970), pp. 445–502.

14. Raúl Trejo Delarbre, "El movimiento obrero: Situación y perspectivas." In *México, hoy,* 5th ed., ed. Pablo González Casanova and Enrique Florescano (Mexico City: Siglo XXI, 1981), pp. 128–130.

15. Dale Story, *Industry, the State, and Public Policy in Mexico* (Austin: University of Texas Press, 1986), pp. 105, 195. See also John J. Bailey, *Governing Mexico: The Statecraft of Crisis Management* (London: MacMillan, forthcoming), ch. 6.

16. On intellectuals, see Roderic A. Camp, *Intellectuals and the State in Twentieth-Century Mexico* (Austin: University of Texas Press, 1985); on public universities, see Daniel C. Levy, *University and Government in Mexico: Autonomy in an Authoritarian System* (New York: Praeger, 1980).

17. While this case cannot settle the debate over whether national political democratization requires democratizing society's associational life, it is pertinent that Mexico's mass-based organizations are notoriously undemocratic. For example, both labor and peasant elections are controlled and corrupt. Practice varies among the associations of more privileged classes; many media, intellectual, and student associations are far from open and free. See, for example, Camp, *Intellectuals,* p. 225.

18. See especially Sergio Zermeño, *México: Una democracia utópica: El movimiento estudiantil del 68* (Mexico City: Siglo XXI, 1978). My views and further citations are found in Levy, *University,* pp. 28–33, 39–41.

19. In Frank Brandenburg's apt label for the regime, "liberal Machiavellian," "liberal" refers to tolerance more than the Dahl/O'Donnell-Schmitter sense of contestation. Brandenburg, *The Making of Modern Mexico* (Englewood Cliffs, NJ: Prentice Hall, 1964), pp. 141–165. Disturbing evidence of intolerance has long come from brutal repression of peasant actions and, recently, from reports about human-rights abuses including torture.

20. Jorge G. Castañeda, "Mexico at the Brink," *Foreign Affairs* 64 (Winter 1985–1986): p. 293.

21. Richard Fagen and William Tuohy, *Politics in a Mexican Village* (Stanford, CA: Stanford University Press, 1969).

22. Levy and Székely, *Mexico,* ch. 4.

23. González Casanova, *Democracy,* p. 68.

24. Alvaro Arreola Ayala, "Elecciones municipales." In *Las elecciones en México: Evolución y perspectivas,* ed. Pablo González Casanova (Mexico City: Siglo XXI, 1985), pp. 330–336. While some observers find local political participation minimal, others see competition within the PRI that includes citizen support for political wings or for candidates proposing popular policies (e.g., improvement of water or electrical systems).

25. Brian Latell, *Mexico at the Crossroads: The Many Crises of the Political System* (Stanford, CA: Hoover Institution, June 1986), pp. 23–25; Miguel de la Madrid, *Los grandes problemas nacionales de hoy* (Mexico City: Editorial Diana, 1982), p. 139.

26. Bailey, *Governing,* ch. 4. See also, on presidential power, Jorge Carpizo, *El presidencialismo mexicano,* 3d ed. (Mexico City: Siglo XXI, 1983).

27. Fernando Henrique Cardoso, "On the Characterization of Authoritarian Regimes in Latin America." In *The New Authoritarianism in Latin America,* ed. David Collier (Princeton, NJ: Princeton University Press, 1979), pp. 42–43.

28. Kevin J. Middlebrook, "Political Liberalization in an Authoritarian Regime: The Case of Mexico." In O'Donnell, Schmitter, and Whitehead, *Transitions from Authoritarian Rule: Latin America*, p. 140.

29. Norman Cox, "Changes in the Mexican Political System." In *Politics in Mexico*, ed. George Philip (London: Croom Helm, 1985), p. 20; Scott, *Mexican Government*, pp. 267–271.

30. A prominent recent source is David Ronfeldt, *The Modern Mexican Military: A Reassessment*. Monograph Series 16 (La Jolla, CA: Center for U.S.–Mexican Studies, University of California at San Diego, 1984).

31. Gustavo Ernesto Emmerich, "Las elecciones en México, 1808–1911: Surfragio electivo, no reelección?" In González Casanova, *Elecciones*, pp. 54–64.

32. Luis Javier Garrido, *El partido de la revolución institucionalizada 1929–45* (Mexico City: Siglo XXI, 1982); González Casanova, *Democracy*, p. 34.

33. This class has been comparatively distinct from the nation's economic elites, despite greatly overlapping interests. Martin C. Needler has compared it to the East European "new class" described by Djilas, except that it has more legitimate and effective in its ownership of state power. See Needler, *Mexican Politics: The Containment of Conflict* (New York: Praeger, 1982), pp. 131–133. Intertwined with the official party, the political class has lacked career service and merit characteristics, but its strength has been tied to its politicization. Recently, however, the class's coherence has been weakened by a surge of technocrats who rise to high posts based on special educational credentials rather than apprenticeship with the party, elective office, public universities, mass organizations, and so forth. See, for example, Roderic A. Camp, "The Political-Technocrat in Mexico and the Survival of the Political System," *Latin American Research Review* 20, no. 1 (1985): pp. 97–118. Additionally, economic opening and diminishing ratios of state expenditures to GDP could mean diminished resources to reward and sanction (e.g., through subsidies and protectionism).

34. Bailey, *Governing*, ch. 7.

35. Implemented reforms have been limited to measures such as selecting candidates with local appeal and varying selection methods. PRI candidates for some 1984 municipal posts were selected after open party assemblies or secret votes rather than just by appointment from above. See Cox, "Changes," p. 28. The PRI has issued some statements critical of government economic policy.

36. On leftist weaknesses and platforms, see, for example, Barry Carr, "The PSUM: The Unification Process on the Mexican Left 1981–1985." In *Mexican Politics in Transition*, ed. Judith Gentleman (Boulder, CO.: Westview Press, forthcoming).

37. Congressional opposition parties unanimously voted against the 1986 legislation, calling it more marginal maneuvering than democratization. For details on the 1977 reform, see Luis Villoro, "La reforma política y las perspectivas de democracia." In González Casanova and Florescano, *México, hoy*, pp. 355–357. On the 1986 reform, see Juan Gerardo Reyes, "Iniciativa de MMH al Congreso," *Excélsior* (November 4, 1986). PR was first authorized in 1963, but the opposition could barely qualify.

38. Villoro, "Reforma," pp. 355–357; and Middlebrook, "Political Liberalization," pp. 126–128. Middlebrook concludes (p. 143) that the regime operated "from a position of strength." That is true in comparison with many transitions in Latin America, but his own analysis properly identifies challenges to which the Mexican regime felt compelled to respond.

39. Some states then chose reform anyway. See Jorge Madrazo, "Reforma política y legislación electoral de las entidades federativas." In González Casanova, *Elecciones*, pp. 293–302.

40. Terry Lynn Karl, "Petroleum and Political Pacts: The Transition to Democracy in Venezuela." In O'Donnell, Schmitter, and Whitehead, *Transitions: Latin America*, p. 217.

41. Advertisement in *Proceso* (September 1, 1986). On Chihuahua, see, for example, Francisco Ortiz P., "Baeza, acorralado," *Proceso* (June 8, 1987).

42. 1980 data from Bela Belassa, et al., *Toward Renewed Economic Growth in Latin America: Summary, Overview, and Recommendations* (Washington, DC: Institute for International Economics, 1986), pp. 56–57. For 1985, see Inter-American Development Bank, *Economic and Social Progress in Latin America, 1986 Report* (Washington, DC: IDB, n.d.), p. 314 (on Mexico); see also Table 1.1 herein.

43. Miguel de la Madrid Hurtado, "Cuarto informe de gobierno," *Comercio Exterior* 36, no. 9 (1986): p. 760.

44. See, for example, Daniel C. Levy, *Higher Education and the State in Latin America:*

Private Challenges to Public Dominance (Chicago: University of Chicago Press, 1986), pp. 114–170.

45. World Bank, *World Development Report, 1980* (Washington, DC: World Bank, 1980), pp. 156–157.

46. Gabriel A. Almond and Sidney Verba, *The Civic Culture* (Boston: Little, Brown, 1963); Ann L. Craig and Wayne A. Cornelius, "Political Culture in Mexico: Continuities and Revisionist Interpretations." In *The Civic Culture Revisited,* ed. Gabriel A. Almond and Sidney Verba (Boston: Little, Brown, 1980), p. 375. See also Fagen and Tuohy, *Political,* pp. 38–39, 136–137.

47. The three respective explanations of acceptance are emphasized in, for example, Paz, *The Other,* Fagen and Tuohy, *Politics,* and Almond and Verba, *Civic Culture* (1963). Observers are divided on whether there has been a significant increase in civil disturbances.

48. Susan Kaufman Purcell and John F. H. Purcell, "State and Society in Mexico: Must a Stable Polity Be Institutionalized?" *World Politics* 32, no. 2 (1980): pp. 204–205. See Craig and Cornelius, "Political," pp. 341, and 385–386, fn. 35, on the different positions. A prominent recent example of the causal political-cultural approach, bitterly denounced in Mexico, is Alan Riding, *Distant Neighbors: A Portrait of the Mexicans* (New York: Knopf, 1985).

49. John Booth and Mitchell Seligson, "The Political Culture of Authoritarianism in Mexico: A Reexamination," *Latin American Research Review* 19, no. 1 (1984): pp. 110–113. The authors report uniformly strong democratic values, though less among women, the less-educated, and the working class than in the middle class. But their data come from developed urban areas known for dissent from the PRI–regime. Also, expressed values do not seem quite so at odds with the system when one acknowledges that it permits some degree of free expression, demonstration, etc.; it does not permit organized alternatives, and the one issue on which the authors report a majority of undemocratic responses was on critics seeking office. Craig and Cornelius, "Political," pp. 348–350, report conflicting data regarding "working-class authoritarianism." Finally, the *New York Times,* November 17, 1986, reported that a poll of 1,576 Mexicans showed "envy" of U.S. democracy and economic strength, but in fact only 16 percent cited democracy as the main point.

50. Rafael Segovia, *La politicización del niño mexicano,* 2d ed, (Mexico City: El Colegio de México, 1982); Craig and Cornelius, "Political," p. 369. Family socialization and interrelations are often described as intolerant and undemocratic. However, the introduction of more participatory educational practices (e.g., Montessori schools) may have a democratizing influence.

51. In a sense, then, elites have developed a degree of "trust" in their pacts even though interpersonal trust is low. On the generally low degree of trust in Mexican society, see Craig and Cornelius, "Political," p. 372.

52. Robert Dahl, *Polyarchy: Participation and Opposition* (New Haven, CT: Yale University Press, 1971).

53. Guillermo Bonfil Batalla, "Los pueblos indígenas: Viejos problemas, nuevas demandas." In González Casanova and Florescano, *México, hoy,* pp. 100–107.

54. Juan J. Linz, "Totalitarian and Authoritarian Regimes." In *Handbook of Political Science,* vol. 3, ed. Fred I. Greenstein and Nelson W. Polsby. (Reading, MA: Addison-Wesley, 1975).

55. Respective quotations from Larissa Lomnitz, "Social Structure of Urban Mexico," *Latin America Research Review* 16, no. 2 (1982): p. 69; and Purcell and Purcell, "State and Society," p. 226.

56. Elite autonomous organizations do not usually serve as "training grounds" for democracy. The public university is the best example of a substantially autonomous organization that has trained most of Mexico's (undemocratic) political elite. Relevant skills are the ability to mobilize and manipulate mass groups, bargaining, and leadership.

57. Bailey, *Governing,* Table 6.1.

58. Gabriel A. Almond and Robert J. Mundt, "Crisis, Choice, and Change: Some Tentative Conclusions." In Almond and Mundt, *Crisis,* pp. 635, 637.

59. The Mexican case is pertinent to the ongoing debate about the role of oil in Venezuela's success with democracy. Levine's chapter in this volume is certainly accurate in asserting that oil is not enough. Mexico was one of the world's top producers in the 1920s and has been again recently. In fact, oil may have helped save Mexico's undemocratic system. But it may also contribute to pressures for democracy and, as in Venezuela, oil and growth could potentially help democratic rule consolidate.

60. Perhaps Mexico's unequal socioeconomic development has facilitated autonomous political participation for some privileged groups alongside mobilized participation by mass groups.

See Samuel P. Huntington and Joan Nelson, *No Easy Choice* (Cambridge, MA: Harvard University Press, 1976). Such a view appears consistent with this chapter's corporatist-pluralist contrasts.

61. I give my views on how Mexico's foreign policy has contributed to stability and on the growing challenges that policy faces in "The Implications of Central American Conflicts for Mexican Politics." In *Mexico's Political Stability: The Next Five Years*, ed. Roderic A. Camp (Boulder, CO.: Westview Press, 1986), pp. 235–264.

62. On prospects for stability, see especially Camp, *Political Stability*.

63. Whether "success" by itself would ever undermine an authoritarian regime, particularly a well institutionalized one, is an interesting but perhaps remote question. More pertinent is whether success sets the general conditions for democracy to the point that crises (economic disaster, military defeat, scandal) leading to instability, or at least turmoil, may in fact lead to democratization.

64. Guillermo O'Donnell, "Introduction to the Latin American Cases," pp. 5, 15; and Luciano Martins, "The 'Liberalization' of Authoritarian Rule in Brazil," p. 72, both in O'Donnell, Schmitter, and Whitehead, *Transitions: Latin America;* and, especially, O'Donnell and Schmitter, *Transitions From Authoritarian Rule: Tentative Conclusions About Uncertain Democracies* (Baltimore: Johns Hopkins Press, 1986), pp. 48–72; also, Alfred Stepan, "Paths Toward Redemocratization: Theoretical and Comparative Considerations." In O'Donnell, Schmitter, and Whitehead, *Transitions from Authoritarian Rule: Comparative Perspectives*, pp. 72–74.

65. See Lamounier's chapter in this volume, and also Martins, "Liberalization," pp. 72–74.

66. The theoretical argument is developed in Adam Przeworski, "Some Problems in the Study of the Transition to Democracy." In O'Donnell, Schmitter, and Whitehead, *Transitions*, pp. 47–63; and in O'Donnell and Schmitter, *Transitions*, pp. 7–16, 48–49.

67. Wayne A. Cornelius, "Political Liberalization in an Authoritarian Regime: Mexico, 1976–1985." In Gentleman, *Mexican*.

68. Carlos Monsiváis, "La ofensiva ideológica de la derecha." In González Casanova and Florescano, *México, hoy*, p. 315. This underscores Przeworski's point ("Some Problems," pp. 50–53) that perceptions of alternatives as well as of the present regime are critical to choices about pushing for transition.

69. Laurence Whitehead, "International Aspects of Democratization." In O'Donnell, Schmitter, and Whitehead, *Transitions: Comparative Perspectives*, pp. 20, 44. Whitehead also writes (p. 43): "Mexico provides a particularly significant litmus test of American priorities. Does it not remain an open question in that country how much democracy of the conventional liberal democratic variety would be tolerable to Washington policymakers?" It does, but when will Mexico put the United States to that test?

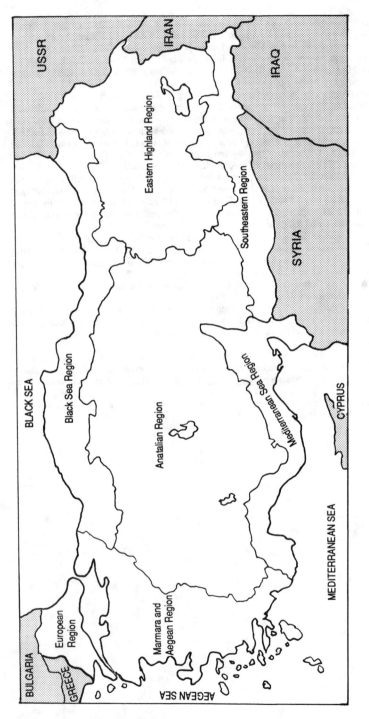

TURKEY

CHAPTER FIVE

Turkey: Crises, Interruptions, and Reequilibrations

ERGUN ÖZBUDUN

The record of democratic development in Turkey has been somewhat mixed. On the one hand, Turkey has remained committed to a democratic regime for the last forty years with only relatively brief interruptions. Presently it is the only democratic country in the entire Middle East (with the single exception of the very special case of Israel), as well as in all of Eastern and Southeastern Europe (with the single exception of Greece, whose post-World War II democratic record has not been appreciably brighter than Turkey's). By most socioeconomic indicators, Turkey is a middle-rank, developing country, with a per capita income of about $1,200. In view of the positive overall relationship between socioeconomic development and political democracy, Turkey is one of the few countries that are more democratic politically than they ought to have been according to the level of their socioeconomic development. However, Turkey's democratic process has been interrupted thrice in the last quarter of a century, which indicates a rather high degree of political instability. At best then, Turkey can be placed in the category of unstable democracies.

If the record of democratic development in Turkey is mixed, so are the factors that may have a bearing on Turkey's overall degree of success with democratic government. Culturally most Turks, elite and nonelite, seem to be committed to a democratic regime; yet this commitment does not always seem to be based on a set of profoundly felt concomitant democratic values, such as tolerance, compromise, and respect for individuality. The military shares the society's commitment to democracy, yet it also displays certain elitist attitudes and a tendency to see itself as the true guardian of the national interest. The major political parties have been nonideological and committed to democracy; yet their leaderships have not always shown a propensity for compromise and accommodation even in the face of a grave and imminent threat to the regime; furthermore, they have not been immune to polarizing influences, as was the case in the 1970s. The society is relatively homogeneous and well-integrated; yet ethnic or sectarian conflict can sometimes, if rarely, become violent. The rate of economic growth has on the whole been quite respectable; yet economic inequalities have also increased and are continuing to do so; moreover, there seem to exist serious obstacles to sustained economic growth in the future.

<h2 style="text-align:center">• THE DEVELOPMENT OF REPRESENTATIVE AND DEMOCRATIC GOVERNMENT •</h2>

The Ottoman Empire

Turkey differs from most of the developing countries of today in that it never experienced a colonial past. On the contrary, the Ottoman Empire—which at its zenith at the end of the sixteenth century comprised the entire Middle East (excluding Iran), North Africa, Southeastern Europe (including Hungary), and southern Russia—left a powerful legacy not only in the contemporary politics of its principal heir, the Republic of Turkey, but also upon those of other "successor states" to the empire.[1] A study of the development of democracy in Turkey cannot therefore be attempted without reference to its Ottoman past.

It is generally agreed that the Ottoman state conformed much more closely to a "bureaucratic empire" than to a European-style feudal system.[2] The Ottoman society was divided into two major classes. The *askeri*, literally the "military," included those to whom the sultan had delegated religious or executive power, namely officers of the court and the army, civil servants and *ulema* (religious functionaries). The *reaya*, on the other hand, comprised all Muslim and non-Muslim subjects who paid taxes but who had no part in the government. "It was a fundamental rule of the empire to exclude its subjects from the privileges of the 'military.' "[3] This accorded well with the fundamental concepts of state and society in the Ottoman Empire, which held that the social order was of divine origin and hence immutable. It was the sultan's duty to maintain this order, assisted by the members of the *askeri* class, by keeping everyone in his appropriate social position. Thus the state was above and independent of the society. Political power did not derive from the society, but was imposed upon it by the will of God (in effect, by conquest) from outside.[4] It was this primacy of politics over society that was to affect the nature of social and political changes in the Ottoman Empire for many centuries.

Two features of the Ottoman system reinforced the rigid dichotomy between the ruler and the ruled. One was the recruitment (*devsirme*) system, which was a periodic levy on the male children of Christian subjects, reducing them to the status of slaves and training them for service to the state. Since these slaves legally became the sultan's property, and he could take their lives and confiscate their wealth without legal process, they were in no position to challenge his authority. Furthermore, their removal from their former social environments prevented the development of locally entrenched, semiautonomous elements in the provinces.

A second feature, which was also instrumental in maintaining a strong central authority over the large territories of the empire, was the Ottoman land tenure system. This system vested in the state the original ownership of all the land, and limited the rights of the fief holders (*sipahi*) to the collection of taxes and the supervision of peasants under their jurisdiction. In return for the land grant, the *sipahi* were expected to recruit, train, and support a local contingent of soldiers; the fiefs were granted by the central government and could be taken away by it. Furthermore, the largest fiefs (*hass*) were perquisites of office. "The Ottoman feudal system seems to have differed from that of Western Europe chiefly in that the principal feudatories held their lands temporarily, in virtue of their offices. Hence the monarchy was exposed to little danger from the rivalry of this class of its tenants-in-chief."[5]

Two other significant social groups were the *ulema* (the class of religious scholars), and the merchants and artisans. Although part of the ruling class, the *ulema* differed from the "military" proper and the administrators in that it consisted of freeborn Muslims. However, the *ulema* did not constitute a hierarchy independent of government, since the most important among its members held appointive posts and hence were completely dependent on the state. As for merchants the Ottoman state, unlike its Western European counterparts, did not pursue mercantilist policies and did not favor the emergence of a powerful merchant class. Another factor that hindered the growth of a politically influential merchant class was the "ethnic division of labor." Non-Muslim minorities took the lead in mercantile activities, especially in international trade. But this group, so important in the development of early mercantile capitalism in Western Europe, was barred from the opportunity of converting such economic power into a significant political role because of the Islamic character of the state.

Thus, with no feudalism comparable to that of Western Europe, no hereditary aristocracy, no independent church hierarchy, no strong and independent merchant class, no powerful guilds, no self-governing cities, and with a ruling institution (i.e., the administration and the army) staffed with slaves, the Ottoman Empire represented a close approximation of an Oriental despotism. In the West, nongovernmental intermediary social structures operated relatively independently of government and played a cushioning role between the state and the individual. The Church was the foremost of these corporate structures such as the guilds, free cities, and the like. These had no parallels in the Ottoman Empire.

Islamic law does not as a rule recognize corporate entities. For all the theoretical supremacy of the *sharia* (Islamic law), even the religious class does not have a corporate identity. At least in Sunni (orthodox) Islam it forms part of the state bureaucracy, dependent upon the state for its appointments, promotions, and salaries. Similarly, in the Ottoman Empire, neither the cities nor the artisan guilds played any autonomous role comparable to their counterparts in Western Europe.[6] This dichotomy between the ruler and the ruled led to a class consciousness very different from that of the West, "that of *askeri* on the one hand and of their opponents on the other. . . . The saliency of these strata replaced the European saliency of strata connected with the production and distribution of goods and services."[7]

The bureaucratic nature of the Ottoman state and the concentration of political power in the hands of the sultan and his military and civilian bureaucrats explain the absence of representative institutions throughout the history of the empire until the last quarter of the nineteenth century. This contrasts sharply with the feudal tradition in Western Europe, which contained within itself the germs of representative and constitutional government. Western European feudalism implied a legally defined division of powers between a relatively weak central authority and local centers of power. It also implied some idea of representation for the estates, regardless of the frequency with which assemblies of estates were actually called. To this was added the corporate autonomy of the Church, the cities, and the guilds. From this medieval social and political pluralism and division of powers, it was a relatively easy step to modern constitutionalism, the rule of law, and modern representative institutions.

The Ottoman state, however, was not entirely devoid of the idea of "consultation" in the conduct of governmental affairs. It was an established custom for the Ottoman government to convene an assembly of leading civilian, military, and religious officials to discuss important matters of policy especially in times of stress. While it clearly had no representative character, this body nevertheless gave support to the notion that important policy decisions should be based on deliberations and consultations in a broader council. Such a consultative assembly was institutionalized in 1838 by Mahmud II, in the form of the "Grand Council of Justice." Mahmud's successor, Abdulmecid I, the council was given the responsibility of discussing and drafting new laws on matters of civil rights and taxation. In practice it "successfully operated as the principal Ottoman legislative organ. . . . All the important *Tanzimat* [Reform] decrees and regulations were prepared by it and over ninety percent of its recommendations were promulgated without change."[8]

In the next few decades, known as the "Reform" period in the Ottoman Empire, the development of representative institutions followed two different routes. One was the increasingly important role of the central legislative council and the effort to broaden its social base without, however, introducing the elective principle. The second was the establishment of local administrative councils based on limited elections. The elective principle in local administration was introduced in the Danube Province in 1864 and then extended in 1867 to the rest of the country. This provided for the election of only the lowest level of local officials (commune headmen) but attached semielected administrative councils to the centrally appointed governors of the each of the three tiers of local administration. A somewhat more representative institution was the "general assembly" created for each province. It was indirectly elected with largely advisory powers.[9]

The First Ottoman Parliament (1876–1878)

The next step was to be the linking of the effective principle adopted at the local level with the practice of nonelective legislative councils at the center. The first Ottoman legislature based on elections came into being with the constitution of 23 December 1876. Interestingly, Midhat Pasha, the leader of the constitutionalist faction, hoped to be able to convene a parliament even before the constitution was officially promulgated. Therefore, a Provisional Electoral Regulation was promulgated on 28 October while the constitution itself was still being debated in the drafting committee, which was composed of high-ranking civil servants.

Despite the limited and indirect nature of the suffrage and certain incidents of interference in the electoral process by provincial governors, it is generally agreed that the first legislative elections in the Ottoman Empire produced a Chamber of Deputies broadly representative (in a sociological sense) of various national and religious communities. While the Muslims, who outnumbered non-Muslims by a considerable ratio in the country, had a majority in the chamber, the Christians and the Jews were proportionally much better represented. The Turks as an ethnic group were a minority of the deputies as a whole, sharing the Muslims seats with Arabs, Albanians, Bosnians, and others. Although a large percentage of the deputies were former government officials, there were also many others representing other professions.[10]

The Chamber of Deputies had two sessions between 19 March 1877 and 14 February 1878, when it was indefinitely prorogued by Sultan Abdulhamid II. Although officially the fiction was maintained that the constitution was still in force, the Chamber of Deputies was not reconvened until the Young Turk revolution of 1908 forced Abdulhamid to do so. It is impossible to analyze here the full political context of the first experiment with constitutional government in the Ottoman Empire

or the reasons for its failure. Suffice it to say that the introduction of
constitutional and representative government was the work of a very
small group of reformist government officials and intellectuals; it was
based neither on broad support, nor on organized political parties.
Consequently, Abdulhamid's prorogation of the chamber did not lead
to any strong public reaction. On the contrary his absolutist rule, emphasizing the Islamic character of the state, seems to have been quite
popular with the conservative, anti-Western mood of public opinion.

The fundamental political cleavage in the Ottoman Empire until the
nineteenth century can be described as a center-periphery cleavage
between the political ins and outs. The ins were "the incumbents of the
Ottoman institutions. The outs were people who were excluded from
the state."[11] Beginning in the eighteenth century, this cleavage was
complicated by another one that resulted from the efforts of Westernization. The adoption of, first, Western military technology and, then,
Western laws and administrative practices was strongly opposed by the
old religious and military elites. This opposition was motivated not only
by religious grounds, but also by the fear that such reforms would
undermine their power and status in the society. In contrast to the older
center-periphery cleavage this one was located at the very center. The
Westernization movement undertaken by bureaucrats fractured the old
intraelite unity, and produced a conflict that remained for many years
one of the principal cleavages in Turkish political life. The political
implications of this culture change, first under the Ottoman reformers
and then under the leadership of Kemal Ataturk, will be discussed more
fully below.

The first Ottoman experiment with constitutional government reflects the emergence of yet another line of cleavage. This one pitted the
constitutionalists (called the "Young Ottomans") against the supporters
of monarchic autocracy. This was also an intraelite conflict, since both
the constitutionalists and the autocratic *tanzimat* reformers came from
the ranks of the Westernized, official elite. The Young Ottomans did
not represent either the local notables or urban merchants. However,
their advocacy of a parliament put them in a dilemma, one that was to
be faced by many generations of future modernizers: the modernizers
wanted to have a parliament as an alternative (and modern) source of
legitimacy. But they soon realized that when a parliament was con-
vened, it "did not increase the power of modernizing officials vis-à-vis
the Sultan, but that it rather increased the power of notables against
state officials."[12] In fact, the Young Ottomans were often bitterly critical
of the abuses of local notables, and charged them with repressing the
countryside. The short life of the first Ottoman Parliament provided
clear manifestations of the deep conflict between the central bureaucratic
elite and the local (peripheral) forces.[13] It is also a good example of

unanticipated and undesired consequences democratization poses for modernizers in traditional or developing societies.

The Second Constitutionalist Period (1908–1918)

The electoral process was reinstated in 1908 after thirty years of absolutist monarchical rule when military-popular uprisings in Macedonia compelled Abdulhamid II to restore the constitution. This was a victory for the reformist-constitutionalist wing of the official bureaucratic elite organized in the underground Society for Union and Progress, which in time transformed itself into a political party. Indeed the second constitutionalist period witnessed, for the first time, the emergence of organized political parties and party competition. The 1908 elections gave the Society for Union and Progress a comfortable majority in the Chamber of Deputies. Of the other two elections held in this period, only that of 1912 was relatively competitive. Because of the administrative pressures exerted by the Unionist government and restrictions on opposition activities, this election came to be known as the "big stick election." The 1914 election was not contested by any opposition party.[14]

The democratic experiment of the second constitutionalist period is generally too easily dismissed as one that quickly degenerated into an internecine struggle poisoned by coups and countercoups, political assassinations and martial law courts, government manipulation of elections and repression of the opposition, becoming finally an outright party dictatorship. While this diagnosis contains a great deal of truth, the same period (especially until the Unionists' coup of 1913) also provided the first extended Turkish experiment with competitive elections, organized political parties, and the parliamentary process. The beginnings of mass politics in Turkey should also be sought in this period. Unlike the earlier military, bureaucratic, intellectual cliques, the Union and Progress, "had too broad a social base and too heterogeneous a class structure to be elitist. . . . The Committee was the first political organization in the Empire to have a mass following and this gave the politics of the day a populist basis."[15] Finally, under the crust of virulent and mutually destructive political struggles of the period, one can discern the beginnings of "issue-oriented politics," which pitted the modernizing, unifying, centralizing, standardizing, nationalist, authoritarian, and statist Union and Progress against three types of opposition: the liberals who favored parliamentary democracy, administrative decentralization, more reliance on private initiative, and a more Ottomanist policy (i.e., a policy aimed at creating an "Ottoman" identity around the common fatherland and dynasty, regardless of religion, language, and ethnicity); religious traditionalists who were opposed to the secularist aspects of the Unionist policies; and the non-Turkish minorities (whether Muslim or non-Muslim) who felt threatened by the nationalist and centralizing drive of the Union and Progress.[16]

The National Liberation Period (1918–1923)

With the defeat of the Ottoman Empire in World War I, the Ottoman government collapsed in fact, if not in theory. While the Istanbul government maintained a shaky existence during the Armistice years (1918–1922) under the control of the Allies' occupation armies, a new governmental structure was developed in Anatolia by the nationalists resisting the occupation.

The era of national liberation is a most interesting period in Turkey's constitutional history, and is full of constitutional innovations. Following the arrest and deportation of many deputies with nationalist sympathies by the Allied occupation forces and the consequent dissolution of the Chamber of Deputies on 18 March 1920, Mustafa Kemal, the leader of the nationalist forces in Anatolia, called for the election of a new assembly "with extraordinary powers" to convene in Ankara. This body, called the "Grand National Assembly," was fundamentally different from the Ottoman Parliament in that it combined legislative and executive powers in itself. It was a real constituent and revolutionary assembly, not bound by the Ottoman constitution.

The Grand National Assembly enacted a constitution in 1921. This was a short but very important document. For the first time it proclaimed the principle of national sovereignty, calling itself the "only and true representative of the nation." Legislative and executive powers were vested in the assembly. The ministers were to be chosen by the Assembly individually from among its own members. The Assembly could provide instructions to the ministers and, if deemed necessary, change them.

In the entire Turkish history, the political influence of the legislature reached its peak during the period of national liberation. The theory of legislative supremacy was also followed in practice. The Assembly closely supervised all aspects of administrative activity. Under the most difficult external and internal circumstances, Kemal and his ministers ruled the country in close cooperation with the Assembly and never attempted to ignore it.

In the months following the victorious termination of the War of Independence and the abolition of the sultanate in the fall of 1922, Mustafa Kemal formed a political party based on populist principles, which was named the People's Party (later the Republican People's Party, or RPP). In the 1923 elections it won almost all of the Assembly seats. However, the newly elected Assembly was also far from being an obedient instrument of the leadership. Disagreements on constitutional and other questions soon became manifest. In November 1924, twenty-nine deputies resigned from the People's Party and formed the Progressive Republican Party. The new opposition party was led by some prestigious generals closely associated with Kemal during the War of Independence. In its initial manifesto the party emphasized economic and particularly political liberalism, including a commitment to "respect religious feelings and beliefs." The manifesto stated its opposition to despotism, and stressed individual rights, judicial independence, and administrative decentralization. It promised not to change the constitution without a clear popular mandate. The Progressive Republican Party was strongly supported by the Istanbul press, and started to set up local organizations in big cities and in the eastern provinces.

Behind these publicly claimed policy differences also lay the personal estrangement of the Progressive leaders from Kemal, and their concern about his growing personal power. At a more fundamental level, however, their opposition reflected a more conservative mentality that Frey sees as typical of postindependence crises in developing countries. Behind all the ideas of the Progressive Republican Party, he argues that "there lay the conservative aim of making the new Turkey—if there was ever to be a *new* Turkey in any basic sense— conform as far as possible to the customs and traditions of the old. Change was to be gradual and evolutionary, not swift and revolutionary in the Kemalist mode."[17]

The Consolidation of the Republic

Justification for crushing the Progressive Republican Party was found in the Seyh Sait rebellion that erupted in eastern Anatolia in February 1925. The rebellion quickly reached serious dimensions. Consequently, the more moderate government of Fethi was replaced by a new one headed by Ismet Inönü, who favored more radical methods to deal with the rebellion. Legislation passed in March gave the government broad powers to ban all kinds of organization, propaganda, agitation, and publications that could lead to reaction and rebellion or undermine public order and security. Martial law was declared, and the Independence Tribunals (revolutionary courts created in 1920 to deal with treasonable activities) were reactivated. The Progressive Republican Party was shut down on 3 June 1925 by a decision of the Council of Ministers, which implicated it in the revolt, although no concrete proof of such connection was established. The suppression of the opposition party and much of the independent press marked the end of the first, semipluralistic phase of the Kemalist regime.

The following period can be characterized as the consolidation phase of the new republican regime. Between 1925 and 1945 the country was ruled by a single-party regime, with the exception of a brief and unsuccessful attempt to introduce an opposition party, the Free Republican Party in 1930. This was a period of radical secularizing reforms such as the banning of religious orders; the adoption of the Swiss civil code to replace the *sharia*; acceptance of other Western codes in the fields of penal, commercial, and procedural law; the closing of religious schools; the outlawing of the fez; the adoption of a Latin alphabet and the international calendar; the repeal of the constitutional provisions that made Islam the official religion of the state, etc. This consolidation of single-party rule, however, did not involve a doctrinal repudiation of liberal democracy or of liberal values. Extraordinary measures were justified by temporary needs to protect the state and the regime against counterrevolutionaries.

Although the regime's authoritarian tendencies were somewhat intensified after the failure of the Free Republican Party experiment in 1930, most of these tendencies were checked or arrested by the more liberal or pluralistic countertendencies within the single party, the Republican People's Party (RPP). Organizationally the RPP never approached a totalitarian mobilizational party model. Ideologically, it did not provide a permanent justification for an authoritarian regime. Authoritarian practices and policies were defeated not on doctrinal, but on purely pragmatic and temporary grounds. A liberal democratic state remained the officially sanctioned ideal. Institutionally attempts were made to partially open up the nomination and election processes starting from the 1931 elections, such as leaving some parliamentary seats open for independent candidates.[18]

As for its social bases, the RPP has often been described as a coalition between the central military-bureaucratic elite and local notables, the former clearly being the dominant element especially at the level of central government. This alliance was, at least partly, dictated by the circumstances of the War of Independence. These two groups were the only ones capable of mobilizing the peasant majority into a war of national liberation. After the consolidation of the republican regime this cooperation continued, since the Kemalists' emphasis on secularizing reforms did not pose a threat to the interests of local notables. Thus the RPP represented the old center, i.e., the world of officialdom, with some local allies in the periphery. But in contrast to mobilizational single parties, it did not attempt to broaden its social base or to mobilize the periphery.

The Kemalist regime was highly successful, on the other hand, in creating a set of new political institutions, among which the RPP itself and the Turkish Grand National Assembly (TGNA) stand out as the most important. Elections were also institutionalized and regularly held. The forms, if not the substance, of constitutional government were carefully maintained. All these political institutions survived with minimal changes in the multiparty era once such a transition was made in the late 1940s. Indeed, political institutionalization under the aegis of a single party provided a kind of "democratic infrastructure" that eventually facilitated the transition to democratic politics.[19] In this sense, the RPP regime can be described as a case of low political participation (mobilization) and high political institutionalization.

Other features of the Kemalist regime in Turkey might have also provided facilitating conditions for eventual democratization. First, the loss of all Arabic-speaking provinces at the end of World War I and the exchange of populations with Greece following the termination of the War of Independence made the new Turkish republic a much more homogeneous state. It thus facilitated the basing of its corporate identity on Turkish nationalism instead of Islamic religion or loyalty to the Ottoman dynasty. Indeed, a reason for the relative failure (compared, for example, with the Meiji restoration in Japan) of Ottoman modernization reforms in the nineteenth century might well have been that such reforms could not possibly have produced sufficient social integration and social mobilization in a multinational and overextended empire. The second facilitating condition was the complete secularization of the governmental, legal, and educational systems under the Kemalist rule. By strictly separating religion from politics the Kemalists created at least a precondition for liberal democracy, i.e., a rationalist-relativistic, rather than an absolutist, notion of politics. Thus it should be no accident that Turkey is the only predominantly Muslim country that is both democratic and secular. Obviously there is a link between Kemalist reforms and those of the nineteenth-century Ottoman modernizers, especially the Young Turks. But the speed, intensity, and scope of the secularizing reforms of the republic clearly surpass those of the earlier eras.

Regarding the relationship between the Kemalist reforms and the development of democracy in Turkey, a counterargument can be made to the effect that the traumatic experience of such a momentous culture change, and the deep cleavage between radical secularists and Islamic traditionalists[20] would make a stable democracy very unlikely. It should be stressed, however, that despite the radical nature of Kemalist secularism, it never intended to eradicate Islam in Turkey. It was anticlerical, to be sure, but not antireligious. It aimed at individualization or privatization of Islam, attempting to make it a matter of individual conscience rather than the fundamental organizing principle of the society. Consistent with this, freedom of religion at the individual level was always respected, while organized political manifestations of Islam were strictly forbidden. Judged by these criteria, the ultimate aim of Kemalism seems to have been accomplished, since a majority of believing and practicing Turkish Muslims are now distinguishing between their religious beliefs and their public and political lives, as evidenced by their voting behavior. Indeed, during the 1970s, fundamentalist Islamic political parties have been able to gain only a small minority of votes.

Transition to Multiparty Politics and the Democratic Party Period

The transition from authoritarianism to competitive politics in Turkey is highly exceptional in that it took place without a *ruptura*, i.e., a break with the existing institutional arrangements. On the contrary, it is a rare example of *reforma*, where the transition process was led and controlled by the power holders of the previous authoritarian regime.[21] This transition started in 1945 when the RPP regime allowed the formation of an opposition party, the Democratic Party (DP), by some of the dissident members of its own parliamentary group. Despite some ups and downs on the road, the process proceeded relatively smoothly and ended in the electoral victory of the DP in the free parliamentary elections of 1950.

It is beyond the scope of the present study to give full account of the transition or to assess its probable causes.[22] While such a momentous change cannot be explained by a single factor, it appears that the potentially democratic aspirations of the RPP regime and President Inönü's firm personal commitment to democratization provided the crucial impulse behind the move. In fact, whenever relations between the RPP old guard (the "bunker") and the DP opposition grew tense, Inönü intervened personally to soften the atmosphere and to reassure the opposition. The most significant of these interventions was his statement on 12 July 1947 after several rounds of talk with the hard-line Prime Minister Recep Peker and the opposition leader Celâl Bayar. The declaration included a promise by Inönü that the opposition party would enjoy the same privileges as the party in power and that Inönü himself would remain equally responsible to both parties as the head of the state.

Inönü's commitment to democratization, in turn, has to be explained by the structural and doctrinal characteristics of the RPP regime. The Kemalist regime evolved into a single-party model without, however, having a single-party ideology. No component of the RPP doctrine provided a permanent legitimation for the single-party system. On the contrary liberal democracy remained the ideal, and authoritarianism was justified only as a temporary measure arising out of the need to defend the Kemalist revolution against counterrevolutionaries. Kemalism as a doctrine was much closer to nineteenth-century liberalism than to the authoritarian and totalitarian philosophies of the twentieth century. Communism and fascism were never seen as models to be imitated. One reason for this might have been that the Kemalist regime was born in the immediate post-World War I period when democratic ideas and values were at the height of their appeal and legitimacy for the new nations.

The timing of the decision to democratize the Turkish system could have been influenced by favorable changes in the international environment. The victory of the democratic regimes in World War II, and Turkey's need for a rapprochement with the West in the face of the Soviet threat, no doubt provided an additional incentive for transition to democracy. Changes in the structure of Turkish society—notably the growth of commerical and industrial middle classes who favored a democratic regime in which their own party would have an excellent chance to win—on the other hand, do not seem to have played a decisive role in the transition. First, it is not clear why the commercial-industrial middle classes suddenly began to feel fettered under the RPP's statism, if statist policies really worked so much to their benefit. Second, assuming that this was indeed the case, there is no evidence that such internal pressures forced the RPP leadership into this decision. The experience of the Mexican PRI suggests that a pragmatic single party is capable of showing sufficient adaptability to accommodate newly emerging groups.

The DP came to power with a landslide electoral victory on 14 May 1950, also won the 1954 and 1957 national elections (Table 5.1), and remained in power for ten full years until it was ousted by the military coup of 27 May 1960. Socially the DP, led by a group of politicians who played fairly important roles in the single-party period, was a coalition of various types of oppositions to the RPP. It brought together urban liberals and religious conservatives, commercial middle classes and the urban poor, and more modern (mobilized) sections of the rural population. The RPP, on the other hand, retained the support of government officials, some large landowners, and a substantial portion of the more backward peasantry still under the influence of its local patrons. The heterogeneous character of the DP coalition suggests that the dominant social cleavage of the era was cultural rather than socioeconomic in nature. The common denominator of the DP supporters was their opposition to state officials. In this sense, the rise of the DP was a victory of the periphery over the center.

The ideological distance between the RPP and the DP was not great. They differed significantly from each other, however, in their underlying attitudes toward the proper role of the state, bureaucracy, private enterprise, local initiative, and toward peasant participation in politics. While the RPP-oriented central elite had a more tutelary concept of development, the provincial elites around the DP emphasized local initiative and the "immediate satisfaction of local expectations."[23]

Despite the nonideological nature of the partisan conflict relations between the two major parties quickly deteriorated. Especially after the

Table 5.1   Percentage of Votes (and Seats) in Turkish Parliamentary Elections (1950–1977)

Party	Elections							
	1950	1954	1957	1961	1965	1969	1973	1977
DP/JP	53.3	56.6	47.7	34.8	52.9	46.5	29.8	36.9
	(83.8)	(93.0)	(69.5)	(35.1)	(53.3)	(56.9)	(33.1)	(42.0)
RPP	39.8	34.8	40.8	36.7	28.7	27.4	33.3	41.4
	(14.2)	(5.7)	(29.2)	(38.4)	(29.8)	(31.8)	(41.1)	(47.3)
NP	3.0	4.7	7.2	14.0	6.3	3.2	1.0	—
	(0.2)	(0.9)	(0.7)	(12.0)	(6.9)	(1.3)	—	—
FP	—	—	3.8	—	—	—	—	—
	—	—	(0.7)	—	—	—	—	—
NTP	—	—	—	13.7	3.7	2.2	—	—
	—	—	—	(14.4)	(4.2)	(1.3)	—	—
TLP	—	—	—	—	3.0	2.7	—	0.1
	—	—	—	—	(3.3)	(0.4)	—	—
NAP	—	—	—	—	2.2	3.0	3.4	6.4
	—	—	—	—	(2.4)	(0.2)	(0.7)	(3.6)
UP	—	—	—	—	—	2.8	1.1	0.4
	—	—	—	—	—	(1.8)	(0.2)	—
RRP	—	—	—	—	—	6.6	5.3	1.9
	—	—	—	—	—	(3.3)	(2.9)	(0.7)
Dem. P	—	—	—	—	—	—	11.9	1.9
	—	—	—	—	—	—	(10.0)	(0.2)
NSP	—	—	—	—	—	—	11.8	8.6
	—	—	—	—	—	—	(10.7)	(5.3)

Note: In the first row of figures for each party are percentages of the popular vote and in the second row (in parentheses) are the percentages of seats won.
Abbreivations: DP, Democrat Party; JP, Justice Party; RPP, Republican People's Party; NP, Nation Party; FP, Freedom Party; NTP, New Turkey Party; TLP, Turkish Labor Party; NAP, Nationalist Action Party; UP, Unity Party; RRP, Republican Reliance Party; Dem. P., Democratic Party; NSP, National Salvation Party.

1957 elections the DP responded to its declining support by resorting to increasingly authoritarian measures against the opposition, which only made the opposition more uncompromising and vociferous. The last straw in this long chain of authoritarian measures was the establishment by the government party in April 1960 of a parliamentary committee of inquiry to investigate the "subversive" activities of the RPP and of a section of the press. With this, many opposition members were convinced that a point of no return had been reached and that the channels of democratic change had been clogged. The ensuing public unrest, student demonstrations in Istanbul and Ankara, and clashes between the students and the police led to the declaration of martial law. This put the armed forces in the unwanted position of suppressing the opposition on behalf of a government for whose policies they had little sympathy. Finally, the military intervened on 27 May 1960, with the welcome and support of the opposition. The National Unity Committee, formed by the revolutionary officers, dissolved the parliament, banned the DP, arrested and tried its leaders, and set out to prepare a new and more democratic constitution.

What is to be blamed for the failure of this first extended experiment of Turkey with democratic politics? One reason lay in the very nature of the DP, which was a coalition of diverse anti-RPP forces. This convinced the DP leadership that the party "could retain its unity only by keeping its ranks mobilized against the RPP. This was realized partly by accusing the RPP of subverting the government through its hold on the bureaucracy, and partly by raising the specter of a return of the RPP to power."[24] A second factor was that the DP leaders, having been socialized into politics under the RPP rule, had inherited many attitudes, norms, and orientations that were more in harmony with a single party than with a competitive party system. These included a belief that a popular mandate entitled the government party to the unrestricted use of political power. Coupled with the Ottoman-Turkish cultural legacy, which hardly distinguished between political opposition and treasonable activity, this attitude left little room for a legitimate opposition.

Perhaps an even more potent factor that eventually led to the breakdown of the democratic regime was the conflict between the DP and the public bureaucracy. The bureaucracy, which was the main pillar of the single-party regime, retained its RPP loyalties under multiparty politics, and resisted the DP's efforts to consolidate its political power. In the eyes of the DP leaders, this amounted to an unwarranted obstruction of the "national will." The bureaucrats, on the other hand, saw it as their duty to protect the "public interest" against efforts to use state funds for political patronage purposes. They were also deeply troubled by the DP government's careless attitude toward the "rule of law," as well as by its more permissive policies toward religious activities, which they considered a betrayal of the Kemalist legacy of secularism. These negative attitudes were shared by civilian officials and military officers alike.

Finally, all bureaucratic groups (again both civilian and military) not only experienced a loss of social status and political influence under the DP regime, but were also adversely affected in terms of their relative income. The DP's economic policies consisted of rapid import-substitution-based industrialization and the modernization of agriculture, largely through external borrowing and inflationary financing. Although a relatively high rate of economic growth was achieved in the 1950s, income distribution grew much more inequitable. Particularly badly hit because of the inflationary policies were the salaried groups. The 1960 coup found therefore an easy acceptance among military officers and civilian bureaucrats for economic as well as other reasons.

Turkey's Second Try at Democracy (1961–1980)

The 1960 coup was carried out by a group of middle rank officers who, upon assuming power, organized themselves into a revolutionary council named the "National Unity Committee" (NUC), under the chairmanship of General Cemal Gürsel, the former commander of the army. The NUC declared from the beginning its intention of making a new democratic constitution and returning power to a freely elected civilian government. In spite of the efforts by some NUC members to prolong military rule, the committee kept its promise and relinquished power in 1961 following the parliamentary elections held under the new Constitution and the Electoral Law.[25]

The constitution of 1961 was prepared by the NUC and a coopted Representative Assembly dominated by pro-RPP bureaucrats and intellectuals, reflecting the basic political values and interests of these groups. On the one hand, they created an effective system of checks and balances to limit the power of elected assemblies. Such checks included the introduction of judicial review of the constitutionality of laws; the strengthening of the Council of State, which functions as the highest administrative court with review powers over the acts of all executive agencies; effective independence for the judiciary; the creation of a second legislative chamber (Senate of the Republic); and the granting of substantial autonomy to certain public agencies such as the universities and the Radio and Television Corporation. On the other hand, the constitution expanded civil liberties and granted extensive social rights. Thus it was hoped that the power of the elected assemblies would be balanced by judicial and other agencies that represented the values of the bureaucratic elites, while the newly expanded civil liberties would ensure the development of a free and democratic society.

The 1961 elections, however, gave a majority to the heirs of the ousted Democrats (Table 5.1). The pro-DP vote was fragmented among the Justice Party (34.8 percent), the National Party (14.0 percent), and the New Turkey Party (13.7 percent), while the Republicans obtained only 36.7 percent of the vote. Following a period of unstable coalition governments, the Justice Party (JP) gradually established itself as the principal heir to the DP. In the 1965 elections, it gained about 53 percent of the popular vote and of the National Assembly seats. The JP repeated its success in 1969, when it won an absolute majority of the Assembly seats with a somewhat reduced popular vote (46.5 percent). Thus Turkey appeared to have achieved, once again, a popularly elected stable government.

Toward the end of the 1960s, however, the Turkish political system began to experience new problems. Partly as a result of the more liberal atmosphere provided by the 1961 Constitution, extreme left- and right-wing groups appeared on the political scene. This was followed by increasing acts of political violence, especially by extremist youth groups. The crisis was aggravated by the activities of various conspiratorial groups within the military. These radical officers, frustrated by the successive electoral victories of the conservative JP, aimed at establishing a longer-term military regime ostensibly to carry out radical social reforms. In fact the military memorandum of 12 March 1971, which forced the JP government to resign, was a last-minute move by the top military commanders to forestall a radical coup.

The so-called 12 March regime did not go as far as dissolving the Parliament and assuming power directly. Instead, it strongly encouraged the formation of an "above-party" or technocratic government under a veteran RPP politician, Professor Nihat Erim. The new government was expected to deal sternly with political violence with the help of martial law, to bring about certain constitutional amendments designed to strengthen the executive, and to carry out the social reforms (especially land reform) provided for by the 1961 Constitution. The interim government accomplished its first two objectives. Political violence was effectively stamped out. The constitution was extensively revised in 1971 and 1973, with a view to not only strengthening the executive authority, but also to limiting certain civil liberties that were seen as responsible for the emergence of political extremism and violence. The interim regime failed, however, in its third objective of carrying out social reforms, not only because of the conservative majority in the Parliament, but also because of the purge of the radical officers from the military in the months following the "12 March memorandum."

The 1971 military intervention can be characterized as a "half coup," in which the military chose to govern from behind the scenes instead of taking over directly. If one reason for the intervention was the failure of the Demirel government to cope with political terrorism, a more deep-seated cause was the distrust felt toward the JP by many military officers and civilian bureaucrats. Thus, in a sense, the 1971 intervention still reflected the old cleavage between the centralist bureaucratic elite and the forces of the periphery that commanded an electoral majority.

The interim period ended with the 1973 parliamentary elections, which produced a National Assembly with no governing majority. The RPP emerged, after many years of electoral impotence, as the largest party with a third of the popular vote and 41 percent of the Assembly seats (see Table 5.1). The RPP's rise was due on the one hand to the energetic leadership of Bülent Ecevit, who became the party leader replacing the octogenarian Inönü, and on the other to the new social democratic image of the party. As the 1973 voting patterns indicate, the new image of the RPP appealed to urban lower classes. This change signified a realignment in the Turkish party system, as the old center-periphery cleavage began to be replaced by a new functional cleavage. The RPP increased its vote particularly in the former strongholds of the

DP and the JP, and among those strata that up to that time loyally supported the DP and the JP.[26]

The Right, on the other hand, was badly split in the 1973 elections. The JP obtained only about 30 percent of the vote (Table 5.1). The Democratic Party, a splinter group of the JP, received just under 12 percent of the vote, as did the National Salvation Party (NSP). The NSP combined its defense of Islamic moral and cultural values with a defense of the interests of small merchants, artisans, and businessmen. Another new actor in Turkish politics in the 1970s was the Nationalist Action Party (NAP). Although it won only 3.4 percent of the vote in 1973, the NAP grew in the 1970s under the leadership of ex-revolutionary Alpaslan Türkes (one of the key figures in the 1960s coup) from an insignificant party into a highly dedicated, strictly disciplined, and hierarchically organized political force to be reckoned with. The NAP's ideology combined an ardent nationalism and anticommunism with strongly interventionist economic policies, and its tactics involved the use of militia-type youth organizations seemingly implicated in right-wing terror.

The composition of the 1973 National Assembly made coalition governments inevitable. First a coalition was formed, under the premiership of Bülent Ecevit, between the social-democratic RPP and the Islamic NSP. The coalition collapsed in the fall of 1974 and was eventually replaced by a "Nationalist Front" coalition under Süleyman Demirel, with the participation of the JP, NSP, NAP, and the RRP (Republican Reliance Party, a small moderate party led by Professor Turhan Feyzioglu, a former RPP member).

The 1977 elections did not significantly change this picture, although they did strengthen the two leading parties vis-à-vis most of the minor ones. The RPP, which increased its share of the popular vote by eight points, came close to an absolute parliamentary majority. The JP also improved its share of the vote and of the Assembly seats (Table 5.1). The NSP lost about one-quarter of its votes and half of its parliamentary contingent. The Democratic Party and the Republican Reliance Party were practically eliminated. The right-wing NAP grew considerably, however, almost doubling its popular vote while increasing its small contingent of Assembly seats fivefold.

Following the 1977 elections, a Nationalist Front government was formed again under Mr. Demirel, with the participation of the JP, NSP, and NAP. In a few months, however, the Front lost its parliamentary majority as a result of the defection of some JP deputies. Consequently, Mr. Ecevit was able to form a government with the help of these dissident JP members, who were rewarded with ministerial posts in the new government. The Ecevit government lasted about 22 months, resigning in November 1979, when the partial elections for one-third of the Senate and five vacant National Assembly seats revealed sharp gains by the JP, which won 47.8 percent of the vote while the RPP support declined dramatically (to 29.2 percent). Consequently, Mr. Demirel formed a minority JP government with the parliamentary support of its former partners, the NSP and the NAP. This government had been in office less than one year when it was ousted by the military coup of 12 September 1980.

How can we account for the failure of Turkey's second experiment with democracy? The immediate reason behind the military intervention was the growing political violence and terrorism that, between 1975 and 1980, left more than 5,000 people killed and three times as many wounded (the equivalent of Turkish losses in the War of Independence). Acts of violence, which became particularly acute between 1978 and 1980, also included armed assaults, sabotages, kidnappings, bank robberies, occupation and destruction of workplaces, and bombings. Some forty-nine radical leftist groups were involved in left-wing terror, while right-wing terror was concentrated in the "idealist" organizations with their unofficial links to the NAP. Thus, in a sense, the pattern that had led to the military intervention of 1971 was repeated, only this time on a much larger and more alarming scale. Just as in the early 1970s, the governments of the late 1970s were unable to cope with the problem even though martial law was in effect in much of the country. Martial law under the Turkish constitutional system entails the transfer of police functions to military authorities, the restriction or complete suspension of civil liberties, and the creation of military martial law courts to try offenses associated with the causes that led to the declaration of martial law. Thus it is a constitutional, albeit highly authoritarian and restrictive, procedure. In the crisis of the late 1970s, however, even martial law could not contain the violence. One reason for this was the infiltration of the police forces by right-wing and left-wing extremists. Another was the general erosion of the authority of the state as a result of growing political polarization in the country, as will be discussed below. It should be added here that a harmful side effect of martial law is the seemingly inevitable politicization of the armed forces, or the "militarization" of political conflict, which may pave the way for full-scale military intervention. Indeed, all three military interventions in recent Turkish history were preceded by martial law regimes instituted by civilian governments.

At a deeper level the incidence of political violence reflected a growing ideological polarization in the country. The polarizing forces were the NAP, and to a much lesser extent the NSP, on the right, and many small radical groups on the left. The NSP was not involved in violence, but its use of Islamic themes helped to undermine the regime's legitimacy among those committed to the Kemalist legacy of secularism, including the military. The parliamentary arithmetics and the inability and/or unwillingness of the two major parties (the RPP and the JP) to agree on a grand coalition or a minority government arrangement gave these two minor parties an enormous bargaining—more correctly blackmailing—power, which they effectively used to obtain important ministries and to colonize them with their own partisans. In fact this seems to be crucial for the crisis of the system. An accommodation between the two major parties would have been welcomed by most of the important political groups in Turkey, including the business community, the leading trade union confederation, the press, and the military, and would have been acceptable to a majority of the JP and the RPP deputies. A government based on their joint support would probably have been strong enough to deal effectively and evenhandedly with the political violence. However, the deep personal rivalry between Demirel and Ecevit, their tendency to see problems from a narrow partisan perspective, and perhaps their failure to appreciate the real gravity of the situation made such a democratic rescue operation impossible. As the experience of many countries has shown, antisystem parties can perhaps be tolerated in opposition, but their entry into government tends to put too heavy a load on the system to be handled by democratic means.

The radical left, unlike the radical right, was not represented in the Parliament, but extreme leftist ideologies found many supporters among students, teachers, and in some sectors of the industrial working class. Just as the JP was pulled to the right by its partnership with the NAP and the NSP, the RPP was pulled to the left by the radical groups to its left. Political polarization also affected and undermined the public bureaucracy. At no time in recent Turkish history had the public agencies been so divided and politicized as in the late 1970s. Changes of government were followed by extensive purges in all ministries, involving not only the top personnel, but also many middle- or lower-rank civil servants. Partisanship became a norm in the civil service, which had retained its essentially nonpolitical character until the mid-1970s.

A related phenomenon that contributed to a decline in the legitimacy of the political system was the *immobilisme* of the governments and parliaments in much of the 1970s. The very narrow majorities in the Parliament and the heterogeneous nature of the governing coalitions (be it the Nationalist Front governments or the Ecevit governments) meant that new policies could be initiated only with great difficulty. In the context of pressing economic troubles (such as high inflation, major deficits in the international trade balance, shortages of investment and consumer goods, unemployment, etc.), and international problems (such as the Cyprus crisis and the U.S. arms embargo), the inability of governments to take courageous policy decisions aggravated the legitimacy crisis. To put it differently this lack of efficacy and effectiveness served to delegitimate the regime. Perhaps the most telling example of such governmental failure of performance was the inability of the Turkish Grand National Assembly to elect a president of the republic in 1980. The six-month-old presidential deadlock ended only with the military coup of 12 September. Other examples of lesser deadlocks abounded particularly in matters of economic and foreign policy.

The 1980 Coup and the 1982 Constitution

From the moment it took over the government on 12 September 1980, the National Security Council (composed of the five highest-ranking generals in the Turkish armed forces) made it clear that it intended to eventually return power to democratically elected civilian authorities. It made it equally clear, however, by words and deeds that it did not intend a return to the *status quo ante*. Rather, the council aimed at a major restructuring of Turkish democracy to prevent a recurrence of the political polarization, violence, and crisis that had afflicted the country in the late 1970s, and thus to make the military's continued involvement in politics unnecessary. The new constitution, Political Parties Law, and Electoral Law prepared by the council-appointed Consultative Assembly—and made final by the council itself—reflect these objectives and concerns of the military and indicate the extent to which Turkey's new attempt at democracy is intended to be different from its earlier democratic experiments.

The constitution was submitted to a popular referendum on 7 November 1982. The extremely high rate of participation (91.27 percent) was, no doubt, partly due to the provision that those who did not participate would forfeit their right to vote in the next parliamentary elections. The constitution was approved by 91.37 percent of those who voted. The counting was honest, but the debate preceding it was extremely limited. The council limited debate only to those views expressed with the purpose of "improving the draft constitution" and banned all efforts to influence the direction of the vote. The constitution was "officially" explained to the public by President Kenan Evren in a series of speeches, and any criticism of these speeches was also banned. Another unusual feature of the constitutional referendum was its combination with the presidential elections. A "yes" vote for the constitution meant a vote for General Evren for a seven-year term as president of the Republic, and no other candidates were allowed. It is generally agreed that the personal popularity of General Evren helped increase affirmative votes for the constitution rather than the other way around.

The election of General Evren as president was one of the measures designed to ensure a smooth transition from the National Security Council regime to a democratic one. Another such transitional measure was the transformation of the National Security Council into a "Presidential Council"—with only advisory powers—for a period of six years, starting from the convening of the new Grand National Assembly. Also, during a six-year period, the president has the right to veto constitutional amendments, in which case the Grand National Assembly (GNA) can override the veto only by a three-fourths majority of its full membership. Finally, the constitution provides restrictions on political activities of former political leaders. The leaders, deputy leaders, secretaries-general, and the members of the central executive committees of former political parties are not allowed to establish or to become members in political parties, nor may they be nominated for the GNA or for local government bodies for a period of ten years. A less severe ban disqualifies the parliamentarians of former political parties from establishing political parties or becoming members of their central executive bodies (but not from running for and being elected to the GNA) for a period of five years. These bans were repealed by the constitutional referendum of 6 September 1987.

In addition to such transitional measures, the constitution introduces highly restrictive provisions on political activities of trade unions, associations, and cooperatives. Thus there can be no political links between such organizations and political parties, nor can they receive financial support from each other. Political parties are also banned from organizing in foreign countries (obviously, among the Turkish residents of those countries), creating women's and youth organizations, and establishing foundations. Also the 1982 Constitution transformed the office of the presidency from a largely ceremonial one, as it was under the 1961 Constitution, into a much more powerful one with effective autonomous powers. Although the political responsibility of the Council of Ministers before the GNA is maintained, the president is given important appointive powers (particularly, in regard to certain high-ranking judges) that he can exercise independently of the Council of Ministers. Also he can submit constitutional amendments to popular referenda and bring about a suit of unconstitutionality against any law passed by the GNA. The constitution did not go as far as the "French" 1958 Constitution, however, in strengthening the presidency. The system of government remained essentially parliamentary rather than presidential.

The National Security Council regime also adopted a new electoral law which retained the "d'Hondt" version of proportional representation with some important modifications. The d'Hondt formula is also known as the highest-average system. Briefly, it ensures that in a constituency no reallocation of additional seats would take place to increase proportionality. The "d'Hondt" system, in its classical version, slightly favors larger parties, but the modifications introduced by the new law made such effect much stronger. The most consequential novelty of the new

TURKEY   197

law is a national quotient (threshold) such that political parties obtaining less than 10 percent of the total valid votes cast nationally will not be assigned any seats in the GNA. This provision is designed to prevent the excessive proliferation of political parties which, in the opinion of the council, contributed significantly to the crisis in the 1970s. The ruling council indicated on various occasions that it preferred a party system with two or three parties, which would ensure stable parliamentary majorities. Another novelty of the Electoral Law is the "constituency threshold," according to which the total number of valid votes cast in each constituency is divided by the number of seats in that constituency (which varies between two and six), and those parties or independent candidates that fail to exceed the quotient are not assigned any seats in that constituency. The combined effects of national and constituency thresholds favor larger parties.

Return to Competitive Politics and the 1983 Elections

The provisional article 4 of the Law on Political Parties gave the National Security Council the right to veto the founding members of new political parties (all former political parties had earlier been dissolved by a decree of the council). The council made use of this power in such a way that only three parties were able to complete their formation formalities before the beginning of the electoral process and, consequently, to compete in the GNA elections. Notably, two new parties that looked like credible successors to the two former major parties (namely, the True Path Party as a possible successor to the JP and the Social Democratic Party to the RPP) were thus eliminated from electoral competition, although both parties were allowed to complete their formation after the nomination process was over. Earlier, another successor party, the Grand Turkey Party, established or joined by a large number of former high-ranking JP figures, had been banned outright by the council. The provisional article 2 of the Electoral Law also required parties to have established their organizations in at least half of the provinces in order to qualify for electoral competition.

As a result of such qualifications, only three parties could contest the GNA elections held on 6 November 1983. These were the Motherland Party (MP), the Populist Party (PP), and the Nationalist Democratic Party (NDP). The MP is led by Turgut Özal, an engineer and economist who occupied high technocratic positions under Demirel, including the post of undersecretary in charge of the State Planning Organization. Özal became the deputy prime minister in charge of economic affairs in the Bülent Ulusu Government during the National Security Council rule. The PP was led by Necdet Calp, a former governor and undersecretary in the prime minister's office. The NDP leader, Turgut Sunalp, was a former general who served, after his retirement, as the Turkish ambassador in Canada.

The November 1983 elections resulted in a clear victory for Mr. Özal and his party. The MP won 45.2 percent of the total valid votes cast and 52.9 percent of the 400 assembly seats. Although a majority of the MP votes presumably came from former JP supporters, it appears that the MP also received votes from the supporters of the former NSP, NAP, and even the RPP. The PP came out as the second largest party with 30.5 percent of the vote and 29.3 percent of the seats, which was a better result than most observers expected. The PP appears to have gained the votes of a large majority of the former RPP voters. The main loser in the elections was the NDP. Despite the high expectations of its leadership, the NDP finished a poor third with 23.3 percent of the vote and only 17.8 percent of the seats. This seems to be related to the fact that most voters perceived the NDP as an extension of military rule, or as kind of a "state party," an image that the party leadership did not try to dispel. By contrast the MP was seen as the most spontaneous or the least artificial party of all three. In this sense, the election outcome can be interpreted as reflecting the desire of a majority of Turkish voters for a rapid normalization and civilianization.

The transition process proceeded smoothly following the elections. The legal existence of the National Security Council came to an end, the council members resigned their military posts and became members of the new Presidential Council. Mr. Özal was duly invited by President Evren to form the new government, and he received a comfortable vote of confidence from the GNA. Despite the speculations to the contrary, the new MP government did not include any independent ministers close to or favored by the military. Another MP deputy, Mr. Necmettin Karaduman, was easily elected speaker of the GNA, again disproving speculations that Mr. Ulusu (a former navy commander and the prime minister during council rule) was favored by the military for that prestigious post. Once in office, Özal started to put his economic liberalization program into effect with characteristic speed and boldness. One of the first laws passed by the GNA allowed all established parties (including the True Path and the Social Democratic parties) to contest the local government elections held in the spring of 1984. These elections confirmed the popularity of the MP. Thus, with the 1983 elections, civilian government has been restored and a new phase in Turkish politics has started.

An Appraisal

On the basis of the above historical analysis, Turkey's overall degree of success with democratic government can be described as "mixed" or "unstable." Democracy has been the rule in the last forty years, but has been interrupted thrice since 1960. Democratic rule is now in place, however, and there appears to be no immediate threat to its existence. A more positive evaluation is also suggested by the fact that of the three interruptions one was only partial, and the other two were of relatively short duration. Furthermore, in both cases, the military rulers declared from the beginning their intention to restore democracy. That they faithfully kept their promises is even more significant. Thus the democratic process was interrupted not by fully developed authoritarian regimes, but by interim military governments that aimed to effect a "reequilibration of democracy." The overall trend then has been *not away but toward* democratic government.

The transition in 1983 followed the pattern of *reforma* rather than *ruptura* or even *ruptura-pactada, reforma-pactada*, as did the transitions in the periods of 1946–1950 and 1960–1961. In fact it was even a purer case of *reforma* than the earlier ones. In the 1946–1950 transition the RPP government and the DP opposition at least agreed upon a new electoral law prior to the crucial elections of 1950. In 1960–1961 period the military government actively collaborated with the two opposition parties in making the new constitution and the electoral law. In the most recent transition, on the other hand, the National Security Council excluded all organized political groups from any meaningful role in the transition. The 1982 Constitution was prepared by the National Security Council itself in collaboration with an all-appointed, no-party Consultative Assembly, and the November 1983 elections were held under conditions carefully controlled by the council.

This process of transition and the new constitution as its product have been questioned by important sectors of Turkish public opinion. Of the three present major parties the MP is the strongest supporter of the new regime, although it has indicated that it was not against certain relatively minor constitutional amendments. The True Path Party of Mr. Demirel favors more substantial constitutional changes. The Social Democratic Party (which became the Social Democratic Populist Party after its merger with the Populist Party) strongly criticizes restrictions on civil liberties and union rights, and advocates a more rapid normalization. There is substantial agreement, however, that the transition to democracy is genuine (although to some, yet incomplete), and that the 1982 Constitution may serve as the basis of the new Turkish political regime with some (more or less important) modifications.

• THEORETICAL ANALYSIS •

What are the historical, cultural, social, economic, and political factors that favored or impeded the development of democratic government in Turkey? Since Turkey is a case of mixed success, it stands to reason that the following list is also a mixed one.

Political Culture

Two important features characterized the Ottoman political culture. One was the predominance of status-based values rather than market-derived values.[27] This was the outcome of the "bureaucratic" nature of the Ottoman Empire, which was described above. Briefly stated, the fundamental relationship under Ottoman rule between economic power and political power was essentially the reverse of the European historical experience: instead of economic power (i.e., ownership of the means of production) leading to political power (i.e., high office in the state bureaucracy), political power provided access to material wealth. However, the wealth thus accumulated could not be converted into more permanent economic assets because it was liable to confiscation by the state. Despite the growth of a substantial commercial and industrial middle class under the republic and especially in the last forty years, such status-based values still persist. The impact of this historical-cultural legacy on the development of democratic government in Turkey has been, on the whole, negative, since the predominance of status-derived values contributes to the strengthening of an all-powerful centralized state and hinders the development of a "civil society."

Another feature of the Ottoman cultural legacy has been the dichotomy resulting from the cultural division in Ottoman society between the palace (great) culture and the local or provincial (little) cultures.[28] They represented two very distinct ways of life, with different operational codes, different symbols (state versus village and tribe), different languages (highly literary and stylistic Ottoman versus simple spoken Turkish), different occupations (statecraft versus farming and artisanship), different types of settlement (urban versus rural), different literary and artistic traditions (*divan* literature and court music versus folk literature and music), and sometimes different versions of Islam (highly legalistic orthodox Islam versus often heterodox folk Islam). The nineteenth-century reforms and the Westernization movement did not eliminate, but perhaps further exacerbated, this cultural dualism by making the elite culture even more alien and inaccessible to the masses. Linguistic differences even among the Muslim subjects of the empire further contributed to this cultural fragmentation. Finally, the *millet* system that gave the ecclesiastical authorities of non-Muslim communities substantial control over their communal affairs without, however, granting them participatory rights meant that these communities maintained and developed their own cultures quite autonomously from the central or "great" culture. All this led to a low level of social and cultural integration of the Ottoman society.

To be sure, the republic made important strides in bridging the gap between elite and mass cultures. In particular, the last forty years of multiparty politics helped to integrate the mass electorate into national political life. "The distributive and the redistributive functions of government received increasing emphasis, while the prevalence of the extractive function began to decline. Second, as an outcome of the first point, the citizens became more interested in national political life and came to identify themselves more closely with national political institutions of which political parties were the main example."[29] Still, the lingering elitist attitudes within sectors of the centralist bureaucratic elite have produced tensions in the political system and remain dysfunctional for the development of democratic government.[30]

There are other features of the Ottoman-Turkish political culture that are also incongruent with a democratic political system. It has been argued, for example, that "there is an element in Turkish political culture to which the notion of opposition is deeply repugnant." Turks have shown a predilection for organic theories of the state and society, and solidarist doctrines found easy acceptance among the Young Turk and Kemalist elites. The Kemalist notion of "populism" meant a rejection of class conflict and a commitment to establish a "harmony of interests" through paternalistic government policies. This "*gemeinschaft* outlook," present in both elite and mass cultures, finds perhaps its most poignant political expression in the excessive "fear of a national split." Indeed, one of the most frequent accusations party leaders hurl at each other is "splitting the nation."[31] Thus it appears that the notion of a loyal and legitimate opposition has not been fully institutionalized at the cultural level. The line separating opposition from treason is still rather thin compared to older and more stable democracies. The tendency to see politics in absolutist terms also explains the low capacity of political leaders for compromise and accommodation. Whether such low tolerance for opposition is comparable in the long run with the institutionalization of liberal democracy is open to question.

A related tendency is the low tolerance shown for individual deviance and heterodoxy within groups. In other words Turkish political culture attributes primacy not to the individual but to the collectivity, be it the nation, the state, or one of its subunits.[32] Individuality and deviance tend to be punished, conformity and orthodoxy rewarded in bureaucratic agencies, political parties, and even voluntary associations. Finally, most social institutions (families, schools, trade unions, local communities) display authoritarian patterns in their authority relations. This tends to create incongruences with the democratic authority patterns in the governmental sphere and to undermine stable democracy.[33]

On the more positive side, however, there seems to be a widespread consensus that the legitimacy of government derives from a popular mandate obtained in free, competitive elections. A democratic system is seen as the natural culmination of a century-old process of modernization and especially of the Kemalist reforms, the purpose of which was to create a Western type of secular, republican, modern state. In addition to this long-standing elite commitment to democracy, the peasants and the urban lower classes have come to see competitive elections as a powerful means to increase socioeconomic equality and to promote their material interests. A survey among some Istanbul squatters demonstrated, for example, that a substantial majority of them believed in the importance of voting and found political parties useful especially as channels of communication with government.[34] This attitude reflects a realization that a noncompetitive system would be less responsive to their group demands. Although there was a great deal of public anxiety over increasing political polarization and violence in the late 1970s, a majority of Turkish voters do not seem to hold the democratic system responsible for the crisis. Furthermore, in spite of such polarization, a centrist political orientation has remained strong among Turkish voters. In a 1977 preelection survey, 26.8 percent of the respondents placed themselves at the center, 27.7 percent at the left of center, and 24.6 percent at the right of center. About a fifth of the respondents (20.9 percent) claimed that they had no opinion on this question. If we assume that "don't knows" indicate a lack of interest in ideological politics, then close to half of all Turkish voters can be placed at the center.[35] While few people would like to go back to the circumstances that prevailed before the 1980 coup, there does not seem to be broad popular support for a prolonged authoritarian solution.

Historical Development

Certain historical factors favor the development of democratic government in Turkey. As the first part of this chapter demonstrates, the first movements toward representative and constitutional government started more than a century ago. Even if we discount the brief periods of

democratic government under the Ottoman Empire and the early republic, the present competitive political system has been in existence for forty years with relatively short interruptions. A generation born in the multiparty period and socialized into democratic values has already reached positions of authority in governmental as well as nongovernmental spheres. Following Huntington we may argue that such longevity, or "chronological age," has helped to institutionalize democratic organizations and procedures.[36]

That Turkey did not have a colonial past, unlike most of the Third

World countries, is also a favorable historical factor for democratic development. Democratic institutions were not imposed from outside, but are seen as a natural outgrowth of internal political processes, which tends to increase their legitimacy in the eyes of the elites and the masses.

One may argue that some sequences of political development favor the emergence of democratic institutions more than the others. It has been posited, for example, that the optimum sequence is to establish national unity (identity) first, then central government authority, and then political equality and participation.[37] Turkish political development followed this optimum course. Simultaneously with the creation of the Turkish Republic in place of the multinational Ottoman Empire, the question of identity was effectively solved in favor of a Turkish national identity. The already highly developed central governmental institutions of the Ottoman state were further strengthened under the republic and penetrated more deeply into the society. The expansion of political participation took place a generation later in the mid-1940s, and proceeded within the already existing institutional framework of elections, legislatures and parties.

Class Structure

The distribution of wealth and income appears to be highly unequal in Turkey. It is markedly so between the agricultural and nonagricultural sectors, within each of these sectors, between cities and rural settlements, and among geographic regions. A substantial proportion of the Turkish population has been, and remains, in a condition of low-end poverty. A study estimated that in 1973 38 percent of all Turkish households were below the subsistence level. Ownership of land is also highly unequal. Another 1973 study found that 22 percent of rural households were landless. About 42 percent of all rural households own very little land or no land at all, and the land owned by this 42 percent makes up less than 3 percent of total privately owned land. Conversely, households with 1,000 or more acres of land, constituting only 0.12 percent of all rural households, own 5.27 percent of total privately owned land. Land distribution is particularly unequal in the eastern and southeastern regions, which display markedly feudal features.[38] Overall income inequality seems to have further increased in the late 1970s and the early 1980s.

On the more positive side one may cite the existence of a rather substantial educated urban middle class of entrepreneurs, professionals, and bureaucrats, as well as a large group of middle-sized farmers. Under the liberal labor legislation that followed the 1961 Constitution, the number of unionized workers rose rapidly from less than 300,000 in 1963 to over 2.2 million in 1977. Thus the percentage of unionized workers reached 14.8 percent of the total economically active population and 39.8 percent of all wage earners.[39] Other alleviating factors ("dampening mechanisms") included the relatively high rate of economic growth (see below) and the availability of "exit" possibilities. Apart from more than a million Turkish workers (over 2 million together with their dependents) who have emigrated to Western Europe and to a much lesser extent to Middle Eastern countries, mass rural-to-urban migration helps to ease distributional problems in rural areas and reduces the propensity to resort to the "voice" option, that is, corrective political action.[40] Also contributing to the general lack of effective collective action aimed at income redistribution in rural areas are the strong in-group feelings and the absence of class-based politics among Turkish peasants who still compose roughly half the labor force. In some of the least developed regions (e.g., the east and the southeast), where land and income inequality is greatest and redistributive action is most needed, the low level of social mobilization and the strength of patron-client relationships tend to make peasant political participation more mobilized and deferential than autonomous and instrumental. In some areas (e.g., central Turkey), relative equality of landownership together with overall poverty also works against emergence of class cleavages among peasants by producing a "corporate village" pattern. This may explain why the social democratic RPP, which has based its appeal on the promise of a more egalitarian income distribution and has greatly increased its urban strength between 1969 and 1977, has not been able to achieve nearly the same degree of success in rural areas.[41]

National Structure (Ethnic and Religious Cleavages)

The breakup of the Ottoman Empire at the end of World War I made the present day Turkey an ethnically, linguistically, and religiously much more homogeneous country than its predecessor. Over 99 percent of its population profess Islam; an estimated 15 percent belong to the Alevi (Shiite) sect, the rest are Sunnis. The Alevis are concentrated in the east central region and have tended to support the RPP. The Unity party, formed in 1968 to represent the Alevis, has not fared well electorally. Its vote declined steadily from 2.8 percent in 1969, to 1.1 percent in 1973, and 0.4 percent in 1977. In the atmosphere of political polarization in the late 1970s, this sectarian cleavage led to violent clashes in several localities, the worst of which was the Kahramanmaras incident in which about 100 people lost their lives. The only large linguistic minority is the Kurdish-speaking minority (again an estimated 10 percent to 15 percent), which is concentrated in the eastern and southeastern regions. Although a few thousand separatist guerillas are currently active in the region, a very large majority of Kurdish speakers seem to be well integrated into Turkish society. There is no political party that specifically represents the interests of the Kurdish-speaking population. The voting patterns in these regions are not markedly different from the rest of the country except that personalistic and clientelistic influences are much stronger there because of economic underdevelopment and feudalistic social structure. Sectarian and linguistic cleavages do not coincide and mutually reinforce each other, however, since most of the (minority) Alevis are Turkish speakers, and a large majority of Kurdish speakers are Sunnis. Furthermore, neither of them coincide with class cleavages except that the eastern regions are in general much poorer than the rest of the country.

State Structure and Strength

One of the principal legacies of the Ottoman Empire is the strong and centralized state authority. The political center composed of the sultan and his military and civilian bureaucrats sought to eliminate all rival centers of power. The resulting situation has been referred to as the "absence of civil society," which means the weakness or absence of corporate, autonomous, intermediary social structures. The number of voluntary associations in Turkey rose tremendously in the multiparty era from a mere 802 in 1946 to 37,806 in 1968.[42] Yet organizational autonomy and the level of organizational participation in such associations are still much lower than in Western European and North American democracies. The relative ease with which interim military regimes abolished parties, restricted union rights, co-opted or neutralized professional associations, and curtailed the autonomy of universities testifies to the weakness of corporate structures.

The weakness of civil society is also evident in the weakness of local governments. The vast territories of the Ottoman Empire were ruled not by local bodies, but by centrally appointed governors. The first semielected, local administrative councils came into being, as we have already seen, only in the second half of the nineteenth century. As for the cities the Ottoman state had no tradition of independent, autonomous municipalities. Nor did the republic attempt to change this centralized system. Although a law passed in 1930 enabled local communities to establish municipal governments, the whole system of local administration remained highly centralized. Local governments, especially municipalities, gained some vitality in the multiparty era. Nevertheless, their autonomous powers have been very limited, central control over their activities (called "administrative tutelage") exceedingly strict, and their financial resources totally inadequate. In this sense both provincial administrations and municipalities have had to depend very heavily on the central government.[43]

Historically the state has also played a dominant role in the economy. This Ottoman legacy was further reinforced under the republic when the Kemalist regime initiated a policy of economic interventionism (statism) in the 1930s. Statism meant the direct entry of the state into the fields of production and distribution. Public economic enterprises started to be created in those years and grew rapidly. Despite the greater emphasis on the private sector in recent decades, such enterprises still produce about one-half of the total industrial output. Both under the Ottoman state and the early republic, private accumulation of wealth depended, in large measure, on position in or access to the state.

This combination of factors, namely the absence of powerful, economically dominant interests able to capture the state and use it to serve their own purposes, and the weakness or absence of corporate intermediary structures, had important consequences for subsequent modernization. First, it led to what is known as the "autonomy of the state," meaning that the state apparatus is not the captive or the handmaiden of any particular social class, but possesses sufficient autonomy to make decisions that can change, eliminate, or create class relationships. This autonomous state, unhampered by established class interests and strong corporate structures, has a high capacity to accumulate and expand political power and to use it for the economic and social modernization of society. The implications for the development of democratic government are not, however, nearly as positive. As has been argued above, an autonomous, bureaucratic state is much less likely to develop democratic political institutions than a postfeudal society in which feudalism and the system of representation of estates left a legacy of autonomous groups with corporate identity and rights.

The nature and autonomy of the state in Turkey also means that the costs of being out of power are extremely high. Because of the high degree of governmental centralization and the large role of the Turkish state in the economy, "those in government have access, directly or indirectly, to an immense amount of resources in relation to the resource base of society, which they can distribute."[44] Conversely, a party that is out of power tends to get weakened since it does not have access to political patronage resources.

The Turkish state, strong and centralized as it is, has generally been effective in maintaining public order. When it was faced with widespread terrorism and violence as in the late 1970s, however, it had to turn to the army by declaring martial law. This may be related to the fact that police forces, being within the direct jurisdiction of the Ministry of Interior, are more susceptible to political influences and, sometimes, even to infiltration by extremist groups, as was the case in the late 1970s. Especially in a politically charged atmosphere, therefore, police action is not considered as impartial and as legitimate by the public as military action.

Indeed the Turkish armed forces are broadly representative of the society as a whole. They are not dominated or controlled by any particular social group or political force. They are strongly committed to the legacy of Atatürk and to a modern, national, secular, republican state. More so than in many Latin American countries, they also have been committed to democratic principles, as attested by their voluntary and relatively rapid relinquishment of power to freely elected civilian authorities after each intervention. They display, however, certain ambivalent attitudes toward democracy, characteristic of the military in other developing nations. In the elitist tradition described above, they tend to see themselves as the true guardians of the national interest, as opposed to "partial" interests represented by political parties. They also consider themselves the protectors of national unity that, in their opinion, is often endangered by the divisive actions of political parties. These attitudes, which signify a deep distrust of parties and politicians, are clearly reflected in those provisions of the 1982 Constitution aiming to limit the power of political parties. Similarly, the constitution's numerous restrictions on trade unions and voluntary associations suggest that the military's conception of democracy is more plebiscitary than participatory. In short the military, reflecting the larger society's somewhat ambivalent values toward democracy, seem to share both a belief in its general appropriateness and desirability for Turkey, and some of the antiliberal, antideviationist, intolerant attitudes embedded in the Turkish political culture.

Political Structure

Some aspects of the political structure in Turkey have been positive in their implications for democracy but others have been negative. On the positive side the major political parties have been moderate and non-ideological. Despite the polarization in the late 1970s, the ideological and social distance between the two major parties has not been great. Major political parties have not sponsored or condoned acts of political violence, nor have they called for military intervention. However, the JP's coalition partnership with the NAP in the late 1970s forced it to be reticent about the right-wing terror.

Extremist parties, such as the NAP and NSP, have not had a significant electoral following. However, those parties played an important role in the 1970s because of the peculiar parliamentary arithmetic that resulted from the system of proportional representation. Although there were only four significant parties in the 1977 National Assembly, the system displayed the functional properties of extreme multipartism. Instead of the centripetal drive of moderate multipartism, the basic drive of the system seemed to be in a centrifugal direction. Standards of "fair competition" fell significantly and there was a corresponding increase in the "politics of outbidding."[45]

No major interest group is excluded from representation in the political system through a party or party faction. The constitution states, however, that the "constitutions and programs of political parties shall not be incompatible with the territorial and national integrity of the state, human rights, national sovereignty, and the principles of a democratic and secular Republic." To this is added a more specific provision banning parties that aim at establishing the sovereignty of a particular class or group, or a dictatorship of any sort. Thus the constitution excludes from political competition communist, fascist, religious, and separatist parties. Political parties that violate these bans shall be closed by the Constitutional Court. Trade unions are also prohibited from establishing political linkages with political parties. They cannot engage in political activities, nor can they support or receive support from political parties.

A strong and independent judiciary has developed, including a Constitutional Court with full powers to declare an act of parliament unconstitutional. The 1961 Constitution took special care to safeguard the judiciary vis-à-vis the legislature and the executive. The 1982 Constitution broadly maintained the same principle with some, relatively minor, modifications. Security of tenure for judges and public prosecutors has been recognized by the 1982 Constitution in identical terms as those of its predecessor, according to which "judges and public prosecutors shall not be dismissed or retired before the age prescribed by the Constitution; nor shall they be deprived of their salaries, allowances, or other personal rights, even as a result of the abolition of a court or a post." Personnel matters for judges and public prosecutors, such as appointments, promotions, transfers, and disciplinary actions are within the exclusive jurisdiction of the Supreme Council of Judges and Public Prosecutors, itself composed primarily of judges nominated by the two high courts in the country and appointed by the president of the republic.

A vigorously free and independent press strongly committed to democratic principles has developed. The press has, in general, maintained its independent attitude and commitment to democracy even in times of interim military governments, although martial law entailed severe restrictions on the freedom of the press. With the transition to a civilian regime in November 1983 and the subsequent lifting of martial law, the press has strongly reasserted itself. It has shown willingness to publicize domestic and foreign criticism of human rights practices.

On the basis of the preceding observations we may conclude that, of our set of variables, that which pertains to political structures is probably the most favorable one to democratic government in Turkey.

Political Leadership

Turkish political leaders have, in general, been committed to the democratic process, and have denounced acts of violence and disloyalty against it. They have also, in general, been reasonably effective and honest in governing. On the other hand, as our historical analysis has demonstrated, they have not, as a rule, shown a high capacity for accommodation and compromise in containing political conflict and managing political crises and strains. On the contrary their failure to do so seems directly responsible for both the 1960 and 1980 military interventions. In 1960, the deterioration of relations between the government and the opposition parties led to widespread public unrest that in turn triggered off the coup. Similarly, prior to the 1980 intervention, a coalition government based on the two major parties, or at least some broad understanding between them, would probably have satisfied the military and held off their intervention. This unwillingness to compromise seems partly a function of the political cultural characteristics and partly of the high costs of being out of power in Turkey.

Development Performance

The rate of economic growth in Turkey has been comparatively high, if somewhat uneven. In the 1950s and the 1960s the average annual rate of real GNP growth has been about 7 percent. Turkey was hard-hit, however, by the oil shock in 1974 and the subsequent "worldwide recession, concomitant with deteriorating terms of trade and continuation of trade policies geared more toward import substitution than export encouragement, including an exchange rate regime that discouraged inflows of capital and workers' remittances." Thus the GDP growth rate fell 2.4 percent in 1978, and declined further 0.9 percent in 1979, and 0.8 percent in 1980. Moreover, the rate of inflation reached 70 percent in 1979 and above 100 percent in 1980.[46] With the introduction of comprehensive reform measures in January 1980, whose chief architect was Turgut Özal (then the director of the State Planning Organization), economic growth has resumed at a modest rate of about 5 percent. These new policies aimed at greater reliance upon market forces and an easing of governmental interventions in the economy. They continued to be pursued by the military regime of 1980–1983, under which Özal was made the deputy prime minister in charge of economic affairs, and obviously since November 1983 when he came to power at the head of his new Motherland Party.

The relatively high rate of economic growth since the transition to competitive politics has been one of the "dampening mechanisms" that discouraged the political participation of low-income strata. It seems, however, that the benefits of growth have been quite unevenly distributed across regions, economic sectors, and social classes. Nevertheless, it is not the case that the rich got richer and the poor got poorer; rather they both got richer, but the rich got richer at a faster rate.[47] The implications for the future of democracy of this economic development performance will be discussed in the next section.

International Factors

Turkey's close alliance with the West since the end of the World War II has generally, but only indirectly, supported democratic developments in the country. Turkey has become a member of the NATO, of the Council of Europe, and an associate member of the European Community. These relations have meant linkages between Turkish political parties, parliaments, trade unions, business and professional associations, armed forces, and their Western European and North American counterparts. Over two million Turks living in Western Europe (a very large majority in the Federal Republic of Germany) provide another, and vitally important, link between Turkey and the West.

While all these relations and linkages provide stimuli for democratic development, their effects have been far from decisive. Turks are proud and nationalistic people who do not like to be dictated to from abroad. A good example of this is that criticisms by the European Community, or the Council of Europe, or individual Western European governments of certain undemocratic practices during and after military rule usually create unfavorable reactions, even among those Turks who may be similarly critical of the same practices. The point is often made that Turkey will remain a democracy not to please its European allies, but because its people believe that this is the most appropriate form of government for their country. Nevertheless, the thought lingers no doubt in the minds of many Turkish leaders that an authoritarian Turkey, isolated and excluded from the club of European democracies, will probably experience greater difficulties in its international relations. The breakdown of authoritarian regimes in Greece, Portugal, and Spain in the 1970s makes the position of a pro-Western but authoritarian European country extremely lonely and uneasy.

• FUTURE PROSPECTS AND POLICY IMPLICATIONS •

Policies Promoting the Growth of Civil Society

In view of the positive and negative factors discussed above, what kinds of policies and political/economic developments would be most likely to support, nurture, and sustain democratic government? If one of the most serious obstacles to democratic development in Turkey is the historical legacy of an exceedingly centralized, overpowering state and the concomitant weakness of civil society, then policies that aim at establishing a healthier balance between the state and the society will clearly be functional for democratic development. One obvious area where the state's role can, and probably should, be reduced is the economy. The market-oriented economic policies of Mr. Özal are important steps in that direction. Greater reliance on market mechanisms, greater emphasis on expanding exports instead of an inward-turned, import substitution economic strategy, realistic exchange rates, and a sharp reduction in bureaucratic controls over private economic activities are the main ingredients of the new economic policy. Bold and far-reaching as these innovations are, one should not expect a sudden and radical diminution in the state's role in the economy. The state economic enterprises, which presently produce almost half of the entire industrial output, will be there to stay in the foreseeable future. If, however, their management is somehow given sufficient autonomy and left outside the scope of direct government intervention, this will help to lower the stakes of politics and reduce the winner-take-all, zero-sum character of political competition.

Another set of policies promoting the growth of civil society would be the strengthening of local governments. One recent positive development in this regard has been the substantial increase in their revenues after 1980 through the allocation of a greater share of public funds. If local governments are seen with less suspicion by the central government and given greater powers and responsibilities, they will no doubt play an important role in socializing people into democratic values. Such a development will also mean a more effective power sharing between the central and local bodies and, consequently, an effective check on the power of the central government. Finally, it will lower the stakes of political competition, since an opposition party that controls important municipalities will be able to render some patronage services to its constituents and thus maintain a certain level of political influence.

A third group of policies with the same overall effect would be those that would promote the growth of voluntary associations. As we have pointed out above, the number of voluntary associations increased very rapidly during the years of multiparty politics. The impact of this development on democratic government has not been entirely functional, however, since many associations displayed a propensity for overpoliticization. Instead of articulating the common interests of their members, many of them came to be dominated by small, politically motivated cliques, and became instruments of polarized political struggle. It was not a rare occurrence in the 1970s to see the members of the same professional group (including even the police forces) divided between extreme right and left-wing "professional" associations. Some of the restrictive provisions of the 1982 Constitution on voluntary associations, which may well seem excessive from a liberal democratic point of view, are understandable on the basis of this past experience. One may conclude, therefore, that the constitution aimed at a certain "depoliticization" of the society in general and associational activities in particular. Whether this aim can be accomplished without impeding democratic development remains to be seen. On the one hand, a vigorous life of voluntary associations and professional organizations is a prerequisite for democratic development. On the other, the overpoliticization of such associations has been a polarizing factor in recent Turkish politics. The optimum combination for democratic development would be some middle course between the two.

Policies Promoting Governmental Stability and Efficiency

It has been pointed out that the crisis of democracy in the late 1970s was due, at least in some measure, to the fragmentation of the party system and to the resulting fact that parliamentary balance was held by small antisystem parties. To this was added the incapacity of the political system to initiate new policies to meet new challenges, because of the narrow and heterogeneous governmental majorities in parliament. Two sets of institutional measures taken by the military regime of 1980–1983 may prove to be helpful in preventing the recurrence of a similar situation. One is the change in the electoral system. The adoption of a 10 percent national threshold for representation in the Grand National Assembly, together with various other features of the electoral system that favor major parties, make it extremely difficult for more than three significant parties to be represented in parliament. Given the tendency of the Turkish party system to coalesce around two major and non-ideological parties, this change is likely to remove one major polarizing factor.

The 1982 Constitution has also taken certain measures to increase governmental stability by strengthening the Council of Ministers vis-à-vis the Assembly. For example, while the vote of confidence taken following the formation of a new Council of Ministers does not require more than an ordinary majority, a vote of censure requires an absolute majority of the full membership of the Assembly. Furthermore, in a vote of confidence only negative (meaning no confidence) votes are counted (articles 99 and 111).

A much more consequential novelty of the constitution designed to increase governmental stability concerns the scope of the power of dissolution. The 1961 Constitution permitted the executive branch to call new elections for the National Assembly only under very exceptional circumstances. This limited right of dissolution did not offer any help in cases of protracted government crisis when no majority coalition could be formed. The 1982 Constitution empowers the president to call new elections when a government cannot be formed within forty-five days either at the beginning of a new legislative assembly or after the resignation of a government. The constitution has also adopted a new procedure in the selection of the president of the republic to prevent the kind of deadlock witnessed in 1980.[48]

Finally, the broadening under the 1982 Constitution of the law-making powers of the executive is designed to increase the efficiency of government. This power was given to the Council of Ministers for the first time by the 1971 amendment of the constitution, under which the Council of Ministers could issue ordinances or decrees that could amend existing laws. The 1982 Constitution further expanded the power to issue such ordinances. The enabling act of Parliament defines the purpose, scope, and principles of ordinances and prescribes the period during which they can be issued. In contrast to the 1961 Constitution, the enabling act does not have to specify which provisions of the existing legislation can be amended or repealed by ordinance. The 1982 Constitution also empowers the executive to issue a special kind of law-amending ordinances during periods of martial law or state of emergency. They differ from ordinary ordinances in that they do not require a prior enabling act and, even more important, they are outside the scope of review by the Constitutional Court. Both ordinary and emergency ordinances are subject, however, to review by the assembly.

Policies Promoting Economic Growth and Equity

It has already been mentioned that the relatively high rate of economic growth in the 1950s and the 1960s has been one of the positive factors supporting democratic development. However, the dominant economic development strategy of the era presents a close resemblance to the one pursued by some relatively developed Latin American countries, notably Brazil and Argentina, during the populist semiauthoritarian regimes of Vargas and Peron, with the same negative implications for democracy. In both cases, economic development strategies were based more on import substitution (of essentially consumer goods) than on export encouragement. One reason given for the emergence of military-bureaucratic-technocratic regimes in these countries in the 1960s and the 1970s is the economic difficulties and bottlenecks associated with this kind of development strategy (industrial dependence on imported inputs and government protection; inability to export, leading to foreign exchange shortages, and then to unemployment and economic stagnation).

As the economic pie got smaller, political conflict became more virulent, the populist coalition broke down, and the middle classes came to see the demands of the popular sector as excessive. The resultant military-technocratic regimes tended to restrict political participation by suppressing or deactivating the urban popular sector, and to follow growth policies that increased socioeconomic inequality.[49]

Thus similarities between the Turkish case on the one hand, and the Argentine and the Brazilian ones on the other are unmistakable, with the exception that the military regime was of much shorter duration in Turkey. The most appropriate policy to avoid a repetition of this vicious circle seems to be an economic growth strategy encouraging exports and export-oriented, internationally competitive industries, combined with an effort to increase equity. While Mr. Özal's economic policies have been highly successful on the first front, they have not been marked by a strong concern for equity. Thus the concluding remarks of an earlier study on the political economy of income distribution, still seems valid:

> With the equity tensions rising, it is abundantly clear that any optimistic scenario for distributional politics in the near and medium terms must be premised on a speedy, confident resumption of economic growth. Only with an expanding pie can the reslicing due to be demanded be reasonably peaceful and satisfying. An optimistic scenario, then, would posit such growth resumption . . . . But then it would also posit a leadership that would add to growth policies far more vigorous and sweeping redistributive reforms than have been yet accomplished. Failing this, the outlook appears to us bleak—along either of the two courses we see events branching. Either the forces favoring redistribution will strengthen their hold on political power and, lacking growth, will force a more equitable sharing of poverty. Or, alternatively, a more authoritarian regime [probably of a military variety] will intervene to repress both redistributive and participatory demands. The first of these less attractive cases, absent growth, would be very likely to induce a switch to the second. And whether the resort to it were immediate or delayed, it would thwart, for an uncertainly long time, Turkey's reach toward a more just and democratic system. Our profound hope is that both can be avoided—by a timely and bold adoption of the growth-with-equity alternative.[50]

Conclusion

As stated above, Turkey is one of the few countries that are more democratic politically than they ought to have been according to the level of their socioeconomic development.[51] This should be explained mainly by the strong elite commitment to democracy and the relatively favorable political structural factors, the elite commitment was the major factor in the crucial transition from authoritarian rule in 1946–1950 period. It was also instrumental in keeping the three military interventions either partial or of relatively short duration. Indeed, interruptions in the democratic process were more in the nature of reequilibrations of democracy than full-blown authoritarian interludes.[52] Thus normalization proceeded more rapidly after the elections of November 1983 than most observers expected at the time. All four parties banned by the military regime have now been revived under new names, with the difference that the two old major parties have two competing heirs each (the Motherland and the True Path parties for the JP; the Social Democratic Populist and the Democratic Left parties for the RPP). The new electoral system with its high national threshold, however, is likely to force similar parties into merger in the long run. Given the fact that the pre-1980 polarization was the work mainly of small extremist parties and groups, their elimination from representation in Parliament may well turn out to be a stabilizing factor. The constitutional ban on the political activities of trade unions and on their establishing linkages with political parties, on the other hand, is not viewed as desirable or legitimate by the social democratic parties. It is to be expected that the most likely course of events in the next few years would be the consolidation of democracy, with the expansion of civil and union rights by means of relatively minor changes in the constitution.

• NOTES •

1. A comprehensive continuing study sponsored by the Center of International Studies of Princeton University attempts to analyze the legacy of the Ottoman Empire upon its successor states.

2. For the differences between bureaucratic and feudal states, and the implications for their developments, see Samuel P. Huntington, *Political Order in Changing Societies* (New Haven and London: Yale University Press, 1968), ch. 3.

3. Halil Inalcik, "The Nature of Traditional Society: Turkey," in Robert E. Ward and Dankwart A. Rustow, eds., *Political Modernization in Japan and Turkey* (Princeton: Princeton University Press, 1964), p. 44. The following analysis borrows extensively from my *Social Change and Political Participation in Turkey* (Princeton: Princeton University Press, 1976), pp. 25–29.

4. Niyazi Berkes, *Türkiye'de Cagdaslasma* (*The Development of Secularism in Turkey*) (Ankara: Bilgi Yayinevi, 1973), pp. 27–28.

5. H. A. R. Gibb and Harold Bowen, *Islamic Society and the West*, vol. 1, part 1 (London: Oxford University Press, 1950), p. 52.

6. Şerif Mardin, "Power, Civil Society and Culture in the Ottoman Empire," *Comparative Studies in Society and History* 2 (June 1969): passim; Clement Henry Moore, "Authoritarian Politics in Unincorporated Society: The Case of Nasser's Egypt," *Comparative Politics* 6 (January 1974): pp. 204–208.

7. Şerif Mardin, "Historical Determinants of Social Stratification: Social Class and Class Consciousness in Turkey," *A. Ü. Siyasal Bilgiler Fakültesi Dergisi* 22 (Aralik 1967): p. 127.

8. Stanford J. Shaw, "The Central Legislative Councils in the Nineteenth Century Ottoman Reform Movement before 1876," *International Journal of Middle East Studies* 1 (January 1970): pp. 57–62.

9. Roderic H. Davison, *Reform in the Ottoman Empire, 1856–1876* (Princeton, N.J.: Princeton University Press, 1963), pp. 147–149, 167.

10. Robert Devereux, *The First Ottoman Constitutional Period: A Study of the Midhat Constitution and Parliament* (Baltimore: The Johns Hopkins University Press, 1963), pp. 126–148.

11. Engin Deniz Akarli, "The State as a Socio-Cultural Phenomenon and Political Participation in Turkey," in Akarli and Gabriel Ben-Dor, eds., *Political Participation in Turkey: Historical Background and Present Problems* (Istanbul: Bogaziçi University Publications, 1975), p. 139. See also, Şerif Mardin, "Center-Periphery Relations: A Key to Turkish Politics?," *Daedalus* 102, no. 1 (Winter 1973): pp. 169–190; Metin Heper, "Center and Periphery in the Ottoman Empire, with Special Reference to the Nineteenth Century," *International Political Science Review* 1, no. 1 (1980): pp. 81–104.

12. Akarli, "The State as a Socio-Cultural Phenomenon," p. 143.

13. Kemal H. Karpat, "The Transformation of the Ottoman State, 1789–1908," *International Journal of Middle East Studies* 3 (July 1972): pp. 263, 268–270.

14. Feroz Ahmad, *The Young Turks: The Committee of Union and Progress in Turkish Politics, 1908–1914* (Oxford: Clarendon Press, 1969), pp. 143–144.

15. Ibid., pp. 161–162.

16. Özbudun, *Social Change and Political Participation*, pp. 38–41.

17. Frederick W. Frey, *The Turkish Political Elite* (Cambridge, Mass.: M.I.T. Press, 1965), p. 326.

18. For details, see my "Turkey," in Myron Weiner and Ergun Özbudun, eds., *Competitive Elections in Developing Countries* (Durham, N.C.: Duke University Press, 1987), pp. 328–368.

19. Ilter Turan, "Stages of Political Development in the Turkish Republic," (Paper presented to the Third International Congress on the Economic and Social History of Turkey, Princeton University, 24–26 August 1983), pp. 6–11.

20. Nur Yalman argues, for example, that the dispute between rationalism and tradition "happens to be especially bitter in Turkey. It is rare to see such virulent opposition to a country's own traditions and history." "Islamic Reform and the Mystic Tradition in Eastern Turkey," *Archive européene de sociologie* 10 (1969): p. 45.

21. Juan J. Linz, "The Transition from Authoritarian Regimes to Democratic Political Systems and the Problems of Consolidation of Political Democracy," (Paper presented to the IPSA Round Table, Tokyo, 29 March to 1 April 1982), pp. 23–41.

22. For details see my "Transition from Authoritarianism to Democracy in Turkey, 1945–1950," (Paper presented at the IPSA World Congress, Paris, 15–20 July 1985).

23. Frey, *The Turkish Political Elite*, pp. 196–197.

24. Turan, "Stages of Political Development," p. 17.

25. Ergun Özbudun, *The Role of the Military in Recent Turkish Politics*, (Cambridge, Mass.: Harvard University Center for International Affairs, Occasional Paper in International Affairs, 1966), pp. 30–39.

26. Özbudun, *Social Change and Political Participation*, passim; Özbudun, "Voting Behaviour: Turkey," in Jacob M. Landau, Ergun Özbudun, and Frank Tachau, eds., *Electoral Politics in the Middle East: Issues, Voters, and Elites* (London: Croom Helm, 1980), pp. 107–143.

27. Mardin, "Power, Civil Society and Culture," pp. 258–281.

28. Ibid., pp. 270–281.

29. Turan, "Stages of Political Development," p. 29.

30. Ibid., pp. 52–55.

31. Şerif Mardin, "Opposition and Control in Turkey," *Government and Opposition* 1 (May 1966): pp. 375–387.

32. Turan, "Stages of Political Development," pp. 46–47.

33. Harry H. Eckstein, *A Theory of Stable Democracy*, (Princeton: Center of International Studies, Princeton University, Monograph no. 10, 1961).

34. Kemal H. Karpat, *The Gecekondu: Rural Migration and Urbanization* (Cambridge: Cambridge University Press, 1976), pp. 205–211.

35. Üstün Ergüder, "Changing Patterns of Electoral Behavior in Turkey," (Paper presented at the IPSA World Congress, Moscow, 12–18 August 1979), pp. 13–15.

36. Huntington, *Political Order*, p. 13.

37. Eric A. Nordlinger, "Political Development: Time Sequences and Rates of Change," *World Politics* 20 (1968): pp. 494–520; Dankwart A. Rustow, *A World of Nations* (Washington, D.C.: The Brookings Institution, 1967), pp. 120–132; Robert A. Dahl, *Polyarchy: Participation and Opposition*, (New Haven and London: Yale University Press, 1971), ch. 3.

38. Ergun Özbudun and Aydin Ulusan, "Overview," in Özbudun and Ulusan, eds., *The Political Economy of Income Distribution in Turkey*, (New York: Holmes and Meier, 1980), pp. 10–12.

39. Maksut Mumcuoğlu, "Political Activities of Trade Unions and Income Distribution," in Özbudun and Ulusan, eds., *The Political Economy*, pp. 384, 404–405.

40. Albert Hirschman, *Exit, Voice, and Loyalty: Responses to Decline in Firms, Organizations, and States*, (Cambridge, Mass.: Harvard University Press, 1970).

41. Özbudun and Ulusan, "Overview," pp. 17–18.

42. Ahmet N. Yücekök, *Türkiye'de Örgütlenmis Dinin Sosyo-Ekonomik Tabani (The Socioeconomic Basis of Organized Religion in Turkey)* (Ankara: A. Ü. Siyasal Bilgiler Fakültesi, 1971), p. 119.

43. Michael N. Danielson and Ruşen Keleş, "Allocating Public Resources in Urban Turkey," in Özbudun and Ulusan, *The Political Economy*, p. 313 and passim.

44. Turan, "Stages of Political Development," pp. 55–60.

45. Giovanni Sartori, *Parties and Party Systems: A Framework for Analysis*, (Cambridge: Cambridge University Press, 1976), pp. 139–140; Ergun Özbudun, "The Turkish Party System: Institutionalization, Polarization, and Fragmentation," *Middle Eastern Studies* 17, no. 2 (April 1981): p. 233.

46. *Turkey: The Problems of Transition* (Bath: A Euromoney Special Study, 1982), pp. 49–50; Zvi Yehuda Hershlag, "Economic Policies," in Klaus-Detlev Grothusen, ed., *Türkei* (Göttingen, 1985: Vandenhoeck and Ruprecht), pp. 346–369.

47. Özbudun and Ulusan, *The Political Economy*, passim.

48. As under the 1961 Constitution, if no presidential candidate obtains a two-thirds majority of the full membership of the Grand National Assembly on the first two ballots, an absolute majority of the full membership will suffice on the third ballot. But under the new procedure, a fourth ballot, if necessary, will be held only between the two leading candidates, and if the fourth ballot does not produce an absolute majority, the Assembly will dissolve automatically and new general elections will be held immediately (article 102).

49. Especially Guillermo O'Donnell, *Modernization and Bureaucratic Authoritarianism: Studies in South American Politics* (Berkeley: Institute of International Studies, University of California, 1973); Samuel P. Huntington and Joan M. Nelson, *No Easy Choice: Political Participation in Developing Countries* (Cambridge, Mass.: Harvard University Press, 1976), pp. 23–24.

50. Özbudun and Ulusan, "Overview," p. 20.

51. See, for example, Tatu Vanhanen, "The State and Prospects of Democracy in the 1980's," (Paper presented at the IPSA World Congress, Paris, 15–20 July 1985). Vanhanen hypothesizes that "the fundamental factor affecting the nature of political systems is the relative distribution of economic, intellectual and other crucial power resources among various sectors of the population." He measures such distribution by a composite index called "Index of Power Resources" (IPR) and finds a strong correlation between the IPR score and political democracy. Turkey's calculated IPR score is 7.8, considerably lower than those for some South European and Latin American democracies: Greece (20.2). Spain (15.0), Argentina (15.7), Uruguay (17.0), Venezuela (11.0), etc. It should also be pointed out that the IPR score itself seems to be strongly correlated with the more conventional indicators of socioeconomic development.

52. See especially, Juan J. Linz, *The Breakdown of Democratic Regimes: Crisis, Breakdown, and Reequilibration*, (Baltimore and London: The Johns Hopkins University Press, 1978), pp. 87–97.

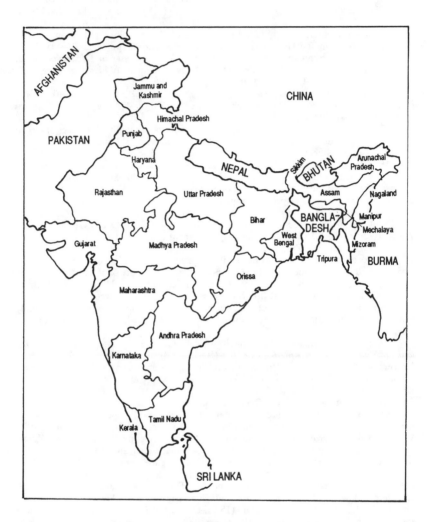

INDIA

CHAPTER SIX

India:
Democratic Becoming and
Combined Development
JYOTIRINDRA DAS GUPTA

Developing countries are not supposed to offer conducive settings for democratic political systems. India's choice of democracy in a setting of poverty, ethnic diversity, and immense complexity of developmental problems must utterly puzzle any theorist of democratic politics. Anyone can imagine how precarious was the prospect of Indian democracy at the moment of its beginning. Four decades of continuous development of constitutional democratic government in India may then call for two kinds of interpretation. Either democracy in India is a misnomer and the pessimistic expectation did not go wrong, or the theorists of democracy were wrong in writing off the possibility of democracy's compatibility with the most stringent tasks of both economic development and political integration in developing countries.

Before we settle for one or the other interpretation, it would be more appropriate to examine the nature of the last four decades' development of democratic politics in India. This will call for, in the first place, an understanding of some of the basic ideas permeating the nationalist movement. The unfolding of these ideas through organizational practice in preindependence days covers a fairly long period. Indeed, the fact that the national ruling party is now more than a hundred years old may offer some solace to those theorists who worry about immature players taking chances with a sophisticated game like democratic politics in developing countries. For our purpose it is important to consider the inheritance of ideas and institutions that prepared the foundation of the new state. We will examine how a set of imported ideas were progressively indigenized to serve large-scale movements and enduring organizations that contributed to the subsequent development of democratic institutions. The second part of our discussion will examine the evolution of the major democratic institutions after independence. This will be followed by an examination of the performance of these institutions with respect to economic development, political participation, and national cohesion. Finally, an attempt will be made to analyze the significance of democratic development for India in terms of national and comparative implications.

The Colonial Period

Nationalist fascination with liberal ideas and organized associations began in India by the first quarter of the nineteenth century. The initial stirrings were mainly directed to internal investigation of the working systems of religion, social organization, and education.[1] Colonial domination of the coastal areas had already enforced a new exposure to the ways of the victors. This was, however, a selective exposure. The terms of selection were largely determined by the rules of consolidation of the colonizing power. The imposed constraints may explain why early nationalist liberation in India chose to stay close to moderate reformism.

Modern nationalism in India began with the notion that Indians should reexamine the very foundation of their existing organization of religion, society, and education. The architects of modern reforms believed that grave weaknesses in these organizations had to be overcome before Indians could seriously strive for active opposition to the colonial rulers. Since the problem of nationalism was perceived to be primarily internal, the immediate target of nationalist action was to be their own society and not the foreign rulers'. The emphasis on internal decay was rather unusual for a nationalist ideal and it turned the focus of the reforms to several unspectacular but patient organizational constructions.

Rationalism and Liberalism

Ram Mohun Roy (1772–1833), and the intelligentsia of his generation, felt that the most impressive aspect of the strength of the West lay not in its hardware and firepower, but in its development of rational thought. In fact, Roy welcomed the British rule as a replacement of Moghul rule because it offered an opportunity for the Indians to challenge and reconstruct their superstitious modes of social order in favor of a rational reordering. He had no doubt that such a society should be based on "civil and political liberty."[2] But he did not leave this transformation to the chance that the colonial rulers might extend their domestic spirit of liberty to liberate the colonized people. Rather, he worked on the assumption that the window on the West would make possible an organized political education, which would enable Indians to recall their original, rational libertarian philosophy. A combination of indigenous and received principles would thus aid the construction of a politically free and socially transformed order.

Ram Mohun Roy's faith in liberal political education was impressed in a number of modern voluntary associations set up by him and his urban followers in the fields of religious renovation, social reform, and educational modernization. Their constructive initiative was directed toward language reform, legal reform, establishing a vernacular press, defending the freedom of the press, and articulating the rights of women, particularly widows.[3] The associational activities spread to different parts of India during the 1860s and 1870s. By this time railroad and telegraph lines had facilitated national communication, and the regional isolation of political consciousness was giving way to an expanding network of public associations concerned with social reform and political protest across the country.

These efforts, however, lacked popular appeal. The liberal appeal to reason and scientific discourse could expand more smoothly only if the pace of introduction of modern education was made faster than what the alien rulers cared for. This pace was dictated by the colonial need for a supply of educated servants of the regime. A unique opportunity for educating the public was missed because the colonial rulers felt educational expansion would threaten their own security.[4] In fact, the abysmally slow growth rates of literacy and education made it easier for the conservative nationalists to gain support from the less educated public on the basis of traditional symbols of solidarity derived from religion, caste, locality, and speech community.

Nationalist politics in India took a new direction following the extensive armed rebellion of 1857. This revolt was effectively suppressed but it left some deep scars on both the rulers and the ruled. Henceforth, India came directly under Crown rule. Strategies of selective favors and suspicions were now used by the regime to deliberately fragment the national perception of British action along religious lines. While this put a premium on religious solidarity for both the favored and the unfavored alike, it seriously damaged the prospects of rational and liberal national mobilization.

Setbacks for Liberalism

The original appeal of liberal ideas in underdeveloped countries consisted of an admiration for the value of the individual and his reasoned preferences unhindered by traditional ties. It is interesting that the historical timing and fascination with liberal ideas in Japan and India were not very far apart. Paradoxically, it was the perceived threat from the liberal West that moved Japanese nationalism toward preemptive militarist modernism, while the colonial rulers in India positively weakened the growth of liberalism by an intensified racialist policy. This hastened the development of reactive communalism, whereby each religious community increasingly came to depend on exclusive mobilization to defend its members' interests.[5]

It is easy to argue that the structural features of Indian society could account for the use of traditional symbols for exclusive mobilization in Indian politics of this time. This, however, would ignore the critical role of the political rewards, punishments, and prohibitions used by a newly centralizing effective power—Crown rule in India. For the strategists of Crown rule the need for Indian manpower offered an excellent opportunity to create a loyal base of support for the expanding colonial regime. Discriminatory preference seemed to offer a special dividend for the new rulers in a country where modern education and political consciousness was historically developing in an uneven spacial and ethnic distribution.

The strategy of selective preference deliberately encouraged the formation of particularistic organizations in Indian politics. The military component of this strategy was aided by a racial theory of graded competence—competence judged by loyalty and not by skill or achievement—whereby Sikhs, Rajputs, and Dogras were placed at the top of the scale of preference for recruitment and trust. The economic component of this preference meant a replacement of precolonial notables in the agrarian property structure by intermediaries drawn from groups promising loyalty to the regime. New revenue settlements (from the days of Permanent Settlement in eastern India to other types instituted in the rest of the country) created a rentier class innocent of productive needs but eager to strengthen the order and finance of the regime. The political component demonstrated, for example, a process of actively supporting the Aligarh movement for Muslim reformism against the antiforeignism of the Muslim fundamentalists and for Muslim exclusivism against non-Muslims. Similarly, exclusive ethnic politics was actively encouraged. Dravidian sentiments were promoted to drive a wedge between northern and southern Hindus and, at the same time, the less advantaged Hindus in all regions were encouraged to press their claims against their superiors in rank.

By the end of the nineteenth century, it seemed clear that the strategy of colonial security and the scramble for new economic opportunities would leave no chance for the growth of secular liberal nationalism. However, two elements came to the aid of the latter. One was the *ideological affirmation* that modernization necessarily calls for a larger political and economic coalition in order to attain both national advancement and individual enhancement. The other was the *pragmatic assessment* of the benefits of a nationally extended market for enterprise, commodities, and employment. What is more important to recognize is the linkage between the two. The promise of extended profitability may not melt all segmental coins but it can soften many for a strategic transition. Nationalist ideological affirmation was expected to facilitate such a transition.

Learning by Organizing

Mutual need more than abstract altruism provided the first major springboard for the construction of a national political platform. Thus when the Indian National Congress was created in 1885, it began as a platform of convenience. With various degrees of attachment to liberal principles, political associations that had grown up in the regional isolation of Bengal, Bombay, Madras, and other areas sought to build a coalition. Since the effective political authority in the country was centralized, it was natural to assume that a national bargaining instrument was necessary to augment the power of the constituents. Thus during the last quarter of the nineteenth century, the Indian Association of Calcutta, the Poona Sarvajanik Sabha, the Madras Mahajana Sabha, the Bombay Presidency Association, and a host of other active associations and individuals helped to form a national political organization that gradually evolved from pleas, petitions, and protest actions to one of the largest and most enduring mass organizations in human history.

During its formative decades, the Indian National Congress performed a number of important functions for democratic political development. It laid the foundation of a national political discourse that facilitated the formulation of political goals and demands in the public arena. It served as a forum for processing conflicting ideas regarding national goals and priorities. Democratic rules of procedure, tolerance of adversaries, and reconciliation of conflicting claims became part of the political education of the participants. From the very inception of the organization the founding leaders were eager to demonstrate their adherence to these democratic norms. Referring to the first phase of the Congress organization one perceptive historian writes that "even though the Congress's democratic procedures were more symbolic than substantive, they indicated a commitment both to representative institutions and to an accommodation of India's pluralism in a future Indian constitution. This commitment was enunciated clearly at the first session of the Congress in 1885, and it remained central in Congress thinking through the drafting of India's constitution after independence in 1947."[6] The founding leaders were highly successful professionals in their fields who did not have to live off politics. They were also aware of their distance from the Indian masses. In their attempt to speak for the people they recognized that their role was one of preparing the ground for popular self-expression and not one of formulating a corporate national will.

Their basic objective was to create a coherent national forum for representing what they perceived as nationalist interests. They were acutely aware of the social, regional, and religious diversities of the country, and the new organization was visualized as a medium for communication and coordination. That they demonstrated an eager commitment to representative institutions can perhaps be explained by a number of factors. Most of them were trained lawyers who were fascinated by the new legal culture and its linkages with liberal notions. Even those who were not in the new legal profession, including business professionals like Dadabhai Naoroji, appeared to be serious about preparing intellectually defensible cases for Indian representation based on empirical evidence. Thus the careful studies of the nature of Indian underdevelopment by scholars such as Naoroji, Ranade, Gokhale, and R. C. Dutt, using the modes of rational investigation normally employed by recognized intellectuals of the colonial home, set a rigorous standard of liberal discourse.[7] Few nationalist movements have yielded such a rich diversity of perspectives on the nature of underdevelopment and the sources of national misery. If Naoroji's work anticipated a dependence notion of underdevelopment, the others heavily emphasized the internal roots of mass poverty. No easy explanation was allowed to lend support to facile antiforeignism.

One positive result of these patient empirical investigations was the gradual evolution of a consensual strategy of democratic development during the early phase of Indian nationalism. Ever since Ranade's essay on Indian political economy insisted on separating political liberalism from orthodox notions of laissez faire, the nationalist leaders generally agreed about the crucial need for an active intervention of a democratic state for a coordinated development of agriculture, industry, and education.[8] It is not surprising that the continuity of this consensus has served as a basis for democratic economic planning since independence.

Repression and Radicalization

The turn of the century brought some major changes in the course of nationalism. Although the Congress leaders had succeeded in establishing a viable organ of national representation, the increasing repression and racial arrogance of the colonial regime had made it clear that it was in no mood to listen to voices of dissent or demand. The ruling lords felt secure enough by 1900 that the bureaucratic personnel and the armed forces could be relied upon to deliver the required goods—more revenue squeezed from an already famished country and the use of India as a springboard for mounting expansion of the empire.

If the immediate interests of the colonizer were realized, the long-term prospects of liberal nationalism in India and elsewhere also at the same time suffered a severe setback. The year 1905 marks a turning point in Asian history. By this time more radical nationalists were ascendant and the old liberal leadership was losing ground in the Congress and the nation. The arrogance and repression of the regime offered a prize incentive to militant nationalism. In the ensuing struggle between brutal imperialism and militant nationalism, whichever gained, liberalism was the loser.

Japan's victory over Russia in 1905 created a new wave of self-confidence all over Asia. This coincided with intensified repression in India and enforced mobilization of Indian resources for British expansionism in Asia. Together these factors strengthened a radical response. Desperation drove the new course of struggle to employ emotional appeals based on highly evocative symbols of solidarity derived from literature, religion, and selective recall of history. Often the intensity of emotional activism erased the distinction between the methods of peaceful resistance and violent adventure. As more people joined the nationalist movement, with the attendant deepening of its social base, the process also paid a high price of creeping cleavage in the nascent nation.

Incentives for Diversion

Radical success using Hindu symbols and recalling the glory of the Hindu heroes mobilized larger numbers but also increased the distance between Hindus and Muslims. Muslim loyalists used this opportunity to carve out a separate road for exclusive religious nationalism. Democratization of the national movement by social deepening through popular mobilization, paradoxically, opened a wide opportunity for attack on both secular mobilization and the principles of democratic politics. The idea of a composite secular nationalism represented by the Congress was challenged from 1906 onward by the exclusive claims to representation based on religious community by the Muslim League and Hindu revivalists. This diversion from the major secular movement for national representation, of course, came in handy for the colonial rulers. Henceforth the political system also actively encouraged a divided system of representation, which reinforced incentives for segmental mobilization on ethnic lines. Beginning in 1909 and in a more elaborate form in 1935, a system of communal representation was introduced by colonial legislation to institutionalize separate electorates for specified ethnic groups.

Besides weakening the national challenge to colonial rule, official encouragement to ethnic solidarity also devalued the case for democratic politics. If the Congress language of democratic politics was embarrassing for some liberals in the administration, the open rejection of democratic politics by the founders of Muslim nationalism must have been a great relief for the regime as a whole. Sir Syed Ahmad Khan had struck the right note equally for the regime and minority religious separatism when he said that a democratic future for India would merely bring Hindu hegemony and oppression.[9]

Exclusive claims to represent a religious community were of course based on the idea that religious communities were homogeneous. The lines of division separating all religious communities in India among caste, language, socioeconomic class and regional groupings could not, however, be easily erased by the leaders' rhetoric. But religious nationalists were not entirely wrong in pointing out the appeal of religion in India. The timing was also appropriate for building separate constituencies in each religious community by intensifying their rivalry for economic opportunities within the colonial regime. The emphasis, however, was entirely on dividing whatever pie the colonial strategists were prepared to concede and not on strengthening the movement for expanding the size of the total pie.

Social Deepening and the Gandhian Phase

Secular nationalists were not unfamiliar with national heterogeneity. Their case for a secular movement seeking to represent people across ethnic boundaries was based on the notion that an individual is not exhaustively identified by his ethnic markers. They were also sensitive to the crosscutting nature of ethnic identities characterizing the Indians: major religious communities are split into many language communities, which in turn are stratified into caste and class formations. Thus Hindi speakers constituted only about a third of the Hindus, while among the Muslims, Bengali and Punjabi speakers outnumbered the Urdu speakers. Given plural identities, the politically interesting affiliations are rarely derivable from social affinities. In fact, an eagerness to utilize one affinity by a political leadership that seeks an easy constituency of popular support may encourage other leaders to exploit the other affinities of the same individual. Thus, for example, the easier course of exclusive Hindu mobilization, by seizing upon the Hindi language loyalty in northern India, created negative political reactions among Hindus who spoke other languages. Similarly, Muslim nationalists' mobilization using the symbols of Urdu language community often left the much larger number of Muslims cold and uncomfortable. Again, religion, language, caste, and other affinities have to compete with the economic affinities developing among people locked into similar stations of both disadvantage and advantage.[10]

It was the common cause of the greatest number that the secular nationalist leaders wanted to use as the foundation of national struggle. However, neither the moderate politics of protest nor sporadic radical movements in regions (as conducted until the end of World War I) had been able to generate mass participation in a common struggle on a nationally significant scale. To be sure, both the moderate and radical styles had helped build an organized arena for nationalist struggles. But it remained for the Gandhian leadership to generate and coordinate mass-based political movements into an effective threat to the colonial adversary.

Probably, the best-known contribution of the Gandhian leadership was to socially deepen the base of the national movement by active incorporation of support from peasantry, labor, and other occupational groups in rural and urban areas. Mass mobilization helped nationalist leaders build a political coalition of social groups to challenge alien rule by peaceful struggle. In doing so, these leaders recognized their mutual differences regarding the future issues of centrality of the state, domain of bureaucracy, role of industrialization, agrarian reorganization, control of production, and pattern of distribution. Gandhi's idealization of peasant production, for example, sharply contrasted with Nehru's idealization of centrally planned industrialism.[11] Moreover, significant support existed for more straightforward concepts of capitalist and socialist industrialization. In fact, during the three fateful decades of the ascendance of Gandhi's leadership, what kept the prominent leaders and groups together was a prudent sense of tolerance of fundamental disagreements rather than any significant agreement on specifics of ideology.

This pragmatic process of inclusion meant that from the second decade of this century the Congress organization increasingly drew sustenance from organized labor, peasantry, trading communities, nationalist business (big and small), students, and professionals. The initial impulse of unionizing labor or organizing peasants and other occupational groups did not always begin under the Congress leadership. However, Congress leaders in different regions gradually either joined the wave or brought the autonomous organizers into a close relationship with the Congress organization. Thus began an inclusionary process of linking mass participation in economic and political action into an institutionalized national organization.

Progressive success in incorporating interest groups called for a delicate task of balancing contradictory interests that was hardly easy for a political organization far from formal power. What made the task more difficult was the frequent need for complex conciliation of the conflicting interests of Indian owners and workers. When both the owners and the workers were aligned with the Congress, the latter could use its influence to mediate in cases of dispute. The joint pursuit of encouraging demands and containing demands by conciliation, in the larger interest of the national movement, helped train a leadership over decades in the art of managing conflicting interests in both the industrial and the agricultural sectors of the economy.[12]

Authority Formation and Coherence Creation

This transition from an elite-induced forum of protest to an institutionalized organization incorporating a broad spectrum of interests gradually endowed the Gandhian leadership with national authority long before it acquired state power. The readiness of this leadership to accommodate contending ideologies and interests, so long as their advocates were prepared to strengthen the common cause of national struggle and development, was a product of the conviction that consensus regarding national priorities is more important than either exclusive ideology or interest. For Gandhi this was much more than simply a matter of reiterating the primacy of the national collectivity over its smaller constituents. The way of accommodation was a part of his basic philosophy of *satyagraha* ("truth force"), or nonviolent resistance. In other words, this was not merely an issue of strategic prudence. Gandhi's strict philosophy of nonviolent resolution of disputes—where forsaking violence is never allowed to serve as a rationalization for acquiescence or submission to oppression—presupposed a theory of truth. According to this theory all that an advocate can claim for his case is incomplete knowledge. Arenas of contest enable rival advocates of incomplete knowledge to test their positions and to arrive at a new composition based on a creative resolution of dispute.[13]

While Gandhi's fellow Congress leaders were often uncomfortable with his strict adherence to nonviolence, they lost no time in recognizing the pragmatic value of consensus formation. The leaders close to Gandhi could use this consensus for strengthening their control of the growing organization, whereas others could at least hope to thrive on the assurance that dissenters would not be thrown out. Thus Gandhi's emphasis on nonviolence and peaceful resolution of conflict simultaneously served the purpose of generating organizational coherence and offering a novel technique of anticolonial resistance. His choice of targets and his capacity to channel isolated points of popular struggle toward a nationally converging course demonstrated an order of skill far superior to that of his colleagues. In addition, his detachment from office within the Congress not merely helped allocate a relatively smooth distribution of prized positions among his colleagues, but also impressed the importance of separation between power and authority.

Another aspect of the authority formation process actively pursued by Gandhi and his colleagues was the preemptive cooptation of outlying mass movements. This served both as a process of political education and a source of support. When Mohandas Gandhi began his political career in India in 1915, he had already earned a reputation for his political skill and moral saintliness during his two decades in South Africa. He used this reputation to gradually influence the Congress leadership, as well as to seek an entry into mass movements that were growing outside the Congress initiative. In fact, his successful conversion of local peasants' grievances against landlords in Champaran, Bihar, rural revenue agitation in Kaira, Gujarat, and a major industrial dispute in Ahmedabad into nationally significant resistance movements provided him with unique political capital from 1917 on.[14] These were followed by a succession of moves to enter, redirect, and nationally focus a diverse field of mass action that otherwise might have remained isolated efforts of limited import. Thus he succeeded in linking the national movement and religious demands of Muslim groups in the Khilafat movement, Sikh temple reforms, and Hindu lower-caste temple entry movements.[15] This process extended horizontally to areas that had never tasted an involvement in national movement and vertically to peasants, lower castes, and poor urban workers.

Although most successful in the practice of preemptive cooptation, Gandhi was not alone in its pursuit. Leaders like Nehru, although lacking Gandhi's rural insight, supplemented his moves by inducing the support of more urban-based groups that were fascinated by the Western idioms of socialism and industrial development. These contrasting styles and idioms held together the growing support groups with contradictory future interests and perspectives through a conciliatory system maintained by the Congress through the fateful three decades before independence. This is where the Gandhian transformation of earlier liberalism into a strategy of inclusionary participation, progressively channeled within a frame of rules of peaceful conflict and organized collaboration in and with the Congress, helped build an important historical foundation for future democratic development.

This mass incorporation, however, brought the challenge of providing national incentives sufficient to preserve new elements in an enduring structure of solidarity. While Gandhi appealed to the moral imperative, he also recognized that it calls for unusual dedication and patience. Most of his colleagues had more use for mundane power and interest. Organizational expansion also required attention to the issue of sustenance of different levels of leaders and workers. Increasing access to local governing institutions and legislatures, although strictly limited by colonial needs, opened new doors to Indian aspirants.

From 1919 on politics had to make room for these new temptations. The constitutional reforms of 1909 had conceded limited Indian representation, but the extension of the franchise and the responsibility of the elected members were severely circumscribed. The reforms of 1919 provided for a relatively large measure of responsibility at the local and provincial levels in subjects such as education, health, and public works that were not "reserved" or deemed crucial for colonial control.[16] However, even these limited concessions were immediately followed by utterly repressive laws known as the Rowlatt Acts of 1919. Growing nationalist resentment against such dubious packaging of reforms eventually led to another round of reforms encoded in the Government of India Act of 1935. While this package conceded an extended electorate based on property qualification to cover about one-sixth of the adult population, it offered no effective concessions for self-government at the center. But it did provide for responsible government in the provinces subject to the discretionary powers of the appointed governors.[17]

Although these hedged reforms evoked strong negative reactions from the nationalist leaders, the latter were at the same time reluctant to miss the opportunities offered by the new institutions and their promise of public and private power. Despite initial resistance by the Gandhian leaders to the temptations of limited power, pressures both within and without the Congress made them participate in the limited elections. In 1937 the Congress swept the provincial elections for general seats and formed ministries in seven (eight in 1938) of the eleven provinces.[18] Such electoral success during the preindependence decades helped the Congress organization accumulate valuable experience in constitutional, competitive politics and offered access to office and patronage.

Electoral reforms based on limited franchise were not, however, designed to offer instruction in democratic participation. The communal system of representation fashioned by these reforms put a premium on exclusive ethnic mobilization and collaboration with colonial rulers. The use of religious symbols in opposition to civic culture was now made doubly remunerative by the prospect of prizes for legislative access and colonial collaboration. The latter was made easier because of the bridge between the legislative and the executive arms of government in the British parliamentary system. The corrosive intent and effect of this colonial chemistry was not unanticipated by the Gandhian leadership, which tried to minimize these effects by several means. They scored impressive victories in Hindu as well as Muslim majority provinces and, at the same time, kept up the pace of mass movements in the form of active resistance and civil disobedience campaigns. Besides mass movements, they also extensively built up a network of constructive enterprises in the form of cooperative, small-scale industries and educational institutions and actively encouraged Indian initiative in large-scale industry and commerce. These constructive efforts provided sources of financial support both at individual and organizational levels and of productive engagement for organizational personnel during downswings of political agitation. But the taste of even limited parliamentary and executive access intensified an impatience for formal power. If Gandhi and a few other leaders could afford patience, most leaders found the decolonizing impulse following World War II to offer an opportune moment to settle for the prize of immediate power—even at the cost of a disastrous partition of the subcontinent.

• EVOLUTION OF THE DEMOCRATIC SYSTEM •

Political reconstruction in India since 1947 has been remarkable for its consistent and continuous use of constitutional methods for generating national coherence, political stability, and the development of economic resources and political freedom.

The special properties of democracy in developing countries call for an understanding of a complex process of combined political, social, and economic development. Unlike the historically established democracies, which benefited from a sequence of social mobilization and economic development preceding political democratization, democratic systems in developing countries have the unenviable task of simultaneously and rapidly developing the polity, economy, and society. The task gets all the more difficult because public assessment at home and abroad tends to concentrate on a partial development at any point in time without considering the set as a whole. Thus, for example, cursory examination of a slow pace of economic development in isolation may easily mislead one to a negative judgement when, in fact, this might be due to a transitional diversion of resources from efficient performers to under-privileged beginners in order to spread the process of social and political development in a more even manner.

Political Inheritance and Renovation

The initial moments of a new regime can be critical. Ironically, the timing of Indian independence earned largely by nonviolent popular movement coincided with an unusually violent moment in the country's history. The architects of the new state soon realized the complex legacy left in 1947 by the departed rulers. The nation was in disarray. Partition of the subcontinent brought mutual insecurity and suspicion between India and Pakistan. A large part of new India was under princely rule. The most important problems on the agenda of reconstruction were political order and territorial integration. One can imagine the severity of the test these imposed at the moment of Indian independence. It is no wonder that few observers writing in those early years could summon enough faith in democratic development to foresee that the Indian system would survive the test. Fortunately the Indian leadership was aided by three important factors. The peaceful transfer of power made for a continuity of leadership and institutional structures. A professional bureaucratic system, already manned mostly by Indians, was available for immediate use and required expansion. Above all, the development of the Congress organization into a nationwide political institution, reaching remote corners and incorporating major political segments of the population representing diverse occupational groups, made for a unified exercise of power. Fortunately as well, this power was already endowed with a sense of authority earned in the course of the nationalist movement. Evidently, the partition of the country and the formation of Pakistan appeared to strengthen the legitimation of power in new India by eliminating a major challenge to nationalism and helped establish a new linkage between the Congress party and the Muslim population. But the new leaders did not take their nationalist legitimation for granted. They sought to create a constitutional system that would institutionalize an authoritative democratic system of representation, competition, and exercise of power.

A comfortable Congress majority in the elected Constituent Assembly made for a largely consensual reiteration of some of the basic democratic principles enunciated in the earlier decades. The Constitution of India, operative since 1950, offered a complex coverage of elaborate legal and moral provisions, in the longest document of its kind, to a largely nonliterate people.[19] The basic principles enshrined in the justiciable part of the document provide for a parliamentary democratic system of government, fundamental rights, federalism tempered by a preeminent center, and secularism. The nonjusticiable part encodes a series of mild democratic socialist guidelines for the state. While codifying the rules of democratic government, the constitution carefully avoided the Gandhian principles of direct democracy, decentralized authority, and debureaucratization. The Gandhian leaders now needed Gandhi's mantle only for ceremonial legitimation.

In many ways the constitutional text could also be read as a developmental document, for it registered the basic aspirations of the members of a consensual intelligentsia to mold the country according to their tastes and preferences. An idealized blending of Western notions of liberal justice and indigenous notions of self-realization and social welfare had already become a part of nationalist culture that was widely shared by the educated classes. Constitutional encoding of these ideas satisfied their collective pride and reminded them of the social task ahead. Public responsibility was assumed to be mainly one of choosing the right legislators. The rest of the responsibility was now supposed to devolve on the state.

Accordingly, constitutional democracy in independent India cleared the way for an active state appropriate to the realization of simultaneous development on many fronts. A well-knit party, securing majorities in the national parliament and in a majority of state legislatures, on the basis of elections held every five years, can pursue extensive intervention in the social, economic, and political spheres to generate and direct resources for national development. The power of the government is subject to several limitations. The federal provisions of the constitution, the fundamental rights, judicial review, various statutory commissions and, of course, the legalized opposition may serve as sources of curbs, limits, and warnings. However, these provisions are subject to considerable muting in cases of overriding "public purpose," which can be invoked with fair ease if the government can obtain the required majority support, simple or complex as specified by the constitution.

Besides providing for cabinet-style authority armed with legislative support, the constitution also offers some directions and perspectives for national development. Part four of the constitution spells out the duties of the state, but these articles are not binding on the state. It says that the fundamental principle of governance shall include the duty of the Indian state to promote the welfare of the people by securing "as effectively as it may" a social order in which justice—social, economic, and political—shall inform all the national institutions. A following specification reads like a catalogue of objectives that would be congruent with an ideology of a socialistic welfare state that carefully steers clear of revolutionary socialism.[20]

What is left out, however, is any sense of priority or urgency among the preferred objectives. The basic law of the country, then, has authorized the state to adopt a course of moderate reforms, but at the same time its amendment procedures ensure that a confident popular mandate can enable a responsible executive to go ahead with more radical reforms. The crucial issue was not what the legal language expressed but rather what the nature of the democratic development in an inexperienced country would make of it.

Democratic Practice and Political Development

Between the first general election held on the basis of universal adult franchise in 1952 to the eighth held in 1984, the Indian electorate has demonstrated a growing capability that was hardly expected in the country and elsewhere. The turnout rate began with the relatively low figure of 45.7 percent in 1952 and moved fairly steadily to a 60.0 percent range in recent elections (see Table 6.1). Many observers had reservations regarding the capacity of largely nonliterate voters to exercise mature choice. In the course of all these elections, Indian voters have proved that they cannot be taken for granted either by the ruling or the opposition parties. At the national level the Congress party has been generally favored with substantial electoral pluralities, which (because of the single-member-district electoral system) have been translated into large, and sometimes overwhelming, parliamentary majorities (see Table 6.1). But when the same party was found to misuse the basic rules

Table 6.1   Summary Electoral Data: National Parliament and State Assembly Results from Eight Indian Elections, 1952–1985

	1952	1957	1962	1967	1971–72	1977–78	1980	1984–85
Electorate (in millions)	171.7	193.7	216.4	249.0	274.1	320.9	355.6	375.8
Voter turnout (in percent)	46	47	55	61	55	60	57	63
Congress party percentage share of popular vote								
Parliament	45	48	45	41	44	34	43	49
State Assembly	42	45	44	40	45	34	—	—
Congress party percentage share of legislative seats								
Parliament	74	75	73	55	68	28	67	79
State Assembly	68	65	60	49	60	16	48[a]	57[b]

Sources: Government of India, Press Information Bureau, *Lok Sabha Elections 1984*, 1984, pp. 1, 2; Lloyd I. Rudolph and Suzanne H. Rudolph, *In Pursuit of Lakshmi* (University of Chicago Press, 1987), pp. 130–131; Robert L. Hardgrave, Jr., and Stanley A. Kochanek, *India: Government and Politics in a Developing Nation* (New York: Harcourt, Brace, Jovanovich, 1986), p. 302; and others.

[a] Based on elections held at different times between 1979 and 1983.

[b] As of 1986; share reduced since the 1987 elections in five states.

of the constitutional system it was served with a crushing defeat in 1977.[21] The Janata party rule that followed also ended because of the electorate's dissatisfaction in 1980, and the Congress party was brought back to power. Dissatisfaction with the Congress party was seething on the eve of the eighth election when the intervening Punjab crisis and the assassination of the prime minister called for an unambiguous mandate for effective stewardship, and the electorate responded overwhelmingly in 1984. However, the same voters refused to give the Congress party a similar extent of support in the state-level elections that took place only a couple of months later. In fact, over the years, the dominance of the Congress party at the national level has not prevented the persistence of non-Congress parties in power in a number of states. The fragmentation and realignment of national opposition parties often persuade the voters to try them for ruling at the state level while refusing to support them at the national level. Since independence, and particularly in recent years, the Congress party has usually held a significantly smaller share of state assembly than national parliamentary seats (see Table 6.1).

By May 1987, when after a twenty-month rule the Akali party government was replaced by central rule in Punjab, the party distribution of state-level power was shifting away from the Congress party. Following the state elections in March and June 1987, the ruling party at the center lost control over about half of India's twenty-five states. The victory in Nagaland in November 1987 came as a poor consolation for the Congress. By that time the pattern of opposition party control of major states revealed this picture: the Communist Party (Marxist) and its allies ruling in Kerala, West Bengal, and Tripura; the Janata party in Karnataka; Assam Gana Parishad in Assam; Telugu Desam in Andhra Pradesh; All-India Anna Dravida Munnetra Kazhagam (AIADMK) in Tamilnadu; Lok Dal in Haryana; and the National Conference in coalition with the Congress party as junior partner in Jammu and Kashmir. As of early 1988 the Congress party did not command a single southern state but it did control the relatively larger states of northern, central, and western India, as well as Orissa in the east.[22]

The assured dominance of the Congress party during the first two decades following independence was rudely shaken by the results of the 1967 elections, when about half of the states chose to stay with the opposition parties.[23] When the Congress party split into two organizations in 1969, it was clear that the nationalist mantle was no longer sufficient to hold together a consensual organization for national reconciliation of dominant interests.[24] The subsequent realignment of the party signified a victory of the leadership that controlled formal power at the federal level of government. Indira Gandhi, the architect of this Congress party, increasingly transformed the nature of the organization from an institutional mode of accommodation to an electoral instrument beholden to a ruling leadership. The other Congress party, while continuing the older style, slowly disintegrated because of its distance from the state power and patronage. Neither the nature of the new dominance nor the pattern of the party system could ever be the same again.

When the vulnerability of the hegemonic role of the Congress party was demonstrated in the critical interlude between 1967 and 1970, political rivalry could no longer be contained within the old institutional structure of one dominant organization. A cynical game of changing allegiance and party alignment signified a transition toward a new mode of institutionalized party system. The Congress split of 1969 left Indira Gandhi's Congress without a majority and consequently dependent on the Communist Party of India and the regional party of Tamil nationalism, Dravida Munnetra Kazhagam (DMK), to continue in power. The other Congress led by the older organization men frantically sought help from opposition parties. This game of coalition politics put a premium on buying immediate support to stay in power, as against building support to win durable power. Indira Gandhi, as prime minister of the federal government, which controlled the strategic points of the economy, and as leader of the larger Congress party, could command larger resources to buy support than her opponents. She confidently went for new elections in 1971 and won the national vote on the basis of a populist rhetoric that enthused the disadvantaged groups without threatening the most advantaged groups in the society and the economy. Her party won a commanding majority in national parliament and in 1972 it won impressive victories in state-level elections. Meanwhile, she won widespread national admiration during the war in 1971 that led to the independence of Bangladesh.[25]

All this appeared to restore a pattern of Congress dominance, except that the institutional basis of this new dominance was different. This time the party was less a national institution of interest reconciliation than a central organization for mobilizing endorsement for the leadership and its hierarchical apparatus. Patronage resources at the top made sure that the successively lower echelon leadership was recruited on the basis of loyalty to the apparatus and capacity to cultivate demonstrative support for it. This plebiscitarian transformation left little scope for sustained building of interest-based support or systematic incorporation of diverse interests within the party. It resembled more a state-dominated party lacking an autonomous institutional authority of its own.[26] In fact, the old system of the Congress party, which had encouraged regional and local leaders to build sustained social bases of support, was now perceived as a threat to the plebescitarian organization. The old idea of a party-based state was now transformed into a state-based party.

This shift from relative autonomy of party to its dependence on the state obviously placed a new burden on the state. By emasculating the institutional system of interest incorporation previously performed by the party, it now had to assume the burden directly. By reducing the chief ministers of the states to a band of prime minister's men bereft of secure regional support and power the sites of regional conflict of interest were increasingly transferred to the national state. If the old structure could afford to reduce the intensity of disaffection by distributing its targets in a polycentric arrangement of institutions, the new system proceeded to concentrate the targets in a monocentric space. The conventional distinction between official and public authority was virtually erased. The prime minister's directorate now combined the official authority of the governing system with the public authority of the dominant party system.

Unfortunately for the new leaders, the problems of the early 1970s were too acute in terms of their depth, magnitude, and simultaneous demand on authority to make the new structure work. The refugee trail of the Bangladesh War, severe drought, energy crisis, and economic failures occurring together offered the most trying test for a newly reorganized authority. As resources were precariously depleted, mounting factional war within the ruling party and public protest against the government rocked the country. The opposition parties were aided by dissident factions within the ruling party and a convergence of nonparty political formations expressing popular disaffection. As the regionally initiated movements of unrest widened, the new ruling authority repressed them as an attack on the nation. This repression further polarized politics into a battle between an increasingly nervous ruling apparatus and an expanding coalition of opposition groups and parties.

Opposition Mobilization and the Emergency

History now presented an opportunity to the opposition that it had never tasted before. As we have seen, the single-member plurality system of electoral representation had discounted the electoral prospects of fragmented opposition parties. Extraelectoral politics of agitation now offered an incentive for these parties to mobilize popular discontent, form a coalition among them, and widen the scope of the coalition by inducting into it popular action groups from many regions, most notably Bihar and Gujarat.[27] The latter regions, in particular, could make use of the national prestige of leaders like Morarji Desai and especially Jayaprakash Narayan, whose Gandhian socialist credentials and continued ability to stay away from the small-time clash of economic and ethnic interests had won wide admiration. These ideologically diverse leadership resources helped forge a national unity of discontent although, inevitably, the nature of the coalition left a potential for rift. The goal of this national movement, as expressed in particular by Narayan, was to organize a popular initiative to replace a ruling leadership that was widely perceived as socially oppressive and politically authoritarian.[28]

While the pressure of the popular movements kept growing, the legal standing and the political stature of Prime Minister Indira Gandhi suffered a severe setback because of a conjunction of two critical events. Her own election of 1971 was invalidated in June 1975 by a high court decision on a case of electoral malpractice lodged by her socialist opponent.[29] Besides losing office, this conviction also entailed debarment from elected office for six years. The Supreme Court, however, awarded a conditional stay of the judgement that temporarily allowed her to retain office, without the right to vote or participate in the proceedings of Parliament, pending consideration of a full-scale appeal. Meanwhile, a coalition of opposition parties in Gujarat scored a decisive victory in the state elections in the same month. Her spirited campaign in the state was of no help to the sagging Congress party in the face of the widespread popular movement against her rule.

Indira Gandhi had a comfortable majority in Parliament. Her cabinet included several leaders of national stature and fairly impressive political and administrative record. She could wait for the conclusion of the legal proceedings and, meanwhile, let another leader of her party exercise formal power without much reasonable fear of losing long-term grounds. Ever since the Congress split, her faction-ridden colleagues had owed their political stature considerably to her populist appeal. However, she did not have confidence in a patiently drawn institutional strategy to utilize her populist appeal in a manner that would strengthen both her party and her democratic authority. Instead, she opted for a system of extraordinary powers by invoking the internal emergency provisions of the constitution.

The Indian constitutional system was designed to serve the country in normal and crisis situations. It was assumed during the making of the constitution that internal and external stresses faced by a newly developing country would require certain temporary deviations from normal procedures to tide the system over a crisis. Thus a complex set of emergency provisions permit comprehensive or partial use of special executive powers, depending on the specific situation.[30] External aggression or grave internal political disturbance permit comprehensive use, while political crises confined to state levels or financial crisis on a national level may warrant limited use of these abnormal provisions. Many of these provisions have been frequently used before and after Indira Gandhi's emergency phase. In fact, the possibilities of a constitutional dictatorship utilizing these provisions were discussed in the constitutional literature on India from the very beginning.[31] But until June 1975, the actual pattern of use of the enabling powers did not entail systematic subversion of constitutional, democratic government on a national scale. This is the crucial point that should help us distinguish between the use of specific emergency powers and an emergency regime that deliberately seeks a transformation of the basic democratic structure into an authoritarian mode of government.[32]

Indira Gandhi's choice of the emergency option was based on her claim that there was a deep conspiracy to destroy civil order and economic development processes in the country.[33] The equation between her own political crisis and national crisis was hardly convincing. In order to register her point she set out to dismantle the democratic system of persuasion and replace it with an authoritarian mode of creating and enforcing public assent. Thus the emergency episode was marked by mass arrests, suppression of civil rights and all opposition voices, elaborate censorship of the media, and a carefully orchestrated campaign to celebrate the virtues of collective discipline promoted by the leader, her son Sanjay, and their nominees. A meek majority in Parliament endorsed the executive orders issued by the prime minister's inner court and the judicial system was emasculated by amending the constitution. These amendments also ensured the supremacy of the prime minister's role, thus formalizing a system that, as we have discussed, was already in process since 1971.[34]

Much was made of the logic of disciplined economic development, which presumably called for a strong state to guide the economy to serve the nation and especially the poor masses. With all the fanfare surrounding the new regime's twenty-point program—later collapsed into five points—this strong state failed to deliver a rate of progress strikingly different from previous or subsequent regimes.[35] Some of the early gains in grain production were due more to climatic favor than organizational changes. Extensive labor repression and the favor shown to terms of discipline dictated by employers helped register some gains in industrial production, but the overall process of economic development served the rich better than the poor. In any event the populist appeal increasingly wore off as the regime stepped into its second year. By early 1977 Indira Gandhi was confident that her party could get a fresh mandate by appealing once again to the people through parliamentary elections.

Emergency measures were relaxed before the elections. The opposition parties accomplished a rare measure of unity in the form of the Janata party, based on the alliance brought about in the course of the Bihar and Gujarat movements. The March 1977 elections turned out to be a landmark event in the history of India's democratic becoming.[36] The Janata party and its allies won an overwhelming victory over Indira Gandhi's Congress party. That the Janata government did not endure beyond two years does not diminish the fact that the party system in India revealed a valuable reserve capacity to mobilize the political resources to replace the dominant system by a more competitive one in a time of democratic crisis.[37] This interesting case of institutional latency may reflect a deeper civic disposition to support a democratic system than what the manifest level of party competition would suggest.

Sources of Popular Mobilization

Political space in India has not been exhausted by the nationally or regionally organized parties or even interest groups of the conventional kind. At many critical moments of Indian politics, when these conventional formations failed to articulate popular grievances, the latter found their expression in relatively durable coalitions of public groups. Popularly known as "movements" in Indian politics, these serve as mobilizing platforms bringing together various parties, groups, and concerned publics.[38] These issue-oriented civic movements need to be distinguished from conventional social movements like labor, peasant, or student movements. While the latter represent persistent political formations organized for long-term interests of occupational or class groups, the short-term civic movements focus primarily on citizenship roles cutting across social groups.

Besides political parties, a wide variety of voluntary associations have offered durable organized vehicles for expressing popular interests and objectives. Industrial labor, organized in nationally extensive trade unions, and peasant associations have remained close to political parties.[39] The traditional dominance of the ruling, as well as the opposition, parties over these organized interests have been increasingly challenged by new leadership groups putting higher emphasis on economic issues, but their success has usually been limited to regional scales. Strong national combinations of industrial workers, white-collar employees and agrarian groups have provided Indian parties with bases of continuous support and stable manpower. Larger student associations have usually aligned themselves with political parties. Business associations have been more prominent in large-scale industry.[40] Their quiet pressures are usually more effective than many unquiet public agitations.

However, organizing rural peasants and workers, despite a long history predating independence, has not proved to be easy. Although the incidence of poverty is highest among agricultural labor and marginal income groups, including tenants and smallholder peasants, their mobilization into organized associations has been hampered by wide variations in agrarian property systems, ecological contexts, social authority patterns (mainly exemplified in caste systems), technological diffusions, and policy approaches.[41] Thus radical mobilization, although initially successful in the 1960s in a few southern districts in Tamilnadu and Kerala under the auspices of two Communist parties, gradually veered toward a wider, multiclass agrarian coalition, which lent an important base of support for the parliamentary radicalism of the dominant Communist party, the Communist Party (Marxist), or CPM. The frequent induction of the Communist parties into power at the state level in Kerala and, more durably, in West Bengal can be understood in terms of their ability to forge a still wider coalition between urban and rural groups with varied class interests.[42] The gains of democratic incorporation, not surprisingly, have also been the loss of rural and urban radical espousal of exclusive causes of the most deprived classes.[43] Access to democratic power, as it were, has served to highlight the compulsion for inclusive combination rather than exclusive mobilization of particular classes. Moreover, this same broadband combination has encouraged shifting reformist coalitions between middle- and lower-caste formations in north Indian states, whereby status-based mobilization has gained precedence over class-based mobilization.

Ethnic Affirmation

Representation or even politicized mobilization of functional interests occupies only part of the politics of participation in contemporary India. The right of association and its active pursuit has given rise to another system of pressures that often cuts across class or functional stations in the society. These associations succeed in recruiting intense loyalty of large segments of the population by seeking to promote exclusive interests based on language, religion, region, caste, and other cultural or ascriptive affiliations. Most observers have interpreted these forms of participation as expressions of primordial loyalty inconsistent with modern democratic politics. A developmental view of this participation may, however, offer a different picture. These are deliberately created political instruments of mobilization that freely utilize the logic of ethnic exclusiveness in order to bargain for certain advantages. How the symbols of ethnicity, to take one example, are used with strategic flexibility for competitive political advantage can be clearly seen in the Assamese movement that hit the headlines in the early 1980s.

Assam is one of the poorer states of eastern India, but it is also endowed with rich resources like oil, tea, and timber. Revenue from these resources, however, largely flows to other parts of India, including the central government. A keen sense of unjust deprivation of the Assamese people was initially enunciated by an Assamese literary association.[44] Poets, novelists, and musicians helped direct the resentment to the non-Assamese people and gradually articulated a notion of Assamese authenticity. College students sharpened the edge of the movement to the extent that it cut deep into the security and livelihood of the non-Assamese population in the state. Elected governments in Assam made use of the movement but increasingly failed to contain it.[45] The national government initially ignored it, and subsequently wanted to teach it a lesson by using the instruments of coercion, manipulation, and election. The forcing of an election in 1983 led to the eruption of mass violence of unprecedented proportion.[46] The massive scale of violence unnerved both the movement and the government. The internal contradictions of the movement were now more clearly exposed. Earlier Assamese authenticity had meant a language-based unity that was supposed to be shared by Hindu and Muslim members of the same speech community. Later the movement sought to rewrite the scope of Assameseness to exclude a substantial number of Muslim speakers of the language on the grounds that they were illegal immigrants from neighboring Bangladesh. Non-Hindi speakers drifted away from the movement and, after 1983, could be used by the elected government to its advantage. The convergence of an adroit leadership in state government and a more compromising national administration under Rajiv Gandhi facilitated a negotiated settlement in 1985.[47] The movement leaders also decided to convert themselves into a political party and to participate in the electoral process.

Clearly, the emergence of the Assamese movement and regional language movements in other parts of India including Punjab could have been avoided if the dominant party in the state and the nation had not written them off initially as irritants and, subsequently, as destructive. What is more important for our purpose is the lesson that an electoral mandate can mislead people in power to discount important sensitivities regarding issues of conspicuous disadvantage that, in the Indian case, have encouraged new political formations. The latter often began as small-scale associations outside the frame of conventional politics. These eventually widened into a mass base and led to large-scale associations, which grew stronger by increasingly establishing themselves as speakers for popular issues omitted from the agenda of normal democratic government. The expansion of popular participation encouraged by these populist ethnic movements could be consistent with democratic incorporation—as they had been in the course of two decades in most regions in India—if the inclusionary instincts of the dominant formal authority were not overcome in the early decades by Caesarist complacency. That the process of democratic inclusion need not be confused with incorporation in the dominant Congress party has been amply demonstrated in Tamilnadu, Andhra Pradesh, and elsewhere. The cases of the Tamil and Andhra movements also show how the displacement of Congress rule has enabled the democratic system to expand to incorporate new groups at the state level and also how the newly incorporated groups can be coordinated at the national level.[48]

When leaders like Nehru condemned their rivals as threats to modernity, democracy, and integration, they ignored the importance of progressive socialization of new forces to expand the political resources of a developing democracy. While they took roles ranging from disciplining schoolmasters to colonial policemen, they often lacked the political art of using a receptive state in a developing country to offer assurance to the new competition that it too is equally entitled to access and power. When the persistent hearing problems of these leaders were corrected by the shock treatment of violence, they discovered that accommodation helped to induct new groups with democratic schooling into the competition. The lessons of the 1960s in the Nehru phase were again ignored in the later years of the Indira phase when manipulative craft increasingly replaced the art of cultivating political support. Indira Gandhi's failure was dramatized by the fires that engulfed Assam in 1983 and Punjab in 1984. When her successor, Rajiv Gandhi, succeeded in bringing about workable accords in Punjab and Assam in 1985, it became evident once again that democratic institutions and behavior may be necessary to develop and manage a nation of India's size and complexity. However, the new prime minister has demonstrated greater skill in generating accords than in making them work, particularly in the case of Punjab as of early 1988.

• DEMOCRACY, PLANNING, AND DEVELOPMENT •

Strategy and Organization

Political democratization, in order to endure, requires a rapid development of economic and social resources so that expanding public demands can be effectively satisfied. But can a democracy in a developing country succeed in generating the required rate of development in a sustainable fashion? This is a question that should be distinguished from one that concerns ideal or spectacular rates of development. The difference in phrasing the question obviously stems from a difference in basic values. A concern for an ideal rate can ignore the issues of how it is brought about and with what cost to freedom, stability, and national autonomy. Those who cannot afford to ignore these issues may, however, opt for an optimum rate consistent with other valued accomplishments. But, it is not necessary to assume that such an optimum cannot approximate or even surpass the maximum attained elsewhere. The linkage problem simply reminds us that the crucial issues to consider with respect to comparative economic development are not, after all, simply economic.

The idea of democratically planned development was pursued by the nationalist leaders long before independence. Gandhian strictures on centralization, large-scale industrialization, and bureaucratic management of development did not prevent the emergence of a wide area of agreement among other leaders regarding the importance of centrally coordinated planning for rapid industrialization. In 1938 Subhas Chandra Bose, the only major leader in Congress history who openly admired fascist discipline, became the president of the Congress and Nehru became the chairman of the party's national planning committee. Immediately after independence the Congress, as the ruling party, appointed an advisory planning board. As the first prime minister, Nehru initiated the Planning Commission and became its first chairman; he encouraged a process of thinking that assumed that economic development was a matter of scientific problem solving.[49] Nehru's admiration for scientism was not shared by his party men.

How has planned development fared? The country experienced seven five-year and three one-year plans. During this period the economy registered a fairly steady, although unspectacular, rate of growth, experienced a partial renovation of agricultural production leading to self-sufficiency in food, developed a structure of industrialization that produces most of what the country needs, expanded the supply of educated and technical personnel able to execute all levels of sophisticated tasks, consistently held down the level of inflation to one of the lowest in the world, and in the process ensured a level of self-reliance and payment ability that kept it away from debt crisis. At the same time disturbing poverty persists, inequality hurts, technology languishes, the second economy thrives, and a number of shadows haunt the economic scene. And yet the popular report cards on the new government leadership in 1985, based on national polls, showed overall public confidence to be higher than expected.[50] But the polls can be misleading and confidence can erode. For a long-range perspective, it is more important to look at how development has prepared the required base for rapid enhancement of the people's capabilities to solve their problems. This will entail a wider view of development than the one that narrowly concentrates on material product alone.

The notion of people's capabilities, when applied to India, necessarily directs one to the rural situation. This is where the weight of decades of agricultural stagnation and technological obsolescence had dragged the largest segment of the nation's population to poverty and human incapacity. The most urgent task was to ensure a priority for rural development over everything else. Such a priority would have called for extensive intervention in the agrarian property structure in the form of land reform followed by investment in productive support, technological change, and improvement in human resources. And yet this is where the record of development has been discouraging. Land reform, initiated immediately after independence, still remains largely unrealized in terms of its redistributive goals. As late as 1984 Planning Commission documents giving an advance taste of the seventh five-year plan kept reminding the policy makers that a good part of the redistributive work of land reforms remains to be accomplished.[51] Drastic intervention in the rural property structure was, in fact, consciously avoided by leaving the reforms to the discretion of state-level legislation. The slow pace of land reform demonstrated a preference for a strategy of promoting production by offering financial and technical support to the relatively better-off segments of the rural population. The proportion of plan investment—implying mostly public investment—directed toward agriculture declined from the first through the second and third plans, the end period of which was accompanied by a severe crisis resulting from extensive drought.[52]

During this period public investment through planning was based on a preferred strategy of industrialization that encouraged considerably higher investment for developing organized industries, mining, power, and communications. A socialistic rhetoric was employed mainly to equate social progress with capital goods production under state control.[53] Scarce national resources were increasingly diverted to pursue import substitution under the leadership of the state. The use of foreign aid increased from a modest 10 percent of the first plan outlay to 28 percent in the third plan. At the same time the increasing self-empowerment of the national-level state through its expanding control of capital, strategic industries, power generation, communication networks, and employment created an impression that the ascendance of state capitalism was irresistible. Command over national, as well as external, resources and the apparatus of planned control of investment and enterprise by now had endowed the state with a degree of power that could be used to induce collaboration from larger private owners of resources in industry and agriculture. Indeed the prospect of such a collaboration could minimize the dependence of the ruling party on the poorer rural groups. Actually, as the ruling party's pursuit of industrialization strategy progressively intensified, its pursuit of the art of cultivation of mass support and its conciliatory coordination declined. A tired generation of Congress leaders appeared now to rely more on the formal instrument of the state, its tightly organized bureaucracy, its patronage powers, and its capacity to subsidize inefficient enterprise in order to consolidate and enjoy its power.

This was largely what one may call the Nehru phase of planned development. During his lifetime Nehru's influence welded the Congress party to a level of coherence sufficient to maintain a semblance of united pursuit of planned development. Nehru's death in 1964 was followed by Shastri's conciliatory style of coordination of major factions and regions. If his capacity for consensus generation ensured a stable transition in politics, the new phase simply succeeded in maintaining the earlier developmental policy frame. No major departures were expected either. The consensus style, however, increasingly emboldened the chief ministers at the state level to assert their role in national policy implementation. A process of regionalization of authority was already developing even during the Nehru phase, and during Shastri's brief tenure it grew stronger. The strength of the chief ministers of states within the party was dramatically revealed when, following Shastri's death in 1966, they helped elect Indira Gandhi as the third prime minister over the candidate of Congress organization leaders at the national level.

Indira Gandhi's style was inconsistent with a federalized system of authority within the party, but in 1966 consolidation was more important for her than anything else. The years 1966–1967 brought a severe crisis to the economy and the polity. Disastrous drought, legacies of wars with neighbors, economic debacle, and a close call in the 1967 elections appeared to offer the Congress party an impetus for rethinking. However, although five-year planning was temporarily dropped, no radical reorganization of the premises of planning came about. The only major innovation was intensive modernization of agriculture with stepped-up investment for selected crops and regions aimed at national self-sufficiency in foodgrain production.[54] Again, the major goal was immediate production promotion and not the wider objectives of raising the long-term capability of the rural poor who composed the majority of the country. Neither the subsequent consolidation of Indira Gandhi's power from 1971, including the phase of emergency, nor her recovery of the popular mandate in 1980 following a non-Congress interlude were used as occasions to question the earlier priorities. The Janata party rule, meanwhile, did raise some questions but its brevity of tenure weakened the effectiveness of its revision of priorities.

Human Base and Food Security

Indian planning began in a social context where nearly 85 percent of the population was rural, the national literacy rate was 12 percent, the majority of school-age children did not attend school, and for most people life was ruled by poverty, oppression, and morbidity. The state of the economy was equally dismal. Orderly management of the colonial economy during the five decades preceding 1950 had registered less than half-a-percent growth rate of per capita real output. Perhaps the only points of relief for the people were that life expectancy was short and the mortality rate was exceedingly high.[55] Clearly, something more than modest economic development was called for to make even a small step to alter such a nonhuman, level of existence.

How does the record of democratic development stand as a response to that challenge? From the moment of independence in 1947 through the subsequent four decades, the people have lent an unexpectedly mature degree of support to the democratic process of economic development. What has this process yielded in terms of altering their level of living? How does it compare with the record of other developing countries following similar or different roads to development? Some basic indicators, despite their imperfection, can be revealing. Expectation of life at birth around 1940 was 32.1 years for Indian males and 31.4 years for females, and on the eve of planned development, around 1949, remained at 32.4 and 31.7 respectively. During the years of development, these figures rose to 41.9 and 40.6 in 1960, 46.4 and 44.7 in 1970, and 50.9 and 50.0 in 1980. A recent report puts the corresponding figures for 1985 at 57 and 56. By historical standards this rapid progress can be counted as encouraging. But by comparative contemporary standards, India's performance leaves room for considerable improvement because many other developing countries have done so much better during the same period. Sri Lanka, largely following a democratic path, succeeded in reaching respective figures of 68 and 72 by 1985, and China, following another path, scored 68 and 70. China's score is particularly interesting because twenty-five years earlier its base figures (41, 44) were close to India's and substantially lower than those for Sri Lanka (62, 62).[56]

Similarly, the mortality rate for infants (under age one) was 165 per thousand live births in 1960 for both India and China. By 1985 China had reduced the rate to 35 and Sri Lanka to 36, while India's rate was 89.[57] Sri Lanka's success dramatically showed that it does not take either a violent revolution or a high national income to bring about an unprecedented rate of improvement of human resources. India's average, of course, conceals the fact that within the same country there have been different rates of progress in different states. In Kerala both the life expectancy and infant mortality rates have registered improvements comparable to China's.

Food security, in the sense of general availability and the assurance of access to the stock of foodgrains, has been the most important issue facing the people. Indian planning began with the inherited base of production yielding barely fifty million tons. Production of foodgrains steadily rose until the crisis years of 1966–1967, when lower growth necessitated a sharp increase in imports, which in 1966 constituted 14.4 percent of total quantity available.[58] The drop in production and drag of foreign dependence pushed the state to begin a renewed effort to modernize agriculture, resulting in a big change on the food front. Production of foodgrains crossed the 100 million ton mark from 1971 and imports steadily declined. Dependence on imported food ended in 1978. In the subsequent three years, no food imports were needed. From 1980 to 1984 a small amount was imported mainly to augment the buffer stock. Production of foodgrains exceeded 150 million tons in 1983–1984—a big jump over the earlier peak of 133 million tons in 1981–1982. Net import of food from 1985 to 1987 was negative, and yet the size of the reserve stock of the state remained comfortable except for 1987 which turned out to be the worst year of drought since Independence. But the ability of the economy to cope with the drought was demonstrated by the fact that unlike the previous drought years of 1965 and 1979, this time the rate of growth of the national product was positive. Indeed, the capacity of the food security system and the general economy to resolutely tide over the crisis that usually accompanies droughts of this magnitude was a new experience for the country.[59]

Success in generating self-sufficiency in foodgrains was accompanied by extensive state action to ensure that demands from the deficit states of the federation were met by transferring the surplus stock of other states in a coordinated manner. The role of the federal government in procurement and public distribution of foodgrains can be crucial for ensuring food security. In the absence of it, there would be no assurance that nationally available food will actually reach the neediest regions and groups. The magnitude of state involvement in procurement and distribution is indicated by the fact that from the mid-1960s, on an average, close to 10 percent of foodgrains has been annually procured and distributed.[60] This has enabled the state to maintain price levels consistent with general planning needs and, at the same time, reasonable access for needy areas. And yet public ability to transfer food to deficit regions does not assure access to it at the lowest income levels in rural areas. This is a weakness that production promotion policies, without the benefit of deeper structural reorganization, will find hard to overcome.

A recent World Bank report on sub-Saharan Africa justifies optimism for Africa from the fact that, while contemporary despair about Africa was matched by a comparable feeling about India just two decades ago, the latter now "has emerged from despair to hope in the eyes of the world."[61] The elimination of famines in India since independence contrasts not merely with their catastrophic recurrence during the colonial years, but also with revolutionary China, where severe famine conditions claimed fifteen million lives during 1959–1961.[62] The experience of democratic planning has demonstrated that democratic instruments can be made to deliver impressive results by a mutual reinforcement of popular voice and prudent policy. But that experience also shows that the reactive type of prudence, as distinguished from anticipatory prudence, can extract a heavy price from the country and especially from the poorer population before a crisis shakes the policy planners.

Thus innovations on the food front should be judged also in the context of the fact that the per capita availability of food has registered only modest progress and that the actual access of the poorer people still remains lower than in many developing countries. The daily calorie supply per capita as a percentage of requirement for India in 1981 stood at 86, while the weighted average of thirty-four lowest income developing countries was 97. The corresponding figure for China was 107, Burma 113, and Sri Lanka 102. If the national average figures are disaggregated by income groups, lower-income groups in India will show worse scores than their counterparts in those three countries.

Nutritional deprivation in India does not stand alone. Progress in providing mass education has been discouraging despite tremendous strides at the higher and technical education levels. The adult literacy rate in India in the eighties has been less than 40 percent. In contrast, the developing countries of East Asia have exceeded 70 percent. The average rate for sub-Saharan Africa in 1970 was lower than that of India in the same period. Now India's rate lags behind that average. Primary school enrollment figures tell us an unexciting story.[63] If the premise of industrial priority explains the uneven emphasis on higher education and gross neglect of rural education at lower levels, it is difficult to imagine how comprehensive industrialization can be compatible with

poor quality of labor. Fortunately, this disparity in educational investment was reduced by the end of the 1970s, indicating a better sense of
balance among levels of schooling. India's earlier failure to coordinate
these components may deprive her industrialization of critical pace and
depth. If the human base is left weak, what will be the impact of such
weakness on overall economic and political development? We need to
examine the pattern of industrialization before we can seek answers to
this question.

Induced Industrialization

The dominant intellectual climate in the 1950s could leave no doubt in
the minds of any forward-looking leader of a developing country about
the virtues of state-induced industrialization.[64] Industrialization,
modernity, and efficient use of resources were universally equated, just
as agriculture, traditionalism, and inefficiency were believed to go
together. To imagine a situation of inefficient industry wasting resources
and modernized agriculture offering a better return on investment and a
sounder preparation for the future would have been a heresy unpardon-
able in the liberal, as well as revolutionary, West and, therefore, among
educated people in India. If the heresy has reversed in many sophisticated circles in the 1980s, we should not forget the charm of the original
equation.

Indian planning for industrialization was based on the assumption
that a rapid rate and a comprehensive pattern of industrial growth can
be obtained by assigning priority to the production of capital goods. If
this called for going slow on agriculture and consumption goods, it was
justified by the promise of future benefits for the nation as a whole.
Expanded capacity in the capital goods subsector was supposed to lay
the ideal foundation for subsequent production of consumption goods
and absorption of labor. Such an expansion was beyond the capability of
the private sector. Thus the logic of industrialization also provided a
logic of centralization, extensive regulation, and a strategic role for the
state in entering production, controlling supplies of inputs needed by
private enterprise, directing crucial financial resources, administering
key prices, and becoming the largest employer in the country. This logic
satisfied the educated middle classes' sense of national mission for a
number of reasons. It held a promise of national power and prosperity
at the same time that an expanded public control offered a moral
gratification. For here was an opportunity to use a socialistic language to
control resources in the name of long-run public interest. After about
thirty years, it is time to ask, where has industrialization arrived?

Judging in the 1980s, it is apparent that India has acquired a comprehensive structure of industrial production (see Table 6.2). It has pur-

Table 6.2   India: Selected Growth Indicators: 1950/51 to 1985/86

Item	Unit	1950–51	1960–61	1970–71	1980–81	1985–86	Annual percent increase 1950–51 to 1985–86
Population	Million	359	434	541	679	756	2.2
Literacy	percent total pop.	16.7	24.0	29.5	36.2	NA	NA
Real national income:	1950–51= 100						
aggregate		100	145	204.7	283.4	351.9	3.6
per capita		100	119.9	135.8	150.1	168.1	1.4
Gross domestic capital formation	percent of GDP	10.0	16.9	17.8	24.5	25.5	12.6
Foodgrain output	million tons	55.0	82.3	108.4	129.6	145.0	2.8[a]
Industrial production	1970–71= 100	29.7	54.3	100	150.7	206.8	5.7[b]
Village electricity	percent of total villages	0.5	3.8	18.5	47.3	66.0	15.2
Consumer price index (average)	1960=100	81	100	186	401	620	6.0
Government expenditure	percent of GNP	10	19.5	22.1	30.5	35.6	13.6
Foreign exchange reserves[c]	10 million rupees	755	245	438	4,822	7,384	6.7

Source: Center for Monitoring Indian Economy, *Basic Statistics Relating to the Indian Economy* (Bombay, August 1986), Table 8.1–4. For more details and annotation see the source.

[a] Compound annual growth rate between triennia centered on 1950–51, 1960–61, 1970–71 and 1983–84.

[b] Official calculation using a new base (1980–81=100 states that the growth rate accomplished by the industrial sector was 8.7 percent in 1985–86 and 9.1 percent in 1986–87. See Government of India, *Economic Survey, 1987–88*, (New Delhi: 1988).

[c] Excluding gold and SDRs; March to end of year.

sued a planned policy of import substitution that may be distinguished from the nonplanned variants followed by many other developing countries.[65] Unlike Brazil, to take one example, the planned variant in India made it possible to develop heavy and light industries simultaneously despite a higher emphasis on the former. The Latin American cases of gradual exhaustion of import substitution in light industries and then desperately scrambling for heavy industries, which led to political and economic crisis, involved a pattern that was not shared by the Indian case, spanning about the same period of history. In fact, India's policy of early emphasis on heavy industries may have allowed it to taste early and then to gradually cope with exchange crisis. Planned import substitution has also facilitated a pattern of industrialization that has endowed the Indian case with a degree of self-reliance rare among noncommunist developing countries acquiring a broad structure of industrialization during the same period of history. The structure of capital goods industries in India is comparable to that of China, but unlike China, a diversified base of consumption goods industries was allowed to develop. Yet a strict regulation of the latter left room for few luxury goods, so that the flood of durable consumption goods characterizing so many industrializing countries was not reproduced in India.

These gains in industrial development were balanced by significant disappointments, however. India's average annual percentage growth rate of industrial production during the period of 1960–1970 was 5.4 followed by 4.3 in 1970–1982.[66] China's rates were 11.2 and 8.3, Mexico's 9.4 and 7.2, and South Korea's 17.2 and 13.6 respectively. Neither self-reliance nor comprehensiveness can serve as factors inhibiting high rates. Can India's planners take the cover of democracy to explain their disappointment? That will not do because democratic developing countries like Malaysia and perhaps Sri Lanka have a better average record. They have to admit that, with all their devotion to industrialism as the key to rapid development, India's performance on many important counts has moved slower than the average rate for developing countries and for the world as a whole.[67]

The growth rate of industrial product may, however, be less important than the diversification of output indicating the creation of sophisticated capacity that makes an economy poised to move on its own. Between 1951 and 1960, sophisticated machinery and metal industries grew at a compound rate of 14.2 percent against the aggregate industrial rate of 6.4 percent, but during 1960–1970 the lead considerably narrowed, while between 1970 and 1983 the two converged around a low rate of 4.5 percent. The 1980–1985 figures actually indicate the former rate lagging behind the aggregate rate.[68]

Clearly something was wrong: India's industrialization was slowing down when other developing countries were moving faster. This was strikingly evidenced in the steel industry, where per capita production fell way behind that in many industrializing countries.[69]

At the same time, however, the national investment rate in India has not been so depressing. Gross domestic investment as a proportion of gross domestic product was about 10 percent in 1950–1951.[70] By 1980 India's percentage share of investment stood at 24, compared to 25 in middle income countries, 21 in low-income countries, and 27 in China. Whereas foreign financing of capital formation accounts for a quarter of the total in low-income countries and about a tenth in middle-income countries, it has substantially declined in India; since 1978 it has rarely exceeded 4 percent of the total.

So far Indian planning has tended more to raise savings than to make better use of capital resources. Persistent inefficiency of the public sector—the share of which in total capital formation rose to 50 percent in the mid-1960s and has remained close to 45 percent since then—largely accounts for the inefficient use. Lower capacity utilization, higher waste of capital and labor, and widespread subsidization of inefficient public sector enterprises have cost the process of industrialization so dearly that the original claims of national mission are now interpreted by the public as a euphemism for the private mission of groups in power to enrich themselves at the cost of national development.

No easy choice, however, awaits the democratic public in India. Not just the Congress party, but all major political parties in the country have misused the public enterprise. Public enterprises have rapidly expanded at the federal as well as state levels within the federation. The record at the latter level is much worse than at the federal level. A number of parties opposing the Congress party at the national level have ruled over these state-level public enterprises. These include regionalist parties in southern India and Communist parties in the south and the east. The paradox of public enterprise in India then can be under-standable. Everybody knows their wastefulness and yet virtually no political group seriously asks for their immediate displacement.

Is this predicament a product of democratic development? Hardly so, since authoritarian China had been meanwhile stuck with a much more extensive public sector, which has recently been subjected to reform precisely on the ground that command from the top alone costs the nation efficiency and productivity.[71] Brazil's military regime rapidly expanded the public sector during the 1960s and 1970s, as the state encouraged and subsidized the largest expansion of durable luxury goods production in the developing world while plunging the country into massive foreign debt.[72] Democratic development in India has thus shared its inefficiency with socialist and capitalist authoritarian modes of development, but unlike them it established a pattern of parliamentary and public responsibility that has not merely kept open the channels of informed criticism, but also the possibility that public enterprises can be curbed and reformed, if not selectively displaced.

At least, public accountability has made sure over all these decades that the composition of commodities produced by these enterprises or through the encouragement of public sector as a whole remains com-patible with the developmental needs of the nation rather than with the luxury demands of an exclusive class. For example, in the early 1980s—despite the attainment of one of the largest industrial and capital goods capacities in the developing world—India's ownership of passengers cars was only 1.3 per thousand population compared to an average of 14.3 for all developing countries and 15.0 for the Ivory Coast. Similarly, India had only 1.7 television sets per thousand population, whereas all developing countries in aggregate averaged 28.4 and the Ivory Coast 38.0.[73] Moreover, none of these products had to be imported to India, and most of the capacity created in automobile and communication industries were directed to serve production or defense needs.

Evidently democratic planning has enabled the country to develop an extensive structure of industrialization where quantitative expansion of capacity has not kept pace with qualitative increase in efficient utilization of productive resources. If this were consistent with the foundational logic of self-reliant industrialization in a large country well-endowed with natural resources and a potentially large internal market, a failure to make a timely transition to a more intensive system of industrialization could be self-defeating. This intensive phase would call for elaborate technological change, organizational improvements, and upgrading the quality of products to standards of international marketability. Obviously this would also require major political initiatives to renovate the old systems of planning, controls, management, and incentives. It would be too simple to subsume all these tasks under a blanket category of liberalization, for a mere dismantling of an inefficient system of regulation does not automatically make for an efficient system of resource utilization in a developing country. For example, if infrastructural investments have not paid the right dividends because of inefficient public enterprise management, the mere removal of the latter would not invite stepped-up efficiency and investment, presumably from private investors waiting in the wings for a liberal signal.[74]

The issue for India is more complex. Can democratic planning learn from its internal experience and external exemplars from developing countries well enough to make this crucial transition without violating the basic conditions that have historically sustained the democratic process? One can, of course, settle for simpler issues of industrial growth or efficiency and go for some ideal economic solutions while ignoring or condemning real political practice.[75] Since we are interested in democratic possibilities, the easier option in this case is obviously ruled out. India's experience suggests that industrial policy has not been a simple function of privileged pressures. If that were so, neither the capital goods emphasis nor the luxury goods deemphasis would have ruled for four decades. Rather, industrial policy has served as a democratic legitimating device that enables certain leadership groups to beat others.[76] Nehru's definition of national mission at least served him well in his leadership competition, just as Indira Gandhi's desperate spree of nationalization and imposition of control systems over organized industry were moves to outbid rivals inside and outside her party. If all these moves have inevitably strengthened the state, what will prevent another set of adventurous leaders from weakening selected groups of vested interests in and around the state by negotiating with foreign investors or donors or some internal radical publics to build new constituencies of support? After all, old constituencies of support may breed rivals while innovative new ones may have the virtue of preempting them.

All this is merely to indicate that multiple, although not unlimited, policy possibilities can exist within a democratic system, and these can be effectively utilized by creative or desperate state leaderships. Intensive industrialization would threaten a big chain of patronage but at the same time might open up opportunities for a larger chain of beneficiaries. In a democratic setup, where numbers count, and in a slowly developing country, where because of limited resources state-dispensed patronage soon threatens to peter out or close the routes of access, the promise of a shift of beneficiaries may yield appropriate support for new moves. Crisis in external relations, internal economy, or international alignments can make the moment of change more opportune. The point is that a democratic state need not be viewed as a passive system of receiving and reconciling vocal interests, it can also generate counter-interests to rival, if not beat, them. Particularly in a developing country like India, where privileged formations tend to be structurally, regionally, and ethnically fragmented, flexible support seeking by national political leaders seems to be all the more feasible. On the other hand, we should not underestimate the misgivings of the underprivileged economic or ethnic groups about policies that might diminish the subsidies and protections they have come to enjoy in the labor market.[77] A shift of industrial policy toward export substitution would naturally strengthen these concerns because of the imperatives of competition. But the increased income and employment opportunities can be used to allay such misgivings. Issues of welfare and justice need not necessarily contradict the case for intensive industrialization in the process of democratic development. When they do so, it signals more a poverty of leadership, mobilization, and policy than a poverty of democracy.

Welfare, Autonomy, and Justice

Democracy offers a unique opportunity to the disadvantaged groups in India to express their priorities regarding developmental values. This freedom of expression and the legitimation of appropriate popular mobilization have raised a number of interesting issues. National development priorities can be understood in terms of an abstract aggregation of collective aspirations imposed by the state, or in disaggregated terms, implying expanding access of less-advantaged groups to resources they need to enhance, if not to equalize, their social and economic opportunities.[78] Democratic states in developing countries cannot hope to arbitrarily impose priorities without violating their democratic nature. They have to work out a collective agreement from the welter of competing priorities expressed in the political arena by diverse disadvantaged groups. Not all of these groups are mobilized at once or in one convergent direction either to support or oppose the national state. This is what makes the linkage between development and justice difficult and yet possible in a developing democracy.

Demands for reversal of disadvantage have assumed a bewildering variety of forms. The nation itself was perceived as one disadvantaged community confronting the advanced states of the world, and thus poised for a prolonged struggle for self-reliance since the early years of the nationalist movement. But the very logic of autonomy also spilled over to subnational groups even before independence. As we have seen, Muslim separatism, leading to the partition of the subcontinent, was a prominent divisive expression of this sentiment. Political movements to reorganize states following independence, at times, began with secessionist threats. Soon, however, most of these threats proved to be strategies of bargaining for autonomy rights within the federal structure. The case for a southern separatism expressed by the Dravidistan movement gave way to several reorganized states in the region.[79] Cultural mobilization of the southern states had to compete with the language rivalry of each with the other, and when they peacefully settled for state-level autonomy, their language-based mobilization was substantially challenged by leaders who used caste- and class-based mobilization to gain access to power and privilege within each state.

Regional articulation of disadvantage or claims for autonomous rights have used horizontal mobilization of people who themselves are vertically divided into highly stratified social formations like castes or economic formations like classes. Whenever regional mobilization has confronted the national state, it has diverted attention from the deep structures of division underlying regional communities. Consequently, whenever the national state has refused to negotiate with regional leaders, it has strengthened the domination of the better-off regional elites over worse-off lower-status and class groups. Fortunately, sustained pressures from the regional mass movements have usually succeeded in realizing their autonomy, beginning with the creation of Andhra Pradesh in 1953 for Telugu-speaking people. This was followed by several phases of the states' reorganization leading to the creation of the twenty-fifth state in 1987.[80] In most cases the creation of autonomous states within the federation has facilitated a transfer of the targets of popular movements from the national state to the regional state. Mobilization at this stage has affirmed either subregional disaffection based on the disadvantages of the poorest areas of these states, as in the case of the Telangana movement in Andhra Pradesh, or wider lower-caste rights movement, as in Maharashtra.[81]

Federal accommodation of regional rights by inclusionary negotiation has in this way succeeded in incorporating into the national polity popular movements representing new political aspirants. By the early 1980s, however, the plebiscitarian mood of the populist leadership as described earlier in this chapter led to exclusionary responses played through manipulative or coercive craft, which drove the Assam and the Punjab regional movements to explosive proportions.[82] That the leadership was not beyond learning the lesson that such a strategy can destroy democratic rights and national cohesion at the same time was exemplified by the unprecedented Assam and Punjab accords signed by Prime Minister Rajiv Gandhi in 1985.[83] The following Assam and Punjab elections clearly demonstrated that the regional parties that came to power were less threatening to democracy and national cohesion than the national leadership that had earlier weakened both processes by their disjunction. If in Assam the accord had worked better, and in Punjab twenty months of the Akali Party rule has been succeeded by a dissolution of the legislative assembly, it certainly calls for a more imaginative implementation. If the Akali Party's pursuit of the accord was weak, it was not strengthened in any way by the sluggishness of the national leadership in implementing it.

Regional and ethnic justice issues inevitably bring in their trail the poverty and inequality issues that call for redistribution of resources among social and economic groups. Tamil, Telugu, or Sikh power often facilitates the case for internal social and economic competition. If the elites can use their communities against the central authority, the lower formations within them can use the same means to claim their share. The cascade effect of mobilization at successively lower layers of power and economic resources indicates how the class potential of ethnic struggles may be realized.

The limits of the ethnic movements to ensure a just sharing of developmental benefits are set by the fact that the major beneficiaries of successful incorporation have been the educated middle castes and classes. Democratic mobilization and incorporation have enabled them to displace the formerly privileged groups from political power without destroying their economic power. Expanded political mobility and access to state power have encouraged the new leaders to serve their constituencies by offering protected employment, preferential access to education and patronage, and expanded welfare provisions.[84] These measures have benefited the more advanced groups of the relatively backward castes and have only lightly touched the wider segments of the lowest castes and classes, including the scheduled castes and tribes. Yet it is interesting to note that the few states in India in which lower-status groups have registered discernible social advancements also happen to be the ones where ethnic politics has played a large part.[85] In fact the Hindi belt states closely associated with the national leadership, or for that matter the national average of all states in India, would reveal a generally poorer record of performance in economic growth or lower-caste or class advancement when compared with the major states where ethnic and regional mobilization have been salient.[86]

These gains, however, may be small consolation for the country as a whole where the shadow of absolute poverty haunts more than 40 percent of the population.[87] Statistical measures of income distribution in the mid-1970s indicate less inequality than in many developing countries. For example, the Gini coefficient for India was 0.38, showing slightly greater inequality than in China and Sri Lanka, which stood at 0.33.[88] However, income statistics can be notoriously misleading with respect to mass poverty and lower-class and status deprivation. Movements for social justice and redistribution of resources thus have a long way to go where demands for egalitarian and fair access suffer from the fact that caste, class, and regional stratification often compete for attention. Measures of protection and welfare, when extended to the lowest *castes*, may not take care of the lowest *classes*, or the worst-off region, or the most vulnerable ethnic groups. Competing and dispersed bases of deprivation and the consequent demands for competing norms of justice and equalization appear to strengthen the need for democratic political competition, for in the absence of it there may be little assurance that one issue of justice will not overwhelm other valid claims for justice. Plural justice thus requires combined pursuit of regional autonomy, progressive reduction of inequality of status, class and ethnic honor and security, and a pace of economic development consistent with but not overriding these objectives. Any fair assessment of democratic development in India has to wrestle with this stubborn complexity.

• THEORETICAL REVIEW •

Liberal democratic theories, as conventionally stated, are more preoccupied with political mechanisms for contestation and articulation than with what these mechanisms can accomplish for society. Such an emphasis on contest may be appropriate to societies where reasonable levels of living have been already accomplished or where crucial functions of development need not call for sustained collective endeavor. By excluding development from its charge, the state can simply be assigned some regulative and protective functions. But is this limited preoccupation justified by even the history of Western democracies? Perhaps the limited focus on *being* a democracy diverts our attention from the more complex historical issue of *becoming* democratic.[89] When the issue of active becoming is analyzed, it may show that there are more things in common between democratic evolution in the advanced and developing countries than is commonly assumed in the conventional literature.

Democracy in developing countries can hardly be appreciated merely in terms of degrees of contestation and expression, as many studies have sought to do.[90] A better way would be to focus on the gradual process of active cultivation of ideas and institutions contributing to the installation and strengthening of a democratic system, through a simultaneous development of social, economic, and political resources. This would imply an emphasis on the transformative role of the state as a collective instrument. The basic issues here, during a critical transition, would be less about formal mechanisms of checks and balances, rights and obligations, and more about the authority of political movements, the strength of operative (if not ideological) consensus, the weight and distribution of actual and latent opposition, and the ability of the system to evoke legitimating sentiments on the basis of performance. For, in a fragile moment of beginning, rules can be easily violated by a state that comes to control most resources in the name of the public. But the same state will more often respect the rules where the absence of such rules may deplete, if not defeat, the economic and social power of the ruling leaders.

The rules of democratic legitimation and incorporation have served the ruling groups rather well in India during their four decades of operation. Unlike in neighboring Pakistan, which emerged from exactly the same colonial experience, the Indian leaders benefited from an early process of converting nationalist support into electoral support. Continued electoral support allowed them to dominate the developing civil society through state control over economy, education, communication, coercion, and extensive systems of patronage and subsidy. The dominant economic classes in industry and agriculture generally found the system profitable and conducive to a stable set of expectations in a national market of vast potential. If occasionally, as in the staggered sequence of modest reforms of land tenure and private enterprise control, some threats were posed to the highest propertied classes, compensatory avenues of gains were maintained for them through formal or informal channels.

Moreover, new entrants to privileged formations were encouraged through the use of public sector financing, licensing, and tax policies in industries, and by promoting relatively affluent peasant entrepreneurs. At the same time, the promise of expansion of privilege offered a mobility incentive to a wider number in rural and urban areas who developed a sense of stake in the system more on the basis of aspiration than accomplishment. The successful incorporation of regional aspirations in a federalized polity created another important constituency of support for this legitimated democratic system. If all this was not enough to impel the leaders to maintain the rules of the regime, the negative reactions of wide segments of the public threatening the brief interlude of rule violation during the emergency could make them fall in line. Besides, the gains of abiding by the rules were also appreciated by the opposition leaders when they realized—as in Kerala, West Bengal, and other states—that access to power, and its prolonged use in cooperation with other parties ruling in the center, would not be denied. When leaders of capitalist and communist persuasion develop and sustain a democratic system of rules with equal eagerness there must be something more to it than a mere veneer on class rule or a chance gift of colonial history.

All these leadership sets have worked through fairly structured organizational systems with relatively durable organizations and modes of mutual interaction. This organizational system has worked best when it has encouraged incorporation of multiple interests from civil society, including ethnic expressions. Such voluntary associations have also served as latent sectors of potential political leadership in moments of crisis as, for example, discussed earlier in the context of plebiscitarian adventures of central leadership. It is true that there have been occasions when the organizational system in the country witnessed disturbing challenges. These threats have always been limiited in time and territorial extension. Thus communist insurrectionary challenge in the early 1950s and late 1960s remained confined to a few districts, separatism of the DMK or the hill peoples' secessionism failed to expand or converge, and religion-using Sikh separatism in the 1980s had to contend with its own rivals in a community that composes 2 percent of the nation's population. All these widely dispersed threats were also widely staggered over time, and in most cases yesterday's adversaries were turned into next day's partners.[91]

This resilience or absorptive capacity has been considerably aided by an ideological consensus (evolving since the nationalist period) regarding liberal means of resolving conflict, the basic premises of self-reliant planned development, and the directive as well as responsive functions of the state in society. Thus no matter which political party has ruled at the center or at the state level, its functioning pattern has shared a degree of similarity that would have been hard to anticipate from its rhetoric before capturing power. This ideological consensus reinforces the consensual readiness of political actors to play by mutually accepted rules.

How deep is the foundation of support for the system? Studies of advanced democracies show that basic agreements among articulate groups seem to be more decisive than their wider penetration among the masses.[92] Empirical studies of Indian political perception indicate a degree of penetration that clearly goes beyond this minimal requirement. By 1967 70 percent of Indian adults identified with a party, compared to 60 percent in the United States in 1972. The attitudes of nonliterates and those with minimal education demonstrated strong commitment to parties, in fact considerably stronger than comparable U.S. cases. A high correspondence was demonstrated between party identification and party issue preference.[93] Another empirical study has found that partisanship is "not only associated with more [system] supportive attitudes, the attitudes themselves are richer and more basic to the viability of competitive institutions in India."[94] These studies also reveal that the perception of party differences among Indian partisans is informed by a remarkable tolerance of the ideologies of other partisans, who are rarely regarded as radical threats to the system.[95] Democratic political development has apparently not been constrained by the slow development of the so-called social and economic requisites of democratic being.[96]

Indian democracy can be understood as a deliberate act of political defiance of the social and economic constraints of underdevelopment. In fact it has been an adventure in creating a political system that would actively generate the social and economic development it lacked at its moment of foundation. This creative exercise in the autonomy of political initiative and inducement to reverse the expected sequence of democratic development called for a simultaneous treatment of multiple issues like national cohesion, economic development, social justice, citizen efficacy, and human development. The requirement of combination also presupposed that exclusive attention to one objective could be self-defeating. Rather, divided attention implied that the system could benefit from a plurality of expectations from various publics. For example, success in managing challenges to national cohesion and promoting agricultural development may reduce the intensity of adverse reaction to the slow implementation of land reform. Thus it is not surprising that aggregate public confidence in the democratic system has not depended on the performance of particular governments in exclusive issue areas. When the "sons of the soil" or the backward castes are enthused to support a regime that offers them special mobility through a protected job market or job reservations, the system obviously gains allegiance at the cost of economic efficiency.[97] But the consequent gains in the political efficacy of the system may allow it to promote efficiency in other areas of economic action.

Admittedly such balancing acts are favored by the nature of social divisions, structural diversities, and the ecological differences in a complex country like India. It is also clear that these acts have been performed well enough to sustain the regime so far. But the limits should not be ignored. Success in balancing requires an imaginative leadership, which no system ensures. Worse still, as one author had put it in a related context, it may be "a good net to catch allies, but one highly vulnerable to anyone with sharp teeth."[98] The art of balancing, even if forthcoming, may become vulnerable to resolute adversaries having independent access to crucial resources, particularly at a point when the resources of the state are dangerously depleted. Moments of economic crisis, international disturbance, tides of internal populism, or desperate actions by dominant classes to break a perceived stalemate may effectively challenge the hard-earned resilience of four decades.

Rapid development of the democratic state's resources of production, organization, distribution, communication, and legitimation can best preempt such danger. Unfortunately this art of balancing practiced in recent decades, by Congress as well as non-Congress leaders at federal and state levels, has thrived more on distributive skills—largely displayed in patronage, subsidy, and welfare promotions—than on rapid creation of resources.[99] It is tempting to believe that this is inherent in the process of democratic becoming in an inhospitable society. It is equally tempting to ask if the same society, with its compulsion for combined development, can be served better by alternatives to democracy, particularly at this point of development when the progressive taste of democratic becoming would scarcely make the people settle for anything less. However, neither logic nor the historical lessons discussed here would warrant a conclusion that democratic development in a context like India's must necessarily be more self-destructive than self-regenerating.

• FUTURE PROSPECTS •

Barely a decade after the launching of independent India's constitutional democracy, a major Western work on Indian politics confidently warned that "the odds are almost wholly against the survival of freedom and that...the issue is, in fact, whether any Indian state can survive at all."[100] Now that the structure of freedom and the state itself have survived such dire predictions for four decades, the issue can admit a somewhat different statement. The analysis in this chapter implies that the successful maintenance of democracy in India has ensured the stability of the new state and reasonably steady development, achieved with a degree of self-reliance and relative freedom from world economic oscillation that is rare in contemporary history. The processes of democratic becoming have crossed a threshold of reasonable success in a world which has witnessed, especially in the 1980s, a resurgence of interest in democratic development. As the appeal of the "glamorous" alternatives to democratic development wear off, more realistic assessments of the enterprise of what I have called the role of democracy in combined development will be possible.[101]

This is not to deny that the political accomplishments of Indian democracy can pose their own problems that can and should worry us. The mass mobilization in the late 1980s against the secular rules of the state on the part of Sikh, Muslim, and Hindu revivalists, to take one example from the ethnic agenda of Indian politics, indicates that democratic opportunities of expression do not rule out an attack on either secular rationality or democratic reason itself.[102] In fact, the social deepening of democracy can strengthen antidemocratic social and political forces in a manner even more threatening than the adventurous emergency regime of 1975–1976. After all, that adventure did not challenge the rationality of secular democracy. Neither did it create social dissension in the bureaucracy and the armed forces. And the adventure was short, shaky, and unsure of its own norm. Its continuity with some of the original elements of nationalist consensus may set it apart from the new moods of fundamentalism shared by a generation that can dispense with the basic values of the system as long as it can squeeze the system to its favor. Fortunately even the biggest potential danger to the system (i.e., Hindu revivalism) is likely to defeat itself if it chooses extreme courses, because of its own horizontal and vertical cleavages of region, language, caste, and class. The danger, however, cannot be minimized in view of the fact that a long evolution of Hindu inclination to avoid exclusivism has been the strongest pillar of secular rationality sustaining Indian democracy, as we have touched upon at the beginning of this chapter.

Although values alone cannot sustain a democracy in a developing country they need an emphasis in our story, in addition to that which we have given to structure, institutions, leadership, and performance. Democracy is about choice, and the citizens' choices are not inexorably determined by economic or social structural factors. As we have seen, many choices are made that cannot be explained by structural constraints alone, just as the advance creation of the political inclination to settle for some issue outcomes as opposed to others is a function of the art of creative and farsighted leadership. India has had its share of artful leadership and citizen choices consistent with democratic becoming. This is not simply a question of more visible national leaders enjoying or exploiting office—it refers to the larger issue of leadership at all levels of political life, including state and district levels. When the issue is posed whether the present state of democratic being can reproduce at least enough political and economic resources to continue the country's democratic becoming, we can do well to recall how the larger networks of political combination and leadership across parties and citizen groups have worked in recent years. This may afford us more optimism than by unreasonably locking our sight on those who, at the moment, happen to be in the limelight.

• NOTES •

1. For an early history of associations in India see, for example, B. B. Majumdar, *Indian Political Associations and Reform of Legislature (1818–1917)* (Calcutta: Firma K. L. Mukhopadhyay, 1965), ch. 2–5. See also S. Natarajan, *A Century of Social Reform in India* (Bombay: Asia Publishing House, 1962).

2. See Stephen Hay, "Western and Indigenous Elements in Modern Indian Thought: The Case of Ram Mohun Roy," in Marius B. Jansen, ed., *Changing Japanese Attitudes Toward Modernization* (Princeton: Princeton University Press, 1965), p. 318.

3. For details see J. Das Gupta, *Language Conflict and National Development* (Berkeley: University of California Press, 1970), pp. 78ff.

4. When the nationalists sought to persuade the ruling authority to introduce compulsory primary education, their move was turned down. As late as 1911 only 1 percent of Indians would be considered as literate in English and 6 percent in vernacular languages. According to high-ranking British administrators Indian "power to stir up discontent would be immensely increased if every cultivator could read." See Sumit Sarkar, *Modern India, 1885–1947* (Delhi: Macmillan, 1983), pp. 66–67.

5. For a discussion of preemptive militarism in Japan see Akira Iriya, "Imperialism in Asia," in James B. Crowley, ed., *Modern East Asia: Essays in Interpretation* (New York: Harcourt, Brace and World, 1970), pp. 122ff. Increasing racialism in colonial rule was typified in a comment like "we could only govern by maintaining the fact that we are the dominant race...," quoted in Sumit Sarkar, *Modern India*, p. 23.

6. John R. McLane, *Indian Nationalism and the Early Congress* (Princeton: Princeton University Press, 1977), pp. 94–95.

7. Dadabhai Naoroji, *Poverty and Un-British Rule in India* (Delhi: Publications Division, Government of India, 1969 [originally published in 1901]), p. 116. For a collection of others' writings see A. Appadorai, ed., *Documents on Political Thought in Modern India*, vol. 1 (Bombay: Oxford University Press, 1973).

8. See W. T. deBary, ed., *Sources of Indian Tradition*, vol. 2 (New York: Columbia University Press, 1963), p. 140, and A. Appadorai, *Documents on Political Thought*, vol. 1, p. 163.

9. See deBary, ed., *Sources of Indian Tradition*, vol. 2, pp. 194–195.

10. For a detailed discussion see Das Gupta, *Language Conflict and National Development*.

11. Gandhi's ideas are discussed in R. Iyer, *The Moral and Political Thought of Mahatma Gandhi* (New York: Oxford University Press, 1973). For Nehru's ideas see M. Brecher, *Nehru: A Political Biography* (New York: Oxford University Press, 1959). See also Ronald J. Terchek, "Gandhi and Democratic Theory," in T. Pantham and K. L. Deutsch, eds., *Political Thought in Modern India* (New Delhi: Sage, 1986), pp. 307–324, and B. Parekh, "Gandhi and the Logic of Reformist Discourse," in B. Parekh and T. Pantham, eds., *Political Discourse* (New Delhi: Sage, 1987), pp. 277–291.

12. The complexity of the job involved in keeping multiple interests together, and yet not exclusively serving a dominant interest due to populist compulsions of the movement, is discussed in C. Markovits, *Indian Business and Nationalist Politics, 1931–1939* (Cambridge: Cambridge University Press, 1985), pp. 180–181.

13. These ideas are analyzed in detail in Joan Bondurant, *Conquest of Violence* (Berkeley: University of California Press, 1965), esp. pp. 190ff.

14. See, for example, Judith M. Brown, *Gandhi's Rise to Power* (Cambridge: Cambridge University Press, 1972). For a detailed analysis of these movements, esp. pp. 52–122.

15. Ibid., especially pp. 190–249.

16. For a background of the 1919 reforms see S. R. Mehrotra, "The Politics Behind the Montagu Declaration of 1917," in C. H. Philips, ed., *Politics and Society in India* (New York: Praeger, 1962), pp. 71–96.

17. The Act of 1935 and its working is analyzed in A. Chatterji, *The Constitutional Development of India: 1937–1947* (Calcutta: Firma K. L. Mukhopadhyay, 1958), pp. 3–25.

18. The general seats were those that were not specifically designated for Muslims, Europeans, Anglo-Indians, Indian Christians, or Sikhs. For most purposes these would imply constituencies for Hindu candidates.

19. The official version of the constitution was in English. In late 1987 a Hindi translation of the document was approved by a constitutional amendment. Thus the fifty-sixth amendment relatively enlarged access in a country where most people cannot read English. Hindi reading ability extends to about one-third of the country's population.

20. See *The Constitution of India*, commemorative edition (New Delhi: Ministry of Law and Justice, Government of India, 1974), pp. 17–18.

21. For an analysis of the 1977 election see Myron Weiner, *India at the Polls: The Parliamentary Elections of 1977* (Washington, D.C.: American Enterprise Institute for Public Policy Research, 1978).

22. The first quarter of 1988 also witnessed the end of communist rule in Tripura, where a Congress-dominated coalition came to power. Meanwhile, the AIADMK rule in Tamilnadu failed to survive the succession crisis following the death of the party's most popular leader, M. G. Ramachandran.

23. This turning point and its aftermath is discussed in Richard Sisson, "Party Transformation in India: Development and Change in the Indian National Congress," in N. S. Bose, ed., *India in the Eighties* (Calcutta: Firma K. L. Mukhopadhyay, 1982), pp. 1–23; and Stanley A. Kochanek, *The Congress Party of India* (Princeton: Princeton University Press, 1968), especially pp. 407–447.

24. The idea of the Congress party as a national reconciler of interests has been extensively treated in many works, of which at least two may be noted: Myron Weiner, *Party Building in a New Nation: The Indian National Congress* (Chicago: University of Chicago Press, 1967); and Rajni Kothari, *Politics in India* (Boston: Little, Brown, 1970).

25. For details of the politics of the 1970s and its impact on the 1980s see Robert L. Hardgrave, Jr. and Stanley A. Kochanek, *India: Government and Politics in a Developing Nation*, 4th ed., (New York: Harcourt Brace Jovanovich, 1986), p. 204ff.

26. See Myron Weiner, "Political Evolution—Party Bureaucracy and Institutions," in John D. Mellor, ed., *India: A Rising Middle Power* (Boulder: Westview Press, 1979), especially p. 32f.

27. For the Bihar and Gujarat agitations see Ghanshyam Shah, *Protest Movements in Two Indian States: A Study of Gujarat and Bihar Movements* (Delhi: Ajanta, 1977). See also Geoffrey Ostergaard, "The Ambiguous Strategy of J. P.'s Last Phase," in David Selbourne, ed., *In Theory and Practice: Essays on the Politics of Jayaprakash Narayan* (Delhi: Oxford University Press, 1985), pp. 155–180.

28. Jayaprakash Narayan explained his position in these words: "I am aiming at a people's movement embracing the entire nation. A movement cannot have a clear-cut program. The main purpose of a movement is to articulate people's wishes." See his collected writings published under the title *Total Revolution* (Bombay: Popular Prakashan, 1978), vol. 4, p. 141. Positive programs favored by him and the core groups of this movement in Bihar are stated in pp. 165ff. These include political accountability of the elected legislators to their constituencies, devolution of decision making authority, and implementation of agrarian reforms through peoples' committees. See ibid., pp. 168–170.

29. The opponent was Raj Narain, who defeated Indira Gandhi in the election of 1977. The court case and the events following it are described in K. Nayar, *The Judgement: Inside Story of Emergency in India* (New Delhi: Vikas, 1977).

30. These provisions and their use in 1975 are discussed in Zubair Alam, *Emergency Powers and Indian Democracy* (New Delhi: S. K. Publishers, 1987), pp. 94–103. The 59th amendment of the constitution passed by parliament in March 1988 empowers the federal government to impose emergency in Punjab.

31. See, for example, A. Gledhill, *The Republic of India: The Development of its Laws and Constitution* (London: Stevens, 1951), pp. 107–109.

32. This distinction is discussed in detail in J. Das Gupta, "A Season of Ceasars: Emergency Regimes and Development Politics in Asia," *Asian Survey* 18, no. 4 (April 1978): pp. 315–349.

33. Why she ended up choosing this option has been subject to extensive speculation. A good analysis of possible reasons and explanations is in P. B. Mayer, "Congress [I], Emergency [I]: Interpreting Indira Gandhi's India," *Journal of Commonwealth and Comparative Policies* 22, no. 2 (1984), pp. 128–150. How the emergency leaders defended this case is exemplified in D. V. Gandhi, ed., *Era of Discipline: Documents on Contemporary Reality* (New Delhi: Samachar Bharati, 1976), p. 2 and passim.

34. The constitutional changes, as intended and executed, are discussed in detail in Lloyd I. Rudolph and Suzanne H. Rudolph, "To The Brink and Back: Representation and the State in India," *Asian Survey* 18, no. 4 (1978): especially pp. 392–399.

35. The developmental implications of emergency are analyzed in Das Gupta, "A Season of Caesars," pp. 332ff.

36. See Myron Weiner, *India at the Polls*, for a detailed analysis.

37. The political implication and the economic record of the Janata rule is analyzed in J. Das Gupta, "The Janata Phase: Reorganization and Redirection in Indian Politics," *Asian Survey* 19, no. 4 (1979): pp. 390–403.

38. Some of these mobilization processes are discussed by Ghanshyam Shah and J. Das Gupta in their papers included in Atul Kohli, ed., *India's Democracy* (Princeton: Princeton University Press, 1988): pp. 144–168 and 262–304. See also Barnett R. Rubin, "The Civil Liberties Movement in India," in *Asian Survey* 27, no. 3 (1987): pp. 371–392.

39. The literature on labor unions in India is extensive. For surveys of the role of trade unions in Indian politics, see S. Jawaid, *Trade Union Movement in India* (Delhi: Sundeep, 1982); and R. Chatterji, *Unions, Politics and the State* (New Delhi: South Asian Publishers, 1980), esp. pp. 27–86. For a survey of peasant associations see A. N. Seth, *Peasant Organizations in India* (Delhi: B. R. Publishing, 1984); and K. C. Alexander, *Peasant Organizations in South India* (New Delhi: Indian Social Institute, 1981).

40. See Stanley A. Kochanek, *Business and Politics in India* (Berkeley: University of California Press, 1974), especially part 3.

41. These are discussed in detail in an excellent analysis of the pertinent literature by Lloyd I. Rudolph and Susan H. Rudolph, "Determinants and Varieties of Agrarian Mobilization," in M. Desai et al., eds., *Agrarian Power and Agricultural Productivity in South Asia* (Berkeley: University of California Press, 1984), pp. 281–344.

42. The support bases in Kerala are discussed in T. J. Nossiter, *Communism in Kerala* (Berkeley: University of California Press, 1982); those in West Bengal are discussed in Atul Kohli, *The State and Poverty in India (Cambridge: Cambridge University Press, 1986)*, ch. 3.

43. As one study of Kerala points out, "It seems that the agricultural labor movement...has now been integrated into the existing system. The reduction in militant struggles, the increasing institutionalization of collective bargaining and parliamentary politics are all indicative of this." See Joseph Tharamangalam, *Agrarian Class Conflict: The Political Mobilization of Agricultural Laborers in Kuttanad, South India* (Vancouver: University of British Columbia Press, 1981), p. 98. Another more empirical survey conducted in Tamilnadu reaches a similar conclusion. See Marshall M. Bouton, *Agrarian Radicalism in South India* (Princeton: Princeton University Press, 1985), p. 310.

44. The role of a literary association like the Assam Sahitya Sabha in generating a popular movement was not unique to Assam. Similar cases of organized literary initiative in different states of India remind us of the political significance of nonpolitical associations. For a discussion of this association and its alliance with the All Assam Students' Union see my "Language, National Unity, and Shared Development in South Asia," in William R. Beer and James E. Jacobs, eds., *Language Policy and National Unity* (Totowa, N.J.: Rowman and Allanheld, 1985), pp. 208ff.

45. For a chronological survey see T. S. Murty, *Assam: The Difficult Years* (New Delhi: Himalayan Books, 1983).

46. On 18 February 1983 a mob of about 12,000 people killed 1,400 men, women, and children.

47. The Assam accord was announced by Prime Minister Rajiv Gandhi on 12 August 1986. It was described by newspapers as a balancing trick that left "no winners or losers." See, for example, *India Today*, 15 September 1985, international edition, p. 27.

48. The organizational durability of the DMK, and later of its breakaway part, the AIADMK (which ruled Tamilnadu until early 1988), and that of the Telugu Desam (which rules Andhra Pradesh), as well as their record of cooperation with national parties, were hardly anticipated at the time of their inception.

49. For a discussion of his ideas on planning see Bruce F. Johnston and William C. Clark, *Redesigning Rural Development* (Baltimore: Johns Hopkins University Press, 1982), p. 24.

50. For one example see *India Today*, international edition, 15 November 1985, pp. 8ff. This is actually an assessment of the prime minister's record. A reasonably discounted value can, however, be assigned to his government by implication. A similar positive result was recorded in another poll conducted by *The Telegraph*, Calcutta, 31 October 1985. By early 1988 the prime minister and his leadership continued to enjoy more public confidence than the national level alternative leadership despite the growing disappointment with his performance. See *India Today*, international edition, 29 February 1988, pp. 17–23.

51. See *The Approach to the Seventh Five-Year Plan, 1985–90* (Planning Commission, Government of India, July 1984). Center for Monitoring Indian Economy edition, p. 9.

52. The proportion of plan outlay devoted to agriculture was 14.8 percent in the first plan (1952–1956), 11.7 percent in the second plan (1955–1961) and 12.7 percent in the third plan (1961–1965). The corresponding figures for organized industry and mining were 2.8 percent, 20.1 percent, and 20.1 percent. See the *Statistical Outline of India, 1984* (Bombay: Tata Services, 1984).

53. For a critique of Indian plan strategies see John W. Mellor, *The New Economics of Growth: A Strategy for India and the Developing World* (Ithaca: Cornell University Press, 1976), especially pp. 274ff. For a sophisticated analysis defending the plan strategies see S. Chakravarty, *Development Planning* (Oxford: Clarendon Press, 1987), pp. 7–38.

54. This refers to the agricultural policies that have acquired the popular label of "green revolution."

55. For an account of this colonial legacy see Dharma Kumar, ed., *The Cambridge Economic History of India*, vol. 2 (Cambridge: Cambridge University Press, 1983), pp. 947ff.

56. See the *World Development Report, 1987* (New York: Oxford University Press, 1987), p. 258.

57. Ibid.

58. John Wall, "Foodgrain Management: Pricing, Procurement, Distribution, Import, and Storage Policy," in *India: Occasional Papers*, World Bank Staff Working Paper no. 279, May 1978 (Washington, D.C.: The World Bank, 1978), pp. 88–89.

59. See Government of India, *Economic Survey, 1986–87* (New Delhi, 1987), pp. 8 and S-15, and *Economic Survey, 1987–88* (New Delhi, 1988), pp. S-23-24 and *passim.*

60. In 1985 and 1986 the procurement rates were 16 and 15 percent of new foodgrain production respectively. Even in the worst drought year of 1987, this rate exceeded 12 percent. *Economic Survey, 1987–88* (New Delhi, 1988), p. S-24.

61. *Toward Sustained Development in Sub-Saharan Africa* (Washington, D.C.: The World Bank, 1984), p. 2.

62. See Amartya Sen, *Resources, Values and Development* (Cambridge: Harvard University Press, 1984), p. 501ff, for an interesting comparison of the scale of famines in colonial India and socialist China.

63. Primary school enrollment as percent of age group for sub-Saharan Africa in the early 1980s was 77.6 percent, for East Asia 113.0, and for India 90.0. Compiled from The World Bank, *World Tables*, vol. 2 (Baltimore: Johns Hopkins University Press, 1984 edition), pp. 158–159, *World Development Report 1984* (New York: Oxford University Press, 1984), p. 226, and *World Development Report, 1987*, p. 262.

64. For an idea of how the leading economists of the 1950s thought about desirable strategies of development and how in the 1980s they assess their earlier thoughts, see Gerald M. Meier and Dudley Seers, eds., *Pioneers in Development* (New York: Oxford University Press, 1984).

65. Jagdish Bhagwati's distinction of several variants of import substitution would help one to place the Indian policy in a clearer perspective. See his "Comment" on Prebisch in ibid., pp. 201–202.

66. I have used total industrial growth rates because of easier availability, but growth rates in manufacturing are not very dissimilar. See The World Bank, *World Development Report 1984*, p. 220.

67. Thus one estimate suggests that the annual percentage rate of growth of industrial product in India was 4.1 compared to 6.3 for nonsocialist developing countries and 4.3 for the nonsocialist world. See S. J. Patel, "India's Regression in the World Economy," in *Economic and Political Weekly*, 28 September 1985, p. 1652. How seriously such estimates need to be taken is an issue that may be controversial. See, for instance, K. N. Raj, "Economic Growth in India, 1952–55 to 1982–83," in *Economic and Political Weekly*, 13 October 1984, p. 1804.

68. From *Basic Statistics Relating to Indian Economy* (Bombay: Center for Monitoring Indian Economy, August 1984), Table 14.9–2, and August 1986, Table 14.11–2.

69. With all the affection for steel, per capita steel consumption in India increased from five kilograms in 1952 only to seventeen in 1982, whereas in China it grew from two kilograms to fourty-one. By 1982 per capita steel production in India and even China—two cases of relatively self-reliant planning—remained way behind compared to South Korea (339), Taiwan, Mexico (114), Argentina (121), and Brazil (105). *World Economy and India's Place in It* (Bombay: Center for Monitoring Indian Economy, October 1986), Table 8.8.

70. Data in this section has been compiled from sources cited in note 68 (including also Table 22.3) and World Bank, *China: Socialist Economic Development*, vol. 1 (Washington, D.C.: The World Bank, 1983), p. 120.

71. For some details of economic reforms in China, see W. Byrd, et al., *Recent Chinese Economic Reforms*, World Bank Staff Working Papers no. 652 (Washington, D.C.: The World Bank, 1984).

72. For an account of the Brazilian public sector's expansion and the attendant problems, see *Brazil: A World Bank Country Study* (Washington, D.C.: The World Bank, 1984), especially pp. 30ff. The strong preference for luxury goods production catering to the upper 20 percent of the population in a country of high inequality is discussed in Alain de Janvry, "Social Disarticulation in Latin American History," working paper for Giannini Foundation of Agricultural Economics, March 1984.

73. Compiled from The World Bank, *World Tables*, vol. 2.

74. Critical works on contemporary industrial policy discuss some of these issues. In spite of their different perspectives, they agree on the crucial public role in infrastructural investments. See Isher Judge Ahluwalia, *Industrial Policy in India* (Delhi: Oxford University Press, 1985), pp. 168–169; and Pranab Bardhan, *The Political Economy of Development in India* (Oxford: Basil Blackwell, 1984), p. 24.

75. Ahluwalia's *Industrial Policy in India* does not entirely ignore the contingency of compromising growth objectives (p. 172), but its detailed treatment is not included in the scope of this work. Pranab Bardhan seeks to account for the avoidance of "hard choices" by the current leadership in terms of its ties to proprietary classes. See especially pp. 73–74 of *The Political Economy of Development in India*.

76. The ideological issues are discussed in Myron Weiner, "The Political Economy of Industrial Growth in India," in *World Politics* 38, no. 4 (July 1986): pp. 604ff. For a discussion of room to effect policy change in the Indian context see John Toye, *Dilemmas of Development* (Oxford: Basil Blackwell, 1987), pp. 132–133.

77. See Barnett R. Rubin, "Economic Liberalization and the Indian State," in *Third World Quarterly* 7, no. 4 (October 1985): pp. 954–955.

78. We need not discuss in detail the implications of the different criteria proposed by various authors, e.g., primary goods (Rawls), basic capabilities (Sen), or resources (Dworkin). For our purpose it is enough to distinguish the aggregative from the disaggregative approaches to defining priorities. For a useful treatment of these criteria see John Roemer, "Exploitation, Property Rights, and Preferences," in Tibor R. Machan, ed., *The Main Debate* (New York: Random House, 1987), p. 365ff. See John Rawls, *A Theory of Justice* (Cambridge: Harvard University Press, 1971), p. 62ff, where the notion of primary goods includes basic rights, power, economic resources, and self-respect. See also Amartya Sen, *Resources, Values and Development*, p. 315ff and Ronald Dworkin, "Equality of Resources," in *Philosophy and Public Affairs*, Fall 1981, pp. 283–345.

79. See Robert L. Hardgrave, Jr., *The Dravidian Movement* (Bombay: Popular,

1965) for a general background of the movement in the south; and J. Das Gupta, *Language Conflict and National Development*, pp. 268ff for its linkage with democratic representation.

80. Maharashtra and Gujarat statehood followed in 1960 and that of Punjab and Haryana in 1966. The secessionist movement in Mizoram was transformed into an autonomy movement within the federal system and statehood was conceded in 1986. Earlier, in 1963 the state of Nagaland was created in response to secessionist threat. A decade later several new states were created in the northeastern region. The latest new state is Goa, promoted from the intermediate status of union territory to full statehood in 1987.

81. These processes are discussed in the context of a number of regions in A. Majeed, ed., *Regionalism: Developmental Tensions in India* (New Delhi: Cosmo, 1984), esp. pp. 89–114 for Maharashtra. See also G. Ram Reddy and B.A.V. Sharma, *Regionalism in India, A Study of Telangana* (New Delhi: Concept Publishing, 1979, pp. 24–35).

82. The Assam case has been discussed earlier. For a short account of the Punjab situation see D. Gupta, "The Communalizing of Punjab, 1980–1985," in *Economic and Political Weekly*, 13 July 1985, pp. 1185–1190. For details see A. Singh, ed., *Punjab in Indian Politics: Issues and Trends* (Delhi: Ajanta, 1985), and A. S. Narang, *Democracy, Development and Distortion: Punjab Politics in National Perspective* (New Delhi: Gitanjali, 1986), esp. pp. 136–189.

83. This was unprecedented because this was the first time that the prime minister signed a statement of accord with nonofficial political organizations. Even as of early 1987 the transfer of Chandigarh to Punjab, one of the elements of the 1985 accord, was not implemented by the national leadership. This obviously weakened the elected chief minister of the state and also the chances of peaceful solution in this area. See "The Bungled Accord," in *India Today*, international edition, 15 February 1986 for a discussion of the political problems of implementing the accord. See also Francine R. Frankel, "Politics: The Failure to Rebuild Consensus," in Marshall M. Bouton, *India Briefing, 1987* (Boulder: Westview Press, 1987), pp. 31–35.

84. Problems of preferential access are treated in Myron Weiner et al., *India's Preferential Policies* (Chicago: University of Chicago Press, 1981).

85. See Roderick Church, "The Pattern of State Politics in Indira Gandhi's India," in J. R. Wood, ed., *State Politics in Contemporary India* (Boulder: Westview Press, 1984), pp. 236–237.

86. Of the six major states gaining autonomy as a result of regional movements four have attained the highest per capita income level in the country. If we take the annual rate of percentage increase in per capita income at constant prices (1970–71) between 1971–72 to 1981–82, again (among fifteen major states) Punjab scores the highest rank, Maharashtra ranks third, Andhra Pradesh and Haryana rank fourth (tie), Gujarat ranks sixth, and Tamilnadu, seventh. Recent poverty level estimates show lower average poverty compared to the national rate in five of these six states. These comparative data are from *Basic Statistics Relating to the Indian Economy*, vol. 2 (Bombay: Center for Monitoring Indian Economy), September 1985, Tables 14.1 and 14.9.

87. The comparable figure for South Korea is 15 percent and Sri Lanka, 23 percent. See S. Mukhopadhyay, *The Poor in Asia* (Kuala Lumpur: Asian and Pacific Development Center, 1985), p. 8.

88. These comparative figures are from The World Bank, *China: Socialist Economic Development*, vol. 1, p. 94. In addition the share of income of the poorest 20 percent of households was greater in India (7.0 percent) than in any other developing country for which the World Bank reports data, while the share of the highest 20 percent is among the lowest. See The World Bank, *World Development Report 1986*, pp. 252–253.

89. Tocqueville's idea that Americans have come to democracy without having endured democratic revolution and that they are born equal, instead of becoming so, may have implications for impressing such bias. Some of these implications are discussed in another context in Albert O. Hirschman, "Rival Interpretations of Market Society: Civilizing, Destructive or Feeble?," in *Journal of Economic Literature* 20 (December 1982): pp. 350ff.

90. See G. Bingham Powell, Jr., *Contemporary Democracies* (Cambridge: Harvard University Press, n.d.), for some samples, pp. 3ff.

91. The taming of the leading Communist parties, the DMK, the Telugu Desam, the

Assam Movement, the National Conference of Kashmir, and the Mizo rebels are some examples.

92. See M. Mann, "The Social Cohesion of Liberal Democracy," in A. Giddens and D. Held, eds., *Classes, Power and Conflict* (Berkeley: University of California Press), pp. 388ff.

93. This congruence was revealed for all major parties and not just the Congress party. Samuel J. Eldersveld and Bashiruddin Ahmed, *Citizens and Politics: Mass Political Behavior in India* (Chicago: University of Chicago Press, 1978), especially pp. 80, 90, 104.

94. John Osgood Field, *Consolidating Democracy: Politicization and Partisanship in India* (New Delhi: Manohar, 1980), p. 288. This work is based on data collected in 1966 as part of a cross-national project.

95. Ibid., p. 292.

96. See, for example, Seymour Martin Lipset, "Some Social Requisites of Democracy: Economic Development and Political Legitimacy," in *American Political Science Review* 53, no. 2 (1959): pp. 69–105.

97. Backward caste demands usually benefit middle castes more than others. See Francine Frankel, "Middle Castes and Classes in Indian Politics: Prospects for Political Accommodation," in A. Kohli, ed., *India's Democracy*; and Myron Weiner, *Sons of the Soil*.

98. Adam Przeworski, "Some Problems in the Study of the Transition to Democracy," in Guillermo O'Donnell, Philippe C. Schmitter, and Laurence Whitehead, eds., *Transitions From Authoritarian Rule: Comparative Perspectives* (Baltimore: Johns Hopkins University Press, 1986), p. 63.

99. I have excluded the issue of corruption. It is a long story and most recently both the national and regional leaders have been involved. The issue of the Bofors arms deal in 1987 and N. T. Rama Rao's case in 1988 are just a few instances. But the corruption issue needs to be seen in the light of the fact that democracy has encouraged and, at the same time, exposed corruption. But exposure does not necessarily eliminate corrupt leaders from politics. Popular toleration of corruption is a problem that cannot be wished away. See, for example, K. S. Padhy, *Corruption in Politics* (Delhi: B.R. Publishing, 1986), esp. pp. 212–213.

100. Selig S. Harrison, *India: The Most Dangerous Decades* (Madras: Oxford University Press, 1960), p. 338.

101. Barrington Moore, Jr., who has inspired many scholars to defend "glamorous" options through his landmark work, *Social Origins of Dictatorship and Democracy* (Boston: Beacon Press, 1966), has recently observed: "political glamour can be a disaster that produces enormous amounts of suffering.... If humanity is to work its way out of its current plight...there will have to be leaders...who can turn their backs on political glamour and work hard for [barely] feasible goals rather than glamourous ones." *Authority and Inequality Under Capitalism and Socialism* (Oxford: Clarendon Press, 1987), p. 125. Not surprisingly, compared to his earlier work, *Social Origins*, Indian democracy comes out in a positive light in this new work (p. 123).

I have used the notion of *combined development* in the sense of the political compulsion to pursue simultaneous or at least multiple objectives in a multi-ethnic developing country interested in comprehensive national development. This use should not be confused with other uses of the term in the literature (notably, Leon Trotsky's use to convey the advantage of historic backwardness). For an elaboration of the latter use see J. Elster, "The Theory of Combined and Uneven Development: A Critique," in J. Roemer ed., *Analytical Marxism*, (Cambridge: Cambridge University Press, 1986), pp. 54–63.

102. The danger of recent Hindu mobilization can be appreciated if one follows the "*sati* incident," i.e., mass reactions in favor of the widow-burning case in Rajasthan in 1987. See I. Qadeer and Z. Hasan, "Deadly Politics of the State and its Apologists," *Economic and Political Weekly* 22, no. 46 (14 November 1987): pp. 1946–1949. The limits of Hindu confessional politics in the contemporary context are discussed in L. I. Rudolph and S. H. Rudolph, *In Pursuit of Lakshmi*, (Chicago: The University of Chicago Press, 1987), pp. 36–47.

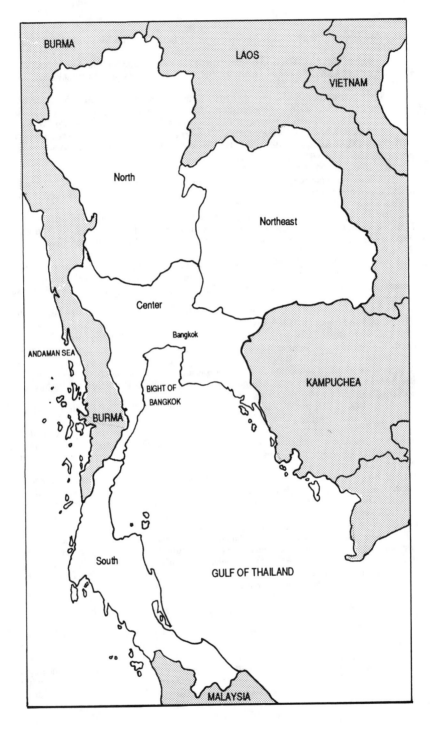

BURMA

LAOS

VIETNAM

North

Northeast

Center

Bangkok

ANDAMAN SEA

BIGHT OF
BANGKOK

KAMPUCHEA

BURMA

South

GULF OF THAILAND

MALAYSIA

THAILAND

CHAPTER SEVEN

Thailand: A Stable Semi-democracy
CHAI-ANAN SAMUDAVANIJA

• HISTORICAL REVIEW •

Alone in Southeast Asia Thailand was never colonized, maintaining its independence through the height of the Western imperial presence in the region. Traditionally the Thai political system has relied on the monarchy as the basis for its legitimacy. The monarchy reigned and ruled and was the focus for the loyalty, love, respect, and religious faith of the Buddhist populace. The king and the dynasty were central to both the ideology and reality of political rule. This was a classic centralized hierarchy, in which the entire focus of legitimacy and status emanated downward from the king through the royal elite to the ordinary citizen, and outward from the palace in Bangkok through the provincial towns to the villages.

Independence in Thailand means that it never experienced the imposition and transfer of institutions from the West that took place in many developing countries. The absence of colonialism also means that traditional structures, particularly the monarchy, the Buddhist Sangha (monastic order), and the military and civil bureaucracy were not disrupted. Although Thailand did not benefit from the process of democratization through the transfer of colonial institutions, neither did it suffer the kind of destruction of the social fabric that many European colonies in the Third World experienced. Because King Chulalongkorn (1868–1910) and his advisors were able to respond effectively to the colonial threat the country also escaped the necessity of overthrowing its colonial yoke. Since no independence movement was necessary the institutions and ideology concomitant with independence movements around the world—especially political parties and mobilized mass movements—never emerged. The Buddhist Sangha, which is the social and religious institution closest to the masses, was therefore not politicized like its counterparts in Burma, Sri Lanka, and Vietnam. Its traditional linkage with the monarchy was not disrupted, but instead has been fostered so that the two institutions have remained complementary to each other.[1] In this sense Thailand faced only a limited political challenge. This allowed the country to defer its true political development to the present.[2]

Democracy as a system of government was adopted in Thailand in June 1932 by a group of junior army, navy, and civilian officers calling themselves the People's Party. Prior to this, constitutionalism and democracy had been discussed among the Thai intelligentsia for a long time. In 1887, a group of princes and officials submitted a lengthy petition to King Chulalongkorn outlining the immediate problems facing Siam and suggested that a constitutional monarchy be instituted.[3] In the late 1880s Tienwan, a commoner and Buddhist scholar, argued in his magazine, *Tulawipak Pojanakit*, that the most effective way to promote justice was to institute a parliamentary form of government.[4] In the 1910s a group of lesser army officials attempted unsuccessfully to stage a coup to replace the absolute monarchy with a republican government. In 1917 Prince Chakrabongse submitted a memorandum to the king suggesting that it was time to grant some kind of constitution to the people. From the latter 1920s to May 1932—a month before the end of the absolute monarchy—the question of whether a democratic form of government was suitable for Siam was one of the major concerns of the regime. Starting from the reign of King Vajiravudh (1910–1925) the monarchy, as an institution, began to be questioned and criticized openly. With the increasing suffering from the Great Depression in the late 1920s, the desire for change was more pressing and resulted in growing awareness of the anachronism of the absolute monarchy.

The reactions of the kings to political reforms were quite similar.[5] Not all of them rejected constitutionalism and democracy as an ideal or a concept of governance, but the appropriateness of the model and practices were questioned. It had always been maintained by the old regime that while constitutional government might be desirable and even inevitable, it was still premature to establish such a system in Siam. The main reasons against the establishment of a constitutional government expressed by foreign advisors, the king, and senior princes were:[6]

1. There was no middle class in Siam. The Siamese peasants took little or no interest in public affairs. Most of the electorate were uneducated; hence to set up a parliament with real power without an educated electorate to control it would only invite trouble and corruption.

2. Parliamentary government was not suitable for the Siamese people, and it was even possible that there must also be certain racial qualities that the Anglo-Saxons possessed and the Siamese did not have to make democracy a successful form of government.

3. Not only was a real democracy very unlikely to succeed in Siam,

it might even be harmful to the interests of the people. The parliament would be entirely dominated by the Chinese.[7]

4. The great bulk of the people of Siam were as yet not trained in political or economic thought.[8] As for the students who returned from Britain, Europe, and the United States, their idea of democracy was half-baked, and their Western ideas were often superficial and misunderstood.

It is clear that the arguments against the adoption of a constitutional government were not so much concerned with democracy as a concept but rather as a form of government, especially its political implications.

Yet it was admitted that Siam would ultimately be forced by circumstances to adopt a democratic form of government, and hence the regime should be well prepared to direct this change gradually. King Prachatipok, however, cautioned that the main danger and the obstacle to this gradual experiment lay in impatience.[9]

Those who were impatient were the Western-educated military and civilian bureaucrats. In the absence of a sizable middle class, a large and strong bureaucracy became the locus of power in the new institutional arrangements. Thai politics after 1932 have therefore been dominated by the bureaucrats, as best described by David Wilson:

> Some 30 years ago the bureaucracy—much strengthened by the reorganization and development of the previous 40 years and by the new techniques of communications and control imported from the West—was cut free of the restraints of absolutism. As much as the leadership of the Thai revolution might have wished things to be otherwise, it was not able to muster much popular interest outside the bureaucracy upon which to base itself. As a result, politics has become a matter of competition between bureaucratic cliques for the benefits of government. In this competition the army—the best organized, most concentrated, and most powerful of the branches of the bureaucracy— has come out on top.[10]

It is ironical that soon after the success of the Westernized elites in their seizure of power from the monarchy, constitutional idealism gradually eroded into formalistic constitutionalism.[11] Since 1932 the bureaucratic elites have been the prime movers in political institutional arrangements under different constitutions. Because of periodic changes in the rules of the game, the scope of political competition, the level of political participation, and the extent to which civil and political liberties are guaranteed have varied according to the nature of the regime.

It should be noted that from 1932 to 1945 the only formal political institution in Thailand was a unicameral legislature composed of two categories of members—half elected and half appointed. The People's Party did not find it necessary to transform itself into a political party since its leading members and supporters were already appointed members of the National Assembly. Political parties in Thailand, therefore, emerged as late as 1946 and were only recognized as legal entities nine years later in 1955. What was institutionalized instead was the political role of the bureaucratic elites. The new leadership relied upon the bureaucracy to play a leading role in educating and mobilizing the mass to participate in elections, as well as to learn about democracy through the symbol of constitution.

Since half of the assembly members were mainly military and civilian officers, the legislative process became an extended arm of, and provided an additional function for, the bureaucracy. Although the new military-bureaucratic elites formed the only organized political group in society, they were not united. On the contrary, soon after June 1932 the young military faction within the People's Party emerged and was, by 1938, able to eliminate the senior members. And since the civilian faction of the People's Party did not develop itself into a broadbased political party, its power and influence gradually declined while that of the military faction rapidly increased, especially after its leader Luang Pibul became defense minister in late 1934 and prime minister in 1938.

From the beginning of constitutional rule, the role of the elected members of parliament was oriented toward internal legislative activities rather than to act as a major political institution for participation and competition for major positions of government power. Hence the electoral process in Thailand, which began as early as 1933, did not lead to the recruitment of political leadership at the top. It was only a tool to legitimate the political system and process in which competition for power was not linked with the electorate but with the factions in the military.

It seems that the objective of the constitution was to establish and strengthen the power position of the new regime rather than to develop a truly democratic political system. The constitution and constitutional symbols were utilized to distinguish between the *ancien* and the *new* regime. In 1933 the National Assembly passed a bill on the protection of the constitution. In the same year it passed another bill establishing a special court to deal with 238 persons who were involved in the Baworadej rebellion. The special court had no provision for appeals or petitions.

The passage of the Protection of the Constitution Act and the special court legislation reflected the ability of the People's Party to control the National Assembly, as well as to utilize it in legitimating their power. Although there was an effort to educate the masses in democratic rule, such an effort was highly formalistic and symbolic rather than substantive.

The 1932 Constitution, therefore, provided considerable stability for the regime, as evidenced by the fact that factional rivalry and competition for power among the military did not result in the abolishment of either the constitution or the parliament. Although there were eight cabinets in a period of six years (1932–1938), there were only two prime ministers, compared with the much more turbulent period three decades later (1969–1979) when there were ten cabinets with six prime ministers under four constitutions.

Political parties were not allowed to function in the first fifteen years of constitutional rule, and the voting method in the first election was indirect. (Each village elected its representatives; the village representatives chose those of the districts, who in turn chose the representatives of the province.) Political participation was a mobilized action in which officials of the Interior Ministry at the village and district levels played a significant role, a pattern not dissimilar to that existing in contemporary Thai politics. Hence early universal suffrage in Thailand did not lead to meaningful political participation or the emergence of political organizations, as happened in other societies. It should be pointed out also that universal suffrage was given to the people when they were not familiar with the principles and the workings of the new system. It is not surprising therefore that constitutional rule was finally replaced by an authoritarian military rule—first by Field Marshal Pibul, and later by Field Marshal Sarit and Field Marshal Thanom respectively.

Pibul's cabinets from 1938 to 1944 marked the high point of rule by the army. During this period, there were seven cabinets with a yearly average of 51 percent military men in the cabinets. Also in this same period, the yearly average of the percentage of military expenditure to total national spending increased to 33 percent, compared with 26 percent during the 1933–1937 period. With the rise to power of Pibul heroism and ultranationalism, with emphasis on leadership, began to develop. Such developments finally led to militarization, especially before the outbreak of World War II. In 1942 the government amended the constitution to extend the tenure of the parliament for two years, and in 1944 the tenure was extended for another two years.

Although Pibul's rise to power did not in any way affect the constitution, his leadership style and ultranationalistic policies greatly affected civil liberties. His *ratthaniyom* marked the first and most systematic intervention of the state into the lives of the Thai citizenry. The Thai people were told what to do and what not to do by their "great leader." The state assumed its role in remolding the values and behavior of the citizens by imposing several orders, rules, and regulations. The nationalist drive also resulted in a number of discriminatory policies against the Chinese minority. Strangely enough, there was no challenge to the government's policies as being unconstitutional, either by the parliament or by the press. This reflected the weakness of democratic values and the inherently autocratic traits in Thai society, which were utilized to a great extent by Pibul and his principal political adviser.

Before the outbreak of World War II the Pibul Government was mainly controlled by members of the 1932 junior clique, including

Pridi—a prominent civilian leader who was the chief ideologist of the 1932 coup group. World War II brought about a major conflict between Pibul and Pridi. The former chose to ally with the Japanese and the Axis Powers while the latter identified himself with the Allied Powers. When Thailand declared war against the Allies Pridi formed an underground movement against the Japanese and the Axis Powers. The defeat of the Japanese and the Axis resulted in the collapse of Pibul's military government.

Postwar Politics

Postwar politics was largely a matter of struggle among three groups for dominance. One was the military group that supported Pibul and was based mainly in the army. The second group, at first centering on Pridi, was rooted in parliament and the civil service. The third group, considerably smaller, was traditionalist and royalist in character. This group was led by Khuang Aphaiwong and Seni Pramoj.[12]

After Pibul's resignation in July 1945, which coincided with the Japanese surrender in the following month, the National Assembly began to play a dominant role in the political system for the first time. Political parties were formed in late 1945 and early 1946. A new constitution was drafted and promulgated to replace the 1932 Constitution in May 1946. The new constitution was an attempt by the temporary civilian coalition of Pridi and Khuang to establish new institutional arrangements to minimize the power of the military. It provided for a bicameral legislature: the House of Representatives, to be elected directly, and the Senate to be elected indirectly by the House. At the first election of the Senate, most of the candidates were the appointed members of the former National Assembly who were Pridi's supporters.

Politics during this civilian interregnum was highly unstable. From August 1945 to November 1947 there were eight cabinets and five different prime ministers. Competition among civilian politicians, together with charges of corruption, economic hardship as the result of the war, and the mysterious death of King Ananda, led to a military coup in November 1947. The coup group abolished the 1946 Constitution and replaced it with an interim constitution, resulting in the January 1948 elections in which the Democrat Party won a majority. However, after less than two months of his premiership the leader of the Democrat Party, Khuang, was forced to resign by the army, and Field Marshal Pibul was installed as the new Premier in April 1948.

In March 1949 a new constitution was promulgated. This constitution provided for a bicameral legislature like that of the 1946 version, but with an appointed Senate instead of an elected one. The new constitution barred officials from being members of the National

Assembly, thus separating the once-powerful military and civilian bureaucrats from active involvement in politics. Such arrangements antagonized the military and finally led to the "silent coup" in November 1951 by the same officers who organized the 1947 coup.

The coup group reinstated the 1932 Constitution, which provided for a unicameral legislature with two categories of members—half elected and half appointed. Ninety-one (or 74 percent) of the total 123 appointed in the 1951 parliament were military members, of whom 62 were army officers, 14 were navy, and 15 were air force officers. It is also noteworthy that 34 of them were the younger generation of middle-ranking officers (major to colonel). As David Wilson pointed out, with the reestablishment of the 1932 Constitution the principle of tutelage was again imposed on an assembly that had been free of it for six years. The government was therefore able to control the legislature through its appointed members and no longer faced serious difficulty in organizing a majority group to support it.[13] In February 1952 an Emergency Law providing the government with wide powers of arrest and press censorship was passed. In November of the same year an Anticommunist Law was approved by parliament by an almost unanimous vote.[14]

Following their consolidation of power in the 1951 "silent coup," the 1947 coup group became deeply involved in politics and commercial activities. They built up their economic base of power by setting up their own business firms, got control over state enterprises and semigovernment companies, and gained free shares from private firms mainly owned by Chinese merchants. This active involvement in business ventures resulted in the division of the group into two competing cliques—popularly known as the "Rajakru," under the leadership of Police General Phao Sriyanond, and Sisao Deves clique, under the leadership of Field Marshal Sarit Thanarat. Each controlled more than thirty companies in banking and finance, industry, and commerce.[15] This split between Phao, the police chief, and Sarit, the army chief, was seen as an attempt by Pibul to maintain his power by manipulating and balancing off these two factions. However, the events of 1955 to 1957 culminated in the coup of September 1957 in which Sarit ousted both Pibul and Phao. This coup mainly concerned a succession conflict; "When a situation of considerable tension had developed in the Bangkok political scene, the Sarit clique moved with the army to take over the government and 'clean up the mess.'"[16]

After the September 1957 coup the constitution was temporarily suspended, resulting in the dissolution of the parliament. The coup group appointed Pote Sarasin, the former Thai ambassador to the United States, as the premier of a caretaker government. A general election was held in December 1957 in which no party won a majority in the parliament. Lieutenant General Thanom Kittikachorn, a leading member of the coup group, was chosen as the prime minister in January 1958. However, as a result of the inability of the government to control the internal strife within its supported party as well as deteriorating economic conditions, Sarit staged another coup in October 1958. This time he abrogated the constitution, dissolved the parliament, banned political parties, arrested several politicians, journalists, writers, and labor leaders, declared martial law, and imposed censorship on newspapers. In 1959, an Interim Constitution was promulgated establishing an all-appointed constituent assembly whose main function was to draft a new "permanent constitution." The interim Constitution also gave tremendous power to the prime minister. From 1958 to 1963 Sarit used the power given by article 17 of that constitution to execute without trial eleven persons—five for arson, one for producing heroin, and four on charges of communism.[17]

Sarit's rule (1958–1963) has been characterized as a dictatorship, as a benevolent despotism, and as military rule. However, as a noted scholar of this period observed, Sarit's 1958 coup marked the beginning of a new political system that endured until at least the early 1970s. What Sarit did in effect was to overthrow a whole political system inherited from 1932, and to create one that could be termed more "Thai" in character.[18] Apart from his strongly anticommunist policy and his initiation of a National Development Plan that opened the way for the tremendous developmental activities of the following decades, the most significant change Sarit brought to the Thai political system was the activation of the role of the monarchy. As Thak rightly pointed out Sarit made it possible, without perhaps so intending, for the monarchy to grow strong enough to play an independent role after his death. The relative political weakness of Sarit's successors brought the throne even more clearly to the center of the political stage.[19]

After Sarit's death in 1963 Thanom became prime minister and commander of the army. In 1968 a new constitution was promulgated after ten years of drafting. The familiar vicious circle of Thai politics, evident in earlier periods, recurred. A semiparliamentary system was established with a two-house legislature. Two years after that conflicts developed within the government-supported party, leading to a military coup in November 1971. Another interim constitution was promulgated, providing for a single constituent assembly composed entirely of appointed members, most of whom were military and civil bureaucrats.

The Breakdown of Military Rule

After the 1971 coup a new and ambitious strongman emerged: Colonel Narong Kittikachorn, the prime minister's son and Deputy Prime Minister Praphat's son-in-law. Narong was appointed assistant secretary-general of the National Executive Council, the supreme body of government administration after the 1971 coup. Apart from being the commander of the powerful Bangkok-based Eleventh Infantry Regiment, he acted as head of a new Committee to Suppress Elements Detrimental to Society, and was also made deputy secretary-general of a new anti-corruption agency. Narong was seen as the heir apparent to the prime ministership. This kind of dynastic succession, never before seen in the Thai military, generated tremendous discontent and criticism from the general public.

Leaders of the student movement were well aware that the growing popular animosity to Narong and the military offered a potentially unique opportunity to put pressure on the military for political reforms, a new constitution, and an elected parliament. On 6 October 1973 student leaders and political activists were arrested while they were distributing leaflets demanding immediate promulgation of a new constitution. The government announced that the police had uncovered a communist plot to overthrow the administration.

From 6 October through 13 October hundreds of thousands of students and others gathered to support the cause of the jailed students. Although the government agreed to release the students and promised to quicken the drafting of the new constitution, riot police on the morning of 14 October clashed with a group of demonstrators in front of the royal palace, thereby sparking violence in other parts of the city. In the meantime a deep split was developing within the military's own leadership. General Krit Sivara, army commander-in-chief, began to adopt a position independent from the Thanom-Praphat group. General Krit's intervention rendered further military suppression untenable, leaving Thanon, Praphat, and Narong no alternative but to flee the country, after being personally ordered by the king to do so. The king appointed Professor Sanya Thammasak, former chief justice of the Supreme Court and rector of Thammasat University, as the prime minister.

The Failure of Democracy, 1974–1976[20]

The student-led uprising of 14 October 1973 brought back once again the period of open politics and democratic experimentation. The 1974 Constitution was patterned after the 1949 Constitution. It limited the number of senators to only 100, with much less power than the elected House of Representatives. Government officials elected to the House or appointed to the Senate had to resign their bureaucratic posts; votes of no confidence remained the sole prerogative of the House; and the prime minister had to be a member of the House of Representatives. These provisions set the stage for a more open political system based on party and pressure group politics.

From 1974 to 1976 the political climate in Thailand became highly volatile. Pressure group politics, mobilization, polarization, and confrontation replaced the usual political acquiescence and the achievement of consensus through bargaining between established patron-client factions. The students, labor unions, and farmer groups were most active in expressing grievances and making demands, which led them into conflict with government officials, business interests, and landowners.

Primarily because the previous governing elite (especially the army) was discredited, and because the abrupt departure of Thanom, Praphat, and Narong had damaged existing patron-client linkages, no single government political party emerged. Several factional groups formed, each composed of members of earlier government parties. Progressive elements also were unable to coalesce into a coherent political party, instead splintering into numerous competing groups. Fragmentation and political polarization of both Left and Right characterized Thai politics during this period. The Democrat Party, the nation's oldest, was divided into three competing factions; each formed its own political party to contest in the 1975 elections. The members of the defunct government party were also split into several competing groups, which subsequently led to the formation of four identifiable parties, namely, the Thai Nation Party, the Social Nationalist Party, the Social Justice Party, and the Social Agrarian Party. These parties were linked with the business community and the military-bureaucratic factions. Apart from these parties, there were two new parties in the center-left spectrum, the Social Action Party and the New Force Party, and two leftist parties, the United Socialist Front and the Socialist Party of Thailand. Although forty-two parties contested the 1975 election, only twenty-two gained seats in the House. The Democrat Party, which had the largest number of seats in the House (72 out of 269), formed a ninety-one-seat minority government in February 1975, but the House on 6 March voted no confidence in the newly formed government. The Social Action Party under the leadership of Kukrit Pramoj, with only eighteen seats in the House, together with three other major parties and ten minor parties, formed a new coalition government. However, this government had a built-in instability because of the lack of trust among leaders of the various parties. Each party, aware of the possible dissolution of the House at almost any moment, focused on building its own small empire. As 1975 progressed, the pace of political maneuvering accelerated. On 12 January 1975—two days before the Democrat Party's scheduled vote of a no confidence motion—Kukrit dissolved the parliament. In the April 1976 election four major parties—the Democrat, Thai Nation, Social Justice, and Social Action—emerged as the dominant powers, compared with the multiplicity of small parties in the House elected fifteen months earlier.

The election results, shown in Table 7.1, demonstrated several continuing features of Thai politics. The national average voter turnout was slightly reduced, 46 percent compared with 47 percent in 1975. Only 29 percent voted in Bangkok, compared with the 33 percent that had voted fifteen months earlier. Leftist parties suffered a humiliating defeat as the electorate displayed a strong conservative tendency in its overall orientation, a preference for political safety over political development. The two socialist parties dropped from twenty-five to three seats, or in percentage terms from 10 to 1 percent of the House as a whole; the progressive New Force Party declined from twelve to three seats. Thus the perceived radical alternative so touted in the months after October 1973 was obliterated by the results of a free election. The Socialists won even fewer seats in April 1976 than in the House elected under military rule in February 1969.

These election results confirmed certain basic trends. One fact was clear: while conflict between the political forces committed to change and those committed to maintenance of the status quo was continuing to escalate, most citizens long for the stability and security of an earlier, easier era. As they reflected on the extremes of violence that had become commonplace over the preceding months, many Thais were seriously asking familiar questions: "Can representative political institutions really survive in Thailand under these pressures?" And, of course, "When will the Army finally intervene?"

The Democrat Party's leader, Seni Pramoj (brother of Kukrit), took over as prime minister on 20 April, at the head of a grand coalition comprising the Democrat, Thai Nation, Social Justice, and Social Nationalist parties. Together these four parties controlled 206 of the 279 seats in the new House of Representatives. However, due in large measure to the weak and vacillating leadership of its aging head, the Democrat Party had by 1976 become divided into two sharply opposing factions, one progressive and the other conservative. The conservative faction, in alliance with other rightist parties, ultrarightist groups, and the military, attacked the progressive faction as being leftist and communist. The factionalism and the weakness of civilian leadership coincided with the growth of leftist ideology and political polarization. Amid these situations came the fall of South Vietnam, Laos, and Cambodia to the Communists. Hence, when a crisis occurred in October 1976 following Field Marshal Thanom's return to Bangkok, the weak and faction-ridden civilian government was unable to control the violent and chaotic situation. On 6 October 1976 the military once again intervened.

The Resumption of Military Rule

The 1976 coup resulted in a familiar autocratic political pattern with even more extremist overtones. The 1974 consitution, parliament, and all political parties were abolished; martial law was proclaimed. The coup group appointed Thanin Kraivichien, a staunchly anticommunist judge, as the new prime minister. Over the months that followed, Thailand was immersed in intense reactionary rule. Several thousand students were arrested while others fled to join the Communist Party of Thailand in the hills.

The ultrarightist policies of the Thanin government—especially its stipulated twelve-year plan for political development, its obsession with communism, and unnecessary aggressiveness toward communist regimes in neighboring countries—resulted in increasing polarization of the Thai society.[21]

Thanin's anticommunist zeal brought about rigorous indoctrination of civil servants, repressive educational control, pressure on labor unions, severe press censorship, and a rigid foreign policy. The military leaders, especially the emerging "Young Turks" in the army, became convinced that Thanin was leading the country to disaster, that his extremist policies were having a most divisive effect and were indirectly strengthening the Communist Party of Thailand (CPT). On 20 October 1977 the Thanin government was overthrown by the same group that had staged the coup that brought Thanin to power one year earlier.

The coup group eased social conflicts and political tension by abolishing the 1977 Constitution and replacing it with a more liberal one. A bicameral legislature with an elected lower House was again introduced and a general election was held in April 1979. However, the new military regime, like its predecessors, maintained its control over the legislature through the appointed Senate to ensure political stability.

The new government adopted a liberal policy toward the problem of communism by granting amnesty to the students and others who were arrested in the 6 October incident as well as to those who had fled to join the CPT. This move, together with other subsequent political measures and reduced support of the CPT by China, led to a diminution of the insurgency in the mid-1980s.

A significant political development from 1977 to 1980 was the rise to political influence of the "Young Turks" within the military establishment. The emergence of these young colonels as a pressure group coincided with the fragmentation of power among army generals. Their political importance stemmed essentially from their strategically important positions within the army organization, which provided a power base for the coup group and the government formed after the coup. Since parliamentary politics after the 1979 election was still unstable because of the proliferation of political parties and interplay conflict in the coalition government, and the military was still deeply split at the higher echelons, the Young Turks were able to exert pressure for changes in leadership. In 1980 they withdrew support for General Kriengsak's government, forcing the prime minister to resign, and installed General Prem Tinsulanond in his place. However, the Young Turks became frustrated a year later with the premier's choice of certain ministers (in a cabinet reshuffle occasioned by interparty conflict in the coalition government). On 1 April 1981 the Young Turks tried and failed to capture state power, despite their overwhelming military forces. The failure of their coup attempt was due largely to their inability to get the tacit approval and support of the king, who openly supported Prem. The Young Turks' power and influence thus ended abruptly.

As a result of the failed coup thirty-eight officers were discharged, leaving a power vacuum in the army. At the same time Major General Arthit Kamlange—who was responsible for the suppression of the 1 April 1981 coup attempt—rose rapidly to the rank of full general and became commander of the army in October 1982. Although he attempted to prove himself as a new strongman and as a successor to Prem, General Arthit found it difficult to advance his political career in that direction. The military's failure to amend the constitution in 1983 to allow permanent officials to hold cabinet positions made it impossible for General Arthit to enjoy the status his predecessors had as commanders of the army. As the army suffered a big split after the 1 April 1981 coup attempt, and the dismissed officers still maintained considerable influence among their troops, there was deep concern and widespread fear of a possible countercoup if a coup was carried out.

In September 1985, while the prime minister was in Indonesia and General Arthit was in Europe, Colonel Manoon Roopkajorn, the leader of the Young Turks, and a group of officers in the Armored Cavalry Regiment still loyal to him, staged an unsuccessful coup. Two former commanders-in-chief of the armed forces (General Kriangsak Chommanan and General Serm Na Nakorn), two former deputy commanders-in-chief, and a serving deputy commander-in-chief of the armed forces (Air Chief Marshal Arun Promthep), were put on trial together with thirty low-ranking officers, while Colonel Manoon was allowed to leave the country. The September 1985 coup created a wider rift between the prime minister and General Arthit since the premier's advisers suspected that the latter was behind the unsuccessful bid for power. Subsequently relations between General Prem and General Arthit became increasingly strained. On 1 May 1986 the government decree on diesel-fueled vehicle registration was voted down in the House, leading the prime minister to dissolve the parliament.

The dissolution of the parliament led to the formation of new political parties that openly declared their hostility toward General Prem. The scheduled election on 27 July 1986 was four days before the retirement date of General Arthit, and it was speculated by the premier's aides that General Arthit could make use of his positions as commander-in-chief of the armed forces and commander-in-chief of the army to influence the outcomes of the election. On 27 May 1986 the premier removed General Arthit as army commander-in-chief and appointed his former aide, General Chaovalit Yongchaiyuth, to the post.

Table 7.1   Comparative Election Results, January 1975 and April 1976, for the Largest Parties in Thailand

	January 1975		April 1976	
	Percent of Popular Vote	Percent of Seats	Percent of Popular Vote	Percent of Seats
Democrat	18.0	26.8	25.4	40.9
Social Justice	14.8	16.7	10.7	10.0
Thai Nation	12.2	10.5	18.1	20.1
Social Action	11.4	6.7	17.8	16.1
Social Agrarian	7.7	7.1	4.3	3.2
Social Nationalist	7.1	6.0	3.3	2.9
New Force	5.9	4.5	7.0	1.1
Socialist	4.7	5.6	1.9	0.7
Socialist Front	3.8	3.7	1.0	0.4
Peace-Loving People	3.5	2.9	—	—
Thai Reformist	2.0	1.1	—	—
Thai	1.7	1.5	—	—
People's Justice	1.7	2.2	—	—
Democracy	1.7	0.8	0.3	0.4
Labor	0.9	0.4	0.8	0.4
Agriculturist	0.7	0.4	—	—
Sovereign	0.6	0.7	—	—
Thai Land	0.5	0.7	—	—
Free People	0.5	0.4	—	—
People's Force	0.4	0.7	4.0	1.1
Economist	0.3	0.4	—	—
Provincial Development	0.2	0.4	0.5	0.7
Dharmacracy	—	—	1.4	0.4
Protecting Thailand	—	—	1.2	0.4
Democratic Front	—	—	1.0	0.4
Thai Society	—	—	0.7	0.4
New Siam	—	—	0.4	0.4
Progressive Society	—	—	0.1	0.4
Total	100.3	100.2	99.9	100.4

Sources: Chai-Anan Samudavanija and Sethaporn Cusripituck, *An Analysis of the 1975 Election Results (Kan wikrorh phon kan luak tang samachik sapha phu tan ratsadorn B.E. 2518)* (Bangkok: National Research Council, February 1977); Rapin Tavornpun, "Popular Votes in 1976 Elections," *The Nation Weekly*, 15 July 1976).
Note: Popular votes totaled 17,983,892 in 1975 and 18,981,135 in 1976. Seats totaled 269 in 1975 and 279 in 1976.

The 27 July 1986 general election did not drastically change the political situation prior to it. Although the Democrat Party won the largest number of seats in the parliament (100 out of 374), there were another fourteen parties elected with representation ranging from one to sixty-three seats (Table 7.2). It was therefore inevitable that a coalition government be formed, and it is interesting to note that this has been the pattern of government since 1975. The only difference is that coalition governments after 1983 have been more stable than their counterparts during 1975–1976 and 1979–1982.

Table 7.2   Results of the Thailand General Elections 1983, 1986

	1983		1986	
	Number of Seats Won	Percent of Seats	Number of Seats Won	Percent of Seats
Democrat	56	7.3	100	28.8
Chart Thai (Thai Nation)	73	22.5	63	18.2
Social Action	92	28.4	51	14.7
Prachakorn Thai (Thai Citizen)	36	11.1	24	6.9
United Democratic[a]	—	—	38	10.9
Rassadorn (People's party)[a]	—	—	18	5.2
Community Action[a]	—	—	15	4.3
Ruam Thai (United Thai)[a]	—	—	19	5.4
Progressive	3	1.0	9	2.6
National Democratic	15	4.6	3	0.9
Muan Chon (Mass party)[a]	—	—	3	0.9
Liberal[a]	—	—	1	0.3
New Force	—	—	1	0.3
Puang Chon Chao Thai (Thai people)	—	—	1	0.3
Democratic Labor	—	—	1	0.3
Independents[b]	49	15.1	—	—
Total	324	100.0	347	100.0

Notes: [a] Parties formed after 1983.
[b] In the 1986 election candidates had to belong to political parties in order to be qualified to contest.

The outcome of the 1986 election did not affect the pattern of leadership succession. General Prem, who did not run in the election and does not belong to any party, was invited by seven political parties (Democrat, Thai Nation, Social Action, People's Community Action, Thai Citizen, and United Thai) to head the government. It is clear that the support from the military was the key factor in the decisions of political parties to nominate him as the premier. This confirms our assertion (see below) that the semidemocratic system is still the most accepted political arrangement in Thailand.

The present Thai political system can be called neither a democracy nor an authoritarian system. It falls between the two political modes and has been termed a semidemocratic government in which the bureaucratic elite have made certain concessions to the nonbureaucratic forces to allow participation in the political process. The semidemocratic system is a political compromise—made possible through distinctive constitutional arrangements—between the bureaucratic and the nonbureaucratic forces.

• HISTORICAL ANALYSIS •

Constitutional Structure and Change

During the half century from 1932 to 1987, Thailand has had thirteen constitutions, thirteen general elections, sixteen coups (nine of which were successful), and forty-three cabinets. There have been sixteen prime ministers, of whom six were military officers and ten civilians. During this period military prime ministers have been in power altogether for forty-four years, while their civilian counterparts were in office for a total of only eleven years. Moreover, some civilian prime ministers were simply fronts for the military.

Successful military interventions usually resulted in the abrogation of constitutions, abolishment of parliaments, and suspension of participant political activity. Each time, however, the military reestablished parliamentary institutions of some kind. This reflects the concern for legitimacy of every military group that came to power after 1932. But because of the weakness of extrabureaucratic forces and the lack of broadbased support for political parties, what has occurred in Thailand since 1932 is referred to as factional constitutionalism.[22] This explains why there have been as many as thirteen constitutions and seven constitutional amendments in a period of fifty-five years. It also explains why democracy in Thailand has many versions and is still being interpreted differently by various groups.

In Thailand a constitution does not normally provide for the general and neutral rules of the game to regulate participation and competition between political groups. On the contrary, it has been used as a major tool in maintaining the power of the group that created it. What Thailand has experienced is not constitutionalism and constitutional government, but rather different kinds of regimes that adjusted and readjusted institutional relationships between the executive and the legislative branches according to their power position vis-à-vis their opponents.

Constitutional arrangements have basically presented three main patterns. One is the democratic pattern, which takes as its model the British parliamentary system, in which the elected legislature and political parties have dominant and active roles in the political process. Under such a system the prime minister must come from a major political party and is an elected MP. An upper house may be maintained but the number of its members is relatively small and its power minimal. In this model military leaders have no opportunity to become prime ministers and bureaucrats are not allowed to take political positions. The second, a semidemocratic pattern, favors a strong executive vis-à-vis the legislative branch. The prime minister does not have to be an elected member of the parliament; the upper house is composed mostly of military and civilian bureaucrats with more or less equal powers to the lower house; and the total number of senators is almost equal to the number of elected representatives.

The third, the undemocratic pattern, has no elected parliament. A legislature is maintained but its members are all appointed, and it acts as a mere rubber stamp on executive decisions that require enactment into laws. Under this system political parties are not allowed to function; hence no elections are held.

Table 7.3 shows the types of constitutions and the periods in which they were in effect.

The most important aspect of a Thai constitution is not the provision and protection of civil and political liberties, but the extent to which it allows the elected House of Representatives to participate in the political process. While, theoretically, the constitution is the highest law of the land, the constitution limits its own power by stating that citizens have political and civil rights and liberties "except where laws otherwise so stipulate." Thus laws, executive decrees, etc. have precedence over constitutional rights and liberties. Such laws limiting rights and freedoms are framed in terms of national security, public order, public morality. Seldom, if ever, is a law challenged on the basis of unconstitutionality. Even if a constitutional issue were to be raised, it would not be decided by an independent judiciary but by a Constitutional Tribunal composed of three ex officio officers (president of parliament, chief justice of the Supreme Court, and director-general of the Department of Prosecutions) and four jurists appointed by parliament. Thus, while the form and structure of constitutional government is visible, in reality the game is fixed; the political deck is stacked in favor of the executive.[23]

In other words constitutionalism was not designed so much to constrain the rulers as to facilitate their rule. The constitutions therefore did not prescribe the effective norms of political behavior, but were used to cast a cloak of legitimacy over the operations of succeeding rulers and to set the stage for a play to be enacted by the extrabureaucratic performers—parliaments, political parties, electors.[24]

Having an elected House of Representatives means that a mechanism must be devised and agreement reached between elected politicians and nonelected bureaucratic politicians (military included) on the sharing of power in the cabinet. Whenever this relationship is strained the tendency has always been to abolish the constitution so that the elected House of Representatives will be automatically terminated. Similarly, having an entirely appointed assembly means that such mechanism and agreement have to be arranged among the bureaucratic elites, especially among the military.

Out of 13 constitutions, only 3 can be classified as "democratic" while 6 have been "semidemocratic" and 4 have been "nondemocratic" (Table 7.3). From 1932 to 1987, "democratic" constitutions were in

Table 7.3   Constitutions in Thailand: June 1932–December 1987

Consti-tution	Types of constitution					
	Demo-cratic (number)	Years in effect	Semi-demo-cratic (number)	Years in effect	Undemo-cratic (number)	Years in effect
1932[a] (provisional)			✓	5 months 12 days		
1932[b]			✓	13 years 5 months		
1946[c]	✓	1 year 6 months				
1947[d]			✓	1 year 4 months 13 days		
1949[e]	✓	2 years 8 months 6 days				
1932[f] (amended 1952)			✓	6 years 7 months 12 days		
1959[g]					✓	9 years 4 months 23 days
1968[h]			✓	3 years 4 months 28 days		
1972[i]					✓	1 year 9 months 21 days
1974[j]	✓	2 years				
1976[k]					✓	363 days
1977[l]					✓	1 year 1 month 13 days
1978*[m]			✓	9 years		
Total[n]	3	6 years 2 months 6 days	6	34 years 3 months 5 days	4	13 years 3 months 25 days

*   Still in effect as of 21 December 1987

Notes:[a] 27 June 1932–10 December 1932; [b] 10 December 1932–9 May 1946; [c] 10 May 1946–8 November 1947; [d] 9 November 1947–22 March 1949; [e] 23 March 1949–29 November

effect for only 6 years and 2 months while the "semidemocratic" and "undemocratic" have been in effect (through December 1987) for 34 years, 3 months and 13 years, 4 months respectively. (No constitution was in effect for 1 year, 8 months.) In other words, during these fifty-five years there were only six years when political institutions could operate within the democratic rules of the game. Moreover, these six years were thinly spread out among three different short periods.

Political Institutionalization

The weakness of the democratic pattern of rule can be attributed to the low level of political institutionalization in Thailand, which is the consequence of three important factors: the frequency of coups d'état, the discontinuity of elected parliaments, and the weaknesses of political parties.

Military coups in Thailand are a means by which political leaders alternate in power. Therefore it is not necessary that political, social, and economic crises be preconditions for a military intervention, although they could facilitate the intervention, particularly when the civilian government's supporters are very strong and active. From 1932 through 1987 there have been altogether sixteen military interventions, nine of which were successful.

As military interventions have become more frequent the commitment of the military to democratic institutions has declined. This is indicated by the fact that in all the five coups during the 1932–1958 period the coup groups changed only the governments in power but did not abolish the constitution. Elections were held and political parties were allowed to function, although their roles in parliament were limited by the presence of the appointed members of the assembly. After 1958, however, military interventions usually resulted in the abolishment of the constitutions and the "freezing" of participant political activities. In the following period of twenty years (1958–1978) there were altogether seven constitutions, only one of which can be classified as "democratic" (1974 Constitution); the rest gave vast powers to an executive branch that was dominated by bureaucratic elites. The high frequency of military interventions in Thailand has had diverse negative effects upon democratic political institutions and has bred more instability within the political system as a whole.

While democratic political institutions suffered setbacks and

Notes to Table 7.3 *continued.*
1951;[f] 8 March 1952–20 October 1958;[g] 28 January 1959–20 June 1968;[h] 21 June 1968–17 November 1971;[i] 15 December 1972–6 October 1974;[j] 7 October 1974–6 October 1976;[k] 22 October 1976–20 October 1977;[l] 9 November 1977–21 December 1978;[m] 21 December 1978 to present.   [n] Excludes a total of 1 year, 8 months, 22 days when no constitution was in effect.

discontinuity, the military has greatly strengthened its organizations and expanded its roles in several areas. During the 1976–1982 period the defense budget averaged about 20 percent of the total government expenditure. The military has also been granted each year a considerable secret fund, which could be used for intelligence operations but has also been widely used for internal security and political purposes. Several civic action programs, political education projects, and rightist movements have been financed from this fund.

Most of the mass communication media, particularly radio and television stations, are under the control of the military—which has undoubtedly reinforced its political potency. Out of 269 radio stations— all of which are government-owned—the military stations account for some 57 percent, while 33 percent are operated by the Public Relations Department and the rest by other ministries and educational institutions. The army also runs two television stations.[25] The military can utilize radio and television programs for psychological warfare and/or mobilizing mass movements in times of political crisis. For instance, the Armored School Radio played a very active role during 1975 and 1976 in mobilizing the rightist movement against the student demonstrators, which eventually led to the coup on 6 October 1976.

In recent years the military has adopted a standpoint that serves to strengthen its legitimate role in politics. It has been emphasized that the military as an institution (or "national armed forces") is the principle machine of the state; therefore when a government composed of political parties fails to solve national problems, the military is entitled to use its own policies to solve those problems.[26]

In a country where participant political institutions are weak, the military can effectively rally public support by pointing to the instability of government and ineffective administration of state affairs by party politics. In their thinking, politics and government administration are inseparable; hence government officials could hold political positions, such as cabinet offices, concurrently with their administrative positions in order to ensure national security.

Historically, therefore, the military and civilian bureaucratic elites represent the most dynamic political forces in Thai society. They were prime movers in most of the events and changes. They are the most powerful political machine in the country, and have been able to control the political game fairly well. The circulation of the military and the bureaucratic elites is also worth noting. The control and command of military positions, especially those at the top of the pyramid and also at the politically important posts, can be utilized for multipurpose activities ranging from getting themselves appointed to the National Assembly to the chairmanship or membership of the public enterprise boards.

Unlike Malaysia and Singapore, where tenures of parliaments last without interruption, only four parliaments in Thailand completed their tenures; the rest were disrupted by coups d'état. While discontinuity of elected parliaments is a fact of political life, the appointed assemblies have been continued without disruptions. It is therefore not surprising that some military officials, such as General Prem, have been members of the appointed assemblies since 1958, while the majority of members of elected parliament in 1980 served in the House of Representatives for the first time.

When parliaments could not complete their tenures several bills proposed by the members had to be resubmitted, thus delaying the process of socioeconomic reform in response to the rapidly changing condition of society during these interim periods. Legislative supporting organizations such as legislative reference and research units were only established in 1974 and could not function effectively because of the lack of support from the government. Members on parliamentary standing committees keep changing from one parliament to another, preventing MPs from developing expertise in their chosen fields.

These consequences of parliamentary discontinuity have weakened the power of the legislative branch vis-à-vis that of the executive and prevented the legislature from becoming a potent force in the Thai political system.

Discontinuity of elected parliaments has had adverse effects on political parties in several aspects. Party organizations could not be developed and political mobilization could only be at best ad hoc. From 1946 to 1981 143 parties were formed but only a few survived throughout these years. All of the parties are urban based with weak rural organization, and party branches are not very well organized.

When political parties were allowed to function they suffered from lack of discipline among their members, who pursued factional and individual interests rather than abiding by party policies. Usually political parties in Thailand are primarily groupings of individuals or networks of patrons and clients who are forced to be together by a political party law requiring candidates to contest elections under party banners. After elections almost all of the parties have no significant programs that would link them with the masses.

Unlike Singapore and Malaysia, which are one-party-dominant states, in Thailand no single party has ever dominated the political scene. When government parties won a majority in parliament, factionalism within them usually led to political crises, culminating in military interventions. From 1975 to 1976, parliamentary seats were shared by from eight to twenty-two parties, resulting in highly unstable coalition governments.

Apart from the above-mentioned factors inhibiting the strength of political parties in Thailand, the development of a party system is affected by the hostile attitude of bureaucratic elites toward the role of political parties. As Kramol Tongdhamachart observes, "the bureaucratic elites often perceived political parties as the cause of national disunity and political instability and also as the political entity that could threaten their power positions."[27] When political parties were allowed to function, the bureaucratic elites usually imposed obstacles on their formation and performance, making it difficult for the parties to mature at a natural rate of growth. The 1981 Political Party Law requires the potential party organizers to fulfill several requirements before their parties can be registered and legally perform their functions. For example, they must recruit a minimum of 5,000 members with residence in five provinces in each of the four regions of the country. In addition, each province must be represented in the potential party with a minimum of fifty persons.[28]

To encourage a strong party system, the present constitution requires that, in the general election, parties must field candidates numbering not less than half of the total number of members of the House of Representatives. Except for the Bangkok Metropolis, which is divided into three constituencies, every other province is regarded as one constituency. The method of voting is to be that of a party slate system; political parties are to submit lists of the candidates supported by them to stand in the constituencies, for the voters to decide on the whole slates.[29] All these measures were made in the hope that they would eliminate small parties so that a two-party system would finally emerge. Naturally such measures have created a tremendous need for major political parties to mobilize funds for their campaigns. It is estimated that to be able to support candidates in a general election, a political party would need at least 50 million baht for campaign funding (U.S. $1 = 25 baht in 1987).[30]

The need for campaign funds has led to a closer relationship between political parties and business interests. Some prominent businessmen have thus become either deputy leaders or executive members of political parties, whereas in the past these people maintained relatively distant relationships with leaders of political parties. At the provincial level local businessmen are also more actively involved in politics both as candidates and as financial supporters of political parties. At the national level most of the businessmen who are party financiers prefer not to run in the election. However, because of their financial contributions, they are given cabinet portfolios in the coalition governments. Conflicts, therefore, usually arise between the elected politicians and the party financiers who are executive members of the parties and are given cabinet posts. The elected politicians call these party financiers "political businessmen," distinguishing them from the "grassroots politicians." Hence, although there has been more involvement from the private sector in the Thai political system, this development has created especially destabilizing effects. This is because, apart from cabinet positions, political secretaries to ministers, and a limited number of executive positions in public enterprises, there are no other significant official positions to which party financiers could be appointed. The competition for limited positions between these two groups of people in various political parties has markedly contributed to the overall instability of the system.

It is fair to say that most of the businessmen still prefer not to be formally identified with any political party. This is because party politics are not yet institutionalized, while bureaucratic politics provides more certainty. However, if there is continuity in the parliamentary system it is natural that compromises would be made between "grassroots politicians," who claim to represent a broader spectrum of national interests, and the "political businessmen," whose interests are more parochial. At present only the privileged groups have access to the formal political institutions through their alliances with political parties and lobbying. The underprivileged groups, i.e., the workers and farmers, have no formal links with political parties and take political actions independently. In other words, while all groups articulate their interests, only the interests of privileged groups are effectively aggregated by political parties.

Major political parties in Thailand have more or less similar policies. They can be classified as moderate and nonideological. Political parties in Thailand have not yet reflected any clear-cut economic interest. Although every major political party has many prominent businessmen on its executive committee, these people became involved in party activities because of their personal relationships with leaders of the parties rather than because of their economic interests. Since parliamentary politics have suffered from lack of continuity, it has not been possible for different economic interest groups to identify their interests along party lines. Parliamentary politics, whenever they are allowed to function, have enabled politically minded businessmen to participate in the competition for power. Short-term parliamentary politics make political and economic alliances highly dynamic and fluid. It is too soon, therefore, to classify Thai political parties by using a criterion of specific economic interests they represent.

Like other problems concerning the weakness of political institutions, the impotence of parliament and political parties in Thailand is unextricably linked with the perennial issue of the conflict between bureaucratic power and that of participant political institutions. Problems facing political parties must therefore be analyzed in a broader perspective and not restricted to internal characteristics of party organizations. It is impossible for any political party to develop its organization and to effectively perform its functions in a political system where coups d'état have become more or less institutionalized.

In historical perspective, democratic development in Thailand suffered setbacks because of certain unique circumstances. In the pre-1973 period, when extrabureaucratic forces were weak and political competition was limited to a few personalities and their cliques, the commitment to democratic values among the political elite gradually declined. This is understandable because those who were committed to democratic principles had no effective base of support, and had to engage in the same game of power play. Hence in the 1930s, the leaders of the People's party sought support from the armed forces in their competition for power. After being drawn into politics new generations of army officers quickly realized their indispensable role. The army officers who staged the coup in 1947 and remained in power until 1973 were not only uncommitted to democratic ideals, they also had strongly antipolitical attitudes. Hence, when extrabureaucratic forces became strong and began to play active roles in politics, they were regarded as destabilizing factors in national development. The military perceived legitimate politics in a very limited sense, involving activities centered in the parliament and not outside. As General Lek Naeomalee (former interior minister) commented: "When people in our country want to have freedom or liberty, they are going to create confusion and disorder—in our democracy we have members of parliament, but what do we get from having a parliament. Can members of parliament help make our country stable?"[31]

It is evident that "democracy" perceived by military men is quite different from the liberal democratic tradition. Its scope begins with a general election and ends at the legislature that is not necessarily an entirely elected body. It is democracy without pressure groups and is conflict-free. In other words there are another set of values higher than liberal democratic values. These values are national security, stability, and order. The attachment to these values is still strong among military officers, and the increased activism of newly emergent groups has further convinced them that full-fledged democratic rule would be detrimental to national security.

Another factor that impeded political development is that rapid socioeconomic changes coincided with the growth of the Communist Party of Thailand. This contributed to the weakening of the overall political system, since any democratic movement that aimed at mobilizing and gaining support from the masses was usually suspected of being communist-inspired. It is therefore unfortunate that significant socioeconomic changes did not lead to a stable pluralist democracy. Ideological polarization during the 1973–1976 period was too extreme and intense. Moreover, political parties were unable to establish linkages to politically active groups such as student, labor, and farmer groups. As a result political participation under the full-fledged democratic rule in the mid-1970s was close to anarchy. The military was therefore able to exploit the situation, suppressing radical elements and co-opting the moderate and conservative sections of these pressure groups.

Economic Development and Social Change

Thailand's economy has grown rapidly over the past two decades, with an average per capita income growth of almost 5 percent per annum between 1960 and 1980. (In 1961 per capita income was 2,137 baht compared with 12,365 baht in 1980. U.S. \$1 = 22 baht in 1980). Over the same period there was a rapid transformation in the structure of production, with the share of agriculture in total value added declining from 40 percent in 1960 to 25 percent in 1980. However, it was estimated that 76 percent of the Thai population still remained in rural areas, a decline of only about 10 percent since 1960. This labor force and population distribution reflects the unusually extensive pattern of Thai agricultural growth and the pervasive rural nature of the Thai economy and society. After two decades of development Bangkok still remains the primary city. While about 9.7 percent of the Thai population lived in Bangkok in 1980, 32.7 percent of total GDP in Thailand originated in Bangkok. Although the overall incidence of poverty was reduced from 57 percent in the early 1960s to about 31 percent in the mid-1970s, poverty remains largely a rural phenomenon.[32] It is estimated that in 1980 11 million people in the rural areas were living in poverty. The benefit of growth was not evenly dispersed but has widened the gap between the rich and the poor, and between the rural and the urban sectors.

The manufacturing sector expanded rapidly as a result of the policy of import substitution. Its share in the GDP rose from 10.5 percent in 1960 to 18 percent in 1980. The number of factories increased fivefold between 1960 and 1980. Figures in 1980 show that there were 3.6 million workers in industrial and service sectors. Apart from workers in privately owned factories, there was also a rapid increase in the number of workers in state enterprises, which rose from 137,437 in 1973 to 433,649 in 1983. Labor unions in state enterprises have been more politically active than labor unions in the private sector. In 1983, there were 323 labor unions in the private sector while there were 91 state enterprise labor unions. However, the former had altogether only 81,465 members compared with 136,335 members in the latter. Public enterprise workers in the Electricity Authority, the railways, and the Water Supply Authority are the most organized; their political significance is due to their control of public utility services in metropolitian areas, which gives them considerable bargaining power. Hence socioeconomic changes in Thailand are marked by the highly urban character of the society, with major potent political forces concentrated in the capital city.

By far the most important change in the Thai economy since the 1960s has been the rapid expansion of the "big business enterprises" (those with assets of more than 500 million baht). According to a 1979 study the value of capital owned by the big business enterprises amounted to nearly 74 percent of the GNP that year.[33] This growth of monopolistic capital was made possible by government development policies during the authoritarian regimes in the late 1950s and throughout the 1960s that favored the development of industrial capital outside agriculture. Such policies were aimed at creating a production base capable of transforming agricultural surplus into manufacturing commodities. As a result, policies of import substitution and trade protection were implemented. During the same period government after government pursued the policy of price controls in favor of urban communities at the expense of the agricultural work force. Prices of rice paddy have been kept low for the sake of city dwellers and consumers while farmers have to purchase chemical fertilizers at extra high prices as a result of additional transportation costs.[34]

In sum, economic development in the past two decades has resulted in the concentration of economic power in the capital city and has created a large urban working class. At the same time this development witnessed the growth of the bureaucracy, which, while remaining highly centralized, penetrated more into the rural areas. By 1980 the number of government employees (excluding military forces) reached 1.4 million, making the ratio between population (46 million) and government employees 33 to 1. In the same year, government expenditure on personnel services accounted for 35% of total government expenditures.[35] Bureaucratic expansion also resulted in a rapid increase in the number of students during the late 1960s and throughout the 1970s. This expansion, unprecedented in Thai political history, resulted from the heavy stress placed on education by the first three national development plans (1961–1976) and provided more than 30 percent of the total government funds each year to education at all levels. Most significant politically was the rapid expansion in the number of university students, which rose from 15,000 in 1961 to 50,000 in 1972, and has since increased greatly.[36]

As discussed earlier, in the early 1970s latent demands for participation were escalating exponentially. The student-led unrest in October 1973 and its aftermath were direct results of the frustrations and unfulfilled aspirations associated with this large and growing gap between change in society at large and stagnation in its political institutions. Although new nonbureaucratic groups emerged, most of them were anomic entities while the better-organized ones, such as the students and workers, were either destroyed or infiltrated and finally controlled by the government.

The Consolidation of a Bureaucratic Polity

It is indisputable that socioeconomic changes led to the emergence of new groups in society, but whether the existence of these groups would lead to a pluralist democracy is another matter. In the case of Thailand socioeconomic changes occurred under situations of semi-imposed development. In this pattern of development political and administrative structures such as the military and the bureaucracy have been able to grow alongside the growth of the private sector. In fact, they have been able to create new institutional structures of their own or to adjust existing structures and functions (or even the "style") to cope with pressures coming from extrabureaucratic groups. The military and bureaucratic groups may "lose" the first battle, especially when intraelite conflicts are high. However, as they had more and more experiences with new environments and situations, their advantage in controlling political resources, especially the use of legitimate violence, made it possible for them to gradually gain control over extrabureaucratic forces.

Rapid socioeconomic changes often create uncertainties and sometimes instability and disorder. In fact, democratic values and norms brought about by these changes are the antithesis of and pose great challenges to traditional values of the military elites, who welcome modernization and development as long as stability and order can be simultaneously maintained.

In the past five decades military interventions in the political process has taken only one form—a coup d'état. But recently, the military has been more sophisticated in developing a national strategy that has helped to expand its legitimate role in the political system. It has adjusted its strategies and tactics in dealing with emergent social forces. Cooperation and co-optation have replaced intimidation and suppression. The experience the military has gained in the past two decades was not from its participation in conventional politics, but from its encounter with the Communist party of Thailand in rural areas. The new generation of military leadership in the 1980s has been politicized in a manner totally different from that of its predecessors. Their experience in organizing the masses in rural areas to counter political activities of the CPT convinced them that the most effective way in dealing with pressure groups is not to suppress them but to find ways and means to control them. This approach is evident in the prime minister's orders No. 66/2523 and No. 65/2525. The former was known as the policy to defeat the Communist party of Thailand, which stated that to destroy the CPT it was necessary to establish a truly democratic regime. Individual rights and liberty should be guaranteed and democratic groups encouraged to actively participate in politics. The army's role in implementing this order is therefore not only to suppress the CPT, but also to act as an instrument to solve political and socioeconomic problems. In a 1983 lecture on "The Changed Situation of the CPT and the Strategy to Defeat the Communists in 1983" Lieutenant General Chaovalit Yongchaiyuth,[37] deputy chief of army staff and the brain behind Order No. 66/2523, stated:

> Nowadays, Thailand has two policies to solve national problems. There is the political party policy, proposed to the Parliament by the government, and the policy of the National Army, the policy to defeat the Communists. These two policies, however, have conflicting contents since one policy is formulated by the political parties but the other by the National Army. But facts, reasons and theory prove that the National Army can solve national problems, namely to win over the CPT, while the political party policy has not succeeded in solving any problems.[38]

From this statement it is clear that the military has taken another step in redefining and reinforcing its role in society. The open criticism of political parties reflected the attitudes of army leaders on the roles of participant political institutions. In fact the military leaders are raising some very important questions, for example, the legitimate role of political parties, whether they really represent the people, and the extent to which parties could successfully cope with national problems.

In mid-January 1983 Major General Pichit Kullavanijaya, First Division commander, warned on a television program that the new electoral system would only result in bringing the "capitalists" into parliament, and, if there was no change in the constitution, the military might well have to "exercise" (to step in) to protect the security of the nation and the interest of the people.[39] He also pointed out that the military has been an important force in society for 700 years and has to be given a proper role in politics.

Order No. 65/2525 reflects a tendency toward a limited pluralist system, especially points 2.3 and 2.4 of the order which state:

> 2.3 Popular participation in political activities must be promoted to enable the people to have more practical experience which can serve to strengthen their attachment to and understanding of the principles of sovereignty. This must be done by involving the *tambon* councils, village committees and cooperatives,... encouraging the use of political parties as a means of promoting their own interests at the national or local level in accordance with the principles of democracy....
> 2.4 Activities of pressure groups and interests groups must be regulated. Pressure and interest groups can act either to reinforce or to obstruct the development of democracy. Therefore, to ensure that their role be a constructive one and to deter any such group from hindering this development, their activities must be regulated....[40]

Order No. 65/2525 (1982) identified six major groups that ought to be regulated: economic groups, the masses, students, progressive groups, the mass media, and the armed forces. While the first five groups were treated at length, the last—the armed forces—was given a very short guideline: "They should have a correct understanding of democracy and preserve this system."

In the same order it is stated that the personnel who will be the main instrument for achieving democratic development are to be "*government* officials" in every agency, as well as ordinary people with idealism who are prepared to *cooperate* to bring about a model democracy (italics added). Hence the Thai military in the 1980s has gone one step further; that is, in the past it only criticized civilian regimes, but now it has set the framework for the development of democracy.

Both the military and the bureaucracy compete with political institutions in organizing and mobilizing the masses in several ways. Although there are several private and voluntary associations, and interest groups, they are mainly Bangkok-based while the great bulk of people in rural areas are organized into groups by the military and the bureaucracy. At the village level the Ministry of Interior is in control of the village councils through the offices of village headmen and district officers. The army, through its Civilian Affairs Department, has not only organized and mobilized masses into groups such as Village Defense Volunteers, but has also infiltrated and taken over certain initially legitimate pressure/interest groups—e.g., student groups, labor, farmers, the media—and created polarization within these movements, weakening them as effective political forces. It was pointed out earlier that political parties had weak links with pressure groups and the masses. With the military's stand and approach to the groups mentioned above, it is very difficult for political parties to establish a closer and more viable relationship with these groups. Political parties are thus reduced to ad hoc electoral organizations, rather than being a meaningful participant political institution.

The present political system is therefore a unique one, in which the leadership of the military has not formed or openly supported any political party as it did in the past. The military and the bureaucrats, however, have their "informal political party," which is the appointed Senate.

The Senate is dominated by military officers and civil servants, with a few businessmen and intellectuals. Military officers are appointed to the Senate according to their seniority and positions (for example, all commanders-in-chief of the army, navy, and air force, chiefs of staff, divisional commanders) as well as for their loyalty to the prime minister. As for civil servants, the undersecretary of every ministry and those of equivalent stature are members of the Senate. These senators have a military whip, the army chief of staff, and a civilian whip, the under-secretary of the prime minister's office. Through their coordinating Committee on Legislative Affairs senators get slips recommending how to vote on various issues both in the Senate and in the joint sessions with the House of Representatives.

The role of the House of Representatives has been constrained by several provisions and procedures of the 1978 Constitution and parliamentary rules. For example, until recently, members of parliament could not freely propose legislative bills unless the Committee on Legislative Bills endorsed the bills. This committee was composed of seventeen members—three appointed by the cabinet, six by the Senate and eight by the House of Representatives. This provision of the 1978 Constitution was lifted in 1983.

Senate control over the House is exercised through the requirement in the constitution that the following matters are considered by a joint session: consideration and passage of The Budget Bill, motion of the no confidence vote, and consideration and passage of legislative bills concerning national security and economic aspects. Under the same constitution, the president of the Senate is president of the National Assembly, the agenda of the meetings is prepared by him and he chairs the joint sessions. The Senate is therefore an instrument for control of the political process—the legislative arms of the bureaucracy.

The semidemocratic pattern of rule described above is the outgrowth of the interplay of social, economic, and political forces in Thai society. It evolved from the nation's unique conditions that have existed for centuries. This semidemocratic pattern is a compromise between two sets of forces that have coexisted since 1932. One set of forces emanates from military and bureaucratic institutions, and values and norms associated with them. The other originates from more recent nonbureaucratic political institutions. These two forces operate within and adjust themselves to changes in the socioeconomic environment. In the Thai situation, changes resulting from social and economic modernization have not automatically strengthened voluntary associations and political groups because the military-bureaucratic structures, rather than the party system, have been able to incorporate and co-opt these new social groups, which then have their interests represented through bureaucratically created and controlled mechanisms. In other words, socioeconomic changes in Thailand have enabled the nonbureaucratic groups to participate more in bureaucratic politics rather than to fundamentally change the nature of the Thai political system from that of a "bureaucratic polity" to that of a "bourgeois polity."

In recent years economic development has brought increased criticism of the bureaucratic polity and of military domination of politics.[41] Ansil Ramsay has observed that political participation in decision making in

Thailand has recently extended to "bourgeois middle-class groups," especially the business elite, who have begun to play a major role in Thai cabinets and in economic decision making. Other groups from middle-class backgrounds, such as leading academics and technocrats, also have increased their access to decision making.[42]

But it is too early to conclude that the bureaucratic polity has already evolved into a "bourgeois polity." One obstacle to this development is the reluctance of these emerging middle-class elements to be politically independent. Moreover, despite the optimism that there have been more businessmen serving in the cabinets than in the past, they make little impact in policy matters. Their participation in the executive branch is usually counterbalanced by the use of advisers and technocrats as practiced under General Prem's governments. Such limitations on the role of the private sector and its leadership are due to the distrust of businessmen's direct involvement in politics on the part of the military and bureaucratic elites. The military, as pointed out earlier, has expressed its concern about the danger of "capitalist interests." Businessmen who have served as cabinet ministers often complained that they could not implement their policies because the bureaucrats did not give enough support.

It seems that the most significant political change in the relationship between bureaucratic and nonbureaucratic groups is that in the 1980s the latter have found a workable partnership with the former through the leadership of a former army general who has an interest in maintaining a semidemocratic system. In the past military leaders formally engaged themselves in parliamentary politics by becoming leader or sponsors of political parties. When conflicts arose between military factions, they were carried over into the arena of parliamentary politics. Political parties and elected politicians were brought into the power play and consequently suffered when conflicts were heightened, which lead to military coups. Under the present system, however, the prime minister is not directly involved in party and parliamentary politics. Indeed General Prem does not consider himself a politician. Also, the leadership of the military has no formal links with political parties. A balance has thus been achieved under the semidemocratic institutional arrangements. Since election campaigns in recent years have involved tremendous funds, the elected members of parliament are naturally concerned with the preservation of the system so that their tenure can be completed. The four parties in the coalition government are satisfied with the portfolios they were given, but the prime minister also appointed former technocrats, retired senior military generals, and a few intellectuals to his cabinets. Hence political power is being shared between bureaucratic and nonbureaucratic forces both at the executive and legislative levels.

It is clear that the military-bureaucratic dominance in the Thai political system is not waning, although it is evident that new and more subtle strategies and tactics have had to have been adopted to cope with social change.

The present state of Thai politics can therefore be described as "politics of contentment" or "politics of satisfaction." Thus continuation of the Prem government in the interest of stability may be viewed as a triumph for the democratic process, but rather as satisfying interests of the bureaucracy, the army (or certain factions in it), political parties, and the monarchy. However, pressure groups, although increasingly more vocal and demanding over the past decade-and-a-half, have remained on the periphery of this political circle of contentment.

• THEORETICAL ANALYSIS •

Politics have taken the shape of a vicious circle in Thailand. A constitution is promulgated and elections are held for legislative seats. A crisis is precipitated, and this triggers a military coup; the military then promises a constitution. Thus the process of democratization in Thailand has been cyclical; authoritarian regimes alternate with democratic or semidemocratic ones. In this situation neither authoritarian nor democratic structures are institutionalized.

Why, despite the social and economic changes that have occurred, is democracy in Thailand still unstable and why has there been the institutionalization of only semidemocratic rule? This is because a differentiated socioeconomic structure does not necessarily lead to the control of the state by societal groups. In Thailand socioeconomic change has occurred under conditions of semi-imposed, forced development, rather than being led by an autonomous bourgeoisie. An activist bureaucratic state competes with participant or nonbureaucratic actors, and this leads to greater bureaucratization, rather than democratization, as the state expands its development role.

The ability of the state to expand and adapt its role to changing situations and environments explains why emergent autonomous forces have failed to challenge the power of the military and the bureaucracy. Although there exists a sizable middle class in Thailand, it is mainly composed of salaried officials and other nonbureaucratic professionals whose interests are not institutionally linked with any of the participant political institutions. The capitalist and commercial class, which is predominantly Sino-Thai, is just beginning to take an active but cautious role in party politics. Neither the farmers nor the laborers, who together compose the majority of the lower class, have yet developed into a class for itself. Although there were some peasant and worker groups that developed consciousness of class antagonisms, they were easily suppressed by the authorities. This underprivileged class is not effectively represented by any strong political party, and is therefore a rather impotent political force in society. Moreover, the military and the bureaucracy have provided an important ladder for social mobility in the past century for many middle-class and lower-class children. This explains why there has been little class antagonism in Thai society despite distinct class divisions. The bureaucracy has therefore been able to function not only as the state mechanism, but also as a social organization.

It should be pointed out that Thai authoritarianism is not very repressive. Authoritarian regimes that attempted to be too repressive usually met with strong opposition from various sections of society. Once an authoritarian regime extended its controls and suppression to the general populace, it was usually opposed by the press, which has been one of the freest in Asia. An independent and long-standing judiciary is another institution that has always been safeguarding the encroachment of civil liberties. It is an autonomous body not subjected to the control of the military and the bureaucracy, but has its own independent recruitment and appointment procedures. The independence and integrity of the judiciary branch is reflected in the appointment of a senior judge to head a government in times of crisis.

The existence of countervailing forces such as an independent judiciary, a free press, and some favorable social conditions such as relatively little class antagonism or ethnic and religious cleavage, are necessary but not sufficient conditions for a viable democracy in Thailand. These conditions do serve as important factors in preventing an authoritarian regime from becoming extreme in its rule. In other words they soften authoritarian rule and, to a large extent, contribute to the maintenance of semidemocratic rule.

The most legitimate institution, which has greatly contributed to social and political stability in Thailand, is the monarchy. It took the monarchy only three decades to slowly but firmly reestablish its prestige, charisma, power, and influence in the Thai political system. By 1985, after almost four decades of his reign, King Bhumibol Adulyadej has become the most powerful and respected symbol of the nation. This is not surprising. He has survived seven constitutions, nine general elections, and over thirty cabinets with eleven different prime ministers. While politicians, military leaders, and civilian prime ministers had come and gone, the king has remained the head of state, the focus of his people's loyalty and cohesion, the fount of legitimacy. Because of the continuity of this institution in contrast to others in Thailand—especially elected legislatures and political parties—the king has gained political experience and developed mature insights into the country's problems.

It has been overwhelmingly accepted, especially since 1973, that the king remains the final arbiter of a national crisis. In 1984, and once again in 1986, in the midst of the conflict between General Prem, the prime minister, and General Arthit, the commander-in-chief of the army, the monarchy played a decisive role in restraining many an ill-advised move by the military.[43]

In this sense, the monarchy performs a highly important substituting function for other political institutions in bringing together national consensus, especially when there is a crisis of legitimacy. It has increasingly played the role of legitimater of political power, supporter/legitimater of broad regime policies, promoter and sanctioner of intraelite solidarity, and symbolic focus of national unity.[44] The social stability of Thailand, despite its periodic coups d'état, can be explained by the existence and positive role of the monarchy. As long as the bureaucratic-military leadership is supported by the monarchy the problem of legitimacy is, to a large extent, solved. Hence it has been observed:

> If any significance emerged from the eventful and volatile political developments of 1984, it was perhaps that the highest institution in the land, the monarchy, revered as a symbol of justice and authority, is likely to be the single most important force capable of holding the country together during times of chaos and crisis and of assuring the viability of a democratic process in Thailand. With a clear commitment of the monarchy to a constitutional government, democracy Thai-style ultimately may have a chance to take root.[45]

This view merits further analysis. What kind of democracy is it that "may have a chance to take root" in Thai society? Democracy Thai-style has been identified in this chapter as a semidemocratic one. Is there any chance for a pluralist democracy or a polyarchy to take root in Thailand?

One of the most important conditions for the development of a pluralist democracy is the more or less neutral "umpire" role of the state. In the case of Thailand, however, the state and its machineries have always played an active and dominant role in society. It should also be noted that the state's principal machinery, the bureaucracy, has been able to adapt its role to changing conditions, most notably by utilizing the ideology of development to expand and legitimate its presence in society.

Although new forces have emerged as a result of socioeconomic changes in the past two decades, they have been under close surveillance by the bureaucratic elites. The privileged organized groups, such as the Bankers' Association, the Association of Industries, and the Chamber of Commerce, have been given access to the decision-making process in economic spheres, but their participation is of a consultative nature rather than as an equal partner. Likewise, labor unions have also been given a limited consultative role in labor relations, while the bureaucracy still firmly maintains its control over farmers' groups through the Ministries of Interior and Agriculture.

Although there were general elections again in 1983 and 1986, popular participation remains relatively low. Where turnouts were high the successes were due to active mobilization by officials of the Interior Ministry rather than to voters' interest in political issues.

The Thai military and bureaucratic elites are by no means united but, despite factional strife and rivalry, they share a common negative attitude toward elected politicians. They are willing to tolerate the elected politicians only to the extent that the latter do not pose a threat to their interests.

The Thai case is different from the U.S. situation where elites are committed to democratic values. In the United States democratic values have survived because the elites, not masses, govern; and it is the elites, not the common people who are the chief guardians of democratic values.[46] Numerous studies on Thai political culture confirm that anti-democratic tendencies have a positive correlation with a high level of education.[47] It has also been reported that people who have high socio-economic status, high educational levels, and good access to political information tend to have a higher degree of political alienation than other groups of people.[48] Furthermore, there is no difference in attitudes toward elections among voters with lower socioeconomic status. Electoral participation by the masses is ritualistic or mobilized participation rather than voluntary political action.[49]

It is fair to conclude that a dynamic balance is currently maintained among various forces, each of which can not possibly afford to dominate the political process on its own strength alone. The semidemocratic model seems to work quite well because, on the one hand, it permits formal and ritualistic political participation through a general election that produces an elected parliament, but, on the other, the real center of power is in the executive branch, which is controlled by the military-bureaucratic elites who, in recent years, have begun to carefully select some business elites to join their regime on a limited basis.

A pluralist democracy is unlikely to develop from an entrenched bureaucratic polity, especially where that bureaucratic polity is not a static entity, but can utilize the ideology of development to redefine its role, and where it exploits traditionally powerful social institutions to further legitimate its dominance by evoking fears of communism and instability emanating from external threats (such as Vietnam and the Soviet Union). While socioeconomic changes have led to the growth of newly emergent forces, they could at best restrain the bureaucratic power rather than capture it and replace it with a group-based bargaining and mutual adjustment system. As for the masses, the persistence of the bureaucracy and lack of continuity in the functioning of political parties have greatly affected their socialization in the sense that they have been bureaucratically socialized rather than politically socialized. This is particularly true in the case of the rural population since they have to rely on the delivery of services from the bureaucracy, and therefore have to learn to survive or to get the most out of what is available from the bureaucracy and not from the parties. The politics of who gets what, when, and how in Thailand is in essence a bureaucratic allocation of values rather than a politically authoritative distribution of benefits.

In conclusion, it should be pointed out that the failures of the April 1981 and September 1985 coups do not mean that Thai politics has developed into a mature democratic system. Military leadership elements continue to view the coup—however difficult it may be to implement—as an acceptable technique to transfer political power. However circumscribed the power of the military may be (due to factionalism), and however expansive may be the growth of nonbureaucratic forces, the result can not be interpreted as signifying a steady development of parliamentary democracy. The major constituencies of government remain outside the arena of its citizenry at large. The balance of power has not shifted to the democratic party system, but to the monarchy, whose charisma and grace enables it to control political power allocation and balance and referee often conflicting political power interests.

• FUTURE PROSPECTS •

In the past, democratic development primarily involved changes in the constitution to make it more democratic by giving more powers to the legislative branch. Such efforts usually led to the instability of the constitutions and the governments because formal political arrangements did not reflect the real power relationships in society. The problem of politics in Thailand is not how to develop a democratic system, but how to maintain the semidemocratic system so that a more participatory system of government can evolve in the long run. In other words, under the semidemocratic system in which an elected parliament is allowed to function, political parties and parliament could utilize the continuity of the political system (which is very rare in Thai political history) to strengthen their organizations. One of the least controversial and most practical aspects of democratic development is the development of the research and information capabilities of political parties and the parliamentarians. The strengthening of the supporting staff of parliamentary committees, as well as research capabilities of political parties, would greatly enhance the role of the parliament in the long run. A well-informed parliament can act more effectively in exercising its countervailing force vis-à-vis that of the bureaucracy.

The continuity of participant political institutions will have great impact upon local politics in the sense that elections for local government bodies, such as the municipalities and the provincial and the village councils, could continue to be held and allowed to operate alongside national politics. In the long run, it would be possible for political parties to extend their infrastructure to rural areas and mobilize support not only in national elections, but also in local elections. It is expected that as long as the elected politicians are willing to make a compromise by not demanding the abolishment of the Senate or insisting that all ministers must be members of the elected parliament, there will be no major disruption in the overall political system. This means that to be able to survive, participant political institutions have to share power with the military and bureaucratic elite.

It seems that the most significant change in Thai politics since 1981 has been the absence of a coup d'état. Some observers regard this as a progressive movement toward a more democratic system because of the more pluralistic nature of society. This led one scholar to conclude that the present Thai polity's strength is its ability to accommodate the demands of a wider range of groups than could the bureaucratic polity.[50] However, the stability and the strength of the present polity might, on the other hand, be attributed to its ability to accommodate the demands of the military and technocratic elites. In this sense, any change in the institutional framework that would upset the existing power relationships would precipitate a coup, because however difficult it might be to implement, military leadership elements continue to view the coup as an acceptable technique to transfer political power. It is their decision not to use this instrument at a particular point in time. When their interests are no longer accommodated and if they overcome factionalism within the army itself, then a coup becomes possible.

This does not mean that the Thai polity will maintain its semi-democratic pattern of rule forever. On the contrary, in the long run, when participant political institutions have the chance to prove their usefulness to the people, their image and credibility will be gradually strengthened. In the meantime, elected politicians should concentrate on their efforts in developing party organizations (such as party branches), and on improving the capabilities of the parliamentary research unit and committee staff so that their already accepted roles could be institutionalized. The improvement of legislative research and reference sections of the parliament and the strengthening of parliamentary committee staff aids are less controversial than the proposal to reduce the number of senators. But such "internal" political reforms will have great effect in the long run. Another recommendation is state financing of political parties in order to reduce the dependency of elected politicians on nonelected party financiers. The German method of reimbursing political parties for their campaign expenses provided that they get more than 5 percent of the votes cast in the election should be adopted in Thailand.

Under the present political situation where there are many active voluntary associations and interest groups that seek to influence government decisions and policies, the parliament should create a new standing committee to act as a channel for the expression of interests and opinions of various pressure groups. In this way groups would operate within the framework of the legislative process, and would reduce their perceived activist role play, which is not acceptable to the military. Instead of putting pressure on the cabinet through strikes, demonstrations, and protests, which so far have not been very effective in redressing grievances, pressure-group politics could best be legitimated through the provision of an institutional mechanism for their interactions with the government and the legislators. In the long run viable relationships would develop between political parties and interest groups.

The above-mentioned recommendations are likely to be acceptable to the military and the bureaucratic elites because they do not directly threaten the existing power relationships. The idea of bringing group actions into the legislative arena is also likely to be welcomed by the military, which has been staunchly opposed to political activism outside formal political institutions and processes.

It is unrealistic to propose any drastic change in the constitution since such a move would induce a military coup. The most important issue in Thai politics is how to avoid the repetitive pattern of political change that I have described as the "vicious cycle of Thai politics." The main reason explaining the persistence of the semidemocratic system, or "authoritarian constitutionalism," is the nature of authoritarian rule in Thailand, which has often been characterized by moderation, flexibility, and careful avoidance of confrontation. As Somsakdi Xuto aptly observes,

> The general public, in particular, has been relatively little affected by exercise of authoritarian power. In short, Thai authoritarianism has been somewhat softened by the personal characteristics of pragmatism and accommodation. Thus harshness or extreme measures typically associated with authoritarian rule in other countries have remained relatively absent, particularly as applied to the general public.[51]

The idea of keeping the elected parliament viable within the semidemocratic system is, of course, a second-best alternative. In the past decade it was impossible for any government to effectively implement its programs because of its preoccupation with surviving. The absence of a coup in the 1980s has enabled the government and the elected parliament to perform their functions without disruption, which is very important in meeting the increasing challenges and uncertainties coming from international political and economic communities. Perhaps improvement of the Thai political process has to begin by accepting existing politics for what they are and not what they should be.[52] It may be worthwhile to accept the role of the military in Thai politics by recognizing its sphere of influence expecially in internal and external security matters. It also means that their participation in the legislative process through the Senate has to be tolerated by the elected politicians. Improvements of internal mechanisms of participant political institutions as suggested above would gradually strengthen these institutions and prepare them well for the more important tasks in the future. A viable and responsible government that would emerge in Thailand may not be exactly like the British parliamentary model that has been followed in form since 1932. It may be a mixed system in which the military-bureaucratic elites and the elected politicians share powers and each side competes for support from the masses in their responsible spheres of influence. The peculiarity of the Thai polity is that, apart from the institution of the monarchy, no other political institution can claim legitimacy on its own account.

It seems that accommodation and compromise, to preserve political stability at whatever the cost, has led to stagnation rather than development in both the political and economic spheres. It has become a question of stability for stability's sake rather than a foundation on which to build progressive reform.

This social stability has enabled Thailand to sustain its economic and social development despite periodic coups d'état. However, as Seymour Martin Lipset rightly pointed out, in the modern world the prolonged effectiveness that gives legitimacy to a political system means primarily constant economic development.[53] Thailand, like other ASEAN nations, has embarked upon the strategy of export-led development in order to minimize its economic dependency on the agricultural sector. The problem is that such efforts will be hampered by increasing trade protectionism, as currently practiced by the United States and Japan. If the effectiveness of a political regime depends upon its economic performance, the export-led development strategy will not be very helpful in furthering the pace of political development in Thailand because it will create economic instability that will lead directly to political instability. As long as the protectionist sentiment remains pervasive in major industrialized countries, there is less hope for Thailand to utilize its export-led development strategy to sustain its economic growth. This problem is aggravated where Thai exports such as textile goods compete with U.S. textile and garment-manufacturing interests.

Because of the increased openness of the Thai economy and its heavy dependence on imported oil, Thailand will continue to face economic problems such as balance of payments squeezes, serious exchange rate fluctuations, accelerating inflation, and increased reliance on foreign borrowing.[54] This would have adverse effects on the performance and credibility of the political system. It is expected that the failure to successfully implement the export-led development strategy would finally lead to economic nationalism and the maintenance of the semi-democratic regime.[55] If economic problems emanating from fluctuations in the world economy worsen it is possible that the military may resort to the adoption of a new corporate state model in order to mediate conflicts among various groups in society. Judging from the past record of political behavior of the Thai military the Western type of pluralist democratic model will not be favored, for it not only threatens the power of the military technocratic elite alliance, but is highly unstable in a society where the economy is very much dependent upon external forces.

In the case of Thailand rapid development has expanded the private sector, but the strength and autonomy of the bourgeoisie have not grown correspondingly to the extent that it could counter the political weight of the military and bureaucracy. This is because the bourgeoisie is largely composed of Sino-Thais who have been under the control of the military bureaucracy for several generations. However, it is likely that the present generation has shown its desire to be more independent by joining political parties and by beginning to be in the forefront by running in the elections. It would, however, take some time before this generation of the bourgeoisie could become a leading political force in society. This is due to the fact that the military has also sponsored a number of political parties to counter the growing extrabureaucratic forces. No matter how rapid the rate of urbanization, political participation in Thailand can never be truly autonomous, but will remain partly bureaucratically mobilized. In conclusion, democracy in Thailand is not regarded as a purely political rule and process, but a political system in which the military and bureaucratic forces largely determine the role as well as the mode of participation of the nonbureaucratic forces. It should be remembered that the Thai parliament is not, and has never been, the center of power. In recent years, as there have been fewer disruptions in the political system, the parliament is only now becoming a new source of power, struggling very hard to institutionalize its legitimacy.

A stable political system—Thai-style—is therefore a semidemocratic system where the bureaucratic and nonbureaucratic forces share political power and continually engage in bargaining and adjusting their strategies to maximize their powers.

• NOTES •

1. On Buddhism and politics in Thailand see Somboon Suksamran, *Buddhism and Politics: A Study of Socio-Political Change and Political Activism of the Thai Sangha*

(Singapore: Institute of Southeast Asian Studies, 1982), and S. J. Tambiah, *World Conqueror and World Renouncer: A Study of Buddhism* (Cambridge: Cambridge University Press, 1976).

2. For more details on Thai political development before 1932 see Chai-Anan Samudavanija, "Political History," in Somsakdi Xuto, ed., *Government and Politics of Thailand* (Singapore: Oxford University Press, 1987) pp. 1–40.

3. Chai-Anan Samudavanija, *Thailand's First Political Development Plan* (Bangkok: Aksornsumphan Press, 1969) (in Thai).

4. On Tienwan see details in Chai-Anan Samudavanija, *Selected Works on Tienwan* (Bangkok: Posamton Press, 1974) (in Thai).

5. See Chai-Anan Samudavanija, *Politics and Political Change in Thailand* (Bangkok: Bannakit Press, 1980).

6. Benjamin Batson, *Siam's Political Future: Document from the End of the Absolute Monarchy* (Ithaca: Cornell University Southeast Asia Program, Data Paper no. 96, July, 1974).

7. Ibid., p. 45.

8. Ibid., p. 10.

9. Ibid., p. 49.

10. David Wilson, *Politics in Thailand* (Ithaca, New York: Cornell University Press, 1962), p. 277.

11. Toru Yano, "Political Structure of a 'Rice-Growing State' " in Yaneo Ishii, ed., *Thailand: A Rice-Growing Society* (Monographs of the Center for Southwest Asian Studies, Kyoto University, English-language Series no. 12. 1978), p. 127.

12. Wilson, *Politics in Thailand*, p. 22.

13. Ibid., p. 20.

14. Thak Chaleomtiarana, *Thailand: The Politics of Despotic Paternalism* (Bangkok: Social Science Association of Thailand, 1979), p. 102.

15. See details in Sungsidh Piriyarangsan, "Thai Bureaucratic Capitalism, 1932–1960" (Unpublished M.A. thesis, Faculty of Economics, Thammasat University, 1980).

16. Wilson, *Politics in Thailand*, p. 180.

17. Thak, *Thailand: The Politics of Despotic Paternalism*, p. 201.

18. Ibid., pp. 140–141.

19. Ibid., p. 334.

20. For more details on Thai politics in this period see David Morell and Chai-Anan Samudavanija, *Political Conflict in Thailand: Reform, Reaction, Revolution* (Cambridge, Mass.: Oelgeschlager, Gunn and Hain, Publishers, Inc., 1981).

21. J. L. S. Girling, *Thailand: Society and Politics* (Ithaca, N.Y.: Cornell University Press, 1981), pp. 215–219.

22. Wilson, *Politics in Thailand*, p. 262.

23. I am indebted to Dr. William Klausner for his observation on this point.

24. Fred W. Riggs, *Thailand: The Modernization of a Bureaucratic Policy* (Honolulu: East-West Center Press, 1966), pp. 152–153.

25. Sethaporn Cusripitak and others, "Communication Policies in Thailand," (A study report submitted to UNESCO, March 1985), p. 37.

26. See details in Lieutenant General Chaovalit Yongchaiyuth, *Lectures and Interviews by Lt. General Chaovalit Yongchaiyuth 1980–1985* (Bangkok: Sor. Sor. Press, 1985).

27. Kramol Tongdharmachart, "Toward a Political Theory in Thai Perspective," (Singapore: Institute of Southeast Asian Studies Occasional Paper no. 68, 1982), p. 37.

28. Ibid., pp. 37–38.

29. This electoral system and voting method were changed to that of multiple constituencies and individual candidacy in the constitutional amendment in 1985.

30. A candidate uses about 800,000 baht in an election campaign although the election law permits a candidate to spend not more than 350,000 baht. In highly competitive constituencies a candidate spends as much as 5 to 10 million baht to win a seat.

31. *Matichon*, 16 September 1979.

32. See details in *Thailand: Managing Public Resources for Structural Adjustment* (A World Bank Country Study, Washington, D.C.: The World Bank, 1984), pp. 1–13.

33. Krirkkiat Phipatseritham, "The World of Finance: The Push and Pull of Politics," (Paper prepared for the seminar on National Development of Thailand: Economic Rationality and Political Feasibility, Thammasat University, 6–7 September 1983), p. 21.

34. Saneh Chamarik, "Problems of Development in Thai Political Setting," (Paper prepared for the seminar on National Development of Thailand: Economic Rationality and Political Feasibility, Thammasat University, 6–7 September 1983), p. 38.

35. Chai-Anan Samudavanija, "Introduction," in the *Report of the Ad Hoc Committee to Study Major Problems of the Thai Administrative System* (Bangkok: National Administrative Reform Committee, 1980), pp. 6–7.

36. Frank C. Darling, "Student Protest and Political Change in Thailand," *Pacific Affairs* 47, no. 1 (Spring 1974): pp. 6–7.

37. Lieutenant General Chaovalit was promoted to chief of army staff and became a full general in October 1985. In May 1986 he was appointed to the position of army commander-in-chief.

38. Lieutenant General Chaovalit Yongchaiyuth, "Guidelines on Planning to Win Over the CPT in 1983," Royal Military Academy, 21 June 1983.

39. I.e., the party slate system requiring the electorate to choose the whole slate of candidates proposed by each political party.

40. Translated by M. R. Sukhumbhand Paribatra in *ISIS Bulletin* 1, no. 2 (October 1982): pp. 14–18.

41. Ansil Ramsay, "Thai Domestic Politics and Foreign Policy," (Paper presented at the Third U.S.-ASEAN Conference, Chiangmai, Thailand, 7–11 January 1985), p. 4.

42. Ibid.

43. Suchit Bunbongkarn and Sukhumbhand Paribatra, "Thai Politics and Foreign Policy in the 1980s," (Paper presented at the Third U.S.-ASEAN Conference, Chiangmai, Thailand, 7–11 January 1985), p. 18.

44. Thak, *Thailand: The Politics of Despotic Paternalism*, p. 334.

45. Juree Vichit-Vadakan, "Thailand in 1984: Year of Administering Rumors," *Asian Survey* 26, no. 2 (February 1985): p. 240.

46. Thomas R. Dye and L. Harmon Zeigler, *The Irony of Democracy: An Uncommon Introduction to American Politics* (Belmont, Calif.: Duxbury Press, 1971) pp. 18–19.

47. See, for example Suchit Bunbongkarn, "Higher Education and Political Development" (Unpublished Ph.D. diss., Fletcher School of Law and Diplomacy, 1968); and Surapas Tapaman R. T. N., "Political Attitudes of the Field Grade Officer of the Royal Thai Army, Navy and Air Force" (Thesis submitted for the Degree of Master of Political Science, Chulalongkorn University, 1976).

48. Pornsak Phongpaew, "Political Information of the Thai People," (Unpublished research report submitted to the National Research Council, Bangkok, 1980), p. 131.

49. Pornsak Phongpaew, *Voting Behavior: A Case Study of the General Election of B. E. 2526* (1983), Khon Kaen Region 3 (Bangkok: Chao Phya Press, December 1984), pp. 155–156.

50. Ansil Ramsay, op. cit., p. 9.

51. Somsakdi Xuto, "Conclusion" in Somsakdi Xuto, ed., *Government and Politics of Thailand*.

52. Ibid.

53. Seymour Martin Lipset, *Political Man*, (London: Mercury Books, 1963), p. 82.

54. Thailand's reliance on foreign capital has reached the unprecedented level of 6 to 7 percent of the Gross National Product in 1984.

55. Dr. Ammar Siamwalla, a leading economist, suggested that the government could transfer resources to the agricultural sector by diverting budgetary allocations from other sectors to improve agricultural productivity. He also observed that if there should emerge public opinion to the effect that Thailand should detach itself from the present world economy, the agricultural sector would be the first to be hard hit. See details in *The Nation* (Bangkok), 21 July 1985, p. 1.

CHAPTER EIGHT

South Korea: Politics in Transition
SUNG-JOO HAN

Since 1948, when an independent government was established, South Korea has gone through several stages of political evolution: (1) the "First Republic" (1948–1960) under the government of President Syngman Rhee, which became increasingly dictatorial; (2) the democratic period of the "Second Republic" (1960–1961), which was ousted by a military coup d'état; (3) the semiauthoritarian period (1961–1972) under President Park Chung Hee; (4) the highly authoritarian Yushin ("revitalizing reforms") period (1973–1979), which ended with the assassination of President Park; and (5) the authoritarian period (1980–1987) of the government of President Chun Doo Hwan. Throughout the entire postindependence period, there has always been a very strong and intense aspiration for democracy. Yet, except for a brief interlude of nine months during the 1960–1961 period, South Korea did not enjoy democratic politics. Those in power resorted to undemocratic means to sustain their rule—rigging elections, oppressing the opposition, altering the constitution by illegitimate means, and restricting basic political freedoms. As the opposition to authoritarian rule—hence the demand for democracy—grew, successive governments had to resort to increasingly repressive and harsh, if sophisticated, measures. These in turn brought about even more intense opposition.

After four decades of predominantly authoritarian rule, South Korea is now undergoing a rapid political transition. Authoritarianism has generated so much opposition from all sectors of the society that, regardless of its possible merits for a developing society, it has been rejected as a viable system for South Korea. The demand and aspiration for democracy have been so intense and forceful that even the supporters of an authoritarian government have come to admit the inevitability of democratization. However, it is an open question as to whether there has been enough change in the substance and significance of those factors—political, social, cultural, economic, and international—that have supported an authoritarian system in South Korea in the past for them now to foster and sustain full-fledged democracy.

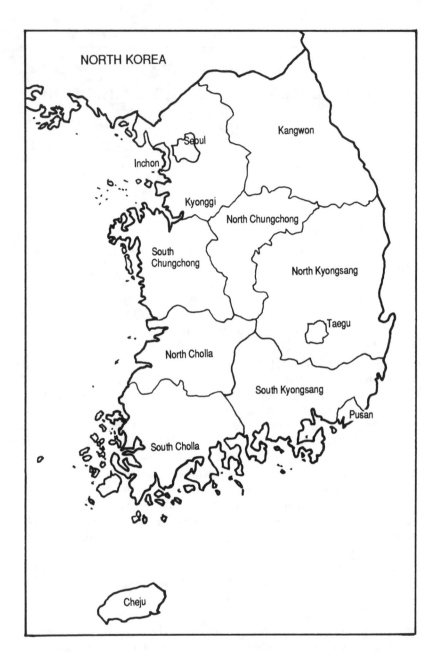

NORTH KOREA

Seoul

Inchon

Kyonggi

Kangwon

North Chungchong

South
Chungchong

North Kyongsang

Taegu

North Cholla

South Kyongsang

Pusan

South Cholla

Cheju

SOUTH KOREA

Contemporary South Korean politics can be characterized as semi-authoritarian, with strong democratic pressures and promises. Whether those promises will be fulfilled depends upon the answers to be given to a series of questions. What are the explanations for the failure of democracy to be instituted and take root in South Korea in the past? How strong and stable are the factors and forces for authoritarian politics? What are the factors and forces that would now work for or against democracy? What are the likely processes by which democratic development and consolidation would take place? These questions will be explored in the following pages.

• HISTORICAL REVIEW AND ANALYSIS •

Democratic Experiments

In May of 1961, a coup d'état by a group of military officers in South Korea put to an end the nine-month-old government of Prime Minister Chang Myon. It also meant the end of the Second Korean Republic, established in July 1960 after Syngman Rhee's ouster in the wake of student uprisings three months earlier. The relative ease with which the coup was carried out was matched by the absence of any overt sign of resistance to the military takeover on the part of the general population. The end of the "Second Republic," as the Chang period was to be called later, marked the second failure of the Koreans to create and preserve a democratic government.

Korea's first democratic experiment ended in failure during the Syngman Rhee period. The first Korean republic was established in 1948 after a thirty-five-year Japanese colonial rule followed by a U.S. military occupation government. It was the product, in large measure, of the determination and persistence of Syngman Rhee, a venerable leader of the independence movement, and his conservative nationalist supporters. They opposed the trusteeship plan of the allied powers (the United States, the Soviet Union, and the United Kingdom) for all of Korea—north and south—and insisted on the immediate establishment of an independent government in the south even if it meant the loss, perhaps permanently, of the northern half of the peninsula to rule under a communist government.

The new government was born with a democratic constitution and with the expectation that it would usher in democratic politics for South Korea. But the Rhee government became increasingly arbitrary and dictatorial. Above all, Rhee was determined to remain in power—for life—which required several constitutional changes, election rigging, and repression of the opposition. Rhee was able to establish his personal dictatorship by making use of the state power as exemplified by the national police.

Many factors contributed to the formidable power of the state and the police: the general proclivities of the great majority of the Korean people at the time for obedience to the state and conformity with others; the absence of strong social organizations that could challenge the prerogatives of the state; the highly centralized and well-disciplined nature of the police organizations; and the existence of a communist threat from the north, as well as from within South Korea itself. The absence of nationwide social organizations other than the police and the administrative bureaucracy greatly contributed to the supremacy of state power, and the prior existence of a well-organized police and bureaucratic apparatus presented a serious obstacle to the development of effective political parties in Korea. And all these gave an insurmountable advantage to the incumbent president and his supporters, who proceeded to undermine the democratic process to perpetuate their rule.

But Rhee's dictatorship, based primarily on coercive force and to some extent his personal charisma, was heading toward a confrontation with the political public, who were being increasingly alienated from his government. When the Korean government was established in 1948, belief in democratic values and practices was not widespread among the people at all levels of the society. However, increasingly large numbers began to demand "free and fair" elections as the actual performance of the government became increasingly less democratic. The rise in democratic consciousness among the public was largely the result of extensive democratic education and rapid urbanization following the Korean War. "Education in democracy" was taken very seriously in both the elementary and secondary schools. Extensive exposure of the highly literate urban and semiurban population to the mass media was instrumental in convincing many Koreans of the virtues of democracy. The positive results of this democratic political education are seen in the fact that in many surveys young people were found to be more "democratically oriented" than their elders.[1]

The polarization of political forces into the progovernment Liberal Party and antigovernment Democratic Party by the mid-1950s made it easier for voters to identify whom to vote for and whom against, depending upon the level of their political consciousness. For the relatively mobilized population the only easy and obvious way to uphold their newly acquired democratic values was to vote against the candidates and party of a government acting undemocratically, and for those opposing the government. Thus in a political setting in which ideological diversity was not tolerated and thus all major political parties were essentially conservative, the only choice for the voters was between a party that was against democracy and one that was for democracy. A large-scale election fraud in March 1960 resulted in massive student uprisings in April and ultimately the fall of the Rhee regime, as the military that had been mobilized to defend it refused to use violence against the demonstrators.

South Korea failed with its first democratic experiment because of the abuse of power by its leader, Syngman Rhee. The second experiment that followed the fall of the Rhee regime ended when a military coup d'état ousted the democratically elected government of Chang Myon only nine months after its inauguration. One obvious reason for the fall of the Chang Myon government (1960–1961) was its inability to detect and destroy a plot within the army. More important, however, the democratic government of Chang Myon was unable to deal with serious ideological and social cleavages effectively, and consequently lost much of the support with which it came to power and gained little new support or loyalty for the regime.

Two sets of conflicts stood out during this period: the social and ideological polarization between the conservative and radical political groups and that between the pro- and anti-Syngman Rhee groups. First, the Chang Myon government, with its indecisiveness and inconsistency regarding punishment of former leaders of the Rhee regime, alienated itself from both the supporters and opponents of the Rhee regime. Second, given the acuteness of the conflict between the anti-Communists and the radical groups within the country, any government committed to political toleration ultimately would have fallen victim to one of these conflicting groups. In this it was difficult to achieve liberal democracy in its true sense. A regime would have survived at the time only by means of alliance with one of these groups and suppression of the other.

Concerning the division between supporters and opponents of the Rhee regime, it can be stated that the first group consisted of Syngman Rhee's immediate subordinates in the Liberal Party, police and bureaucratic personnel, military officers (especially the top-ranking ones) and businessmen, while their opponents included the opposition politicians of the Democratic Party, the intellectuals in the "university-press nexus," and the students. Thus the April "revolution" could be understood as a successful challenge to and overthrow of the rule of the first group by the second.

The Chang Myon government, which owed its creation to a loose coalition of intellectuals, newspaper writers, liberal students, and anti-Rhee politicians, was expected to satisfy the immediate aspirations of the anti-Rhee forces—namely, the "revolutionary" punishment of former officials of the Rhee government. The Chang government's commitment to due process and liberal democracy was largely responsible for its initial failure to fulfill this task. This failure, however, alienated many of its coalition partners from the Democratic government. Subsequent punitive legislation against former Rhee supporters in turn served to alienate from the Chang government those conservative groups that had supported the Rhee regime and that could conceivably have been wooed to the side of the Democratic regime by offering them protection. As a result, the Chang government not only lost the support of its electoral and intellectual constituencies, but also succeeded in neutralizing the effectiveness of its administrative and law enforcement apparatus.

The dilemma of liberal democracy in South Korea was especially acute in the Second Republic because of the presence of powerful groups strongly committed to oppose any form of leftist radicalism. The division of the country between the communist-controlled north and anticommunist south was primarily responsible for the intolerant anti-communist attitude among key groups in South Korea, such as the armed forces, the police, the bureaucracy, and most party politicians. Communist agitation in South Korea during the immediate postliberation period, "red" and "white" terror during the Korean War, and the threat of North Korean subversion and attack accounted for the development of such a rigid anticommunist attitude in South Korea.

During the First Republic, Syngman Rhee and his regime dealt with the ideological conflict by ruthlessly suppressing any leftist movement as "communist-controlled" or "communist-inspired" conspiracies. Such a policy proved to be quite effective because of the support it received from the powerful anticommunist sectors, which feared the prospect of a real social revolution in South Korea in the event of a leftist takeover. The relatively liberal political atmosphere following the collapse of the Rhee regime provided leftist politicians and other political groups with an opportunity to organize and advocate their "radical" views without the same type of pressure they had felt in the past. The radical move-ment after the collapse of the Rhee government was supported not only by former leftist politicians, but also by many college students and school teachers who felt the need to correct what they considered to be socioeconomic injustice at home, and to achieve national unification, which they believed was being hindered by the presence of foreign powers on Korean territory. However, the leftist politicians and parties experienced a near complete defeat in the July 1960 election, perhaps the most open and fair one in South Korean history, revealing that a significant gap existed between them and a great majority of the voters. The ideologically conservative nature of the urban voters and culturally traditional nature of the rural voters made the electoral success of the leftist candidates almost impossible. As a result of its failure in electoral process, the leftist movement turned its emphasis from parliamentary to nonparliamentary politics.

The leftist agitation in turn helped to mobilize the anticommunist elements in the society, who discredited the Chang government because of its failure to firmly suppress the leftists. Furthermore, when the choice was between a radical leftism and a radical anticommunism, most supporters of liberal democracy, such as the leading members of the opposition New Democratic Party, chose the latter, as shown by their acquiescent attitude toward the military coup d'état.[2]

Throughout the Second Republic the military continued to be a key factor in Korean politics. Despite the pervasive factionalism among the top-ranking officers, the military constituted the only nationally effective organization with the capacity to exercise coercive force during the post-Rhee period. The military was thus capable of preventing a radical change in the status quo and suppressing the rise of any significant leftist or other revolutionary groups if necessary. When the conservative politicians appeared unable to carry out that task most of the military officers refused to commit themselves to defending them against their enemies, making it easier for organizers of the May coup d'état to accomplish their goal.

Obviously many factors contributed to the fall of the Chang Myon government. The failure of his liberal democratic government to survive and provide a foundation for democracy in South Korea can be explained by South Korea's socioeconomic "immaturity," its undemocratic authority patterns, and the constitution that provided for a weak cabinet government. Yet the most immediate source of the Chang Myon government's problems appears to have been the social and ideological cleavages. Because of its liberal character, these cleavages and conflicts were more visible during the Second Republic than at any other period after the establishment of the Korean republic in 1948. This visibility of conflicts, however, became one of the most important reasons for the government's downfall.

Given the acute nature of the social conflict, the government faced the necessity of allying itself with one of the antagonists and suppressing the other. This, however, would have been diametrically opposed to what a liberal democracy should stand for, and the Chang government was both unable and unwilling to abandon its commitment to liberal procedures and institutions to insure its own survival. Such was the tragedy of liberal democracy in South Korea in 1961.

The Authoritarian Legacy of South Korean Politics

South Korean politics during the twenty-six-year period between 1961 and 1987 can be characterized as basically authoritarian.[3] Even during the height of political oppression in South Korea, opposition parties, elections, policy debates, and the subsystem autonomy of various official and nonofficial groups and institutions have existed and have been meaningful, although only to a limited extent. Elections since 1963 have generated competition and debate mostly *within* the government and opposition parties, but not *between* them. Because of the built-in safeguards (for the incumbents) in the electoral system, the opposition parties have not won the presidency or a majority in the National Assembly. Serious and lively debates on public policy issues have been allowed to be conducted within and outside of the government and its party, but only as long as they did not question the nature of the governing system or of the top leadership. Yet social groups and institutions generally have been left free from intense ideological indoctrination or politicization. What the state has exercised in an effective way is a *negative* control aimed at preventing antigovernment activities rather than a *positive* control of the totalitarian type designed to elicit explicit and total support for the government or party in power.

Although there are both historical and sociological explanations for the authoritarian trends in Korea, much of the structural and practical applications of authoritarian politics can be traced to the eighteen-year rule of the Park Chung Hee government (1961–1979). Thus understanding the nature of the Park period is essential for an analysis of contemporary South Korean politics.

Major General Park Chung Hee came to power in May 1961 after toppling the constitutionally established government of Chang Myon, accusing the latter and the civilian leadership of being corrupt, incapable of defending the country from internal and external threats of communism, and incompetent to bring about economic and social transformations. Upon taking over power, General Park pledged to transfer the government to "fresh and conscientious politicians" when the tasks of the revolution had been completed. During the ensuing two years, Park made preparations to assume the leadership of the future "civilian" government by (1) banning for at least six years more than 4,000 politicians of the previous regime from political activities; (2) consolidating his own position within the ruling group of primarily military leaders by purging the recalcitrant elements and potential rivals; (3) having a new constitution providing for a strong presidential system with a weak legislature adopted by a national referendum; and (4) building a party (the Democratic-Republican Party) to aid him and his supporters in presidential and legislative elections.

Following a series of political crises that resulted from Park's reluctance to relinquish the military rule, a presidential election was held in November 1963 under pressure from the United States and political forces at home. Park, who had formally retired from the military at the end of August to participate in the campaign, won the election, considered to have been conducted in a reasonably fair atmosphere. Park received in the election 46.7 percent of the votes cast over his major civilian opponent's 45.0 percent. Park's support was weak in the urban areas; he also failed to receive strong support from the so-called military areas along the demilitarized zone.[4] In the legislative election that immediately followed, Park's party won a large majority, 110 seats out of the total of 175. Park was reelected in 1967 by a more comfortable plurality of 49 percent of the votes cast over his chief opponent's 39 percent (the anti-Park and antimilitary vote was split between two major civilian candidates). In the second half of the 1960s, all appeared to be going well for President Park's continued stay in office except for two elements. One was the agitation of the students who opposed the Park government for its "military" character and the "reactionary" nature of its foreign and economic policies; the other was the constitutional restriction on the presidency of two four-year terms.

The first major outbreak of student demonstrations since 1961 took place in 1964 against the proposed Korea-Japan normalization treaty. Many students believed that South Korea had made too many concessions to Japan and that it was negotiated in a "humiliating" manner. They were demonstrating not only against the treaty but also against what they considered were many failures of the Park government. The government initially attempted to mollify the students through postponement of the signing of the treaty and a cabinet reshuffle. However, as the protest grew in size and intensity, the government, well aware of the consequences of the April 1960 student uprising, sternly suppressed it by declaring a state of martial law and arresting several hundred students. Large-scale demonstrations occurred many times since then during the Park regime; in 1965 against the ratification of the Korea-Japan treaty; in 1967 against allegedly unfair National Assembly elections; in 1969 against the constitutional revision that permitted a third-term presidency for Park Chung Hee; and after 1972, against the Yushin (revitalizing reforms) Constitution. In the face of a mounting threat to the regime caused by student disturbances, President Park tightened the legal ban against student activism. In October 1971 the president ordered, among other things, the expulsion from school of the leaders of demonstrations, rallies, sit-ins, strikes, or other "disorderly activities," the disbandment of all nonacademic circles and groups in the campuses, and the prohibition of all "unauthorized" publications by students. A presidential decree of April 1974, later repealed, provided for punishment up to the death penalty against student protest activities.

When the 1969 constitutional amendment—achieved through a referendum—enabled the president to run for his third term in 1971, the move became another serious impetus for agitation by the students, which in turn necessitated further and heavier penalties for their anti-government activities. The 1971 presidential election, in which Park's chief opposition candidate Kim Dae Jung received 46 percent of the votes cast, indicated to Park that his continued stay in office could be threatened under the existing electoral system despite enormous advantages he enjoyed in elections as the incumbent.

It seems that, except for the KCIA (Korean Central Intelligence Agency) activities and the suppression of student political activism, many of the oppressive features of the regime did not begin to appear in full force until 1972. There was relative freedom of the press, speech, and opposition activities. All three presidential elections held prior to 1972 were rather close ones that could have gone the other way with a little more unity, popular appeal, and astuteness of the opposition. The question arises as to what might have happened if Park had actually lost one of those elections. Kim Se Jin, a student of Korean military politics, pointed out the irony of Korean democracy: "Park's victory [in 1963] was in fact a blessing for the future of democracy in Korea. Had the military lost, it can be safely assumed that the military would have ignored the electoral outcome and continued to rule even though such rule would have meant a total destruction of constitutionalism."[5]

During the 1970s the restrictions on opposition activities and limitations to effective political competition were legally prescribed. Until 1979, when the Park government collapsed following his assassination, the key legal instrument for this purpose was the Yushin Constitution, which was adopted in a referendum held under martial law in November 1972. The Yushin Constitution had been proposed by the Park government, assertedly to facilitate national unification, to cope with the changing international situation, and to effectively carry out the country's socioeconomic development. It provided for an indirect election of the president by the locally elected (and thus more easily subjected to the influence of the government) National Conference for Unification; appointment by the president of one-third of the 219-member National Assembly (the rest of the membership being elected in seventy-three two-member districts); an unrestricted number of six-year terms for the president; reduction of the powers of the legislature and the judiciary; and curtailment of civil and political rights by presidential decrees.[6] In the face of mounting criticism and protest, the Park government promulgated a series of "emergency measures" in 1974 banning all criticism of the Yushin Constitution and demand for its revision. A March 1975 revision of the criminal code provided for heavy jail terms for any citizen at home and abroad who "insults, slanders or harms by rumors or other means the government or its agencies." Student demonstrations and rallies were strictly prohibited by law and presidential decrees under penalty of imprisonment and expulsion from school.[7]

An overall assessment of President Park's legacy and contribution to Korean political development would indicate both negative and positive aspects. One of the Park regime's negative contributions was its failure to provide for an institutional and political framework within which an orderly succession could take place following his departure from the political scene, voluntarily or otherwise. He left the nation with a constitution that was highly unpopular and unworkable after his death. Park needed the Yushin Constitution to prolong and strengthen his presidency. But it had been tailor-made only for him, making a major constitutional revision inevitable. When President Park died the country did not even have a legal framework within which a new leader or government could be chosen in an orderly way.

Second, the Park regime played a negative role in institutionalizing political parties and a party system within which a new generation of leaders could emerge and which could bring various forces and interests into the political process. Park was personally suspicious of both the progovernment and opposition parties and considered them as a necessary evil at best and a threat at worst. Neither his own Democratic-Republican Party nor the opposition New Democratic Party was given a proper opportunity to develop the necessary leadership structure and to cultivate grassroots support. Neither party could attract the participation of high-caliber individuals or induce strong identification with it by the electorate or major social groups. As a result, political parties failed to become the main medium by which struggles for power and influence could be carried out following Park's death.

Third, in the course of his prolonged rule, President Park had generated so much opposition to and alienation from not only his own rule, but also the sociopolitical system as a whole that, once he departed from the scene, piecemeal changes and peaceful transition became almost an impossibility. Various individuals and groups sought radical solutions and tried to "settle old scores" immediately. In addition, during President Park's tenure, much of the top elite circulation took place horizontally and within a limited circle of supporters, thus frustrating the power aspirations of ambitious individuals both within and outside of his own party. This intensified the intraparty, as well as interparty, power struggles following President Park's death in 1979.

Another negative legacy was the increased propensity and capability of the military to play a political role. In large part because of the way the Park government came to power and also because it depended heavily on the military for staying in power, the military became prone to intervening in politics when it would feel there was the need and the justification. Finally, as Park became increasingly unpopular, he made political use of the security issues with the unfortunate result of weakening its credibility. Many people, particularly the students, acquired the habit of showing cynicism toward South Korea's security problems, which were nonetheless genuine. At the same time, the political involvement of some of the government law enforcement and intelligence agencies compromised their effectiveness in performing their tasks and caused them to lose credibility.

Against the "negative" legacy discussed above, a few political consequences of a positive kind should also be mentioned. As a result of his persistent drive for rapid economic development, President Park succeeded in creating a substantial economic class that could become the mainstay of a democratic political system if and when it were established. A democratic government in power would be able to count on the support of this class as long as it could provide continued economic growth, social stability, and security from external threats. A related consequence of Park's rule was the regularization of government procedures and the institutionalization of executive power. It is true that these were accompanied by excessive bureaucratization of the government and the proliferation of authoritarian practices surrounding the presidency. However, they could also be seen as serving positive purposes by making the exercise of administrative power by the government and its leaders more economical, predictable, and effective. It could provide continuity and stability of the government even when democracy requires rather frequent changes of government.

Thus at the time of President Park's death, Korean society had a potential for acute polarization and power struggles, but the necessary leadership structure and institutional mechanisms by which such struggles could be managed without necessitating violence or social disorder were lacking. These were the very sociopolitical conditions that induced and enabled a group of military leaders to step in and take over the reins of power in the political vacuum that followed the death of President Park in October 1979. The restoration of democracy in South Korea thus had to be postponed until after another round of authoritarian politics was to complete its cycle.

Explaining the Authoritarian Trend in the 1970s

Concerning the authoritarian trend in Korea during the 1970s, various explanations have been offered by critics and apologists for the government, as well as observers purporting to be objective. Neo-Marxist writers argue that the South Korean government has had to resort to repressive measures in order to collaborate with and serve the economic interests of international capitalism led by the U.S. and Japanese multinational corporations.[8]

On a more general level, scholars have pointed out factors such as (1) the centralizing and hierarchical nature of Korea's social structure and political culture; (2) ideological cleavages between the "rightists" and the "leftists," as well as between the "authoritarians" and the "liberal democrats"; and (3) the unbalanced development of political institutions—i.e., the "overdevelopment" of the output institutions such as the bureaucracy and the military relative to the input institutions such as political parties and interest groups.[9] Other explanations include the political leaders' personal penchant for power and the legacy of Korea's recent history, especially the Korean War, which has left the society militarized and lacking in civil values.[10]

Comprehensive as the above listing of the explanations might appear, it is not quite adequate in two respects. First, it does not distinguish between what might be called the "permissive" factors that constitute the general background to authoritarianism on the one hand, and the "causal" factors that act as the direct moving force in what might be called an authoritarianizing process" on the other. Second, the explanations do not adequately address themselves to the question of why the process of authoritarianization was accelerated in South Korea from around the end of the 1960s.

It seems that the general-level explanation—sociocultural, ideological, institutional, and historical—provided a permissive environment for authoritarian rule. The "militarized" nature of the society—a large number of military personnel and veterans, diversion of huge amounts of resources to defense, priority given to military considerations in foreign and domestic policy making, and a permanent emergency atmosphere—as well as the support that the Park government received from the military, bureaucratic, and business sectors, also contributed to creating a political setting that permitted the authoritarianizing process to proceed.

The most important and immediate impetus for the emergence of an oppressive regime, however, came from the Park government's realization that elections under the existing system (pre-Yushin) would not guarantee continued victories for the DRP candidates and that, should a favorable outcome be engineered by illegal means to give the incumbent an election victory, it would provide the government's opponents with a rallying point against it, as such an action had provoked Syngman Rhee's opponents to collective action in 1960. The 1969 constitutional amendment, which enabled President Park to run for a third term, can be considered to have been a turning point in the government's ability to maintain the electoral support necessary to keep the president in office indefinitely. Many of those who had held a reasonably favorable attitude toward the Park government and had a high regard for its achievements were disappointed by its tampering with the constitution to prolong Park's presidency. Since the 1969 amendment only permitted a third term for the incumbent, a further stay in office beyond the term would have required another change in the constitution, which in turn would have cost the Park government more popular support.

It seems certain that during the several years following his narrow election victory in 1963, President Park succeeded in increasing his support levels, primarily because of the successful implementation of the government's economic development plans. In elections he and his party were also aided by the availability of disproportionately large amounts of campaign funds, which were of crucial importance in Korea.[11] However, as the situation was changing substantially after 1969, a significant restructuring of the legal and governing system was deemed necessary if a transition of power either within the government party itself or to the opposition were to be prevented from happening.

On its part the government argued that, by eliminating for practical purposes the interparty electoral competition, much "waste" of resource and energy that had been an indispensable part of electioneering by both parties could be eliminated; that the government, through its system of so-called administrative democracy—which places emphasis on identification, articulation, and representation of interests by administrative means and mechanisms—could more effectively concentrate on solidifying the nation's defense and achieving social and economic development without interference from "politics"; and that the country would not be turned over to a weak government that could easily be toppled by another military coup d'état. Apologists for the government also argued that an authoritarian, but humane and benevolent, government was not adverse to Korea's political-cultural tradition and was therefore not unacceptable to a great majority of the Korean people.[12] Regardless of the validity of these arguments, however, opposition to the authoritarian regime was growing at a rapid rate and the government was losing legitimacy as well as ability to maintain social stability and effective governance.

Politics in the 1980s: Democratization Postponed

The authoritarian system of Yushin collapsed in 1979 with the assassination of President Park Chung Hee by his chief intelligence aide, who claimed that his action against Park was motivated by his desire to spare the nation from a "bloodbath" that might have resulted from growing protest against the Park regime and its strong reactive measures. It is not certain if the Park regime would have collapsed soon by growing opposition to it had the assassination not taken place. It is clear, however, that serious strains began to appear in the regime, and the polity was heading toward instability and a major crisis. Its popularity was at an all-time low, measured even by the results of elections heavily interfered with by government power. For example, Park's Democratic-Republican Party had suffered a serious loss in December 1978 when it obtained only 31 percent of the popular vote in the National Assembly election.

Large-scale riots took place toward the end of his regime in such major cities as Pusan and Masan.

Park's death was greeted with the expectation that authoritarian rule would come to an end and full democracy be restored. However, a period of active anticipation and lively political activity by various groups and individuals was followed by the declaration of full martial law in 1980 and the assumption of power by General Chun Doo Hwan who had headed the Military Security Command under the Park government. Authoritarian rule in South Korea received another lease on life and democratization suffered another setback and postponement. With the support of key military leaders, Chun first took over the post of chief executive as acting president in August, after which the rubber stamp National Conference of Unification elected him as president. In October a new constitution, which retained many of the key features of the Yushin Constitution, was put to a national referendum that approved it by an overwhelming vote. Under the new constitution, Chun was elected president without competition for a seven-year term in January 1981.

Upon assuming power Chun disbanded all political parties of the previous regime, purged their leaders, and placed under political ban hundreds of politicians and other activists. In addition to his own Democratic Justice Party he allowed the formation of several parties by political personalities and organizations that could not challenge the ruling group in any effective way. Instruments of "power and control," such as the KCIA (renamed the National Security Planning Agency) and the Military Security Command were retained or strengthened. The new National Assembly and the interim Legislative Council that had preceded it in 1978 enacted laws that enabled effective control by the government of the press and labor movement. In short, another cycle of authoritarian rule devoid of political competition and civil rights had begun.[13]

There was nothing inevitable about the fact that in 1980 South Korea's democratization process would face another serious setback and authoritarian rule would be restored. It is possible, however, to offer a few explanations as to why the transition to democracy that had been so ardently and overwhelmingly aspired to by South Koreans after nearly two decades of authoritarian rule had to be postponed once again.

First, it may be pointed out that even though Park had died, the power structure—the military, the bureaucracy, and other groups that had a vested interest in the status quo—remained intact. Only the ruling Democratic-Republican Party was seriously weakened, although it did not collapse. This was in contrast with the post-Rhee period, when few organizations or groups remained supportive of the political or socio-economic system that the Rhee regime had left behind. Thus the remnants of the Park governments, as an organization if not as individuals, including the interim cabinet of Choi Kyu Hah (who had been Park's prime minister before his death and who had temporarily succeeded him), were able to hold off the pressures and demands of the anti-Park forces to implement the democratization process immediately. They bought enough time for those who had a stake in the authoritarian system to regroup among themselves and render support for a regime that was likely to be more favorable to their interests than a democratic one.

Second, the party politicians, particularly of the opposition, lacked effective leadership and unity. The chasm was especially evident between the incumbent leaders of the New Democratic Party, the principal opposition party during the Park period, and the forces represented by and supporting Kim Dae Jung, who had been imprisoned and deprived of the right to participate actively in politics. Being certain that their turn to assume power had come, and preoccupied with struggle and competition among themselves, the democratic politicians of the opposition allowed the antidemocratic forces outside of party politics to gain control of events and ultimately supersede party politics.

The radical and vengeful image of certain groups, particularly among dissident students, intellectuals, and progressive Christians, as well as the politicians who were supported by them, also contributed to a certain degree of acquiescence that the general public exhibited when authoritarian rule was restored by Chun. Even though riots broke out in certain cities such as Kwangju when martial law was extended throughout the nation in May 1980, citizens began to show as much concern about the social instability and disorder accompanying the democratization process as about its delay. Such concern became more poignant as student demonstrations intensified and after large-scale riots by miners and steel mill workers broke out in April. The "middle class," to the extent that their existence could be ascertained and delineated, had grown during the Park regime with its economic developmental efforts to the extent that it had a vested interest in socioeconomic stability and continuity. But it was still too insecure about its political and economic status to opt decisively for political freedom and democracy at the risk of sacrificing its country's continued economic growth and its own newly secured socioeconomic status.

A fourth explanation for the relative ease with which Chun and his military associates could take over power can be sought in the nature of the South Korean military itself. It was with General Park Chung Hee's military coup d'état in 1961 that the Korean military began directly intervening in politics. Until then President Syngman Rhee had skillfully kept the military under control and away from political involvement. It was only during the last few days of the Rhee government that the military played a decisive role in the political outcome when it refused to use violence against the anti-Rhee demonstrators. But by coming to power by a coup d'état, and by staying in power primarily through the support of the military, the Park government contributed greatly to politicizing the military. Top officers came to believe they had a claim, and indeed an obligation, to involve themselves in South Korea's politics by virtue of their position as defenders and protectors of a society under constant threat of external invasion and internal subversion. After all the military was getting a disproportionate share of the national budget and manpower, and the society had been highly militarized in terms not only of its resource priority, but also of the mentality and ways of life. Furthermore, although the Korean military had lacked cohesion among the high-ranking officers and between the higher and lower officers during the earlier (Rhee and Park) periods, by 1980 the core and mainstream of the South Korean military came to consist of regular graduates of the Korean Military Academy, among whom there was a strong sense of camaraderie, shared interest, and sense of responsibilities. Thus it is not a mere coincidence that General Chun represented Class One of South Korea's regular military academy and that his military colleagues were able to secure the acquiescence, if not support, of a substantial part of the middle- and lower-ranking officers (colonels and captains) in their takeover of the government.

Finally, a contributing factor in the collapse of the democratization process was the absence in South Korean society of individuals, groups, and institutions such as a monarch or respected political elders who could act as a mitigating, mediating, and moderating force among and between the contending political forces. Political conflicts therefore tended to be of a naked, confrontational and zero-sum nature. In this normative vacuum there was no one person or institution that could bestow upon or deprive a person or group of legitimacy. Neither could anyone authoritatively endorse or deny someone else's claim to power even when it was clear that fair and due process was ignored and popular aspirations betrayed.

Knowing that he had come to power without popular mandate Chun devised a novel definition of democracy, arguing that its most important ingredient was a "peaceful transfer of power" at the end of the president's prescribed term, something that had never happened in South Korea's post-World War II political history. Thus he repeatedly stressed his determination to step down at the end of his seven-year term in early 1988. Clearly, this gesture was far from adequate to mollify the anger and frustration of those who saw their democratic aspiration and struggle nullified by a group of ambitious military officers. The antigovernment, democratic movement in due course picked up where it had left off upon the death of President Park. Only this time it was to be better organized, more forceful, and more widely spread than before. As it became clear toward the end of the Chun government that his idea of "peaceful transfer of power" was to be within the "power group" rather than to the civilian opposition, antigovernment activities intensified to the extent that the Chun government came to have only the choice between total suppression by mobilizing all the coercive instruments of power, including the military, and making substantial concessions to the opposition to begin the democratization process.

The End of an Authoritarian Cycle

From the outset the government of President Chun Doo Hwan lacked legitimacy and was beset with opposition. He came to power after squelching the democratic hopes and expectations that had been aroused in the wake of President Park's death. His ascendance to power was accompanied by the tragedy of the Kwangju uprising in which several hundred citizens were killed. In addition his government inherited all the hostility and antagonism toward a military-authoritarian government that had been generated during the Park government. The mainstay of President Chun's power was the military. As such, he saw little need for and thus gave insufficient effort in becoming a popular leader. Even if he had, Chun probably would not have succeeded as his lack of prior experience in political life made him inept in mass politics. That Chun was not a good politician was perhaps a blessing in disguise for South Korean democracy, as it made authoritarian rule vulnerable and the democratic movement stronger.

Having secured the legal basis of power through the adoption of the new constitution, Chun and his supporters attempted to strengthen their basis of power by devising a party system that would give the government an overwhelming advantage over the opposition. They thus tried to establish a multiparty system in which the dominant (government) party would be opposed by several minor parties. Furthermore, in this plan there was to be scarcely any competition within the dominant party. Such a scheme seemed to be having some success as, in the first National Assembly election held after the establishment of the Chun government, the ruling Democratic Justice Party (DJP) received 36 percent of the votes cast while the rest was shared by twelve other parties, including the opposition Democratic Korea Party (DKP), which obtained 21 percent, and the National Party (which was formed by individuals with close connections with the defunct Park government) with 13 percent of the votes.

This was only a temporary phenomenon, however. As the political ban on former politicians was lifted for the most part, there was a coalescing of opposition forces into a single party. The parliamentary election of February 1985 brought about a basic realignment of political power and parties. In that election, the New Korea Democratic Party (NDP), formed largely by politicians who had been placed under political ban in 1980 by the Chun government, made an impressive showing, winning sixty-seven of the 184 elective seats. This compared with only thirty-five for the existing Democratic Korea Party that, even though it had acted as the main opposition party during the preceding four years, was seen by the electorate as being accommodating to the Chun government. The new opposition party's electoral success led to a mass defection of the KDP members to the NDP, with the result that a virtual two-party system emerged. Now the battle line was clearly drawn—between the government party, which insisted on the legitimacy of the government as well as the existing constitution by which it came to power, and the opposition party, which argued that the government lacked legitimacy and the system as it stood favored the incumbent party, because in an indirect election of the president the electoral college is susceptible to government influence.

As the government party had a clear majority in the National Assembly, however, the battle—with constitutional revision as the key symbolic as well as substantive issue—was waged in the streets and campuses and largely by the *chae-ya se-ryok* ("forces in the field"), consisting of dissident student leaders, intellectuals, and progressive Christians. Even Cardinal Stephen Kim, who headed the 3-million-strong Korean Catholics, joined those who called for a constitutional change. In the face of large-scale demonstrations, mostly by university students, continuing social instability and pressure from various groups including the church, intellectuals, and lawyers, as well as the United States, the Chun government decided in February 1986 that the constitution after all would be revised before the expected transfer of power in 1988. It was perhaps not a mere coincidence that only a few weeks earlier, the Marcos government was ousted by "people power" in the Philippines.

As the debate on constitutional revision continued through 1986, it became clear that the opposition was determined not to retreat one step from its demand for a presidential system of government in which the president was to be elected by a direct, popular vote. The government, on its part, proposed a parliamentary system of government in which the chief executive would be elected indirectly by the legislature.

Several reasons prevented the opposition from entertaining the idea of compromising with the government in the constitutional revision. First, there was so much distrust of the government by the opposition that any move, even apparently a conciliatory one, was seen as mere maneuvering by the ruling military group to perpetuate itself in power. It suspected that Chun was simply trying to buy time.

Second, the opposition was divided internally so that a leader could give the appearance of accepting a compromise solution only at the risk of being accused of selling out and betraying the cause of democracy. This was especially true in view of the fact that the opposition leader, Kim Dae Jung, who was technically still under political ban and therefore carried something of a moral authority within the opposition, remained adamant about the proposal for direct popular election of the president. Under these circumstances even an opposition leader with the stature of Kim Young Sam, who had previously advocated a parliamentary system for South Korea, could not even suggest the possibility of a compromise. In 1987 a leading proponent of compromise, NDP leader Lee Min Woo, would pay a heavy price for acting on his inclinations.

Finally, in the Korean political culture and under the existing rules of the game, compromise is not seen as a sign of rationality and good will but as a signal of weakness and lack of resolve not only by one's adversaries, but by one's allies as well. This leads the power players to chronically overestimate their own strength and underestimate that of their rivals. Any gesture toward compromise is likely to be met by further demands by the adversary, which tries to take advantage of the opponent's perceived feebleness. Politics in Korea usually takes the form of a zero-sum game in which winning is more important than keeping the game playable and productive. It was for this very reason that the government refused to entertain the idea of accepting the opposition proposal. It accepted the opposition proposal only when it was forced to do so in the face of a massive show of force by student demonstrations, which were often accompanied by violence.

1987—The Beginning of a Democratic Cycle?[14]

By any measure 1987 was a momentous year for South Korean democracy. Running against the political clock of the end of President Chun Doo Hwan's seven-year term in February 1988 and the international clock of the Seoul Olympics in the summer of 1988, events moved briskly—from massive protests in the spring to government capitulation in June and from the negotiation for and adoption in October of a new constitution, to the election of a president in December by a direct popular vote. The economic situation seemed to favor South Korea's difficult but inevitable transition to democracy.

The year began inauspiciously for President Chun Doo Hwan and his Democratic Justice Party. As the deadlock between the ruling party and the opposition New Korea Democratic Party on the issue of constitutional revision remained unresolved and antigovernment student demonstrations persisted, the country learned in mid-January that Park

Chong Chol, a Seoul National University student, had died of torture under police interrogation. The revelation of the incident, which was confirmed by the government, could not have come at a worse time for the DJP, as it was trying to persuade the opposition to accept its proposal for a parliamentary form of government in return for certain democratic reforms. The opposition on its part had been in disarray, split from within among those who were adamant about their proposal for a presidential system with a direct popular vote and those who were willing to compromise. The torture death of Park Chong Chol not only gave the antigovernment movement in and outside of party politics a rallying point, but also contributed to strengthening the position of hard-liners within the opposition who now regarded the government as weak and vulnerable.

The actual power and leadership within the opposition were held by Kim Young Sam and Kim Dae Jung. Kim Young Sam, on his part, insisted that the party's 1985 election pledge for direct presidential elections was the very basis of the party's existence. As noted above his political rival for leadership of the opposition, Kim Dae Jung, took an even more hard-line stand. The two Kims succeeded in quashing an initiative by nominal party leader Lee Min Woo, who offered to consider the DJP's constitutional formula in exchange for seven major political reforms, including the release of political prisoners, press freedom, and the restoration of Kim Dae Jung's political rights.[15] Nonetheless, the squabbling within the opposition did not subside, and in early April the two Kims split from the NDP to form a new party. Sixty-six of the NDP's ninety lawmakers followed the Kims' breakaway lead and, on 1 May formally inaugurated the Reunification Democratic Party (RDP) with Kim Young Sam as its president. The humiliated Lee Min Woo, on his part, merged the remnants of his party with the People's Democratic Party (PDP), which had split from the NDP in early 1986, to form a twenty-six-seat bloc in the National Assembly.

But the origin of political drama in 1987 can be traced directly to President Chun Doo Hwan's declaration on 13 April of his "grave" decision to suspend debate on constitutional reform. Only a few months earlier the Chun government had seemed quite capable of maintaining its authoritarian system with only modest concessions to the opposition and to democracy. The opposition was split between those who were, although silent for the most part, willing to accommodate and those who were not. Student protest, although continuing, was losing sympathy and support among the general public because of its radical and extremist tendencies. Thus, if it had wanted to, the government could have tried to pass a constitutional amendment embodying its own proposal. The opposition leadership could not and would not have accepted it. But if it had been accompanied by a program of genuine democratic reforms, the passage of a new constitutional draft as required by the existing constitution might have elicited, while not perhaps enthusiastic acceptance, at least a fair degree of acquiescence among the public.

In a classic case of miscalculation the Chun government decided to push its luck, and announced that constitutional revision, after all, would not take place and the next presidential election would be held under the existing—unpopular—constitution. In defending the measure the DJP argued that the opposition (badly splintered) could not act as a responsible negotiating partner and that time was running out; continuing political uncertainty and instability would hurt the chances for successfully crossing South Korea's twin hurdles of 1988: the change of government and the Seoul Olympics. Rather than bringing about certainty and stability, however, Chun's decision was met with near universal disapproval by the South Korean public, and provided new momentum to student protest, which was losing sympathy and support among the general public because of its radical and extremist tendencies. The government was placed in an even more embarrassing position following disclosures in mid-May of a cover-up in the Park Chong Chul incident. Chun's cabinet shake-up of May 26, dropping three of his closest aides (Prime Minister Lho Shin Yong, Home Minister Chung Ho Yong, and the director of the Agency for National Security Planning, Chang Se Dong) did little to cool the anger of the protesters.

Street violence reached its peak after 10 June when the DJP, in an audacious act of political insensitivity and imprudence, formally nominated Roh Tae Woo as the party's presidential candidate to become Chun's handpicked successor under the existing unpopular constitution, which provided for an indirect election of the president. Thousands of students poured into the streets, many hurling firebombs. The riot police, which responded mainly with massive tear gas attacks, was hopelessly outnumbered by the demonstrators, often joined in and cheered by middle-class citizens. Several hundred people were injured and one student died in the clashes. The central districts of Seoul, the capital city, were turning into what the *New York Times's* Clyde Haberman depicted as a "war zone."[16]

In the face of massive, prolonged, and often violent antigovernment demonstrations, the choice for the Chun government and the DJP was narrowed to one between, on the one hand, mobilizing the troops to quell the demonstration and risking large-scale violence and possibly a civil war and, on the other hand, making a wholesale concession to the forces of democracy and risking the loss of power. Chun tried to mollify the opposition by proposing a meeting with Kim Young Sam. At the meeting, which took place on 24 June, Chun indicated to Kim that he was willing to allow a resumption of parliamentary negotiations on constitutional reform. Sensing that Chun's position had weakened, however, Kim rejected Chun's offer, insisting instead that the government should agree to an immediate national referendum to choose between a parliamentary system and a presidential system with a direct popular vote, to release all political prisoners, and to restore the civil and political rights of Kim Dae Jung.

In a dramatic turn of events Roh Tae Woo, the DJP's presidential candidate and a former military colleague of President Chun's, surprised both the supporters and opponents of the government by announcing on 29 June a democratization plan that embodied a wholesale acceptance of the opposition's demands, effectively ending the "spring of discontent."[17] Roh's eight-point proposal, which was subsequently accepted and endorsed by President Chun, pledged "the speedy amendment" of the constitution, allowing for direct presidential elections, and amnesty for Kim Dae Jung and the restoration of his civil rights. The opposition in a rare show of approval welcomed Roh's action. A democratization process finally began.

The immediate results of the Roh declaration were the restoration of Kim Dae Jung's political rights, release of political prisoners, and the start of negotiations on constitutional amendments. Kim Dae Jung, the man who unsuccessfully ran against Park Chung Hee in the 1971 presidential election, was considered as a perennial anathema to the successive regimes of Park and Chun. He had been kidnapped from Japan by agents of the Park government in 1973 and incarcerated until 1979, when Park was assassinated. After a brief period of active politicking in the spring of 1980, Kim was arrested by the martial law command in May 1980 on charges of inciting riots. He was subsequently sentenced to death by the Chun government, which eventually commuted the sentence to a twenty-year prison term. Kim was then allowed to travel to the United States, where he stayed for two years before returning to Korea in February 1985. After the restoration of his political rights in July 1987, Kim Dae Jung officially became an adviser to the RDP while sharing on an equal basis effective power within the party with party president Kim Young Sam.

But no sooner did power seem to be within reaching distance than trouble started in the marriage of convenience between the two Kims. Each Kim saw himself as the hero of South Korea's political drama, and plainly thought the other was behaving unreasonably in refusing to pull out. Kim Young Sam claimed he appealed to a broad cross section of increasingly middle-class Koreans. This made him not only very electable, in his view, but also a much more suitable figure, once elected, to unite a politically fractious nation. Kim Dae Jung saw things differently; after exile in the United States and repeated jailings and house arrests in Korea over the years, he had suffered more in the cause of democracy, he claimed. His failure to run in the presidential election, he warned, could churn up anger and frustration among his many supporters and reignite the potentially dangerous regional antagonisms that had always bedeviled Korean politics. After meeting a few times, the two Kims failed to agree on a single candidacy, and both of them eventually decided to run, even at the risk of defeating themselves. After the formal adoption of the new constitution on 22 October, Kim Dae Jung formed a new party—the Peace and Democracy party—and declared himself a presidential candidate.

The new constitution, which was adopted by a national referendum following a series of negotiations between the government and opposition parties, was the fruit of a long struggle by the two Kims, who insisted on a direct popular election of the president. But it was also a product of political convenience and expediency. Working against the political clock, representatives of the two parties negotiated for a constitution that provided for a direct, popular election of the president. The most problematic aspect of the new constitution was that it allowed the election of the president by simple plurality. The three presidential aspirants, but particularly Kim Dae Jung and Roh Tae Woo, knew that they would have difficulty in obtaining a majority of the votes and thus their chances of winning would be maximized in a situation of multiple candidacy.[18] The constitution also failed to provide for a vice-presidency, making it even more difficult for power contenders within the same party to compromise and remain united.

Joining the three-way race of Roh Tae Woo (Democratic Justice Party), Kim Young Sam (Reunification Democratic Party), and Kim Dae Jung (Peace and Democracy Party), was Kim Jong Pil, former prime minister under President Park Chung Hee, who ostensibly wanted the people's vindication of the record of his defunct Democratic Republican Party (1963–1980). Since each candidate knew he could win by securing firm support from a minority, campaigns were conducted to maximize regional and partisan appeal. Roh Tae Woo, who promised political stability and continued economic growth, had his largest support in the southeastern provinces, among the middle-class voters, and in the rural areas. Kim Young Sam, who called for an end to decades of military rule in South Korea, also appealed to voters in the southeast and to the middle-class voters, although his support was particularly strong among the urban white-collar voters. Kim Dae Jung, who enjoyed solid support in his native southwest, tried to maximize this support among the underprivileged and young voters. The role of Kim Jong Pil, who was strong in his native Chungchongdo provinces, was essentially that of a spoiler, drawing votes from the upper middle classes, which could have gone to either Roh Tae Woo or Kim Young Sam. (See map at the front of this chapter.)

Regional rivalries, often expressed in violent disruption of campaign rallies by candidates from rival provinces, were most conspicuously manifested between the southeast and southwest. Many of Kim Dae Jung's supporters in the southwestern Chollado provinces felt that their region had been discriminated against by the successive regimes dominated by leaders from the southeastern Kyongsangdo provinces. Citizens of Kwangju, in particular, felt that their city had been the object of regional oppression in 1980 at the time of the "Kwangju uprising" in which more than 200 people were killed. Ultimately, the level of voting support for each of the candidates closely coincided with his regional background; Kim Dae Jung received more than 90 percent of the votes from his home provinces and less than 5 percent from the southeastern provinces.

Localism played an especially important role in the 1987 election because of the particular combination of candidates, which tended to magnify the rivalries and animosities between regions. The strong regional identification that the candidates, particularly Kim Dae Jung, fostered ensured that the campaign was to be divisive and emotional. The newly adopted electoral system allowed the election of a president by a mere plurality of votes, thus encouraging multiple candidacies. This in turn led the candidates to conduct a parochial campaign with the result that each of them alienated a large segment of the general population. By casting themselves as regional champions they also tended to promote regional rivalries. Although localism will continue to be a salient factor in South Korean politics, its importance will probably decrease in future elections with a change in the composition of the candidates and the emergence of new campaign issues. It is thus unlikely that regional rivalries will constitute a serious obstacle to Korea's future democratization process.

The 29 June declaration by Roh Tae Woo brought about a brief hiatus in student political activities. Soon, however, the activists went to work, demanding the release of all "political prisoners," and accusing the Chun government of scheming to rig the election. Small-scale demonstrations continued throughout the fall. As the election approached in December, however, the students decided to concentrate on working to ensure a fair election, having organized themselves in teams of election and ballot watchers.

One development that served as a key factor in the campaign was the controversy surrounding events on 12 December 1979. On that day several military leaders, including Generals Chun Doo Hwan and Roh Tae Woo, had mobilized troops, apparently without proper authorization, to overpower and arrest General Chung Sung Hwa, who was then the army chief of staff and martial law commander. General Chung, it had been argued, was suspected of complicity in Park's assassination. During the election campaign, General Chung joined the Kim Young Sam camp and publicly accused the Chun-Roh group of having carried out a "mutiny." The public revelation of details of the 12 December incident was a serious setback for Roh Tae Woo's effort to present a nonmilitary image of himself, although the extent of damage done to his election campaign was impossible to ascertain.[19]

Despite charges of irregularities, the voting took place as scheduled on 16 December and Roh Tae Woo, the DJP candidate, was elected with 36.6 percent of the votes cast. Kim Young Sam, the more moderate of the "two Kims," was second with 28.0 percent, while Kim Dae Jung came in third with 27.0 percent of the votes. Although the losing candidates charged the government with an unfair election campaign and "frauds" in ballot counting, it was clear that the main reason for the defeat of the opposition was that its vote was split almost evenly between the two major candidates. A divided opposition not only brought its own defeat, despite the fact that the two Kims together received a majority (55 percent) of the votes, it also produced a minority government that would face challenges to its legitimacy.

The December presidential election and the events of 1987 that led to it have contributed to resolving, at least in part, the thorny question of legitimacy that had loomed large throughout the period of the Chun Doo Hwan government. Although the DJP candidate won by a mere 37 percent of the vote and there were charges of serious election irregularities, most people accepted that the election of the president by a direct popular vote passed the test of due process, particularly in view of the fact that it was the opposition that defeated itself through its own internal divisions—specifically, its inability to agree on a single candidate. Furthermore, it seemed inevitable that, no matter who was elected, the democratization of Korean society would continue apace. The next government promised to be more democratic than any of its predecessors—if by democratic is meant a government chosen by an open and competitive election that respects the basic freedoms of expression, assembly, and organization. The candidates campaigned unhindered by government restrictions, and each of them, including the government candidate, was subjected to spirited debates and tough questioning. The government that was to emerge from this process would have no choice but to keep the momentum going, the alternative being popular opposition on a massive scale.

One of the most serious problems in the aftermath of the election was the continuing and worsening disarray within the opposition, which remained divided. It appeared incapable of reshaping itself into a political force that could compete effectively in future presidential elections. A majority of the voters, who supported the opposition candidates, were frustrated with the election results and angered by the opposition, which in effect threw the election away. In the absence of a strong, united opposition that could provide the necessary checks and balances on the government, there appeared to be no chance of early and complete democratization as the consequence of an electoral victory by political forces that fought against authoritarian rule. It appeared, instead, that continuing democratization of South Korea would have to depend on the good faith and sound judgement of a government party that would see its own interest to be in fulfilling the commitment to bring about democracy.

Why the Authoritarian Cycle Came to an End

It is impossible to tell whether South Korea's transition to democracy will be successfully completed and consolidated. There is one certainty, however: the latest cycle of authoritarian rule has come to an end. How did this come about? One obvious explanation is the persistence, strength, and determination of the opponents to the Chun government, including the opposition politicians, antigovernment students, and ideological dissenters. More important, however, authoritarianism lost whatever remained of its usefulness and mandate. In 1980 Chun's authoritarian government came to power out of turn, following an eighteen-year rule by Park's authoritarian rule. The Chun government inadvertently further helped the democratic cause with its ineptness in dealing with the opposition politicians and the constitutional revision issue. It helped to unite the opponents of the government with its indiscriminate policy of oppression and rigidity. It lacked logic and consistency in its approach concerning the constitution, and could not retain existing supporters or convert new ones. The personal unpopularity of the president also helped to strengthen antiauthoritarian movement. With a more popular and charismatic leader the authoritarian cycle might possibly have lasted longer.

It may also be argued that certain successes of the authoritarian regime actually contributed to limiting its options when it was confronted with a massive and widespread protest movement. Mobilization of troops, in addition to the uncertainty that it could actually restore order, was certain to have disastrous consequences for the South Korean economy, which was performing well, and for the hosting of the 1988 Olympic Games, for which the regime took so much credit and pride. In addition the urban "middle class," which in 1980 lacked confidence in its economic status and political position, became large and strong enough to assert political rights and expectations. Although its new attitude was not demonstrated by participation in antigovernment activities for the most part, its government was certain to lose its support and acquiescence; its endurance and patience simply wore too thin.

Finally, the pragmatic attitude and approach of South Korea's military leaders and military-turned-politicians should be pointed out. Faced with an overwhelming show of force by the demonstrators and political opponents, the military leadership—including President Chun and the DJP presidential nominee, Roh Tae Woo—decided to accommodate, rather than to mobilize troops and risk a breakdown of the political system and a resultant plunge in the country's economy and international standing. It is also possible that the United States, with which South Korea is allied and which counseled prudence and restraint, particularly on the part of the military, was instrumental in their decision to try the democratic route. Equally important, perhaps, was their assessment that, given the factional divisions with the opposition forces, the DJP had at least an even chance of winning the next presidential election even with a direct popular vote. In fact the DJP made every effort to boost the image of its nominee by giving him the sole credit for the democratization gestures of the DJP and the government. Indeed it is ironic that the ruling party of an authoritarian government, unless it is forcibly ousted, will agree to democratization measures only if it has a reasonable prospect of winning the next democratic election.

• THEORETICAL ANALYSIS •

What are the factors that promote democracy in South Korea on the one hand and those that hinder it on the other? The preceding analysis of political evolution in South Korea during the post-World War II period points to several factors that promote democratization in South Korea: democratic socialization among the highly literate populace; the growth of the "middle class," whose members are becoming increasingly confident with the economic achievement and political rights; the high cost of repression resulting from a rapidly growing democratic movement; the national desire to be accepted and recognized by the outside world as a modern democratic nation, a status that is becoming increasingly important in continued economic expansion; and the peculiar externality of South Korea as a nation closely allied with the United States for its acute security needs.

Underneath the social changes that have pushed for democratization is the rapid economic growth that South Korea has achieved during the past two decades. Between 1967 and 1987, the South Korean economy grew at an average annual rate of over 7 percent, moving it from an underdeveloped, low-income country to what has come to be called a newly industrializing country with a per capita income of nearly $3,000. The rapid economic growth has brought about social changes that not only increase the pressure for democratization but also facilitate that process. First of all, it meant an increase in the size of the middle-income group that is politically conscious, interested, and assertive. A 1987 survey showed that as much as 65 percent of Koreans identify themselves as members of the middle class, indicating the emergence of a social base upon which democratic politics can be built.[20]

Rapid economic development has also been accompanied by increasing complexity and pluralization of the society, in which social groups and organizations require, demand, are capable of, and become accustomed to autonomy in management and decision making. The result has been a social environment in which excessive state involvement in the private sector is resented and resisted. Furthermore, industrialization is accompanied by rapid expansion in the means and modes of communication and transportation, facilitating the exchange of information and people. This makes it difficult if not impossible to sustain a government that is weak in popular support and legitimacy. Finally, for a country such as South Korea, which has placed the utmost importance in the promotion of exports, expansion of external relations is an inevitable consequence as well as a requirement of economic growth. In due course the government and the people realize that democratization is the necessary ticket for membership in the club of advanced nations. This provides a strong incentive for political, as well as economic, liberalization at home.

On the other hand rapid industrialization and economic growth can also hinder or delay democratization, at least in the short to medium term. Successful economic development may serve as a useful justification for the continuation of an authoritarian regime, as was the case with the Park Chung Hee government in South Korea. By providing economic benefits and creating a class of people who depend on the government for their economic well-being and privileges, the government finds a useful *raison d'être* as well as an important support base. This enables it to forego or delay any measure that would hasten democratization. The increasing amount of economic means at the government's disposal also enables it to deal effectively with its potential opponents and critics both at home and abroad. Advanced communication and transportation, public relations skills, organizational capabilities, and other techniques of persuasion can work to the advantage of an authoritarian regime that tries to remain in power without having to resort to democratic elections. At the same time rapid industrial development often results in the problem of unequal distribution of wealth and privileges, both real and perceived, and is accompanied by socioeconomic dislocation. This creates the danger, at least in the minds of the middle and upper classes, of radical ideologies and movements, inclining them to support the authoritarian status quo rather than risk the uncertain future of democracy.

The democratization process in South Korea is also hindered by other factors, which include the following: the highly centralized socio-political structure with a minimum degree of social pluralism; uneven development of political institutions in favor of the "output" institutions; authoritarian social patterns and values; ideological polarization between the "authoritarians" and "democrats" on the one hand and between the "rightists" and the "leftists" on the other; and genuine security problems that require a large military establishment and a certain degree of social militarization in values and behavior patterns. More immediate obstacles to democratization have included such factors as the personal ambitions of those in the power game, which make accommodation and gradual evolution difficult; corporate (such as of the military) and regional interests as well as loyalties; the ideologically radical nature of significant parts of the opposition, which provides justification for the authoritarian reaction of the power holders; and the retribution factor, which has become more salient as rapid economic growth has provided opportunities of corruption for those in power.

Institutionally, the failure of a stable party system to take root presents one of the most serious problems for democratization in South Korea. There are several reasons for the weakness of political parties and party systems. First, a serious imbalance that exists between the bureaucracy (including the military) and political parties has hampered the development of the latter. Power holders in Korea generally tend to favor and depend more on the bureaucracy, which is readily available and generally dependable, than political parties, which are often hindrances to unquestioned and unchallenged power. The large and well-developed military bureaucracy magnifies the problem of bureaucratic supremacy, which is the result of a long Confucian tradition as well as Japanese colonial rule.

Second, parties have not been able to cultivate a stable following among the voters because, in the post-1948 period, there has been no room for ideological deviation from the officially accepted line on virtually all important issues, including unification, national defense, socioeconomic development, and management of wealth. This insistence on ideological consensus is the result not only of traditional preoccupation with orthodoxy under Confucianism but, since 1948, the physical and ideological confrontation with communist North Korea. Ideological uniformity has thus deprived the parties of opportunities to offer meaningful policy choices and to effectively reach and organize sectors of the society that are yet to be mobilized for electoral support and party activities. This is becoming an increasingly serious problem, as political challenge to the governmental and socioeconomic systems is growing among those who are opposed to the government on ideological grounds. Emphasis on economic development and export-led industrialization, it is argued, render social gaps and contradictions more serious—between the rich and the poor, the industrial and nonindustrial sectors, and the international and national orientations. "Socioeconomic justice" and "national identity" have become catch phrases with which dissenters who oppose the entire system join the antiauthoritarian "democrats" in their antigovernment activities.

A third reason for the weakness of the party system can be found in the many changes of regimes and constitutions that took place, usually through extraordinary measures by governments that came to power by nondemocratic means. No party—neither government nor opposition— has survived long enough to claim the loyalty and support of the public. Instead, parties and their leaders have often been purged and discredited after one or another of the uprisings, coups, or other upheavals South Korea has frequently experienced.

Still another obstacle to the development of a strong party system is the private nature of South Korean politics. Personal, factional, and regional rivalries are still deeply embedded in Korean political behavior. Factions and personal ties are often formed on the basis of provincial origins, school ties, the same graduating class (as in the case of the military ties), common experience in the past, or a common patron who had assisted the members in financial and other matters. Personal ties (*inmaek*) constitute an extremely important political factor even under circumstances of curtailed political activities. In contrast with political factions in Japan, which in some way contribute to stable party policies, Korean political factions and groupings tend to be fragmented, amorphous, and often lacking in strong personal leadership.

Finally, the government's occasional banning of existing leaders from active political participation, as happened during the early Park as well as the Chun periods, makes institutionalization of parties extremely difficult. Certain other legal measures, including regulations controlling political activities, have reduced the chances for party continuity and stability.

The Korean party system, for all its unstable and fragile nature, has exhibited an enduring tendency since the 1950s. It is partly due to the presidential system of government that the country has had for the most part the proclivity of the politicians to gather around two major parties—one for and the other against the government. This is exactly what happened in the wake of the February 1985 election. The ruling party had no choice but to accept the situation although its own preference was obviously a multiparty system in which the opposition would be divided among several parties. Until the two Kims went their separate ways in the 1987 presidential election, the two-party system survived in its basic form even when the opposition party split between the hard-liners and the "accommodationists," as most of the opposition members then joined the splinter Reunification Democratic Party.

Various social and political groups play important roles—both negative and positive—in the democratization of South Korea. What role the workers and farmers play in the democratic institutionalization depends very much upon the government's ability to sustain economic vitality and expansion and to channel their demands and aspirations through an orderly and legitimate process. The serious labor disturbances in the spring of 1980, as well as in the mid-1980s, indicate that there is a potential for further problems in case the workers' demands are not adequately responded to and/or there is a limit in the government's ability to control and establish order. With a very young population entering the labor market in large numbers workers will become increasingly assertive and susceptible to ideological mobilization. Since the early 1960s successive regimes have limited, through legal and extralegal means, the organizational activities of the workers. With political democratization the scope of their organization, activities, and demands is likely to expand radically. Unless institutional means (primarily parties) are found to represent their interests and channel political aspirations, worker participation will take place in large part outside of the regular political process, seriously straining the effort to consolidate democracy.

The farmers are not likely to resort to collective disorderly actions, but their continued positive support for the existing government—even if it is an authoritarian one—has been indispensable for any government party in sustaining an electoral majority in South Korea. For all the emphasis on economic growth and industrialization the Park Chung Hee government had a strongly agrarian orientation, emphasizing the need to provide benefits to the rural areas. Even under the Chun government, which has paid more attention to industrial and urban problems, rural areas have been the mainstay of political support for the ruling party. It is one of the many ironies of South Korean democracy that assurance of electoral success in the rural areas has been an important condition for the party in power to implement measures that enable meaningful political competition, the key element in political democracy.

Because of the large number and concentration of university students in major cities, their political role has been and will continue to be very important for some time to come. Their agitation has made the continuation of authoritarian rule difficult. Similarly, however, student activism will prove to be a major challenge to a democratic government in its consolidation, as their extrainstitutional political participation will not only immobilize the government but also give foes of democracy a justification to take over power through undemocratic means. A combination of political, social, psychological, and organizational factors makes and keeps the student situation in South Korea fluid. Student protest is becoming increasingly well organized, ideological, and violence-prone.

Generally speaking there are three ways of looking at student political activism in Korea. Some regard it as an essentially passing phenomenon at a certain stage in industrial development. According to this view student activism will run out of steam on its own accord and normalcy will be restored after a period of unrest, as it seems to have been the case, for example, in Japan. Others argue that student activism in Korea is a response to a particular combination of socioeconomic and international circumstances, so that no matter what kind of a government is in power it is likely to pose a serious political problem for a considerable period of time. An eclectic view would agree with the second view in that it regards as inevitable the existence of an ideologically committed minority of students who will seriously challenge the existing socioeconomic system under any kind of politics—authoritarian or democratic—as long as the basic socioeconomic structure is maintained. The third view differs from the second in arguing that these radical students are able to take advantage of antiauthoritarian sentiments and mobilize the support of a large number of students only when the political system is not democratic.

If the third view is accurate, with the passage of time and as the democratization process proceeds, radical and activist students will be deprived of the most important justification for mobilizing the support of other students. But this will be only a slow and gradual process that will involve many setbacks and detours, particularly in view of accumulation of the grievances of several generations of students who have opposed, and suffered under, successive authoritarian regimes. Nonetheless, in due course, and with improved situations in both economy and politics, the "student problem," as it is called in South Korea, will become far less serious than it has been so far.

The military plays a crucial role in politics, indirectly by providing or witholding support for a government and directly by taking over power. In a country that devotes a disproportionate amount of human and material resources to defense and security, the military can easily prevail upon the civilian sector in carrying out a political role for itself. The military may temporarily retreat from active involvement in politics, under pressures from the sentiments and forces against military-dominated authoritarian government. But it will always lurk over the shoulders of a civilian regime, either as a supportive force or a potential threat to its existence. As we have seen, the increased propensity and capability of the military to play a political role was a legacy left by the Park government. Thus the military became ready to intervene when it felt there was the need and opportunity. After several decades of direct and indirect intervention, however, the military is now acutely aware that a government cannot rule in South Korea without the consent of the governed. It is thus not likely that the military will intervene in politics without major provocation. Experience in other countries such as Brazil has shown that the military can agree to take a back seat on its own accord when the civilian sector offers a moderate alternative.

• CONCLUSION: SOUTH KOREAN DEMOCRACY AT A CROSSROADS •

With the rapid increases in social complexity and affluence, political awareness, and international involvement, South Korea faces growing pressure for more pluralistic and democratic politics. However, democratization and its consolidation will encounter many difficulties and take time.

Korea is a modernizing society undergoing rapid socioeconomic change. Thus one must consider the problem of democracy in Korea, above all, within the context of political consequences of social and economic modernization. Modernization entails social mobility, industrialization, rational and secularized thinking, and political awakening. On the negative side for political stability secularization undermines traditional bases of political authority. Furthermore, increased awareness creates demands and expectations that cannot be met by the government. Industrialization will tend to create new social and ideological cleavages and conflicts. Social mobility and urbanization would make people more susceptible to ideological agitation and disorderly mass action. On the positive side for democracy rational thinking will make more feasible and necessary electoral choice of the government. Improved communication and greater awareness will make it difficult to maintain an authoritarian government. Economic growth and social development will contribute to social groups such as the middle class, which would support a democratic system of government.

Given these general tendencies, what actually happens to the politics of a modernizing society during a particular period in its history will depend upon the following several factors: (1) the nature of the traditional society; (2) the ways in which social change (modernization) has come about—for example, whether it has taken place in a controlled or uncontrolled manner; (3) the timing of the period in question in the modernization process; (4) the external environment of the country; and (5) the ways in which benefits of socioeconomic change are distributed and such distribution perceived.

Turning first to the traditional legacy, before the process of modernization began in the late nineteenth century, Korea had been an authoritarian society ruled by a highly centralized bureaucracy under an autocratic monarch. This was in sharp contrast with such feudal societies as traditional Japan that, although equally authoritarian, had maintained a pluralistic and decentralized polity. The concentration of power in the central government in Korea was further heightened in the twentieth century during Japanese rule, which imposed on Korea a highly centralized colonial administration. Until the end of World War II, Koreans had experienced only a highly centralized executive power that was neither checked nor balanced by countervailing power groups such as regional lords or elected representatives. In South Korea today there is still a highly unbalanced development of political institutions—that is, the "overdevelopment" of the output institutions such as the bureaucracy and the military as opposed to the "underdevelopment" of input organizations such as political parties and interest groups.

Second, social change in Korea took place in an uncontrolled and indiscriminate way. During the colonial period the traditional elite lost its power and social status; much of its values were discredited, and its practices were discarded. Korea experienced a total dismantling of its political institutional and authority structures. Socioeconomic modernization was introduced to Korea by a foreign elite who had no interest in preserving its traditional institutions. Thus, when Koreans had the opportunity to form their own government after their liberation from Japanese colonial rule, they had to build their political structure from the very beginning. They had not preserved any traditional mechanisms by which loyalty to the new government could be generated; excessive burdens would be placed on new means of legitimacy such as elections, which are yet to be fully institutionalized.

What kind of politics a modernizing society is likely to experience at a given time period depends in part upon how much time has elapsed after the modernization process began. South Korea's experiments in modern politics had their beginning only four decades ago. It did not have satisfactory results with either the "charismatic" leadership of Syngman Rhee or parliamentary democracy during the 1960–1961 period. Such an unsatisfactory experience with other systems might be called "legitimacy by default"—that is, the acceptance, albeit without enthusiasm, by the people out of the feeling that other alternatives were not much more desirable. A governmental system that would have been rejected if it had been attempted before experiments with other systems were made might be deemed acceptable because of the unhappy experience with the earlier ones. Now authoritarianism has had its turn—a long one at that—and has been decidedly rejected as a suitable system for South Korea today.

As for the fourth factor, South Korea has been under constant and acute security threat since 1948, a devastating war having taken place in the 1950–1953 period. For this reason it has had to maintain a large military establishment, a government capable of mobilizing national resources for defense purposes, and a society oriented toward maximizing security against internal subversion and external attack. Such requirements have tended to favor the rise of a "firm" and strong state. Indeed a substantial portion of the people seem to feel that a "soft" state will not be able to cope with the security problem nor to handle the task of economic development that is deemed necessary for security. A corollary of this argument is that a strong state is not compatible with a democratic system of government.

Finally, the dilemma of liberal democracy has been especially acute in South Korea because of the serious social and ideological cleavage between the conservatives and the radical Left. The division of the country between the communist-controlled north and anticommunist south has been primarily responsible for the intolerant, anti-Left attitude among key groups in South Korea such as the armed forces, the police, the bureaucracy, and individuals in the "establishment." On the other hand radicalism has grown, particularly among the students and those who consider themselves belonging to the "deprived" groups, to the extent that it is seen by the conservatives as posing a genuine threat to the survival of the nation, not to mention to the existing socioeconomic order.

Radicalism in Korea exhibits traits of strong nationalistic and egalitarian beliefs.[21] The appeal of radicalism derives from the perception among many of an uneven distribution of the benefits of socioeconomic change and of the country's excessive dependence on foreign powers. Radical activists thus demand a complete overhaul of not only the political system but also the socioeconomic structure itself. This, however, hinders the democratization process. As the defenders of the socioeconomic status quo see it, the choice is between revolutionary change and defending the existing socioeconomic order rather than between liberal democracy and dictatorship. The result can be a vicious circle of oppressive measures and radical demands, leaving little room for democracy.

Nevertheless, Korea is at the threshold of an evolutionary process by which democracy is restored and takes root. The society's growing complexity and international involvement will result in increasing demand and pressure for pluralism, openness, and competition in politics. More important the political public, both in and out of the government, is anxious to achieve progress in democratization, even if it is a slow and sometimes a socioeconomically costly process. Whether the various factors that work against democratization can be successfully overcome by those factors that work for it will depend upon whether the polity as a whole can avoid confrontational politics and learn the necessary lessons from the unhappy experiences of the past.

• NOTES •

1. See, for example, Yun Ch'on-ju, *Han'guk chongch'i ch'egye* (*The Korean Political System*) (Seoul, 1981), pp. 189–248.

2. President Yun Po-son, who was a leading member of the New Democracy party, reportedly declared after learning about the coup: "The inevitable has come!" See Yun Po-son, *Kugugui kasibatkil* (*Thorny Road Toward National Salvation*) (Seoul, 1967), p. 110.

3. Juan Linz defines authoritarian regimes as "political systems with limited, not responsible, political pluralism; without elaborate guiding ideology (but with distinctive mentalities); without intensive or extensive political mobilization (except at some points in their development); and in which a leader (or occasionally a small group) exercises power within formally ill-defined but quite predictable limits." See Juan Linz, "Opposition in and Under an Authoritarian Regime," in Robert A. Dahl, ed., *Regimes and Oppositions* (New Haven: Yale University Press, 1973), p. 185.

4. Se-jin Kim, *The Politics of Military Revolution in Korea* (Chapel Hill, N.C.: University of North Carolina Press, 1971), p. 135.

5. Ibid., p. 136.

6. Chae-jin Lee, "South Korea: The Politics of Domestic-Foreign Linkage," *Asian Survey* (January 1973): pp. 99–101.

7. Sung-joo Han, "South Korea: The Political Economy of Dependency," *Asian Survey* 15 (January 1975): pp. 43–45; John K. C. Oh, "South Korea 1975: A Permanent Emergency," *Asian Survey* 16 (January 1976): pp. 74–75.

8. See, for example, Herbert P. Bix, "Regional Integration: Japan and South Korea in America's Asian Policy," in Frank Baldwin, ed., *Without Parallel: The American-Korean Relationship Since 1945* (New York: Pantheon Books, 1973), pp. 179–232; Gerhard Breidenstein, "Capitalism in South Korea," ibid., pp. 233–70.

9. Gregory Henderson, *Korea: The Politics of the Vortex* (Cambridge, Mass.: Harvard University Press, 1968); Edward Reynolds Wright, ed., *Korean Politics in Transition* (Seattle, Wash.: University of Washington Press, 1974); and Sung-joo Han, *The Failure of Democracy in South Korea* (Berkeley: University of California Press, 1974).

10. See U.S. House of Representatives, *Human Rights in South Korea: Implications for U.S. Policy*, Hearings before the Subcommittee on Asian and Pacific Affairs of the Committee of Foreign Affairs, 93rd Congress, 2nd Session (Washington, D.C., 1974).

11. Chang Won-jong, "Son'go Kyongje ron," ("Electoral Economics"), *Shin Dong-a* (June 1971): pp. 98–111.

12. Pyong-choon Hahm, "Toward a New Theory of Korean Politics: A Reexamination of Traditional Factors," in Wright, ed., *Korean Politics in Transition*, pp. 321–356.

13. For an excellent description of events in 1980, see Chong-Sik Lee, "South Korea in 1980: The Emergence of a New Authoritarian Order," *Asian Survey* 21 (January 1981): pp. 125–143.

14. This section borrows substantially from my article, "South Korea 1987: The Politics of Democratization," *Asian Survey* 28 (January 1988).

15. *Far Eastern Economic Review*, 5 February 1987, p. 16.

16. The *New York Times*, 22 June 1987, p. 1.

17. *Far Eastern Economic Review*, 9 July 1987, p. 8.

18. For example, Kim Dae Jung wrote after declaring candidacy that "the candidacy

of Kim Young Sam, my colleague in the opposition, increases the size of my lead."
International Herald Tribune, 11 November 1987.

    19. Wolgan Chosun, *Monthly* (December 1987): pp. 189–225.

    20. Ibid.

    21. For a definition of "radicalism" in Korea, see Sungjoo Han, *The Failure of Democracy in South Korea*, p. 5.

CHAPTER NINE

Nigeria: Pluralism, Statism, and the Struggle for Democracy

LARRY DIAMOND

The Nigerian experience with democracy has been paradoxical and even schizophrenic. Twice the country has undertaken to govern itself under liberal democratic constitutions, following carefully staged transitions. Both these efforts were ruined by antidemocratic behavior and then ended by popular military coups. And yet, Nigeria has never been content with authoritarian rule, and no military regime that has not committed itself to a transition to democracy has been able to survive. Through their country's turbulent quarter-century of independence—which has encompassed eight governments, five successful military coups, a civil war, and a dizzying economic boom followed by a crushing depression—Nigerians have maintained a profound commitment to personal freedom and political participation. Amidst the continual drama of political crisis and economic disarray has been the quiet but steady growth of the social infrastructure of democracy—a free press, a rapidly expanding educational system, a sophisticated legal system, and a diverse array of autonomous social, cultural, and economic organizations. Moreover, although the ethnic complexity of the country has generated intense and sometimes catastrophic political conflict, it also represents an irrepressible social pluralism that cannot be effectively managed by authoritarian means. But over these promising currents of pluralism falls the growing shadow of a swelling state, feeding political corruption and instability. In the struggle between pluralism and statism the search for a viable system of democratic government continues.

• HISTORICAL REVIEW •

Developments Before Independence

Nigeria has an enormous diversity of ethnic groups, as indicated by the presence of some 248 distinct languages.[1] Many of these linguistic groups are tiny and politically insignificant. But three comprise collectively two-thirds of the population: the Hausa-Fulani (two peoples who are typically grouped together

351

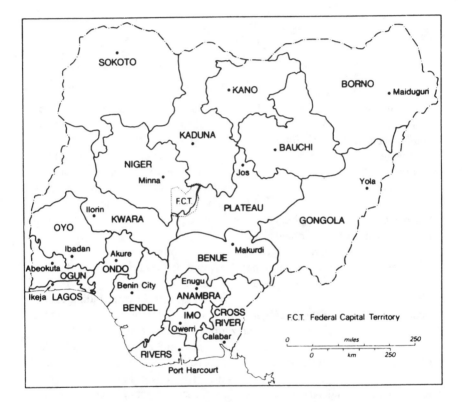

SOKOTO

KANO

BORNO
Maiduguri

KADUNA

BAUCHI

NIGER
Minna

Jos

Yola

Ilorin
KWARA

F.C.T.

PLATEAU

GONGOLA

OYO

Ibadan

Akure

Makurdi

BENUE

Abeokuta
OGUN
ONDO

Benin City

Enugu
ANAMBRA

Ikeja LAGOS

BENDEL

IMO

CROSS
RIVER

Owerri

Calabar

RIVERS

Port Harcourt

F.C.T. Federal Capital Territory

0   miles   250

0   km   250

NIGERIA

because of their substantial cultural and political integration), the Yoruba, and the Igbo (see Table 9.1). In this respect, Nigeria has what Horowitz would term a relatively "centralized" ethnic structure, which presents a greater challenge to ethnic harmony.[2]

Although there were significant democratic traditions among the more decentralized and acephalous of Nigeria's ethnic groups (such as the Igbo and Tiv), and mechanisms for limiting power in the constitutional monarchies of the Yoruba, the history of democratic government in Nigeria must begin with the history of the nation itself, which was the creation of British colonial rule. For half a century—from the time that separate protectorates were declared for Northern and Southern Nigeria in 1900 to the Constitutional Conference of 1950—Nigeria was ruled in essentially authoritarian fashion by the colonial power. But that fashion was not uniform across the country. Even after the formal amalgamation of the two protectorates in 1914, the British continued to rule Nigeria, in effect, as two countries. In the North, a native authority system was constructed to rule indirectly through the centralized and steeply hierarchical structures of traditional authority in the Muslim emirates. In the South, where power was more dispersed and there was more accountability of rulers to ruled, indirect rule worked poorly and even broke down in places. At the same time, Western (European) education and religion were permitted to spread rapidly in the South but heavily restricted in the Muslim North, creating enormous disparities in economic and technological development. In addition, political

Table 9.1   Distribution of Nigerian Ethnic Groups, 1952–1953 and 1963

Group	Percent of Population[a]	
	1952–1953	1963
Hausa	18.2 ⎫	
Fulani	9.9 ⎬ 28.1	29.5
Kanuri	4.2	4.1
Tiv	2.5	2.5
Nupe	1.1	1.2
Yoruba	16.6	20.3
Edo	1.5	1.7
Igbo	17.9	16.6
Ibibio-Efik	2.7	3.6
Ijaw	1.1	2.0
Total: Hausa-Fulani, Yoruba, and Igbo	62.6	66.4

Source: Etienne Van de Walle, "Who's Who and Where in Nigeria," *Africa Report* 15, no. 1 (1970).
[a] The census has been a subject of continuing scholarly debate and political conflict in Nigeria for three decades, and hence no set of figures can be accepted as precise. Because the 1963 census was ensnarled in intense controversy, the 1952–1953 figures, compiled by the more neutral colonial administration in a less politically charged atmosphere, may represent more accurately the demographic balance of peoples.

354 DIAMOND

participation was permitted earlier in the South. From 1923 until 1947, only Southern Nigerians were allowed to elect members of the Legislative Council (advisory to the British governor).[3]

The separate character of development in Nigeria, and the political tensions to which it gave rise, were rooted in the regional structure created by the British. In 1939, Nigeria was divided into four administrative units: the colony of Lagos, and the Western, Eastern, and Northern Provinces. The power of these provinces grew, and in 1951 they were designated "regions," becoming constituent units in a quasi-federal system. The boundaries of these regions coincided with and reified the primary ethnic division in the country: the Igbo were the dominant group in the East, the Yoruba in the West, and the Hausa-Fulani in the North. But each region also contained significant minorities of other ethnic groups that feared and resented the domination of these "big tribes." Despite the intense lobbying for separate states by ethnic minority groups throughout the decade, and the profound concerns of Southerners about a system in which one region, the North, was more populous than all the others combined, the British were unalterably committed to this regional structure, and "after 1948 every effort was made to encourage 'regional thinking.'"[4]

The decisive first step toward self-rule and popular participation came in 1948, with several reforms in response to rising nationalist agitation. Africani-

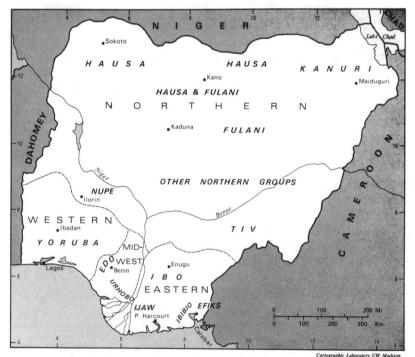

Cartographic Laboratory UW-Madison

Figure 9.1 Nigeria: Ethnic Groups and Four Regions
From Crawford Young, *The Politics of Pluralism,* University of Wisconsin Press.

zation of the senior civil service was accelerated. The native authority system was democratized, and scrapped altogether in the East, in favor of a hierarchy of elected councils. Primary and secondary education were rapidly expanded and colonial efforts were extended to higher education.[5] Most important, a process of constitutional revision was launched that entailed extensive and unprecedented popular participation.

Out of this two-year process came the 1951 constitution, which launched the first period of full-scale electoral politics in Nigeria.[6] This provided for regional assemblies elected indirectly through a system of electoral colleges and a central legislature (half from the North) elected by the regional assemblies. No provision was yet made at either level for elected executives.[7]

The 1951 constitution made the regions the more important locus of political life. Through the end of colonial rule and the life of the First Republic, the growing regional emphasis was to tilt the national political balance decisively in favor of conservative forces, as the British had no doubt intended. Growing regional autonomy protected the position of the aristocratic Northern ruling class from the challenge and infiltration of better educated and more cosmopolitan Southern elites and from any interference by the central government.[8] Moreover, the Northern Region's absolute population majority in the country made it likely that its dominant class would also be the dominant political force in Nigeria. But inherent in this strange federal structure was an explosive contradiction between the political power of the North and the socioeconomic power of the South, which generated deep insecurity and recurrent conflict.[9]

The regional system made control of regional government the *sine qua non* for both traditional and rising elements of the emergent political class.[10] This put an enormous premium on the 1951 regional elections. Given the coincidence of regional with ethnic group boundaries, it was virtually inevitable that these first elections would see the organization of political parties along ethnic and regional lines. Hence, although the leading nationalist organization, the National Council of Nigeria and the Cameroons (NCNC), had sought with some success to reach out beyond its Igbo core to construct a multiethnic, national base, it was able to win only the election in the Eastern Region. In the West and North, power was captured by openly regionalist political parties formed by ethnic elites for the express purpose of winning regional power against the challenge of the Igbo-led and better organized NCNC.[11] In the West, the formation of the Yoruba-dominated Action Group (AG) followed years of intense competition between Yoruba and Igbo elites.[12] In the North, the transformation of the Northern Peoples' Congress (NPC) from a sagging cultural organization into a modern political party was in defense of both class and ethnic interests.[13]

The aggressive mobilization of Southern parties and groups stirred a "political awakening" among a new generation of Northern elites whose exposure to Western education had bred reformist inclinations and who had become alarmed to discover their region's massive and pervasive disadvantage in every aspect of modernization.[14] The social dominance of the traditional ruling class of the Northern emirates (the *sarakuna*) was threatened by political competition not only from militant and culturally alien Southerners, determined to dismantle the "feudalistic" structures of the emirates, but also from radical young Northern commoners (*talakawa*) similarly pledged to sweeping reform. Stunned by victories of the radical party, the Northern Elements Progressive Union (NEPU), in the early stages of the 1951 Northern elections, the "awakened" Northern elites revitalized the NPC just in time to win a sweeping victory in the final stage of voting.[15]

The 1951 victories of the NPC, the AG, and the NCNC in their home regions established a close identity between region, party, and ethnicity that was to heighten over the course of the 1950s. The constitution of 1954 not only created a genuinely federal system, but gave enormous autonomy and control over resources to each of the three regions. As the regions became the primary centers of power and wealth in Nigeria, the struggle between their ruling parties for socioeconomic resources came to dominate Nigerian politics. This struggle was manifested in repeated political conflicts over such issues as the timing of self-government, revenue allocation, and the NPC's effort to purge southerners from the Northern bureaucracy and economy. But most of all, it was evinced in electoral competition.

Political competition during colonial rule peaked in the federal elections of 1959. By then, Nigeria had conducted three regional elections in the East, two each in the North and West, and one in the federation as a whole. The subsequent regional elections had tightened the grip of the ruling parties, but in the 1954 federal elections, the NCNC won not only in the East, but also (narrowly) in the West, joining the NPC in a coalition of expedience at the center. When the office of federal prime minister was created in 1957, NPC President Sir Ahmadu Bello chose (revealingly) to remain the premier of the North, and the party's vice-president, Abubakar Tafawa Balewa, became prime minister. He then constructed a coalition cabinet embracing all three major parties. But this grand coalition would last only until the 1959 elections, which would produce the first fully elected national government and the one that would lead the country to independence the following year.

As with previous campaigns of the decade, the 1959 campaign was characterized by blatant appeals to ethnic prejudice and vituperative rhetoric, which completely drowned out the substance of party programs and proposals. Also, violence and repression marred the democratic character of the campaign. Repression was most prevalent in the North, where the NPC regularly used its control of traditional systems of justice and administration to obstruct, harass, and punish opposition candidates and their supporters. This repression reached new levels in 1959. Perhaps because electoral outcomes were not so much secured through institutional means of repression in the South, the campaigns were much more violent there. From the inception of electoral competition in 1951, parties fielded bands of thugs to disrupt, intimidate,. and attack the opposition, and injuries in the hundreds were not uncommon. In the high stakes of the 1959 election, such violence spread to the North as well, frequently victimizing Southern and NEPU campaigners.[16]

Despite the significant antidemocratic currents in the 1959 election, the "steel frame" of colonial administration maintained some semblance of political order and electoral integrity, and the keen anticipation of independence produced a postelection spirit of accommodation. Although battered by the extraordinary bitterness of the campaign, the tacit preelection alliance between the NPC and the NCNC matured into a coalition government led by the former, which was only a few seats short of an absolute majority in Parliament. The alliance was facilitated not only by the NCNC's desire to bridge the North-South divide on the eve of independence, but also by both parties' resentment of the AG's aggressive efforts to mobilize ethnic minority groups in their regions.

The First Republic

Nigeria thus achieved independence on 1 October 1960 with a functioning parliamentary system. Legislative power was vested in an elected Parliament, especially in the powerful lower chamber, the House of Representatives, which was responsible for the laws and finances of the federation. Executive power was vested in a cabinet, headed by a prime minister, who was to be appointed by the governor-general (and, after 1 October 1963, when Nigeria became a republic, by the president) upon demonstrating majority support in the House. Judicial power was vested in an independent court system, including a Federal Supreme Court with power to decide cases involving the constitutions and laws of the federation and the regions.[17]

Constitutionally, the system was democratic. Power was distributed between three branches of government. Regular parliamentary elections were required at least every five years. The primary restriction on adult suffrage and eligibility for elective office was in the North, where these political rights were restricted to males. Otherwise, political and civil liberties were formally guaranteed in the constitution's detailed chapter on fundamental rights.

There were also other democratic features of the political landscape. A number of political parties competed for power. Their contestation was increasingly flawed, but still it existed. And although plagued by zealous partisanship, inexperience, irresponsibility, and economic and political pressure from the parties and governments that owned most of the newspapers,[18] the Nigerian press was a significant source of political pluralism and critical inquiry. In fact, some outside observers saw it as "the most potent institution supporting democratic freedom in Nigeria."[19]

In other dimensions, however, Nigeria fell much wider of the democratic mark. Loopholes in the constitution facilitated abuse. Each provision on human rights excepted laws that were "reasonably justifiable in a democratic society" in the interest of national defense, public order, etc. These exceptions could be widened much further during a state of emergency, which could be declared by a simple majority vote of each house of Parliament. In addition, the constitution enabled Parliament (by a two-thirds vote of each house) to take over the law-making functions of a regional government. In a system where parliamentary opposition was regionally based, this created enormous potential for intimidation.

More troubling was the actual performance of political actors. In all three regions, regional powers were used increasingly to harass and repress political opposition. In the North, "the freedoms normally regarded as essential if a two-party system is to work simply [did] not exist."[20] Genuine political competition was becoming constricted to the federal arena, as one-party states emerged in each region. In the regional elections of 1960 and 1961, each ruling party significantly consolidated its dominance, leaving the opposition shattered and demoralized.

Beyond escalating the insecurity in the federal system, the regional elections exposed again the shallow commitment of political elites to democratic norms of tolerance and fair play. These antidemocratic currents make it difficult to classify Nigeria at independence as a democracy. It was a quasi-democracy struggling to establish fully democratic government.

The assault on the edifice of democracy continued relentlessly over the five and a quarter years of the First Republic. During these years, the political system was buffeted by a succession of five major crises that heightened ethnic and regional polarization, intensified political violence and intolerance, and heavily eroded the popular legitimacy of the regime.

The first crisis began as an internal conflict within the ruling party of the Western Region, pitting the AG national leader, Chief Obafemi Awolowo, who resigned as premier in 1959 to lead the party's federal campaign, against his successor as premier, Chief S. L. Akintola. The conflict was partially personal and factional, but also heavily ideological. Long committed to a moderate socialist program, Chief Awolowo moved, after the AG's sweeping 1959 defeat, to a much more radical stance, vowing to replace the regional system with a structure of multiple states and to forge a political alliance against the NPC. A transformation of the regional system threatened not only to unravel the social and political dominance of the Northern ruling class, but also to weaken the political classes of the Eastern and Western Regions, since smaller regions would mean smaller bases of patronage for the ruling parties and very likely different ruling parties in some of the new regions. Regionalism thus coincided with the conservatism of the Akintola faction while Awolowo's antiregionalism was the logical spearhead of his radical challenge to the status quo.[21]

In a federal system with only three regions, no serious political conflict could long remain contained within a single region. When the Awolowo faction succeeded in deposing Chief Akintola as premier, the NPC/NCNC Federal Coalition took action. Seizing upon internal disorder in the Western Region House, it declared an emergency and prevented the Awolowo faction from taking power. After six months of heavily biased emergency rule, Chief Akintola was reinstated as premier at the helm of a new party. By the time the full effects of federal emergency rule had been felt, a fourth region (the Mid-Western) had been created out of the Western Region, Chief Awolowo and his close associates had been convicted of treason and sentenced to prison, and the AG had been destroyed as a national political force. The crisis not only alienated a large segment of Nigerian youth and intelligentsia who had been attracted to Awolowo's radical egalitarian appeals, but it also left the Yoruba feeling victimized as a people.[22]

The second crisis partially overlapped the first. By 1962, Nigerians were being mobilized intensively for the national census. With the distribution of power and resources between the regions hanging on its outcome, the census became the object of heated political competition. Controversy flared when the initial results revealed much larger population increases in the South—sufficient to end the North's population majority—and demographic tests showed some of the Eastern Region's figures to have been "grossly inflated." When the North then claimed to have discovered eight million people more in a "verification check" (thus preserving its population majority), the ensuing crisis forced Prime Minister Tafawa Balewa to cancel the census and order a new one for later in 1963. But now that the census had been blatantly established as an instrument of ethnic and regional competition, mass political mobilization was even more intense and mutual suspicion even more profound. The result was an even greater fiasco—an "altogether incredible" national increase of 83 percent in ten years and a continued Northern population majority.[23] Despite bitter rejection by the Eastern Region's NCNC government, the NPC used its parliamentary power to win official acceptance of the figures.

The census crisis not only heightened the salience of ethnicity and region in politics, but it also marked the beginning of fiercely polarized competition between the NPC and the NCNC, who were both looking toward the critical federal election due before the end of 1964. With the decimation of the Action Group, the political system was realigning around a bipolar struggle: as progressive elements of the NCNC and AG began to unite, Chief Akintola's party moved closer to the NPC. But before these sectional tensions could cumulate in the electoral struggle, a third crisis erupted.

Late in 1963, wage laborers in Nigeria began to focus their indignation over declining real income and gross economic inequality into militant demands for government attention and higher pay. For the next year, the severely fractured trade union movement united in a concerted challenge to the country's political class. Following months of government arrogance and procrastination, the unions launched a devastating general strike in June of 1964, which brought the economic life of the nation to a standstill for thirteen days. In addition to the overwhelming support of Nigerian workers, both organized and unorganized, the strike also drew widespread popular support, especially in the cities.[24] This came in response to the larger political issues in the strike: the enormous disparities in the official wage structure and the glaring corruption and extravagant consumption of the nation's political elite. The strike also drew some support from progressive AG and NCNC politicians, but it was really an expression of disgust with the entire political class. Although the government was finally compelled to make significant concessions, the effect of the strike was to further weaken the regime's legitimacy and to expose the weakness of its authority.[25]

By the time the strike was over, the two leading parties were busy organizing contending alliances for the 1964 federal election. The NCNC first formed an alliance with the Action Group, which was joined on 1 September by NEPU and the minority party of the Christian lower North in the United Progressive Grand Alliance (UPGA). Meanwhile, the NPC drew in Chief Akintola's party and various minor Southern parties to form the Nigerian National Alliance (NNA). These alliances—dominated by the Igbos of the East and the Hausa-Fulani of the North—reduced national politics to a bipolar struggle along the great cumulative divide of ethnicity, region, and party, reinforced by the ideological cleavage between progressive, antiregionalist forces (in UPGA) and conservative, regionalist forces (in the NNA).

With the entire distribution of national power and resources at stake, electoral conflict became more abrasively tribalistic and more violent than ever before. The class consciousness of the June general strike was drowned in an emotional resurgence of ethnic attachments,[26] and the democratic character of the 1964 election was obliterated by organized political thuggery and official obstruction and repression of opposition campaigns.[27] This led UPGA to boycott the election, provoking a tense showdown between the NPC prime minister and the NCNC president of Nigeria in which, for several days, the specter of secession and possible civil war loomed large. Wishing to avoid mass bloodshed, and unable to win military and police support, President Nnamdi Azikiwe finally yielded, and the NPC returned to the federal government more powerful than ever, with the NCNC obtaining a reduced role in a new and even more superficial coalition government. For the third consecutive time, the NPC had triumphed totally in a decisive confrontation with a Southern party.

This pattern prevailed through the final crisis of the First Republic, the October 1965 Western Region election, which pitted Chief Akintola's ruling party and the Action Group in a "do-or-die" struggle for control of the West. Hated for its corruption, extravagance, neglect, and collaboration with the "oppressor" of the Yoruba people, the Akintola regime was compelled to employ massive coercion as a substitute for legitimate authority. Still, it had to resort to wholesale electoral fraud to salvage a claim to reelection. With the announcement of this preposterous result, the Western Region erupted into popular rebellion. The wave of violence and destruction made the region effectively ungovernable. This only further accelerated the process of political decay, which had been advanced earlier in the year by a spate of scandals involving federal government corruption and by a growing consciousness of the degree to which official corruption swollen salaries, waste, and recurrent political crises were squandering the nation's resources. These developments combined to rob the regime of what little legitimacy it still retained, especially among the educated "counter-elite" in the intelligentsia, the civil service, and the military.

Military Rule, 1966–1975

On 15 January 1966, a group of young army majors and captains overthrew the First Republic, assassinating the prime minister, the premiers of the Western and Northern Regions, and a number of high-ranking military officers. Although an ethnic motive has been deduced from their predominantly Igbo composition and the fact that leading Igbo politicians were spared, the coupmakers struck primarily "to end a corrupt and discredited despotism that could only be removed by violence."[28] Their disgust with the First Republic was shared by a broad cross-section of the population, which welcomed the coup in an effusive outpouring of joy and relief. However, the young coupmakers failed fully to execute their plans, and governmental power was wrested from them by one of their intended victims, Major General J. T. U. Aguiyi Ironsi, General Officer Commanding of the Nigerian army, who—like most of the plotters—was Igbo.

Initially, General Ironsi struck swiftly against corruption and graft, detaining a number of former political office holders. He also promised an early return to civilian rule, appointing panels to draft a new constitution and to study problems of the judiciary and economy. But in administering the country, Ironsi tended to confirm mounting fears and suspicions (especially in the North) that the coup had been designed to impose Igbo hegemony on the country.

As concern grew over Igbo bias in his military promotions and choice of political advisers, Ironsi blundered disastrously on 24 May 1966. "Without waiting for the report of his constitutional study group or submitting their report to the promised constituent assembly," he announced a new constitution abolishing the federal system and unifying the regional and federal public services.[29] For Northerners, who had long feared that their educational disadvantage could open the way for Southern domination of their civil service (and the entire state system), this was anathema. Within days, hundreds of Igbos were killed in riots in Northern towns. Although Ironsi backed away somewhat from his original plan, Northern alarm and bitterness persisted, culminating in a bloody countercoup by Northern officers in July, which killed Ironsi and many other Igbo officers and soldiers. Out of the chaos and uncertainty, the army chief of staff, Lieutenant Colonel Yakubu Gowon, a Northern Christian from a minority ethnic group, emerged as a compromise choice for head of state.

At first, Gowon also spoke in terms of an early return to civilian rule. After reinstating the old regional system, he organized meetings of regional opinion leaders to prepare the groundwork for a constitutional conference. There support gathered for a stronger central government and creation of more states. But Gowon could not bridge the years of enmity and suspicion, nor heal the wounds of two bloody coups. With the Eastern Region's governor and military commander, Colonel Chukwuemeka Ojukwu, refusing to recognize Gowon's authority, and with Eastern Region delegates insisting on extensive regional autonomy, the deliberations stalled, and were abruptly ended in early October 1966 by a new wave of Igbo massacres in the North. Subsequently, more than a million Igbos poured back into the Eastern Region while Ojukwu ordered all non-Easterners to leave.

The soldiers proved even less adept than the politicians at managing the country's explosive divisions. Amid rising secessionist pressure in the East, efforts to negotiate some kind of compromise, confederal arrangement failed. With centrifugal pressures also growing in the West and Mid-West, the Northern emirs finally agreed to the creation of additional states as the only hope for preserving the federation. On 27 May 1967, Gowon announced the division of the country into twelve states (six in the North, and three each in the East and West). This at once broke the monolithic power of the North and granted the longstanding aspirations of ethnic minorities, who along with the Yoruba, found their commitment to the federation renewed. But the alienation of the Igbo was now irreparable. Three days later, Ojukwu announced the secession of the Eastern Region as the Republic of Biafra, and in early July the Nigerian civil war began.

Short of total defeat in war, there is probably no greater trauma for a nation than civil war. For the East in particular, which suffered immense destruction and hundreds of thousands of military and civilian fatalities, the thirty-month war was a horrific experience. Nevertheless, Nigeria emerged from the experience with a hopeful future, owing in part to General Gowon's magnanimous policy of reconciliation with the defeated East, and in part to the development of oil production, which, by the end of the war in January 1970, was beginning to generate substantial revenue. With the specter of national disintegration now definitively laid to rest and a more effective federal system in place, attention turned to two overriding national problems: postwar reconstruction of the economy and society, and political reconstruction of civilian democratic government.

The war period had seen the imposition of stern authoritarian measures, including strict controls on trade unions, a ban on strikes, and a crackdown on movements for new states. Although these "had all been accepted as part of the necessary restrictions on a nation at war,"[30] democratic aspirations remained strong. Some continuity with civilian rule was maintained by the presence in the wartime government of prominent civilians, led by the previously jailed Chief Obafemi Awolowo.

With the end of the war, Nigerians eagerly awaited the announcement of a program for transition to civilian rule. Not until ten months later, on 1 October 1970, was it announced. The military was to remain in power for another six years while it pursued a nine-point program of reconstruction. The armed forces were to be reorganized, the economy rebuilt and revived, corruption eradicated, a new census conducted, a new constitution drafted, and the thorny questions of additional states and revenue allocation settled. Following this, genuinely national political parties would be organized and elections conducted. Although many Nigerians, not least the former politicians, were stunned and disappointed by the length of the transition, the setting of a definite date for return to civilian rule met with popular favor.

As oil production reached two million barrels a day in 1973 and oil prices quadrupled during 1973 and 1974, Nigeria entered a breathtaking economic boom. Ironically, this was when the popular consensus behind Gowon's rule began to unravel. Once more, the census generated a damaging political crisis, as it produced not only an incredible total count but bitterly disputed state results. With the North preserving its population majority by an even larger margin than in 1963, the census drowned in charges of fraud and ethnic domination, and the results were never formally adopted.

Alarmed by the resurgence of ethnic conflict, realizing that little progress had been made on most of the points of his transition program, and pressured by an increasingly venal circle of military officers who sought to extend their control over the juicy resources of power, Gowon shocked the nation on 1 October 1974 by announcing an indefinite postponement of the return to civilian rule.[31]

At the time of his announcement, General Gowon committed himself to new reforms: a new constitution, new states, new military governors, and new federal commissioners. But no progress was forthcoming on any of these fronts in the subsequent ten months. Popular disillusionment sharply intensified as the twelve state governors became ever more entrenched, and arrogant and brazen in their corruption, while venality and mismanagement exacted a mounting toll on the national economy as well. The inept handling of the Udoji Commission's proposals for large wage increases for government workers brought a steep rise in inflation that actually reduced the purchasing power of urban workers. Strikes crippled banking and health services. Shortages of essential commodities occurred. The ports became hopelessly jammed with ships waiting to offload fantastic amounts of cement inexplicably ordered by the government. And in yet another scandal, severe shortages of gasoline mysteriously developed, forcing dawn-to-dusk queues. General Gowon became increasingly remote not only from public opinion and protest, but from military officers outside his narrow ruling circle, who worried increasingly that the corruption and mismanagement of his regime were dragging the entire armed forces into disrepute.[32]

The Transition to the Second Republic

On 29 July 1975 (nine years to the day he assumed power), General Gowon was overthrown in a bloodless coup while attending an OAU summit. The coup was engineered by reform-minded senior officers determined to clear out the rot in the government and bureaucracy and return the country to civilian rule. The new head of state, Brigadier Murtala Muhammed, moved swiftly and boldly to achieve these goals. To great popular acclaim, he removed the twelve state governors within hours of taking power. Over the following weeks, more than 10,000 civil servants at every level of government were dismissed for abuse of office or unproductivity. Following this, the army itself was purged, and plans drawn up to reduce its size from 250,000 to 100,000. Commissions were appointed to investigate several major scandals and the assets of public officers, to study and make recommendations on the creation of new states, and to explore the possibility of moving the federal capital from impossibly congested Lagos.

Most significant of all, Murtala Muhammed responded forthrightly to the mounting pressures for a transition to democracy. Through the previous decade of military rule, democratic aspirations had remained alive. These were sustained in part by the vigor of the Nigerian press, which, despite repressive. decrees and continuous threats, harassment and arrests, managed to preserve its freedom and integrity to a considerable degree.[33] "In the absence of a democratically elected Parliament, newspapers found themselves playing the role of a deliberative assembly, reflecting the feelings of the people [about] . . . government policies and actions. . . ."[34] Risking imprisonment, journalists and editors had taken the lead in exposing and denouncing corruption; in demanding the release of political detainees, the lifting of press restraints, and the restoration of other liberties; and in criticizing government policies and performance.[35] Through repeated strikes, boycotts, declarations, demonstrations, and other means of mass mobilization, university students also played a crucial role in demanding accountability, responsiveness, and basic freedoms from the Gowon government.[36]

On 1 October 1975, General Murtala announced a precise deadline and detailed timetable for the restoration of civilian, democratic government. In five stages over a period of four years, a new constitutional and political foundation was to be carefully laid. First, the issue of new states would be resolved and a Constitutional Drafting Committee would be given twelve months to produce a draft constitution. Second, local government would be reorganized and new local governments elected, to be followed by the election of a Constituent Assembly to review and amend the draft constitution. Stage three would lift the ban on political parties by October 1978. Stage four would elect state legislatures and stage five a federal government, in time to transfer power to "a democratically elected government of the people" by 1 October 1979.[37]

Despite the tragic assassination of Murtala Muhammed in a failed coup attempt on 13 February 1976—when he was riding the crest of an unprecedented wave of national popularity—and despite a bitter debate within the Constituent Assembly over whether to establish an Islamic *Sharia* court of appeal at the federal level—which threatened explosive religious and regional polarization until it was resolved by compromise and skillful mediation[38]—Murtala's timetable was implemented faithfully and skillfully by his successor, General Olusegun Obasanjo.

Several aspects of the transition process appeared to augur well for the future of democracy in Nigeria. The volatile issue of new states, which had been the focus of intense ethnic and subethnic political mobilization, was tackled early and decisively with the creation of seven more states in April 1976 (implementing one of Murtala Muhammed's final policy announcements). In addition to creating several new ethnic minority states, the major Yoruba state was broken in three and the major Igbo state was split in two. The new nineteen-state system—containing four predominantly Hausa-Fulani states, four Yoruba, two Igbo, and nine ethnic minority states—seemed likely to weaken the ethnic and regional solidarities that had cursed the First Republic and to generate a more fluid and shifting pattern of alignments, with state interests representing an independent and, at least occasionally, crosscutting line of cleavage.[39]

The concern for generating crosscutting cleavages was also evident in the new constitution, which explicitly prohibited sectional parties and required broad ethnic representation in each party as a condition for recognition.[40] Constitutional provisions for an executive presidency, and requiring a presidential candidate to win at least a quarter of the vote in at least two-thirds of all the states in order to be directly elected, had a similar purpose. Together with the creation of a powerful Federal Electoral Commision (FEDECO) to certify parties and regulate campaigning, these innovations in "institutional architecture" seemed to produce a more durable political foundation.[41]

The new constitution was an elaborate and carefully crafted document. Closely modeled after the U.S. system, it provided for an elected president and vice-president (eligible for no more than two four-year terms); a bicameral National Assembly (with five senators from each state, elected by district, and 450 members of the House of Representatives, elected from federal constituencies of equivalent population); an independent judiciary, headed by a Supreme Court and State High Courts, with courts of appeal below them; and a detailed chapter on "fundamental human rights," guaranteeing not only life, liberty, and due process, but essential freedoms of expression, association, peaceful assembly, movement, and the press. In addition, contained in the constitution's Fifth Schedule was another significant innovation: an extensive Code of Conduct for Public Officers, along with a bureau and tribunal for monitoring and enforcing compliance with its provisions.

Also auspicious was the widespread popular participation in the transition process. In the six months following the presentation of the draft constitution in December 1976, the country became consumed with a free and vigorous debate on its provisions, which continued in the deliberations of the elected Constituent Assembly.[42] The thoroughness and freedom of the public debate and the national consensus behind its result suggested that "Nigeria's Second Republic was established upon a genuinely popular foundation"[43] that gave legitimacy to its political institutions.[44]

The process of transition did not give the same careful attention to the development of political party institutions, however. Not until three of the four years had passed was the ban on political parties lifted. Aspiring political parties then had only three months to apply to FEDECO for registration. In this brief period, they had to establish a national network of local and state branches, elect party officials, and conduct national conventions. After thirteen years of prohibition of political parties, this severe compression of the period for political cal party development had precisely the consequences the military hoped to avoid: most truly fresh political formations either fractured into more familiar forms or died stillborn. Only nineteen of some fifty emergent parties were able to file papers by the mid-December (1978) deadline, and of these only five were certified by FEDECO.[45]

These five new parties bore a strong resemblance to the parties of the First Republic, in part because of significant continuities in their leaderships and regional bases. Thus the Unity Party of Nigeria (UPN), strongest in the Yoruba states and led by Chief Obafemi Awolowo, struck many as the reincarnation of the Action Group. The National Party of Nigeria (NPN), based most powerfully in the far North and led in the presidential elections by former NPC Minister Alhaji Shehu Shagari, was widely seen as the successor to the NPC. The Nigerian Peoples Party (NPP), reduced primarily to an Igbo base after a damaging split cost it much of its Northern support,[46] and then nominating Dr. Nnamdi Azikiwe as its presidential candidate, was seen to reproduce the NCNC. And the Peoples Redemption Party (PRP), also based in the emirate North and led by Mallam Aminu Kano, seemed to reincarnate the radical NEPU, which he had led in the First Republic. Only the Great Nigerian Peoples Party (GNPP), which split from the NPP when its leader, Waziri Ibrahim, refused to step aside for Dr. Azikiwe as presidential candidate, could not be obviously linked to a major party of the First Republic.

In fact, each of these parties was broader than its supposed antecedent in the First Republic. In particular, the NPN represented the broadest ethnic base ever assembled by a Nigerian party, perhaps the first truly "national" party in the nation's history. Although party power was based on the aristocratic and modern technocratic elites of the Muslim upper North, Yoruba, Igbo and minority political and business elites played strategic roles in the party's formation, and the NPN showed signs of becoming the predominant party of an increasingly integrated and cohesive Nigerian bourgeoisie. Even after its traumatic split, the NPP continued to draw critical support from Christian areas of the "Middle Belt" (or lower North) that had never been associated with the NCNC, and the GNPP showed strength through much of the Muslim North and also in the minority areas of the southeast. While the UPN and PRP were more regionally based, they were the sharpest and least parochial in their substantive programs, seeking to build national constituencies around social democratic and socialist ideologies respectively.[47]

Nevertheless, in the brevity of the period for party development and under pressure of imminent elections, politicians tended to retreat into convenient and familiar ethnic alignments, and new political entrepreneurs were forced to look to established politicians for leadership. This not only snapped some significant crosscutting alignments—especially that represented by the original NPP—it also produced "a sad level of regional and tribal correlation in voting behaviour."[48] And it brought together politicians of such disparate ideological inclinations that their associations were bound to become sorely strained.

The Second Republic

The Second Republic was born in the elections for state and federal offices that took place in five rounds during July and August of 1979.[49] Although largely successful, their legitimacy was tarnished by charges of administrative bias and, in particular, by a serious controversy over the presidential election. Pro-NPN bias was suggested by the pattern of disqualification of candidates by FEDECO, on the grounds of nonpayment of income tax.[50] The actual conduct of the voting was also disputed. Predictably, "the various parties complained of fraud, victimization, and all kinds of electoral malpractices in places where they had not won."[51] Numerous malpractices were in fact documented, and election tribunals did order some new elections, while courageously upholding the disputed election of the PRP candidate for governor of strategic Kaduna State. On balance, the 1979 elections were relatively free and fair in their conduct.[52] Parties were free to campaign and the results in most states seemed to reflect apparent political trends. Moreover, in contrast with previous elections, the 1979 contest was impressively peaceful, due in no small measure to the active efforts of the military government to check political thuggery.

However, a truly serious challenge to the legitimacy of the 1979 elections—and of the new republic—grew out of the ambiguous result of the last round of voting for the presidency. Although the NPN candidate, Shagari, had won a plurality of the vote, the runner-up candidate, Chief Awolowo, and his UPN insisted Shagari had not satisfied the second condition for direct election because he had won 25 percent of the vote in only twelve, and hence not quite two-thirds, of the nineteen states. The ruling of the electoral commission that he was elected because he had won 25 percent in "twelve and two-thirds states" (i.e., a quarter of the vote in twelve states and two-thirds of a quarter in a thirteenth) was bitterly challenged by the UPN, but upheld by the Supreme Court. The controversy engendered lasting political enmity between the NPN and UPN that was to heavily color subsequent political developments.[53]

This tension congealed rather quickly into competing political alliances. Building upon patterns of electoral cooperation, the nine elected governors from the UPN, GNPP, and PRP began meeting late in 1979 as a kind of coordinating committee for the political opposition to the NPN. The self-styled "nine progressive governors" denounced what they alleged was repeated abuse of constitutional authority by the NPN federal government. Initially, this was countered by two alliances on the NPN side. One gave the NPP, by formal agreement, a share of executive and legislative offices in return for its legislative cooperation. The other, a *de facto* arrangement, drew into the NPN's expanding and patronage-rich political network a growing number of NPP, GNP, and PRP federal legislators (mostly senators), who were constitutionally prohibited from crossing the carpet but who gave the president reliable and often pivotal legislative support.

The NPN-NPP accord never worked as intended. Disappointed with the lack of consultations and patronage, the NPP withheld legislative support on several critical issues. By mid-1981, the accord completely collapsed, and several (but not all) NPP ministers honored their party's call to withdraw from the government. Gradually, the NPP drew closer to the opposition alliance; later in 1981, the "nine progressive governors" became twelve when they were joined by the three NPP governors. These twelve states represented the full range of Nigeria's ethnic diversity: four predominantly Yoruba, two Igbo, two Hausa, and four ethnic minority states. Meanwhile, the informal alliance became more important for the NPN, and this also cut sharply across region and ethnicity: many of the tacit collaborators with the NPN came from the two Igbo states and from elsewhere outside the party's far Northern base. These developments raised the possibility of a historic realignment in which two new political parties, one more conservative and one more progressive, would contest for power on a national basis.

Despite the increasing polarization between the ruling NPN and the UPN-led opposition, there was some cause for hope in the fact that this cleavage was far less centered on ethnicity and region than was political conflict in the First Republic. As a result of not only expanding education and communication, but also the deep inequalities and contradictions engendered by the oil boom,[54] class and ideology were coming to play a more significant role in political conflict.[55] This was particularly so in the two states carried by the PRP in 1979—Kano and Kaduna, part of the core of the old emirate system. As these states became the focus of political conflict, crosscutting cleavage became increasingly salient.

Three interrelated crises developed along this line in 1980 and 1981. The first was a deep split in the leadership of the PRP, not unlike that in the Action Group in 1962, save that the stance of moderation and national political accommodation was espoused by PRP President Aminu Kano and his aides, while it was the two elected governors of Kano and Kaduna who favored confrontation and a more radical, ideological approach. The latter faction was the larger of the two, containing most of the PRP's youth support, founding intellectals, and legislative representatives. They supported the participation of the two governors in the meetings of the nine opposition governors, while the party establishment opposed it and ordered it to cease. Out of the mutual expulsions, two opposing party structures emerged, each claiming to be the genuine PRP. In a controversial decision early in 1981, FEDECO officially recognized the Aminu Kano faction, further eroding the legitimacy of that crucial regulatory body.

Aggravating this internal division was a deepening stalemate within Kaduna State between the radical PRP governor, Alhaji Abdulkadir Balarabe Musa, and the NPN-controlled legislature. This reflected the widening class cleavage in the far North, as a new generation of radical intellectuals and professionals sought to mobilize the peasantry in a struggle to dismantle the entire structure of traditional class privilege and power, based on land and the emirate system. Even though the legislature was controlled by his political and class opponents, Balarabe Musa plunged ahead with his socialist program, abolishing exploitative local taxes, investigating land transactions, and inaugurating a mass literacy campaign. When he persisted in the face of intense legislative opposition, the NPN majority in the State Assembly, with the support of the establishment PRP, impeached him and removed him from office in June 1981. With opposition forces around the country bitterly condemning the nakedly partisan action as undemocratic and unconstitutional, the legitimacy of the Second Republic suffered. At the same time, speculation grew about a four-party alliance to wrest power from the NPN in 1983, which was further encouraged by the rupture of the NPN-NPP accord two weeks after the impeachment.

Just a few weeks later, on 10 July 1981, conflict in Kano State erupted into violence on a massive scale, burning down much of the physical infrastructure of the Kano State government and killing the political adviser of the PRP governor, Mohammed Abubakar Rimi. The immediate precipitant of the riot was an offensive letter from Governor Rimi to the Emir of Kano implying his possible removal for acts of disrespect to the state government. But the systematic character of the destruction, and considerable other evidence, indicate that the riot was organized to embarrass and intimidate the PRP administration and derail its agenda for change. Supporters of the governor and the radical PRP were convinced that the NPN and the PRP were responsible—seeking to do by violence in Kano what could not be done by impeachment, given Governor Rimi's overwhelming support in the state legislature. The massive destruction had a traumatic and deeply polarizing effect on political conflict, heightening opposition fears that the NPN and its allies were not prepared to "play by the rules." In retaliation some months later, the radical PRP impeached the deputy governor of Kano, who had backed the PRP establishment faction.

The mere fact of conflict—even recurrent and intense conflict—between the ruling NPN and the congealing opposition forces was not in itself an ominous development for democracy. Nor did the occasional heavy-handedness of the NPN federal government represent a really grave threat to democracy: despite the opposition charges of "creeping fascism," basic freedoms remained largely intact and a number of controversial government actions were reversed or enjoined in the courts.[56] What was dangerous was the aura of desperation and intolerance that infused these conflicts and the violence that often attended them. These danger signals were noted with increasing alarm by the nation's press, which repeatedly condemned "the politics of bickerings, mudslingings,

. . . lies, deceit, vindictiveness, strife and intolerance that are again creeping back into the country's political scene."[57]

Of particular concern to independent observers and opinion makers was the growing trail of violence. Even in the first two years of the Second Republic (when the 1979 elections were history but well before the 1983 election campaign had begun), casualties mounted from the repeated clashes between thugs of rival politicians, parties, and party factions. In Borno State alone, the count had run to 39 dead, 99 injured and 376 arrested by May 1981.[58] As the 1983 elections approached, violent clashes proliferated between supporters and hired bullies not only of rival parties, but also of rival candidates for party nominations, especially within the NPN and the UPN. In many states, escalating political violence brought temporary bans on public meetings and assemblies. In some communities, thuggery reached a point where people became concerned for their physical safety. Reflecting the growing public cynicism, weariness, and disgust, the press repeatedly warned of the impending danger:

> We are tired of celebrating politics as a rite of death. . . . If politics cannot inspire recognition and respect for fundamental human rights, the credibility of the captains of our ship of state is certainly at stake. . . . We can ask to be saved from politicians and their notoriously bloody style of politicking.[59]

But political violence and intolerance were not the only sources of public disillusionment. From the very beginning, concern was also manifest over the opportunistic and self-interested behavior of the politicians, as reflected in the prolonged debate over legislative salaries and perquisites that dominated the initial deliberations of the National Assembly. Cynicism was bred by the constant stream of suspensions, expulsions and defections from the various political parties, which split not only the PRP, but later the GNPP and, to a lesser extent, the NPP as well. And within states controlled by each of the five parties, state assemblies became absorbed in bitter conflicts over leadership positions or threats to impeach the governor. The tremendous instability in party structures and identities suggested a general lack of substantive commitment among the politicians, whose main motivation was the personal quest for power and wealth.

Most of all, public disillusionment was bred by the unending succession of scandals and exposés concerning corruption in government. In 1983 alone, these included the mishandling of $2.5 billion in import licenses by the minister of commerce, the alleged acceptance by legislators of large bribes from a Swiss firm, the rumored apprehension in London of a Nigerian governor trying to smuggle millions of naira into Britain, and the revelation by a federal minister that the country was losing close to a billion dollars a year in payroll fraud. The issue was dramatized in January 1983 by a shocking fire that destroyed the 37-story headquarters of the Nigerian External Telecommunications in Lagos. The fire, condemned by a leading newspaper as "a calculated act, planned and executed to cover up corruption and embezzlement in the company,"[60] symbolized the rapaciousness of the ruling elite and visibly quickened the pace of political decay. Students took to the streets in several cities, carrying signs calling for the return of the military.[61]

Such incidents and revelations only reinforced the evidence in virtually every state and community of venality, insensitivity, failed promises, and callous waste: the skeletons of unfinished hospitals and schools, the treacherous craters in ungraded roads, the abandoned bulldozers, the rusting pumps beside the undrilled boreholes. These phenomena had spread malignantly since the oil boom, but seemed to assume a wholly new and reckless momentum with the return of the politicians.

The devastating effects of corruption at all levels of government—which, by most estimates, drained billions of dollars from the Nigerian economy during the Second Republic—were compounded by the precipitous decline in oil revenue, from a peak of $24 billon in 1980 to $10 billion in 1983. As corruption and mismanagement prevented any kind of disciplined adjustment, the economy was plunged into depression and mounting international indebtedness. Imports of industrial raw materials and basic commodities were severely disrupted, forcing the retrenchment of tens of thousands of industrial workers and sending the prices of staple foods and household necessities skyrocketing. Shortages were further aggravated by hoarding and profiteering (especially of rice) by the powerful and well-connected. Sucked dry of revenue by the corruption, mismanagement, and recession, state governments became unable to pay teachers and civil servants or to purchase drugs for hospitals, and many services (including schools) were shut down by strikes. Everywhere one turned in 1983, the economy seemed on the edge of collapse. Still the politicians and contractors continued to bribe, steal, smuggle, and speculate, accumulating vast illicit fortunes and displaying them lavishly in stunning disregard for public sensitivities. By its third anniversary, disenchantment with the Second Republic was acute, overt, and remarkably broad-based.[62]

As the rot deepened, so did the popular aspiration for change. Beyond the chimera of popular rebellion (of which some leftist intellectuals dreamed and in fear of which the paramilitary wing of the police was rapidly expanded), only two possible avenues were open: to change the incumbents in power in the five weeks of national and state elections due in August and September 1983 or to displace the political system altogether and bring back the only alternative, the military. A large proportion of the Nigerian electorate had come, by 1983, to favor the latter option. My own preelection survey in Kano State, the largest and most volatile in the country, showed a majority of the state's electorate and two-thirds of the voters in Kano city to favor a military government. Probably an even larger proportion of the intelligentsia and the military had come to favor the systemic change, out of deep skepticism that reform from within was possible. Nevertheless, this group waited to see if change could come by constitutional means, viewing the elections as the last chance for the Second Republic to redeem itself.[63]

From the beginning of the process, the elections were gravely troubled. The two-week registration of voters during August 1982 ended amid widespread protests of incompetence, partisanship, and fraud. When the preliminary register of voters was displayed in March 1983, with millions of names missing, mangled, or misplaced, opposition fears heightened. These hardened into outrage and disbelief with the release (just ten days before the election) of the final register, which showed not only an absurd total of 65 million voters (certainly in excess and possibly twice the legitimate total) but the largest increases in NPN states.[64]

Even more troubling was FEDECO's refusal to register a new and powerful opposition alliance that sought recognition as the Progressive Peoples Party (PPP). Bringing together the NPP and the largest factions of the PRP and the GNPP, the PPP seemed clearly to have satisfied the constitutional requirements. In fact, with control of seven state governments (as many as the NPN), the PPP was at least the second largest and broadest political formation in the country. But FEDECO even denied the NPP's request to change its name to PPP. Such rulings (hailed by NPN officials) badly tarnished the integrity of FEDECO and of the election.[65] Although the other party factions subsequently merged into the NPP, their Northern campaign was to suffer from widespread identification of the NPP as an "Igbo" and "Christian" party—a major theme of the NPN campaign in the Muslim North. Anxiety further mounted as the election neared and FEDECO proved unable to cope with the staggering logistical preparations for five successive elections with tens of millions of voters in nineteen states.

Biased and incompetent administration was not the opposition's only concern, however. With full control of federal patronage and an extraordinarily well-financed national political machine, the NPN was a formidable national contender, even with its sorry performance in office. Probably the only hope for an opposition victory in the presidential election lay in uniting behind a common ticket. But months of negotiations between the UPN and the NPP (and their PRP and GNPP allies) under the rubric of their Progressive Parties Alliance (PPA) failed to produce agreement. Neither of the surviving political giants—Azikiwe of the NPP and Awolowo of the UPN—would step down for the other. As they divided the opposition vote, the Shagari campaign was able to brand them in the North as champions of alien ethnic and religious interests. Still, as they campaigned relentlessly against the corruption and mismanagement of the NPN administration, the two gathered new support around the country, including Northern, Muslim states they had previously failed to penetrate in their long careers.

Although it was apparent that the division of the opposition might enable President Shagari's reelection with a weak plurality, changes were widely expected at other levels. In particular, a number of massively corrupt and negligent governors figured to be booted out. Certainly no one was prepared for the scale of the NPN landslide, and even the most hardened skeptics were astonished by the degree of electoral fraud. Ballots were obtained in advance and thumbprinted en masse. Electoral officials at every level were bribed to falsify returns. Whole communities were disenfranchised. Although all the parties engaged in malpractices, those by the NPN were the most systematic and brazen. In many Northern states, NPN agents collaborated with electoral officials and police to prevent opposition party agents from observing the polling and vote counting.[66] In the absence of this crucial check (guaranteed in the electoral law), unbelievable returns were reported and announced. Not only was President Shagari reelected decisively—and by incredible margins in some states—but the following week, the NPN increased its governorships from seven to thirteen, scoring shocking upsets in several opposition states while comfortably reelecting even its most venal incumbents. Subsequently, it was to increase its standing in the National Assembly from a small plurality to two-thirds, but, by then, the credibility of the elections had been shattered and most of the electorate was no longer bothering to vote.

Despite numerous appeals, few of the results were overturned in court. All but one of the most controversial gubernatorial outcomes were upheld. In that lone case, a defeated UPN governor was found to have been reelected by more than a million votes.

As they had in 1965, the people of the Yorbua states, where the rigging had been most outrageous, exploded in a frenzy of violent protest following the gubernatorial elections. More than 100 people were killed and $100 million in property destroyed.[67] Violent protest erupted in other states as well, claiming more than thirty lives. Both Awolowo and Azikiwe charged that the election was stolen and pronounced the country "on the brink of dictatorship." A pregnant calm returned by the inauguration on 1 October, after which the reelected president took some steps to upgrade his cabinet and launch tough new austerity measures. But by then it was too little and too late.

The Second Military Interregnum

Like the first coup eighteen years before, the coup that brought the military back to power on 31 December 1983 was widely welcomed and celebrated around the country.[68] The reasons for the coup were largely apparent in the declarations of the coupmakers: to redeem the country from "the grave economic predicament and uncertainty that an inept and corrupt leadership has imposed" on the country. The new head of state, Major General Muhammadu Buhari, added to the economic indictment the rigging of the 1983 elections. Observed a former army chief of staff, "Democracy had been in jeopardy for the past four years. It died with the elections. The army only buried it."[69] If there was any hesitance at all on the part of senior officers after the election, it was surely removed by the continued rapid deterioration of the economy (which saw food prices skyrocket between September and December) and the realization that militant junior officers, from whose ranks had come several unsuccessful coup attempts over the previous four years, could not indefinitely be kept at bay.

The government of General Buhari and his second-in-command, Major General Tunde Idiagbon, moved quickly to punish corruption and eliminate waste. More than 300 top officials in the civil service, police, and customs were dismissed or retired. Hundreds of former politicians were detained—including the president, vice-president, and prominent governors, ministers, and legislators. Huge sums of cash were seized from the homes of leading politicians, and the accounts of detained and fugitive politicians were frozen. Imports and travel allowances were slashed, black market currency operations raided, and government contracts placed under review.

These initial moves were highly popular, especially with the interest groups—students, trade unions, businessmen, professionals—that had been most disgusted with the civilian regime. Newspapers and intellectuals also supported the professed intention of the new regime to restore accountability to public life. But early on, it became apparent that the Buhari regime viewed accountability only in retrospective terms, and had no more intention than the Gowon regime of allowing itself to be scrutinized and questioned. With unprecedented harshness, arrogance, and impunity, the Buhari regime turned on the constituencies that had welcomed its arrival.

Political problems crystallized in March 1984 with the announcement of several controversial decrees. Decree Number 3 provided for military tribunals to try former public officials suspected of corruption and misconduct in office. The announcement of investigations and trials was popular, but protest arose over the severity of the penalties (a minimum of twenty one years in prison) and in particular over the procedures, which placed the "onus of proving" innocence on the accused, prohibited appeal of the verdict, and closed the proceedings to the public. These provisions led the Nigerian Bar Association to boycott the trials.

In the subsequent year, Nigerians were gratified to see the conviction and sentencing of some of the country's most corrupt politicians, including former governors from a majority of the nineteen states. Acquittals of some other officeholders suggested that the tribunals were capable of fair and independent verdicts. But concern mounted over the continued detention without trial of politicians who had not been formally charged. Consternation also grew over the dearth of convictions of the most powerful kingpins of the NPN, especially those from the party's Northern power base. Given, as well, the heavily Northern composition of the Supreme Military Council, the regime came increasingly to be derided as the "military wing of the NPN."

The disenchantment was fed not only by the narrow ethnic base of the regime, but also by its increasing repressiveness and arrogance, as manifested in its assault on the press. Decree Number 4 forbade the publication or broadcast of anything that was false in any particular or that might bring government officials into ridicule or disrepute. Under this and the internal security decree (Number 2) announced in January, several prominent journalists and editors were arrested. Although journalists continued to test the regime's narrowing limits, the decrees and arrests had a chilling effect on news coverage and editorial commentary and alienated the intelligentsia.

Under Decree Number 2, which provided for the detention of any citizen deemed a security risk, the Nigerian Security Organization (NSO) was given a virtual blank check to arrest and intimidate critics of the regime. Some of Nigeria's most forceful and popular social commentators were imprisoned without trial. Others fell silent in a growing climate of fear.

Politics in the sense of articulation and representation of interests did not cease. As it had previously during military rule, mobilization continued by a panoply of assertive and clamorous interest groups. Repression became the reflexive response of the regime. Public declarations were discouraged and obstructed, meetings were forcibly dispersed, and group leaders were detained by the NSO. In addition, prominent interest groups, including the National Association of Nigerian Students and the Nigerian Medical Association were banned. Toward the end, even public discussion of the country's political future was banned.

Public disaffection was intensified by the growing economic hardships, which followed from the severe austerity measures imposed by the Buhari government. Although these brought considerable progress toward balancing Nigeria's external payments, they came at the price of deepening recession. During 1984, an estimated 50,000 civil servants were retrenched, retired, or dismissed. Tens of thousands more industrial workers also lost their jobs as factories remained desperately short of imported raw materials and spare parts. Severe shortages pushed inflation to an annual rate of 40 percent. After three years of decline in GDP by an estimated 10 percent, the 1985 budget forecast only one percent growth, cutting imports again by more than half while assigning 44 percent of foreign exchange to debt service. At the same time, credible reports spread of renewed corruption in high places, including (incredibly, given its role in the demise of the Second Republic) the allocation of import licenses.

Escalating repression not only engendered deep resentment and bitterness among a people who cherished their personal freedom, it also dangerously cut the regime off from popular sentiments and relieved it of any need to be accountable for its conduct. In trying to impose a monolithic order on Nigeria's irrepressibly pluralistic society, this narrowly based dictatorship was risking a convulsion of enormous proportions. Rumors of failed coup attempts from the junior ranks circulated anew. Perhaps most fatally for the regime, its arrogance led it to ignore critical opinion and the imperative for consensus even within its senior military ranks.

What was coming to be viewed around the country as an inevitable military coup finally happened on 27 August 1985. It was led by army chief of staff Major General Ibrahim Babangida, who became the first of Nigeria'a six military rulers to take the title of president. From its initial statements and actions and the enthusiastic popular reception it received, the Babangida coup appeared to mark a decisive rejection of the previous authoritarian trend. In his maiden address to the nation, Babangida announced an immediate review of the status of political detainees and the repeal of Decree Number 4, vowing, "We do not intend to lead a country where individuals are under the fear of expressing themselves."[70] Shortly thereafter, all journalists in detention and dozens of politicians who had not been charged or tried were released, many to heroes' welcomes. The detention centers of the NSO were exposed to public view, and a thorough probe and restructuring of the dreaded organization was undertaken. Forceful and opinionated civilians were chosen to head crucial cabinet ministries, and the ruling military council was reorganized to disperse power. Babangida also promised to present a program of political transition, beginning with the revitalization of local government.

In perhaps his most extraordinary move, the new military president opened the most sensitive and controversial policy question facing his administration—whether to take a loan from the IMF—to a vigorous public debate. Negotiations with the IMF for a $2.5 billion, three-year adjustment loan had been dragging on since well before the December 1983 coup; and upon assuming office, Babangida indicated his intention to complete an IMF agreement. On strictly economic grounds, the case for the loan seemed urgent and compelling. With foreign debt having swollen further to $22 billion and oil prices and production still sagging, the country was desperately in need of the foreign exchange that would come from the IMF loan, and from other international loans and credits that an IMF agreement would unlock. Moreover, the austerity measures attached to the loan—a steep devaluation of the currency (by more than half), trade liberalization, and substantial cuts in petroleum and other consumer subsidies—enjoyed strong support from economists in and outside the country.

But the politics of the IMF loan simply would not fly. The debate brought forth a tidal wave of popular, intellectual, and interest group opposition to the loan, not only because of the harshness of the policy measures and the diminution of national sovereignty it would imply, but also because of widespread public cynicism that such a large new infusion of cash would be managed responsibly. Babangida therefore set aside his original plans and rejected the IMF loan. Nevertheless, he proceeded to implement the IMF's harsh austerity prescriptions and to reap some of the benefit not only from the consequent economic adjustments, but also from the increased receptivity of other multilateral and private international lenders. A radical new phase of economic adjustment was thus inaugurated.

Under Babangida's ambitious and courageous program, the Nigerian economy finally began to make the adjustments long considered essential if the country is ever to build a basis for self-sustaining economic growth. Moreover, these painful changes were accepted with surprising understanding and farsightedness by the population and showed signs of improving the country's economic performance (see the last section of this chapter). But as President Bab' ngida won support for his economic policies, his commitment to liberal and accountable government became increasingly tarnished. On the issue of accountability, the process of trying and punishing the corrupt conduct of the former politicians ground to a halt. Some of this was in a liberal, consitutional spirit: in response to recommendations of two judicial tribunals appointed in late 1985, the regime reduced the sentences of more than fifty convicted former officeholders and acquitted twelve completely. Forty-nine were banned for life from seeking public office, including the former president and vice-president when, several months later (in July 1986), they were finally released from detention. At that time, 100 other politicians were also cleared of all charges, some to the dismay of a skeptical press and public, while 800 were ordered to be tried for corruption. One year later, nothing had come of these new corruption trials, and there was growing skepticism that they would ever be held.

More disturbingly, there were growing indications of a reassertion of the repressive climate that prevailed under Buhari and Idiagbon. Many believe the principle of accountability was unjustly distorted when President Babangida, in mid-1986, banned *all* of the former politicians from future political involvement for a period of ten years.[71] Many groups also objected to the decision—rescinded under pressure from the bar and the press—to extend from three months to six the length of time a person could be detained without trial (for reasons of "state security") under Decree Number 2, which was never repealed.

Two events registered particular damage to the regime's liberal image. On 23 May 1986, police went on a rampage at Ahmadu Bello University in Zaria, killing several students (perhaps over twenty) and injuring many more. The news of this indiscriminate shooting, by police who had been summoned in response to peaceful student protests, provoked widespread popular outrage and sympathy demonstrations on other campuses, leading to further confrontation and violence.[72] The government's response over subsequent months was to quash a planned sympathy demonstration by the Nigerian Labour Congress and detain its leaders, to dissolve all student unions for the remainder of the academic year, and to reject its own commission's recommendation that police not be sent to campuses in the future with lethal weapons.

In perhaps the most shocking development to date under military rule, one of Nigeria's most talented, admired, and fearlessly independent journalists, Dele Giwa, was assassinated by a parcel bomb in October 1986. Giwa was the founding editor-in-chief of the country's leading weekly news magazine, *Newswatch,* which had become widely celebrated for its biting commentaries and aggressive investigative reporting. Just before his death, Giwa had been questioned intensely by the deputy director of the new State Security Service, who charged the liberal and nonviolent Giwa with plotting to import arms and foment a socialist revolution. These preposterous charges combined with a wealth of other circumstantial evidence to fix public suspicion on the state's security apparatus as the party responsible for Giwa's murder.[73] This suspicion was deepened by the government's refusal to launch an independent investigation and the failure of the police, nine month later, to record any progress. All of this again cast a chilling shadow over the Nigerian press. In April 1987, this shadow lengthened when the government banned *Newswatch* for six months after it published an extensive analysis of the leaked report of the political bureau Babangida had appointed to consider the country's constitutional future. The ban was strenuously condemned by the Nigerian Bar Association, the Association of Nigerian Authors, the Nigerian Union of Journalists, and numerous other groups.[74]

The continuing tension with the press and popular interest groups reflects perhaps a growing strength of the authoritarian impulse in Nigeria. It appears that a number of key military and security officials remain apprehensive about any liberalization, and particularly the mobilization by trade union, student, and other popular organizations that it might unleash. These officials would prefer to see such interest groups tightly controlled and licensed by the state through some kind of authoritarian corporatist arrangement. They share with some intellectuals and bureaucrats a deep distrust and dislike for the turmoil and divisiveness of a multiparty system. They value order and stability over freedom, and would probably wish to institutionalize some kind of "bureaucratic-authoritarian" regime along the lines of the South American regimes of the 1970s.[75]

A Summary Assessment of the Nigerian Experience

Twice in Nigeria's twenty-five years of independence, elaborate democratic constitutions have been overthrown by the military after several years of unsuccessful and unpopular operation. In this sense, democracy in Nigeria has failed. But most Nigerians are not inclined to accept this failure as inevitable or enduring. Although the disgust with politicians was still palpable four years after the demise of the Second Republic, most Nigerians, especially the educated, want their country eventually to return to some form of civilian, democratic government. Moreover, authoritarian rule has been more fundamentally unsuccessful in Nigeria, because it has been rejected not only in its actual performance, but in its moral and political logic. Somewhat lost in the drama of a quarter century of political turmoil has been the gradual emergence of an increasingly broad and sophisticated democratic infrastructure, including a vibrant and maturing press, an extensive university system, a rich array of independent business and professional associations, and a judiciary with some significant autonomy. These groups and institutions constitute a powerful constituency demanding the preservation of basic freedoms. Together with the nation's complex ethnic divisions, this growing social pluralism makes the country, in a practical sense, very difficult to govern by authoritarian means. For all these reasons, Nigeria retains considerable promise for democratic success if the structural roots of the previous failures can be identified and altered.

• ANALYSIS OF THE HISTORICAL DEVELOPMENTS •

We seek now to explain Nigeria's political development over its quarter century of independence. Specifically, why did the two attempts at democratic government fail, and why did authoritarian rule not implant itself as an alternative? We begin with the failure of the First Republic.

Why the First Republic Failed

The proximate causes of the downfall of the First Republic were manifest in the statements of the coupmakers and have been widely acknowledged by students and observers of that experience. They included first, the succession of intense political crises, the deepening polarization, the incessant political instability and strife; second, related to this, the style and tone of political behavior and conflict, the violence, repression, and failure to play by the rules of the game; and, finally, the "ten wasted years of planlessness, incompetence, inefficiency, gross abuse of office, corruption," and resulting lack of economic development.[76] These phenomena progressively destroyed the legitimacy of the republic.

It is tempting to attribute this decay and failure to an undemocratic *political culture,* lacking appreciation for "the conventions or rules on which the operation of western democratic forms depend."[77] To be sure, most Nigerian politicians manifested a weak commitment to democratic values and behavioral styles, as witnessed in the vituperation, intolerance, repression, violence, and fraud characteristic of electoral politics. But political values were far from uniformly undemocratic. Many Nigerian political leaders manifested a considerable pride in the democratic system and a sincere desire to make it work. A number of them had studied in Britain or the United States and had acquired a sophisticated intellectual and moral commitment to democracy. Moreover, the traditional political practices and values of many Nigerian peoples had significant democratic features. But values and beliefs do not wholly determine behavior. In Nigeria, democratic currents in the political culture were overrun by imperatives in the social structure. Political culture, in itself, cannot explain why political competition became a kind of warfare.

The most common conception is that the First Republic failed because of *ethnic conflict,* and, on the surface, this is indisputable. But this, again, can be a superficial and misleading explanation in itself. Certainly there were deep cultural divisions, and these were heightened by the centralized structure of ethnicity in Nigeria. But it was hardly inevitable that ethnic groups would contend in mortal political combat. This, too, must be viewed as in intervening variable, resulting from the interaction of ethnicity with social and political structures. Even the stimulus to ethnic conflict generated by the competitive pressures of modernization[78] provides only a very partial understanding of why ethnicity became so heavily politicized. Here we must make reference to three other factors: the establishment of political party competition in the absence of other crosscutting cleavages; the role of the federal structure in reifying the major, tripartite ethnic cleavage and heightening ethnic insecurity in general; and the role of the class structure in encouraging "tribalism"—the deliberate mobilization of ethnic suspicion, fear, jealousy, and hostility.

By any reckoning, the peculiar *federal structure* heavily contributed to the failure of the First Republic. Indeed, one may question the very use of the term "federal" for a system in which one region was larger and more populous— hence more powerful—than all the others combined. The additional fact that the Southern regions had huge advantages in their levels of technologial and educational development made for an "acute contradiction" prone to "political upheaval."[79] Further destabilizing was the authoritarian social structure of the Northern emirates, which the federal structure was pivotal in preserving. The polarization and bitterness of national politics owed significantly to the Northern aristocracy's determination to control the federal government at all costs not only to secure regional and ethnic interests, but also to preserve its class dominance against the mobilization of radical commoners and the winds of change whipping up from the South.[80]

Polarization was also advanced by the small number of constituent units in the federal system, enabling the tripolar structure to collapse into a bipolar struggle. That ethnic minorities lacked the security of their own regions added to the persistent tension. And with so few regions, each was compelled to exploit the internal conflicts of the others. There were simply too few regions to permit the federal system effectively to decentralize conflict and to insulate the politics of the periphery from the politics of the center.

Finally, the federal structure heavily contributed to one of the most powerful structural problems of the First Republic, the close *coincidence of major cleavages:* region, ethnicity, and party. Instead of complicating and crosscutting the centralized character of the ethnic structure, the federal structure heightened it by making the Yoruba, the Igbo, and the Hausa-Fulani, in effect, governmental as well as ethnic categories. This made the organization of political parties along this divide virtually inevitable. When every election and political conflict became a struggle for supremacy not just between parties but between ethnic groups and regions as well, everything was at stake and no one could afford to lose.

The polarizing effect of coinciding cleavages was compounded by the *cumulative pattern of conflict* it helped to produce. Until independence, some relief was provided by the shifting of alignments over time in a three-player game. But with the destruction of the Action Group in 1962-1963, conflict was reduced to a running struggle between the NPC and its Southern antagonists, with the Northern party prevailing decisively over the AG in 1962, over the NCNC in the census crisis, and over the combined forces of Southern progressives in the 1964 and 1965 elections. This pattern, constituted the maximum formula for polarization: each successive conflict involved the same cumulative line of cleavage, the same configuration of actors, and the same predictable outcome. Given that the triumphant party lacked any support in half the country, and was also feared and hated in parts of the other half, it is not surprising that it was ultimately toppled through a wholly different process.

The most basic cause of the failure of the First Republic had to do with the *structures of class and state*. Nigerian society in this era was a prime example of Richard Sklar's argument that, in the emergent states of Africa, "dominant class formation is a consequence of the exercise of power."[81] Colonial rule left in place a modern state that dwarfed all other organized elements of the economy and society. State control was firmly established over the greatest source of cash revenue in the country, cash crop agriculture, and the greatest source to be—mineral mining.[82] In addition, state monopolies were established in many other sectors, private indigenous enterprise was discouraged, and the parastatal sector was rapidly expanded.[83] In the classic sense of a class of autonomous capitalist producers, there really was no native bourgeoisie. By 1964, 54 percent of all wage earners were employed by some level of government, and most of the rest (38 percent) were employed by foreign capital.[84] Moreover, with the spread of Western education, media, and consumer goods, colonial rule fostered the rapid growth of materialist values.

In the South, material wealth became the mark of what Sklar termed the "new and rising class." Government power became the primary means for individuals to accumulate wealth and enter the rising class, and for the ruling parties to weld diverse profesional, business, and traditional elites into a new dominant class.[85] In the Northern emirates, state power became the indispensable instrument for preserving class domination by reconstituting it on a modern foundation and broadening it through the incorporation of commercial and ethnic minority elites.[86]

The brutality and intolerance of political conflict followed from the sweeping nature of the stakes in controlling state power. Political and bureaucratic offices offered not only high social status and handsome salaries and perquisites,[87] but also vast opportunities for accumulation through bribery, embezzlement, favoritism, and other types of corruption.[88] Moreover, given the scarcity of private resources and opportunities, those who did not hold state office heavily depended on those who did. Political office could deliver or block the licenses, contracts, and public loan and investment funds that could make a new enterprise or a quick fortune, as well as the scholarships, government jobs, and military commissions that could quickly lift an individual from poverty into the middle class. By the same token, the loss of political office or access threatened an abrupt plunge in socioeconomic status. Few Nigerian politicians (or their clients) had alternative careers that could offer anything like the material and status rewards of state power. At the level of the group, state power was just as indispensable to material advancement. For communities, both rural and urban, it was the source of schools, roads, clinics, pipe-borne water, electricity, factories, markets, and almost every other dimension of material progress. For cultural groups, it could be the primary threat to or the primary guarantor of their cultural integrity.

Because of this enormous premium on political power, the competition for state control became a desperate, violent, zero-sum struggle. To lose political power was to lose access to virtually everything that mattered. Hence, political actors—even those committed in principle to democracy—were willing to use any means necessary in order to acquire power. This breakdown of constitutional norms, in the context of the high premium on state control, in turn generated a high level of political anxiety—"the fear of the consequences of not being in control of the government, associated with a profound distrust of political opponents."[89] In these circumstances, it was exceedingly difficult for elite accommodation and compromise to bridge the polarization and attenuate the bitterness of political conflict because these were so deeply rooted in the relationship between state and society.

This relationship is also crucial to understanding the politicization of ethnic conflict. Although each ethnic group had a real cultural and psychological stake in its own communal identity and progress, "tribalism" was not a primordial force. Rather it was generated "by the new men of power in furtherance of their" class interests.[90] These rising and traditional class elements had to control the democratic state. To do this, they had to win elections, and in a largely illiterate, multiethnic society, with relatively scant crosscutting solidarities or national ties, no electoral strategy seemed more assured of success than the manipulation of ethnic pride, jealousy, and prejudice. As they appealed relentlessly to ethnic consciousness, the politicians inflamed group suspicion and fear to the point where ethnic mobilization assumed an explosive momentum of its own.

In two other senses as well, tribalism was significantly a product of the class structure. First, it functioned as a "mask for class privilege."[91] By focusing politics on ethnic competition for state resources and by distributing patronage to their ethnic communities, politicians diverted attention from their own class-action and precluded effective class-based mobilization against it. Second, in mobilizing mass ethnic bases, tribalism became an instrument of competition within the emerging dominant class for the limited spoils of the developing state.

The extreme dependence of class formation on a swollen state is also crucial to understanding the escalating corruption that helped to delegitimate the First Republic. Even with the princely official salaries and perquisites, the accumulation of truly sizable wealth required the illicit manipulation of political resources. Moreover, as politics became organized into hierarchical networks of patrons and clients, in the absence of effective political institutions, corruption was necessary to maintain and extend the proliferating chains of clientage.[92]

Why the Second Republic Failed

Of the two structural causes underlying the failure of the First Republic, one was understood and rectified in the subsequent period of military rule, while the other was not. By creating first twelve states in the 1967 and then nineteen in 1975, the military governments dramatically reorganized the structural imperatives toward ethnic polarization. Innovations in the 1979 constitution further encouraged the development of crosscutting political cleavages. But the problem of statism and its corollary phenomena—corruption, clientelism, and waste—only grew worse during military rule. In this failure to alter the relationship between the state and society lies the primary reason for the failure of the Second Republic.

Despite the widespread disillusionment over that second democratic failure, it is important to appreciate the significant political progress that was achieved. Although ethnicity remained the single most important basis for political identification and alignment, the identity between party and ethnicity was perceptibly weaker in the Second Republic, and was beginning to decompose in historic ways when the system unraveled in 1983.[93] In this sense, the revisions in the 1979 constitution forbidding ethnic political parties and requiring visible evidence of crosscutting support as a condition for party registration must be credited with some real success. In particular, the much more complicated federal system made a profound difference. Although the Yoruba and Igbo states tended to vote as a block in 1979, the NPN made visible inroads there in subsequent years. In the North, the Hausa-Fulani heartland became a major political battleground, with the NPN and PRP splitting control of the four key states in 1979. As had been envisioned, the ethnic minority states became the swing factor in national politics (and a powerful pressure group within the NPN), and their political alignment was the most fluid and hotly contested. And, on some issues, such as revenue allocation—where the oil states lined up against the oilless states—the nineteen-state system did generate crosscutting cleavage.

It is a matter of immense significance that the kind of ethnic and regional polarization that savaged the First Republic did not emerge in the Second Republic. There was ethnic mobilization. There were charges of "big tribe chauvinism." There was North-South tension. There were all the traditional ethnic rivalries and hostilities. In fact, ethnicity remained the most salient political clevage. But it was much more fluid and decentralized. *National* political conflict did not polarize around ethnic divisions. Rather, the experience of the Second Republic demonstrated that in a democracy, deep cultural divisions, even a centralized ethnic structure, do not inevitably produce mass ethnic conflict. Cultural complexity can be managed and centrifugal forces contained by effective political structures.

And yet, politics were not significantly less violent, vituperative, and chaotic in the Second Republic than they had been in the First Republic. This was because the relationship between the state and the class structure had not changed. State power remained the primary locus of national wealth, the chief route of access to the resources and opportunities of class formation. If the articulation of the private sector since 1966 opened possibilities for upward mobility outside the state that had not existed in the First Republic, so the petroleum boom opened possibilities for accumulation of wealth in office that could not have been imagined then. In fact, these possibilities were so fantastic that they brought an important change in the character of economic life, what Sayre Schatz has described as a shift from "nurture capitalism" to "pirate capitalism." "For the most vigorous, capable, resourceful, well-connected and 'lucky' entrepreneurs (including politicians, civil servants, and army officers), productive economic activity . . . has faded in appeal. Access to, and manipulation of, the government-spending process has become the golden gateway to fortune."[94] In other words, power has replaced effort as the basis of social reward. Under such circumstances, "a desperate struggle to win control of state power ensues since this control means for all practical purposes being all powerful and owning everything. Politics becomes warfare, a matter of life and death."[95] From this continuing enormous premium on political power followed the familiar consequences of political chaos, intolerance, and instability: the impeachments, decampments, expulsions, thuggery, rioting, arson, and massive electoral fraud that did so much to drain the Second Republic of the considerable legitimacy with which it began.

Perhaps no less than the above, political corruption also served to delegitimate and destroy the Second Republic. The continuing expansion of the state and the paucity of private economic opportunities has steered the entrepreneurial and acquisitive spirit into all kinds of political corruption. The heavily clientelistic character of party politics has further served to increase the spread of corruption during civilian rule. But significant responsibility must also be attributed to the failure of the legal system to restrain corrupt conduct in office. Corruption in Nigeria has offered not only immense opportunities for reward, but virtually no risk of sanctions.

The makers of the 1979 constitution understood that the conduct of public officers must be carefully circumscribed, monitored, and, if necessary, punished in order to reduce corruption. That is why the constitution contained a strict code of conduct and an elaborate enforcement machinery. The code required every public officer to declare all his assets at regular intervals to the Code of Conduct Bureau, which was empowered to monitor compliance and refer charges to the Code of Conduct Tribunal. The latter, a quasi-judicial body, had the authority to impose serious penalties on offenders, including vacation of office, seizure of assets, and disqualification from public office for ten years. But neither of these bodies ever worked as intended, because the National Assembly, upon which the constitution made their activation and supervision dependent, buried the enabling legislation. Without this legislation, the bureau was unable to hire any permanent officers, or to investigate suspicions and complaints. In fact, most public officials went several years without declaring their assets. The bureau never really functioned. The tribunal never sat.

This was indicative of a fundamental flaw in the 1979 constitution. Crucial regulatory functions, on which the legitimacy of the Second Republic heavily depended, were left open to manipulation, sabotage, and abuse by the politicians. As a result, other sensitive regulatory institutions—the Federal Electoral Commission, the police, and, to some extent, even the judiciary—behaved or were perceived to behave as partisan instruments of the ruling party. The problem is unlikely to be resolved by the traditional checks and balances between the three branches of government. The integrity of the legislature and executive is so suspect, and the pressures for abuse so powerful, that some wholly new type of institutional check is necessary (see this chapter's last section).

Other factors also contributed to the demise of the Second Republic. A significant problem was the chaotic party system. The military architects of the transition to civilian rule appear to have drawn precisely the wrong lesson from the failure of the First Republic. Suspicious and mistrustful of party politics, they delayed the lifting of the ban on political parties as long as possible, after the Constitutional Drafting Committee passed on Murtala Muhammed's invitation to "feel free to recommend . . . some means by which Government can be formed without the involvement of Political Parties."[96] With so little time for new parties to develop coherent identities, broad-based constituencies, and fresh leaderships, it was highly likely that the old political divisions and leaders and anxieties would resurface in a dominant role.

The character of political leadership was also a problem. It would have been difficult even for the strongest and most heroic leaders to contain the political violence and corruption generated by the high structural premium on state power. But President Shagari never put that propositon to a test. A weak leader prone to governing by consensus, he was unable to control the venal tendencies of his party machinery and closest advisers. The meetings of his cabinet and party councils became grand bazaars where the resources of the state were put up for auction. Hence, although Shagari was not a polarizing leader, and was more inclined than most to seek some reconciliation of differences, he could not deliver effective and accountable government. Most of the elected political leaders were corrupt, and organized or at least condoned the political violence. But it is misleading to attribute these fatal excesses of the Second Republic to the failings of its political leaders. It is doubtful that a new generation of political leaders will behave differently in a Third Republic unless the relationship between state and society is altered.

Similarly, it would be simplistic to blame the failure of the Second Republic on the economic depression brought on by the collapse of the world oil market. Even in the best of circumstances, this would have sorely strained an emergent democratic system. But the economy could have adjusted to this reality—painfully, but without the degree of dislocation and consumer hardship that occurred—if governmental capacity and resources had not been so relentlessly

drained by corruption. With honest and effective government that was otherwise considered legitimate, the Second Republic could probably have survived
this difficult period of adjustment. On the other hand, even with continuing economic boom, it would probably have been brought down by the corruption, mismanagement, deepening inequality, and political instability.

Why Authoritarian Rule Has Not Survived

To the extent that political culture has autonomous explanatory value for
Nigeria's political development, it better accounts for the failure of authoritarianism than the failure of democracy. Nigerians value personal freedom;
with the expansion of education, the mass media, and political participation in
the past quarter century, this commitment has heightened. Because of the relatively liberal character of British colonial rule, a vigorous press, and a vibrant
associational life were able to develop with modernization, independent of state
control. By the time of the first military interregnum, these autonomous interest
groups and associations had established sufficiently broad constituencies and
deep roots so that they could not have been eliminated without a level of violent
repression that no Nigerian military regime—even that of Buhari and Idiagbon—has dared attempt. In this sense, the Nigerian case supports the classic
pluralist argument that autonomous intermediate groups "provide the basis for
the limitation of state power" and make society less "likely to be dominated by
a centralized power apparatus."[97]

Similarly, Nigeria's volatile ethnic and religious diversity has made it difficult to institutionalize authoritarian rule. It is very difficult to manage this
complex cultural cleavage by authoritarian means because of the tendency for
various groups to view any regime, and particularly a nonparticipatory one, as
weighted against them. When there are institutional means for rotating national
leaders, changing the composition of the federal government, and electing local
and state leaders and representatives, each group can develop some degree of
security and retain some hope of improving its position. But in an authoritarian
regime, the ethnic identity of the few top leaders assumes exaggerated importance, and the distribution of power and resources takes on an aura of perma-
nence, which makes it much more fundamentally threatening to groups that feel
excluded or inadequately included. Thus, it is under authoritarian rule that centrifugal tendencies are most likely to be unleashed. The floating of proposals for
confederation during the Buhari regime by prominent Yoruba and Igbo leaders
was only the most recent demonstration of this danger.

Because of these various currents of social complexity, authoritarian rule
could probably only endure if it pursued some strategy of institutionalization—
most likely through the mechanism of a single party—that evolved some means
both for the stable division of resources and for the regular rotation of leadership
positions (among not only individuals but ethnic groups), and that provided
some outlet for popular participation, criticism, and debate. Independent of

whether such a system could withstand Nigeria's pluralist pressures and liberal aspirations (even if it governed more effectively), it would require an effort of political institution-building perhaps no less demanding than the reconstruction of a liberal democratic system. No Nigerian military regime has yet seriously contemplated such a task.

It is revealing of the nature of the society and its political culture that every Nigerian military regime has committed itself, at least verbally, to an eventual return to civilian rule, and no regime that has seemed to betray this democratic commitment has been able to survive. Although military rule has been the norm in Nigeria—having governed for almost two-thirds of the time since independence—it continues to be viewed as an aberration or correction, a prelude to something else. When it has lingered too long or governed too harshly, the institutional reputation and integrity of the armed forces have begun to suffer serious damage, and shrewder officers have intervened to rescue them.

· THEORETICAL CONCLUSIONS ·

From the preceding analysis, *the relationship between the economy and the state* and the resulting *character of class formation* constitute the most basic reason for the failure of democracy in Nigeria and the most important obstacle to its future success. In part, this supports the proposition that stable democracy is associated with an autonomous, indigenous bourgeoisie, and inversely associated with extensive state control over the economy. But the logic of this association is not simply that economic and political pluralism tend to go together or that a hegemonic state is inherently undemocratic. Even more so, it is that democracy requires moderation and restraint. It demands not only that people care about political competition, but also that they not care too much, that their emotional and tangible stake in its outcome not be so great that they cannot contemplate defeat. In Nigeria, and throughout much of Africa, the swollen state has turned politics into a zero-sum game in which everything of value is at stake in an electon, and hence candidates, communities, and parties feel compelled to win at any cost.

This is not to say that the commonly presumed bane of democracy in Africa—*ethnic conflict*—is not a crucial variable in the Nigerian case. But the difference between the experiences of the First and Second Republics highlights the importance of the *federalism* in managing deep ethnic divisions. A structure that ensures some degree of group autonomy and security while crosscutting major ethnic solidarities can do much to prevent the polarization of politics around ethnicity. A flawed federal structure or unitary system can do much to generate it. Similarly, electoral regulations and structures can either reinforce or complicate, and so gradually soften, ethnic solidarities. Moreover, if ethnic conflict does degenerate into mass violence and civil war, this tragedy can serve as a learning experience, pressing ethnic elites toward structures and styles of accommodation and intergroup cooperation. This helps to explain the concern for ethnic balancing in the structures and institutions of the Second Republic and the efforts to make it work. Thus, the Nigerian case indicates that democracy in developing countries is not incompatible with even deep and complex ethnic divisions. The effect of ethnicity on democracy is mediated by other variables.

Political culture was also found to be a significant intervening variable. The style of political behavior, the willingness to play by the rules of the democratic game, heavily affects the performance of the constitutional system and the popular perception of its legitimacy. Values, beliefs, and cultural traditions all influence behavior but their importance should not be overstated. The degree to which political actors are inclined toward tolerance, compromise, moderation, and restraint is also powerfully affected by structural inducements and constraints. Values and beliefs appear to have had greater independent influence in precluding the institutionalization of authoritarian rule in Nigeria and pressuring for renewal of democratic government.

Other features of the institutional landscape have helped sustain the commitment to democracy, even though they have not succeeded in sustaining its actual practice. The role of the *judiciary* has been somewhat positive, although not nearly as much as it could be potentially. During the Second Republic, several notable judicial decisions served to limit the power and reverse arbitrary actions of the NPN government, and so reduced the fear of opposition forces that federal power would be massively abused to undermine and eliminate them. This points to the crucial role of an independent judiciary in developing a system of mutual security between competing parties. Unfortunately, the judiciary performed much less impressively in the more urgent test of the 1983 elections, failing to overturn many patently fraudulent election outcomes. The scale of the rigging was probably too great for the judiciary to play an effective balancing role, but part of the problem lies in the degree to which the corruption and inefficiency of a statist society have infected all public institutions, including the judiciary. This infection has been made more acute by the judiciary's lack of adequate autonomy from the executive and legislative branches. The latter two control not only the appointment and number of judicial personnel, but also the funding of the judiciary. Since independence, the extreme financial dependence of the judiciary on the other two branches, and its inadequate salaries, facilities, and staff, have been important causes of its weakness and vulnerability.[98]

A maturing and pluralistic *press* has been an important democratic force in Nigeria. The press played a largely positive role during the Second Republic, both in relentlessly exposing corruption, mismanagement, and abuse of power, and in warning, forcefully and repeatedly, of the dangers of political violence, intolerance, and misconduct. Unfortunately, the politicians blithely ignored these warnings. These positive contributions were counterbalanced but not outweighed by some continuing tendency toward irresponsible sensationalism and the proclivity of some newspapers, especially those owned by state governments, to reflect and accentuate the polarization of partisan loyalties. More effectively, but at greater risk to its practictioners, the press has kept alive the commitment to democracy and has sought to establish some kind of accountability during periods of authoritarian rule. Today, Nigeria has more than twenty daily newspapers. Two of the largest are controlled by the federal government, but there are four privately owned dailies with wide readerships, and several other private newspapers compete at the state level with those owned by the state governments. Since the fall of the Second Republic, several privately owned weekly news magazines have also begun to have an important impact on an information-hungry and opinion-rich public. Increasingly, the most popular and dynamic publications are in private hands. Despite the constitutional monopoly by federal and state governments over radio and television, this enormous pluralism in the print media is one of the most favorable conditions for democracy.

Similarly, the prospects for democracy in Nigeria are strengthened by the increasing pluralism of *associational life*. Although they have not been immune from politicizing pressures, professional and other interest groups, along with more loosely organized networks of intellectuals and opinion leaders, have constituted a significant source of pressure for democratic and accountable government. During periods of authoritarian rule, many of these groups have bravely asserted their interests in the face of intimidating power and sometimes coercive repression. Prominent on this organizational landscape have been the Nigerian Bar Association, the Nigerian Medical Association, the Nigerian Labour Congress, the Nigerian Chamber of Commerce, the Academic Staff Union of Universities, the National Association of Nigerian Students, the Nigerian Union of Journalists, and women's organizations such as Women in Nigeria and the National Organization of Nigerian Women Societies. At the local level, a growing number of interest groups abounds, both as constituent units of the above and as independent entities. Most of these are independent of state control, but even those, such as the trade unions, sanctioned by it have dared to confront it on occasion.

As should be expected, the *political party system* has played a significant role in the Nigerian experience with democracy. The coincidence of party cleavage with region and ethnicity produced destructive political polarization in the First Republic, while the banning of ethnic political parties and requirements for broadly based party organizations were one of the more hopeful developments of the Second Republic. The Nigerian case strongly supports the proposition that parties should crosscut other major cleavages unless a full-blown consociational strategy is attempted.[99] It is neutral with respect to the ideal number of political parties since it has never had more than a few significant ones, and the problem with them has been not their number but their nature. Political parties have been extremely shallow, fragile, and weak. Lacking the coherence, complexity, autonomy, and adaptability that are the mark of institutionalization, they have behaved as little more than associations of expedience for the capture of power.[100] Their incessant divisions, crises, defections, and recombinations have heightened popular cynicism about the political process.

Historical developments, in particular the *colonial legacy*, have also had important effects on Nigeria's experience with democracy. This was particularly so for the First Republic, in which the inherited federal system figured so negatively. The British could also be faulted for waiting so long to begin developing a modern democratic system, as a result of which the whole process of party development and political learning was compressed into a single decade. But while the colonial legacy still weighs heavily in some senses, such as the continued state dominance over the economy, it has been overcome in others; after a quarter century of independence, the utility of attributing political failures to colonial legacies becomes increasingly dubious. Moreover, it should not be forgotten that the commitment to democracy and individual liberties has been enriched by contact with Britain and other Western nations. While it had its authoritarian and exploitative side, British colonial rule also witnessed the development of the first modern newspapers, interest groups, trade unions, and political parties in Nigeria, and this liberal side of the colonial experience may, in the long run, constitute the more important legacy.

Although the analysis here has centered on socioeconomic and political structures, individuals cannot be absolved of historical responsibility for their actions. The repeated failure of democracy in Nigeria must be attributed, in part, to the choices and behavior of *political leaders*. Nigerian political leaders have been, for the most part, lacking in integrity and commitment to the democratic system. Their behavior has tended to be highly shortsighted and self-interested. Sadly, there have been few political leaders able to rise above the pressures and temptations of the system. But analytically, this behavior cannot be divorced from social structure. As long as the premium on political power in Nigeria remains so high, it would be unrealistic—and dangerous—to expect that a generation of more committed democratic leaders will emerge.

Development performance has also affected democracy in Nigeria, as theories of democracy would predict. A primary reason why democracy has twice lost legitimacy and been overthrown is because it has not delivered the goods. Economic growth sagged during both democratic experiences, with no plan or promise of development progress. By the time of the Second Republic, the agricultural sector (which continued to employ more than half the labor force) had precipitously declined, even in real terms,[101] and economic growth had become almost entirely dependent on the isolated stimulus of oil, through government spending. It was the double misfortune of the Second Republic to have inherited such an "inert economy,"[102] along with all of the other distortions of the oil boom, and to have been the victim of falling global demand for oil in 1981. But the federal government did nothing effective to restructure the inert economy or to cushion, manage, and reverse the economic slide. Rather, governments at every level deepened the depression through massive corruption, gross mismanagement, and callous indifference and waste. To a lesser extent, these phenomena also sapped development potential in the First Republic. In both experiences, they also heightened inequality in a highly visible way, directing particular resentment at the self-aggrandizing and conspicuously extravagant "political class."

Two factors magnified the effect of these development failures on democracy in Nigeria. First, because both republics were new regimes, their legitimacy was more heavily contingent on the effectiveness of their immediate performance.[103] Second, these development performances have been especially poor relative to the high popular expectations in each instance—generated in the First Republic by the great promise of national independence and in the Second Republic by the high rate of aggregate economic growth (averaging 7.5 percent during the 1970s) and the huge infusion of cash from the oil boom. But while the oil boom made possible rapid expansion of the educational system and the middle class, it also generated numerous distortions. Beyond those already mentioned, it eroded moral values, deepened inequality, increased inflation, displaced rural labor, discouraged entrepreneurship, distorted planning, and fostered corruption and waste.[104] On balance, both for democracy and development, oil has probably been more of a curse than a blessing for Nigeria, and for other developing countries as well.[105]

It is primarily through the nexus of oil production that the *international environment* has affected democracy in Nigeria. The resulting economic dependence has made the political system extremely vulnerable to changing conditions in the global economy. But the link between economic prosperity and political stability can easily be overstated. Gowon was overthrown at the peak of the oil boom. The Second Republic would have been overthrown even if there had been no glut in the global oil market. The effect of the international environment on the democratic prospect in Nigeria is probably particularly important at the moment, when deep indebtedness and a slack oil market have tied the country's economic future—and so, indirectly, the prospect and timing of a transition back to democracy—to the decisions of the international banking and trading community. As it did during colonial rule, the international environment also had a certain cultural and political influence on the Second Republic. Increasing identification with the United States had not only the positive effect of nurturing the return to democratic rule, but also the negative effect of encouraging the adoption of a constitution modeled too closely on the U.S. system. This experience should caution the established democracies against pushing their own constitutional arrangements as a solution to the problems of democracy in the Third World.

A few of the variables in our theoretical framework have not had any particular impact on democracy in Nigeria. Unlike in Latin America, the polarization of *class cleavage* has not figured prominently in the failure of democracy in Nigeria. There are several reasons for this. First, although economic inequality has been substantial and growing more extreme, this has been crosscut and overtaken by ethnic cleavage, and the politics of tribalism and patronage have tended to distract and eclipse emergent class consciousness. Second, because land has historically been communally owned in most Nigerian (and African) villages, Nigeria has not had the grotesque inequalities in land distribution and the huge class of landless peasants that have characterized many Latin American societies. Finally, because of the low level of economic development, the urban proletariat remains limited in size and continues to have close family ties to the hinterland.

However, all of these factors are changing. The number of organized urban laborers has grown considerably since the 1960s, and despite the efforts of earlier military regimes to incorporate and contain the trade union movement, it has become increasingly militant. Rural inequality is increasing as a number of large-scale agricultural development schemes are being implemented. This not only accelerates migration to cities that cannot meet the demand for jobs, but may also be giving rise to a class of landless peasants.[106] In both the countryside and the cities, there have been signs of growing class consciousness.[107] During the Second Republic, class cleavage was beginning to appear quite strikingly in the politics of the area where stratification has historically been most steeply graded—the emirate North. Partly for this reason, political conflict was especially intense there and antidemocratic behavior especially prominent. Thus, deepening class cleavage could become a serious threat to a Third Nigerian Republic if economic development does not generate improved livelihoods and better living conditions for small peasants and urban workers.

Finally, the institutional structure and character of the *armed forces* cannot be identified as a significant factor in the failure of democracy in Nigeria. In both instances of democratic breakdown, military intervention came after civilian regimes had thoroughly discredited themselves. Personal ambitions and institutional considerations may have been contributing motives of individual coupmakers, but these did no more than facilitate an intervention that was compelled by the malfunctioning of the political system. Hence, both the January 1966 coup and the December 1983 coup—and, probably, most military coups that overthrow democratic regimes—fit within the category of what Horowitz terms "reconstitutive" coups, in that they are occasioned primarily by systemic rather than institutional, sectional, or personal factors.[108] However, there are some indications of an emergent "bureaucratic-authoritarian" mentality in the military, modeled on the more repressive regimes of recent Latin American experience, and sharing the Latin American military's sense of "institutional mission" to eliminate the internal enemies of national order and progress. In this sense, the repressiveness of the Buhari-Idiagbon regime might represent only a modest precursor of what could follow the failure of a third attempt at democratic government in Nigeria.

• POLICY IMPLICATIONS AND FUTURE PROSPECTS •

Two broad policy implications follow from the analysis above. First, although the Second Republic made impressive progress in redesigning the "institutional architecture" of democracy, further institutional innovations are needed to check the powerful tendencies in contemporary Nigeria toward the abuse of power and the desecration of the rules of democratic competition. Second, economic and social changes are needed to attack the *source* of this tendency toward political abuse. As I have argued repeatedly throughout this chapter, such changes must reduce the premium on political power. This implies, in part, a reduction in state control over the economy.

Restructuring the Political System

At the beginning of 1986, President Babangida renewed the debate over Nigeria's constitutional future by announcing a return to democratic, civilian rule in 1990 and appointing a seventeen-member Political Bureau to initiate and lead what he termed the "collective search for a new political order." This "Politburo" (as it ironically came to be known) was asked to identify the reasons for Nigeria's previous political failures, to propose a basic philosophy of government, and to gather, collate, and evaluate opinions from Nigerians around the country. In the subsequent nine months, the members of the bureau crisscrossed the country during a vigorous national debate that elicited a broad outpouring of popular and elite opinion.[109] On 27 March 1987, they submitted their report to the government.[110] This was followed on July 1 by the release of the government's white paper.[111] Together, these two documents represent a kind of blueprint for the country's constitutional future.

Among the most impressive features of the Political Bureau's report was what it did not contain. The bureau—and even more so the government—resisted the impulse to propose wholesale changes in the country's political structure. In particular, the Political Bureau rebuffed many original, provocative, and ill-conceived proposals to do away with political parties, to recast (or in effect eliminate) the federal system, and to give the military an institutionalized role in government. Yet it did not shy away from proposing significant changes.

Reflecting perhaps the strongest point of political consensus in Nigeria today, the bureau urged and the government embraced retention of a multistate federal system. Rejecting proposals to eliminate state governments, or to drastically reduce or increase their number, the bureau opted for something close to the current nineteen-state system. A majority favored creation of a few more states (from two to six) to settle long-standing ethnic and political tensions (within the existing Kaduna and Cross River States), to give the system a better ethnic balance (by creating a third Igbo state), and to bring development closer to the people (in dispersed areas of the middle North "too remote" from their current state capitals "to feel the impact of meaningful development"). A minority favored no change at all. The government accepted in principle the creation of (a few) more states.[112]

This powerful federalist sentiment reflected an appreciation of the considerable success the multistate federal system achieved during the Second Republic in breaking up the hegemony of the three largest groups, decentralizing ethnic conflict, dispersing development activity, fostering crosscutting cleavages, exposing intraethnic divisions, and generally containing the immense centrifugal pressures inherent in Nigeria's ethnic composition.[113] But, at the same time, the bureau identified an aspect of Nigerian federalism in need of strengthening.

One of the Political Bureau's most significant proposals was to deepen the federal system by enhancing the power and resources of local governments. Since the onset of the oil boom, government authority and finances have become increasingly concentrated in the central government. The changes proposed by the bureau and largely accepted by the Babangida government would reverse this trend. Viewing local government as "the basic unit for the administration and development of the country," they give Nigeria's 301 local government areas (and also the states) substantially greater responsibility over economic development activities and social services, increase local governments' share of the federation's revenue allocation pool from 10 to at least 20 percent, and allow them greater latitude to collect revenue from diverse sources.[114]

Such decentralization figures to strengthen Nigerian democracy for several reasons. First, because the locality is the level of government closest to the people in any democratic system, giving it more power and resources figures to enhance popular control. But local government is not only a vital arena of action and initiative in a federal system; it can also be a school for the development of citizen awareness and political skills. In this sense, it may help realize the bureau's goal of mobilizing and educating the citizenry at the grassroots as "the greatest deterrent to bad government such as we have had in the past."[115] Moreover, decentralizing government power and resources also means dispersing the political stakes, which could help to reduce the tremendous premium on controlling the central government in Nigeria.

Another significant institution to be retained from the Second Republic will be the presidential system of government. In fact, the government rejected even the limited changes proposed by the bureau in this regard. Once again, the president, and vice-president, and state governors will serve four-year terms, renewable once (rather than the single five-year terms proposed by the bureau). The national legislature will remain bicameral, because—in contrast to the bureau—the government recognized the value, within a federal framework, of having an upper house drawing representation equally from all states and a lower house based on population. The government also rejected the majority view of the bureau that legislative representation be based only on local government areas, which would satisfy neither of the above principles of representation.[116] The bicameral national and unicameral state legislatures will again have four-year terms, and the local government councils three-year terms.

No doubt, there are strong arguments to be made on behalf of a parliamentary system. Particularly in a polity (like Nigeria's) highly prone to polarization, a parliamentary system offers greater flexibility, more scope and pressure for compromise and coalitions, and hence less of a zero-sum game in politics.[117] However, a presidential system makes more sense for Nigeria, not only (perhaps not even) because of its presumed "merit of unity, energy and despatch," to quote the bureau,[118] but because it has become an important instrument in Nigeria's strategy of managing ethnic conflict through the fostering of crosscutting cleavage.

In the presidential system of the Second Republic, the requirements for breadth of national support forced the parties and the presidential candidates to organize and mobilize across ethnic boundaries, and made of the president, in particular, a panethnic figure whose constituency was "all of multi-ethnic Nigeria." However, as Donald Horowitz has noted, the system suffered from a damaging internal contradiction, in that the method of electing national legislators from single-member (and mostly ethnically homogeneous) territorial districts meant that the National Assembly members behaved "as delegates of their ethnic groups."[119]

This may argue for innovation in the method of electing a National Assembly to give it more of the national, panethnic character of the presidency. An electoral system based on proportional representation from national party lists would move in this direction. On the advice of the bureau, the government decided to retain the single-member-district, first-past-the-post electoral system, with its closer ties between legislators and electorates. (Indeed, it even chose to retain the very same constituencies used in the Second Republic). However, the integrative potential of proportional representation should not be dismissed.

A possible compromise might be something along the lines of the West German system, in which half of the representatives would be elected by district and half by proportional representation from national party lists. In fact, the Political Bureau took a step in this direction by proposing that women and labor each be allocated 5 percent of the legislative seats, with the candidates to "be nominated . . . by the political parties in the ratio of their relative numerical strengths in each legislature."[120] This principle of functional group representation was denied by the government. However, Nigeria could innovate by allowing political parties to take these and other groups, crosscutting ethnicity, into account in selecting lists of candidates from whom some portion (10 to 20 percent, at least) of the National Assembly would be elected by proportional representation. Such a mixed electoral system would not only give the legislative branch a more transethnic character, it would also encourage the development of more coherent and vigorous national party organizations.

It was the issue of party structure that presented the Political Bureau with one of its most vexing problems. Mistaking the instrument of political instability for the cause (as had the Murtala-Obasanjo regime), many intellectuals advanced proposals for a zero- or one-party system. And in its open meetings around the country, as well, the bureau encountered tremendous popular cynicism with party politics. Still, the bureau recognized that the political party is an indispensable instrument for the articulation, aggregation, mobilization and representation of interests in a modern democracy. Further, it perceived the dangers of authoritarianism and regimentation of opinion intrinsic to one-party systems. But the bureau apparently was not unaffected by the antiparty sentiment, and it settled on the strange hybrid of a mandatory two-party system, which was accepted by the government. Both of the parties must subscribe to the national philosophy—although this will not be the "socialism" recommended by the bureau but a set of principles so general as to be acceptable to virtually all but the most extreme and explicit antidemocrats. As in the Second Republic, each party must also "reflect the federal character" of Nigeria by being ethnically balanced in its internal structures.[121]

Mandating a two-party system presents a number of problems. Practically, it is not clear how the new National Electoral Commission (NEC) will choose if more than two political associations meet the various requirements (including demonstrated breadth of organization across states and ethnic groups). In principle, it may be seen as a diminution of democracy to limit the number of parties arbitrarily to two, even if others satisfy reasonable and objective criteria for recognition. This too could have practical consequences, weakening the commitment to democracy of excluded groups and even inducing them toward violent, antisystemic means to express their interests. It could also be seen as undemocratic to require each party to subscribe to the same basic philosophy, although again, the government's version is now so vague as to reduce, in essence, to "democracy and social justice."[122] Perhaps the greatest argument against such an arbitrary limit on the freedom of political organization and contestation is that it is unnecessary. The political system of the Second Republic was moving perceptibly toward realignment into two predominant parties. With the absence from the scene of the historic ethnic political leaders—whether through banning, retirement, or death (which took Chief Awolowo in May 1987)—a Third Republic would figure to resume this progress quickly.

Whatever the party system, however, the principal challenge of political structure in a Third Nigerian Republic will be to devise more original and far-reaching mechanisms to check, balance, and distribute power. Both of the previous attempts at democracy were sabotaged by the abuse of constituted authority and the violation of the rules of democratic competition. Crucial procedural institutions were compromised by partisan manipulation and pressure: the electoral administration, the judiciary, the police, the census, and the code of conduct machinery. Constitutional provisions for the autonomy of the executive bodies overseeing these functions have been clearly inadequate.

If the democratic process is to work in any kind of predictable and orderly fashion, and if the contending parties are thus to develop confidence in its integrity, such procedural institutions must remain above party conflict and independent of party control. The failure of conventional provisions for separation of powers points to the need in Nigeria for a new body—almost a fourth branch of government in its autonomy—that would have exclusive authority for the appointment, funding, and supervision of those executive bodies in charge of crucial procedural functions. The scope of authority for such a national council should include the Federal and State Electoral Commissions, the Code of Conduct Bureau and Tribunal, the Federal and State Judicial Service Commissions, the Police Service Commission, and the National Population Commission. New regulatory institutions, such as a network of federal and state ombudsmen and a general accounting office (designed, like the GAO of the U.S. Congress, to monitor government inefficiency and fraud) might also be included.[123]

The most difficult problem in designing such a new regulatory structure is figuring out how it can be constituted to ensure its independence from control by political parties or the executive or legislative branches. One method that has attracted some favor in Nigeria would be to give this function (and perhaps others) to the military.[124] While opposing any major institutional role for the military—because of the danger that it might politicize the military and so destabilize the country—the Political Bureau nevertheless gestured in this direction by proposing that the military nominate two of its members to serve on the election commission and that two other high-ranking officers serve on the National Population Commission. The rejection of any military involvement in the political process (even in these limited forms) represents one of the most interesting and surprising—and in the long run probably one of the wisest—of the Babangida Government's intentions for the new political system.[125] The evidence from Asia and Latin America shows quite graphically the risk of enduring and undemocratic politicization of the armed forces that comes with giving the military any institutionalized role in government.

The Political Bureau proposed that the Council of State (which includes high federal officials plus the state governors) be given increased authority over the election and judicial commissions and over judicial appointments (and, more significantly, that the judiciary be given independent control over its own recurrent expenditure).[126] However, the government rejected most of these changes. And in any case, even though this approach would have reduced direct presidential control, the involvement of politicians (who form the great bulk of the Council of State, even as the bureau proposed to alter it) in such an oversight body is precisely what must be avoided.[127]

If it is to be effective, a national oversight council must be composed of civilians not involved in or beholden to political parties. One way to do this would be to have a number of Nigeria's independent interest groups each nominate a member of the council. These groups might include the bar and medical associations, the Nigeria Labour Congress, associations of students, journalists, manufacturers, traders, women, peasants, and other groups—autonomous from both the parties and the state—that represent important collective interests.

It is beyond our scope here to review all of the important issues in constitutional design (not to mention all of the bureau's political recommendations and the government's views). But certainly one of the most crucial issues is the structure and timing of the transition to democracy. A distinguishing feature of the Political Bureau's report, and even more so of the Babangida government's response, was the concern to devise a more deliberate and gradual transition to democratic government than occurred during the previous military withdrawal. Although the Murtala-Obsanjo transition had several phases, the resurrection of competitive politics and transfer of power happened quite rapidly, in the space of less than a year. Because most of its members felt bound to President Babangida's announced target of a handover of power in 1990, the bureau actually did not allow much more time for the reconstruction of partisan political life. It proposed to begin the transition in 1987 with the creation of new states, election of local government councils, appointment of a constitution-drafting panel, and establishment of the election, population, and code of conduct commissions. This would have been followed by a census in 1988, the lifting of the ban on political parties (along with new local government elections) in 1989, and first state and then federal elections in 1990.[128]

The chief problem with this formula was that, once again, it did not allow sufficient time for political parties to develop free from the pressures of an imminent election (or series of elections) in which virtually all political power would be at stake. The clear lesson of the Second Republic is that political parties need more time to develop fresh political identities and complex, coherent organizational structures. They need time, as well, to develop between them relations of mutual tolerance and trust, which will give them the confidence that defeat will not mean political obliteration and victory will be tempered by conciliation. Such a system of "mutual security" can only grow gradually over many years and several elections, although elites can do much at the beginning to initiate it.[129] This is one reason for staggering elections, so that state and federal offices are not contested all at once. It is also an argument for phasing in elections gradually, from the bottom up, to give parties time to get accustomed to competing with one another and to internalize the rules of the democratic game, beginning at levels where the stakes are small and the risks low.

Such a strategy of phased transition of course requires extending the period of partial military rule, particularly military control over the executive branch of the federation, beyond what would the country might prefer (or even tolerate). But, during this period of phased withdrawal, the military would serve as a more effective guarantor of procedural integrity and autonomy than would any ruling party (witness the difference between the 1979 and 1983 elections). This would remove the greatest danger during the transition to stable democracy: that "when conflict erupts neither side can be entirely confident that it will be safe to tolerate the other."[130]

In his address to the nation outlining his government's transition program, President Babangida quoted from the Political Bureau to emphasize the need for "a broadly spaced transition in which democratic government can proceed with political learning, institutional adjustment and a re-orientation of political culture, at sequential levels of politics and governance beginning with local government and ending at the federal level."[131] This concern for space, deliberation, sequence and political learning led the government to pospone the final transfer of power to 1992 (as a minority of the bureau had recommended). This extended timetable gave the government the last part of 1987 and the first part of 1988 to establish the most important regulatory commissions and bodies, to inaugurate a constituent assembly, and to hold (nonpartisan) local government elections. It then allowed the remainder of 1988 for these structures to begin operating, while consolidating the task of economic adjustment and renewal. And yet, still it allowed more than three years, rather than one, from the lifting of the ban on party politics to the election of a national president. Although it entailed five elections in three years, the government's timetable introduced the crucial innovation of phasing in the electoral struggle for power at progressively higher levels, permitting the competitors after each leap into the uncertain to pause, take stock, adjust their strategies and remobilize. The final three years of this timetable were as follows:

- 2nd quarter, 1989: lifting of the ban on party politics
- 3rd quarter, 1989: recognition of two political parties
- 4th quarter, 1989: partisan local government elections
- 1st-2nd quarters, 1990: election of state legislatures and governors
- 3rd quarter, 1990: convening of state legislatures
- 4th quarter, 1990: swearing-in of state executives
- 1st-3rd quarters, 1991: census
- 4th quarter, 1991: local government elections
- 1st-2nd quarters, 1992: National Assembly elections and convening
- 3rd-4th quarters, 1992: presidential election and inauguration and final military disengagement

While much more spaced, this timetable is still quite rushed—so much so that it may defeat much of the purpose of the spacing. On the other hand, it also probably represents the best compromise realistically attainable between the needs for deliberation and phasing and the popular impatience for a return to civilian, democratic rule.

The still-hurried character of this new transition underscores the urgency of getting crucial institutions working quickly. In particular, it is crucial that the military administration begin to set some standards for democratic performance by holding itself to standards of accountability and responsibility under law. Two limited steps here would be of enormous significance as a legacy for the future. First, the military could commit itself to abide by an explicitly articulated bill of individual rights that the judiciary would have the supreme power to interpret and enforce. Second, the military must establish by example that incumbent governments can be held accountable to standards of probity. Hence, the Babangida government must, as the bureau proposed, get the Code of Conduct Bureau and Tribunal operating before it leaves office and must require that all the incumbent political officeholders comply with the code's provisions, including the declaration of assets.[132] Perhaps no single development would augur more hopefully for the future of a Third Nigerian Republic than the prior establishment of a code of conduct machinery, which would have by the inauguration of the new democratic regime sufficient independence, experience, and organizational momentum (including some convictions and sentences) to effectively deter political corruption.

Reorganizing the State-Society Relationship

Partly in response to the request for it to recommend a new "national philosophy of government" and partly, perhaps, in response to its own ideological impulses, the Political Bureau dealt extensively with economic and social questions in its report. Weighing the competing merits of capitalism, socialism, Islamic theocracy, and African communalism, the report recommended a socialist system for Nigeria. State ownership would be extended throughout the "commanding heights" of the economy, including not only public utilities and enterprises involving the nation's political integrity and security, but also all those involving heavy capital expenditures or monopoly conditions. The private sector would not be abolished, but would be limited to agriculture and small to medium-scale enterprises.[133]

This is not the place to quarrel with the bureau's condemnation of capitalism for the mass poverty, ignorance, and disease it supposedly fosters, nor with the realism of its vision of a socialist "Eldorado where human want is eliminated but freedoms are guaranteed."[134] Nor is it necessary here to point to the generally poor performance of state enterprises in Africa. Whether or not further nationalization of the economy and constriction of the private sector will bring economic and social progress and greater national autonomy, one consequence is indisputable: it will increase state control over economic and social resources. And this can only increase further the premium on getting and keeping control of the state itself. It was probably more because of its own ideological and policy orientation that the government largely rejected the bureau's socialist agenda, but, whatever the reason, democratic politics will be more viable as a result.

The statist orientation of the Political Bureau's report was apparent as well in its recommendations on the press. Fearing control of the press by wealthy individuals, it recommended that government ownership of much of the print media continue, along with the state's monopoly over radio and television. Further, it suggested "abolishing private ownership of mass media except by organisations."[135] The government, in response, was notably less wary of statism with regard to control of the press.[136]

There was a certain tension in the bureau's report over the state-society relationship. While distrusting private control of the mass media, it called for strengthening press freedoms, including "the right to receive and disseminate information and protect the source of such information."[137] Similarly, the bureau favored (and the government accepted) a more direct state role in building a new political culture through the establishment of a "national directorate of social mobilisation and political education." Yet, this will also be supplemented by greater democratic involvement of voluntary associations such as cooperative unions, women's groups, youth and student organizations, and village, ward, and clan councils.[138]

This tension is not peculiar to the "Politburo's" intellectual debates and political recommendations, nor to the government's response. It is deeply embedded in the current Nigerian situation. Pluralism is vigorously established and increasingly assertive in the country's ethnic structure, associational life, and information order. But the state elite, including influential elements of the intelligentsia, continue to push the expansion of state control. This tension between pluralism and statism may constitute the country's most pressing contradiction. Certainly it is the one with the most profound implications for the future of democracy.

It is not only for political reasons that economic statism, or its graduation into a full-blown socialism, must be questioned. There is growing understanding in the international community (by no means just among the bankers and policy makers of the First World) of the economically dysfunctional consequences of state control over the economy.

This understanding was the major impetus behind the rather daring economic adjustment program launched by the Babangida government in October 1985. Through sharp cutbacks in petroleum and other consumer subsidies, decreases in government spending and employment, a more realistic exchange rate, and elimination of import licensing and exchange controls, Babangida sought to open up the economy to competition, to reduce state interference, and to get the country to begin living within its means. These developments, it was assumed, would increase productivity and investment in "real" economic activity, foster national self-reliance, and reduce corruption and waste. The leading element of this adjustment program was an effective devaluation of the naira by about two-thirds through the creation of a "Second-Tier Foreign Exchange Market" (SFEM), which exposed the value of the naira to market forces.

Before long, these historic initiatives began to yield some impressive results. In his 1 January 1987 budget message, President Babangida reported that the SFEM had boosted government revenues and increased the competitiveness of Nigeria's agricultural exports. Industry, which had been starved of desperately needed raw materials and spare parts under import licensing, also began to rebound. For consumers, times were hard, as import prices increased dramatically, but these hardships were balanced at least somewhat by greater availability of many goods.

Most of all, perhaps, the Structural Adjustment Program began to alter economic incentives and so to direct into productive activity (especially agriculture) the entrepreneurial energy that had previously been diverted toward the huge returns and low risks of government contracts and licenses. Hence, despite the steep sacrifices exacted by an austerity program much harsher than even the IMF had asked for, Nigerians responded positively, and there appeared "a dramatic release of creative energy for internal solutions."[139]

Of course, this was only a beginning. After two years of economic adjustment, it was not clear how long austerity could remain politically viable in the face of heavy international indebtedness and slack oil prices. But the internal reforms did give the regime some significant leverage with the international banking community, enabling it to negotiate new loans and extend old ones. Although trade unions and other groups demanded higher wages and more investment in social services, Nigerians generally seemed willing to give the program a chance.

The key question for future policy is how much further reform can go in the face of entrenched interests. The government has pledged to privatize more than 100 public sector enterprises, but this is intensely opposed by political and bureaucratic elites who do not wish to relinquish the economic control of which they are assured in a statist economy. Resistance comes especially from much of the Northern establishment, which fears that wholesale privatization would deliver the economy into the hands of the much larger, richer, and better organized Southern bourgeoisie.

There are ways of organizing the privatization process to take account of these concerns. The Babangida government has pledged to give special encouragement and preference in the purchase of parastatals "to groups and institutions like trade unions, universities, youth organizations, women societies, local governments and state investment companies."[140] Certainly, regional and ethnic balance can be a consideration in the sale of government companies, even at the price of some restrictions on the competitiveness of bidding. If this gave a one-time bonanza to certain groups and inviduals who could not otherwise afford to purchase these companies, this would be better for the economy and polity than the continuing bonanza that perpetually accrues to the incumbents of state power.

If it is to succeed in the long run, privatization must not only decrease state control over the means of production, it must also increase and stimulate indigenous private ownership of productive enterprises. The Political Bureau reflected in its report the fear that privatization might open a new wedge for expansion of control by foreign capital. This is partly because of the comprador character of the bulk of the Nigerian bourgeoisie, which has preferred the quicker, easier returns of intermediary trade and relatively passive participation (including fronting as owners) in foreign-dominated enterprises. As Thomas Biersteker has argued, state fiscal policies can be designed to make ownership of shares or partnerships in these transnational enterprises less profitable for

Nigerians than new enterprises which they might be induced to initiate in needed sectors or areas with income tax credits and other incentives.[141] Food production and processing is one sector with immense potential. A strong case could also be made for permitting (if not encouraging) private ownership of broadcasting stations (at least radio, initially), not only for economic reasons, but to promote greater pluralism of ideas and information sources.

Clearly, none of this is to suggest that the state can or should withdraw from the economy altogether. Nothing like a pure reliance on markets is feasible politically, and, in any case, even a laissez-faire development strategy requires active and effective government support (e.g., provision of credit, agricultural inputs, improved transport, and other infrastructure).[142] But if there is to be any basis for self-sustaining growth and peaceful, democratic politics, there must be a transition (in Schatz's terms) from pirate capitalism to a more sophisticated and effective nurture capitalism. Nigeria must develop, for the first time, a basis of production and accumulation outside of oil and outside the state.

This will require the development of a real bourgeoisie—both grande and petite, agricultural and industrial—that will not depend on the state for its survival, and hence that will be able to view the electoral struggle with some degree of detachment. If, at the same time, real risks and penalties begin to attach to the pursuit of wealth through political corruption, the linkage between political power and class formation will have been seriously undermined, and the stakes in the struggle for power measurably reduced.

The Democratic Prospect

Nigeria stands today at a crucial and possibly decisive crossroads in its political development. It is torn between its deep commitment to personal freedom and responsible government, and its revulsion with the corruption, violence, and self-interestedness that have twice consumed promising attempts at democracy. It further suffers a deepening contradiction between the pluralism of its social and cultural life and the statism that suffocates the economy and perverts the polity. The aspiration for democracy remains sufficiently strong to make it likely that there will be a transition to a Third Republic, if not by 1992 then probably not long thereafter. However, it is unlikely that a third democratic failure would leave the country poised, despite its frustration, for another try.

The conjunction of the huge challenges of political reconstruction and economic adjustment makes this a time of unique opportunity for Nigeria. But it is also a time of great danger. The contradiction between pluralism and statism will not remain at a standoff indefinitely. If Nigeria cannot develop and maintain a democratic political system, its liberal and pluralist impulses could come under intense and possibly violent challenge from any one of several forces.

There is, as has been mentioned earlier, a growing repressive mentality in the security establishment that could, at some point of acute political polarization, exhaustion, and despair, unleash a much more brutal and zealous authoritarianism than Nigeria has ever known. There is also growing sentiment for a much more radical break with the status quo on the left, which might seek by coup or rebellion a socialism (or at least a measure of social justice) that was denied it democratically. To some extent, these two pressures feed upon one another, carrying the potential for the "Latin Americanization" of Nigerian politics. In addition, one cannot ignore the growing incidence of religious mobilization, extremism, and violence in Nigeria, which could become a growing outlet for popular frustration and cynical elite exploitation if a pluralistic democracy cannot be made to work. In a country that is roughly half Muslim and half Christian, with a bloody ethnic civil war in its past, such religious conflict must raise profound alarm.

In short, the stakes in political engineering have never been higher. Nigeria cannot afford to fail in its next attempt at democratic government. Its social pluralism, cultural values, federal system, and even perhaps the political learning from the Second Republic offer real hope for the development of democratic government. If it can reduce the economic premium on political power and institutionalize powerful, autonomous mechanisms of public accountability, the prospects for consolidating democratic government would appear to be good. But if it should fail, it might well be a generation, with much blood and bitterness behind it, before the opportunity would come again.

• NOTES •

1. James S. Coleman, *Nigeria: Background to Nationalism* (Berkeley: University of California Press, 1958), p. 15.

2. Donald L. Horowitz, *Ethnic Groups in Conflict* (Berkeley: University of California Press, 1985), p. 39.

3. Coleman, *Nigeria*, p. 50.

4. Ibid., p. 323.

5. Ibid., pp. 308–318.

6. In addition to James S. Coleman's classic work, the indispensable studies of this inaugural era of party politics in Nigeria are Richard L. Sklar, *Nigerian Political Parties: Power in an Emergent African Nation* (Princeton: Princeton University Press, 1963, and New York: NOK Publishers, 1983); and C. S. Whitaker, Jr., *The Politics of Tradition: Continuity and Change in Northern Nigeria, 1946–66* (Princeton: Princeton University Press, 1970). Other important works on this period are B. J. Dudley, *Parties and Politics in Northern Nigeria* (London: Frank Cass & Co, 1968); and K. W. J. Post, *The Nigerian Federal Election of 1959* (London: Oxford University Press, 1963). The following historical review of politics in the 1950s and the First Republic draws from Larry Diamond, "Class, Ethnicity and the Democratic State: Nigeria, 1950–66," *Comparative Studies in Society and History* 25, no. 3 (1983); and *Class, Ethnicity and Democracy in Nigeria: The Failure of the First Republic* (London: Macmillan, and Syracuse: Syracuse University Press, 1988).

7. Michael Crowder, *The Story of Nigeria* (London: Faber and Faber, 1978), p. 231.

8. Whitaker, *The Politics of Tradition*.

9. Richard L. Sklar, "Contradictions in the Nigerian Political System," *Journal of Modern African Studies* 3, no. 2, p. 209.

10. Sklar, *Nigerian Political Parties*.

11. Ibid., pp. 88–112.

12. Coleman, *Nigeria*, pp. 332–352.

13. Whitaker, *The Politics of Tradition*.

14. Coleman, *Nigeria*, pp. 353–366.

15. Whitaker, *The Politics of Tradition*, pp. 361–362.

16. Post, *The 1959 Nigerian Election*, pp. 276–292; and John P. Mackintosh, *Nigerian Government and Politics* (Evanston, Ill.: Northwestern University Press, 1966), p. 525.

17. Oluwole Idowu Odumosu, *The Nigerian Constitution: History and Development* (London: Sweet and Maxwell, 1963), pp. 193–197; and Frederick A. O. Schwarz, *Nigeria: The Tribes, the Nation or the Race—The Politics of Independence* (Cambridge, Mass.: MIT Press), pp. 196–211.

18. Ernest Adelumola Ogunade, "Freedom of the Press: Government-Press Relationships in Nigeria, 1900–1966" (Ph.D. diss., Southern Illinois University, 1981), pp. 165–218.

19. Frederick Schwarz, *Nigeria*, p. 162.

20. Mackintosh, *Nigerian Government and Politics*, p. 538.

21. Richard L. Sklar, "The Ordeal of Chief Awolowo," in Gwendolen Carter, ed., *Politics in Africa: Seven Cases* (New York: Harcourt, Brace and World, 1966), p. 156; and "Nigerian Politics in Perspective," in Robert Melson and Howard Wolpe, eds., *Nigeria: Modernization and the Politics of Communalism* (East Lansing, Mich.: Michigan State University Press, 1971), pp. 47–48.

22. K. W. J. Post and Michael Vickers, *Structure and Conflict in Nigeria* (London: Heinemann, 1973), pp. 88, 90.

23. Walter Schwarz, *Nigeria* (New York: Frederick A. Praeger, 1968), p. 158.

24. Robert Melson, "Nigerian Politics and the General Strike of 1964," in Robert I. Rotberg and Ali A. Mazrui, eds., *Protest and Power in Black Africa* (New York and London: Oxford University Press, 1970), pp. 771–774, 785.

25. A. H. M. Kirk-Greene, *Crisis and Conflict in Nigeria*, vol. 1 (London: Oxford University Press, 1971) p. 20; and Robin Cohen, *Labour and Politics in Nigeria 1945–71* (London: Heinemann, 1974), p. 168.

26. Robert Melson, "Ideology and Inconsistency: The 'Cross-pressured' Nigerian Worker," in Melson and Wolpe, *Modernization and the Politics of Communalism*, pp. 581–605.

27. Post and Vickers, *Structure and Conflict*, pp. 141–149; and Mackintosh, *Nigerian Government and Politics*, pp. 576–579.

28. N. J. Miners, *The Nigerian Army*, 1956–66 (London: Methuen and Co., 1971), p. 178.

29. Crowder, *The Story of Nigeria*, p. 269.

30. Kirk-Greene, *Crisis and Conflict in Nigeria*, p. 4.

31. Anthony Kirk-Greene, "The Making of the Second Republic," in Kirk-Greene and Douglas Rimmer, *Nigeria Since 1970: A Political and Economic Outline* (New York: Holmes and Meier, London: Hodder and Stoughton, 1981), pp. 5–7; and Crowder, *The Story of Nigeria*, pp. 278–280.

32. Kirk-Greene, "The Making of the Second Republic," pp. 7–9; Crowder, *The Story of Nigeria*, pp. 280–281; and Billy J. Dudley, *An Introduction to Nigerian Government and Politics* (Bloomington: Indiana University Press, 1982), pp. 80–82.

33. Decree Number 53, for example, made it a criminal offense to publish or report "anything which could cause public alarm or industrial unrest"; granted the police and armed forces heads the right of arbitrary detention; and suspended the writ of habeas corpus. Victor A. Olorunsola, *Soldiers and Power: The Development Performance of the Nigerian Military Regime* (Stanford: Hoover Institution Press, 1977), p. 102.

34. *West Africa*, quoted in Olorunsola, *Soldiers and Power*, p. 88.

35. Olorunsola, *Soldiers and Power*, pp. 86–101; and Lateef Kayode Jakande, "The Press and Military Rule," in Oyeleye Oyediran, ed., *Nigerian Government and Politics Under Military Rule* (London: Macmillan and New York: St. Martin's, 1979), pp. 110–123.

36. Olorunsola, *Soldiers and Power*, pp. 60–76.

37. Statement of General Murtala Muhammed, quote in Kirk-Greene, "The Making of the Second Republic," pp. 13–14.

38. David D. Laitin, "The Sharia Debate and the Origins of Nigeria's Second Republic," *Journal of Modern African Studies* 20, no. 3 (1982): pp. 411–430.

39. Jean Herskovits, "Dateline Nigeria: A Black Power," *Foreign Policy*, no. 29 (Winter 1977/78): p. 179.

40. *Constitution of the Federal Republic of Nigeria 1979* (Reprinted by New Nigerian Newspapers, Ltd., Kaduna, 1981), p. 65, sections 202–203; and Richard Joseph, "The Ethnic Trap:

Notes on the Nigerian Elections, 1978–79," *Issue* 11 (1981): p. 17.

41. C. S. Whitaker, Jr., "Second Beginnings: The New Political Framework," *Issue* 11 (1981): pp. 2–13; and Claude S. Phillips, "Nigeria's New Political Institutions, 1975–79," *Journal of Modern African Studies* 18, no. 1 (1980): pp. 1–22.

42. W. Ibekwe Ofonagoro, ed., *The Great Debate* (Lagos: Daily Times of Nigeria, 1981).

43. Richard L. Sklar, "Democracy for the Second Republic," *Issue* 11 (1981): p. 14.

44. Whitaker, "Second Beginnings," p. 7.

45. Phillips, "Nigeria's New Political Institutions," p. 15.

46. Richard Joseph, "Parties and Ideology in Nigeria," *Review of African Political Economy* 13 (May-August 1978): p. 82; and "The Ethnic Trap," p. 18.

47. Larry Diamond, "Social Change and Political Conflict in Nigeria's Second Republic," in I. William Zartman, ed., *The Political Economy of Nigeria* (New York: Praeger, 1983), pp. 35–39. For a fuller review, see Joseph, "Parties and Ideology in Nigeria."

48. Martin Dent, *West Africa*, 6 August 1979, p. 1406; see also Joseph, "The Ethnic Trap," p. 20.

49. This section draws from several of my previously published works: "Cleavage, Conflict and Anxiety in the Second Nigerian Republic," *Journal of Modern African Studies* 20, no. 4 (1982): pp. 629–668; "Social Change and Political Conflict"; "A Tarnished Victory for the NPN?" *Africa Report* 28, no. 6 (1983): pp. 18–23; "Nigeria in Search of Democracy," *Foreign Affairs* 62, no. 4 (1984): pp. 905–927; and "Nigeria: The Coup and the Future," *Africa Report* 29, no. 2 (1984): pp. 9–15.

50. The most affluent party, the NPN, suffered by far the fewest disqualifications (6 percent), while its radical and much more humble Northern challenger, the PRP, suffered the most numerous (49 percent). Moreover, the PRP and NPP presidential candidates were not finally certified to run until less than three weeks before the election, when the courts overruled FEDECO's provisional disqualification. Haroun Adamu and Alaba Ogunsanwo, *Nigeria: The Making of the Presidential System 1979 General Elections* (Kano: Triumph Publishing Company, 1983).

51. Ibid., p. 199.

52. Ibid., pp. 255–256; Walter I. Ofonagoro, *The Story of the Nigerian General Elections 1979* (Lagos: Federal Ministry of Information, 1979); and Larry Diamond, "Free and Fair? The Administration and Conduct of the 1983 Nigerian Elections" (Paper presented to the 26th Annual Meeting of the African Studies Association, Boston, 7–10 December 1983), p. 25.

53. Richard Joseph, "Democratization under Military Tutelage: Crisis and Consensus in the Nigerian 1979 Elections," *Comparative Politics* 14, no. 1 (1981): pp. 80–88; and Whitaker, "Second Beginnings," p. 13.

54. Richard Joseph, "Affluence and Underdevelopment: The Nigerian Experience," *Journal of Modern African Studies* 16, no. 2 (1978): pp. 221–239; Henry Bienen and V. P. Diejomaoh, eds., *Inequality and Development in Nigeria* (New York and London: Holmes and Meier, 1981); and Michael Watts and Paul Lubeck, "The Popular Classes and the Oil Boom: A Political Economy of Rural and Urban Poverty," in Zartman, ed., *The Political Economy of Nigeria*.

55. Diamond, "Social Change and Political Conflict."

56. Prominent government actions overturned by the courts included the president's signing into law of the 1981 Revenue Allocation Bill after it was adopted only by a Joint Senate-House Committee; the jamming of Lagos State Television by the Nigerian Television Authority; and the deportation to Chad by the Ministry of Interior of a prominent GNPP leader in Borno State.

57. *Daily Star* (Enugu), 22 July 1981.

58. *National Concord* (Lagos), 26 October 1982.

59. *Punch* (Lagos), 31 March 1983.

60. *New Nigerian* (Kaduna), 25 January 1983.

61. Diamond, "Nigeria in Search of Democracy," pp. 906–908.

62. Newspaper interviews with a wide cross-section of Nigerians revealed a profound exhaustion and disgust with the greed, corruption, opportunism, thuggery, "witch-hunting and character assassination" that had "polluted" the political system. *New Nigerian*, 3 October 1982.

63. This interpretation was later confirmed by one of the key architects of the coup that overthrew the Second Republic, Major General Ibrahim Babangida. He revealed that the army had considered staging a coup as early as July 1982, but did not want to be fixed with the blame for preventing elections, and so decided to let them proceed. With the rigging of the elections they realized that that the chance for self-correction had been lost. (*Nigeria Newsletter,* 28 January 1984, p. 12). In

addition, a confidential source in the Shagari administration informed me that the president was warned in the spring of 1983 by a group of high-ranking military officers that a coup was inevitable if basic changes in the substance and style of government were not forthcoming.

64. For an extensive analysis, see Diamond, "Free and Fair?," pp. 43–52.

65. Another controversial FEDECO decision reversed the election sequence from 1979 so that the presidential election would be held first. This maximized the chances of an NPN bandwagon through the five rounds of voting.

66. See Diamond, "A Tarnished Victory for the NPN?" and "Free and Fair?"

67. Diamond, "A Tarnished Victory for the NPN?," p. 22.

68. This section draws on several of my previous articles: "Nigeria in Search of Democracy"; "High Stakes for Babangida," *Africa Report* 30, no. 6 (1985): pp. 54–57, "Nigeria Update," *Foreign Affairs* 64, no. 2 (Winter 1985/86): pp. 326–336; and "Nigeria Between Dictatorship and Democracy," *Current History* 86 (May 1987): pp. 201–204 and 222–224.

69. Diamond, "Nigeria: The Coup and The Future," p. 13.

70. *West Africa,* 2 September 1985, pp. 1791–1793.

71. Ibid., 7 July 1986, pp. 1403–1406.

72. Ibid., 2 June 1986, pp. 1144–1146; 9 June 1986, pp. 1196–1197; and 16 June 1986, pp. 1247, 1250–1251.

73. *Newswatch* (Lagos), 3 November 1986, pp. 13–25; and 10 November 1986, pp. 15–22; *New African,* February 1987, pp. 13–15.

74. *West Africa,* 20 April 1987, pp. 748–749.

75. On bureaucratic-authoritarian regimes in Latin America, see David Collier, ed., *The New Authoritarianism in Latin America* (Princeton: Princeton University Press, 1979).

76. Lt. Col. Ojukwu, quoted in Kirk-Greene, *Crisis and Conflict in Nigeria,* p. 146.

77. Mackintosh, *Nigerian Government and Politics,* pp. 617–618.

78. Robert Melson and Howard Wolpe, "Modernization and the Politics of Communalism," in Melson and Wolpe, *Nigeria: Modernization and the Politics of Communalism.*

79. Sklar, "Contradictions in the Nigerian Political System," and "Nigerian Politics in Perspective."

80. Whitaker, *The Politics of Tradition,* p. 402.

81. Richard L. Sklar, "The Nature of Class Domination in Africa," *Journal of Modern African Studies* 17, no. 4 (1979): p. 536.

82. Robert H. Bates, *Markets and States in Tropical Africa* (Berkeley: University of California Press, 1981), pp. 12–13; Claude Ake, *Political Economy of Africa* (London: Longman, 1981), pp. 63–65; Uyi-Ekpen Ogbeide, "The Expansion of the State and Ethnic Mobilization: The Nigerian Experience" (Ph.D. diss., Vanderbilt University, 1985), pp. 37–44.

83. E. O. Akeredolu-Ale, "Private Foreign Investment and the Underdevelopment of Indigenous Enterprise in Nigeria," in Gavin Williams, ed., *Nigeria: Economy and Society* (London: Rex Collings, 1976); Sayre P. Schatz, *Nigerian Capitalism* (Berkeley: University of California Press, 1977); and David Abernethy, "Bureaucratic Growth and Economic Decline in Sub-Saharan Africa" (Paper presented to the 26th Annual Meeting of the African Studies Association, Boston: 7–10 December 1983, pp. 12–13.

84. Diamond, *Class, Ethnicity and Democracy in Nigeria, pp. 178–179.*

85. Sklar, *Nigerian Political Parties,* pp. 480–494.

86. Whitaker, *The Politics of Tradition,* pp. 313–354; Coleman, *Nigeria,* pp. 353–368; and Sklar, *Nigerian Political Parties,* pp. 134–152.

87. Richard Sklar and C. S. Whitaker, Jr., "The Federal Republic of Nigeria," in Gwendolen M. Carter, ed., *National Unity and Regionalism in Eight African States* (Ithaca, N.Y.: Cornell University Press, 1966), p. 122; and Abernethy, "Bureaucratic Growth."

88. Schatz, *Nigerian Capitalism,* pp. 190–195, 208–209, 231–232; and Larry Diamond, "The Social Foundations of Democracy: The Case of Nigeria" (Ph.D. diss., Stanford University, 1980), pp. 556–582.

89. Claude Ake, "Explaining Political Instability in New States," *Journal of Modern African Studies* 11, no. 3 (1973): p. 359.

90. Richard L. Sklar, "Political Science and National Integration—A Radical Approach," *Journal of Modern African Studies* 5, no. 1 (1967); p. 6.

91. Ibid.

92. Robert H. Jackson and Carl G. Rosberg, *Personal Rule in Black Africa: Prince, Auto-*

crat, Prophet, Tyrant (Berkeley: University of California Press, 1982); and Richard Joseph, "Class, State and Prebendal Politics in Nigeria," *Journal of Commonwealth and Comparative Politics* 21, no. 3 (1983): pp. 21–38.

93. See Diamond, "A Tarnished Victory for the NPN?"; and especially *Nigeria in Search of Democracy* (Boulder: Lynne Rienner Publishers, forthcoming), chapters 3 and 4.

94. Sayre P. Schatz, "Pirate Capitalism and the Inert Economy of Nigeria," *Journal of Modern African Studies* 22, no. 1 (1984): p. 55.

95. Claude Ake, Presidential Address to the 1981 Conference of the Nigerian Political Science Association, *West Africa*, 25 May 1981, pp. 1162–1163.

96. Murtala Muhammed, Address to the Constitution Drafting Committee, App. II, *Constitution of the Federal Republic of Nigeria 1979*, p. 123.

97. Samuel P. Huntington, "Will More Countries Become Democratic?" *Political Science Quarterly* 99, no. 2 (1984): p. 203.

98. Dan Agbese, "The Courts in the Dock," *Newswatch*, 26 May 1986, pp. 15–22.

99. Arend Lijphart, *Democracy in Plural Societies: A Comparative Exploration* (New Haven: Yale University Press, 1977).

100. Samuel P. Huntington, *Political Order in Changing Societies* (New Haven: Yale University Press, 1968), pp. 12–24.

101. World Bank, *World Development Report 1981* (New York: Oxford University Press, 1981), p. 136. Between 1960 and 1979, the contribution of agriculture to GDP fell from 63 to 22 percent.

102. Schatz, "Pirate Capitalism and the Inert Economy."

103. Seymour Martin Lipset, *Political Man* (Baltimore: Johns Hopkins University Press, 1981), pp. 64–70; Robert A. Dahl, *Polyarchy: Participation and Opposition* (New Haven: Yale University Press, 1971), pp. 129–150; Juan Linz, *The Breakdown of Democratic Regimes* (Baltimore: Johns Hopkins University Press, 1978), pp. 16–23.

104. See note 54; also Schatz, "Pirate Capitalism and the Inert Economy"; and Diamond, *Nigeria in Search of Democracy*, chap. 2.

105. Jahangir Amuzegar, "Oil Wealth: A Very Mixed Blessing," *Foreign Affairs* 60, no. 4 (1982): pp. 814–835.

106. Watts and Lubeck, "The Popular Classes and the Oil Boom," pp. 120–126.

107. A striking manifestation of this in the countryside was the violent peasant uprising at the site of the Bakalori Dam in Sokoto State in 1980. Bjorn Beckman, "Bakalori: Peasants versus State and Capital," *Nigerian Journal of Political Science* 4, nos. 1 and 2 (1985): pp. 76–104. For evidence of urban class consciousness, see Paul Lubeck, "Class Formation at the Periphery: Class Consciousness and Islamic Nationalism among Nigerian Workers," in R. L. and I. H. Simpson, eds., *Research in the Sociology of Work*, vol. 1 (Greenwich, Conn.: JAI Press, 1979).

108. Donald L. Horowitz, *Coup Theories and Officers' Motives: Sri Lanka in Comparative Perspective* (Princeton: Princeton University Press, 1980), pp. 200–209.

109. Some statistics suggest the extent of the debate and the breadth of popular involvement. "The Bureau met 149 times, visited all the 301 local government areas in the country, and received a total of 27,324 contributions, among them 14,961 memoranda, 1,723 recorded cassettes and video tapes and 3,933 newspaper articles." *Newswatch*, 13 April 1987, p. 15.

110. The publication by *Newswatch* of a detailed analysis of this report (which was later summarized but not released in full) was the cause of the government's decision to seize all available copies of the 13 April issue and ban the magazine for six months.

111. *Government's Views and Comments on the Findings and Recommendations of the Political Bureau* (Lagos: Federal Government Printer, 1987).

112. Ibid., pp. 60–62; *Newswatch*, 13 April 1987, pp 24–26.

113. Horowitz, *Ethnic Groups in Conflict*, pp. 604–613.

114. *Newswatch*, 13 April 1987, pp. 19, 26; *Government's Views*, pp. 26–29, 59–60.

115. Ibid., p. 31.

116. Government's views, pp. 22–26, 30–31.

117. Juan Linz, *The Breakdown of Democratic Regimes*, pp. 72–74, and "Democracy: Presidential or Parliamentary. Does It Make a Difference?" (Paper presented to the workshop on "Political Parties in the Southern Cone," Wilson Center, Washington D.C., 1984).

118. *Newswatch*, 13 April 1987, p. 17.

119. Horowitz, *Ethnic Groups in Conflict*, p. 638.

120. *Newswatch*, 13 April 1987, p. 18.

121. *Newswatch*, 13 April 1987, p. 20; *Government's Views*, pp. 42–43.

122. Ibid., p. 14.

123. For a fuller discussion, see Diamond, "Issues in Constitutional Design," pp. 215–221.

124. This was in fact my own initial—and I am now persuaded, mistaken—thinking. See "Nigeria in Search of Democracy," p. 913, 916–919.

125. *Government's Views*, pp. 44, 51–52, 57–58.

126. *Newswatch*, 13 April 1987, p. 19.

127. *Constitution 1979*, Third Schedule, Part I, p. 103.

128. *Newswatch*, 13 April 1987, p. 38.

129. Dahl, *Polyarchy*, pp. 10–16, 33–40.

130. Ibid., p. 38.

131. Address by Major General Ibrahim Badamasi Babangida to the Nation, "On Political Programme for the Country," 1 July 1987, p. 5.

132. *Newswatch*, 13 April 1987, p. 32.

133. Ibid., p. 16.

134. The quote is from *Newswatch* Editor-in-Chief Ray Ekpu, ibid.

135. Ibid., p. 31, *Government's Views*, pp. 72–74.

136. Ibid., p. 75.

137. Ibid., p. 73. The government viewed existing constitutional protections as adequate.

138. Ibid., pp. 70–72.

139. *West Africa*, 12 January 1987, pp. 48–9.

140. *Newswatch*, April 13, 1987, p. 33.

141. Thomas J. Biersteker, "Indigenization in Nigeria: Renationalization or Denationalization?," in Zartman, ed., *The Political Economy of Nigeria*, pp. 203–205.

142. Sayre P. Schatz, "Laissez-Faireism for Africa?," *Journal of Modern African Studies* 25, no. 1 (1987).

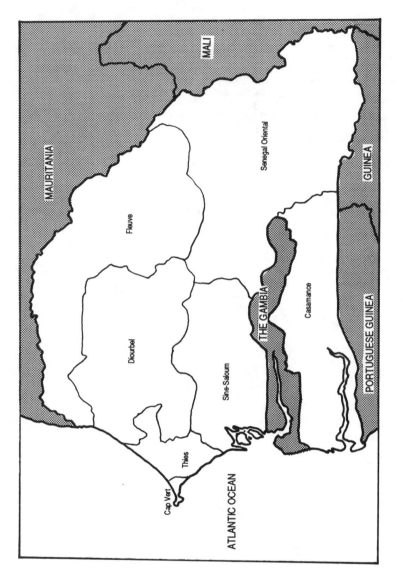

SENEGAL

CHAPTER TEN

Senegal: The Development and Fragility of Semidemocracy

CHRISTIAN COULON

A survey of historical experience in Senegal shows that democracy has had mixed success in that country. To facilitate analysis, three periods, with their own specific characteristics, have been singled out. The first covers the period from the beginning of the century to independence (1960). It is characterized by the progressive extension of rights and liberties within the framework first of colonization and then of decolonization. The second period extends from independence to 1976 and is set off by a *de facto* one-party state. Since 1976, Senegal has embarked little by little on an experiment in democracy that seems daring indeed when compared to the political situation of most countries in black Africa, but which, as will be seen, has had its limits.

It is important to emphasize, as will be pointed out later in more detail, that each of these periods is mixed in nature. Although the "democratic" periods are not lacking in restrictions concerning civil and political liberties, the era of the one-party state cannot be compared to a tyrannical regime, and even less so to a totalitarian one.

Conquering Liberties

Senegal became independent in 1960—at about the same time as most of the other countries in black Africa. Decolonization was brought about quasi-naturally, without violence or revolution, and with the agreement of the various interests. It was the culmination of a political process that began before World War II, tending to reduce political inequalities by encouraging the ever-widening participation of Africans in public matters. On this point, it is necessary to emphasize the specific nature of Senegal's political experience. In Senegal, as elsewhere in Black Africa, political parties came into being after World War II. Unlike in other countries, however, "modern" political practices and elections were not unknown in Senegal before this date, at least for the (very small) percentage of the population that enjoyed French citizenship. Indeed, it

411

is not possible to understand postindependent political development without taking into account this heritage, which has influenced the style of Senegalese political culture.

It is not our purpose here to undertake an analysis of French colonial politics in Black Africa.[1] The ideology of and the experiments in assimilation, however, have left their mark on Senegal. Since the middle of the nineteenth century, a small number of Africans held French citizenship and, as such, participated in the election of a deputy to represent Senegal in the French National Assembly. A little later, when Saint Louis, Dakar, Gorée and Rufisque became townships with full political rights *communes de plein exercice* their inhabitants were called to the polls to elect members of the municipal councils. In 1879, the government set up a General Council in Senegal to be elected by the inhabitants of the four towns.

Democratic rights were limited to the famous four townships. To be a citizen and to participate in these different elections, one had to show proof of having been born in one of the four towns or of having resided there for at least five years. Such people were considered French, enjoyed the right to vote, and were subject to the French civil and penal codes. The other Africans in Senegal were French "subjects" with no political rights. They came under the jurisdiction of customary or Islamic law, as interpreted by the French, which did not prevent colonial administrators from inflicting sentences and fines on these "subjects" without any form of trial. In addition, these "natives" could be enrolled by force in public works projects. Up until the period just after World War II, the number of Africans who could claim citizenship was very small. In 1922, there were 18,000 *originaires* out of a total of 66,000 inhabitants in the four towns and 1,200,000 in the country.

However limited this experience was in terms of the numbers of people concerned, it clearly had an important impact on Senegalese political life. It fostered the habit of political competition, mobilized social forces (business establishments, religious organizations, ethnic-based groups, etc.) around political clans, and, above all, allowed a few Africans to be members of consultative bodies. In the nineteenth century the political class was made up mainly of Europeans and people of mixed blood. After World War I, however, and particularly after the election of Blaise Diagne, the first authentic African to reach the French National Assembly, African leadership became more pronounced and gradually conquered the different representative institutions.[2] In 1931–1932, Blaise Diagne became the first African to hold a cabinet position in a French government (as undersecretary of state for the colonies).

Thus, a class of African politicians developed in Senegal much earlier than in most colonies. They were true political entrepreneurs who controlled important support networks and appeared as real political bosses. If conflicts about factions and money issues often prevailed over questions of electoral platforms, these politicians, nonetheless, had to justify their positions before their African constituencies and defend their specific interests, which were sometimes opposed to the interests of the French colonial office. This democracy "of the few" set the tone for Senegalese political life and contributed to the creation of a class of professional politicians.

After World War II, the French Fourth Republic gave new impetus to the process of democracy in the colonial situation. In 1945, forced labor was abolished. The following year, the status of "native" was dropped and French citizenship granted to all former "subjects." The French constitution of October 1946 that created the French Union called for participation of overseas territories in the central institutions. Henceforth, Senegal sent two deputies to the National Assembly and three senators to the Council of the Republic and to the Assembly of the French Union. Like other territories, Senegal was given a territorial assembly and was included in the regional Council (the Grand Council of French West Africa)—with limited powers, however. Universal suffrage was adopted only progressively, and it was not until 1956 that all adult citizens, male and female, had the right to vote.

Important modifications to this political structure were made when the law of 1956 (called the *loi cadre*) was passed. The law called for a government council in each territory to be elected by the territorial Assembly and to be made up of a number of ministers, one of whom had the title of president of the government council. The road to autonomy was now open.

These constitutional modifications allowed for greater participation and more democratic management of public affairs by Africans. Rural inhabitants who had played no role in public life up to then could, henceforth, participate in public affairs. The sweeping social changes going on in the country—urbanization, upheavals in the rural areas as a result of the development of peanut farming, the emergence of a working class and of a middle class of civil servants—created new situations and new demands that engendered new organizations: associations of all sorts, trade unions, and political parties. Despite the diversity of their aims and ideologies, these movements had the common goal of promoting and defending the interests of Africans. At this time, the trade union movement began to develop, although the unions, and in particular the Senegalese branch of the French General Confederation of Labor (Confédération générale du travail—CGT), had already made themselves felt before the war in fierce strike actions like that of the railway workers in 1938. Regional and ethnic-based movements also started to bloom.

Above all, during these final years of colonial rule, political parties began to flower as well: the Rassemblement démocratique africain, which was the Senegalese section of the SFIO (the French International Socialist Labor Party), and the Mouvement nationaliste africain. At first, it was the SFIO of Lamine Guèye, Blaise Diagne's former lieutenant, that dominated political life. But very quickly, Léopold Sédar Senghor, a young politician who had been elected as deputy to the French National Assembly as a member of Guèye's party, set himself off from his former boss. Senghor accused Guèye and his party of being too tied to the interests of continental France and the French Socialist party, of encouraging assimilation, and of favoring the old elite of the four townships. In 1948, he founded an independent movement, the Bloc démocratique sénégalais (BDS), which wanted more autonomy for overseas territories, sought to pave the way for an "African socialism," and defended the interests of peasants, whom the old politicians of urban areas had tended to treat as second-class citizens.

Senghor's BDS rapidly became the dominant party. It was more rooted than its rival in the rural areas, and although Senghor was a Catholic, it was much closer to the Muslim brotherhoods (*tariqa*) who held tight control over much of the peasantry. It was also much more open to currents of African thought, like negritude and African socialism, with which trade unionists and the new elite of young intellectuals and civil servants easily identified. In 1951, the BDS won the two seats in the French National Assembly. The following year, it carried forty of the fifty seats to be filled in the territorial assembly elections. The elections of 1956 confirmed this position.

The BDS gradually tried to gather rival political movements under its banner. A first attempt in 1956 brought several minor parties into the BDS, which now became the BPS (Bloc populaire sénégalais). The year 1958 witnessed the birth of a "unified party," the Union progressiste sénégalais (UPS), which absorbed Lamine Guèye (who had become reconciled with Senghor) and his partisans.[3]

In was in this context, and after General de Gaulle came to power (1958), that the referendum of the project of the French Community took place. Under this project, African territories were to be granted extensive autonomy. The UPS suffered its first division over this issue. The majority of the party was in favor of de Gaulle's project, but the left wing broke off and founded the Parti du regroupement africain (PRA). The split did not affect the UPS unduly, however, and it won a massive victory in the referendum (92 percent of the votes), thanks to the support of rural leaders and marabouts (Muslim religious leaders). During the 1959 elections for the Senegalese National Assembly, the opposition was completely divided between the Marxist element, the Parti africain de l'indépendance, and the more conservative forces, the PRA and the Parti de la solidarité sénégalaise, and did not win a single seat. With 82.7 percent of the votes, the UPS's victory was absolute.

Thus, when Senegal became independent in 1960, first within the framework of the Federation of Mali and then as a sovereign entity, the UPS had a strong hold on the new country.

The long period we have just surveyed was essentially as a time of formal questioning of the colonial order. To explain these political gains, one must focus mainly on the struggles of the elite and the different movements that sought to give Africans elementary democratic rights—to elect their representatives, to form associations, trade unions and parties, and to have adequate protection under the law. These struggles, of course, were led by a minority—those whose ambitions were frustrated by a colonial situation that only very reluctantly and incompletely encouraged the appointment of Africans to positions of responsibility. In contrast to what happened in Algeria, or to a lesser extent in Cameroon or in Madagascar, there was never any mobilization of the masses against the colonial regime, and even less so any attempt to take up arms against the colonizer.

One of the main explanations for this was that Senegalese peasants, particularly in the regions where peanuts—"the great wealth of the country"—were grown, were under the control of Muslim religious leaders, who exerted a sort of formal and indirect rule over the rural world in their role as middlemen between the "center" and the "periphery." The ties of these very popular religious leaders—and peanut producers—to the colonial system were strong enough to act as a kind of safety valve. The marabouts rendered services of all kinds to the peasants. They also had the charisma (*baraka*) that made them leaders whose protection was sought not only in the here and now, but also in the afterlife. In addition, because of their religion, the marabouts felt very little attraction for, white culture and were, therefore, very reluctant, if not hostile, to accepting any form of assimilation. This religious power was a definite factor of political stability, and the success of Senghor and his party can be explained to a great extent by the relationship of trust he was able to cultivate among this class of religious leaders.

Léopold Senghor, who came from an ethnic group in the interior of the country and loudly proclaimed his African culture, appeared to be the natural spokesman of the marabouts and the peasants. Moreover, his status as an intellectual,[4] his active involvement in the African culture and literary movement of the time, as well as his pioneering efforts to defend "African socialism" attracted the sympathy of a great number of the young elite who could not identify with the older, urban-based leaders whose attitude they felt to be too "French."

Other explanations for the above political gains can be found in the age of political traditions in the country. Despite its status as a colony, Senegal was the only overseas territory to enter into modern political life at such an early date. as early as at the beginning of the century, a number of Africans had begun participating actively in electoral competition and acquired the habit of political debate. African politicians knew how to manage townships, how to make themselves heard in assemblies, and how to build a support network. At the outset, only a minority of the population was involved, and political struggles resembled private quarrels more than ideological debates. But, largely because these political activities took place in the urban arena, they had an impact that extended far beyond the few thousand people who were directly concerned. Hence, when political participation was widened, political "games" were not something new in Senegal. At the time of independence, a great number of leaders were immersed in the culture of political machinery, even if they endeavored to give it a new meaning. This was an inheritance that very few ex-colonies could claim. It made it very difficult to impose restrictions on a people who, for more than a century, had been used to political battles.

From a Dominant Party to a Single Party (1960–1976): Moderate Authoritarianism

In the period following independence, as a result of a series of crises, the regime sought to reinforce its control over society by strengthening the executive and the centralized power structure, and by developing a mass party. This authoritarian tendency was accompanied by restrictions on civil liberties, but, unlike many African countries, the regime never developed into a police state or promoted a situation of state-inspired political violence. Despite the UPS's monopoly over political life, despite many violations of civil liberties, and despite the personalization of power, freedom of speech in Senegal was never throttled. Social and political life in the country was constantly enlivened by debates on issues, by the voicing of opposition, and by the confrontation of clans and of ideas.

Senegal became a sovereign state in September 1960 after a short-lived attempt at union with the former French Sudan (April-August 1960) as the Federation of Mali. Ideological and personal antagonism, as well as differences in history and social structures between these two countries, explain the failure of this experiment.[5]

In August 1960, Senegal adopted a constitution that was inspired, both in spirit and largely in letter, by the French constitution of 1958. The text granted political parties the freedom to compete for the people's vote, on the condition that they respect "the principles of a national sovereignty and democracy." It called for a bicephalous system of executive power, with a president of the republic to be elected for seven years by an electoral college made up of parliamentarians and representatives of municipal and regional councils. As guardian of the constitution and supreme arbitrator, the president insures the continuity of the republic and the regular working of institutions. The president of the Council, or prime minister, determines and carries out national policy and is responsible to the Assembly. Legislative power is invested in a single chamber, the National Assembly, whose members are elected for five years by direct, universal suffrage. The constitution recognized the independence of the judicial branch and set up a Supreme Court that, aside from being the highest administrative jurisdiction, ensures that the Constitution is respected. In sum, then, the constitution called for a liberal, parliamentary democracy in which power is shared and civil liberties are guaranteed.[6]

Such a democratic foundation, however, hardly prevented the authoritarian evolution of a regime that was confronted, from the start, by major political crises. The most important was that of 1962, which brought into conflict the president of the republic and secretary-general of the UPS, Léopold Senghor, and his prime minister, the party's assistant secretary-general, Mamadou Dia. This conflict provoked a profound split between the UPS and the National Assembly that fast turned into a struggle of clans and clienteles, as had always been the case in Senegalese political life. Above and beyond any question of personal or factional rivalry, however, fundamentally different ideological options explain the uneasy co-existence of these two men.

Mamadou Dia supported a strong socialist line and urged rapid, radical reforms in economic and social matters. He wanted to put a stop to the all-powerful French interests, which were backed by their African clients. His idea of democracy was based not on institutional pluralism, but on grassroots action that gives initiative to the "powerless masses" through cooperatives and rural organizations. In order to bring about these changes, he thought it was necessary to build a party of the masses that would have preeminence over constitutional powers. Dia was not so attached as Senghor to the former "motherland," and encouraged the diversification of Senegal's foreign relations, particularly with Eastern bloc countries. His populist brand of socialism drew the favor of young civil servants and rural organizers—in short, of the "radical" wing of the UPS. Conversely, he met with the hostility, not to say hatred, of French businessmen and most Muslim religious leaders and traditional political authorities, who did not take kindly to the idea of radical changes that would reduce their own power. This power elite placed their faith much more in Senghor, whose humanistic form of socialism did not call for such rapid or profound changes. Senghor's lack of dogmatism, his concept of Negritude that encourages cultural contact, and his less "authoritarian" view of the party not only reassured businessmen, but also the marabouts and the dignitaries with whom he had been dealing for so long.

After a series of complicated events, a motion of censure was voted against Mamadou Dia by forty-seven members of Parliament on 17 December, 1962. He was accused of restricting parliamentary liberties and abusing power. Dia tried in vain to put down this parliamentary rebellion by force. The following day, he was arrested by the forces of order loyal to Senghor. In 1963, after a public trial, Dia was sentenced to life in prison, and several of his political friends also received prison sentences of varying lengths. In the period that followed the regime hardened. Executive power was reinforced and the opposition tamed. The man who had given the image of moderate and democratic leadership, who had criticized his adversary's dictatorial tendencies, gradually turned more authoritarian in order to rectify the situation.

After Mamadou Dia was arrested, Senghor initiated a constitutional reform, changing the regime from a parliamentary to a more presidential type. Henceforth, the president of the republic was to be elected by universal suffrage. Presidential power was extended, and in "exceptional circumstances" and for a limited time, the president was enabled to govern without the Assembly. He also had recourse to referenda in order to have legislation approved.

The basis for election to the National Assembly was also modified. Senegal was transformed into a single constituency, and parties were authorized to present candidates at an election only if they offered a complete list of candidates. As G. Hesseling noted, "For the authorities, the ballot by list was supposed to encourage national unity. In reality, it meant that only one party could sit in the Assembly."[7] In 1967, another constitutional reform further increased the powers of the president by giving him the right to dissolve the Assembly.

Opposition groups were gradually eliminated, either by integration into the government party or by repression. The Marxist-oriented Parti africain de l'indépendance (PAI) had been outlawed in 1960. In 1963, Senghor began a major campaign to woo the Bloc des masses sénégalaises (BMS), a party that stood under the banner of African nationalism and was favored by some marabouts of the powerful Muslim brotherhood, the *mourides*. In exchange for two ministerial appointments and some seats in the Assembly, Senghor proposed a merger of the BMS and the UPS. A few members of the BMS accepted the offer, although others refused, including Senghor's great intellectual rival, the historian Cheikh Anta Diop. On October 14 the BMS was outlawed by decree. Its leaders refused to be intimidated and decided to found another political movement, the Front national sénégalais (FNS).

In January 1964, a new law went into force requiring political parties to request a "receipt" from the minister of the interior to be authorized to carry out their activities. A few months later, the FNS was dissolved, having been accused of encouraging violence and of being a cover for the activities of the partisians of Mamadou Dia.

Still, the Parti du regroupement africain (PRA), which had splintered off from the UPS at the time of the 1958 referendum (see above), continued to exist. The PRA was solidly anchored in a few places like Casamance, in the south of Senegal. Senghor attempted to buy out the PRA, and, in 1963, a minority group of the party swallowed the bait. Those who held back were taken to court. But, in 1966, the two parties reached an agreement: in exchange for three ministerial appointments and a few seats in the controlling organs of the UPS, the PRA merged with Senghor's party.

All the parties belonging to the legal opposition had now disappeared. From this point on the "unified party" was a *de facto* single party. In the legislative elections of 1968, the UPS was the only party to present candidates and it obtained 99.4 percent of the ballots cast.

The opposition now had a choice between two channels of expression: clandestine political activity or trade union organizations. But here also, the trend was to unification. In 1962, all Senegalese trade unions had been regrouped into the Union nationale des travailleurs Sénégalais (UNTS), which was linked organically to the UPS. Despite having been bought out in this way, some union organizers did not hesitate to stir things up. Serious strikes took place in 1968 and 1969 as the result of pressure from the membership. Unable to control its rank and file, the UNTS was dissolved and replaced by a union more loyal to the government, the Confédération nationale des travailleurs du Sénégal (CNTS).

In 1973, by virtue of the 1965 law on seditious associations, the government abolished the Syndicat des enseignants du Sénégal (SES), the teachers' union and the second legal organization to openly attack the politics of the government.

The replacement, not to say monopolization, of political power by decisionmaking institutions had its effect on the management of the state and the society. As Sheldon Gellar writes, after Mamadou Dia's departure from power, "the technocratic perspective gained ground over the agrarian socialist perspective of the early 1960's."[8] The cooperatives and the rural organizations that were supposed to revolutionize social and economic relationships in the country were not done away with, but efforts were made to reduce whatever dysfunctional features they might have that would threaten the established order. On the other hand, centralized control of the marketing of peanuts was reinforced through the state marketing agency (set up at the time of independence)—for the simple reason that the sale of peanuts furnished most of the funds necessary for the functioning of the state and the salaries of its civil servants.

By the same logic, the state took steps to extend its control over the governing bodies on the local level. The Ministry of the Interior's power over townships was consolidated, and the latter's budgets were limited. The powers of regional governors were reinforced, and the regional assemblies were reduced to being organs to relay decisions and programs coming from the central state. In short, as Gellar concludes, "the subordination of local government to administration control coupled with the elimination of opposition political parties marked a sharp setback to democratization of Senegalese politics that was not reversed until the mid-1970's."[9]

Thus, throughout this period, one can observe in Senegal, as in most African countries, the setting into place of an authoritarian state and a one-party regime, aimed at concentrating all decisionmaking powers in the hands of the central authorities and at eliminating any group liable to oppose the established power structure. However, in Senegal this process never went so far as to set up an arbitrary or absolute dictatorship. If there were arrests, unlike in Guinea, there were never any concentration camps, nor were politial opponents physically eliminated. Having lived in Senegal during this period, I can testify to the fact that people did not hesitate, even openly, to criticize the government. The political atmosphere was tense at times, but there were no reactions of fear, of silence, or of secrecy. Those who were arrested were regularly tried, even if the courts leaned to the side of the government. The attitude of the government toward the opposition was strict, for Senghor's policy was to "unify" all parties and movements; but such a policy implied the use of the carrot as well as the stick. After all, there were many more leaders of the opposition who chose to join the party in power than those who chose to go into hiding.

Furthermore, the government was (relatively) amenable to negotiation and power plays. In 1968, under pressure from the UNTS, the government agreed to talks on a tripartite basis (government, employers, unions) that resulted in an increase in wages and an attempt to lower the price of staple foods. The principle of authoritarianism never excluded the idea of maneuvers and tactics to come to terms with difficult situations. The strategy of defusing conflicts was not only used for parties and trade unions, but also for Muslim religious leaders who "held" (and who still hold today) much of the country. Rather than eliminate the "feudal enclaves" of the marabouts as Sékou Touré tried to do, the Senegalese government preferred to win them over by meeting some of their demands (particularly in agricultural matters) and by using them to govern the peasants, as the French had done. Such policies lessened, to some extent, the effects of centralization, which, on the other hand, the regime was attempting to reinforce. Strangely enough, the marabouts were an obstacle to the state's absorption of civil society.[10]

Finally, the progressive elimination of the opposition did not prevent power struggles within the government party. Much more than a mass party, the UPS was (and is still) composed of clientele networks that compete for control over the local, regional, and national organization of the party—and, thus, for control of the political resources attached to them. There is a long history of such struggles in Senegal, and they can be violent. This is the case, in particular, when choosing candidates for elections to the National Assembly. The UPS's timid attempts to centralize the mechanisms of the party and to introduce a code of morality were not strong enough to resist this fundamental characteristic of Senegalese political culture. The UPS has remained a political arena in which bosses compete with one another not out of any ideological motivation, but for the spoils they expect to pick up.

Thus, the existence of a single party did not stifle political life, and competition continued to prevail in the choice of party officials. It was very difficult in Senegal for the central party organ to impose a leader on a constituency if he had no local power base. Such practices had no ideological dimension and were but a fiction of real democratic proceedings, but they did serve to limit the all-powerful tendencies of the party and the state. They functioned both as safety valves for the regime, by preventing the crystallization of more radical tendencies, and as obstacles to the abuse of power.[11]

From independence to the middle of the 1970s, Senegal was characterized by a modified one-party state. The government had set up a regime that could be called authoritarian, but the process was never complete because the government either could not or did not want to do so. What factors explain this situation? We will first take into account elements that arose from the situation itself and examine later the structural features of the Senegalese political system.

At the outset, one has to stress the importance of the personality of President Léopold Senghor, the "father of the nation," who left such an indelible mark on the first years of independence. His regime reflected the leadership of a man who is both a great intellectual—one of Africa's most well-known writers and the pioneer of African socialism—and a first-class politician, skilled in political maneuvering and shrewd in his ability to adapt to situations or to predict them.

Senghor can in no way be defined as a dogmatic intellectual or politician. The father of "negritude" is also the man who promoted such ideas as *métissage culturel* (cultural crossbreeding) and *dialogue des cultures* (cross-cultural communication). He borrowed part of his socialist ideas from Marx, but he also endeavored to adapt such ideas to Africa, and even to go beyond them. His humanistic socialism is a far cry from the combative Marxism of someone like Sékou Touré. If he was in favor of the creation of a "unified party" and worked to bring it into being, he never conceived of the party as a monolithic institution, even if he always denounced the "fratricidal" struggle of factions within the UPS. While arguing that the absence of real social classes in Africa (a proposition one could debate) and that the need to promote national unity justified the existence of a single large national party, he never rejected the idea of pluralistic democracy—when circumstances allowed it. And, as we will see, he became the promoter of pluralism in the middle 1970s.

Senghor's international status and his prestige as a writer were important factors in his moderation and liberalism. It was very difficult for the man who has long been thought of as a future Nobel prize winner in literature to behave as a tyrant and as a violator of civil liberties. He has always been very sensitive to the image that Senegal projected abroad, and he did not want to appear as the oppressor of the country's intelligentsia—remarkably large and lively for such a small nation. Whatever love-hate relationships he may have had with fellow artists like Sembène Ousmane, the filmmaker, or Cheikh Anta Diop, the historian—people who did not hesitate to voice their criticisms—Senghor endeavored to turn Senegal into a "black Greece." Such an ideal was incompatible with a hard-line regime suspicious of artistic creation and criticism.

Senghor also turned out to be a first-rate politician who could be firm when he felt it was necessary, but who was amenable to discussion and negotiation. His authority and his "untouchable position," to use a term coined by G. Hesseling, were as much the result of his political art as they were of his intellectual aura.[12] Two very good examples of this political know-how were the ways in which he was able to win the backing of Muslim brotherhoods, despite being a Catholic himself, and to "convince" many opposition leaders to rally to the cause of the government or the UPS.

If Senghor had so much authority and prestige, it was because a whole class of political and intellectual elites identified with him in a certain way, even if a few members of this group had uneasy relationships with him. Senghor was the the "ideal portrait" of the Senegalese elite of the time. A brilliant craftsman of both the written and the spoken word, he was the best symbol of the all-important "master" figure in Senegalese culture. In the subtle and efficient way he played the politician's game, he was a real political boss, a most worthy heir of the great Senegalese politicians who preceded him.[13]

Under these conditions, it is easy to understand why the UPS never became a monolithic party. Local leaders in Senegal were too used to political competition (the "natural" mode of selecting leaders) and to the process of creating a clientele to agree to unite within a closed organization, where they would have to be at the leader's beck and call and where they would have to accept decisions from the top without complaining. Whatever authority Senghor had over his party, he was never able to turn the UPS into a mass party of ideology that toed the line behind him. The UPS remained a political machine, or rather, the sum of a number of political machines.

Nevertheless, Senegal's political and economic situation in the first years after independence gave rise to political and social tensions that pressed toward a hardening and a centralization of power. Although the country appeared to be much further along the road to "political modernization" than many other African countries (with its skilled political elite, electoral tradition, and experience in the management of public affairs, etc.), it was not saved from the structural problems that shook most of these new nations, even if it coped better than the others with these problems.

Between 1960 and 1970, Senegal was buffeted by three major political crises, which resulted in a redefinition of the structures of power and of the state along more authoritarian lines. The first was the short-lived Federation of Mali, whose demise not only put an end to the hope of achieving regional political union in West Africa, but also took its toll on Senegal's political climate. The impossible entente with Modibo Keita's Soudan (now Mali) created tensions within the UPS that led to sanctions against party officials and members who were suspected of encouraging Keita's plans. Emergency measures were taken to "set things in order": the Law of 7 September, 1960 authorized the government to legislate in effect by decree in certain areas. The Decree of 10 October, 1960 restricted the freedom of movement in the country for any person whose actions were judged to be a threat to public order and safety.

The second major crisis was the conflict between Senghor and Mamadou Dia, mentioned earlier. This rift, as well, was followed by purges in the party, a reinforcement of executive power, and the gradual elimination of the opposition. Senghor's aim was to get rid of the rival political clan that was guilty of questioning his supremacy. If the rules of the game of Senegalese political culture allow for struggles between factions, such conflicts must never reach the top of the political pyramid so as to threaten the position of the supreme leader, who is conceived as the ultimate arbitrator. In this sense, one would have to say that competition between political clans cannot lead to any true choice or even to any true alternative sharing of power.

In 1968 and 1969, it was not any struggle at the summit that shook Senegal, but rather a movement of revolt on the part of students and unions. Initially inspired by the French "revolution" of May 1968, the events provoked violent clashes involving a great number of intellectuals, civil servants, and workers who protested price increases and who felt their careers were stifled by the government's timid measures of Africanization in the public and private sectors. As we have seen, the government's response was to pull in the reins on the workers' movements.

Essentially urban phenomena, these crises masked the profound malaise in rural areas resulting from the deterioration of the situation of peanut farmers. Peanut production had declined sharply after the agreements signed between African countries and the European Economic Community, putting an end to the preferential prices France granted Senegal. Moreover, the years of chronic drought in the Sahel had not helped matters any.

The peasants were losing their enthusiasm for growing a crop that paid them less and less and were increasingly devoting their efforts to the cultivation of staple foods. The state, however, was dependent on peanut farming to furnish an important share of its budget. Thus, the government cultivated the influence of local political and religious leaders to hold the rural world in line, but it did not hesitate to resort to force if necessary, carrying out veritable "dragon hunts," in the words of René Dumont, to collect taxes and to force peasants to pay their debts.[14] All these methods served to alienate the state from the rural population, who felt they were being taken back to the worst days of colonization. Thanks alone to the marabouts, who played the role of middleman and safety valve, this situation of structural conflict did not degenerate into a full-scale peasant revolt.[15]

In the final analysis, the growing authoritarianism (in relative terms) of the regime corresponded to the elite's inability, or at least its difficulty, in holding the civil society and its movements in check. It was to correct these shortcomings that the regime changed its course.

Democratic Renewal (1974–1985)

In 1974, Senegal began setting into action a series of institutional reforms that were to modify the nature of the regime profoundly by opening the political arena to multi-party competition, first on a somewhat timid basis and later in total freedom. Judged by outsiders to be exemplary in Africa, these initiatives did not solve the more structural problems of the country. They did, however, guarantee the stability of the political system, at least for some time. But closer analysis shows that this transition to democracy corresponded to an acute crisis between the state and the society that was masked by the often naive expectations generated both inside and outside Senegal by these reforms. Liberalizing the regime was an attempt—whose success must be qualified—to give new life to a state that was up against social, economic, and political constraints that it could hardly control.

This new chapter in the history of Senegal is marked, in the main, by the personality of Abdou Diouf, the chosen successor of President Senghor, who voluntarily resigned from office in 1981. Senghor's decision was motivated by his desire to be seen as a fighter for democracy. More a high-level civil servant than a politician, and more a technocrat than an intellectual, Abdou Diouf had carried out his career in the shadow of Senghor, first as first secretary to the president and then as prime minister. The date of his later appointment, 1971, coincided with a constitutional reform that reinstated the function of prime minister as a means of diluting executive power.

Abdou Diouf's role in the democratization of the country cannot be denied, but it was Senghor who initiated the reforms as early as 1974 by officially recognizing lawyer Abdoulaye Wade's Parti démocratique Sénégalais (PDS), a party that proclaimed its allegiance to the tenets of social democracy. In 1978, a constitutional reform was adopted which put into place a system of "controlled democracy." The number of parties was limited to three, and they were required to belong to one of the following three systems of thought: (1) liberal and democratic; (2) socialist and democratic; (3) Marxist or communist. These restrictive measures were aimed at fostering political rigor and stability and discouraging opportunism and anarchy.

The UPS voted to become a socialist party at its 1978 convention and chose the second option. The PDS agreed, although reluctantly, to define itself as "liberal and democratic." As for the old African Marxist movement, the Parti africain de l'indépendance, it much more willingly accepted the communist label, although internal divisions within Senegal's extreme left wing had led to the proliferation of rival clandestine or semiclandestine groups.

On the other hand, the Rassemblement national démocratique, the party of Senghor's old rival, Cheikh Anta Diop, was rejected from the official political scene. The party had been founded in January 1976 under an essentially nationalistic platform. In 1978, a fourth "conservative" option was recognized, thus allowing Boubacar Guèye's Mouvement républicain Sénégalais (MRS) to participate openly in political life.

The legislative and presidential elections of 1978 were a great success for the Socialist party (which received 81.7 percent of the ballots cast and 82 of the 100 seats in the Assembly) and for President Senghor personally (who won 82.5 percent of the vote). But they also gave the country an official opposition, the PDS, which won eighteen seats in the Assembly, while Abdoulaye Wade received 17.4 percent of the presidential vote. It must be emphasized, however, that the elections were held in a tense climate and organized in a way that threatened the secrecy of the ballot. Furthermore, the rate of participation (63 percent of registered voters) showed a lack of enthusiasm on the part of the people for this experiment in democracy. This allowed the "illegal" opposition—particularly the RND, which had called for a boycott—to claim success in the elections.

With the arrival of Abdou Diouf as head of state in 1981, Senegal seemed to undergo an even greater renewal. While claiming to be Senghor's heir, Diouf set out to give new impetus to political life and to provide better management of state affairs. In his own words, they were to be "transparent" and more open to democratic debate.

Four months after coming to power, Diouf proposed a constitutional reform abrogating the law of 1976, which had set limits to the number of parties and the number of possible ideological banners. This liberalization, to which Senghor declared his opposition, brought forth a multitude of political movements, including Cheikh Anta Diop's RND and the Movement démocratique populaire of ex-Prime Minister Mamadou Dia. Thus, today there are more than fifteen officially recognized political parties in Senegal, including a number of small Marxist groups. This adventure in democracy had its counterpart in the labor movement, and there are currently four trade unions in Senegal: the CNTS, "affiliated," although no longer "integrated" with the Socialist party; the Union des travailleurs libres du Sénégal (UTLS), which has close links to the PDS; a teachers' union, the Syndicat unique et démocratique des enseignments du Sénégal (SUDES), a powerful opposition movement to the government; and the Confederation Générale des travailleurs démocratiques du Sénégal (CGTDS). Likewise, there has been a proliferation of political journals, some more long-lived than others. However, all this has had little effect on either the television authority, the Office de la radiotélévision sénégalaise (ORTS), or on the country's only daily newspaper, *Soleil*, both of which show little tendency to voice other than official opinions.

President Diouf did not stop at the lifting of restrictions on political life that had been initiated by his predecessor. He also wanted to renew both the style and the political practices that had prevailed among the old Senegalese political elite. Speaking first in front of the National Council and then before the convention of the Socialist party, he denounced the corruption, opportunism, and influence peddling that was so common in the party and invited it to open up to "all the winds blowing in from afar" and to the "quickening forces" of the nation. He urged party officials to encourage the initiatives of members, who were often treated as simple clients and who were "glorified in periods of renewal [of party leadership] and pushed to the sides afterwards." In Diouf's view, the free political competition that had been inaugurated should, in turn, incite the Socialist party to renew itself in order to keep its dominant position.

At the same time, Abdou Diouf and his government adopted a policy of dialogue and reform with respect to the social groups that had long been on uneasy terms with the state. Turning to the rural world, he put into place a more liberal policy, less controlled by the state and more heavily dependent on private business. This was designed to appease the peasants, who had become discouraged by unwieldy and ineffective production and marketing structures that were more useful in serving personal and political aims than those of development.[15] In August 1980, when he was still prime minister, he had replaced the official marketing board with a more flexible and less bureaucratic organization. All these measures had the effect of restoring the confidence of both peasants and traders and of encouraging their initiative.

The problems of education on primary, secondary, and university levels were also taken up. These issues had been responsible for much violent discussion, agitation, and unrest since independence. In January 1981, Diouf invited the teachers and their unions, including the SUDES—which accepted despite its well-known hard-line attitude—to attend a vast forum to debate the question of education. The long-running conference led to an extensive, if gradual, reform of the educational system. Politically it reduced tension, for some time, between the government and the teachers and students. For Diouf, it was also a step toward what he called "national reconciliation" as a means of "overcoming old ideological reflexes."[16]

Finally, for the new president, the extension of democracy also called for a healthier management of public affairs in a country that was ailing from corruption, misdoings, and frequent misuse of public funds. It was a question of creating an image of rigor and clarity in the business of running a state. Toward this end, a law was passed in July 1981 punishing the accumulation of illicit wealth. Although few people were actually prosecuted, the law did have the effect of bringing about a rumor campaign against a certain number of politicians, including some ministers, who had no recourse but to resign.

In short, Diouf and his new team projected an image of liberal leadership that aimed to put the affairs of state in order and that was open to dialogue with the social forces in the country.

The legislative and presidential elections of 1983 were to be the most patent sign of democratic renewal in Senegal, as well as a popularity test for Senghor's successor and for his policy of change. Diouf won a large victory over the five rival candidates (receiving 83.5 percent of the ballots cast) and the Socialist party kept absolute control of the Assembly with 80 percent of the votes and 111 seats. The opposition was left with only ten seats (nine for the PDS, one for the RND). But the participation of voters was even lower than in 1978 (58 percent of those registered), and many irregularities in balloting procedures were also officially noted, pointing to the limits and the difficulties of democratic renewal in Senegal.[17]

The fact is, although Diouf has given new life to the regime, many problems remain up in the air and much tension still exists. The enthusiasm generated by the new president and his ministers when they first came to power five years ago has dampened somewhat, and the honeymoon period is over. The liberalization of the economy and, in particular, of the marketing networks for peanuts, have not brought about the hoped-for results, nor have they been able to prevent the illegal sale of seed stock on a large scale. Dialogue and democracy have been powerless in the face of violent regional outbursts in Casamance, the southern part of the country (in 1980, 1982, and 1983), which represent a challenge to the Senegalese nation-state. Nor has the new team managed to channel and control increasingly restless Islamic forces. It would seem as though social forces, expectations, and grievances have been unable to find a means of expression in the structures and organizations that Senegalese democracy has made available to them—a significant reminder (to which we will return) of the gap between civil and political society. Moreover, the Senegalese military expedition into Gambia in July 1981 (in order to save a regime that was up against the wall and to set up a confederation of the two countries) had all the appearances of a power play to gain control of the former British colony. Even if this move plucked a thorn from Senegal's side, one would be hard put to say that it grew out of an authentic democratic desire for regional unity or that it was the result of free choice by the interested groups.

One should, nonetheless, beware of underestimating the extent of the reforms undertaken by Abdou Diouf. Two facts help to explain why the democratic structures that he tried to put into place did not always produce the expected results. First, Senegal's democratic experience is one of the most daring that Africa has seen. Second, many of the obstacles encountered were due to an established political culture and to structures that were based on political bargaining and on networks of clientelism—patterns of behavior, in other words, that are resistant to innovation. To understand the nature, scope, and limits of this experiment in democracy, it is necessary to focus more closely on the factors that explain Senegal's recent evolution, as well as the obstacles encountered.

It is important to recall, briefly, Senegal's situation on the international scene. We have already seen how aware Senegalese leaders (Senghor in particular) were of their country's international image. The reputation of the poet-president's regime, despite efforts at moderation, was a bit tarnished as a result of the *de facto* outlawing of opposition parties and trade unions and the repression of student strikes. Senghor wanted his country to be a model of liberty and democracy for Africa, and he counted on this prestige to attract Western aid and investors, who could not but be impressed by the example of Senegal in an Africa characterized by the widespread degradation of living standards and political mores. Similarly, Senghor wanted his party to be recognized as a full-fledged member of the International Socialist Movement that included many social democratic parties in Europe and Latin America. This membership required the liberation of all political prisoners and the official acknowledgment of a pluralist state. Senghor's idea was that Africa should add its brick to the construction of the socialist ideal in the world. A short time after tri-party structures were set in place, Senegal's Socialist party joined the International Socialist Movement, in which Senghor took on important responsibilities.

Above and beyond the international ambitions of this little country, internal factors led the regime to modify the political structures and climate of a state that was increasingly powerless to do anything, either about the crisis in the countryside or uncontrolled urban development. By 1981, an estimated 31 percent of the population lived in urban areas, especially in Dakar and its outskirts. This had given rise to a veritable parallel society that the political system was not able to keep in check.

Léopold Senghor had managed, by charm or threat, to integrate into his government and his party most of the opposition forces, and, thus, to establish the great "unified party" that he had dreamed of. However, this personal success also had its shortcomings. Far from injecting new strength into the party, the state, and the government, these political maneuvers had the effect of encouraging the growth of clientelism, crony networks, and inefficiency. In the words of Pierre Biarnes, "Senghor found himself at the head of a weakened political movement that was threatened with sclerosis, and the disease finally infected the apparatus of the state itself."[18]

In such conditions, Senghor and his successor were intelligent enough to attempt to regenerate a political system that was running out of breath and increasingly cut off from the realities of the country. Senegal's enormous economic problems made it even more urgent to carry out reforms and to call forth the "living forces" of the country—the class of African businessmen and young managers—that political democratization had neglected up to then. It was also urgent to find new forms of organization and control for this society that were more pluralist in conception, less rigid, and more open to local initiatives. Moreover, the renewal of democratic processes and the reworking of state structures were meant not only to loosen the lines of communication between the government and the civil service on the one hand and the citizens on the other, but also to boost the economy by reinstating confidence in producers.

Reform had also become necessary to deal with the challenge of growing Islamic mobilization. During the 1970s, Islam served as an ideology that mobilized and structured social groups who could not find the answers to their problems and expectations elsewhere. This was all the more true in that the *turuq* (brotherhoods), which were traditionally rooted in the rural milieu, had succeeded in adapting themselves to the urban context. Pushed forward by their followers, the marabouts had become more of a threat to a state that sought, in vain, to isolate them.

Thus, the democratic renaissance must be seen in a much wider context than simply an isolated response to a state of crisis. Democratization and liberalization of the regime and the state are attempts to strengthen the social foundation of the state, to ensure that the legal country and the real country coincide. Political stability in the past had been guaranteed by a mixture of bureaucracy and clientelism that allowed for political communication between the "center" and the "periphery," each of which checked the excesses of the other.

However, the system was less and less able to cope with the changing reality in the country. Challenged by the rise of a young, dynamic elite, old political bosses clung to their positions and privileges. Confronted by rural exodus, economic collapse, and the tragedy of drought-stricken rural areas, as well as by the government's grand development schemes (like those of the Diama and Manatali dams), these older men were drained of their "resources" and left helpless. As for the central government and the civil service, they had gradually given up bureaucratic control of the economy (as we have seen with the reform of peanut-marketing networks) and adopted a new ideology and new institutions aimed at organizing society at the local level and incorporating citizens directly into the state—meaning doing without middlemen such as political "bosses" and marabouts.

In the minds of Abdou Diouf and his "Young Turks," renovating the Senegalese Socialist party, giving free rein to different currents of opinion, and attacking the bureaucratic rigidity of the state were all means of restructuring, within a single, established framework, the centrifugal or parallel forces and movements that the authoritarian and clientelist state had impelled away from the political arena. In so doing, the state also became the main spokesman for both urban and rural masses.

It remains true, however, that the new generation of leaders cannot claim to have the same political backing as the "old barons" of the regime they are replacing, even if the older generation, as we have seen, was somewhat on the decline. Gellar writes:

> Technocrats spending most of their time running the state bureaucracy, they had few close ties with the party faithful at the grassroots levels. The lack of contact with the less educated and more traditionalist rank and file members of the party was largely due to the fact that Diouf and the relatively young, well educated cosmopolitan group around him, defined themselves as members of a national intellectual elite rather than the representatives of local, regional, and ethnic constituencies.[19]

Thus, it is easy to understand that democracy had not become part of everyone's belief system in Senegal. It is identified with the intellectual and professional elite of the country. A large percentage of the people do not play the game at all. They are not interested in partisan competition and channel their demands through other social institutions (religion, local associations, music)—or through violence (the revolts in Casamance). The authoritarian and clientelist, but inert, state counted on middlemen to preserve stability. The new technocratic, democratic, and more ambitious state can no longer call upon these local resources to maintain itself. That makes it all the more vulnerable.

• THE SEARCH FOR EXPLANATIONS •

Having traced the different historical stages of Senegalese politics, we can now step back to consider the explanatory factors behind the regime's mixed success. We will be better equipped, as a result, to open the perspectives that seem to be the most plausible.

Political Culture

Just as the democratic performance of the regime has been a mixed success, so Senegalese political culture partakes of a mixed nature. It is a combination of rather authoritarian values and beliefs, compensated for by a propensity for debate, political gameplaying, and a conception of power that depends more on the interdependence of actors (even if the relationships are unequal) than on organized violence.

It must first be emphasized that the traditional political culture of Senegal's ancient local political systems was far from being locked up in a rigid authoritarianism, even if it was based on political and social hierarchies. Political competition between clans was indispensable for the exercise of power, and the Senegalese certainly did not wait for the birth of modern politics to discover the virtues (and the shortcomings) of political contests—they belong to their "natural" political universe. Moreover, among the Wolof (as among the Tukulor), political power holders were chiefs who were closely watched over by dignitaries, by the people, and, above all, by a whole political code that required them to work for the commonwealth. The Senegalese historian Cheikh Anta Diop has spoken in this regard of "constitutional monarchies."[20] The power of the "king" was limited, shared, and decentralized. It was governed by a political culture that defined a chief as a *samba linguer*, that is, as a man of honor who was supposed to protect those who were living under his authority and to be generous toward them. Dominant groups could not totally exploit or tyrannize their subjects without losing their favor. The "king" had duties toward his people, and if his power became too arbitrary, he could expect to be unseated and replaced. Power was thus held in check, if only because of its potential danger. As a Wolof proverb says, "A king is not a parent"; this means that the self-interested nature of power can lead its holder to sacrifice the interests of his family to his own interests.[21]

If traditional chiefdoms have disappeared today, this political culture has not disappeared with them. It survives, in particular, in the Muslim brotherhoods, whose leaders are viewed on the popular level as the holders of "good power," people whose "resources" profit those who are lacking in them.

The modern political elite has also been marked by these values. Of course, such values have become somewhat twisted in the system of patronage and clientelism that is the backbone of contemporary Senegalese political culture. One has to admit, however, that these kinds of behavior are ambivalent. It is true that they are responsible for the corruption, the prevarication, or at the very least, the manipulation of institutions for personal aims that are features of modern political life. On the other hand, they are also a way to control power. A "boss" who is unable to furnish the benefits expected will be disowned by his rank and file (his clients) in favor of a rival who appears to be more generous.

But the political elite of the present day have not only been nourished by these traditions and experiences. They have also been schooled in the ways of Western democracy. Senegalese leaders, more than others in Africa no doubt, are sons of France. They have learned from the former motherland the arts of politics on the most pragmatic level (political maneuvering), but also on the most noble. Hence, for Abdou Diouf, "knowledge of the other, the refusal to wear ideological blinkers, the search for the truth which leads one to listen to others, the expression of all opinions on acts of power, and the safeguard of the social and moral values of the country are all indispensable conditions for any pluralist democracy."[22]

Modern political culture in Senegal is thus a mixture of *liberalism*, which delights in discussions of philosophy and doctrine and which is hardly compatible with ideological dogmas, combined with a propensity for the *accumulation of power* (the more resources one has, the larger one's clientele, and the means to achieve such ends include compromise, as well as the crushing of rivals). A final element of this combination is the constant concern to convey an *acceptable image to the outside*, for Senegalese politicians have also conceived of their experiences as being models.

These values, however, appear more and more artificial or theoretical to segments of the population whose daily problems have not been solved by the intellectual debates, games of patronage, and pursuit of international prestige of the Senegalese political class. This explains the tendency for some to turn toward other systems of reference, such as militant Islamic organizations that purport to solve the county's problems through ideals of rigor and nationalism. The lack of interest in elections and the growing development of different Muslim brotherhoods and associations attest to an evolution that could lead, in the long run, to radical transformations.

Historical Developments

The historical developments that have left their mark on the Senegalese political system have been noted and analyzed in the preceding pages. The essential features can be summarized here.

Traditional political systems in Senegal, although articulated around unequal power relationships (except in the south, in Casamance, where acephalous types of societies predominate), can be defined more as "constitutional monarchies" that allow for some political competition and control of power. We have shown what remnants of this remain in contemporary political life.

Second, if the colonial experience had sometimes been brutal (slavery, economic, social and political destruction), it was nevertheless conditioned—one is tempted to say "softened"—by two elements: the existence, in the rural world, of a sort of system of indirect rule, based around Muslim brotherhoods that had taken on the role of the precolonial aristocracy; and, in the urban world, the existence of democratic institutions that mobilized the African elite and allowed it to gain access to certain positions of responsibility. This explains to a great extent why independence was acquired without revolutionary struggle. Structured as Senegal was by the marabouts, who had the confidence of the peasants, and by a class of experienced politicians, the conditions were not present for violent anticolonial sentiment to develop—contrary to what happened in the Portuguese colonies or in Zimbabwe, for example. Indeed, one could say that the absence of revolutionary and violent anticolonial struggle in Senegal helped to generate democracy by limiting violence as a method of political expression.

Class Structure

The structure of social classes in Senegal is extremely unequal. Nevertheless, certain social and political mechanisms have limited up to now the disruptive effects of this inequality.

It must be remembered that inequality was an inherent feature of traditional societies in Senegal. Such societies were divided into "orders" (free men, castes of craftsmen, slaves), which themselves were subdivided into several categories (noblemen or simple commoners in the first group, for example). An exception to this, as we have seen, was the south, where the idea of hierarchy in social structures was practically nonexistent, particularly among the Diola. These traditional social distinctions are far from having disappeared. Members of inferior social groups have, of course, been able to climb the social ladder to positions of leadership. But they remain the object of prejudices that depreciate them socially, and it is often difficult for them, in particular, to marry outside the social group from which they originate. In a 1977 interview, Léopold Senghor admitted it was a delicate issue that did come up when making appointments, although he always tried to play down the phenomenon.[23]

Social inequality is, thus, not new in Senegal. However, whereas traditional social ranks were based on differences of social status and not necessarily on wealth, modern hierarchies are much more a matter of differences in income. These gaps are particularly acute between the urban and the rural worlds. The average income of wage earners in the public and private sectors is estimated to be ten times higher than that of farmers, and the income gap between town and country is widening despite the higher prices growers have been getting for peanuts in the last few years.

The upper classes are dominated by the bureaucrats of the civil service, who make up the class of power wielders. "Senegal's proliferating state administration, accounting as it does for almost half of the national total of wage employees and for more than half of the national budget, may properly be called [in local terms] a ruling class."[24] Furthermore, the income the state uses to pay civil servants derives, in part, from trade in peanuts, for "the export monocrop has remained the nation's most readily taxable resource."[25]

Under the influence of the International Monetary Fund, however, the expansion of the public sector has slowed down of late. Since 1980, the Senegalese government has taken a number of measures to limit public spending, creating problems, in turn, for young university graduates who are finding it increasingly difficult to procure employment—although job offers in the private sector have been on the rise in recent years.

The class of Senegalese merchants and manufacturers is still relatively small compared to the powerful foreign interests in the country. During the early years of independence, the state directed its efforts more to expanding the public or semipublic sectors rather than to developing domestic capitalism. It has had to change its position somewhat since the beginning of the 1970s in response to demands from Senegalese businessmen who felt their margin of maneuver between state-run companies and foreign interests was much too narrow. It is a growing category nonetheless—although very dependent on the state—not only for the supply of credit, but also for the marketing of goods.

Many of the most successful businessmen are merchants belonging to the *mouride* brotherhood. Religious networks have been put to use parallel to political networks. Thanks to these two factors, for example, the *mourides* have managed to gain control of the main market in Dakar, Sandaga.

Also among the *mourides* (and, to a lesser extent, the other Muslim brother-hoods) can be found a bourgeoisie of rural religious leaders. Marabouts in Senegal are the only big growers. They have at their disposal a free labor force to work their fields—that of their faithful (*taalibe*)—not to mention the Islamic tithe (*zakat*) that brings to them a share of the harvest from the private farms of other disciples. In exchange, the marabouts must take care of the moral, as well as the material, well-being of their followers: help them in time of need, supply them with fields to work, find them wives, and defend their interests (meaning the price of peanuts) before the state.

Up to now, these structures of patronage between unequal categories have contributed to the stability of the country, for they have allowed a certain re-distribution of wealth. If these structures continue to govern the relationships between marabouts and *taalibe*, however, they work less and less well in the modern sector, even though it is customary in Senegal for a wage-earner to come to the aid of a great number of people. The urban explosion and the crisis in the rural world no longer enable these mechanisms to function on a large scale. Given the degree of peasant discontent, one cannot be sure that the mara-bouts will be able to continue to act as effective buffers. As "peasant leaders" of rural revolts, they may be tempted to make political use of discontent. They may even be led to instigate such revolts.

Ethnicity and Religion

For a long time, Senegal was free of any ethnic and religious tensions that might present a threat to nation building. However, the conflicts that have arisen in Casamance since 1980 are such that, in the long run, ethnic stability might well be upset.

With the ethnic equilibrium that seemed to prevail for many years, Senegal had been relatively privileged compared to other African countries. The Wolof group, with 41 percent of the population, appeared to be the keystone of the edifice. Indeed, their language had gradually become the medium of communi-cation in the whole country. There were several reasons for this: the great number of Wolof living in towns, their weight in the civil service, their domi-nant position among African traders, their geographic mobility, and their posi-tions of leadership in Muslim organizations. Their domination was often viewed as intolerable by other ethnic groups, but at the same time, they appeared as mod-els of social promotion for non-Wolof elites. Moreover, the Wolof domination did not prevent other groups from being present in representative institutions, including the head of the state. Senghor himself was a Serer (14 percent of the population).[26]

Also contributing to the reign of ethnic peace was the fact that the govern-ment never sought to impose Wolof as the only African language. Along with French, the official languages included six national languages: Wolof, Fulani,

Serer, Malinké, Diola, and Soninké. But, on the question of introducing these languages into the educational system, the attitude of the government was much more reserved. The prestige of French was admittedly an inhibiting factor, but so was the Wolof question. Teaching African languages would naturally mean putting Wolof in a privileged position, not only because of the extent to which it is spoken in the country, but also because it has been studied more by linguists and could be immediately operational in school curricula.[27] And although non-Wolofs might well be able to function in that language, they would certainly object to any attempt to impose Wolof as a compulsory official language—for which certain Senegalese nationalist (Wolof) groups have been clamoring.

Another element that must be weighed is the overwhelming presence of Islam as the religion of 90 percent of the Senegalese people. Aside from the question of unifying customs—a point that is too often raised—there is no denying that the Muslim religion has, at the very least, inspired new feelings of belonging to a national and even an international community. The celebration of major Muslim feast days, for example, or the participation of the brotherhoods in the pilgrimage to Mecca, are ways of uniting people of different ethnic origins around common experiences and common symbols, even if, here again, Wolof leadership is an obvious element.

One could point out, of course, that Senegalese Muslims are divided into several brotherhoods (*murridiyya, tijaniyya, qadiriyya*), not to mention the groups of reformists or Islamists who reject or criticize these traditional religious orders and advocate the unity of Islam. However, if such marginal beliefs have sometimes led to friction or even violent outbursts, particularly inside mosques, there is no seed here of any religious war. The leaders of brotherhoods meet upon occasion and adopt common attitudes from time to time. The authorities of the muridiyya do not cry out that the tijanes or the qadirs are heretics. None of these groups excludes the others from the world of Islam. The only problem would seem to arise from the dynamic nature of *mouride* activism, which inspires a great deal of jealousy among the other brotherhoods.

Christians (mainly Catholics—about 5 percent of the population), are found primarily among the Serer and the Diola. Islamic renewal movements in Senegal might raise problems for them one day, if those who advocate an Islamic republic were heeded or came to power. But for the time being, and despite strong pressure from Muslim groups, the government remains firmly attached to the notion of the separation of religion and state.

Religion is a prominent aspect of the specific identity of the people in Casamance. The Diola dominate groups that defend regional interests. Very few Diola are Muslims, and where conversion has taken place, it is often only very superficial. Traditional religions and Catholicism (led by clergy who have a strong sense of ethnic membership) are ramparts against Islamization and militant Islamic movements. Other differences derive from the social and political organization of these societies, which are radically different from those of the northern part of the country. Wolof and Tukulor societies are characterized by the tradition of a central state and by social systems based on a strict hierarchy. Diola society, on the other hand, like that of neighboring peoples, the Balante and Manjaque, is acephalous and egalitarian.

Other factors contribute to the strong sense of frustration in Casamance and the drive to actively proclaim local identity in the face of "internal colonialism." There is Casamance's geographic isolation. It is separated from the rest of Senegal by Gambia. The infrastructure, in matters of health and education particularly, is much less developed in Casamance. Finally, local commerce and civil service jobs are dominated by "northerners." All of this has created, as D. Darbon has written, "a general incapacity of communication between the Senegalese state and the people of Casamance."[28]

The specificity of Casamance was first expressed through the blossoming of prophetic movements, then by the development of opposition parties in the region (the PRA was, above all, a Casamance party, and more recently, the PDS has chalked up much higher scores in Casamance than its national average). Recently, regional demands have become much more radical and violent, and serious troubles have broken out in Zinguinchor and Oussoye resulting in several dozen deaths. On a number of occasions, Casamance was in a state of seige. A Casamance flag appeared along with a clandestine political movement, the Mouvement des forces démocratiques de Casamance (MFDC), led by a Catholic priest, Father Augustin D. Senghor, who is in prison.

In my opinion, there is a real regional movement in Casamance today. It is an expression of the difficulties of communication and presents a real challenge to the Senegalese state. But, above and beyond Diola ethnic identity or Casamance regional identity, what is finally at stake is the kind of relationship that exists between a powerless central state and a "periphery" that has brought a number of mechanisms into play in its efforts to repel an intruding "center" whose actions are perceived as negative.

In sum, Senegal's relative ethnic equilibrium and religious homogeneity have allowed the country to avoid conflicts that would have undermined the political stability necessary to democracy. But, on the other hand, groups who are outside this "natural" national unity, like the Diola, might feel drawn to commit acts of violence to express themselves.

State and Society

The Senegalese state is heir to the French tradition of centralization. Senegal's administrative structures, as well as the national ideology that governs them, have been modeled on the French Jacobin state. Regions are void of power and autonomy, and any manifestation of ethnic difference is rejected, on principle, as being an obstacle to national unity. This tendency to centralization has also been reinforced by the colonial tradition. Finally, Senegal's leaders justify the state's domination as a condition for development. According to them, in order for development to be effective, efforts and initiatives must not be spread out too thinly.

All of these factors, in addition to the state's role as the main employer and the means by which the class of politicians and bureaucrats can accumulate wealth, have resulted in an administration that is omnipresent and that employs a great number of people. With independence, Senegal adopted a system of national planning and set up many state-owned companies, particularly after 1970 (between 1970 and 1975 approximately seventy-five state companies were created). A nationalized system for marketing farm produce was also erected. The central role played by the state in the organization of society, added to the "resource" it commands, has contributed to the forging of a political system based on clientelism and patronage.

The policy of centralization, however, has not been completely effective. First, the state does not have the material means to carry it out. Its budget is not big enough to allow effective presence in all sectors of the society. Its capacity to control and organize society is also limited by the vitality of so-called traditional societies and the presence of local leaders (like the marabouts), who either ignore or marginalize the role of the state or who refocus and deform the structures and initiatives of the "center" that might threaten their autonomy, in order to turn them to their own advantage.

When confronted with such "peripheral" forces, the state is often obliged to make concessions to local systems, for its political legitimacy depends to a very great extent on the support of these middlemen. This is what J. S. Barker calls the "paradox of development": the government is torn between the need for political support that requires it to listen to the demands of the local community and the need to carry out a policy of development that drives it to transform the community.[29] Nevertheless, we have already noted the increasing tendency of the state to do without these middlemen and to communicate directly with the people. As we have seen in Casamance, the political risks of such an undertaking are enormous because of the danger of direct conflict breaking out between the state and the local community.

Recent reforms have attempted to lessen the weight of the administration, particularly in the realm of the economy. The signs of impotence were all too clear. Already heavily in debt, the public sector was also having to pay heavy costs for mismanagement, corruption, and absence of clear lines of responsibility. The IMF agreed to a loan of $66.1 million conditioned on certain reforms: the structure for marketing peanuts was redesigned, subsidies for state companies (almost all in the red) were curbed, and civil service hiring was brought to a halt.

If these measures liberalized the economy, they did not fundamentally change the nature of the Jacobin model. Although a failure from the political and economic point of view, it remained part of the political culture of the power elite. Unable to control society, the state has managed all through this period to maintain order. To be sure, discounting recent events in Casamance, it has never

had to deal with any subversive or terrorist movements. But this absence of destabilizing forces is also because of the relative freedom of expression that political movements enjoyed in Senegal and the concern of Senegalese leaders to
accept the principle of dialogue with members of the opposition. This is what
President Diouf calls a "national consensus." If, in certain circumstances and at
certain points in time, the government took a hard line and made decisions that
were antidemocratic, the use of force was never looked upon as a *long-term*
means of solving problems.

Another consequence of political stability is that the role of the army is
much less noticeable than in the rest of Africa. The government has sometimes
turned to the army for help (in Gambia and in Casamance), but in the last
analysis, it does not owe its survival to military intervention. There is in Senegal
today a tradition of nonintervention by the army in political life (members of the
armed forces do not have the right to vote) that could only be brought into question in the event of grave difficulties.

Although this tradition is conducive to the consolidation of democracy, the
centralizing ideology of the state is a major obstacle in this regard. The failing
is one of communication. Paradoxically, the more the state becomes centralized, the further away appears to be from society, and the greater is society's
tendency to act autonomously. The Senegalese state is not an expression of the
Senegalese society. It aims to control society without taking into consideration
its specific features, its ethnic and cultural diversity, and the movements that
society has engendered. From this point of view, one might agree with Mar Fall
that the Senegalese state is, indeed, sick. It is suffering from the disease of isolation.[30] And the democratic renewal has done very little to modify the situation.

Political Institutions

As we have observed, presidential power has grown since independence. In
Senegal, it is the executive that governs. For many years, the Assembly was a
body where decisions were simply registered. The presence today of a number
of opposition parliamentarians has made the Assembly a political forum, but its
capacity for initiative to legislate or to control the government is extremely limited—in fact, if not by law. All powers are concentrated in the hands of the
Socialist Party, the government, and the president. The judiciary would also
seem to be subservient to the executive branch, even if it appears to have some
margin of maneuver compared to other African states. Here again, there is no
contrast between the two periods. Trials are conducted in a relatively unrestricted manner, but as Gellar notes, "the courts have rarely ruled against the
government in important constitutional cases or political trials."[31]

In the party system, there have been some important changes with the
evolution of a *de facto* one-party state to first a limited multiparty structure and
then a totally unrestricted multiparty system. The government party, however,
continues to play a dominant role in political life, and opposition parties remain

marginal. But distinctions must be made on this point. The PDS and the RND are both movements with a wide social base (their clientele has about the same social profile as that of the Socialist party) and a wide geographical base—although their position is stronger in regions with problems, like Casamance for the PDS. The political philosophy of both parties is also rather moderate. It is, in fact, quite close to that of the Socialist party on many issues, their principal criticism being the Socialist party's incompetence or its unwillingness to carry out its program. The small parties of the extreme left, on the other hand, are much more ideologically oriented and divided by points of doctrine. Their social base is very narrow (teachers, students, and trade unionists), and their influence is practically nil outside of the towns. Yet, all of these groups have contributed in a big way to the development of a very active political press that enjoys great freedom compared to the systematic repression it experienced in the past.

Despite the apparent vitality of political life in Senegal, the party system still remains relatively impervious, as has already been noted, to movements in the rest of society. Politics is much more an arena for politicians than a channel for the expression and defense of new social interests and forces. The low voter participation in elections is one sign of this crisis, and the difficulty of Senegalese political movements in coping with Islamic mobilization is another.[32]

Political Leadership

This last commentary underscores the limits of political innovation in Senegal, as well as the gap that exists between political leaders and the masses, who are looking outside official or institutionalized political channels for solutions to the problems they face. We can see taking hold and developing in Senegal today an informal political system that aims to compensate for the failure of the political system to adapt to social changes—but that also is an obstacle to the initiatives of political leaders. There is a sort of vicious cycle in the dichotomy between the "center" and the "periphery," between the state and what can be called *grassroots movements of political action*. Such movements are channeled through structures like Muslim brotherhoods or village development associations. Their strategy consists either in bypassing official institutions by creating their own organizational networks and schemes of action, or in recouping the benefits of initiatives from on high. Violence sometimes breaks out, as in Casamance, when problems of divison and incomprehension fail to be overcome by passive resistance or manipulation.

It is not a question here of the democratic bent of Senegalese leaders. We have seen throughout this chapter that, even in the authoritarian period, the Senegalese government has been open to dialogue and negotiation. For the most part, compromise and consensus have always been the rules of the game, at least in the long term. They are part of what can be called the political art of

Senegal. The problem is much more that of a state whose centralizing ideology does not mesh well with grassroots dynamics.

Socioeconomic Development

The distance between the state and the society is a factor that has hampered development in the country. Since independence, the Senegalese government has endeavored to carry out what it calls "great development projects" (the building of dams and petrochemical plants, for example). It has given itself the tools that were supposed to free the country from dependence and under-development through the creation of a whole series of state companies and strictly controlled peanut-marketing mechanisms—leaving the door open, however, for foreign investment. But these measures were undermined by bureaucratic structures that left no room for responsible participation on the part of producers or wage-earners. They also carried the threat of gigantic production structures that were not compatible with local traditions, particularly in rural areas. The outcome of these efforts was often financial disaster. In the final analysis, those who profited from these schemes were, above all, the experts hired as advisors and the technocrats. As Donal Cruise O'Brien puts it, when there were profits in the agricultural sector, "instead of being used to support modernization and increased productivity in the rural sector, the surplus was absorbed into costly services, state enterprises and the civil service."[33] And René Dumont, one of the most astute observers of Senegal's economy, has observed:

> What is called rural development seems to have been the development of the bureaucracy rather than of the peasantry. The civil service widened its hold to serve the interests of the various organizations of control or intervention, more than that of peasants who were only alibis . . . In wanting to organise peasants along strict lines without consulting them, the state turned them into welfare cases.[34]

Development has also been hampered by the chronic drought that has prevailed in Senegal for fifteen years, bringing about drastic fluctuations in agricultural production and accelerating the country's food dependency.

It is true that other sectors have been relatively more successful: the phosphate mines, the petrochemical industry (with the refinery at M'Bao), and tourism. But this has not been enough to offset the effects of the slump in agricultural production, which remains the cornerstone of Senegal's economy. The situation is all the more serious in that the sharp rise in the price of oil (a twentyfold increase between 1960 and 1980) has sent the country's national debt skyrocketing.

A few statistics are enough to demonstrate the poor performance of the economy. Between 1965 and 1984, Senegal's annual growth rate of per capita GNP was minus 0.5 percent; and between 1973 and 1984 the GNP grew by 2.6 percent (minus 0.2 percent in agriculture and 6 percent in industry). The deficit in the balance of payments went from $16 million in 1970 to $274 million in 1984. The external debt, which was $131 million in 1970, rose to $1,565 million in 1984.[35]

As Gellar concludes, these development schemes "have failed to raise living standards for most Senegalese or to redistribute wealth and services in favor of the poor."[36] As indicated in Table 10.1 improvements in the quality of life for the average Senegalese over the last two decades have been more modest than the average for low-income countries in the Third World, or even for those in sub-Saharan Africa. In fact, by such revealing measures as life expectancy, infant mortality, and adult literacy, Senegal remains among the poorest countries in the world, with a literacy rate of 10 percent and a life expectancy below fifty. Not only has the economic situation worsened since independence, but inequalities have increased.

Faced with such a disastrous situation, yielding to the pressure of the IMF, and aware also of the political dangers of rural discontent, President Diouf has embarked upon a program of reform and austerity. The state marketing board has been abolished, limits have been set to the growth of state enterprises and of the public sector in general, and their structures have been reformed to make them more competitive and efficient. A liberal economy is supposed to come to

Table 10.1   Socioeconomic Development in Senegal and Other Low-Income Countries

	Senegal		Sub-Saharan African Low Income Countries[a]		Low Income Countries[a]	
	1965	1984	1965	1984	1965	1984
Male life expectancy (in years)	40	45	41	47	44	50
Female life expectancy (in years)	42	48	43	50	45	52
Infant mortality (per 1000 live births)	172	138	155	129	147	114
Adult literacy (percent)[b]	6	10	—	—	23	40
Primary-school enrollments[c] (as % of school-age population)	40	53	37	76	44	74
Secondary-school enrollments[c] (as % of school-age population)	7	12	4	13	9	20

Source: World Bank, *World Development Report 1986* (New York: Oxford University Press), and for literacy, *World Development Report 1983*.
[a] These figures are the averages for each group of countries, weighted by population. The category "Low-Income Countries" includes all 36 countries classified by the World Bank as low-income in 1986, excluding China and India, which are more developed.
[b] These figures are for 1960 and 1980.
[c] These figures are for 1965 and 1983.

terms with all of Senegal's problems—and a liberal philosophy in politics to be a safety valve for the regime.

It is too early to measure the effects of such policies. It is not certain, however, that such measures will not be detrimental to the lower classes and provoke, in turn, more unrest and other forms of inequality (the development of a business bourgeoisie). This is all the more probable, as a policy of "truth in prices" will no doubt increase the price of staple foods—and wage earners of the public sector will not remain indifferent to an erosion of their purchasing power.

To conclude on this point, it is nonetheless surprising to note that, in spite of this disastrous economic performance, Senegal has experienced continuous political stability. This is no doubt because of the function of mediation played by the Muslim brotherhoods and, on a wider level, the practice of clientelism, which has acted as a safety valve. But, as the gap between the state and society grows, one cannot be sure that these networks will continue to maintain a relative and fragile communication between the top and the bottom of the political and social system. One may well ask if the democratic renewal will be able to cope with these frustrations.

International Factors

International relations in Senegal are characterized by two tendencies that, at first sight, are contradictory. The first is the country's extreme dependence on the outside. Despite the efforts of its government to diversify agricultural production and equip itself with a dynamic industrial sector, Senegal's monocrop economic structure remains typically colonial. Seesawing agricultural output (508,000 tons in 1977 and 1,145,000 tons in 1982, for example) and the fluctuating world price of peanuts are grave threats to economic stability and an important contributing factor to Senegal's rising national debt. The situation has been aggravated, as seen above, by the rise in the price of oil. In such a context, French aid, which had solved the problem for a long time, is no longer adequate. To improve matters, Senegal must appeal to the IMF—and agree to its conditions—as well as to other outside sources. Hence, as Gellar notes, "at the beginning of the 1980's the Senegalese economy was more than ever hostage to external economic forces."[37] If France has remained the first supplier of technical assistance (63 percent of such aid in 1980) and Senegal's first trading partner, more and more financial aid and investment comes from other sources, including the European Development Fund and the IMF. The United States is also visibly present in Senegal through USAID and U.S. commercial banks. The aid of Arab countries, in the form of bilateral agreements or multinational business interests, is also on the increase.[38] The influence of France, however, remains preponderant on the political and cultural planes. France still has a military base in Dakar, and Senegal's intelligentsia is the most Parisian in all of Black Africa.

This dependence on the outside is matched by extremely active diplomatic involvement in Africa and the rest of the world. From this point of view, the Senegal of Abdou Diouf is as enterprising as that of his predecessor. Senegal has played a pioneering role in setting up regional economic bodies. The country has been a mediator in many inter-African conflicts (recently in the Western Sahara), and has made important contributions to the Organization of African Unity. Moreover, Senegal has been one of the initiators of the French "Common-wealth" (*francophonie*) and has always been an active participant in international institutions like the United Nations and UNESCO. In the eyes of the world, Senegal is one of the leaders of moderate Africa. If it leans more to the West than to the East, with whom relationships are somewhat distant, Senegal also aspires to be nonaligned.

Senegal's leading role in international relations implies the existence of a political regime that is stable and respectful of human liberties. We have already seen how important Senegal's international image was for Senghor in the past, and how important it still is for Diouf today—particularly as it concerns Western countries that are important sources of aid. This image has two complementary functions: it allows Senegal greater influence on the international scene than its demographic and economic weight would merit; and, by offering reassuring guarantees on the nature and stability of the regime, it helps attract international assistance and private investment.

With Abdou Diouf, however, another image has grown up around Senegal, that of an Islamic country. Senghor developed close ties with certain Arab countries (Saudi Arabia, Kuwait, Iraq, and the Gulf States), and in 1973 he authorized the Palestine Liberation Organization to open an office in Dakar. But, as a Muslim, his successor can go even further in this direction, and Diouf's participation in January 1981 at the Islamic Conference in Saudi Arabia, combined with his pilgrimage to Mecca, have had a considerable echo in Senegal. In openly underscoring Senegal's Islamic character, Abdou Diouf has aimed to encourage Arab aid. At the same time, such moves are also symptomatic of internal aspirations in Senegal, where Islam is increasingly active. But Diouf also wants to control and contain the phenomenon of Muslim renewal, and in 1984 he did not hesitate to close down the Iranian Embassy, just as Senghor, a few years before, had not hesitated to break off diplomatic ties with Libya when it was accused of meddling in Senegal's internal affairs. Thus, as we can see, Senegal's relationships with the outside are closely linked to its internal problems.

Summary

In the last analysis, Senegal appears today to be a semidemocracy. The factors that have played in favor of democracy relate to Senegal's history and political culture, as well as to its relative ethnic equilibrium and religious homogeneity. In addition, one cannot overlook the international image that this little country has tried to project. On the other hand, the weight of the state, economic—and, to a certain extent, political—dependence, and the phenomenon of clientelism have functioned as limits to democracy.

• FUTURE PROSPECTS •

Formal democracy is a political tradition in Senegal, despite a period of about ten years during which some violations were committed. More than elsewhere in Africa, Senegal has used pluralism and negotiation (sometimes accompanied by threats, it is true) to overcome the difficulties it has encountered. There is no doubt that the majority of the political elite strongly favors democratic government. The problem is whether democracy can solve the fundamental issues facing the country.

The first of these concerns Senegal's economic survival. As has been pointed out, despite its efforts to take better advantage of its (scarce) resources, Senegal has been hit head-on by the world recession and the drought. It has also had to face the consequences of the neocolonial structure of its economy, as well as the shortcomings of its political and administrative apparatus—its unwieldiness and lack of flexibility and its clientelist practices. Up to now, public funds, international aid, and foreign investment have served to develop the ruling elite and the bureaucracy rather than the country's productive forces. In such conditions, democracy is fragile and artificial. It can benefit, at the very most, certain elites by giving them channels to express their opinions, but it has not changed the living conditions of the majority of the people. This explains their growing mistrust of institutions and political parties and their lack of interest in electoral, political and public affairs. The success of ideologies and movements outside the formal political scene is thus not very surprising, and the renewal of Islam has to be seen in this light.

Here, then, is the second big issue facing Senegal. It is one of utmost importance, for it reveals the existence of another political culture that may not be fundamentally antidemocratic, as is often thought, but which brings into question the political heritage and traditions that have dominated the intelligentsia and the ruling elite up to now. For a long time, Islam, and especially the brotherhoods that structured it, served as institutions of social, political, and economic mediation. Today, however, Islam has become an ideology of mobilization and protest. The failure of modernization has contributed to the rise of a religion that appears as a weapon in the combat against the West and its values as expressed by the elite of the country. Henceforth, the marabouts are no longer simple clients of the ruling elite and of the state. Riding on the wave of popular opinion that sees Islam as a universal remedy to poverty and decadence, the marabouts have become more demanding partners of the state, setting themselves up as lesson-givers, or even as a counterelite. In this sense, Islam is no longer simply an element of popular culture. It has become an ideology aiming to remodel society and the state. The young, and particularly young intellectuals, as well as members of the frustrated petty bourgeoisie, no longer identify with the values of the West, or with Marxism, but have thrown themselves into Islamic movements.[39]

It is very difficult for the state and for democracy to cope with this dynamic social force. What we are witnessing is the transition from a relatively tolerant and open kind of Islam to an Islam that is setting itself up as an autonomous political force. Whereas the first type was compatible with democracy, the second is more of an obstacle, for it implies a totalitarian vision of society.

The problem of Casamance represents a third challenge for the regime. The revolts that have shaken the southern part of Senegal in the last five years cannot be stopped by mere administrative reforms. I have tried, briefly, to give reasons for this. It must be emphasized that this is not just a rebellion of a particular ethnic group. What is being questioned, above all, is the kind of communication that exists between the "center" and the "periphery." It is the culture of the Jacobin state itself that is under fire, particularly by a people who do not live in the same social and cultural universe as those of the rest of the country and feel they have been ignored for too long.

In short, these three critical issues show the limits of a democracy that has been too much the exclusive concern of a relatively privileged minority and that remains cut off from the realities of the country. The inhabitants of Senegal will only be able to feel concerned about pluralism and liberalism if this minority is able to provide for their security and dignity. As of now, the above problems not only impose limits to the liberalization of the regime, but threaten the country's political stability.

It would be presumptuous of us to claim to have lessons to teach or to have miracle solutions to the crisis facing Senegal today. However, in light of the above analysis, it is possible to indicate a few directions that could allow Senegal to consolidate its democratic gains and to make these gains more meaningful for a greater number of its inhabitants.

The most fundamental point concerns the economic survival of the country, and, more specifically, that of its most underprivileged categories. On the whole, massive state intervention and huge agroindustrial complexes have been failures. Not only have such schemes prevented any grassroots initiative, but they have failed to improve the income of the social groups they were meant to benefit. Worse, the effects have often included a profound breaking down of the groups concerned—and erosion of the legitimacy of a regime that has been unable to meet people's expectations and fulfill promises made.

The recently adopted state policy of economic liberalism is certainly a step forward, but only if two conditions are maintained. First, as proclaimed in a recent government report, it must indeed encourage "real participation on the part of rural inhabitants as well as sharpen their sense of reponsibility."[40] Next, it has to achieve food self-sufficiency for peasant communities and make them less dependent, not only on the state, but also on the world market. This is also the only approach that can stop the rural exodus and the uncontrollable urban spread, both sources of anomie and social frustration and factors of political fragility.

Such steps cannot be carried out simply by limiting the role of the state. It is necessary, above all, to invent a new means of communication between the "center" and the "periphery." And that means that the state has to be more open to local realities. I believe that only a policy of decentralization would be able to put such dynamics into motion and reestablish confidence between the summit and the base, for political pluralism will function in a vacuum if it is not anchored in local societies. Unfortunately, both the Jacobin tradition and the monocratic presidential system work against such transformations, justifying the monopolization of power in the name of "the greatest good." In his contribution to a debate on democracy in Senegal, Pathé Diagne observed that democracy loses much of its meaning when it is structured around a monocratic and centralizing power system that prohibits people "from achieving their full material and cultural potentials by refusing to allow them to set up their own assemblies and local administrations in their own specific context and geographic space."[41]

Decentralization is certainly not a panacea for all the problems in Senegal, and it might even be a threat to national unity, but it can bring institutions closer to the people and thus prevent disastrous clashes, such as might well occur one day in Casamance.

Finally, if decentralization really is to work, both the state and the forces behind it have to anchor themselves more deeply in Senegal's cultural environment. The elite's Westernized consumption patterns and concept of the state only serve to widen the gap between the ruling class and the majority of the people, who live in another universe and who have no means of gaining access to the "superior" culture. Muslim nationalism feeds on this gap. And refocusing the political culture around "indigenous" values, practices, and realities would help narrow and, finally, close this gap, which is detrimental to democracy.

What national or extranational forces might foster such changes?

I have emphasized already the rather large consensus that exists in Senegal around the concept of pluralism. Such orientations, however, could be brought into question by the rising forces of Islam, which are gaining support among certain elites seeking new forms of action and legitimacy. Among the social categories mobilized by the Islamic revival can be found the young intellectuals and, to a lesser extent, the business class, no doubt because they perceive the Muslim religion as a way of setting themselves off from the political and administrative elite that governs the country. As for the latter, it is undermined by a conflict of generations that pits the former political bosses and dignitaries against young technocrats. The older generation has strong local backing but it is incapable of coping with the mutations the country is undergoing, and the younger generation is more competent but less rooted in the "real country."

What they do share, however, is their mutual support for the democratic form of government.

The values and institutions of democracy find much less favor, on the other hand, among the lower social classes, who do not perceive their utility, or rather their effects, on daily life. For these classes the state is often a foreign entity that is ineffective and oppressive. Competition among political parties is a game that does not concern them directly because it cannot solve their problems or fulfill their aspirations. In such conditions, democracy lacks pertinence and cannot throw down roots in the "real country."

The most important task on the international level, I believe, is not merely to consider Senegal as a politically strategic region for the West, but to try to overcome the difficulties that restrict the impact of democracy. From this point of view, any action that limits the state is a necessary, although insufficient, condition, for there is the everpresent risk that giving free rein to economic forces would create new forms of inequality and reinforce the neocolonial structure of the economy. International aid must not only help to develop an entrepreneurial class in the strictest sense of the word. It must allow local communities to have control of their own affairs and give them the means of innovation. Thus, heavy capital outlay or aid schemes for "massive development projects" should give way to an aid emphasis on smaller-scale and intermediate technology, featuring projects that are less ambitious but closer to the people. It bears repeating that any policy that tends to bring the "center" closer to the "periphery" promotes stability and democracy.

On a strictly political level, it is also vitally important that Senegalese political parties not be isolated, but be in constant contact with democratic movements in the world. To be shut off from the outside carries with it the threat not only of political sclerosis, but also of authoritarianism. Anything that facilitates the exchange of experiences and ideas encourages the development of democracy and renewal. Dialogue of this sort could not but help to widen the perspectives of Senegalese political parties.

Finally, the industrialized nations of the West must be reminded that they should not set themselves up as the supreme models of democracy. African history has shown us that the dynamics of African politics can also invent original forms of participation and pluralism. Nothing is more dangerous for the West than to appear to be the sole source of democracy. The West should content itself, on a much more modest level, with facilitating the changes that propose an alternative to authoritarianism and tyranny. From its contact with Africa, the West could also learn to respect differences, which is the very core of the concept of democracy.

• NOTES •

1. On this subject, see Michael Crowder, *Senegal: A Study in French Assimilation Policy* (London: Oxford University Press, 1962).

2. See J. H. J. Legier, "Institutions municipales et politiques coloniales: Les communes du Sénégal," *Revue francaise d'histoire d'outre-mer*, no. 201, p. 445. On this period see also the fundamental work of G. Johnson, Jr., *The Emergence of Black Politics in Senegal: The Struggle for Power in the Four Communes, 1900–1920* (Stanford: Stanford University Press, 1971).

3. On the political life in Senegal in this period, the following works can be consulted: R. S. Morgenthau, *Political Parties in French West Africa* (Oxford: Clarendon Press, 1964); K. Robinson, "Senegal: The Elections to the Territorial Assembly," in J. W. Mackenzie and T. Robinson, eds., *Five Elections in Africa* (New York: Oxford University Press, 1960); P. Mercier, "La vie politique dans les centre urbains du Sénégal: Etude d'une période de transition," *Cahiers internationaux de Sociologie* 6, no. 17, (1959).

4. Senghor was the very first African to pass France's prestigious *agrégation* examination, which allows successful candidates to teach at the higher levels of the lycée and is often a stepping stone to a university career (translator's note).

5. See W. F. Foltz, *From French West Africa to the Mali Federation* (New Haven: Yale University Press, 1965).

6. Among the many studies of this constitution and its different reforms, one may consult the following works: J. C. Gautron and M. Rougevin-Baville, *Droit public du Sénégal* (Paris: Pedone, 1977; 1st ed. 1970); D. G. Lavroff, *Le Sénégal* (Paris: Librairie générale de droit et de jurisprudence, 1966); G. Hesseling, *Histoire politique du Sénégal* (Paris: Karthala, 1985).

7. G. Hesseling, *Sénégal*, p. 247.

8. Sheldon Gellar, *Senegal: An African Nation Between Islam and the West* (Boulder, Colo.: Westview Press, 1982), p. 31.

9. Ibid., p. 41.

10. On this subject, see. my own work, *Le marabout et le prince: Islam et pouvoir au Sénégal* (Paris, Pedone, 1981).

11. On clan struggles, see. in particular, F. Zucarelli, *Un parti politique africain: L'union progressiste sénégalaise* (Paris: Librairie générale de droit et de jurisprudence, 1970); and C. Coulon, "Electious, factions et idéologies au Sénégal," in Centre d'étude d'Afrique noire et Centre d'études et de recherches internationales, *Aux urnes l'Afrique* (Paris: Pedone, 1978), pp. 149–186.

12. G. Hesseling, *Sénégal* p. 137.

13. On Senghor, the following works will be found very useful: J. L. Hymans, *Leopold Sedar Senghor: An Intellectual Biography* (Edinburgh: Edinburgh University Press, 1971); I. L. Markovitz, *Leopold Sedar Senghor and the Politics of Negritude* (New York, Atheneum, 1964).

14. R. Dumont, *Paysanneries aux abois* (Paris: Editions de Seuil, 1972).

15. For a very skillful analysis of peanut-growing policies in Senegal, see N. Casswell, "Autopsie de l'ONCAD: La Politique arachidière au Sénégal," *Politique africaine* 14 (1984): pp. 38–73.

16. See A. Sylla, "De la grève à la reforme: Luttes enseignantes et crises sociales au Sénégal," *Politique africaine* 8 (1982): pp. 61–73.

17. Donal Cruise O'Brien, "Les élections sénégalaises du 27 février 1983," *Politique africaine* 11 (1983): pp. 7–12.

18. Pierre Biarnes, *L'Afrique aux africains (Paris: A. Colin, 1980), p. 130.*

19. S. Gellar, *Senegal* p. 119.

20. Cheikh Anta Diop, *L'Afrique noire précoloniale* (Paris: Présence africaine, 1960).

21. In addition to Diop's work mentioned above, see also A. Sylla, *La philosophie morale des Wolof* (Dakar: Sankore, 1978).

22. Abdou Diouf in the preface to J. M. Nzouankeu, *Les partis politiques sénégalais (Dakar: Edition clairafrique, 1984), p. 7.*

23. *Jeune Afrique*, no. 834–855, 1977, quoted in G. Hesseling, *Sénégal* p. 82.

24. Donal Cruise O'Brien, "Ruling Class and Peasantry in Senegal: 1960–1976," in Rita Cruise O'Brien, ed., *The Political Economy of Underdevelopment: Dependence in Senegal* (London and Beverly Hills: Sage, 1979), pp. 213–214.

25. Ibid.

26. W. J. Foltz, "Senegal," in James S. Coleman and Carl Rosberg, Jr., *Political Parties and National Integration in Tropical Africa* (Berkeley: University of California Press, 1964), pp. 16–64.

27. See Donal Cruise O'Brien, "Langue et nationalité au Sénégal," *Année africaine* (1979) pp. 319–338.

28. D. Darbon, "Le culturalisme des Casamançais," *Politique africaine* 14 (1964): p. 127.

29. J. S. Barker, "The Paradox of Development: Reflections on a Study of Local-Central

Relations in Senegal," in Michael F. Lofchie, ed., *The State of the Nation: Constraints of Development in Independent Africa* (Berkeley: University of California Press, 1971), pp. 47–63. On the same theme, see also the work by Jean-Louis Balans, Christian Coulon and Jean-Marc Gastellu, *Autonomie locale et intégration nationale au Sénégal (Paris: Pedone, 1975)*.

30. Mar Fall, *Sénégal: L'état est malade* (Paris, L'Harmattan, 1985).

31. S. Gellar, *Senegal*, p. 37.

32. I have analyzed the attitude of political movements towards Islamic renewal in my article, "Sénégal" in "Centre des hautes études d'Afrique et d'Asie modernes," *Contestations en pays islamiques* (Paris: CHEAM/Documentation française, 1984), pp. 63–68.

33. Rita Cruise O'Brien, *Dependence in Senegal*, p. 30.

34. René Dumont and M. F. Motin, *Le défi sénégalais* (Dakar: ENDA, 1984), p. 9.

35. World Bank, *World Development Report 1986* (New York: Oxford University Press, 1986).

36. S. Gellar, *Senegal*, p. 63.

37. Ibid., p. 52.

38. Between 1974 and 1981, Senegal ranked fourth among African countries (after Guinea, Zaire, and Mali) in aid received from Arab countries ($397.7 million).

39. I have analyzed the reasons for the nature, and the extent of Islamic renewal in my book, *Les musulmans et le pouvoir en Afrique noire* (Paris: Karthala, 1983).

40. "New Agricultural Policy," report by the Ministry of Rural Development, 1984.

41. Actuel Tekkrur, *Quelle démocratie pour le Sénégal?* (Dakar: Editions Sankore, 1984), p. 48.

CHAPTER ELEVEN

Zimbabwe:
In Search of a Stable Democracy

MASIPULA SITHOLE

While there often is disagreement on whether capitalism is good or bad, as well as on the virtues and vices of socialism or communism, there seems to be universal consensus that democracy is good and dictatorship bad. Where dictatorship is spoken of with any virtue, it is with reference to the dictatorship of the proletariat, or the people, or the majority over the minority. Democracy, however understood, universally connotes a positive value, something to aspire to, or at least to identify with. No contemporary leader, no political regime, and no individual will answer kindly to the description, "dictator." Even those who are dictators and autocrats will, more often than not, seek to justify themselves by the exigencies of the times or situations and not on the argument that dictatorship in itself is not bad. Moreover, the term democracy has fallen victim to the emotive stances adopted in the international ideological and intellectual discourse so that it has come to mean whatever those who have spoken the loudest have wanted it to mean.

In discussing democracy in Zimbabwe, it is important to note that there is no consensus yet as to the meaning of the term. The debate surges about whether the democracy Zimbabwe should have is the Western libertarian type, or the Leninist vanguardist type, or the Third World mass mobilizational type.[1] It is not the place here to discuss these three types of democracy, or which is preferable for Zimbabwe. For one thing, I do not think that MacPherson's three typologies, although of heuristic value, are necessarily legitimate, nor do I accept the implicit and derived suggestion that, *ipso facto*, Zimbabwe is experimenting simply with Third World democracy. Democracy must mean government with the consent or mandate of the governed, whether in the East, West, or the Third World. The tendency to call every political system a democracy deprives democracy of meaning and interferes with its growth and development in those areas of the world where there is dictatorship and tyranny. Democracy's universal character is that those who exercise political authority do so with the explicit consent and genuine electoral mandate of their subjects. This is the criterion I use in assessing the democratic project in Zimbabwe. Thus, where Zimbabwe is a success, it succeeds in democracy and not just in Third World democracy.

ZIMBABWE

Similarly, where Zimbabwe is a failure, it fails in democracy and not just in Third World democracy.

In discussing the democratic experiment in Zimbabwe, one is visited with an immediate problem: where to begin. The easy way out is to start from 1980, when Zimbabwe was born following a "one man, one vote" election. In this way, one would conveniently cover six years of experience with democracy in Zimbabwe. In a way, this is largely my intention. However, anything born is born of something, and this weighs heavily on its potential. To that extent, some historical background as to how democracy in Zimbabwe was born is necessary. As with individual human beings, the past experiences of nations heavily affect the way they see and deal with the present, and this further affects, in some ways, what happens in the future.

Many of the problems and, indeed, prospects for Zimbabwe's experiment in democracy that seemed to emerge after independence were not entirely new. They were either a resurfacing of earlier tendencies or they emanated from the political arrangements that brought independence, and were, themselves, the result of various factors with a long history. This chapter, therefore, reviews the experiences with democracy in both the colonial and the postcolonial periods. The first section reviews the history of intrawhite democracy in the Rhodesian settler state, the development of the African nationalist movement, and the post-colonial democratic regime. The second section analyzes the above historical developments. The third discusses the several theoretical assumptions of this chapter about democracy in an effort to isolate those factors that seem, hitherto, to have been more salient in explaining Zimbabwe's experience with democracy. Finally, the last section considers the future prospects for democratic government in Zimbabwe.

• HISTORICAL REVIEW •

The country known today as Zimbabwe was first organized as a single nation-state and named Rhodesia in 1890, following the conquest of its Ndebele and Shona inhabitants by Cecil John Rhodes's Pioneer Column of the British South Africa Company. Rhodesia was a British colony for the ninety years between 1890 and 1980, when the African people won their struggle for independence and majority rule and renamed the country Zimbabwe. Prior to 1980, white settlers ruled Rhodesia without the consent of the conquered African majority, who were deprived of practically all civil and political liberties. Open competition with African leaders and political parties was so restricted as to be denied. Looked at from the standpoint of the African majority, white Rhodesian settler rule was not democratic; it was an imposed dictatorship of the few over the many, an oligarchy based on color. Whatever African participation there might have been was marginal and peripheral.[2] However, our intention here is not to discuss how whites ruled without the consent of the Africans but, rather, to outline white politics in a Rhodesian settler state that was an "intrawhite" democracy.

Intrawhite Democracy

Many accounts of white Rhodesian settler political history have been written. It is not necessary to detail all of them to establish the point we want to make. But, of particular note for our purpose, is Larry W. Bowman's *Politics in Rhodesia: White Power in an African State*[3]. Bowman's work, more than any before, demonstrates that intrawhite political conflict took place "within a 'democratic' political process."[4]

By the Southern Rhodesia Order in Council of 1898, the British government established a partially elected legislative council for the white settler community. Thus, whites in Rhodesia enjoyed representative government almost from the outset. From 1922, when the settlers opted for self-government under British tutelage instead of joining the Union of South Africa, to 1979, when a short-lived accommodation with the less militant element of the nationalist leadership was reached, the white electorate took part in several crucial decisions regarding the future of Rhodesia. Seven national referenda were held during this period. In 1922, whites voted 64 percent in favor of federation with Northern Rhodesia and Nyasaland (two other British possessions to the north); and, by an impressive 89 percent vote, the white electorate tacitly approved the impending unilateral declaration of independence in the referendum of 1964. In 1969 and 1971, respectively, the white electorate (now with characteristic enthusiasm) approved a republican constitution, and settlement proposals negotiated between Ian Smith and British Foreign Minister Sir Alex Douglas Home. Finally, in 1978, they approved terms of the "internal settlement" negotiated between the Smith government and a "moderate" African nationalist element that, once very popular, was becoming increasingly marginalized.

In addition to national referenda, general elections were held periodically and at regular intervals during the period of colonial rule. There were fourteen such elections between 1924 and 1977. From 1933 to 1962, Rhodesian politics were dominated by a "liberal" element of the settler community led by the United Rhodesia Party (URP), renamed the United Federal Party (UFP) during the period of the federation, 1953–1963. Two personalities, Sir Godfrey Huggins and later his deputy, Sir Roy Welensky, dominated white settler politics during this decade. The URP won the two successive federal elections in 1954 and 1958, and, while federation lasted, the leadership of Huggins and Welensky after him was rarely challenged in intrawhite settler politics. Welensky was seriously and successfully challenged only toward the last years of federation, when the right wing was gaining ascendency in Rhodesia.

The period of federation, however, also witnessed intense factional fights among white politicians within Rhodesia itself. While, in 1953, the quarrel was over the prudence of the proposed federation, in 1958, Garfield Todd, who had become Rhodesia's prime minister in 1953 succeeding Huggins (now on the federal mantle), lost his position as a result of an internal leadership crisis. The government of his successor, Sir Edgar Whitehead, was defeated in the 1962 election for vacillating on African suffrage, and a completely new party, the right-wing Rhodesia Front (RF), assumed control. In 1964, after just two years in power, the RF founding leader Winston Field was replaced by his more militant deputy, Ian Smith. A year later, the latter issued the Unilateral Declaration of Independence (UDI) when negotiations with Britain proved unfruitful. Under the RF, the right wing thus held sway in Rhodesian politics from 1962 to 1978, the eve of black majority rule.

Rhodesia had five prime ministers from 1933 to 1978. However, thirty-six of those years were dominated by two personalities: Sir Godfrey Huggins, who ruled for twenty years before taking on federal politics in 1953, and Ian Smith, who ruled Rhodesia for fifteen years until 1978, when he began to give in to black majority rule—a prospect, ironically, he had sprung to the forefront of Rhodesia politics in 1964 to prevent. The eleven years between Huggins and Smith witnessed leadership instability in white politics: there was, on the average, a new government every three and a half years. By contrast, prefederation and postfederation white politics in Rhodesia suggested a tendency toward one-man rule and, therefore, the one-party state. In 1965, and again in the subsequent and final three elections under white minority rule (1970, 1974, and 1977), the RF captured all fifty white seats in Parliament. In each election, it increased its vote, completely eclipsing white opposition parties.

The period of RF rule under Ian Smith saw the breakdown of democracy within the white community. Although parliamentary elections continued and the regime sought the mandate of white public opinion before taking important political decisions, political repression increased and was extended to the white community. For the first time, white opponents of the government were openly harassed, and organs of the state were used against them. Any white perceived to be sympathetic to black rule was denounced as a "traitor to the white race." Former federal Prime Minister Sir Roy Welensky was denounced as "a bloody Jew, a communist, a traitor, and a coward," and his "liberal" inclinations appeared to compromise white interests.[5] Former Rhodesia Prime Minister Garfield Todd was put under house arrest many times. Many white intellectuals and clergymen were arrested and several were deported during this period. The frequency of these arrests and deportations increased in the 1970s as nationalist guerrilla activity intensified.[6]

Rhodesia's relationship with Britain likewise deteriorated under RF rule. The self-government constitution granted to Rhodesia in 1923 provided for reserved clauses that gave Britain a limited but critical right to monitor constitutional developments in Rhodesia, particularly in those matters affecting Africans. This relationship with Britain progressively became a contentious issue in the late 1950s onwards, when successive white governments in Rhodesia demanded total independence before the African majority was enfranchised.

In 1961, Britain granted Rhodesia a multiracial constitution, which gave Africans fifteen elective seats in a sixty-five-member parliament. In addition, a Chief's Council was created to advise the white government on matters affecting Africans in the so-called "tribal trust lands." Of special note is the fact that the composition of the Chief's Council was based on the principle of ethnic or regional parity between the Ndebele and Shona despite the fact that only about 20 percent of the population was Ndebele (see below). "Liberal" and "conservative" governments alike inflated the political importance of the chiefs throughout the colonial period, in particular during the period of the nationalist movement in the 1960s and 1970s, in an unsuccessful bid to undercut that movement. Moreover, the chiefs were granted representation in all successive attempts to settle the Rhodesian constitutional problem. Even the final solution at the 1979 Lancaster House constitutional conference gave the Chief's Council power to appoint ten chiefs from their members to represent them in the thirty-member Senate. And, significantly, parity was still maintained between Ndebele and Shona representation.

While Britain would not grant sovereign independence to the white minority government in Rhodesia, it did not intervene to prepare Africans for an eventual takeover. Hence, African political advancement practically depended on the attitudes of successive white settler governments, which differed only in minor details of strategy on the question of how best to preserve white supremacy. The "liberals" came up with a deceptive middle-class strategy designed to enfranchise "civilized" and "responsible" Africans who had acquired substantial incomes and a certain level of education while, at the same time, limiting African access to both education and, therefore, to high incomes. The "right-wing" element that dominated Rhodesian politics after federation did not see any virtue in liberal pretentions. The RF leadership was forthright. Ian Smith spoke of "no African government in my life-time," and "not in a thousand years."[7] He went on to declare UDI in 1965, plunging the country into fifteen years of international isolation and bloody civil war. During the 1970s, nationalists hardened their demands as the liberation war expanded.

When Britain would not recognize UDI, it suited the Smith government to continue to seek accommodation. Four unsuccessful attempts were made in 1966, 1968, 1972, and 1978. In late 1979, however, a successful settlement to the Rhodesia impasse was reached at the Lancaster House conference, in which all the parties to the dispute participated.

The Development of the Nationalist Movement

At this point, we outline the historical development of the nationalist movement, its internal and external dynamics, and its outcome to this day with direct implications for democracy in Zimbabwe.

Zimbabwe is racially and ethnically a plural society. Blacks are by far the majority, 97.6 percent of the country's population of over 7.5 million (1982 cen-

sus estimates); whites constitute 2 percent, while the rest, 0.4 percent are col-
oreds and Asians. The black population belongs to about forty different ethnic
groups. However, Murphree and his associates note that "on the basis of ethnic,
cultural and linguistic affinities," the Shona (77 percent) and Ndebele (19 percent) can be further subdivided into several subethnic groups by linguistic
dialect and subculture characteristics.[8] Below is a graphical presentation of the
various ethnic and subethnic groups by percentage of the total population.

The Karanga are the largest of the major black subethnic groups in the country, while the Ndau are the smallest. The Zezuru are the second largest group,
and the Ndebele, Manyika, and Korekore are intermediate in size. Often, the
Korekore have been submerged with the Zezuru, making the Zezuru the largest
subethnic group. Also, the Kalanga in Zimbabwe politics were practically considered Ndebele, thus making the Ndebele the third largest group. Further, the
Ndau were generally grouped with the Manyika, making the latter group fourth
largest. The Rozwi, constituting 9 percent of the population, were the sixth
largest group. However, unlike the other groups, the Rozwi are scattered in
smaller communities all over the country.

Historically, the Rozwi are believed to have been the ruling class among
the Shona groups before the advent of the Ndebele, followed by the white
settlers in the nineteenth century. It is the Rozwi, more than any other Shona
group, who are closely associated with the Monomatapa kingdom and the Great
Zimbabwe ruins from which the country gets its name. The Rozwi are therefore
the remnant of a Shona imperial royalty. While the Shona in general did not
have centralized political institutions and authority, but rather were what Fortes
and Evans-Pritchard called "stateless societies,"[9] Rozwi political organization
was highly centralized.

Figure 11.1   The Ethnic Composition of Zimbabwe's Population

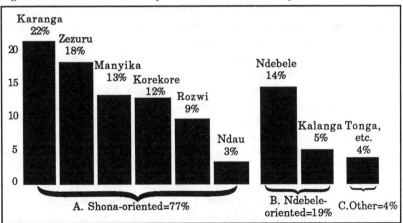

Source: Adapted from M. Sithole, "Ethnicity and Factionalism in Zimbabwe Nationalist Politics,
1957–79," in *Ethnic and Racial Studies*, Vol. 3, No. 1 (January 1980), p. 23. Based on 1969 Census.

The Ndebele migrated from South Africa in the 1930s. Mzilikazi, one of the Zulu King Tshaka's rebellious generals, fled Zululand and led his followers to settle near the present-day city of Bulawayo. It is from this base that he, and later his son Lobengula, conducted further expansionist raids on the surrounding Shona, establishing present-day Matebeleland.

Unlike the Shona, the Ndebele were highly organized around a centralized authority, much in the manner of the Rozwi. They had a highly stratified social system at the top of which was an aristocratic caste, the *zansi*, who were the direct descendants of the original Zulu immigrants. Below the *zansi* were the *enhla*, a group of acculturates whom Mzilikazi accumulated on the long march from Zululand. They were entitled to some limited rights and privileges. The lowest caste was the *holi*, the servant class. These were recruited from among the Shona upon settlement. Until well after the advent of white settlers, "intercaste marriages and intercourse were forbidden."[10] The Kalanga were incorporated into Ndebele society, largely as the *holi* caste, although some became "religious leaders" within the Ndebele superstructure.

Thus, at the time of British occupation in 1890, an unsettled dispute prevailed between the Ndebele and Shona groups over suzerainty and control of the area. This quarrel faded into the background during the period of colonial consolidation and black acquiescence to white rule (roughly 1900 to 1945) but would resurface, albeit in more disguised and subtle forms, during and after the liberation struggle (roughly from the late 1950s to the 1980s).

A nationwide struggle for majority rule in Rhodesia began in earnest in the late 1950s, and, from its very inception, the nationalist movement was conscious of the Ndebele-Shona dichotomy. At a meeting in Harare (then Salisbury) in 1957, the Bulawayo-based African National Congress of Southern Rhodesia, led by Joshua Nkomo, merged with the Harare-based Youth League led by James Chikerema to form a new and expanded organization that retained the name African National Congress (ANC) of Southern Rhodesia.[11] A conscious effort was made to achieve regional or ethnic balance between the Ndebele and the Shona. As such, the reconstructed ANC executive committee was evenly divided between the Ndebele and the Shona. Joshua Nkomo became president of the new organization, and James Chikerema vice-president. An observer of this early balancing act noted that "the Zezuru [Shona] founders of the old African National Congress had invited [Joshua Nkomo] in a bid for unity."[12] The ANC and two other successor organizations, the National Democratic Party (NDP) and the Zimbabwe African People's Union (ZAPU), were banned within a year of each other, notwithstanding the fact that the so-called white liberals were then in power.[13]

The nationalist movement remained united until 1963, when the first major rift occurred. A group of prominent ZAPU executive members led by Ndabaningi Sithole lost confidence in Nkomo's leadership and asked him to step down. When Nkomo refused, they formed their Zimbabwe African National Union (ZANU), which today is the ruling party, ZANU (PF).[14]

The ZAPU-ZANU split of 1963 had far-reaching consequences for politics in Zimbabwe. First, the nationalist movement would remain divided throughout the liberation struggle and after on basically ZAPU-ZANU lines. Second, while it did not take on clearly Ndebele-Shona tribal lines, the split latter degenerated to that, particularly since the 1970s, when intra-ZAPU and intra-ZANU subethnicity was politicized. Although earlier deviant splinter groups were often castigated as "stooge" and "sellout" parties, the ZANU split from ZAPU earned the same labels plus more. Violent methods and tactics were used by ZAPU to liquidate ZANU, and the latter used similar methods to survive. Since then, the use of violence against the opposition has become part of the Zimbabwean political culture. This has implications for democracy in Zimbabwe, which we consider in a later section.

Suffice it to emphasize now that the 1963 split was accompanied by fierce factional fights in most major cities. The ensuing violence involved fists, stones, sticks, knobkerries, knives, axes, and homemade petrol bombs—the only weapons of war readily available to the feuding factions at the time. In the 1970s and after, the feuding factions added to their war paraphernalia all modern weapons of war readily available to them, including armored vehicles. Those factions that did not use modern weapons of war did not have them.

During the mid-1960s, following the ban on ZAPU and ZANU, the theater for Zimbabwe nationalist politics was transferred to exile and progressively took on a new orientation in the form of armed struggle and varying shades of socialist and Marxist-Leninist commitment, particularly in the 1970s. The period between 1965 and 1971 saw a lull in nationalist activity inside the country. However, from 1972 onward, Bishop Abel Muzorewa's African National Council (ANC) filled the apparent vacuum.

What gave rise to Bishop Muzorewa and the ANC was the presence in the country, in March and April of 1972, of the Pearce Commission, which was canvassing African opinion on the acceptability of the 1971 Smith-Douglas Home proposals for a settlement of the Rhodesia independence issue. This event is worthy of note for three reasons. First, it was the first time in the history of colonial Rhodesia that either the British or the white settlers ever sought to sound African opinion on the political future of the country. Second, it was the first time since 1963 that supporters of ZAPU and ZANU united in a joint effort, albeit under a different leader. Third, the subsequent political demise of Bishop Muzorewa, after the release of the better known nationalist leaders, lends credence to our earlier assertion that the fundamental split in the nationalist movement and in Zimbabwe politics has thus far been the ZAPU-ZANU split.

Muzorewa was approached in late 1971 by a team of ZAPU and ZANU officials to lead a new organization in an effort to reject the settlement proposals. He was to be leader *pro tem*.[15] However, after the release of the nationalist leaders in 1974, Muzorewa stayed on at the helm of an independent organization, a gladiator in his own right, until his total eclipse in the 1985 election.

In exile in 1971, the African nationalist movement split further when the Front for the Liberation of Zimbabwe (FROLIZI) was formed amid recriminations in both ZAPU and ZANU involving threats and use of arms to resolve the political difference that had arisen. Important in the formation of FROLIZI was the fact that, for the first time, ethnic conflict between the Shona and Ndebele and among the Shona subethnic groups openly surfaced. Violent exchanges and denunciations of "tribalism," "meetings of clansmen in the dark," and "tribal corruption and nepotism" were openly leveled by principal political gladiators against each other. [16]. When, because of the events of 1971, Chikerema and several other ranking ZAPU officials (mainly Zezuru) left ZAPU, that party then became virtually a Ndebele party. It has retained this stigma ever since and has paid heavily for it at the 1980 polls, and more convincingly in 1985, as we shall demonstrate later. This split also destabilized the political equilibrium in ZANU in a way that has taken that party a long time to recover and to reestablish a new balance of ethnic forces within it. [17] In 1976, in a belated bid to recover his lost support among the Shona, Nkomo asked Robert Mugabe, then on the ascendant in ZANU, to join him in a Patriotic Front that existed tenuously for only three years until the end of the Lancaster House talks in 1979—dashing hopes for a joint campaign in the 1980 election. In his political biography, Nkomo laments that Mugabe abandoned him at the last moment. [18]

By the time of the Lancaster House conference in 1979, there had been a proliferation of political parties on the Zimbabwe political landscape. At their most numerous, they numbered nine. Yet, when the dust finally settled, the residue showed the former ZAPU-ZANU split. Now, however, the scales of dominance had shifted in favor of ZANU, and the leading personality was Mugabe, not Sithole. This proliferation of parties resurfaced on the eve of the 1985 general election, but again the residue showed the centrality of the ZAPU-ZANU cleavage.

Postcolonial Politics

Zimbabwe was born on 18 April 1980, when independence was proclaimed following a general election based on the principle of "one man, one vote," which had long been the basis of the conflict between blacks and whites throughout the political history of white-ruled Rhodesia. In 1979, as a result of the Lancaster House conference involving all the parties to the Rhodesia power dispute, a consensus was reached on a constitution for the new republic. This was the first time that democratic rule in its inclusive sense was established.

Although Zimbabwe is a competitive multiparty state with a single dominant party, there are indications that it is moving to a *de jure* one-party state. The possibility exists, however, that Zimbabwe may still opt to remain a *de facto* one-party-dominant state. We shall discuss this in the concluding section, when we examine future prospects for democracy in Zimbabwe. At this point, we turn to political developments since independence, focusing in particular on the three general elections since 1979 based on the principle of "one man, one vote."

The first one-man, one-vote election was held during the period of Zimbabwe-Rhodesia in 1979.[19]. These elections were held amid both local and international controversy about their authenticity. This stemmed from the questionable legitimacy of the "internal settlement" that authorized the elections while, ironically, excluding the nationalist guerrillas who had brought about the necessary pressure for change.

Following the failure of the 1976 Geneva Conference on Rhodesia, and under increasing pressure from nationalist guerrillas, Ian Smith identified those nationalist factions that appeared out of favor with either the frontline states or the guerrilla forces.[20] He enticed them into a political deal that he hoped would enable them to supersede the Patriotic Front Alliance of Mugabe and Nkomo (then based in exile) while, at the same time, keeping the political outcome securely under white control. This led to the "internal settlement talks," culminating in the "March 3rd Agreement" of 1978 between Muzorewa's United African National Council (the UANC renamed from the ANC of 1971), Sithole's faction of ZANU, and Chief Chirau's ZUPO, on the one hand, and Ian Smith's RF on the other.[21]

The Zimbabwe-Rhodesia constitution spawned by this settlement provided for a president and a Parliament, comprising a House of Assembly and a Senate. The president, who acted on the advice of the prime minister and the Executive Council, was appointed by an electoral college consisting of all the senators and all members of the House of Assembly. The Senate consisted of thirty members, of whom ten were blacks elected by seventy-two black members of the House of Assembly, ten were whites elected by twenty-eight white members of the House of Assembly, and ten were African chiefs elected by the existing Council of Chiefs. Of these chiefs, five were to be from Mashonaland and the other five from Matebeleland—a sort of ethnic balance.

The House of Assembly consisted of 100 members, seventy-two of whom were elected by blacks on a party list system, and twenty-eight by whites on a single constituency basis. At the end of ten years or after the second Parliament, whichever would come later, a commission was to be established to review the question of the retention of the twenty-eight white seats. The franchise was extended to all persons eighteen years or older who were either citizens or had been permanently and continuously resident in the country for at least two years before the election. Provisions were also made in the constitution for the first government to be a government of national unity. To this end, any party winning five seats or more in the House of Assembly was represented in the cabinet in proportion to its seats in Parliament.

In all three elections, parties were represented on ballots by name and by a symbol distinctive to each party. Prior to each election, the government instituted a widespread information program to encourage people to vote and to explain the election process (and, in the case of the 1985 election, the voter registration procedures). Elaborate election procedures were set up for all three elections. Hundreds of polling stations (including mobile units) were established in urban and rural locations to provide as wide a spread of polling as possible. To check that a person had not voted previously, each voter had to dip his fingers in a colorless liquid containing dye visible under ultraviolet light and that stayed on a person's fingers for a week or more. Polling officials were empowered to explain the ballot paper and how a vote should be indicated. Representatives of the competing political parties, international observers, and the press were able to enter polling stations at any time and scrutinize the voting process. They could also be present at the sealing and reopening of ballot boxes and to affix their own seals if they so desired.

An electoral Supervisory Commission was established for all three elections and was charged with ensuring that the elections were free and fair. This feature was required by the constitution, and persons making charges of election fraud were asked in press notices to communicate their information to this commission. It was a democratic process.

Although five political parties ran in the 1979 general elections, only three won seats, with Muzorewa's UANC winning fifty-one of the seventy-two African seats, Sithole's faction of ZANU twelve, and Chief Ndiweni's United National Federal Party (formed only three months before the election) winning nine seats. The voter turnout was 65 percent of the voting population, estimated at 2.9 million.

Although there was disruptive pressure from the Patriotic Front guerrillas, these elections were pronounced to have been "substantially free and fair" by the electoral Supervisory Commission and several international "observer" groups who filed similar reports approving the conduct of the election.[22] All competing parties but ZANU(Sithole) concurred with this assessment. ZANU(Sithole) alleged "gross irregularities" in the conduct of the elections and lodged an unsuccessful petition with the authorities.

The twelve ZANU(Sithole) members initially boycotted Parliament but later took up their seats when it became apparent that no one in the system really believed their story. Also, it became clear that, if they maintained their boycott, they would be excluded from a Zimbabwe-Rhodesia delegation to possible constitutional talks in London. Contrary to expectations, the government formed by Bishop Muzorewa failed to gain international recognition and attracted intensified guerrilla pressure until he and his internal settlement colleagues were summoned to London by the British Government to discuss a new constitution with the leaders of the Patriotic Front late in 1979.

The 1979 Lancaster House conference gave Zimbabwe its current constitution. Thus, since 1980, and most likely until 1990, Zimbabwe government and politics have operated within the framework of a constitution agreed to by all the parties in the dispute. The governmental and electoral provisions of this constitution were similar to those of the Zimbabwe-Rhodesia constitution, already mentioned. There were, however, some important exceptions.

Although the House of Assembly still consisted of 100 members, eighty rather than seventy-two were to be elected by the common roll, while the white seats were reduced to twenty. Further, while the Zimbabwe-Rhodesia constitution required formation of a government of national unity (with proportional representation in the cabinet), the composition of the cabinet was now entirely the prerogative of the prime minister. However, he was still required to choose his cabinet from among those elected to the House of Assembly or Senate.

Another critically important innovation was the way in which nationalist guerrillas were to be handled in the transitional period. During Zimbabwe-Rhodesia, the guerrillas were required to "surrender" to the Rhodesian security forces, but now they would go into "assembly points," where they would remain for the duration of the election. From their number, and from the former Rhodesian army, a new Zimbabwean national army (ZNA) would be created with the help of British military experts. During the transition in early 1980, there were several assembly points throughout Zimbabwe's countryside: in Mashonaland, these assembly points housed ZANU's ZANLA guerrillas, and in Matebeleland, ZAPU's ZIPRA. Eventually, some of these guerrillas were brought into makeshift barracks located within the major cities of Harare and Bulawayo and housed right across from each other in the high-density suburbs of these cities. This worsened existing tensions between the two groups.

Also significant in the Lancaster House agreement was the provision of a British governor charged with responsibility for administering the country during the transition period, supervising the conduct of the elections, and asking the leader of the winning party to form a government. In Zimbabwe-Rhodesia these procedures had been the responsibility of Ian Smith's Rhodesia Front governmental machinery.

Finally, there was the provision of subsection 2, section 75, chapter VII of the constitution, which says:

> The President may give general directions of policy to the Public Service Commission with the object of achieving a suitable representation of the various elements of the population in the Public Service and the Prison Service.

Known locally as the "presidential directive," this clause allowed for the appointment of personnel and lateral entry into any section of the public service if the president (on the advice of the prime minister) deemed it necessary in order to redress past imbalances. This device was particularly important since key public service posts had, hitherto, been staked with "old order" types whom it would take decades to replace on the basis of the normal course of experience.

"Presidential directives" have been utilized to full effect since independence. Ibbo Mandaza, a commissioner on the Public Service Commission observed that, "Were it not for the Presidential Directive, and the fact that qualified Zimbabweans returned home in their numbers at independence, there would have been little change in the structure and direction of this important component of the State machinery."[23] The presidential directive clause not only provided the new leadership with constitutional means for redressing past imbalances, but, more significantly, it enabled the new rulers to meet the aspirations of a highly qualified (if politicized) and potentially critical element of the African intelligentsia. In this way, animosities between blacks and whites were obliterated almost immediately after independence. This facility arrested revolutionary pressures and redirected their energies into implementing bureaucratic procedures in the service of the state.

Among the more significant features of previous constitutions retained in the 1979 Zimbabwe (Lancaster) constitution were the Senate and Presidency. This meant that Zimbabwe would continue to have a parliamentary system, with a two-tier legislature and a basically ceremonial president, much like the British monarchy. Like the House of Lords in relation to the Commons, the Zimbabwe Senate was essentially a vetting, if rubber stamp, body on legislation passed by the House of Assembly. Also noteworthy was the retention of the provision for parity of representation between Ndebele and Shona in the Senate, and the fact that none of the nationalists at the Lancaster talks either advocated or criticized retention of this structure. Once presented, it was accepted as if by conditioned habit.

The 1980 independence elections were held over a period of three days, 27–29 March, with a total of nine political parties contesting (three more than in 1979). However, only three nationalist parties won seats in the 100-member Parliament; Mugabe's ZANU(PF) won fifty-seven, Nkomo's PF(ZAPU) twenty, and Muzorewa's UANC three. The twenty seats reserved for whites were all captured by Ian Smith's Rhodesia Front, which ran unopposed in fourteen of the twenty constituencies. Following his overwhelming victory, Mugabe was called upon by the British governor to form a government.

There were allegations and counterallegations of violent intimidation by all political parties, particularly among the major ones—ZANU(PF), PF(ZAPU), UANC, and ZANU(Sithole)—with the latter three complaining that they could not campaign in any of the rural areas formerly controlled by ZANLA guerrillas. ZANU(PF)'s complaints were mainly directed at Lord Soames (British governor in charge during the transition to majority rule). Soames was accused of bias against ZANU(PF) in favor of the UANC in particular and the other parties generally.[24] Moreover, there were several attempts on Mugabe's life during the 1980 campaign.[25] On the complaint that other parties could not campaign in former ZANLA areas, the ZANU(PF)'s typical attitude was: "Why should any party go where it is not wanted? Why should any party wish to go and reap where it did not sow?"[26] ZANU(PF) was not about to give rival parties safe passage into its areas of dominance. In the big cities, there were numerous clashes between parties and a number of fatalities during the election campaign. However, notwithstanding the various accusations of intimidation and violence, the elections were pronounced by Lord Soames, the electoral Supervisory Commission, and international observers to be a fair reflection of the will and choice of the people.

The independence election of 1980 produced a clear-cut ZANU(PF) victory. But, instead of forming an exclusively ZANU(PF) cabinet, Prime Minister Mugabe invited his former Patriotic Front partners of ZAPU into a government of national unity in an effort to create harmony and a stable democracy. The ZAPU president, Joshua Nkomo, was first offered the position of president, which he turned down, preferring the more powerful post of home affairs minister, responsible for the police. Whites were also included in Mugabe's cabinet in an effort to foster reconciliation between the races. Everything seemed in place for national reconciliation.

Suddenly, in 1982, fighting broke out between former ZANLA and ZIPRA guerrillas stationed around Harare and Bulawayo, culminating in a showdown between the defense forces and former ZIPRA guerrillas in several parts of Matabeleland and the Midlands. Many former ZIPRA personnel defected from the newly integrated national army to form the nucleus of the present dissident activities in Matebeleland. Subsequently, arms caches were uncovered in several ZAPU-owned farms in Matebeleland, whereupon all ZAPU cabinet ministers were sacked, and involved ZAPU properties were confiscated by government authorities. Several ranking former ZIPRA officers in the army were arrested as some defected to join the ranks of dissidents. A renewed state of emergency has existed in many parts of Matebeleland since 1982, the start of serious dissident activities. This remains the biggest threat to the democratic project in Zimbabwe, a theme we shall explore in the next section.

Independent Zimbabwe's most important experience with democracy to date was the general election held on 1–4 July 1985. This election was significant in many respects. It was the first general election Zimbabwe had held as an independent sovereign state; the 1980 election having been held under British supervision. Second, with the exception of some parts of Matebeleland, the 1985 election, unlike the earlier ones, was largely held in an atmosphere of peace. Third, like the 1979 and 1980 elections, the 1985 election was held in a multiparty context, notwithstanding suggestions by the ruling party for a one-party state. Fourth, while the two previous elections were based on the party list electoral system, the election of 1985 was conducted on a single-constituency basis. Finally, although a separate election was again held for the white electorate, the 1985 election brought the end of white unity and fifteen years of Rhodesia Front hegemony in white politics. For the first time in a long while, two white factions (both with a Rhodesia Front background) competed in the white roll elections in 1985.

In 1980, ZANU(PF) had its first experience in running an election campaign; then it was a party out of government. In 1985, it had two onerous responsibilities. As the party in government, it was responsible for the administration and conduct of the general election while, at the same time, it was also responsible for its own campaign for reelection in a contest in which five other parties also sought office, although with varying degrees of vigor and appetite. This dual responsibility placed ZANU(PF) both at an advantage and disadvantage. For the first task, it had gained enormous experience from years of mobilization during the liberation struggle, as well as from the actual election campaign of 1980. For the second task, that of administering a national election, ZANU(PF) had very little prior experience. It had to take the blame for anything wrong about the elections. Moreover, while the black population had prior experience with the party list system of election (1979 and 1980), they had not experienced a constituency-based election. The need for prior administrative experience in conducting elections was manifest throughout the exercise. It was a learning experience.[27]

ZANU(PF) came on top with another brilliant victory. It picked up seven more seats, increasing its 1980 total to sixty-four. It took all the seats in Mashonaland Central, East, West, and Masvingo, as well as in the Midlands, where in 1980 PF(ZAPU) had managed to win four out of the twelve seats. In Manicaland, ZANU(PF) won all but one seat in the Chipinge constituency, stronghold of Sithole's faction of ZANU. PF(ZAPU), shut out in six of the eight provinces, swept all fifteen seats in Matebeleland North and South, defeating two incumbent ministers in Mugabe's cabinet. In the white elections, Ian Smith's Conservative Alliance of Zimbabwe won fifteen of the twenty seats, and the more conciliatory Independent Zimbabwe Group won four seats. One seat was won by a "left-of-center" candidate.

The elections were pronounced "free and fair" by all international observers who came in their private capacities. Independent groups within Zimbabwe itself passed similar judgment of approval, although Nkomo did express disappointment with the results.[28] The electoral Supervisory Commission was also pleased with the conduct of the election. Its chairman, Professor Walter J. Kamba, vice-chancellor of the University of Zimbabwe, commented:

> We were satisfied, beyond doubt, that the elections were conducted fairly at every stage of the process. My commission visited many places in the country observing the election preparations, during the polling period and the counting of votes. We are satisfied that the officials acted and behaved with probity and impartiality. I have no doubt that the electorate expressed its choice at the polls freely. In every area, and in every constituency, people voted for the party or candidate of their choice.[29]

The actual conduct of the election on 1–4 July was peaceful and civil. Everything possible was done to ensure voter secrecy. For four full days, the people quietly cast their secret ballots. Even in dissident affected parts of Matebeleland, relative quiet reigned. According to the registrar-general, the success and orderly conduct during the polling days was attributable to the "prohibition of certain activities, including the wearing of Party Uniform, the banning of canvassing and political activities within 100 meters of the polling stations."[30]

The irony of the 1985 election, however, was the almost unbelievable reaction of many ZANU(PF) supporters, especially women and youth in the urban areas. A few days after the news of the victory, they went on a rampage beating up and evicting members of minority parties from their houses. Whole families and their belongings were thrown out on the streets, and several people were killed in this postelection violence.

Further, there were very strong, if unfamiliar, anti-Nkomo manifestations in several urban communities by some party officials and enthusiasts. At several places, mock funerals were held with people carrying "coffins" of Nkomo and ZAPU for burial. At one such mock funeral in Kadoma, a live bull (the ZAPU election symbol) was actually axed to death in front of a huge crowd to symbolize the death of ZAPU. Although other minority parties were also the objects of similar ridicule, the anti-ZAPU manifestations were many and more pronounced.

Since independence, politics has also been waged at the local government level. The Zimbabwean constitution provides for the establishment of locally elected district and city councils. City mayors are elected from the councils. At the district level, however, district administrators are appointed by the minister of local government. A significant postindependence development was the creation of provincial governorships, one in each of Zimbabwe's eight regions. These governors are appointed by the president on the advice of the prime minister. They coordinate and oversee implementation of government policy in the provinces.

Important to note about politics at the local level is its marked repetition of attitudes shown at the national level. Thus, city and district council elections in Matebeleland tend to be dominated by ZAPU while ZANU controls local councils in the rest of the country. The story is different, however, when it comes to appointive posts such as district administrators and provincial governors. Here they tend to be predominantly ZANU members. In Matebeleland, such appointees have often been targets of dissident violence.

• ANALYSIS OF HISTORICAL DEVELOPMENTS •

At this point we seek to explain the developments outlined above, namely: intrawhite democracy, the development of the nationalist movement, and the development of democracy in Zimbabwe since independence.

Analysis of Intrawhite Democracy

Several questions come to mind regarding intrawhite democracy. Why, in the first place, was there intrawhite democracy in the Rhodesian state? Second, both Godfrey Huggins and Ian Smith ran exceptionally long, uninterrupted regimes—one liberal and the other right-wing. What explains the longevity and stability of these seemingly "different" regimes, in contrast to the apparent regime instability from 1958 to 1964? Finally, why did successive efforts at a peaceful democratic settlement between Ian Smith, the British government, and the African nationalists fail? In other words, could democracy have been achieved without a violent liberation struggle?

Until independence, white Rhodesians were always the more educated and prosperous of the country's population. Moreover, culturally, they were predominantly the offspring of British traditions; as such, the politics of contestation were no stranger to them. The settler economy was basically a free enterprise economy. Most white politicians were wealthy, and had independent status before they rose to preeminence in politics. Huggins, Welensky, and Whitehead were knighted well before entering politics. Todd, Field, and Smith were prosperous farmers long before they became prime ministers of Rhodesia. Politics among whites, therefore, was a vocation rather than a means of livelihood. Among them, it was not a "do-or-die" affair. As each man retired or lost to the other, he had a viable livelihood to return to. Hence, losing an election did not mean losing everything; politics was not a "zero-sum game."

There was, however, a sense in which whites did view politics in Rhodesia as a zero-sum game; this was when politics was perceived in a racial context. Here whites were basically one; regardless of class, ideology, or whether of English or Afrikaner extraction. They all saw African majority rule as inimical to white interests. Thus, the fundamental issue of intrawhite political conflicts concerned the best strategies and policies to follow in order to preserve the system of white privilege through dominance. Decisions to achieve these ends, however, were made in the most democratic way possible within the white community. But why was intrawhite democracy important?

Democracy was important for white Rhodesian politics because it narrowed the perceptual gap between the white political elite and their followers in understanding interests and the strategies necessary to achieve them. This explains why whites were able to maintain unity among themselves, unity that could be broken only after African majority rule had been achieved. Given, in particular, the British cultural legacy and its democratic ethos, democratic consultation was necessary to produce goal consensus and regime legitimacy among whites as they confronted a common enemy in what was perceived essentially as a "do or die" contest between black and white. Without periodic consultations, goal consensus, and regime legitimacy, white rule in Rhodesia would have not lasted as long as it did, and as cohesively.

A second issue of note is the lengthy tenures of the Huggins and Smith regimes. Right from the inception of white rule in colonial Rhodesia, whites saw themselves as a distinct group potentially threatened by Africans. As such, they maintained a basic consensus in the perception of their position throughout the period of white rule. Up until 1958, this consensus was on a philosophy and strategy that viewed relations between black and white in some sort of strange paternalism. Huggins characterized the relationship as one between "junior and senior partners."[31] Whites believed that Africans, formerly a primitive people, felt themselves privileged to be ruled by Europeans—that white rule was a blessing. The fear of the African began during the Federation of Rhodesia and Nyasaland, when the nationalist movement in the two northern territories became increasingly successful amid British acquiescence and an increasingly anticolonial international environment following World War II. White Rhodesia then abandoned its formerly carefree paternalistic disposition and reached a new consensus in the right-wing drift of the RF election of 1962, which was solidified in Ian Smith's ascendency in 1964. The apparent leadership instability of the 1958–1964 period suggests an adjustment period as the white community moved to a new consensus.

It remains to explain why several successive attempts to resolve the Rhodesian constitutional impasse failed until 1979. The simple answer is that the British would not give or recognize independence in Rhodesia based on a constitution that denied the franchise to the African majority. But why would Britain take such a stance, yet not take any tangible steps to enfranchise the Africans?

First and foremost, the international climate after World War II, as we have noted, was hostile to colonialism and racism—both of which Rhodesia typified. Embodied in the United Nations, the international community became activist with regard to democratization and self-determination in the colonies. From the 1960s, the Organization of African Unity (OAU) and other British commonwealth countries effectively discouraged British inclinations to recognize the Unilateral Declaration of Independence. Moreover, Britain had already embarked on granting independence to the other two countries of the federation on the basis of African majority rule, although African resistance there had become more aggressive, and the white population and interests were much less than in Rhodesia. At any rate, Britain could not do otherwise in Rhodesia without being seen as racist in such a double standard.

Finally, and more important, throughout the 1970s, the Zimbabwe African nationalist movement had matured in sophistication and effectiveness and would not settle for any independence formula short of immediate total transfer of power to the African majority. For instance, in 1971, Ian Smith and the British government agreed on a formula for gradually accelerated majority rule. When African opinion was sought by the Pearce Commission in 1972, the proposals were overwhelmingly rejected. Similarly, the 1978–1979 "internal settlement" was denounced by a mainstream nationalist opinion to which the international community now listened.

Given the previous white intransigence, why, then, was 1979 successful? By then, a complex combination of factors had coalesced to induce the white oligarchy to accept inclusive popular democracy. Cumulatively, the international isolation, economic sanctions, intensified nationalist guerrilla effectiveness, political pressure from the African "front-line states" on the nationalists, and from South Africa on the Smith regime all contributed to a conducive climate. Further, there was in London, by 1979, a rather decisive Conservative government with an activist foreign policy. Moreover, there was also that element of luck in the circumstances of the Lancaster House conference whereby all the major power aspirants perceived themselves the likely victor in the proposed elections. Even the whites believed their "black candidates" of the "internal settlement" would win and combine with them in a coalition government.[32]

Finally, was it inevitable that white Rhodesian politics turn to the right as they did, and, therefore, that majority rule be achieved only after an ugly armed struggle? Following the accession to power by the RF in 1962 and by Ian Smith in 1964, it was clear from Smith's pronouncements of "no African government in my life-time" and "not in a thousand years" that armed struggle was inevitable. Simple and "unserious" as they may appear, these statements had tremendous impact on both black and white. The whites received them with reassurance, thereby making them blind and intransigent for fifteen years. On the other hand, such unyielding pronouncements forced African nationalists to reassess their method of struggle, which hitherto had been peaceful and constitutional.[33]

Thus, from 1962 to the attempts at an internal settlement in the 1978–1979 period, Rhodesian politics were extremely polarized between black and white. The two worked at cross-purposes and could find no common ground for a settlement. This, however, suggests that an accommodation was possible earlier, during the "liberal" period. There are two views that suggest why early accommodation did not occur and how such an accommodation might have been achieved, thereby averting further polarization and the escalation of violence.

Early peaceful accommodation presupposes that the liberalism/paternalism of the Huggins, Todd, and Whitehead period was substantially different from the right-wing tendency of the Smith period; that the liberals had it in the back of their minds to see eventual black rule and an independent Zimbabwe. In 1962, right before his electoral defeat, Edgar Whitehead, the last of the "liberals," publicly declared that "there is no doubt that the African will have a majority within 15 years.[34] (Ironically, African majority rule did come soon thereafter, but as the result of armed struggle and not gradual improvements on the 1961 constitution.) However, observers of white Rhodesian politics have commented that the apparent shift to the right was not at all a shift but part of a "continual process of white reassessment" of strategy and tactics in pursuit of white supremacist goals.[35]

We should not, however, lose sight of the possibility that paternalists like Todd, Whitehead, or Welensky might have been philosophical liberals, believing that, ultimately, white interests could only be served by an inclusive multiracial polity. They and others never joined the RF nor were they prominently identified with RF rule. For that reason, one could argue that the fifteen years of polarization and civil war could have been avoided. If, for instance, the British government of the time had been resolute in its commitment to majority rule and had sent unambiguous signals to white settlers that UDI would be treated as treasonable rebellion against which British troops or any other (UN, Commonwealth, etc.) would be unleashed in support of the constitution, the liberals, and other democratic forces, it is conceivable that white opinion in Rhodesia would have been a lot more cautious on UDI. Instead, the British government went on record publicly stating that it would not use force against UDI, and that it opposed the use of violence against an illegal regime by the African nationalists. At UN and Commonwealth forums, the British blocked resolutions to send international troops; such a policy was not attractive to the British government and public because most white Rhodesians were British "kith and kin." Lack of strong commitment to majority rule by the British then fueled tendencies towards further polarization between black and white in Rhodesia. Race interfered with Britain's democratic inclinations.

Analysis of the Nationalist Movement

We have seen that Zimbabwe nationalist movement was fraught with splits and factional in-fighting from the ZAPU-ZANU split of 1963 throughout the liberation struggle. Starting with one organization in 1957, there were nine different parties at independence in 1980. Should this be celebrated as a manifestation of a tendency toward multiparty democracy in the Zimbabwe political culture? Yet, only two of these parties, ZANU and ZAPU, now remain viable. But shall we then celebrate a flourishing of, or prospects for, a two-party democracy in Zimbabwe? No, we cannot, least of all because of the drive toward a one-party state by the present ruling party. What then explains factionalism in the nationalist movement during the liberation struggle and the persistence of division between ZANU and ZAPU after independence?

One theory argues that the incumbent colonialists engineered division and factional in-fighting in the movement to weaken it so that they would either remain in power or in neocolonial control of the emergent government. This is an aspect of the classical "divide-and-conquer" theory. It is difficult, however, to demonstrate how the ZAPU-ZANU split of 1963 was the work of either the white settlers in power or elements external to the movement itself. There were suggestions of "enemy agents" involved in some of the splits in exile in the 1970s.[36] And suggestions that all the "internal settlement" parties of the 1978–1979 period were sponsored, to varying degrees, by the Smith regime have not been disputed. Moreover, more than achieving ethnic parity in the Council of Chiefs, the settler regime hoped to develop or retain Ndebele and Shona consciousness in the polity by always creating structures that weighted the Ndebele as numerically equal to the Shona. But the uneasy relations between these two groups, as we saw, predate colonialism.

It is doubtful that, left to themselves, African nationalists would have inclined toward unity in one party during the liberation struggle. The ZAPU-ZANU split of 1963 was caused neither by white settlers nor by external imperialists. Nationalist leaders disagreed among themselves, and, when they could not resolve their differences, they split and ZANU was formed. Moreover, the major factions involved in the "internal settlement" did not, as we have seen, originate from Ian Smith. They were the result of earlier developments in the nationalist movement itself. In any case, a divided movement, like a divided country, often attracts the attention of its enemies.

A second school of thought argues that factionalism and infighting in the Zimbabwe Nationalist Movement was caused by "unprincipled," "petty bourgeois" politicians hungry for power. According to this argument, as long as the petty bourgeois class led the liberation struggle, splits and factional infighting were inevitable.[37] The suggestion here is that when leadership stems from the working class, splits and factional infighting stop. Such a romantic view of the proletariat is sentimental nonsense.[38]

Finally, a third school of thought argues that a better explanation of factionalism and infighting in the liberation movement and the continued strife after independence is tribalism or the ethnic factor in power contestations.[39] The leaders of political parties and factions within the parties have tended to have an ethnic power base. Hence, when ZANU split from ZAPU, it never made any headway in Matebeleland, Joshua Nkomo's home area. This situation obtains to this day. ZAPU's support among the Shona was mainly among the Zezuru (a Shona subgroup). This was because Zezuru leaders of the Youth League, led by James Chikerema and George Nyandoro, who had formed the ANC with Nkomo in 1957, remained loyal to ZAPU until 1971, when Chikerema and Nyandoro (now in exile) left ZAPU to form FROLIZI. From then on, ZAPU became the largely Ndebele party that it is today. Moreover, when the ZAPU-ZANU split occurred in 1963, Chikerema and others were in detention after the ban on the ANC in 1959. In the 1970s, Chikerema and the bulk of the FROLIZI element rallied behind Muzorewa. As Mugabe (himself Zezuru) emerged as the leader of ZANU in the late 1970s, ZANU became the dominant party for the first time in all Shona-speaking regions.

The three elections we outlined indicate the preponderance of the ethnic factor in postcolonial Zimbabwe politics. The 1985 election epitomized this when the voting patterns revealed an even stronger manifestation of the Ndebele-Shona ethnicity than in 1980. Joshua Nkomo's party won all the seats in Matebeleland, but not because workers and peasants in Matebeleland mistook Nkomo for a worker or peasant. Together with the Ndebele bourgeoisie, they have always known Nkomo loved capital. Similarly, ZANU(PF)'s overwhelming victory in the Shona-speaking areas was not a vote only from Shona peasants and workers. The Shona bourgeoisie also voted ZANU(PF) knowing fully well that Mugabe inclined toward peasants and workers. It could hardly be convincing to argue that the Shona bourgeoisie decided to commit class suicide while Ndebele peasants and workers were not aware of their real class interests.

Further, we have seen that there were subethnic groups among the larger Shona and Ndebele groupings. To what extent has subethnicity been a factor in intraparty infighting? In the 1970s, the internecine fights in the ZANU-in-exile were blamed on emergent hostilities between the Karanga and Manyika Shona subethnic groups. When Chikerema broke away from a coalition with Muzorewa in 1979, he accused the latter of running his party, with a "Manyika

Mafia," while Muzorewa's group denounced Chikerema as leader of a Zezuru "Zvimba clique."[40]. Thus, interethnic alliances in the Zimbabwe nationalist movement have been dynamic and not permanent. If properly understood, such dynamism augurs well for pluralistic democracy in Zimbabwe.

Analysis of Postcolonial Developments

Political developments in Zimbabwe during the postcolonial era were as much a product of the past as they were of new developments. We seek now to explain why democracy has endured in Zimbabwe, however tenuously, over the first six years of independence. But first, let us explain the stresses and strains on democracy during this period.

The first six years of independence were trying times for the new government. Like most countries, Zimbabwe's economy was affected by the world recession, but more important, it was hard hit by a three-year drought (1981–1983) that was the worst in many years. Further, during the same period, Zimbabwe had to deal with a costly conflict in Matebeleland to the west and maintain a military presence to the east, in an effort both to guard a strategic oil pipeline and assist Mozambique's government in its war effort against South African-assisted insurgents destabilizing that country. These were hardly small challenges for people just learning not only how to govern, but also how to lead normal lives after some fifteen years in exile or in detention. Moreover, there was deliberate scrutiny by both the international community and the internal opponents of the new rulers to see how well the new rulers were succeeding in gluing together a country hitherto torn apart by war with its attendant lines of cleavage along race, ethnic, and party-cum-military lines.

However, by far the most difficult and costly problem for the new government was the conflict in Matebeleland. This conflict, as we have seen, dates not only back to the liberation struggle, but into the nineteenth century. It is the central thesis of this chapter that, ultimately, democracy in Zimbabwe depends largely on the resolution of the conflict in Matebeleland.

We stated earlier that a conquering people, the Ndebele, by and large dominated the Shona before the advent of colonialism. This Ndebele dominance in one form or another persisted for some time during the colonial period. It was the result both of history and psychological inertia, as well as settler manipulation of the polity. In Matebeleland, for instance, many Shona families adopted Ndebele names while Ndebeles in Shona communities did not. Further, the deference to and tolerance for nationalist leader Joshua Nkomo among the Shona during the early part of the nationalist movement derived, in large part, from the previous Shona deference to the Ndebele. It is largely this inertia that underlay the conflict in Matebeleland in postcolonial Zimbabwe.

Moreover, ZANLA and ZIPRA, the guerrilla armies of ZANU and ZAPU respectively, developed along ethnic-regional lines. Had the Lancaster House conference not occurred when it did, and had the Smith regime been run out of

Salisbury by ZANLA guerrillas, it is conceivable ZIPRA would have occupied Bulawayo and the two forces would have engaged each other in the Midlands, beginning a worse civil war than the scattered skirmishes witnessed in Matebeleland. ZANLA and ZIPRA guerrillas often wasted their strength upon each other during the liberation struggle. Moreover, it was common knowledge in Zimbabwean liberation circles during the 1970s that ZAPU had adopted a strategy of not engaging its forces in an all-out fight against the Smith regime so that they could engage a worn-out ZANU army at the end of the war. The ZANU leadership had always been suspicious of ZAPU strategy and intentions. Thus, after independence, military maneuvers in ZIPRA assembly points, discoveries of arms caches, and ZIPRA defections from the national army were not only predictable, but anticipated and prepared for by a ZANU leadership that had no reason to trust the ZAPU leadership.[41] A showdown between ZANU and ZAPU was, therefore, inevitable.

Right after the signing of the Lancaster House agreement, ZANU pulled out of the Patriotic Front alliance with ZAPU, dashing Nkomo's hopes that the two would campaign jointly in the impending elections. Why did Mugabe pull out of the alliance, and why was Nkomo interested in running jointly with Mugabe? There are several explanations, but the following we find plausible.

In his political biography, Nkomo argues that he wanted to run jointly with ZANU in order to foster unity and thus prevent the current conflict in Matebeleland, which he foresaw.[42] For its part, ZANU pulled out because it did not trust Nkomo, and, more important, many in ZANU believed ZANU did not need the alliance to win the election and that such an alliance would even be a liability. ZAPU, however, needed the alliance.[43] When this first option was denied, ZAPU then hoped to forge an alliance with the 1978–1979 "internal parties" in a "ganging-up" coalition government in which it would be dominant. Given the possibility that ZANU could well win the election against any other electoral combination and permutation, a third strategy, it would appear, became necessary for ZAPU. This took the form of military confrontation after independence. This would explain the arms caches and defections from the national army.

Several reasons point to why ZAPU strategists would entertain the third option. There was the perception first (not entirely incorrect) that, although extremely popular with the masses, ZANU had been an unstable party suffering more frequent and serious squabbles than ZAPU; second, that Mugabe, who had only just emerged as ZANU leader, had yet to gain control of his fractionalized and unstable organization; third, that the entire former Rhodesian security apparatus, as well as the whites generally, would, under the circumstances, support a move against an infant ZANU government; and fourth, that ZANU's former ZANLA forces would be caught "napping," celebrating their victory and "tired" of war, as had been expected. Moreover, throughout the liberation struggle, ZAPU's ZIPRA army was often cited as "Soviet-trained" for "conventional warfare," as "more disciplined," and, by implication, superior to ZANLA, which was regarded as rather chaotic but whose strength lay in morale and numbers. In addition, there was often a misperception of the Shona of the twentieth century as basically the same as those of the nineteenth century—peaceful and shy of war. Traditionally, fighting was not in the Shona way of life. They belonged to what Ali Mazrui has called the "palaver tradition," while the Ndebele, with their Zulu background, belonged to the "warrior tradition."[44] This misperception has proven costly.

The Shona of the twentieth century is qualitatively different from the Shona encountered by Mzilikazi in the nineteenth century. He is a Shona who believes that he was largely responsible for the defeat of white settler rule with its sophisticated organization and newest weapons of war. Thus, we may be witnessing in the conflict in Matebeleland violence that always arises when society must accept a new balance of forces and a new power equilibrium, much as Marx depicted for changes in modes of production and relations of production.

However, with an arsenal of arms buried in various places in Matebeleland, and a cadre of young men aching to fight, ZAPU had not only the will, but also the capacity to test both Mugabe's will to rule and ZANU's capacity to survive. Postindependence dissident activity then must be seen in terms of this decisive test. It is a test that those intimately connected with the development of the liberation struggle could see coming, and that must fade away as Mugabe's will and ZANU's capacity are effectively demonstrated. It is this conflict in Matebeleland that has threatened the development of democracy in newly independent Zimbabwe as the government has resorted to authoritarian and repressive methods to deal with dissident activity. The agenda to discontinue the state of emergency, introduced during white settler rule, was deferred on account of this conflict. Ronald Weitzer has argued that the repressive powers and institutions of the white Rhodesian state were perpetuated and utilized by the postindependence government.[45] Moreover, the human rights organization, Amnesty International, which frequently cited the Smith government for human rights violation during the liberation struggle, now accuses Prime Minister Mugabe's government of similar infractions.[46]

While Weitzer's well-documented argument cannot be denied by common experience during Zimbabwe's first years of independence, it misses an important point. The Mugabe government faced cruel dangers right from its inception. As shown above, ZANU (PF) came to power in an atmosphere of fear, uncertainty, and mutual suspicion between blacks and whites, as well as among the various black factions. Significantly, the various contending groups had the requisite coercive instruments with which to seize power in pursuit of their aims. Under these circumstances, a premature dismantling of the coercive instruments of the former Rhodesian state was ill-advised. Such a step would have created a power vacuum deliciously attractive to the various centers of power already armed to step in. The alternative to maintaining the instruments of the former Rhodesian state was to create new ones in their place. What, in fact, happened is that new instruments of coercion, such as the Fifth Brigade, were added. This raises the question of whether such an additional instrument

SITHOLE

was necessary. Here again, it does not help much to examine the events and passions of the present without being sensitive to those of the past.

Although Prime Minister Mugabe's government came to power via an election, this was preceded by a war with fractional armies. The creation of a new Zimbabwean national army from these formerly warring armies meant that its political neutrality and loyalty to the new government could not be simply assumed, at least not in the short run. Such an assumption would have been a textbook approach to power. Dissident activity in Matebeleland started almost immediately after independence, and it became necessary for the new government to create the Fifth Brigade because it could not rest its fortunes on an army initially plagued with mutual distrust. Thus, the observations made by many that the brigade (or, as it is emotionally called, *gukurahundi*—"the storm that gathers and clears everything") is highly politically motivated are not mischievous. At independence, Mugabe's government needed the brigade to deal with an equally politically motivated dissident element.

Yet, repression, like many bad things, is habit-forming. There is the real danger in postindependence Zimbabwe that, the longer the state of emergency in Matebeleland continues, the good life and democratic values for which the nationalist struggle was fought might begin to fade from memory and be replaced by a culture of authoritarian rule and violence. Moreover, those involved in prolonged violence are eventually forced to develop a stake in it. Once this happens, there is no end in sight, much like the situations in Northern Ireland and Lebanon. Herein lies the danger for the development of democracy in societies that allow themselves to resort to protracted armed struggles in settling political disputes (a possible lesson for South Africa).

At this point, we attempt to explain why the Zimbabwean government has survived the severe tests of the past six years, and why competitive multiparty democracy has persisted, however tenuously. A number of factors explain why Mugabe's government has survived and stayed committed to democracy during the past six years. First is its *legitimacy*. Mugabe's government is widely viewed as legitimate. It was twice elected by the people in elections internationally acclaimed as "free and fair." Prime Minister Mugabe has ruled much according to the "social contract"—the Lancaster House constitution to which all parties agreed. Any changes to the constitution have been made within the law, and any changes the ruling party might have wanted (such as the one-party state) but that the law does not allow, have not been made. The political elite thus seems committed to the rule of law. The state of emergency the government declared in parts of Matebeleland was generally understood and accepted by the public, given the nature of the problem as outlined earlier. Moreover, the state of emergency was debated and passed by Parliament in accordance with the constitution.

As the government is regarded as legitimate, so the dissidents and the party associated with them, ZAPU, are perceived by the public—particularly the Shona—to be engaged in illegitimate and unacceptable methods of acquiring power, given that ZAPU has always been allowed to participate in the electoral process. It should be remembered that dissident activity started after ZAPU lost the 1980 elections and long before the elections of 1985. This suggests to many that the insurgents are saying that, unless ZAPU is voted into power, they will fight any other duly elected government. Such an attitude is unacceptable.[47]

Further bolstering the legitimacy of the regime is the fact that it has demonstrated its effectiveness not only militarily, but also administratively. It has penetrated many parts of the country with impressive programs, particularly in health, education, and agriculture. As a result, the majority of the population, especially in the countryside, appears today to agree with the statement, "We are better off today than we were five years ago."[48] This view was expressed throughout the country with 78 percent of those asked saying they were better off.[49] Of note is the fact that 69 percent of those sampled in Matebeleland gave the same evaluation. This suggests that the Mugabe government has not been discriminatory in its development and welfare assistance to the various regions, notwithstanding dissident activity. Moreover, it is conceivable that a strategy to win the hearts and minds of the people of Matebeleland would have involved development and welfare assistance. Disaffection in Matebeleland is often expressed against the high-handed methods the army has used, but not that government has neglected the people of Matebeleland in the highly valued areas of agriculture, health, and education.

The ruling party, too, has successfully penetrated the country very effectively, except in Matebeleland where both the carrot and the stick have failed to produce electoral support for it. Sustained effectiveness in the rest of the country is likely to further strengthen the legitimacy of the government. Such sustained effectiveness might also signal a "lost cause" to the disaffected areas. But the reverse is also true. Any loss of ground by the government and the ruling party would encourage dissidents and other sections of the country to question the legitimacy of the government. Thus far, the ZANU (PF) regime has moved from strength to strength both electorally and in maintaining a stable and coherent administration.

Another factor behind the persistence of the democratic system relates to the above. Contrary to expectations, ZANU(PF) has emerged fairly united and cohesive after years of fratricidal tendencies in exile. Moreover, the more ZAPU and the dissidents continue posing a threat, and the more their methods are perceived as illegitimate, the more likely ZANU(PF) will be to sustain its unity and cohesiveness. Related to this is ZANLA unity. Contrary to expectations, former ZANLA fighters now in the national army were not necessarily weary of war. In fact, they had anticipated the conflict in Matebeleland, given the nature and direction of the liberation struggle.

The white community, which largely accepted the hand of reconciliation extended at independence, is another factor encouraging democratic persistence. This removed a sensitive and dangerous strain on the new government. Whites played a critical role in the fairly sophisticated economy the new government inherited at independence. While collapsing economies give rise to revolutions, once they are successful, revolutionary governments are sustained by sound economies. In the short run, the contribution of the whites to economic stability and sustained growth in Zimbabwe was necessary. This could not be achieved by a reckless policy of reprisals against them. On their part, whites accepted Prime Minister Mugabe's hand of reconciliation more readily than did ZAPU and other black parties. The reason for this is obvious. After the struggle for majority rule was won, the question no longer was, "Who will govern, blacks or whites?," but rather, "Who among the blacks will govern?" At this stage, whites were largely peripheral to the arena of politics. However, their role in the economy has been an important stabilizing factor.

Democracy is also commonly associated with a *free press*. In Zimbabwe, radio and television are largely controlled by government as parastatals. The print medium is, however, free in that, unlike radio and television, individuals or companies are free to establish their own newspapers. Moreover, political parties as well can publish their own periodicals.[50] There are two privately owned major journals, *Moto* and *Prize*, which often engage in "constructive criticism." *Moto*, associated with the local Catholic organization, has earned a reputation as probably the most independent and unbiased newspaper in the country. It is widely read by all sectors of the society.

However, Zimbabwe's two main newspapers, the *Herald* and *Sunday Mail*, are owned by the Zimbabwe Mass Media Trust, a parastatal created after independence. The trust bought up South African shares in both newspapers and other regional dailies like the *Bulawayo Chronicle* and *Manica Post*. Yet, although the editors of these newspapers liaise closely with the Ministry of Information, they are not government or party employees and are free to take an independent line on various issues of policy and public concern. The executive director of the newspapers, Elias Rusike, described the relationship with government and the party as follows: "We make a very serious distinction between the government and the ruling party. Though we might support the government, we are not the mouthpiece of the ruling party."[51] However, editors in a fairly ideological and young country might feel obliged to support government and party policy even when this is not demanded by either government or the party. On balance, press pluralism in Zimbabwe augurs well for democracy.

The heterogeneity of the Zimbabwean social milieu is yet another important factor that has helped to sustain some form of pluralist democracy in Zimbabwe. Here, ethnicity has been a contributory factor. In a real sense, continued Ndebele support for Nkomo's ZAPU has slowed down ZANU's speed toward countrywide hegemony and the one-party state. In addition, intra-Shona ethnicity has also kept the ruling party busy patching up differences that have periodically visited it, such as the Hove-Ushewokunze "diatribe" that errupted in the Parliament early in 1986.[52] Moreover, whites still retain residual political influence. Besides their guaranteed twenty seats until 1990, at the latest, opinions of whites and what happens to them invariably catches international attention, particularly in the West, to which Zimbabwe pays particular attention, given the country's colonial history, and sociocultural and economic links.

Further, Zimbabwe lacks class homogeneity, notwithstanding socialist rhetoric. The political class has shown a highly developed appetite for accumulation. Since independence, high-ranking party officials have acquired substantial personal wealth in violation of the party's leadership code, which strictly limits the amount of wealth party leaders may acquire. This embourgeoisement process could, in due course, produce politicians more dependent on their own means of survival and less on the party, thereby increasing independent political opinion. Related to this issue is the peasantry and proletariat, who constitute roughly 74 percent and 20 percent, respectively, of the population. Peasants, more than workers, featured prominently in the liberation war. Although, after independence, the government has paid a lot of attention to the rural areas, peasant policy preferences have, in some instances, tended to contradict party socialist policy preferences. They have, for instance, been more enthusiastic about state-assisted individual peasant farming than collectives.[53]

The labor movement in Zimbabwe is weak and somewhat defensive, feeling guilty for not participating fully in the liberation struggle. There was a wave of strikes in many cities after independence. The workers were quickly silenced and reminded of their complacency during the liberation struggle. Since then, the government has taken what appears to be a corporatist approach to the country's trade union movement. The Zimbabwe Congress of Trade Unions (ZCTU), formed in 1981 with encouragement and assistance of the government, works closely with the Ministry of Labor and Social Services. This is both its source of strength and weakness in that, on the one hand, its favored status gives it advantage over unaffiliated unions, while, on the other, such status compromises workers interests in negotiations with either government or private employees. However, the fact that other independent trade unions can exist gives workers alternatives. This should encourage more dynamism in the ZCTU even under the present corporatist arrangement—a development descernible with the recent election of a new ZCTU leadership. Thus, notwithstanding its initial weakness, there is potential for the trade union movement in Zimbabwe to play a significant role independent of the government or ruling party.

The initially "friendly" attitude of the international community also contributed somewhat to the persistence of democracy in Zimbabwe during the first six years. None of Zimbabwe's neighbors, including South Africa and the superpowers, were overtly hostile to the new government. When not supportive, they adopted a wait-and-see attitude. Moreover, Zimbabwe was well aware it was the focus of attention and scrutiny by the international community, whose principal actors had doubted if democracy in this newest of African countries could endure. Thus, commitment to constitutional rule and to free and fair elections would retain international respectability for Zimbabwe.[54] However, the recent (1986) commando raids by South Africa into Zimbabwe (as well as into Botswana and Zambia), the withdrawal of economic assistance by the United States under the Reagan administration, and, more important, the escalating war in neighboring Mozambique are all likely to frustrate and drive the Zimbabwean government into the authoritarian rule characteristic of any country on a war footing.

Finally, and more important to sustaining democratic rule in Zimbabwe, is Prime Minister Mugabe's personality and leadership ability. Structural factors notwithstanding, personalities matter a lot and may even be the key factor in determining the success of regimes, including democratic regimes. They may prove decisive, for example, in generating loyalty to the system and in getting things done.[55] In contrast to the naive Marxist once jeered at by Nkomo during the liberation struggle as "an upstart who thinks he can win Zimbabwe with a Marxist textbook," Mugabe has emerged as both more pragmatic and shrewder than all his opponents, including Smith, Sithole, Muzorewa, and Nkomo himself—all of them skilled politicians.[56] He is a man of acknowledged integrity who scorns corruption and indiscipline. He respects the country's political institutions, and has not unduly interfered with the country's press or the system of justice.[57] He has allowed the Public Accounts Committee of Parliament to function—investigating, and thus embarassing, some of his cabinet ministers and high-ranking party officials.[58] And, significantly, Mugabe has earned the respect of Zimbabwe's intellectual community; he is one himself in his own right.[59] The support and confidence of the intellectual community is critical for the survival of any regime, even in this age of populism.

• THEORETICAL ANALYSIS •

Zimbabwe, six years after independence, is far too young to fit into theoretical frameworks of democracy in any definitive way. Although the present Zimbabwe government is the result of "free and fair" elections held within a competitive pluralistic party framework, Zimbabwe cannot be classified as completely democratic. The conflict in Matebeleland has resulted in a state of emergency that has placed limitations on civil liberties in the region for a sustained length of time. Zimbabwe can therefore be classified as "semidemocratic" and "partially unstable" because of the conflict. This classification is similar to that by Freedom House's 1985–1986 survey of freedom in the world, which lists Zimbabwe as "partly free."[60] Yet, one must account for the relative success of democracy during Zimbabwe's brief period as an independent state.

This chapter has identified race and ethnicity as the primary factors that have influenced political behavior and, therefore, the experience with democratic politics, first in colonial Rhodesia and then in independent Zimbabwe. While theories of democracy associate it with economic prosperity, this can hardly be said to hold in all cases. Moreover, it is often difficult to establish causality. There may be an association, but causal relationships have not been established. In circumstances where the polity is subjectively divided along lines of race, ethnicity, religion, or any other form of so-called "false conscious-ness," the dominant group may deal with subordinate groups in an authoritarian manner to preserve its dominant position, whether or not the economy is grow-ing. This, in fact, is what happened during the period of colonial rule in Rhodesia. The economic prosperity of the days of federation did not lead to the liberalization/democratization of an essentially racial, authoritarian settler rule; it led, instead to a right-wing trend. Even intrawhite democracy gave in to Rhodesia Front hegemony and authoritarianism within the white community, notwithstanding the white prosperity of the time.

Neither can the performance of the economy be easily linked to the fate of democracy. After independence, Zimbabwe enjoyed a booming economy, fol-lowed in 1981 through 1983 by a severe drought and world recession. As it hap-pened, Mugabe proclaimed a policy of reconciliation between races, parties, etc., from the outset in 1980. Later, however, he sacked ZAPU from his cabinet, and authoritarian rule followed in parts of Matebeleland. This happened in the middle of the drought and economic hardships for the country. However, it would be far-fetched to link dissident activity and repression in Matebeleland to the distressed economy of this period, or the accommodating approach at inde-pendence to the prosperity of the time. Rather, ethnic and political factors were driving these developments. Similarly, it is not the economy (declining or ex-panding) that continues to induce the electorate in Matebeleland to vote ZAPU and in Mashonaland to vote ZANU. Economic hardships were countrywide. Moreover, Matebeleland received special attention from Mugabe's government in the drought relief effort, indeed because of both political and humanitarian dictates. Thus, the electorate in Matebeleland may prosper from government development programs, but still vote ZAPU. The problem between ZANU and ZAPU is not economic. It is at the subjective level.

Neither has class been a salient factor to date in Zimbabwe's political ex-perience. It was not only the lower classes among whites who favored racial domination and authoritarian rule to preserve it, but all classes of whites. Nor was black resistance identified with any particular class; it cut across class lines. The nationalist movement was led by a petty bourgeois element excluded from positions of power and prestige not on account of ignorance and poverty, but because of color. Prior to independence, authoritarian rule and the resistance to it were based on race. Economic inequalities only enhanced the capacity to re-press. Since independence, the central political conflict that threatens the demo-cratic experiment has been based on ethnicity, not class.

As mentioned before, however, there is one sense in which economic per-formance has affected democracy. The relative effectiveness of the Mugabe government in delivering the goods of development in health, education, ag-riculture, and so on, has increased its legitimacy and, by extension, that of the democratic system.

With respect to the relationship between state and society, democracy in Zimbabwe has benefited from the lack of coincidence between wealth and one's position in government in Zimbabwe thus far. Zimbabwe's richest African is not in government, but in the private sector. In fact, in the eyes of many upwardly mobile Zimbabweans, the private sector has more status. Also, one's position in the private sector has, thus far, not been affected by membership in the ruling party. Moreover, opposition ZAPU politicians are not the poorest in the country. Nkomo himself, hardly a peasant, drives in a dark, bulletproof Mercedes-Benz similar to that of the prime minister. (This caught the attention of one of my students who observed: "We are so free in this country that even a leader of the opposition drives like a prime minister!") On the other hand, there is the danger in any society that the private sector could become too powerful vis-à-vis the state and then undermine its authority in the eyes of the people.

In terms of powersharing, the postindependence political structure has not been a salient factor. As noted, Nkomo refused the presidency, which, in fact, pays more than the prime minister's job. When he finally accepted other cabinet posts, he did not complain that they were too few. The problem is neither economic nor structural; it is psychological and, therefore, political. It is mainly at that level that efforts should be concentrated. A very key point to appreciate in this regard is that Nkomo and his ZAPU organization had expected to be in power at independence. They had a central committee and an army ready to govern the whole country, not just part of it in the context of local government. Therefore, not until ZAPU is convinced its goal of winning national power is futile can we expect its leading politicians to take a personal interest in local government.

Structures gain salience when perceptions of their importance crystallize at the local and regional level. To this end, elective governorships would be enhanced in being perceived as powerful and, therefore, attractive to politicians now so focused only on power at the national level. Directly elected mayorships could also be similarly affected.

Political culture is, however, a significant and important variable in Zimbabwe's search for a stable democracy. Zimbabwe's political culture is a product of several factors that weigh differently in influencing political attitudes for or against the politics of contestation. Traditional political attitudes and norms tend to be supportive of one-man and, therefore, one-party state tendencies in politics.[61] This is likely to be stronger in the more rural than urban areas where, prior to colonial rule, no organized political parties existed, and there was only one leader (the traditional chief or monarch). People knew the next chief would come from the royalty, and any competition was therein confined. A sitting or aspiring chief did not go around campaigning among his subjects every five years. Political parties as legitimate means of contesting for power are relatively new in Zimbabwe—only twenty-five years old. Further, they developed under circumstances of white settler rule, which normally would manipulate any otherwise legitimate differences between nationalist leaders and parties. Hence, the various factions and personalities often suspected and denounced each other as enemy agents. Moreover, each believed in the correctness of their approach to decolonization, finding the other's deviation unacceptable.

Colonial authoritarianism itself left an oppressive inheritance that it would be a mistake to downplay. Ninety years of colonial rule must leave a type of mental outlook and political style on the colonized. Common sense should prevent us from expecting Zimbabwe to have rid itself of the psychological burden of a century in only five years. In particular, the intolerance manifested by white settler governments of (black) opposition mobilization, as well as the inclination to repress rather than negotiate, have left their mark on the contemporary political culture. And, as noted earlier, instruments of control and coercion, including some of the institutions, laws, and personnel, were inherited and maintained.

The liberation struggle also left a significant mark on Zimbabwe's political culture. The commandist nature of mobilization and politicization under clandestine circumstances gave rise to the politics of intimidation and fear. Opponents were viewed in warlike terms, as enemies and, therefore, illegitimate. The culture from the liberation struggle was intolerant and violent. Enemies were to be killed; hence, in 1985, a caricature of Nkomo was put in a coffin to the delight of crowds who were quite unaware that tomorrow it could be a party colleague who has a different point of view.

Another factor with impact on the political values of Zimbabwe is the climate of international ideological discourse. The Zimbabwean political elite and cadre consumed a large dose of Marxist-Leninist and Maoist thought during the liberation struggle, particularly in the 1970s. Thus, ideas of the Marxist-Leninist one-party state after independence do not come by accident and without reflection. In addition, the African environments in which the liberation movements were based during exile—mainly Zambia, Tanzania, and Mozambique—were themselves one-party states with variations of socialism, Marxism, and Leninisn. This environment had an impact on the emergent Zimbabwe leadership. Moreover, Marxist-Leninist regimes elsewhere have tended to emphasize political conformity rather than diversity.

Religion is another factor affecting Zimbabwe's culture. Zimbabwe is multireligious and multidenominational. Probably, 60 percent of Zimbabwe's population is traditional in its religious outlook. However, the political elite has been exposed to Christianity. For instance, Sithole and Muzorewa were ordained ministers; Nkomo is a lay preacher; and Mugabe is a practicing Catholic. Despite these differences, Zimbabwe is one of the most religiously tolerant societies. In fact, there has never been a reported case of interreligious fighting. Cooperation between church groups of different denominations has been quite high, notwithstanding the fact that Christianity, like political parties, came in the colonial package. This suggests that the lack of interparty tolerance may have very little to do with the novelty of political parties among Africans. Rather, it is rooted in the perception of politics as a zero-sum game.

Most of these factors—the lack of experience with party politics, the authoritarian colonial legacy, the nature and exigencies of the liberation struggle, the climate of ideological discourse, and, not least, the depth and long history of ethnic divisions—have produced a cultural tendency to view politics as a "do-or-die" struggle, a zero-sum game.

The perception of politics as a zero-sum game is not without limits. After Mugabe had won in 1980, he did offer Nkomo the presidency; when that was declined, he nonetheless included Nkomo and other ZAPU leaders in the first cabinet. Similarly, in 1979, Muzorewa invited Sithole to name four persons for cabinet posts as was then required by the Zimbabwe-Rhodesia constitution. Yet, in both instances, as we have seen, there was a tendency for the main opposition not to cooperate fully with an inclusive approach. It is doubtful whether ZANU(PF) would have cooperated fully had it lost the election to either ZAPU or to some coalition. In fact, given that its guerrilla force controlled a good three-quarters of the countryside, it is reasonable to predict that all hell would have broken out. This tendency thus supports the thesis that, when politicians do not play according to the rules, democracy is greatly compromised.

• FUTURE PROSPECTS •

In conclusion, let us consider future prospects for democracy in Zimbabwe. In the foregoing discussion we have shown how the Rhodesian state practiced democratic decisionmaking within the white community, and argued that such consultation narrowed the perceptual gap between the white elite and their followers, to the effect that they maintained goal consensus and unity until the day of African majority rule. But, because the bulk of the African people were governed without their consent, the legitimacy of the white settler state was challenged, and it was eventually overthrown in hopes of an inclusive and more stable democracy. To be underscored here is the fact that goal consensus between leaders and followers facilitates the stability of regimes. Such consensus on values derives from honest consultation with the people at all levels. As such democracy facilitates rather than undermines the stability of regimes.

Perhaps the most important development in postcolonial Zimbabwe politics has been the continued antagonistic relations between ZANU and ZAPU. Because of this, the new democracy in Zimbabwe remains unstable. In a continuing search for stability, the new leaders have actively advocated a one-party state. To that end, unity talks have been held on and off between ZANU and ZAPU since 1983; the latest in early 1986. Should they succeed, one mammoth party is the likely outcome. Thus, looked at through these events, Zimbabwe's days as a multiparty democracy are narrowly numbered. This, however, need not be the only scenario.

Unity between ZANU(PF) and PF(ZAPU) is an imperative that most people in Zimbabwe welcome. As has been shown, the ZANU-ZAPU division has been the most serious and persistent in the nationalist movement. However, unity between these two parties need not lead to the one-party state. Instead of a *de jure* one-party state, Zimbabwe could have a *de facto* one-party-dominant state as in Botswana or Senegal. In such a system, opposition parties would be free to organize, criticize, and compete for power, even though the breadth of the ruling party's base would assure its electoral dominance.

There are several factors that favor democracy in contemporary Zimbabwe. Ironically, one is the multiethnic nature of its society. Considered in subethnic terms, there are two ethnic groups in Zimbabwe large enough to combine into a majority. There would have to be at least three groups in combination to form a political majority. An awareness of this reality would foster intergroup tolerance as each major group realizes that, by itself, it cannot form a majority. Even in a one-party-dominant context, this multiethnic reality would provide some basis of pluralism, and could enhance tolerance and, therefore, democratic tendencies.

Second, Zimbabwe came to independence six years ago with a fairly sophisticated intelligentsia well aware of the paucity of miracles of the one-party state elsewhere in Africa. Thus, the one-party state is less likely to be accepted with the previous enthusiasm. Moreover, the expanding literacy level is likely to enhance a questioning outlook in the mass public. Under the circumstances, and in the long run, an imposed one-party state is not likely to receive the good will of the intelligentsia, and could survive on fear only temporarily.

Third, the experiences of one-party regimes in the region, as elsewhere in Africa, has put the local political leadership under intellectual strain to advance a coherent argument for this anachronism. The one-party state is no longer as popular an idea today in Africa as it was in the initial period after independence. It has not lived up to its promise of unity, stability, economic equality, and development. Moreover, the seeming move away from the one-man syndrome in Africa—if Senegal and Tanzania are any cases to go by—would suggest that the one-man/one-party tendency may no longer be as popular. Abandoning power might become the more fashionable thing to do. Those willing to relinquish power have no stake in perpetuating the one-party anachronism.

Fourth, leadership is often a critical factor in the genesis of one-party regimes in Africa and elsewhere. Zimbabwe's luck, at least for the time being, is that Prime Minister Mugabe himself shares democratic values and is often acknowledged to be a consultative leader. This characteristic in Mugabe is not new. During the struggle, he was acknowledged as being democratic to the point of weakness. Yet, the manner in which he has consolidated power and steered a precarious state since independence would suggest that the "to the point of weakness" image might have been more circumstantial than substantial. Mugabe has, thus far, been successful in observing key social forces and social-psychological trends and has been fairly good in his choice of action and the timing of it. But there is often the danger that popularity and success in politics can lead to a false confidence, which invariably blinds the good and the well-intentioned. An uncritical commitment to the one-party idea, at this hour in Africa's postcolonial history, would be an error. But, to the extent that the issue of a one-party state and the form it takes is still under open debate in Zimbabwe, it is an error that the ZANU(PF) leadership has not finally committed. And, most important, it is an error that there is no need to make.

Fifth, a continued embourgeoisement of the political class bodes well for the emergence of politicians of independent means; they will be consulted by the leader more on a give-and-take basis, whether in the context of achieving national unity and stability or in maintaining unity within the party itself. This is healthy because it facilitates collective leadership. Also in this group should be included personalities outside the party with independent means and religious leaders who periodically voice a constructive opinion, even in criticism. Moreover, a sustained growth of the middle class increases the number of those with a stake in maintaining stability and democratic values. The expansion of the bureaucracy (bureaucratic bourgeoisie) since independence, and the concomitant Africanization of the private sector, favors the continued growth of the middle class in Zimbabwe.

Sixth, Zimbabwe's nonaligned pluralist approach to relations with other countries, particularly the assortment of countries with which economic, cultural and political relations have been established, has increased pragmatism at the expense of dogma. To the extent that such diversity includes countries committed to democratic values, it reinforces Zimbabwe's own commitment to democracy. This should be encouraged.

Seventh, political tolerance, and therefore democracy, tend to be associated with levels of literacy. Zimbabwe's level of literacy has jumped by leaps and bounds from 25 percent at independence in 1980 to 64 percent in 1985, only five years after independence. This is good for democracy in Zimbabwe. However, here a question is often asked: "Will the government have employment for its thousands of school-leavers every year? Would this not lead to revolutionary pressures and, therefore, to authoritarian responses?" This unfeeling question can be taken to suggest that the masses should remain ignorant. Yet, it is when people are educated and enlightened that they can deal more effectively with both their personal problems and those of the nation. In the long run, democracy is more secure in the hands of people sophisticated enough to know how and why it works.

Finally, let us consider ways of enhancing democracy in Zimbabwe. We have argued that there exists in Zimbabwe a political culture that, because of colonial authoritarianism and circumstances of prosecuting the liberation struggle, tends to be "commandist" and politically intolerant. But, since this political culture was "learned," it can be "unlearned," over time, through efforts by government and other agencies deemphasizing the "commandist" and "subject" political orientations that colonial authoritarianism and the liberation struggle left in Zimbabwe's political culture. A more tolerant "civic" culture, respectful of both legitimate authority and the civil rights of citizens (including minorities), could be inculcated through the school system and other agencies of political socialization such as the family, churches, trade unions, and, indeed, the political parties themselves (both ruling and opposition).

Further, the international community can assist in Zimbabwe's democratic evolution. The international community matters for Zimbabwe as it does for other Third World countries. Both government and those who oppose it read international attitudes and signals, and often count on them. With regard to Zimbabwe, those in the international community (the United States and Britain in particular), who have favored multiparty democracy have tended to be more concerned about the ruling party's pro-one-party state pronouncements than about the illegitimate methods of the opposition, which are clearly outside the Lancaster House constitution they helped to formulate. When the makers of the rules do not disdain those who violate them, they only encourage the culprits to play outside the rules even more. A clear stance by international actors in favor of constitutional government and electoral democracy would, therefore, dispel possible misperceptions. Also in this vein, the escalating civil war in Mozambique has serious implications for democracy in Zimbabwe. There is the real danger that conflict could lead to the introduction of a state of emergency the areas on Mozambique's border. The international community could intervene positively to end that conflict before the arena of democracy in Zimbabwe shrinks further on account of that conflict.

But, more than anything else, the dissident element mentioned earlier militates against democratic prospects in Zimbabwe. In the face of violent dissident activities challenging the authority of a democratically elected government, frustration affects decisionmakers who, in search of possible solutions, are tempted to try the one-party formula. In this way, illegitimate or disloyal opposition tactics often contribute to one-party ideas within ruling circles. The opposition often exaggerates its claim to a share of power, the oppressive activities of the regime in power, and its own superior ability to bring manna from heaven once in power. In Zimbabwe, it is rare to hear the opposition praising anything government does.[62] In its bid to gain power, the opposition in Africa has often overlooked constitutional provisions and tried shortcuts, which turned out to bring very long terms in jail or exile. At worst, they have brought unending civil strife to society.

Authority in the new nations is often nervous. Hence, it tends to be intolerant and perceives deviations as threatening the very survival of the regime. The opposition must appreciate this nervous state of the new rulers. Thus, if the opposition were more constructive in its criticism and more responsible in its posture, it could help to build a climate of mutual trust and tolerance between the parties, which would enhance the prospects for democracy. Most of all, it is imperative that the opposition reject any actions or strategies disloyal to the democratic constitution.

Furthermore, opposition parties have had a propensity for flirting with foreign opponents of the state, and the latter, being precarious, has been extremely sensitive and quick to respond. Moreover, the opposition has often lacked tact in its conduct of relations with the enemies of the state. For instance, in Zimbabwe, one opposition leader, when questioned by state security officials about what he had been doing in South Africa, is said to have replied that it was none of the state's business since, as a Zimbabwe citizen, he was free to go anywhere and to see anyone.[63] Such an insouciant attitude invites authoritarian responses.

The future of democracy in Zimbabwe must lie, in large part, in the resolution of the conflict in Matebeleland. It has been argued in the foregoing pages that a showdown between ZANU and ZAPU had to occur sooner or later, (a) to test the theory that ZANU was an unstable party fraught with factional infighting, and therefore could be toppled, and (b) to test Mugabe's and ZANU's capacity and will to rule. All of this was to test an old hypothesis between the Ndebele and Shona. It is the impression of this author that both tests have been passed. Misconceptions and misperceptions between ZAPU and ZANU had to be settled sooner or later. They had to scale each other in a match of sorts. Two matches have occurred electorally. A military match was, perhaps, also necessary to scale things once and for all—and better sooner than later.

With the resolution of the conflict in Matebeleland, however, a *de jure* one-party state seems neither necessary nor obligatory. If the people in Matebeleland want their own party they should have it, but society obligates them to operate within the law. ZAPU's attitude to constitutional and electoral democracy will help, to a great extent, in deciding where Zimbabwe goes from here. My observation is that the Zimbabwe leadership is committed to observing the rules of the game. I have tried to show how, in fact, it has tried to do so. Hence, once the opposition has reconciled itself to accepting and actually playing according to the rules of the game, Zimbabwe—the whole of it—will be a much freer society.

Still, the ZANU leadership has the ultimate responsibility for steering the young nation along a democratic path. To this end, it should resist the temptation to wield more power than is necessary to run the country. There are a number of instances in the Zimbabwe party and political system where improvements could be made to enhance democracy. Clearly, the selection of district administrators and provincial governors are two such instances. The election of provincial governors would make them accountable to the local provincial electorate. Governors could then appoint district administrators. Such devolution of power would expand the arena of politics, thereby reducing the present fixation with politics at the national level.

Also, in the event of Zimbabwe becoming a one-party state, there is need for institutionalizing democratic mechanisms in the one party. In 1984, ZANU(PF) adopted, for the first time, a Politburo in its structure. The Politburo is the organ that wields any substance of collective power in the party, and can take decisions and make policy on behalf of the party and its Central Committee. It is, however, appointed by the first secretary of the party with advice by the second secretary. Its selection from and by the Central Committee could give it broader accountability.

There is no doubt, even among many in the opposition in Zimbabwe politics, that Prime Minister Mugabe's leadership of both his party and the country has been exercised with outstanding skill. But herein lies the danger. What happens when someone else who is less able and democratically committed inherits strong and powerful institutions that could be easily abused? The concern, therefore, should be with constructing institutions in such a way that they cannot be readily abused.

Most important, the ZANU leadership must accept the task of including all major sectors of society in all important structures of power. In doing this, it may be obligated to include the opposition (ZAPU) in structures of power, whatever the difficulties of the past, because ZAPU represents an important and visible constituency. After all, national unity and consensus must ultimately come from a feeling of belonging. The opposition must be made to feel it belongs. To this end, Dunduza Chisiza's diagnostic prescription made a quarter of a century ago is instructive:

> The main explanation for the friction hinges on the sharing of gratitude and prestige. Before independence, foreign rulers occupy the topmost rungs of the social ladder. With the coming of independence, however, they step down and leaders of parties which have triumphed at the polls step up to fill the vacant rungs, thereby becoming the recipients of gratitude and admiration from their fellow-countrymen for having liberated their countries. Leaders of the opposition parties who may have fought for independence just as valiantly as anyone else find themselves the recipients of practically nothing. Herein lies the rub. It is only human for these people to feel that they have been given a raw deal.[64]

This is to underscore that democratic politics cannot be a zero-sum game and be stable. But, while the opposition must be given a stake in the system, the new rulers must equally be given assurance of the loyalty of the opposition. Precisely because the new rulers are new and the system is not secure, this assurance is most important in the early years of the regime. If neither side will see the necessity of playing its part, then, in the phrase of the Ghanaian writer Ayi Kwei Armah, "the beautiful ones are not yet born."[65] There is need for both the rulers and the opposition in Africa to recast and reorient their thinking regarding relations between them. Otherwise prospects for democracy on the continent are remote indeed.

• NOTES •

1. This distinction is suggested by C. B. MacPherson in his book, *The Real World of Democracy* (London: Oxford University Press, 1966).

2. White settlers never, in fact, intended that Africans should be trained for eventual takeover. Such, however, remained the British policy over which disagreement with the settlers widened in the 1960s onward.

3. Larry Bowman, *Politics in Rhodesia: White Power in an African State* (Cambridge, Mass.: Harvard University Press, 1973).

4. Ibid., p. 3.

5. Reported in the *Rhodesia Herald* (Salisbury), 22 September 1964.

6. Reports on Rhodesia by Amnesty International and the Zimbabwe-based Catholic Commission for Peace and Justice document many of the arrests, detentions, and deportations during this period.

7. These inflammatory statements became part of the political vocabulary of the UDI period in the 1960s and 1970s. See the *Herald* (Salisbury), 11 May 1964, also 6 June.

8. Marshall W. Murphree, et al, *Education, Race and Employment in Rhodesia* (Salisbury: ARTCA Publications, 1975), p. 30.

9. M. Fortes and Edward E. Evans-Pritchard, eds., *African Political Systems* (Oxford: University Press, 1940).

10. Marshall W. Murphree, *Education, Race and Employment*, p. 32.

11. For a discussion of the early African National Congress up to 1959, see Tapera O. Chirau, *The African National Congress of Zimbabwe* (Ann Arbor: University Microfilms International, 1986).

12. From an article "Tribalism on Trial" in the *Sunday Mail* (Salisbury) 10 June 1979, p. 13.

13. For a discussion of the development of the Zimbabwe Nationalist movement, see Wellington Nyangoni, *Zimbabwe African Nationalism* (Washington, D. C.: University Press of America, 1978).

14. For a detailed discussion of the ZANU-ZAPU split, see Nathan Shamuyarira, *Crisis in Rhodesia* (London: Andre Deutsch, 1965), pp. 173–193; and M. Sithole, *Zimbabwe: Struggles Within the Struggle* (Salisbury: Rujeko Publishers, 1979), pp. 27–46, especially the document by Ndabaningi Sithole quoted on pp. 31–34.

15. For an account of the formation of the African National Council, see Abel Muzorewa, *Rise Up and Walk* (Nashville: Abington Press, 1979), p. 94; and Joshua Nkomo, *Nkomo: The Story of My Life* (London: The Chaucer Press, 1984), p. 141.

16. Most literature on the Zimbabwe liberation movement on this period will more likely than not cite such exchanges. See the chapter, "Contradictions in FROLIZI" in M. Sithole, *Zimbabwe Struggles*, pp. 88–97.

17. Ibid., pp. 67–87.

18. See the account in *Nkomo: The Story of My Life*, p. 20.

19. For about a year (March 1979 to February 1980), Zimbabwe was known as "Zimbabwe-Rhodesia," a frivolous compromise name agreed to between the RF government, which preferred the name Rhodesia, and the internally based nationalist leaders who preferred the name Zimbabwe.

20. It was at the Geneva Conference that Smith noticed the extent and magnitude of the factionalization in the nationalist movement and the forces behind them and decided to exploit the situation. He had this in mind when he finally decided to be arrogant and intransigent in his attitude to the talks. He, in fact, promptly left the talks for Rhodesia because "I have a country to run."

21. The "March 3rd Agreement" is the subject of a publication by Ndabaningi Sithole; *In Defense of the March 3rd Agreement* (Salisbury: Graham Publishing Co., 1979). It is articulate but unconvincing.

22. There were in all ten "observer groups" to the 1979 Zimbabwe-Rhodesia election. These were from: The United Kingdom, United States, West Germany, Canada, South Africa, Mauritius, France, Belgium, Australia, and the European Parliament. See *Report of the Australian Parliamentary Observer Group on the Zimbabwe-Rhodesia Common Roll Elections* (May 1979)

23. Ibbo Mandaza, *The Zimbabwe Public Service* (Paper presented at the United Nations Inter-Regional Seminar on Reforming Civil Service Systems for Development, Beijing: 14–24 August 1985), p. 24. (unpublished)

24. Every other party seemed to gang up against ZANU(PF). Some were even speculating on an arithmetic that would deprive ZANU (PF) of victory. See Martin Gregory, "Zimbabwe 1980: Politicization through Armed Struggle and Electoral Mobilization," in *Journal of Commonwealth and Comparative Politics*, 19, no. 1 (March 1981): p. 68, where he quotes some estimates of the Rhodesian Ministry of Home Affairs as "Muzorewa 43 seats, Mugabe 26, and Nkomo 20." Exact on Nkomo, totally off on the rest.

25. One of these incidents took place in the province of Masvingo when Mugabe was on a campaign tour of the area. See the *Herald*, 10 February 1980.

26. Eddison Zvobgo, Director of the 1980 ZANU (PF) campaign, was fond of making such comments at meetings with the Election Directorate where officials of other parties lodged complaints. The author attended the meetings.

27. For a detailed and candid account of the various procedures and problems encountered in administering this election, see the registrar-general's 1985 *General Election Report* (Harare), 13 September 1985.

28. In an interview following announcement of the results, Nkomo said that, "ZANU (PF) rule over the last five years has divided the country into tribal and racial groups. This is a tragedy that has never happened before," *Sunday Mail*, 7 July 1985. This, however, does not deny that the elections themselves were "free and fair." Moreover, "tribal and racial groups" predate ZANU (PF) rule.

29. Interview by author on 4 November 1985.

30. Registrar-general's *Report*, p. 22.

31. Bowman, *Politics in Rhodesia*, p. 18.

32. For an elaborate discussion of these factors, see Jeff Davidow, *A Peace in Southern Africa: The Lancaster House Conference on Rhodesia* (Boulder, Colo.: Westview Press, 1984).

33. At the 1964 First ZANU Congress held in the Midlands city of Gweru (only thirty miles from Ian Smith's farm), Robert Mugabe, then secretary-general of the party, warned that, if our freedom should depend on someone's lifetime, it may be necessary to eliminate that person so that we can be free soon. He was later convicted under the country's "Law and Order Maintenance Act" for making this statement. (I attended the 1964 ZANU congress and followed the subsequent trial).

34. Bowman, *Politics in Rhodesia*, p. 35.

35. Ibid., p. 43.

36. This is the suggestion made by David Martin and Phyllis Johnson in their "unconvincing" book, *The Chitepo Assassination* (Harare: Zimbabwe Publishing House, 1985). See my review of this book in *Journal of Modern African Studies* 24, no. 1 (1986).

37. For such neo-Marxist interpretations, see John Saul, "Zimbabwe: The Next Round," *Monthly Review* (September 1980): pp. 34–35. Also, Owen Tshabangu, *The March 11 Movement in ZAPU: Revolution Within the Revolution for Zimbabwe* (York: Tiger Paper Publications, 1979). Also, Giovanni Arrighi, "Black and White Populism in Rhodesia," unpublished but quoted in John Saul, ed., *The State and Revolution in East Africa* (London: Heinemann, 1979), p. 112.

38. See Masipula Sithole, "Focus On: Class and Factionalism in the Zimbabwe Nationalist Movement," *African Studies Review* 27, no. 1 (March 1984), for a critique of vulgar use of class analysis and romantic view of the proletariat.

39. See M. Sithole, *Zimbabwe Struggles*. Also his "Ethnicity and Factionalism in the Zimbabwe Nationalist Movement 1957–79," in *Ethnic and Racial Studies* 3, no. 1 (January 1980).

40. See the *Herald*, 21 June 1979.

41. A good discussion of the "goings-on" inside the liberation movement is in David Martin and Phyllis Johnson, *The Struggle for Zimbabwe* (Harare: Zimbabwe Publishing House, 1981). See, in particular, chaps. 11–14.

42. Nkomo, *The Story of My Life*, p. 200.

43. David Martin and Phyllis Johnson, *The Struggle for Zimbabwe*, pp. 328–329.

44. Ali Mazrui, speech at the *African Studies Association Annual Conference*, Chicago, Palmer House Hotel, 1974.

45. See his well-documented article, "In Search of Regime Security: Zimbabwe Since Independence," in the *Journal of Modern African Studies* 22, no. 4 (December 1984): pp. 529–558.

46. See "Amnesty International Report," 1985, pp. 115–119.

47. There are two jokes (but with serious implications) about the definition of a dissident in Zimbabwean political humor. The one says, "A dissident is a Ndebele," the other that "a dissident is a person who takes up arms against the state when he has lost an election." The one is tribalistic, while the other suggests strong disapproval.

48. The evidence is from a preelection survey conducted by the author in 1985.

49. However, satisfaction was more pronounced in rural than urban areas.

50. In this respect, both ZANU and ZAPU publish their own party publications, *ZANU News* and *Zimbabwe Review*, respectively. To date, there is no indexed political publication in Zimbabwe.

51. See the article, "Zimbabwe Newspapers: A Unique Experiment," by Colm Foy, in *Africasia* no. 32, 1986. Foy says that Zimbabwe's "new system of press ownership and operation distinguishes the country's newspapers from most others in the Third World."

52. See *Zimbabwe: Parliamentary Debates* (Harare: Government Printers), vol. 12, nos. 44 and 45, 9 and 10 April 1986, respectively.

53. In a brilliant analysis, "Farmer Organizations and Food Production in Zimbabwe," *World Development* 14, no. 3 (1986), pp. 367–384, Michael Bratton shows how small farmer groups improve access to household assets and argues that centralized statist policies often lead to conflict with local communities.

54. An election post-mortem in the ZANU (PF) journal, *Zimbabwe News* (September 1985), would suggest such awareness and preoccupation.

55. In this regard, it is commonly held that Joshua Nkomo, as a personality, has had phenomenal impact on the Ndebele and is almost irreplaceable as their leader.

56. Quoted in W. Walker, *The Bear at the Back Door: The Soviet Threat to the West's Lifeline in Africa* (London: Foreign Affairs Publishing Company, 1978), p. 38.

57. For an informed discussion of the status and role of the Zimbabwe Judiciary since independence, see Richard Sklar, "Reds and Rights: Zimbabwe's Experiment," *Issues: A Journal of Africanist Opinion* 14 (1985): pp. 29–31. In a conversation with the author on 14 November 1985, Zimbabwe's Chief Justice Enoc Dumbuchena categorically stated that government had never brought any undue pressure on him or the justice system as such. "No; never; not once," he said, and agreed to be quoted.

58. In 1986, Dr. Herbert Ushewokunze, ZANU (PF) secretary for the commissariat, member of the Politburo, and also minister of transport, was the object of severe scrutiny by the Public Accounts Committee. The prime minister did not interfere even when the whole affair appeared embarassing to both his government and party.

59. Mugabe has seven university degrees (not counting honorary) most of which he earned by private study during his ten years of detention. In 1985, he received the MSC in Economics from the University of London.

60. Raymond D. Gastil, *Freedom in the World: Rights and Civil Liberties, 1985–1986*, (New York: Greenwood Press, 1986), pp. 399–400.

61. For a discussion of the one-man tendency in Zimbabwe politics, see Masipula Sithole, "Unreal Opposition," in the *Herald* (Harare), 5 December 1983.

62. I once confronted a leader of one of Zimbabwe's opposition parties with the question: "You have never said anything good about Mugabe or the ruling party. Could it be that there is really nothing good in what they say or do? Are the millions who have voted for them that blind? His reply was quite interesting: "The problem with you academics," he said, "is that you see both sides. In politics there is only one side, your side." On reflection he was right. I have never heard leaders of the ruling party say anything complimentary about the opposition.

63. This insoucient attitude earned Bishop Muzorewa several months in detention.

64. Dunduza K. Chisiza, *Africa: What Lies Ahead* (New Delhi: Indiana Council for Africa), 1961, p. 2.

65. Ayi Kwei Armah's book is in fact titled, *The Beautiful Ones Are Not Yet Born* (Boston: Houghton Mifflin), 1968.

• Index •